THE DEEP SOU
Author's Tr
D0407596
Lake Superior
Duluth
Sault Ste. Marie
WIS.
St. Paul
MICH.
L. Michigan
L. Huron
Lansing
Detroit
Madison
Milwaukee
IOWA
Chicago
Gary
ILL.
Des Moines
IND.
Indianapolis
OHIO
Columbus
MO.
Springfield
Kansas City
E. St. Louis
St. Louis
Cincinnati
KY.
Frankfort
Louisville
Charleston
W. VA.
VA.
Cairo
TENN.
Knoxville
Nashville
Chattanooga
Richmond
N.C.
Raleigh
Charlotte
ARK.
Memphis
Little Rock
MISS.
ALA.
Huntsville
Birmingham
Jackson
Montgomery
Selma
Atlanta
GA.
Savannah
S.C
Columbia
Charleston
LA.
New Orleans
Houston
Tallahassee
FLA.
Jacksonville
Cape Kennedy
Tampa
Miami
Gulf of Mexico
Atlantic
Ocean
MAINE
Augusta
Portland
Burlington
N.Y.
N.H.
Concord
Boston
MASS.
L. Ontario
Rochester
Buffalo
Albany
L. Erie
Cleveland
PA.
Scranton
R.I.
CONN.
New York
N.J.
Philadelphia
Atlantic City
Pittsburgh
Harrisburg
MD.
DEL.
Dover
Washington
Norfolk
A.-Annapolis
B.-Baltimore
W.-Wilmington
T.-Trenton
N.-Newark
N.H.-New Haven
H.-Hartford
S.-Springfield
P.-Providence
KAUAI
NIHAU
OAHU
Honolulu
MOLOKAI
MAUI
HAWAII
Hilo
Pacific Ocean
MILES
0 50 100 200
N

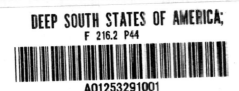

THE *DEEP SOUTH STATES* OF AMERICA

By Neal R. Peirce

THE MEGASTATES OF AMERICA

THE PACIFIC STATES OF AMERICA

THE MOUNTAIN STATES OF AMERICA

THE GREAT PLAINS STATES OF AMERICA

THE PEOPLE'S PRESIDENT

THE

DEEP SOUTH STATES

OF AMERICA

People, Politics, and Power

in the Seven Deep South States

NEAL R. PEIRCE

W · W · NORTON & COMPANY · INC ·
NEW YORK

Published simultaneously in Canada by George J. McLeod Limited, Toronto.
Printed in the United States of America.

FIRST EDITION

Library of Congress Cataloging in Publication Data
Peirce, Neal R
The Deep South states of America.
Bibliography: p.
1. Southern States—Civilization. 2. Southern States—Politics and government—1951–
3. Southern States—Race question. I. Title.
F216.2.P44 917.6'03'4 73-18244
ISBN 0-393-05496-9

1 2 3 4 5 6 7 8 9 0

CONTENTS

FOREWORD

THIS BOOK is a book about the Deep South States, part of a series covering the story of each major geographic region and all of the 50 states of America in our time. The objective is simply to let Americans (and foreigners too) know something of the profound diversity of peoples and life styles and geographic habitat and political behavior that make this the most fascinating nation on earth.

Only one project like this has been attempted before, and it inspired these books: John Gunther's *Inside U.S.A.*, researched during World War II and published in 1947. Gunther was the first man in U.S. history to visit each of the states and then to give a good and true account of the American condition as he found it. But his book is a quarter of a century old; it was written before the fantastic economic and population growth of the postwar era, growth that has transformed the face of this land and altered the life of its people and lifted us to heights of glory and depths of national despair beyond our wildest past dreams. Before he died, I consulted John Gunther about a new book. He recognized the need for such a work, and he gave me, as he put it, his "good luck signal."

But what was to be a single book became several, simply because I found America today too vast, too complex to fit into a single volume. A first book, *The Megastates of America*, treated America's 10 most heavily populated states. The series of eight regional volumes, completing the exploration of all the states in our time, began with publication of *The Mountain States of America* and *The Pacific States of America*, followed by *The Great Plains States of America*. This is the fourth regional volume, and will be followed by a companion book, *The Border South*, and separate books on the states of the Mid-Atlantic, New England, and the Great Lakes.

A word about method. Like Gunther, I traveled to each state of the Union. I talked with about 1,000 men and women—governors, Senators, Representatives, mayors, state and local officials, editors and reporters, business and labor leaders, public opinion analysts, clergymen, university presidents and professors, representatives of the Indian, black, and Spanish-speaking communities—and just plain people. Some of the people I talked with were famous, others obscure, almost all helpful.

I went by plane, then rented cars, made a personal inspection of almost every great city and most of the important geographic areas, and must have walked several hundred miles in the process too, insanely lugging a briefcase full of notes and tape recorder into the unlikeliest places. Usually I got names of suggested interviewees from my newspaper friends and other contacts in new states and cities and then sent letters ahead saying I would like to see the people. From the initial interviews, reference to still more interesting people invariably ensued. Rare were the interviews that didn't turn out to be fascinating in their own way; the best ones were dinner appointments, when the good talk might stretch into the late evening hours.

Altogether, the travel to 50 states took a year and a half, starting in 1969; there were return visits to some states, and telephone follow-up calls to many sources. The writing was complicated by the need to review hundreds of books and thousands of articles and newspaper clippings I had assembled over time. And then each manuscript, after it had been read and commented upon by experts of the state (often senior political reporters), had to be revised to include last-minute developments, and still once more given a final polish and updating in the galley stage.

Amid the confusion I tried to keep my eye on the enduring, vital questions about each state and its great cities:

What sets it (the state or city) apart from the rest of America?

What is its essential character?

What kind of place is it to live in?

What does it look like, how clean or polluted is it, what are the interesting communities?

Who holds the power?

Which are the great corporations, unions, universities, and newspapers, and what role do they play in their state?

Which are the major ethnic groups, and what is their influence?

How did the politics evolve to where they are today, and what is the outlook for the coming years?

How creatively have the governments and power structures served the people?

Who are the great leaders of today—and perhaps tomorrow?

A word of caution: many books about the present-day American condition are preoccupied with illustrating fundamental sickness in our society, while others are paeans of praise. These books are neither. They state many of the deep-seated problems, from perils to the environment to the abuse of power by selfish groups. But the account of the state civilizations also includes hundreds of instances of greatness, of noble and disinterested public service. I have viewed my primary job as descriptive, to show the multitudinous strands of life in our times, admitting their frequently contradictory directions, and tying them together analytically only where the evidence is clear. The ultimate "verdict" on the states and cities must rest with the reader himself. Nowhere is this more true than in the Southern states, so sensitive about their own identity and place in the nation. As a non-Southerner, I approached them with some trepidation, yet soon found myself swept up in the excitement of their rapidly expanding social and political and economic horizons. Yet the millennium in Dixie is still a distant thing, and if some Southerners are offended by unflattering comparisons I have drawn between their states and other parts of the country, I can only quote a born Charlestonian, Chancellor Alexander Heard of Vanderbilt University: "We in the South cannot duck behind the thought that if we show up in the rear ranks in the national ratings, the ratings measure the wrong thing." The exhilaration Southerners should feel today is that for the first time since the Civil War, they have a real prospect of climbing out of those rear ranks and of being distinctive not because they are behind, but because there are areas—especially the development of a civilization of human scale and value—in which they can lead the nation.

For whom, then, is this chronicle of our times written? I mean the individual chapters to be of interest to people who live in the various states, to help them see their home area in a national context. I write for businessmen, students, and tourists planning to visit or move into a state, and who are interested in what makes it tick—the kind of things no guidebook will tell them. I write for politicians planning national campaigns, for academicians, for all those curious about the American condition as we enter the last decades of the 20th century.

From the start, I knew it was presumptuous for any one person to try to encompass such a broad canvass. But a unity of view, to make true comparisons between states, is essential. And since no one else had tried the task for a quarter of a century, I decided to try—keeping in mind the same goal Gunther set for *Inside U.S.A.*—a book whose "central spine and substance is an effort—in all diffidence—to show this most fabulous and least known of countries, the United States of America, to itself."

THE

DEEP SOUTH STATES

OF AMERICA

THE DEEP SOUTH STATES

"FREE AT LAST"?

THE WORDS came from an old slave spiritual; they were used time and again by Martin Luther King, Jr., in his speeches, and now they adorn his tomb in Atlanta: *Free at Last, Free at Last, Thank God Almighty, I'm Free at Last.*

Now King himself is *Free at Last.* But is the South?

A compelling argument may be that it is—or soon will be.

Rapid and liberating change—change more fundamental than in any other region of America—has come to the states of the Deep South in the last two decades.

A second Reconstruction, painful to many white Southerners but far more durable than the first, has overturned ancient racial mores. The black men and women of the South enjoy more liberties than at any time in the three and a half centuries of their life in America. And now the voting power of black people gives them, for the first time, a chance to stand tall in the Southern sun.

By that very change—it is now almost axiomatic to say—the white man is made free too. Spiritually, economically, politically, all Southerners were bound to remain enslaved to a bitter past and bleak present as long as a third of the region's people were denied the most fundamental liberties and opportunities. As the black Southerner expands the horizons of his freedom, so does the white Southerner.

A century of economic depression in the South is ending with a rapid shift from the agrarian economy of old to a new economy based on industry, a shift from ruralism to urbanism, and from unskilled to skilled labor. For the first time, the South is developing cities of distinction, the nerve centers that any society needs for advanced economic and intellectual activity.

The South may also be said to be on the threshold of an exciting new era when it stops neglecting and starts tapping its immense human resources, black and white alike. Southern bodies today are healthier, because nutrition is greatly improved. The vast majority of Southerners have said good-bye to diets of soggy biscuits washed down by greasy "sawmill" gravy, sow belly, molasses, and grits. The scourges of the past that sapped people's strength, making them listless—malaria and hookworm and pellagra and venereal disease—now can be largely controlled by modern medicine.

Southern minds can grow to their full potential because the region's dark age of educational deprivation is drawing to a close. From elementary school classrooms to the universities, an era of adequacy—that may one day reach excellence—has dawned. One reason is that the crippling phenomenon of a dual school system, separate but never really equal, has been brought to an end.

The social profile of the South today shows, for the first time, a substantial middle class between the dwindling (though still substantial) ranks of the underprivileged on one hand and the gentry and mercantile princes on the other. The social changes stem from the breakdown of the feudal-agrarian system, which for so long was buttressed by a Calvinistic religion that led Southerners to believe their social and economic position was predestined, with salvation primarily available in the afterlife, and by a military motif that permeated Southern life and made it clear to the lower classes, in the words of Frank A. Rose, president of the L.Q.C. Lamar Society, that they were "foot soldiers under captains of politics and business" and that to question the established order was "tantamount to treason." Writing in a Lamar Society book, Rose said the ethos of the latest "New South" differs from the past because it symbolizes a South that "wants to be free—free from its past, free from fears, free from wants, free from prejudices."

It is an exhilarating prospect because, as Southern writer John Egerton has observed, "The changes stimulate and reinforce one another: Racism diminishes, industry moves in, and the cross-migration of people accelerates. The educational level rises, and people accustomed to being left out find themselves near the center of things. Confidence rises, and suspicion declines." Confederate nostalgia, the deep regional guilt feelings and alibi psychology that so many writers found endemic to the region, now head for the pigeonholes of history. Southerners are no longer ashamed of their region. They have rejoined the Union.

In the process they have lost some of the things that once stood "as indisputable fact that the South was different . . . the one-horse farmer, one-crop agriculture, one-party politics, the sharecropper, the poll tax, the white primary, the Jim Crow car, the lynching bee." C. Vann Woodward, the distinguished modern-day historian of the South who compiled that list, added that it would "take a blind sentimentalist to mourn the passing" of those monuments to regional distinctiveness.

Quite to the contrary, thoughtful Southerners now tell one of a hope that their region may enrich the United States as a whole by sharing some of its finest qualities. Among these they list civility, a sense of place and community and family, and a feeling for the tragic side of history—values so lacking in the acquisitive and (hitherto) confident North. As Reese Cleghorn, one of the region's fine young writers, observed of Martin Luther King, Jr.: "With the end of old tyrannies, King thought the South might become a redemptive force ('black and white together') against the impersonal, mechanical, amoral forces of our time."

Yet as bright as all these prospects seem, the fact is that there is a dark underside to each, with yawning chasms between the vision and the reality. One must remember that in things material, intellectual, and spiritual, the South entered the years following World War II as a cripple. The region is now less crippled, but it is not yet whole. It is in transition still, and if the shore so dimly seen by Governor Ellis Arnall of Georgia in the 1940s is looming ever closer on the Southern horizon, the fact is that it has not yet been reached—and possibly may not be reached in this century at all. I think of the lines of a very *un*-Southern poet, Robert Frost: "I have promises to keep/And miles to go before I sleep."

The Black Syndrome

Starting with a trickle around the time of World War I, accelerating during the next World War, and then in a mighty flood, one of the greatest folk movements of history, black people have been leaving the Deep South. About 1.3 million went North during the 1940s, 1.2 million in the 1950s, and 1.1 million in the 1960s. In 1900 the population of the Deep South states was 47.3 percent Negro; by 1970, it was only 24.5 percent—6.2 million of the region's 25.2 million people. So if Southern blacks are dwindling so rapidly in comparative numbers, one asks, why make them today the focus of an investigation of the region?

The reason is offered by a native white Mississippian, writer John Osborne, who reflected the theme of scores of books about the South when he wrote: "Negroes in their bondage indelibly marked and molded the society that we call the 'white South.' Almost every quality and attitude that have set the South apart during the two centuries of slavery and the following century of substitutes for slavery may be traced in some degree—and often wholly—to the presence of the Negro." Lerone Bennett wrote: "Racism is the cornerstone of the Southern mystique." One can accept that assertion, I believe, even if one recognizes the richly diverse strands of Southern history brought out by historians like C. Vann Woodward—the fact that alongside the Bourbons there were always the independent yeomen whose systems ran back to Jacksonian democracy, and who became the Populists of the late 19th century, and that alongside the romantic mythos of the region and its garrison mentality there were unheralded Southerners who rightfully damned the North for the crassness and venality of its materialism in the Gilded Age that followed the Civil War. Yet no matter what intellectual bypaths one takes, the race question forever reappears. One reason is that white and black Southerners are so much two peas from the same pod.

An awareness is now dawning, William C. Havard wrote recently in *The Changing Politics of the South,*

> that such important Southern characteristics as love for elaborate rhetoric, an earthy, frontier sense of humor, the will for survival in the face of adversity, the manners of the regional inhabitants, and the hedonistic propensities of the "hell-of-a-fellow" frontier type are shared traits to which neither of the races can lay exclusive claim. And we well know that in the culinary arts, in folk music, and in the creation of the colorful, metaphoric, and highly expressive language of the South, the Negro has been extraordinarily creative.

Yet despite that close association, Havard noted, in the mid-1950s "one could still regularly encounter biblical, biological, and cultural arguments for the unalterable superiority of Caucasians to Negroes." There are undertones of the same in the South today. In 1973, when I gave a speech to the conservatively oriented South Carolina Medical Association, one of the physicians asked me if I denied the inherent intellectual inferiority of black people. But I needed only to refer him to the derisive laughter of his colleagues.

Various aspects of the Southern black and white story will be examined in each of the state chapters which follow—the familiar historic progression from the defense of slavery (which became a regional obsession, drowning out virtually all dissent after 1830), the Civil War itself, the infamous Black Codes, Reconstruction, and the sell-out of Southern Negroes stemming from the disputed Presidential election of 1876. The story continues with the restrictive state constitutions that blotted out the last vestiges of black voting around the turn of the century, the rise of Jim Crow, the Supreme Court's antisegregation decisions culminating in the 1954 *Brown* school case, the era of "massive resistance" and the South's sometimes violent reaction to the federal court orders, the modern-day civil rights movement, and the new liberties for Southern blacks guaranteed in the Civil Rights Acts of the 1950s and especially the 1960s.

The depths of the historic Southern race problem—a problem made national by the folk wanderings of our time—are familiar to most, and I need touch on them only lightly here. It is interesting to note that as late as the mid-1940s, John Gunther was obliged to look to a book by a non-American—*An American Dilemma: The Negro Problem and Modern Democracy,* by the Swedish social scientist Gunnar Myrdal—for an analysis of the broad reaches of the racial situation. It was not until 1941, for instance, that W. J. Cash's classic *Mind of the South* was published. Despite the earlier studies and cries of despair from sociologists like W. E. B. DuBois, Americans as a whole for more than 70 years had chosen to see no evil and hear no evil about the most outrageous blot on their professed democratic beliefs. Gunther himself provided in *Inside U.S.A.* a classic summary of the bestialities practiced on Southern blacks. But even he was taken in by the Southern myth that Reconstruction had been an unmitigated evil inflicted on the region by Northern carpetbaggers and by illiterate blacks. Later revisionist historians have shown that much good came from the Reconstruction governments, including the start of public education in the region, and that they were in fact almost entirely controlled by whites, not blacks.

One should stress that the caste system imposed on Southern Negroes—in their work, their recreation, their associations, their schools, and the places they could eat and sleep and even get a drink of water away from home—was deeply rooted in the history of the region. In fact, Southern whites viewed legally enforced segregation as morally right—a hangover of the earlier belief that slavery was right. The fear of black uprisings, the phenomenon of miscegenation, the concern for inviolate white Southern womanhood—all came down directly from antebellum days. And if the black man, as the codes of slavery had indicated, was something less than human, then even the most refined classes could look in the other direction when 3,441 lynchings were recorded in the South between 1882 and 1959. To their credit, a group of Southern women—the idealized but unheeded sex of the region—organized to fight lynchings in the 1920s. But Southern Senators and Representatives fought tooth and nail to block national anti-lynching legislation, just as they would fight anti-poll tax legislation, voting rights legislation, the opening up of public accommodations, school desegregation, open-housing legislation, and even in the 1970s, the proposed national family income maintenance plan that would have rescued millions of Southern blacks (and poor whites too) from the worst trough of poverty.

Who then can take credit for the climactic changes of the 1960s, the second Reconstruction? For years the groundwork had been laid by litigation filed by such groups as the NAACP Legal Defense and Education Fund (LDF) and the American Civil Liberties Union (ACLU).* The courts in turn responded—not only the Supreme Court but the local federal courts, presided over by judges who often risked ostracism in their own communities to do what they thought was right. Presidents (especially Lyndon Johnson) and Congress deserve great credit. One cannot overlook the role of the young Freedom Riders and other civil rights activists who ventured into the region, often in the face of severe physical danger, starting in the early '60s. But in the deepest sense, this 20th-century Reconstruction was the work of black Southerners themselves. The places where they did it now sound like the honor roll of some great war—Montgomery and Albany and St. Augustine and Birmingham and Selma and the March on Washington. Less heralded were the confrontations at hundreds of dusty crossroads and voting registrars' offices across the South, as black people put their jobs and homes, and even their lives, on the line. It was surely one of the most nobly conducted struggles for freedom in human history. And it was victorious.

One can wonder now if the Movement, as it came to be called, would have gathered the velocity, or had the integrity that it demonstrated, had

* The LDF, a separate body from the NAACP itself, was established in 1940 as the legal arm of the civil rights movement and in the following years won scores of vital cases. The important Supreme Court higher education and school desegregation decisions stemmed from litigation it filed, as well as important voting rights cases, striking down of Jim Crow statutes, and action to defend civil rights workers against illegal arrests, harassment, and violence. The ACLU, especially during the 1960s when Charles Morgan, Jr., headed its Atlanta office, concentrated on cases to desegregate juries, prison systems, and the whole administration of justice. It also took on countless voting rights cases, desegregation of public employment, and antiwar cases during the Vietnam conflict—on the theory, as Morgan put it, that "the war sapped creative energies that could have been applied to civil rights."

Martin Luther King, Jr., not been its leader. But the fact is that King was there, propelled by circumstances and his own eloquence to the forefront of the Montgomery bus boycott of 1955, never again to be a private man. He was a leader such as his people, South or North, had never had. He was of the black elite, but as Max Lerner noted, his roots were in the black folksoil. And he was also, to the roots of his being, a Southerner. He was a Christian preacher, a prophet in the deep Biblical tradition, in a region that had always professed its religious beliefs. That Baptist oratory—"I have a dream . . . I have a dream . . ."—was a recitation of the South, and his vision of the beloved community evoked a higher image of an age-old Southern value.

Even before King's death, as the Northern cities to which so many black people had fled erupted in flames and angry young blacks began to reject the leader's doctrine of nonviolence and his vision of an integrated nation, there was talk that King was passé, an anachronism in his own time. But as time went on, the black racism that some of the militants preached would prove to be as spiritually bankrupt as the white racism that preceded it. King did not need to resort to a hate-filled black power, because in his preachings and demonstrations he was the embodiment of black power—even while he insisted on keeping communication open with the larger culture of America. And it would be remembered that King was a legitimately prophetic figure beyond the cause of black liberation alone. He had proven it with his 1967 declaration at Riverside Church against the Vietnam War—a desperately lonely stand, even among his own colleagues of the civil rights movement, when he made it but a prophetic judgment that most of the nation in time would accept. And in the planning for the Poor People's Campaign in the last year of his life, King was kindling the fire of a militant coalition of the racially and economically and politically abused peoples of the land, a coalition cutting across race and class. One could say the idea was absurd—that blacks and Mexican-Americans and Indians and poor Appalachian whites (and in time King would surely have incorporated the women's liberation movement) could never coalesce. By the early 1970s, they had still not coalesced, but the idea, like the very idea of black freedom during the long years of oppression, lay glowing in the ashes, awaiting its time.

Of all the epitaphs written for King, my favorite is this one, penned for *New South* by his Morehouse College classmate, Samuel DuBois Cook:

> Martin Luther King, Jr., hungered and thirsted for justice, freedom, equality, dignity, and the beloved community. . . . He sought to moralize power struggles, phenomena, and relations. . . . He sought not to "do in" his enemies but to convert them into friends. "Love your enemies" is the most difficult, mind-jarring, ego-transcending, and revolutionary ethical imperative ever uttered. In earnest, Dr. King sought desperately to do just that. . . .
>
> His life made a *creative difference* in history, touching the longings of the human heart and aspirations of the human spirit. He inspired. He moved men, events, institutions, and forces. He led. He combined protest and affirmation, rebellion and solidarity, realism and idealism, power and morality, criticism and construction, vision and technique, love and militance. What a man!

Of course he was not perfect. The stories of his robust manhood were not all fiction. Many of his campaigns—especially in the North—were failures. A profound sadness came over him in the last months of his life, as the anger of the urban black seemed to engulf all else; there are those who say he yearned finally for his own death. Perhaps we are too close to King to see him in true perspective. But it does not seem extravagant to predict that when the history of these times is written, he will emerge as the man for all seasons, the Southerner of the century.

The 1960s did bring momentous change in the life of Southern blacks. Through the hand of the law, terrorism directed against black people was almost eradicated. The era of the rope and the fagot, the fire bombing and the casual racial murder, now passes into history. The Ku Klux Klan and its white-collar corollary, the Citizens Councils, are reduced to a shadow of their former influence.* The segregated bus, the segregated restaurant and rest-room and water fountain, the segregated hotel and motel and movie theater and park are all things of the past. White people no longer shrink from shaking hands with blacks, and blacks no longer have to make way on the sidewalks for white folks. Clerks in stores and banks now address blacks as "Mr." or "Miss" or "Mrs."—no longer by their first names—and many of those clerks are now black themselves. Blacks are finally being let in—and not in the condescending, paternalistic way of old—on the traditional courtesy and friendliness of Southern culture.

The color line remains in a few places—some doctors' waiting rooms, in many bars (not covered by the Civil Rights Act of 1964), and most shameful of all, still in some churches. But where the hand of the law can reach, segregation is dead. And the black has gained a new sense of self-respect—what Dr. King used to call "a new sense of somebodiness." By the end of the 1960s, Pat Watters wrote in *The South and the Nation*, "the civilization of the South was no longer undergirded by law that, in its deepest meaning—dehumanization of Negroes—was based on murder, based on the antithesis of the meaning of law and civilization. That was crucial. Southerners were free at last. They could struggle within the limit of law rather than against it for a just society." Watters, who has continuously felt the pulse of the Southern byways by travel through the region, told me he was especially impressed by what he saw of a new "casual desegregation—people working together in 10-cent stores and groceries and Dairy Queens, people who on both sides of the color line would never see themselves as integrationists. But they are—and they have more in common than the upper classes would with either one of them."

It took more than a decade and a half after the Supreme Court's *Brown* decision, but the dual school system of the South has been virtually terminated—just since the late 1960s, in fact. According to the federal government's own figures, integration is now further advanced in the South than in the North. The process has not been an easy one, even for the blacks it

* The Klan has been tamed not only by a newborn willingness of white law officers to protect black people, but because blacks in many areas have made it clear that violence inflicted on their brothers and sisters would be returned in kind.

was supposed to benefit. There have been countless reports, for instance, of perfectly adequate black schools being closed because whites are unwilling to attend them, of black principals being replaced by less qualified whites, and of every conceivable form of subtle and not-so-subtle discrimination in formally desegregated schools. There are many reports of black children being pushed out for "disciplinary" reasons, and of continuing substandard teaching and curricula. But the segregation academies, to which many whites fled, quickly hit a plateau in attendance, and a shortage of financial resources promises their demise in many communities. They may last the longest in counties with overwhelmingly black populations, or in cities with large-scale school busing to achieve integration. But the Gallup Poll showed a dramatic drop between the early '60s and a decade later in the number of white Southern parents objecting to sending their children to racially mixed schools. What was once unthinkable becomes commonplace, and in the wake of change in the law, attitudes change too. In the early '70s, as sociologists split deeply on the question of whether integration improved academic achievements, a Naples, Florida schoolteacher, Edna McA. Watts, commented: "In 13 years I have seen mutual suspicion and fear change into mutual understanding and tolerance. Bigotry among young Southerners is not merely no longer fashionable; it is socially unacceptable. That accomplishment alone should settle the question." And as discord and occasional violence wracked the schools in response to the final wave of desegregation around 1970, students in school districts across the South said that if parental interference would stop, they would find a way to work out racial tensions themselves.

Desegregation in Southern colleges and universities began earlier and has been highly visible because of the acceptance of black athletes on the football teams of once lily-white schools. Some of the university coaches have engaged in furious competition to snare the best black players—because they need them now if they hope to have winning teams. In a region that takes its football perhaps more seriously than any other in the country, integrated teams mark a huge social departure. The white universities still have a low percentage of blacks compared to the overall population, and the progress will probably remain slow for a number of years because of the vastly inferior basic education so many young black people were receiving up to the late '60s. But for the bright young blacks, the opportunity is there, as never before. One sad note is the plight of private black colleges in the South, which face ever more severe problems in raising enough money to hire faculty of sufficient caliber to assure an education of excellence for the next generation of Southern black leaders.

Of all the changes in the lot of Southern blacks, none may be so important as the newly guaranteed—and enforced—right to vote. For despite every frustration that Southern blacks may face, the ballot means that now, and in time to come, they will be true participants in deciding the shape of the society and their own fate.

In every Southern state, as we will note in the chapters which follow, the era of semielectoral freedom that black people enjoyed in the first postbellum decades was ended when the Bourbon and Populist forces decided to "cleanse" the system of abused and manipulated black votes. Between 1889 and 1902, all the states of the old Confederacy adopted new statutes or constitutions including such devices as the poll tax, increased residency requirements, literacy tests, and the famed "grandfather clause." The intent and effect of all was the same—to keep the black man away from the polls, insuring the continuance of an apartheid society.

Until the Supreme Court invalidated the white primary in 1944, there was not a single Deep South state in which as many as 10 percent of the voting-age Negroes were registered to vote. After that, blacks began to register in some numbers, especially in urban areas. But countless legal impediments remained, and in the rural countryside economic threats and physical violence were enough to hold the black vote to pitifully low levels. In 1958 the U.S. Commission on Civil Rights found 44 Deep South state counties in which not a single black person was registered. Almost invariably, these were also the counties in which Negroes formed a majority of the population, and their vote was feared the most by the white establishments. In 1960 only 5.2 percent of the voting-age blacks were registered in Mississippi, 13.7 percent in Alabama, and 15.6 percent in South Carolina. The highest figure was 38.9 percent in Florida.

The Civil Rights Acts of 1957, 1960, and 1964 made a start at obtaining the vote for broader masses of Southern blacks, and throughout the early '60s black and white civil rights activists were hard at work in the South, trying to break down the walls of official resistance to black voting. But it took the historic Voting Rights Act of 1965, which made literacy tests illegal in low-vote states and authorized federal voting examiners to order the registration of Negroes, to snap the spine of the old system. President Johnson signed the bill in August 1965, recalling that the first slaves landed at Jamestown in 1619.

> They came in darkness and chains. Today we strike away the last major shackle of those fierce and ancient bonds. . . . Today is a triumph for freedom as huge as any victory won on any battlefield. Today the Negro story and the American story fuse and blend.
>
> Let me say to every Negro in this country: You must register, you must vote. And you must learn, so your choice advances your interest and the interest of our beloved nation. Your future, and your children's future, depend upon it.

The major provisions of the 1965 Act were quickly applied to all the Deep South states except Arkansas and Florida, and even there the provisions establishing criminal penalties for interference with voting rights had an effect. The cumulative effect of the legislation and the registration campaigns of the 1960s in the Deep South States was nothing less than momentous—not only in expanding the black voter rolls but in prompting whites, largely in reaction, to increase their registration as well. And the payoff of the new black vote was quickly reflected in the election of blacks to government positions that had been in white hands since Reconstruction. In 1962 there had been fewer than 25 elected black officials in the entire South. But by 1968 there were 248, by 1970 there were 711, and by 1973 there were 1,144—of whom 809 were from the seven Deep South states.

	1960	*1968*	*1971**
Blacks Registered	740,965	1,784,000	2,054,138
Share of Voting-age Population	24.2%	58.4%	54.7%
Whites Registered	6,169,403	7,905,000	8,940,005
Share of Voting-age Population	64.6%	82.8%	74.4%
Black Share of Total Voter Pool	10.7%	18.4%	18.7%

* Percentages of voting-age persons registered in 1971 for both races were lower than 1968, largely because of addition of 18-to-20-year-olds to the potential voter pool.

One could easily belittle the black advances by pointing out that the number of offices won was still only one half of one percent of the elective posts in the region. And most of the Negro officials held quite minor offices—city council and school board posts in particular—with only 38 in the legislatures of the entire seven-state region and only one in the U.S. Congress. A large portion of those elected came from the 80 counties of the region with a black majority, and even then many of the overwhelmingly black counties were still electing all-white officer slates.* Only in a handful of large cities (Atlanta and New Orleans in particular) had blacks been strong enough to force the winning electoral coalitions to give them recognition. In 1970 the Nixon administration—responding to South Carolina's Strom Turmond and the other Dixie allies of its "Southern strategy"—had almost succeeded in stripping the Voting Rights Act of some of its strongest provisions. Even after that, the administration enforced the law in a very lackadaisical way, and especially in rural areas various economic pressures were still applied against blacks who sought to vote, and especially those who sought to become political leaders.

"Black involvement in the general policymaking process of the South is still minimal," George Esser, executive director of the Southern Regional Council, said in a 1973 interview. As an example, he pointed out that blacks were just beginning to get appointments to the state police forces of many Southern states. "It will take a generation after the first integration," he said, "for those black patrolmen to get up to where they are captains and majors of the patrol and influence or control its basic policy. The same is true for similar positions in state health and welfare agencies, and state economic development ventures." The effort of the Nixon administration to close down the Office of Economic Opportunity, and especially its community action programs, he said, would "take away from the black Southerner his major access to policy and administration."

Nevetheless, a vital change in tone had come over Deep South politics as a result of the '60s. John Lewis, director of the Voter Education Project and one-time president of the Student Nonviolent Coordinating Committee, traveled through all the region in the early '70s with Julian Bond, the Georgia

* Mississippi has the most black majority counties (24), followed by Georgia (21), South Carolina (12), and Alabama and Louisiana (9 each).

legislator, encouraging blacks to register and vote. (Bond subsequently organized the Southern Elections Fund to give campaign spending assistance to black candidates.) As a Freedom Rider in 1961, Lewis recalled, he had entered a state like Mississippi and quickly landed in jail. Those were the days when blacks attending rural voter registration meetings would be in mortal fear of a bombing or would be checked and harassed by the local police. But in 1971 the police were the picture of courtesy, and when Bond and Lewis appeared, police escorts were provided in many towns.

"I'll never forget Belzoni, Mississippi, in the heart of the Delta," Lewis said. "It had been a bad town—the place, for instance, where two NAACP officials were killed on the courthouse steps for voter registration activity back in the 1950s. Yet in the summer of 1971, Julian and I were talking in a church there when suddenly the center doors opened and a white man came up the center aisle. He walked straight up front, and he caught Julian on one hand and me by the other, and said, 'Welcome to Belzoni. You two young men are doing a fine job. You're a credit to your race. I'm the mayor of Belzoni.' That would have been unthinkable for any white official to do in Mississippi a few years ago." The explanation was quite simple: the mayor had put on a tie and walked into that sweltering little church at his dinnertime because he wanted to remain mayor, and he needed black votes to win.

The phenomenon of white officials and candidates addressing black groups and appealing for their votes, Lewis noted, was occurring all over the South. Where elections polarized along racial lines—as in George Wallace's 1970 campaign for governor of Alabama, and in many Mississippi races—the blacks were still generally on the losing end. Their political isolation was illustrated most dramatically in the 1968 and 1972 Presidential elections, when they voted overwhelmingly Democratic while the white majorities of the region were strongly for Wallace or Richard Nixon. But there were some races, including several governorship contests, in which the whites seemed to be picking their candidates on issues unrelated to race, so that the blacks could provide the winning edge for moderate candidates. (Many of those moderate white contenders, in fact, might never have gotten into politics at all before the black vote began to "open up" the political process in the region.) Southern executives elected with black support were showing an increasing willingness to consult blacks on policy decisions and to appoint blacks to policymaking boards and commissions. The "nigger-nigger" talk had almost vanished from the region's political rhetoric; instead it was now fashionable for white (and black) candidates to talk of representing "all the people." The election of blacks from predominantly white constituencies was still quite rare—but it was beginning, with the congressional victory, for example, of former Southern Christian Leadership Conference leader Andrew Young from Atlanta in 1972, and even with the election of a few blacks on a city- and countywide basis in Birmingham, Alabama, a city once considered the very embodiment of last-ditch white resistance.

John Lewis noted that there are many writers, black intellectuals, and campus observers who "say that the civil rights movement is dead—perhaps never really existed, and that all the effort really didn't pay off." But when one travels the South, he said—not just the cities, but also the rural areas and small towns—the real fruits of the movement are apparent. "It's not only the changes in the number of people elected, in the breakdowns of barriers in public accommodations and desegregation, or in better jobs for blacks," he said. "It is also the change of attitude, among both blacks and whites. There is a new, recognized sense of black dignity and pride. In many Southern communities you see blacks and whites working together in plants, in poverty projects and the like. In the black communities of states like Mississippi and Alabama, and in south Georgia, you see some of the same people who were involved in 1961 or 1965 still at work today. You may not have the drama of a march from Selma to Montgomery, but you still have the people there. If the movement did nothing more than bring people together and create some viable, ongoing political unit, I think it succeeded."

Many of the black people involved in Southern politics today, Lewis said, "see their involvement in politics as a direct extension of the civil rights movement—they really don't separate the two." Most of the local black groups, he said, are operating without much help from regional or national organizations. The Southern Christian Leadership Conference (SCLC) which Martin Luther King, Jr., founded, seemed about to expire in 1973 when his successor, Ralph David Abernathy, almost resigned with a complaint that blacks who came to occupy "high positions made possible through our struggles" would not support the organization financially. The real reasons, however, seemed to go deeper. During the 1960s SCLC and other components of "the movement" had gone after highly visible targets of segregation or discrimination, and there had been a brilliant clarity about the goals, and real momentum in reaching them. By the 1970s, it was becoming more difficult for blacks—and particularly young blacks—to feel the breeze of momentum in their faces. As H. Brandt Ayers, a Lamar Society leader, pointed out, "the targets are no longer so obvious and neither is the cure so readily at hand." Sophisticated strategies, based on an understanding of complex political and economic factors, were necessary to attack problems like the formation of Southern urban ghettos. But that would take time and patience, and there was real danger that the young blacks graduating from Southern colleges and entering leadership roles in the '70s might not have that patience.

If the eclipse of the SCLC was understandable, it was still regrettable, for there were still so many Southern black communities without real leadership or self-awareness.

The SCLC was not the only Southern rights group that faced problems in the transition from the '60s to the '70s. The Southern Regional Council, a biracial group formed in 1944 to ameliorate the region's racial problems, underwent a crisis of leadership with the resignation of its longtime executive director, Paul Anthony. But by 1972 it seemed back on the track under George Esser, former Southern representative of the Ford Foundation. Out of the 100 Southern leaders who make up the council, Esser formed task forces on economic development, housing, education, and health care. The objective was to get a comprehensive picture of the state of the South, on which Southerners can base action for change, continuing the organization's longtime focus on the plight of blacks and poor people in the region.

Despite the growing urbanization of the South, Esser said in an interview, the focus of the worst social and economic problems its black people face is in the rural regions. In a typical Deep South state like Georgia, rural whites have a per capita income of $2,500—80 percent of the national average. For rural blacks, the figure is about $980—only 30 percent of the average for all Americans. The rural South of the Mississippi Delta and the Alabama and Georgia and South Carolina black belts, John Egerton wrote, refutes the shining image of a "New South." Here, he noted, "countless sharecropper shanties and migrant labor camps and backwoods towns, voiceless poverty and relentless white supremacy are still the norm." One finds rural discrimination against blacks in every conceivable field—economics, education, social services, the administration of justice. It is simply a way of life there. And especially on the economic front, it may get even worse in the next years as the continued mechanization of agriculture forces more hundreds of thousands of black people onto the welfare rolls, or into the cities, or out of the region altogether.

As for the Congress on Racial Equality, another battler in the rights fights of the '60s, it was not working much in the South by the early '70s. SNCC passed out of existence in the late '60s—a victim of its own irrelevance to Southern black ways of thinking when it abjured the principle of nonviolence embodied in its name, ousting Lewis as its president and installing Stokely Carmichael in his stead. That left two other really viable regional civil rights groups—the daddy of them all, the NAACP, with its roots into thousands of Southern communities, and the Voter Education Project. The VEP broke off from its parent, the Southern Regional Council, because of a change in the tax laws, but it remained remarkably vital. Over the years, it funded hundreds of indigenous groups for voter registration—135 in 1972 alone, the largest financial investment of any year in its history. Its work remains cut out for it, because in 1973 there were still 1.5 million unregistered voting age blacks in the Deep South—the majority of them in rural counties, most lacking the rudiments of a decent education.

There have been a few signs of hope for rural Southern blacks in recent years, including the development (often by people out of the civil rights movements) of a handful of farming or handcraft cooperatives that free the blacks from economic control of the local white power structure. Through Head Starts and many other projects, the much-maligned federal poverty programs brought help and interest where none had been before. Some state governments—even in Mississippi—are working on programs to help rural blacks economically. But all such efforts, federal and state alike, are still minor compared to the need. And the Deep South states still have to live with the truism that Alabama's young attorney general, Bill Baxley, uttered about his own state, but which is applicable across the region—that until black people can be brought into the mainstream, "socially and economically," then there is no hope of getting the South back into the real national economic mainstream. Alabama's high level of poverty, Baxley said, can be traced to policies and customs denying opportunities to blacks. "One way to keep a man down in a ditch is to get down there with him," Baxley observed. (Wittingly or not, Baxley was paraphrasing the words of Booker T. Washington: "You can't hold a man down without staying down with him.")

Are Southerners about to climb out of that ditch, black hand in white? There are many reasons to discount the possibility. In the one area where the South was always less segregated than the North—residential housing—there is heavy evidence that the old salt-and-pepper pattern is giving way to the familiar Northern phenomenon of black center cities surrounded by white suburban collars. "Legalized segregation and overt racism may be over," Egerton noted, "but what remains is a style and pace and form of white advantage—a more sophisticated racism—that differs little from South to North to West."

Yet with amazing frequency, one hears the opinion in the South that the region may be able to overcome its racial problems more rapidly than the North. John Osborne spoke of the South's "racial realism" and quoted the late Whitney M. Young, Jr., executive director of the National Urban League, as saying: "If most of the South has a farther way to go than the rest of America, I believe that it is at least going there quicker." A vital sign may be the small countermigration of blacks to the South, first noted in the late '60s. It was limited largely to college-educated, urbane young blacks—coming back, as John Lewis noted, "because of the significant changes in the social, economic, and political climate of the region." Any mass countermigration, he said, would have to await more radical changes in the Southern climate, and it seemed certain that for years it would be less numerically than the continued northward flow of ill-educated, low-income blacks. But for talented young blacks, the South for the first time offered decent jobs and a way to live in dignity; as more of them stayed (or returned), the black leadership of the region would be immensely enriched.

The proposition that "the solution of the race problem will eventually come out of the South" was put most convincingly to me by Gedney Howe, a Charleston, South Carolina lawyer of unusually keen perceptions:

> The Southerner admitted he hated "niggers." Northerners loved blacks only collectively, not individually. Discrimination in the South was total and absolute in every area—but no one ever claimed it was otherwise. In the North, the claim was that blacks were humans. But after that assertion, there was systematic exclusion. One example of that has been the built-in discrimination in the labor unions of the North. But now watch the explosion of skilled Negroes in the South—without built-in unionization to stop their great skills.
>
> Because the civilization and national culture of the nation passed this region by, it was left in a more primitive, uneducated state. And thus it is equipped to make its necessary revolution. The South has enough Negroes to force it to do its thing right. And the result will be a big, viable black culture, as part of the whole.

The South in Congress

"I believe," Harry Truman wrote in his *Memoirs*, "that if [Richard] Russell had been from Indiana or Missouri or Kentucky he may very well have been President of the United States." But he never had a serious chance, Truman said, because he came from Georgia, "where the race issue was so heated." After Russell's death, Richard Nixon echoed the same opinion; others described the patrician Russell as a Senatorial analogue of Robert E. Lee. Friend and foe agreed that in his milieu, the United States Senate, Russell was virtually unmatched in his grasp of parliamentary tactics, of rules and traditions. He played the role of mentor and tutor to several decades of Senators and did more than the world ever knew to start Lyndon Johnson on his road to greatness.

But if the best of the old South—gentility, a noble bearing, a deep sense of honor—were at the core of Richard Russell, so was the worst: an inflexible, everlasting opposition to the cause of equal rights for the black man. Russell was the masterful, often cunning field general of the Southern Senators who met in his office to plan their fights against every bill to aid the Negro, from the anti-lynching bills of the 1940s to the climactic civil rights statutes of the 1960s. He refused to desert his Democratic party to be the Dixiecrat Presidential candidate of 1948, and he never descended to the racial demagoguery of some other politicians of his region. Yet he opposed the civil rights bills, historic in their redemption of the American principle of equality, not only out of duty to the opinion of his constituents but with passion and whole heart. In the end he became bitter, complaining that "the times have passed me by" and speaking of "treason" and "appeasement" on the race issue, promising "they will find me in the last ditch." Thus, one Capitol Hill reporter noted, he was not really so much the martyr to geography as "a victim to his prejudices."

The death of Richard Russell in 1971 symbolized the beginning of the end of one of the most remarkable eras of regional dominance in American congressional history. Reelected in good years and bad, outliving politically their colleagues from more fickle Northern constituencies, absolute masters of their legislative specialties, the Southerners rose to control a majority of all the committee chairmanships in Congress and to impress their views on the laws of the nation.

At this writing, several of this "magnificent breed" still occupy the cockpits of power on Capitol Hill. But as correspondent Richard L. Strout of the *Christian Science Monitor* has noted, the fact that seven or eight members of the old Southern caucus still head committees simply "makes them as conspicuous as the last tall pines left at the top while the loggers level the forest below." And it is not only a possibility but an inevitability that most of the remaining patriarchs will fall in the next few years, ending the South's unique power in Congress for years to come.

The reason lies in the actuarial tables. Of the eight remaining Senate committee chairmen from the states of the Old Confederacy, six will be more than 70 years of age when (and if) they face the voters again. And instead of Southerners, one finds Northerners—men like Edmund Muskie of Maine, Philip Hart of Michigan, and William Proxmire of Wisconsin, elected as liberals during the '50s and early '60s—standing behind them on the seniority ladder. Not a single Deep South Democrat is left who entered the Senate between December 1948 and November 1966—a seniority gap of 252 years cumulative service which, in Kevin Phillips' words, "must exclude the South from major Senate power by the end of the 1970s."

For example, six Northerners, led by Proxmire, follow 74-year-old John Sparkman of Alabama on the Banking Committee. Nine of the next 10 Democrats after 76-year-old John L. McClellan of Arkansas on the Appropriations Committee come from the North, led by Washington's Warren G. Magnuson. Just behind Mississippi's John Stennis, 72, on Armed Services, are Stuart Symington of Missouri and Henry M. Jackson of Washington. Jackson or Muskie would follow North Carolina's Sam J. Ervin, Jr., 76, as chairman of Government Operations. Hart is next in line behind three aging Southerners on the Judiciary Committee—Chairman James O. Eastland, 69, of Mississippi, McClellan, and Ervin. Sparkman is next in line behind 68-year-old J. W. Fulbright of Arkansas on Foreign Relations, but the next six men are Northerners.

When those patriarchs finally relinquish their seats, the South's Senate chairmanships will probably number only two—Russell B. Long of Louisiana, now 55, chairman of the Finance Committee, and Herman Talmadge of Georgia, 60, head of the Agriculture Committee. It will be a great comedown from 1960, when 11 of the 17 major committee chairmen in the Senate were Southerners. And Republicans are likely to benefit, because they will no longer confront the old argument that retaining Democrats in the South's Senate and House seats is necessary to preserve the region's unique congressional power.

In 1973 Southerners still held 11 of the 23 committee chairmanships in the House. But the region's hold on the powerful Rules Committee, circumscribed by reforms in the '60s, was finally ended with the retirement of Mississippi's William M. Colmer in 1972. Several of the remaining Southern chairmen are over 70, including F. Edward Hébert of Louisiana, head of Armed Services. The two key money committees are chaired by men in their mid-60s—Arkansas' Wilbur Mills of Ways and Means, and Texas' George Mahon of Appropriations. But committee chairmen in general are likely to be less powerful in the years to come, as the Speaker and the Democratic Caucus gain more power over the shape and flow of legislation. By the 1970s the hard core of Southern conservatives numbered no more than 50, about half the figure of a decade before. The growing Republican vote, the influence of blacks on Southern elections, and finally congressional redistricting that broke up the old Southern rural redoubts under "one-man, one-vote" rules had all taken their toll.

If the Southern Congressmen were all conservatives today, and could act as a body, it would theoretically be possible for them to switch en masse to the Republican party, making the GOP the majority in both houses of Congress, presumably making a deal to preserve their remaining committee chairmanships in the process. But in fact the region's men in Washington are no longer the definable, conservative bloc they once were. In 1973, in fact, Northern and Southern Democrats were acting in unusual unison to stem the abuses of power—ranging from impounded funds to the Watergate scandal—practiced by the Nixon administration. Civil rights were no longer the burning issue, because the South knew the landmark bills of the '60s would never be repealed, and because Northerners were as perplexed by problems such as school busing as their Southern brethren.

Thus Southern Congressmen move into the national mainstream, and as the old prejudices and regional peculiarities fade, there is reason to believe that a modern-day Richard Russell or "New South" governor, riding the crest of his times instead of fighting a rear-guard action, might become President.

Deep South Politics

No region of America has had politics as complex and perplexing as those of the South. Before the Civil War, there was a fairly clear division—the planter-merchant classes, gathered in the Whig party, who defended slavery with the most fervor, and the rugged white yeomen of the Dixie uplands, whose political loyalties had been formed by the great champion of the plain man on the frontier, Andrew Jackson, and who had little personal stake in the system of slavery. After the war, it would have been logical for the Bourbon Democrats, as most of the old Whig classes came to be known, to form one party and for the poor agrarian masses (white and black alike) to form another. And at times there were indications that might happen. The early Populists wanted to form an alliance of the dispossessed of both races, a vision held by Georgia's Tom Watson in the early 1890s: "You are made to hate each other because upon that hatred is rested the keystone of the arch of financial despotism which enslaves you both. You are deceived and blinded that you may not see how this race antagonism perpetuates a money system which beggars you both."

But it was not to be, because of the success the Bourbons had in manipulating a controlled black vote. Watson and many of the other Populists ended up being the most rabid racists of all. And so, since it was unthinkable (except in a few hill counties which had resisted Confederate conscription the most vigorously) to join the hated Republicans, all the energies and competition were channeled into one party—the Democratic. The South developed a one-party (or really no-party) politics on the state and local level, a kind of stultifying experience in which the voters rarely comprehended the essential issues before them, elections centered on personalities and voting for "friends and neighbors," and the "have-nots" ended up on the short end of the stick.

The emphasis on personalities did have its lighter side. Journalists Reg Murphy and Hal Gulliver wrote:

Why has the South always had such colorful political characters? . . . The answer, of course, is that politics always has been the favorite parlor game of the South. It was expected to be the entertainment, the conversation piece of men's minds, the whatnot that piqued the imagination, the curio that rescued the evening from dullness. Long before electronic entertainment, in the winter days between the time the harvest was home and the rise of the new sap, the political personalities filled the conversation. They became legends, as did Pitchfork Ben Tilden in South Carolina, the Longs in Louisiana, Theodore Bilbo in Mississippi, Kissin' Jim Folsom in Alabama, the Talmadges in Georgia, . . . and a string of others that stretched out to a point where the memory of man runneth not to the contrary.

Most such characters are gone now, though a younger Talmadge still represents Georgia in the Senate, two Longs still represent Louisiana, and the names of George Wallace and Lester Maddox may win niches in Southern folklore. Yet even in a less flamboyant age than that of the old demagogues, Murphy and Gulliver observed, the memory of them (at least for some whites) "assuages and comforts and planes the rough edges of change and future shock."

Change and shock have indeed visited the South in recent years, disrupting the ancient political patterns with final consequences that we can see only dimly. Georgia historian Numan Bartley assembled a list of the factors that gave the South its political distinctiveness, and it is interesting to note that each is now far less salient than before:

- Slavery, defeat in war, and Reconstruction—phenomena now receding far into history.
- A staple-crop economy—gone with the fall of King Cotton.
- Poverty—still serious but being ameliorated.
- Ruralism—fading with the rush to the cities.
- An overwhelmingly Anglo-Saxon white population, Protestantism, and fundamentalist beliefs—all reduced in importance by the movement of non-Southerners into the region and Southerners' exposure through television and military service and travel to other American cultures.
- *De jure* racial segregation—now, for all intents and purposes, a dead letter.
- "Most of all, the persistent white concern for the maintenance of white supremacy in the social order"—now a lost battle, as most Southerners know.

We should also note that malapportionment, the handmaiden of Negro disenfranchisement in the old order, has also toppled because of federal court decisions since the early '60s. The old rotten boroughs were citadels of Bourbon strength. They were broken up under a drumfire of court orders, and as a result many more urban legislators, almost uniformly more moderate in their political outlook, were sent to the state capitols. Now the region is undergoing a "second wave" of reapportionment in which the courts have been ordering election of legislators on a single-member-district basis instead of the countywide system in urban areas preferred by the ruling Democratic establishments. The inevitable result is the election of more blacks and more Republicans, further undermining the conservative politics of the old one-party South.

It is interesting to note that the conservatism of the Bourbon Democrats notwithstanding, the South (except for race matters) was on a rather liberal course during the Depression years of the '30s and indeed clear up to 1950. A great have-not region gladly welcomed TVA, the agricultural reforms of New Deal days, and indeed all the federal programs that poured money into the area. Public opinion polls taken during the '30s showed Southerners more likely than residents of any other region of the country to classify themselves as "liberals" rather than "conservatives." Southern Congressmen led the fight for many of the New Deal reforms. And in the first postwar years, many progressive young war veterans returned to the South to topple corrupt old courthouse rings.

The liberal trend came to a screeching halt when Presidents, starting with Harry Truman, began to take an active interest in the plight of the American Negro. In a region that had habitually given astronomical percentages to Democratic Presidential candidates, the 1948 Dixiecrat movement led by South Carolina's Strom Thurmond presaged the political demise of progressive Southern leaders like Florida's Claude Pepper and Alabama's James Folsom. The Southerners in Congress seemed to lose interest in liberal legislation, putting their first priority on defending their region's racial caste system against outside interference.

For the Republicans, the erstwhile pariahs of Southern politics, the moment of golden opportunity seemed to have arrived. With Dwight Eisenhower leading their Presidential ticket in 1952 and 1956, and Richard Nixon in 1960, they expanded their beachhead from their old pockets of strength in the Appalachian and Ozark mountains to win support of high proportions of voters in the growing cities and suburbs of the South. They failed to win any Deep South state except Louisiana in 1956, however, and their showing on the local level was still dismal. Even after the 1962 elections, they still held only two U.S. House seats in the Deep South—both in Florida—and not a single Senate seat or governorship. Their winnings in the state legislatures and county courthouses were extremely minimal.

It was then that the Republicans first adopted their famed "Southern strategy." Abandoning civil rights in the name of states rights, Barry Goldwater in 1964 got virtually unanimous support from Dixie's delegations to that year's Republican National Convention and then went on to sweep every Deep South state except Arkansas and Florida. Even in those states, he won a majority of the white vote; in fact, for the first time in history, the Republican party seemed to be the "traditionalist" party of the South, led by a man perceived as the candidate of the Southern white man. It is interesting to note that while Goldwater swept the Deep South cities—working-class districts and affluent suburbs alike—his most startling majorities were in the lowland counties, the ancient Bourbon strongholds. Yet the 1964 election underscored the deep division between the Deep South and the rest of the country, because except for Goldwater's own Arizona, there was not one other state that went Republican for President that year.

But the Republican breakthrough failed to go much beyond the Presidential level. The party did pick up five U.S. House seats in Alabama, and one each in Georgia and Mississippi, but the region's House total was still

44–9 in favor of the Democrats, and one still needed a magnifying glass to find Republicans in the legislatures. Local Republicans who ran on a Goldwater-type platform in the following midterm elections of 1966 were equally disappointed, and in 1968 Alabama's George Wallace was able to carry every Deep South state except South Carolina and Florida—seeming proof that the switch was away from the national Democrats, not necessarily to the Republicans.

A new and more refined "Southern strategy" was in the making, however. It was forged, Murphy and Gulliver wrote in a book of that very name, when

> Richard Milhous Nixon, now President of the United States, sat in a motel room in Atlanta in the early spring of 1968 and made his political deal. Senator Strom Thurmond of South Carolina was there.* And there were others. The essential Nixon bargain was this:
>
> "If I'm President of the United States, I'll find a way to ease up on the federal pressures forcing school desegregation—or any other kind of desegregation." Whatever the exact words or phrasing, this was how the Nixon commitment was understood by Thurmond and other Southern GOP strategists.

Thurmond himself gave me six points he said were covered in the Atlanta meeting: Nixon's agreement to maintain "a strong military establishment," "to try and stop the big spending in Washington and deficit spending and use the veto if necessary to do that," a new emphasis on the rights of the states with "a stop to shifting all the power to Washington," a cutback on the growth of foreign textile imports, support for "freedom of choice" school plans and opposition to school busing, and finally "the appointment of strict constructionists to the Supreme Court." Nixon, Thurmond said, expected that his "greatest achievement as President" would be the appointment of "sound judges who would support a strict construction of the Constitution."

The Nixon pledge enabled Thurmond to turn back the appeal of California's Ronald Reagan, to whom the heart of many Southern Republicans belonged, and to win for Nixon 128 of the 176 Deep South votes at that year's Republican National Convention. Nixon immediately showed his gratitude by selecting Spiro Agnew, a man who was to prove very popular in the South, as his running mate. And as early as 1969, the vision of the South as the cornerstone of an *Emerging Republican Majority* in American politics was formulated in a book of that name by Kevin P. Phillips, a onetime aide in the Nixon Administration's Justice Department.

There is no doubt that Nixon, once installed in office, tried to carry out the pledge he had made to Thurmond in that Atlanta hotel room. White Southerners were made to feel, for the first time in many years, that their feelings were being taken into full account by a national administration. To the extent that Nixon and his Attorney General, John Mitchell, felt they could get away with it, enforcement of the civil rights laws and federal court desegregation orders was hamstrung. (Ironically, the most sweeping

* Thurmond had abandoned the Democratic party in 1964, announcing his conversion to "the Goldwater Republican party."

school desegregation was achieved during Nixon's first term—but the courts were chiefly responsible, and the President certainly wanted to take no credit for it.) The President tried to appoint two Southerners to the Supreme Court, but when the Senate in its wisdom rejected them, the President called Mitchell to his side to claim that it had been an "act of regional discrimination" against the South.*

By 1972, Nixon had refined his strategy with the use of antiblack code words including "forced busing" and "quotas." The Deep South was his with a stunning 74 percent of its vote. But one could argue whether the race issue was more than one contributing factor in his Deep South victory, because he also won impressive victories across the country, including states with minuscule black populations.

The Nixon landslide was disappointing to Southern Republicans who had hoped to ride into office on his coattails. For the first time in the 20th century, Republicans held at least one U.S. House seat in each Deep South state—but Democrats still outnumbered them, 41 to 14. Vigorous Republican Senate bids failed in states like Georgia and Alabama, and the GOP still held not a single governorship in the region, having lost the two it held for four years in the '60s—Florida and Arkansas—in the 1970 elections. The cumulative state legislature total for the region was 1,019 Democrats to only 131 Republicans, a GOP advance over the 1,158-to-12 Democratic lead in 1962 but still a disappointing record after so many years of serious Republican effort. County courthouses under Republican control were still a rarity, though the party did hold some important mayoralties (usually won in nonpartisan elections).

There is no question of the *need* for a viable two-party system in the South. Frank Rose has stated that the lack of two-party competition has reduced the pressure on national party leaders to distribute patronage in the region. With a legitimate two-party system, Rose pointed out,

> The general elections, formerly empty ceremonies, are transformed into battlefields of political philosophies, and the voter's sense of participation in government is heightened when he has a chance. Minority opinion becomes more significant in formulating platforms, and interest groups are more evenly balanced. Officials become more conscious of their responsibility to all interests rather than just to those which were fortunate enough to carry the primaries, because promises in a two-party system have to be backed up by performance.

There is also reason to believe that Republicanism will gradually rise in the South, because of the region's traditional social conservatism. Numan Bartley and Hugh Davis Graham wrote in a 1973 book on Southern politics that

> Time and logic, if not the South's tenacious historical legacy, appear to favor the GOP's Southern strategy, as do particularly such explosive racial issues as bus-

* The first appointee, Clement F. Haynsworth of South Carolina, had been rejected ostensibly because as an appeals court judge he had sat on cases linked with his own financial dealings. The second, G. Harrold Carswell of Florida, went down because of a mediocre judicial record and past antiblack statements. In selecting his Southern court nominees, Nixon deliberately avoided selecting any of a group of Eisenhower appointees—Elbert Tuttle of Georgia, Frank M. Johnson, Jr., of Alabama, or John Minor Wisdom of Louisiana—who had shown outstanding skills as jurists and been on the firing line and suffered grievous personal attacks because they chose to enforce the Constitution in ending desegregation. Any one of them would probably have been confirmed by the Senate with ease.

ing, which provoke emotional responses from whites pretty much regardless of socio-economic station or even region, and seem so ideally if not cynically designed to link Southern and Northern whites in a reenactment of the compromise of 1877 that terminated the first Reconstruction.

But are social backlash issues the bedrock on which Southern Republicanism can grow over the long haul? They have, to be sure, been used in a majority of the party's Southern campaigns of the '60s and early '70s. But a great majority of those campaigns failed, as Republicans discovered that they could not be more segregationist than the old Dixie Democrats, or found that the emerging black vote was providing the margin of victory for their opponents. A minority of successful Southern Republicans, ranging from the late Winthrop Rockefeller of Arkansas, a moderate, to Congressman Jack Edwards of Alabama, a strong fiscal conservative, have identified racism as a suicidal course for the party. Even Strom Thurmond and Harry Dent, chief architects of the GOP Southern strategy, have said since 1970 that the Republicans must find a way to get a share of the Negro vote. Without it, Southern GOP candidates start at a severe disadvantage because they must win not just a plurality, but a huge majority of the white vote each time they expect to win. To develop a strong, permanent party base, Southern Republicans may be forced to abjure racism and return to a slower but perhaps surer strategy akin to that of the Eisenhower Southern Republicans in the '50s: combining the small but traditional GOP vote in the rural hill counties with the party's new base in the cities and suburbs, where the party's fiscal conservatism has the most appeal. Party building would also proceed apace in the "black belt" and coastal counties, but the GOP would not rely on the virulent racism of those areas to effect dramatic breakthroughs.

To date, most Republican Southern victories have been built "from the top down"—starting with President, then to the congressional and finally to the legislative level. A mature Southern GOP may have to reverse the process, working much harder at the grass roots. In each election, hundreds of Democratic officeholders still go unopposed in the South. Yet in the words of elections expert Frederick H. Sontag, coauthor of *Parties: The Real Opportunity for Effective Citizen Politics*, "Running candidates for all offices is a prerequisite of building a strong party. Even when a first-time victory is unlikely, vulnerable incumbents have their records challenged and the minority party builds up a cadre of experienced potential officeholders and campaign workers, thus enhancing its future prospects."

The 1972 elections did leave open the question of why the Republicans were able to do so well at the Presidential level but continued to show such meager results in state and local races. There seemed to be a dichotomy in Southern voters' minds. It was acceptable to turn one's back on the national Democratic party in Presidential voting, especially as that party became identified as the party of white liberalism and black interests. The Dixiecrats of 1948 had established the new independence, which was reinforced by the Goldwater, Wallace, and Nixon victories in the region. In local races, on the other hand, a century of Democratic voting left the habit still deeply ingrained. A "Georgia Democrat" or "Mississippi Democrat" did not seem as threatening as a Hubert Humphrey or a George McGovern. The personal ties between the county courthouse rings and the statewide officeholders and the veteran Southern Democrats in Congress all lent stability and continuity to the Democratic party on the state and local level. Most local Democratic contenders in the South managed to avoid the liberal and integrationist tags put on the party's Presidential candidates. Those who did get labeled lost to other Democrats in the George Wallace or Lester Maddox mold, or Republicans like Strom Thurmond and Florida's Claude Kirk. But as the '70s approached, more and more middle-of-the-road Democrats were avoiding that fate. And where elections did not polarize along racial lines, there was an opportunity for the black vote and the small liberal white vote, which was submerged in Presidential races, to occupy a swing position.

Another factor was at work in the elections of the late '60s and early '70s when a widely heralded group of "New South" Democratic governors—men like Reubin Askew of Florida, Dale Bumpers of Arkansas, Edwin Edwards of Louisiana, Jimmy Carter of Georgia, and John West of South Carolina—were elected. Like voters all across the country, Southerners were becoming disillusioned with traditional politics and hackneyed politicians. Without being terribly specific about issues, the new Democrats managed to project themselves as moderate modern-day Populists who would be responsive to the broad masses of the people. Jimmy Carter, after mentioning the hundreds of thousands of hands he had shaken in his prolonged campaign for the Georgia governorship, explained it this way:

> A few years ago the common practice for someone who sought the governorship was to go into a courthouse and speak privately in the back room to the sheriff or judge—or perhaps to go and talk to the local banker, or on a few occasions to the editors. If their reaction was satisfactory, perhaps on election day the votes for that county could be delivered.
>
> That time is gone. This change began when Andrew Young and Martin Luther King and others demonstrated their concept of a new freedom by speaking out for rights which they had lost or never had, and the public heard them, and inequities were corrected. Later on, students did the same thing. And then the peanut farmers and the filling station operators and the taxicab drivers—and all of them may not have agreed with the goals or motivation or the philosophy of the demonstrators—began to say, "If they can exert their influence on government, why can't I?" And there has evolved in the last few years a new impact on public officials of those who were either previously inarticulate or afraid or reticent.

One sensed something quite quixotic about those popular pressures, however—a question of how durable they would be, and whether they would be sidetracked onto racial issues like school busing or begin to focus on the real problems of the South.

Nothing very revolutionary occurred in the region's state governments after the new breed Democrats took office. One looked in vain for rapid action to deal with the problems so well defined by George Esser, executive director of the Southern Regional Council—"issues such as genuine tax reform in a region that taxes the poor much more heavily than the rich, the consequences of land and water exploitation as the price for development, the consequences of a pattern of land ownership that features increasing ownership by corporations and decreasing ownership by individuals who need land as a resource for development, indeed the consequences of an economy that can distribute 43 percent of the region's wealth to the top 20 percent and only 4.5 percent to the bottom 20 percent."

Nevertheless, a subtle but very important change was taking place. The new governors, unlike some of their predecessors, were at least *aware* of the region's problems, and in small ways almost all of them began to chip away at the problems. In practically every one of the states they governed, some amelioration of the inequitable tax burden was begun. More blacks than ever before were being appointed to high posts in state governments. And efforts to revamp the outmoded and unwieldy state governments were underway practically everywhere. Compared to many (but certainly not all) Northern governments, those of the South still seemed mired in a past era. But compared to where the same states had stood just a few years before, the change was nearly miraculous. So in evaluating the South's progress, one is again confronted with the quandary: should one say that the glass is half empty, or that it is half full?

Among those for whom it is still quite empty—the poor of both races—the vision of a radical Populism has never quite died. It remains a distinct possibility in a "postracial" South, and there are glimmerings of it in movements like the alliance of destitute black and white woodcutters in southern Mississippi and Alabama. A revitalized labor union movement in the South, or perhaps the leadership furnished by the modern-day wave of cause-oriented lawyers and community organizers, might provide the focus needed. Populism has always needed *bêtes noires* to attack, and in this case the targets could be the banks, utilities, and monster corporations. But the odds against a quick mobilization of the South's underprivileged people—who themselves share much of the region's social conservatism—appear formidable indeed. It has to start at the grass roots, and as Luther Munford, a young Mississippian, has written, "community organization is not going to be accomplished in a 'Freedom Summer' or a VISTA sabbatical from Scarsdale; organizing a community will take a lifetime."

Class conflict has been endemic to Populism in its past incarnations, and there are many Southern leaders now who would like to effect change in their region in a less disruptive manner. They banded together in 1969 to form what may be the prototypal organization of the present-day New South, the L. Q. C. Lamar Society.* Its membership, according to Ayers, an Anniston, Alabama newspaper publisher and one of the founders, "is composed of the same intellectual, professional, and opinion-making ele-

* Lucius Quintus Cincinnatus Lamar was a firebrand for secession in antebellum Mississippi who later became a spokesman for reconciliation between the races in the South and an Associate Justice of the U.S. Supreme Court. The Lamar Society founders may have been remiss in their historic research when they decided to name their organization after him, however. Lamar was one of the conservative Bourbon Democrats who wanted the Negro to vote to withstand the inroads of the radically-inclined poor whites. They abhorred the Negrophobia of the lower-class whites because Negroes posed no threat to them, and because they viewed Negro-baiting as tasteless and crude. But they did believe that the Negro was inherently inferior.

ments which legitimized the original Progressive movement." Governors, Congressmen, university presidents and professors, lawyers and editors, business leaders and representatives of both races, are included. The organization decided early on not to be involved in actual election contests but to focus on an interchange of information and ideas in areas like economic development, regional planning, environmental protection, and expansion of higher education—all in a way that would be a catalyst for change, in a spirit of moderation and conciliation. The old order, in other words, would be reformed but not overthrown. One of the first projects was a Southern Growth Policies Board, which stemmed from a proposal made by former North Carolina Governor Terry Sanford at the Lamar Society's 1971 meeting in Atlanta.* Another was a series of essays on various aspects of the South's development published in 1972 under the delightful title *You Can't Eat Magnolias*.

There is still a vast gulf between the political passions expressed in the voting booths of Dixie and the rarified, rational atmosphere of a Lamar Society meeting. Perhaps they can never meet fully, though the election of the moderate governors augurs well for the possibility. To the extent that they can relate, the hopes for a demythologized and responsive political order in the South are greater than at any time in the region's history.

The Economy: Up from Destitution

If the South today, as some have said, is like an underdeveloped nation that has reached—or passed—the "takeoff" stage of its economic development, one must first note how far it has come.

Cities like Charleston and Savannah and New Orleans notwithstanding, most of the Deep South was a rough frontier area in antebellum days, and the dirt-poor white farmers far outnumbered the plantation gentility who would later be enshrined in Southern lore. Large tracts of the South were subjected to incredible devastation during the Civil War, and afterwards the ruling classes effected their own return to affluence through exploitation of both the poor white and the Negro. The one-crop cotton economy, marked by high risks and low returns, created a huge sharecropper and tenant farm population and exhausted the soil. Whatever industry there was—cotton mills and logging operations—was of the most decimating kind. Wages were rock bottom and profits went into the hands of a narrow few. The virgin timber stands of the South were destroyed to feed the sawmills in what one expert described as "the most ruthless destruction of forests known in history."

Despite a few spots of major industry, the region remained overwhelmingly rural and bound to the land during the very decades that the rest of the

* The Growth Policies Board could have a major impact on the region because, like the quite successful Southern Regional Education Board, it is a creation of the governors and state legislatures. Working with a policy-oriented staff, it has the potential of formulating common regional positions on problems like the effect of federal transportation policy on urban sprawl and rural starvation. The key question will be whether the governors and legislatures will then be willing to use their political muscle to get the proposed policy directions implemented.

United States was industrializing and urbanizing. In 1930 the vast majority of the Deep South's people lived on farms or in little villages—in Mississippi, the most rural of all, the figure was 83 percent. And the per capita income of the region was only half that of the country as a whole. During the 1920s the boll weevil ravaged Southern cotton crops, and then the Great Depression struck the region like a sledgehammer. As Thomas D. Clark wrote in *The Emerging South:*

> In 1935 vast areas of the rural South were reduced to shabbiness. Farmsteads were cluttered and run-down, reflecting a deepset state of poverty. Rusting implements and vehicles were scattered about in disarray of abandonment. Barns, outhouses, fences, and grounds sagged under the weight of sun and time. Even country churches stood on careening foundations atop ground that receded with the wash of recurring wet seasons. Agricultural backwardness, if not complete failure, was stamped upon homesteads as indelibly as the thrust of the hills and the slash of the streams. From 1865 to 1935 an objective observer could hardly have been favorably impressed with farming and small town existence in the South. There were islands, of course, where land and people helped organize community life in a pleasant manner. . . . [But] between Charleston and Natchez, . . . "nigger house shabbiness" was more descriptive than "Tara," "Rosehill," "Afton Villa," and "Llangollon" splendor.

The historians may never fully agree on whether the South's destitution up to World War II was primarily its own fault or that of the North. Physically, there was nothing to prevent development of a diversified agriculture and a diversified industry in the South. But the federal government did virtually nothing to encourage Southern economic recovery after the Civil War, and even if it had tried, there was always the old plantation-mind set that dictated against new directions. It was true that discriminatory freight rates and low wages paid by Northern-owned mills helped to keep the region in a kind of semicolonial status, but even when Southerners accumulated some capital, they were reluctant to invest it in new industrial efforts in their own part of the country—except, perhaps, for cotton mills. There was a professed belief in diversified industry on the part of Atlanta editor Henry Grady and the other apostles of a "New South" in the late 1800s. One recalls Grady's oft-quoted story:

> I attended a funeral once in Pickens County in my state. This funeral was particularly sad. It was a poor fellow like most Southerners. . . . They buried him in the midst of a marble quarry; they cut through solid marble to make his grave; and yet a little tombstone they put above him was from Vermont. They buried him in the heart of a pine forest, and the pine coffin was imported from Cincinnati. They buried him within touch of an iron mine, and yet the nails in his coffin and the iron in the shovel that dug his grave were imported from Pittsburgh. They buried him by the side of the best sheepgrazing country on the earth, and yet the wool in the coffin bands and the coffin bands themselves were brought from the North. The South didn't furnish a thing on earth for that funeral but the corpse and the hole in the ground.

But the cotton mentality dominated the industrial gospel, and as Frank Rose has pointed out in paraphrasing W. J. Cash, "the effect was to transplant the plantation system from the cotton field to the cotton mill. The owner of the new mill was the new aristocrat, the white working class was the new labor force, and the blacks stayed behind on the farm as tenants or as house servants." The new industry, Cash wrote, would "bear up the tradition of unforfeitable white superiority." Later on, when unions tried to organize in the cotton mills, they would be fiercely—and effectively—opposed.

Reviewing the South's long economic travail, former federal official Clifford Durr of Alabama noted that "we Southerners still blame our fate on the damned Yankees and on Sherman who destroyed our homes. You might say that a hundred years was enough time for us to rebuild on our own. But what we did lose was two or three generations of education. That was what kept the South behind." His own generation, Durr said, was the first to start going back to college in any significant numbers. But when he entered the University of Alabama in 1915, there were only 500 in the student body, and many departments consisted of a single professor. For years, the brightest young Southerners tended to look to the North for top-grade education or for professional opportunities.

Franklin Roosevelt, who had witnessed the poverty of the rural South firsthand during visits to his vacation home at Warm Springs, Georgia, was the first President to take a serious interest in the economic development of the South. The Tennessee Valley Authority, approved soon after he took office, began to provide cheap power and the possibility of industrial development in the northern, hillier region of the Deep South. The various New Deal agencies pumped huge amounts of money into the region. The 1938 federal report which identified the South as "the Nation's Number One economic problem" also said it could be a region of great economic opportunity if the chronic wastage of human and material resources in the South were halted and a serious program of development undertaken.

It was World War II, however, that provided the greatest catalyst for economic expansion in the Southland. Georgia, Alabama, Louisiana, South Carolina, and Mississippi were all recipients of big military camps that provided good-paying jobs for thousands of Southerners and pumped vast sums into the local economies. The federal government spent billions for constructing or expanding chemical, ammunition, and shipbuilding industries in the South. Hundreds of thousands of new manufacturing jobs were added, and by 1950 the average wage of a Southern production worker was 55 percent higher—in constant dollars—than it had been before Pearl Harbor.

The surge of growth occasioned by World War II has yet to abate in the South. One can take any measure—per capita income, the percentage of the working force engaged in manufacturing, the share of the population living in metropolitan areas, and many others—and the picture is consistent. In each decade (and indeed in most single years) the Deep South has advanced dramatically compared to its own earlier levels, and it has continued to close the gap between itself and the rest of the United States. Part of the growth has matched the established patterns of the region—garment and shoe and now electrical appliance assembly plants, located mostly in rural areas where the lowest wages are paid. Following the lead of Mississippi in the 1930s, every Southern state has set up programs of tax abatement, free land, and sometimes even free buildings to draw in industry —"a handshake and handout for any castoff cut and sew operation from New York," as one local cynic put it to me.

But there have been many other aspects to the industrial growth. Pulp and paper mills have multiplied across the region. Food processing has grown consistently. Aluminum plants near New Orleans and in the Tennessee Valley, petrochemicals along the Mississippi River, aircraft in Georgia, shipbuilding along the Gulf Coast, steel in Alabama and South Carolina—the list is long and constantly expanding. To this one can add the huge income Florida gets from retirees and tourists, the continuing income from the South's long list of military bases, and the stimulus that was provided (chiefly in the '60s) from the "space crescent" stretching from Cape Canaveral to Huntsville to the rocket-testing site in Mississippi and New Orleans. Among cities, Atlanta has soared as the transportation, communications, and regional headquarters center of the South. But on a lesser scale, New Orleans and Birmingham and even Jackson, Mississippi, are performing the same functions—not to mention the booming Florida metropolises of Miami, Orlando, Jacksonville, and Tampa-St. Petersburg. Since 1950, the number of people living in metropolitan regions in the seven Deep South states has advanced from 5.2 million to 12.7 million in raw numbers and from 32 percent to 51 percent of the total regional population. And for a fortunate minority of Southerners who live in rural areas and want to avoid being forced to the cities, there is a growing trickle of industries in such fields as electrical equipment and chemicals, paying much better wages than the apparel factories and lumber mills that have favored rural Dixie up to now.

Still, there is grave doubt whether the Deep South states will be able to create a standard of living for their people equal to that of the nation as a whole at any time in the foreseeable future. The problem is that as the region moves toward national norms, it is confronted with a moving target. Per capita income—perhaps the best general measure of people's economic well-being—is a case in point. Except for Louisiana, the seven Deep South states saw an increase of *over 100 percent* in their per capita income between 1961 and 1971, compared to a national increase of 83.5 percent. But compared to the income of Americans as a whole, the people of the region were still very badly off. The figure in Mississippi, $2,766, was still only 67 percent of the national average of $4,138. Five of the region's states—Mississippi, the lowest, plus Arkansas, Alabama, South Carolina, and Louisiana —ranked at the absolute bottom of the 50 states in actual per capita income. Georgia at 34th place among the states and Florida at 24th place were somewhat better off, but even the Florida figure was 5 percent behind the national average. And in terms of the dollar gap between their per capita income and the U.S. figure, all of the seven states except Florida were actually worse off in 1971 than they had been 10 years before. In Louisiana, for instance, the gap had increased from $578 to $890, and in Alabama from $758 to $1,088. Department of Commerce projections to the year 1990 indicate the dollar gap will become even greater. And Mississippians will still be earning only 72 percent of the national average, Arkansans 75 percent, and Alabamians 79 percent.

Another sobering note is that Southerners' income might have shown little gain relative to the rest of the United States in recent years if it had not been for the massive outmigration of black people. Even in the early 1970s, the income of black families in the South was less than 70 percent of the income of white families. The incidence of poverty among Southern blacks is three times as high as that among Southern whites—although in absolute numbers, there are more whites than blacks in the region living under the poverty line. Counting the Border States, the South has almost half the nation's poor people. Poor health—measured by the mortality rate among young children, a lack of prenatal and maternal care, the incidence of disease, the malignant effects of malnutrition, wretched housing and sanitation, and severe shortages of physicians and dentists—remains, sadly, much higher in the South than anywhere else in America. A Citizens' Board of Inquiry into Hunger and Malnutrition in the United States found in a 1968 report that 138 of the nation's 256 "hunger counties" were in the Deep South, and another 82 in the Border South. Yet even by 1973, only half the Deep South's 5.7 million people living below the poverty line were receiving food stamps or surplus agricultural commodities.

Deep South states have always been quite generous in welfare for the aged but stingy in aid for destitute children and younger families. For many years there was conscious policy of holding down welfare levels so that poor Negroes would be forced to move out of the South. The policy was not only morally repugnant but shortsighted, since it drove out the better educated and productive young Negroes while leaving behind the listless, the old, and the helpless. More than half the dollar benefits from the defeated Family Assistance Plan of the early 1970s would have flowed into the South, creating—in the words of *Fortune* magazine—"a revolution in the shanty towns and rural hovels of the Deep South." Only the most charitable observer would say that Southern Congressmen took the leading hand in killing the bill only because of feared abuses or the region's traditional hatred of welfare and fear of expanding federal power. The fact was that the plan would have begun to erase the last traces of the Southern caste system, both economically and politically. Hiring maids and janitors, or even workers for the lowest paying sanitation and mill jobs, might have proven much more difficult. The incentive for Northern migration by destitute blacks might have been reduced. And if local blacks had less fear of losing their jobs or welfare benefits in retaliation for voting, then they might have become more effective politically, endangering the local white power structures.

Farmers forced off the land by mechanization have formed the great labor pool of the South, providing the major share of the region's 100 percent increase in manufacturing payrolls since 1950. But the new industries have been primarily in the low-wage, labor-intensive category, and by one estimate the per capita income of the whole region would be 6 percent higher if it had the same share of capital-intensive, higher-paying industries as the rest of the country. Manufacturing wage levels, which still lag 20 percent behind the national average, have also been held down by the very low rate of unionization, which is reinforced by the anti-union tone of the regional press and right-to-work laws on the books of every Deep South state except Louisiana. The more intelligent leaders of the region recognize the foolhardiness of an economy centered on low-paid, unskilled labor. As Taylor Webb, president of the influential Mississippi Economic Council, told a group of businessmen in 1971:

> It is not in your interest to build an economy around a cheap labor force. It is a disservice to people. A competitive labor force, yes, but if the products manufactured in Mississippi are to be sold nationally at competitive prices, then the employees should be paid a competitive wage instead of the savings in the form of profits leaving the state to those, but not all, nonresident stockholders who are attracted to Mississippi by tax exemptions and cheap labor. The future emphasis should be on upgrading the labor force, thereby offering more productive labor and not human bargains.

In virtually all the Deep South states, major new efforts in education—from the vocational and manpower training area to the advanced degree sector—have been made in recent years. Even George Wallace's governance of Alabama, notably backward in most areas, has been forward looking in vocational education. But despite the region's keen desire for higher-paying (and less polluting) high-technology industries, it continues to lag far behind the rest of the United States in attracting them. The kind of plants the region has drawn up to now have been overwhelmingly in "primary" industry representing a first-stage use of raw materials. In the North and West, by contrast, the shift of recent years has been toward "secondary" industry (which is primarily dependent on inputs from primary industries, rather than raw materials) and toward "tertiary" industry (dependent on research and development). But can a region habitually dependent on outside capital hope to attract the advanced industries and the headquarters complexes that go with them? "Southerners are always talking of 'bringing in' industry, but they rarely talk of 'setting up' industries," Clifford Durr said. "It's part of the South's ingrained psychological attitude." He noted that there was only one "great indigenous Southern industry—Coca-Cola."

That may be changing, however. In Atlanta, in the Florida cities, and even in staid New Orleans, a hustling young entrepreneur class—including many born Northerners—is now on the rise.* To date, most of their efforts have centered on building the skyscrapers and big residential developments which symbolize the region's new vitality. But in time they may shift to larger-scale enterprises, and as they do, the banks of Atlanta and several other Southern cities will be able, for the first time in history, to supply them with the capital to do the job.

The environmental movement was slow to catch fire in the South, but it is now taking hold—especially in Florida, with its delicate ecological balance of water and land, but also in the other Deep South states. One of the first political leaders to sense the issue was Winthrop Rockefeller, who I

* *Business Week* quoted Edward D. Smith, chairman of the First National Bank of Atlanta, as saying: "You can go to any gathering of businessmen in Atlanta, and I'll bet you $5 to a ginger cake that at least 50 percent of them will not be natives."

believe did more to change the course, both economically and socially, of his adopted Arkansas than any other leader of an American state in modern times. Rockefeller saw farther than the state borders, and he put the issue squarely at a Southern Governors Conference: "The danger, in playing economic catch-up, is that we could adopt false definitions of progress. The ultimate cost of such a course—we are reminded by grim evidence to the North, East, and West—would be disruption of the Southland's priceless natural environment. . . . It should be clear to us by now that man cannot, in the name of progress, destroy nature without destroying himself."

There is evidence enough that that destruction has begun in the South, the still broad and inviolate rural stretches of the region notwithstanding. Polluting pulp and paper and steel mills and petrochemical complexes, open sewers, tampering with the natural water courses through channelization that thwarts the natural cleansing action of nature, and the senseless sprawl and auto congestion of the growing Southern metropolitan regions—all testify to the grave dangers. Up to 1973, the region had taken its most effective corrective action in the area of industrial pollution of the air and waters. Some localities had begun to turn away potentially polluting factories. But many of the sins of the Army Corps of Engineers would take years to undo, and statewide land planning, outside of Florida, was still in the talking stages. (Even the Florida approach, regionally oriented with ultimate state veto power over new developments, was still in its trial stages.)

Although half the people of the South now live in metropolitan regions, the proportion is still well below the national average of two-thirds. Because the region was rural for so long, its cities are comparatively new, and they still have some time to learn by horrible examples in the North what they ought to avoid. Dr. Joel Fleishman of Duke University, in *You Can't Eat Magnolias,* pointed to several advantages of Southern metropolitan regions. The cities are generally smaller (and thus more manageable) than those of the North and West. There is a much thinner overlay of proliferating and competing governmental units, and thus greater possibilities for timely annexation and orderly planning. Southern cities are less densely populated and less afflicted (with exceptions like Birmingham) with big, polluting industries. But housing segregation is increasing rapidly. Fleishman suggested that unless Southern cities accept broad school integration (including busing) to reduce the incentives for racially isolated neighborhoods, and unless they move rapidly toward state-assisted urban growth policies and timely mergers and annexations, they would lose a unique opportunity to shape "a more graceful, more humane, and more livable environment than other regions."

A Postscript on Character

In the midst of the tumultuous change of the Deep South today, one senses—and often hears—a concern that the qualities that made the South distinctive are dying out. The nation's most agrarian society becomes urban; the most rigid class system begins to break up; the most ossified political structure becomes fluid. In place of the old isolation, physical and intellectual, one discovers now interstate highways, jetways, movies, and above all, television, with its effect on everything from attitudes to accents. Major new presences loom in the region: big-league sports; transplanted corporate executives; university faculties larded with non-Southerners; organized crime (supplementing the region's high rates of crimes of violence); and the federal government in all its guises. In the early 1970s two social scientists applied a variety of economic and sociological tests to the modern South and concluded that "the South is increasingly becoming indistinguishable from the rest of the United States." Gallup Polls in the early '70s showed no appreciable difference between Southern attitudes and those in other regions on most major issues.

There are those who admit all the objective changes but still claim that the South, through "a thousand and one cultural nuances, ranging from speech peculiarities and food preferences to the tempo of life," will remain a place set apart from the American mainstream. The emphasis on the family and kinship ties, a strong proclivity to fundamentalist religious belief, a lingering veneration of the plantation past, that special belief in one's "Southernness"—all these are still there, sometimes in amazing degree. A few hours before his death in 1970, South Carolina's James McBride Dabbs wrote on the last page of his last book, *Haunted by God:*

> Here is the irony of the whole Southern situation. We have evil and we have had evils beyond compare; I have never denied this. But somehow we've never ceased being haunted by God. Somehow we've remained human. Somehow the stars of kindliness, of integrity, of courage, and indeed, of a strange kind of humility have never gone out.

But how long, one wonders, can such values hold out against the onslaught of what go for national mores in the United States today? Just one example: when one travels through 50 states, as I have in recent years, nowhere does one find skills as raconteurs to match those of the Southerners. Down through the years, the fruit of Southern storytelling has been an outpouring of splendid novels and short stories. Even today, an amazing proportion of the finest reporters on newspapers like the New York *Times* are born Southerners. Mississippi novelist Eudora Welty tells us why:

> Southerners . . . love a good tale. They are born reciters, great memory retainers, diary keepers, letter exchangers, and letter savers, history tracers and debaters, and—outstaying all the rest—great talkers. Southern talk is on the narrative side, employing the verbatim conversation. For this, plenty of time is needed and it is granted. It was still true not so very far back that children *grew up listening*—listening through unhurried stretches of uninhibited reminiscence, and listening galvanized. They were naturally prone to be entertained from the first by life as they heard tell of it, and to feel free, encouraged, and then in no time compelled, to pass their pleasure on.

But, one asks, will there be time for storytelling in an acquisitive, hurry-hurry society, when children (and grown-ups too) spend vast stretches of their life gazing into a television tube? Or what will come of the South's much-heralded sense of "place" when ancestral homes become a rarity and most of the population is raised in carbon-copy ramblers or city apartments? What will become of the region's idolization of Southern womanhood when its women finally detect how long Southern males have held them in bondage, demanding (as the blacks have done) freedom to be their own persons? What might come of the South's patriotic and military traditions if a "postmilitary" age were suddenly to dawn?

The Civil War, Robert Penn Warren wrote,

> claimed the Confederate States for the Union, but at the same time, paradoxically, it made them more Southern. . . . Once the War was over, the Confederacy became a City of the Soul, beyond the haggling of constitutional lawyers, the ambition of politicians, and the jealousy of localisms. In defeat the Solid South was born—not only the witless automatism of fidelity to the Democratic Party but the mystique of prideful "difference," identity, and defensiveness. . . . In the moment of death the Confederacy entered upon its immortality.

Now all that is become unraveled, because the sense of adversity and historic tragedy in the Southern mystique is difficult to maintain if in fact the South is no longer a defeated, impoverished region. One thing that sustains the Deep South's distinctiveness of character today is that it still has a goodly number of economic and political flaws, something to be defensive about. In time, those flaws will pass. Could it be then that the distinctiveness will linger chiefly in modes of speech, in the memories evoked by cities like old Charleston, and in the face of the land? Or in traditional Southern manners and gentility, and a more humane pace of life (provided the worst mistakes of the already industrialized North can be avoided)? We can offer no conclusive answer, but perhaps it is appropriate to start with Louisiana, the state where the "otherness" of Southern landscape and folkways is most striking of all.

LOUISIANA

AN EVOCATION

THE VERY THOUGHT OF Louisiana is evocative. Like a boat on the bayou, moving past cypress hung with Spanish moss on a misty early morning, there is an air of mystery in so many things. Some of it is in the soul of the river; one stands on a levee and watches the Missouri and the Ohio and the Arkansas and all the rest that make up the mighty Mississippi, the very guts of a continent, the course over thousands of miles now finished, moving toward the open sea. And with the flow of ships and men through New Orleans and its port, it is as if one is beside one of the great funnels of a shifting earth, only faintly grasping its complexity.

In the people there is mystery too. Rural Cajuns live in a world apart, in "parishes" * with names like Evangeline and Acadia, still speaking French, trapping muskrat and fishing for crawfish as they have done since they came from Canada two centuries ago. Theirs is essentially a peasant culture; John Gunther called them "Latin hillbillys." But no one should take the Cajuns lightly, for they seem to absorb everybody long in contact with them—a "dominant gene" among ethnic groups, one might say. Then there are the

* The parishes are the equivalent of counties in other states; the term was originally used for the ecclesiastical units into which the Spanish governor divided Louisiana in the late 17th century.

Creoles, that delicate blend of Latin bloodstreams, a bit harder to identify than the Cajuns, though they continue to represent a special kind of aristocracy in New Orleans and other towns of substance.

In New Orleans, one discovers a soft blend of social structures long ingrained, of Mardi Gras, provincialism, worldliness, colorful folkways, Dixieland, and the French Quarter; taken together, as Huey Long once said of himself, they must be considered *sui generis*. And what gentle spirit brings the finest cuisine of the American continent to New Orleans, with its superb blend of French recipes, Spanish seasoning, and American Indian herbs? In these softer graces of man, Louisiana excels.

There is another side, of course. There is nothing soft about Bogalusa and even the state capital of Baton Rouge, both Klan-infested in recent decades. Little mystery surrounds that archconservative oiltown, Shreveport, second largest city in Louisiana.There is not much sophistication about the Plaquemines Parish of the late Leander Perez, run as a feudal island in the 20th century with the black man so long subjugated. The once-inviolate marshlands of the delta, home of waterfowl of every description, have been slashed to pieces by oil fields and gas lines. And the Mississippi's banks from Baton Rouge to New Orleans are lined by refineries and petrochemical plants that often put on a garish display as they burn wastes at night. In the cold light of day they bespeak little more than grim industrialization. Where they stand, a visitor in earlier times would have seen the regal plantation houses and ramshackle tenant cabins of the great cotton and cane thralldoms.

Even if imperiled by "progress," many of the wondrous landscapes of Louisiana live on. All of Louisiana, in fact, lies within the Gulf Coastal Plain. Except for the northwestern part of the state with its pine and hardwood forests akin to those of neighboring Arkansas and East Texas, the essential Louisiana story is one of lowlands, and water, and the River. A great part of southern Louisiana is a jungle of swamps and those devious waterways that pierce them, the bayous. The Mississippi's expansive delta and its great spreading mouth lie entirely within the state, and the river is the reason that the writers of the WPA series on the American states could liken Louisiana's map to "a boot with its frayed toe dipping into the Gulf of Mexico."

No other state is so flat; only Florida, perhaps, is so humid, and moist, and hurricane-prone. The hurricanes, some studies show, are now occurring more frequently than in past centuries; in 1969, Hurricane Camille's 200-mile-an-hour winds destroyed 5,000 homes near the mouth of the Mississippi. If Camille's course had been a few miles more westerly, as many as 150,000 people living around New Orleans might have been drowned in their homes. Yet in contrast to that violence, one must speak of the life-giving qualities of the swamps and marshlands, which include a half million acres of wildlife preserves, homes of hundreds of varieties of birds, from the heron to the marsh wren, the laughing gull to the sandpiper, and North America's greatest wintering area for ducks and wild geese.

Each year, the silty load of the Mississippi creates some thousand new acres at the river's mouth. Hodding Carter sought the spirit of the great stream's last stretches in his book, *Man and the River:*

> Downstream, downstream—the eternal amalgam of water and earth, of lakes and bayous and swamps and *terre tremblante* close by the hungry sea . . . the three mouths of the river . . . the lighthouse faithful to the ceaseless southward flow of water . . . the freighters heading northward with cargoes from the wharves of everywhere, ready to clear their holds and to bear the hoard of the American continents.
>
> And now at land's end, the brown, silt-streaked river begins to meet the sea. The sediment coalesces as the fresh and salt water meet, thrusting into the Gulf the long-borne earth of a mid-continent and removing all trace of the immense scourings from the river's valley within a mile. . . .

One of the greatest challenges to man's ingenuity has been to control the flow of the Mississippi to prevent the mighty floods along the river and the companion waterways of the valley; now, in our time, a complex of levees and pumping stations extends over all of southern Louisiana. Large areas (including the city of New Orleans) are actually under sea level, as the river rolls along behind its levees. In spring 1973, almost all these levees held firm in the face of the worst Mississippi River flooding in more than 20 years. But if the scourge of flooding is ameliorated, new problems have arisen; one is that floodwaters can no longer deposit their load of rich topsoil on the alluvial plain, and the fields no longer receive that rejuvenation. And in the vast Atchafalaya Swamp, to the west of the Mississippi, flood control projects of the Army Corps of Engineers have squeezed off much of the overflow of the Atchafalaya River and vast stretches of swamp have become dry land, imperiling the fantastically variegated plant life and fish and birds and alligators and furred animals alike.

Lumbering of cypress and hardwood, pesticides, oil rigs, and sportsmen's trash have taken a heavy toll too. Sad to report, the state bird, the brown pelican, is virtually extinct, the reported victim of alien chemicals in the waters.

Cultures and History

The historic roots of Louisiana go back not to the westward push of Anglo-Saxons across the continent in the 1800s but rather to the 16th- and 17th-century struggles of Spain and France for ascendancy in the interior of the New World. The story began when Spanish explorers discovered the Mississippi River, apparently between 1519 and 1530, and ended with the Louisiana Purchase in 1803, when President Jefferson obtained for $15 million a vast stretch of interior America, including one-third of the present continental United States, from Napoleon Bonaparte.

The southernmost portion of the purchase land was declared the Territory of Orleans in 1804; eight years later Congress added more land in the southeast (known as the Florida Parishes) and the whole became the state of Louisiana on April 30, 1812. Less than three years later, in the concluding

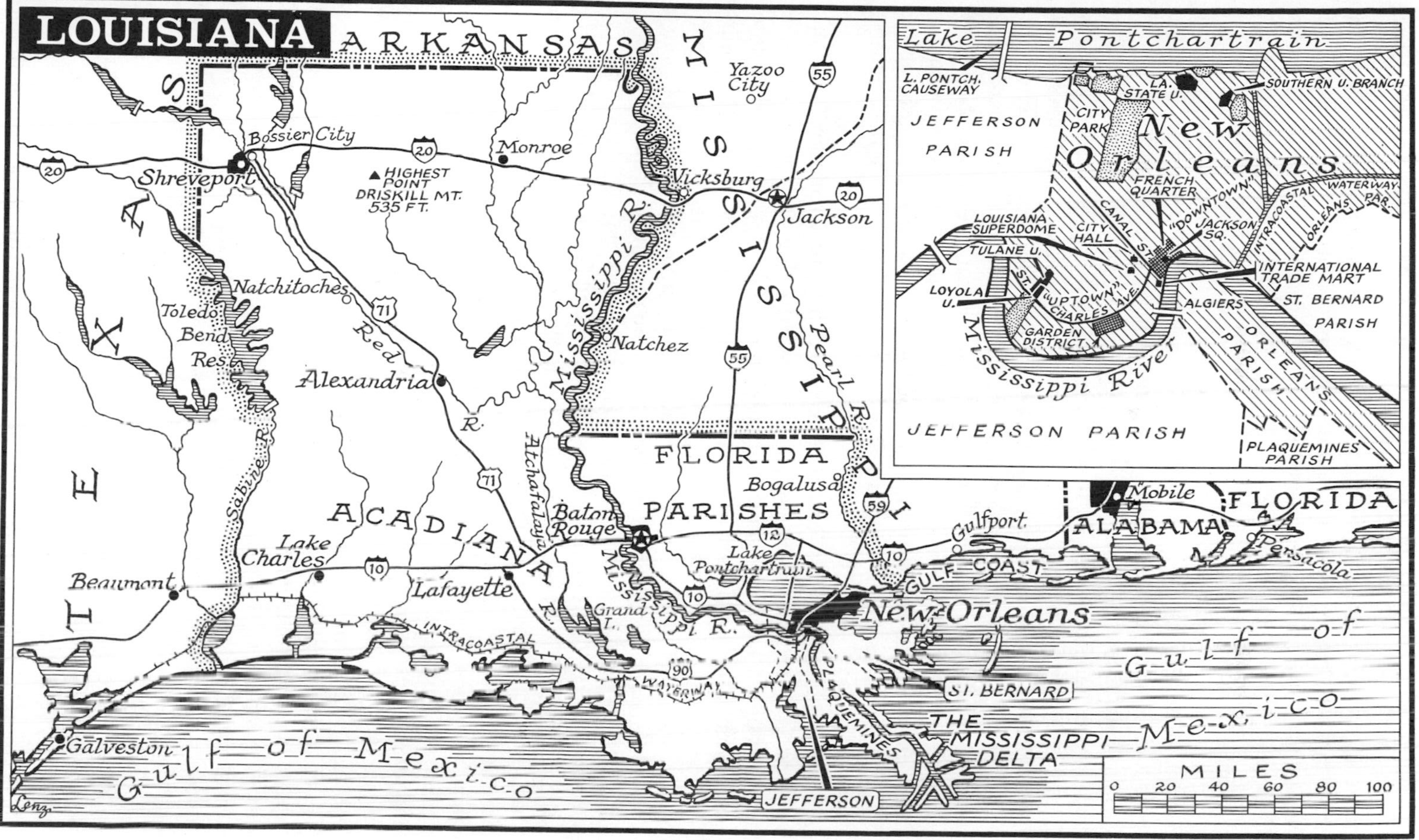
LOUISIANA
ARKANSAS
MISSISSIPPI
TEXAS
Shreveport
Bossier City
Monroe
HIGHEST POINT DRISKILL MT. 535 FT.
Vicksburg
Yazoo City
Jackson
Natchitoches
Toledo Bend Res.
Sabine R.
Red R.
Alexandria
Natchez
Mississippi R.
Pearl R.
FLORIDA PARISHES
Bogalusa
ACADIANA
Atchafalaya R.
Baton Rouge
Lake Charles
Lafayette
Beaumont
Lake Pontchartrain
Grand L.
INTRACOASTAL WATERWAY
New Orleans
GULF COAST
Gulfport
Mobile
ALABAMA
FLORIDA
Pensacola
ST. BERNARD
PLAQUEMINES
JEFFERSON
THE MISSISSIPPI DELTA
Galveston
Gulf of Mexico
MILES
0 20 40 60 80 100
Lenz
Lake Pontchartrain
L. PONTCH. CAUSEWAY
LA. STATE U.
SOUTHERN U. BRANCH
JEFFERSON PARISH
CITY PARK
New Orleans
FRENCH QUARTER
"DOWNTOWN"
INTRACOASTAL WATERWAY
ORLEANS PAR.
LOUISIANA SUPERDOME
CITY HALL
CANAL ST.
JACKSON SQ.
TULANE U.
INTERNATIONAL TRADE MART
LOYOLA U.
ST. CHARLES AVE.
"UPTOWN"
ALGIERS
ST. BERNARD PARISH
GARDEN DISTRICT
ORLEANS PARISH
Mississippi River
JEFFERSON PARISH
PLAQUEMINES PARISH

phase of the War of 1812, the English invaded Louisiana, and General Andrew Jackson led an army of volunteers from Kentucky, Tennessee, and Mississippi, plus a ragtag assortment of Louisianans including Creoles, Choctaw Indians, and free Negroes, in defeating the invaders at the Battle of New Orleans.

This new American state was like none other, one with close to a full century of settled life as a Spanish and French colony behind it. New Orleans had been founded in 1718—when Houston was just a speck on Buffalo Bayou. Lawrence Goodwyn notes that "Congress had to ponder the fact that in the proposed new state of Louisiana, with its Creoles, Acadians, Canary Islanders, Spaniards, Germans and Dominicans, a great majority of the population could not speak a coherent English sentence. . . . The terms of statehood gave striking evidence of the Creoles' tenacity. Louisiana came into the Union trailing the French judicial system, the Code Napoleon, which remains the basis of Louisiana law to this day." For many years, in fact, debate in the legislature could be either in French or English, at the discretion of each member. State laws were published in both languages down to 1898.

A brief digression must be undertaken to define the Creoles of Louisiana. In New Orleans and other cities of the state to this day, one encounters members of old families—white and tan-skinned alike—who insist their forebears were Creole. It does seem certain that there was a French-Spanish aristocracy that adopted this name; it included the settlers and native-born of Louisiana before American governance started in 1804, and of course their children and children's children. The Creoles, in their proud way, resisted the cultural intrusions of the *Américains* who flooded into New Orleans after the Louisiana Purchase. But the Creoles were not all white; historian Joseph G. Tregle, Jr., has written in the *Journal of Southern History* that "in the 1820s and 1830s 'Creole' was generally used in Louisiana to designate any person native to the state, be he white, black, or colored, French, Spanish or Anglo-American." Moreover, a mixture of races most certainly occurred; there were the famous Quadroon Balls of the late 18th and early 19th centuries that led to all manner of alliances, including arrangements by mulatto mistresses for their daughters to make *liaisons sans mariage* with young white men, the daughters being set up in town houses, the children of these unions all carefully taken care of, even while the same white men often had their own legal spouses and families elsewhere in the city. The children were well educated (sometimes in France) and were universally regarded as free men and women, not slaves, when they reached maturity—a race of *les gens de couleur libres* that would have been anathema anywhere else in antebellum (or for that matter, postbellum) South.

Thus down through history came the two groups of Creoles—white and mulatto—and the confusions exist to this day. The late A. P. Tureaud, a distinguished light-skinned Negro who for years was counsel for the NAACP in New Orleans, told this story:

> I'm what you call a Creole. . . . I had a very interesting experience with that very thing and it deals with the Selective Service. I was in Washington at the time

of World War I and when I went to register for the Selective Service I started filling out the application and they wanted to know your race and I put down "Negro." The man looks at me and says, "You aren't a Negro, are you? Where are you from?" I said, "Louisiana," and he says, "What do they call them down there?" And I said, "They call us Creoles." And he said, "Put that down." So I did, and sure enough, when I was called, I was called for a battalion that was all white, because they weren't calling Negroes for anything but labor battalions and quartermaster.

Louisiana grew and thrived in the years between the War of 1812 and the Civil War. The first steamboat went into operation in 1812 and New Orleans became a great port city, the produce of the vast reaches of the Mississippi Valley all brought down river and deposited on its levees, then shipped on to the East and Europe. Recorded tonnage of the port jumped from 67,560 tons in 1814 to 537,400 tons in 1840. By then, New Orleans had 102,193 people and was the fourth largest city in America. This was also the golden age of Louisiana's great sugar plantations, which expanded rapidly along the rivers and bayous, drawing their wealth from the rich river-bottom soil and slave labor. In 1853, Louisiana had 1,500 estates, and some 75,000 slaves were laboring in the cane fields. The planters dominated all aspects of Louisiana life, economic, political, and cultural.

Nostalgia for the plantation era lingers on, even to this day. One feels it in the antebellum plantation houses which still stand, some now in decay, others lovingly restored and maintained, all lovely whispers of a bygone age. It is also a matter of the spirit. Joseph Judge of the *National Geographic* relates the story still told in New Orleans of a Yankee who after the Civil War visited one of the plantations that had escaped destruction. Sitting in a perfumed garden, the visitor remarked on the beauty of the Southern night. An aging servant replied: "You should have seen that moon before the war."

While sugar planters and allied merchants controlled Louisiana politics, the seeds of another Louisiana were being planted in the uplands. The Red River, which flows from northwestern Louisiana, was freed of the driftwood that had obstructed it for centuries, and hardy settlers poured in from the Carolinas, Georgia, Alabama, and Tennessee. Small farmers and Jacksonian Democrats, they quickly lined up against the planter interests of the south. So it was that "redneck" Louisiana was born.

The planter interest propelled Louisiana into the Confederacy, and the state furnished not only a substantial complement of men but several distinguished leaders to the South's side. A Union fleet in 1862 captured New Orleans, and until the end of the war Louisiana had two governments, one federally controlled at New Orleans, the other Confederate at Shreveport. Few states suffered as long and tumultuous a period of Reconstruction. The economy lay in ruins, carpetbaggers poured in from the North, radical Republicans plundered the state and disfranchised Confederate veterans. The whites, in turn, formed vigilante groups including a White League that terrorized Negroes. There was one bloody riot at Colfax, in the course of which three whites and 120 Negroes were killed. Not until 1877 did Reconstruction come to an end.

With the withdrawal of federal troops, bleak years lay ahead for both Negroes and any political cause save that of the dominant white Democrats. There was a flurry of opposition to Bourbon control in 1896, in which a Populist-Republican coalition candidate for governor got 43 percent of the vote. The ruling clique then called a constitutional convention which met in 1898 and instituted stiff new property and educational requirements for voting. All of these would be waived, however, for anyone who had voted before 1867, or his descendants. This infamous "grandfather" clause was intended to save the vote for illiterate and impoverished whites, while keeping Negroes away from the polls. At the close of the convention, its president stated:

> We have not drafted the exact constitution that we should like to have drafted; otherwise we should have inscribed on it, if I know the popular sentiment of this state, universal white manhood suffrage, and the exclusion from the suffrage of every man with a trace of African blood in his veins. . . .

The convention accomplished its purpose. In the immediately preceding election, there had been 164,088 white and 130,344 Negro registrants; by the next Presidential election, only 5,320 Negroes were left registered. Between then and the 1930s, the Negro registration rarely exceeded 2,000. Many whites also lost interest in elections, and the turnout for Presidential elections went down from 63 percent of voting age persons in 1896 to 21 percent in 1900 and 14 percent in 1920.

The oligarchy that ruled Louisiana from Reconstruction into the 1920s was one of the most powerful and heartless any American state has ever seen. Little was done to cope with overwhelming problems of illiteracy and crushing poverty which left most Louisianans with inadequate food, shelter, and clothing well past the year 1900. It was 1898 when the state made its first serious efforts to guarantee free public education and 1916 before a compulsory education law was enacted. Even in the late 1920s, V. O. Key has estimated, the chances are that one out of five white rural men could not read or write. The 1940 Census would show that 15 percent of the white men of Louisiana over 25 years of age had not completed a single year's schooling (compared to only 7 percent in Virginia, the next highest on this index, or 5 and 3 percent in neighboring Texas and Mississippi, respectively).

Admittedly, Louisiana's rulers faced gruesome problems. Each year the boiling springtime crests of the Mississippi threatened to inundate great portions of lowland Louisiana; progress on levees was slow and difficult and one great flood of 1882 swept away miles of levee already constructed. Flood ravages were matched by those of yellow fever epidemics. The worst had occurred in 1853, when 11,000 people died in New Orleans alone and many small towns were almost wiped out. Each year hundreds of Louisianans died from the fever, and it was not until 1905 (when mosquitoes were identified as the carrying agents) that the disease could be brought under control.

Beyond its own special interests, the ruling group did little for the people. V. O. Key points out that the oligarchy included elements not present, at least in the same degree, in the other states of the South:

The New Orleans machine bulked large in state politics and had established itself early. In every respect it was an old-fashioned machine, effective in its control of the vote and, in turn, itself beholden to the business and financial interests. Add to the mercantile, financial and shipping interests of New Orleans, the power wielded by the sugar growers, an interest peculiar to Louisiana, then add the cotton planters of the Red River and the Mississippi. The lumber industry constituted perhaps a more powerful bloc than in any other Southern state and also enacted a spectacular drama in exploitation apparent even to the most unlettered. Later came oil. . . . Add to all these the railroads and gas and electrical utilities, and you have elements susceptible of combination in a powerful political bloc.

Unlike other Southern States, Louisiana never had colorful Populist leaders who could loosen the rule of the oligarchy, even if ever so slightly. Perhaps the cultural and linguistic divisions of the people were too great for a single leader to emerge. The oligarchy was indeed skillful in playing off the Protestant North against the Catholic South. Louisiana became a classic case of arrested political development.

The Longs

When change came, it was volcanic. Its agent was Huey Pierce Long, born in 1893 in a small north central Louisiana town, the eighth of nine children of a hardscrabble farmer. Ethnically, Long's roots ranged from French to Scotch. Ethically, he did much that was questionable. Personally, he was rude and vulgar. He bullied friend and foe alike and ended up with virtually dictatorial powers over his state—more power than any governor in American history has held, before or since. Long carried in him a *hubris* that makes his assassination, in retrospect, seem almost inevitable. But up to that fateful moment in 1935, it was literally true in Louisiana: "L'Etat, c'est Huey."

Politically, Long was from start to finish what he presented himself to be: the champion of the little people against the entrenched interests. In his autobiography, *Every Man a King,* Long quoted a speech he made at St. Martinsville in the French country in his successful campaign for governor in 1927. Standing under the famous oak of Evangeline legend, Long said:

> And it is here, under this oak where Evangeline waited for her lover, Gabriel, who never came. This oak is an immortal spot, made so by Longfellow's poem, but Evangeline is not the only one who has waited here in disappointment. Where are the schools that you have waited for your children to have, that have never come? Where are the roads and the highways that you sent your money to build, but are no nearer now than ever before? Where are the institutions to care for the sick and the disabled? Evangeline wept bitter tears in her disappointment, but it lasted through only one lifetime. Your tears in this country, around this oak, have lasted for generations. Give me the chance to dry the tears of those who still weep here! *

* T. Harry Williams, in his magnificent biography, *Huey Long* (New York: Alfred A. Knopf, 1969), notes that some critics have doubted the authenticity of this speech. But Williams located newspaper accounts which indicated Long had said something very similar.

What set Long apart from other Southern Populist-demagogues was that he kept faith with the people. He did not, as one account puts it, "follow the customary practice of wearing a wool hat when he harangued the mob and a panama planter when he made his political deals with the Bourbons." Instead, he delivered on his promises to the people, letting his antagonists —the oil companies and other vested interests—pay the bill through greater taxation. Free schoolbooks were offered all children, including those in Catholic schools. A great program of highways and free bridges was undertaken. New hospitals rose. A rebuilt Louisiana became a kind of temple to Huey Long.

In the process, Long destroyed the integrity of government in Louisiana. He would brook no opposition. Mayors, judges, or parish officials who fought him were ripped from office or suffered profound economic coercion. Complete fealty was demanded of state legislators. Cecil Morgan, an oil attorney and later dean of the Tulane Law School who was a state legislator in the 1920s, recalls that the same day he refused to back some Long bills to centralize power in the governor's office, his father was fired from the state banking commission. (Morgan was subsequently a chief member of "The Dynamite Squad" that tried, unsuccessfully, to impeach Long. He still tells the story with such vividness that it seems like yesterday.) Two of Long's final deeds, after he had already gone off to Washington to be Sanator and elected a henchman governor, were to get the legislature to put a five-cent-a-barrel tax on refined oil (enraging his old enemy, Standard Oil) and literally taking physical control of New Orleans by use of the National Guard, thus humiliating both the mayor and the old-line Choctaw political faction that still held sway there.

There had been questions aplenty about Long's Robin Hood morality, but after him, it was *le déluge*. As V. O. Key put it:

> Extortion, bribery, peculation, thievery are not rare in the annals of politics, but in the scale, variety, and thoroughness of its operations the Long gang established, after the death of the Kingfish, a record unparalleled in our times. Millions of dollars found their way more or less directly to his political heirs and followers. From the state treasury, from state employees, from gambling concessionaires, from seekers of every conceivable privilege, cash flowed to some members of the inner circle.

Eventually some, though probably not enough, of this group went to prison, and Louisiana politics took on a semblence of bifactionalism (always within the Democratic party, of course). On the one side were the Longs, who would offer venal but people-oriented programs; then there were anti-Longs, who provided relatively honest, unimaginative government in the mold of the gentlemanly do-nothing governors who preceded Huey. Actually, it was never quite that simple. A prominent "anti-Long," Jimmie ("You Are My Sunshine") Davis, elected governor in 1944 and again in 1960, fitted the mold well enough by doing little when he was in office except to defend segregation to the last gasp * and make movies and recording albums in

* In fairness, it should be pointed out that Davis, in his earlier term, backed an equalization of pay for black and white schoolteachers—a revolutionary step at that time.

never-ending succession. But some of his shenanigans hardly measured up on the honesty scale. And not every Long faction candidate spurned the big corporations, and especially the oil companies, as Huey did.

Huey's most colorful successor was none other than his own brother, Earl K. Long, a man of raucous speech and manner. (In 1928 he almost bit off the ear of a political enemy as they fought in a cramped elevator.) Earl exhibited streaks of apparent insanity in his last years of life (while he was still governor) and at one point was actually trundled off to a mental hospital in Texas where he arrived, as he put it himself later, with "not enough clothes on me to cover a red bug, and a week later I was enjoying the same wardrobe." Earl K. did permit pervasive corruption in his administration as governor, but the late Margaret Dixon, managing editor of the *Baton Rouge Advocate* and one of his close friends and supporters, was probably right when she said: "Earl was more sinned against than sinning. He simply lacked any inhibitions. He was a genuinely kind person with a real feeling for the underprivileged; there was none of the element of exploitation in him that Huey showed at times." Mrs. Dixon told me his apparent insanity was due to a series of small strokes affecting areas of the brain. He had, in office, fought for welfare programs, equalized teachers' salaries and upgraded them tremendously, and put the tax screws on "the Standard Oil crowd."

Neither Huey nor Earl Long ever descended to "nigger-baiting"—then so popular—in their campaigns. Huey's strategem was apparently to pose as a segregationist, make a few disparaging comments on Negroes from time to time, and then institute broad programs of social reform which did more to uplift Louisiana Negroes, in their day-to-day life, than anything done for them since the Civil War. T. Harry Williams quotes him as saying "I have been able to do a hell of a lot of things down there because I am Huey Long. A lot of guys would have been murdered politically for what I've been able to do quietly for the niggers." Long did not regard words like "nigra" and "nigger" as offensive, Williams said, and "he was completely without prejudice in his personal relations." In 1934, when the Ku Klux Klan denounced him at its "imperial klonvocation" in Atlanta and the head of the Klan said he would go to Louisiana to campaign against the Kingfish, Long sought out reporters to respond: "Quote me as saying that that Imperial bastard will never set foot in Louisiana, and that when I call him a sonofabitch I am not using profanity, but am referring to the circumstances of his birth." He added that if the Klan leader did come to Louisiana, he would leave with "his toes turned up."

When Roy Wilkins, then a newspaperman, interviewed Long in 1935, Long tried to set the record straight for once and for all. "In your article," he said, "don't say I'm working for the niggers. I'm not, I'm for the poor man—all poor men. Black and white, they all gotta have a chance. They gotta have a home, a job, and a decent education for their children. 'Every Man a King'—that's my slogan. That means every man, niggers along with the rest, but not specially for niggers."

Earl Long got along well with Negroes, too, and in fact they represented his margin of victory in his 1956 campaign for governor. Earl was quoted by A. J. Liebling in *The Earl of Louisiana* as saying just before his death in 1960: "Fellas like [Orval] Faubus and . . . Leander Perez and da rest of da White Citizens and Southern Gentlemen in dis state want to go back behind Lincoln. And between us, . . . we got to admit dat Lincoln was a fine man and dat he was right." On another occasion, Earl is said to have told Leander Perez: "What are you going to do now, Leander? Da Feds have got da atom bomb."

Post-Longian Politics

"I advise anyone who thinks he knows something about politics to go down in Louisiana and take a postgraduate course," the late Senator Tom Connally of Texas said 40 years ago. A. J. Liebling called Louisiana "the westernmost of the Arab states" and observed that its politics "is of an intensity and complexity that are matched, in my experience, only in the Republic of Lebanon. Louisiana is part of the Hellenistic-Mediterranean littoral —sensual, seductive, speculative, devious."

More recently, an observer summed up Louisiana politics as "a spicy combo of race, crime, religion, oil, and horseplay." Sometimes the *leitmotif* is the bizarre duel between the Cajun, Catholic south and the hard-rock Protestant counties of northern Louisiana—a fight that is "as much folklore as politics." Sometimes the issue is corruption, in a state where graft, bribery, influence peddling, and Mafia influence all play an inordinate role. (Louisiana is badly in need of a strong corrupt practices law.) Sometimes the issue is sketched clearly in black-versus-white tones, and sometimes the flamboyance of the candidates overshadows all else. Rarely do elections resolve basic issues of public policy.

In a sense, what Louisiana has been grasping for is some semblance of a two-party system that would offer the voters policy alternatives—and help to expel the incumbent scoundrels in Baton Rouge from time to time. V. O. Key suggested that the competition between the pro-Long and anti-Long factions, both of which demonstrated a high degree of cohesion and continuity—even picking entire "tickets" or "slates" at primary time, a phenomenon unknown in most Southern states—offered Louisiana some of the benefits of a two-party system. There was even the phenomenon of anti-Longs administering Longian programs, because in truth, there never was an attempt to restore Bourbon rule as it had existed before the Kingfish. Writes Dr. Perry Howard of Louisiana State University: "Like the national Republican party [in the wake of the New Deal], the anti-Longs chose not to turn back the clock but to preside over the more efficient administration of agencies and services established through the reform impulse of the opposition. The Longs' welfare system provided hundreds of appointive jobs and anti-Longs learned to live with this source of patronage."

Pro- and anti-Longism had their limits as a substitute for genuine two-party politics, however. Political scientist Alan Sindler has pointed out that the courthouse groupings provided no certain local organization for any statewide faction, much less a solid political base comparable to the continuing grass-roots organizations of established parties. In any event, the governorships of Earl Long and Jimmie Davis drew down the curtain on bifactional politics.

The question of recent years has been whether the Republicans could provide a real alternative for Louisiana voters. But with one big exception—Presidential elections—the Pelican State has remained enthusiastically, obdurately, overwhelmingly Democratic. The Republicans have been trying, of course, but with slim results to date. In the 1964 governorship election, Shreveport oilman Charlton Lyons picked up nearly 300,000 votes, 38.5 percent of the total, running on the Republican ticket. The GOP's David Treen carried several metropolitan areas and most of rural northern Louisiana when he ran for governor in the February 1972 general election. But his 480,000 votes represented only 42.8 percent of the total, still far from victory. In those same 1972 elections, the Republicans rose from one seat to a grand total of four in the 105-seat Louisiana house of representatives. The state senate had one Republican—but he was a turncoat who was elected as a Democrat. Thus the aggregate legislative party balance remained 96.5 percent Democratic.

The Republicans' showing in congressional races is even more dismal. In 1972, David Treen was able to score a 55 percent victory in a new congressional district composed primarily of New Orleans' archconservative suburb, Jefferson Parish. But it was a lonely victory—the first time, in fact, that Louisiana had sent a Republican to the U.S. Congress since the election of Confederate Army veteran Hamilton Dudley Coleman of New Orleans in 1888. The Republicans' record in Louisiana congressional elections is the worst of *any party* in *any state* in the 20th century.

Why have the Republicans done so poorly? The principal reasons seem to be a lack of grass-roots organization (except in a few urban areas) and inflexible ideology often tainted with racism. In 1968, during one of his earlier races for Congress, Treen actually came within a few thousand votes of upsetting the late Democratic House leader, Hale Boggs. Treen was making Boggs' vote for civil rights laws the cardinal issue of the campaign. But Treen needed only 6 percent of the black vote to defeat Boggs. Even in the face of that fact, he refused to make even the most low-keyed bid for black support.

Although blacks account for 21 percent of the voting strength in Louisiana, not a single member of their race was put on the state's full delegate slate to the 1968 Republican National Convention. In 1972, two blacks were included—a breakthrough, some said, though National Committeeman Tom Stagg noted that they probably represented less than a thousand black Republicans in the entire state. Early in 1972, there were only 37,087 registered Republicans of any race in Louisiana—compared to 1,617,191 Democrats. The GOP figure now is closer to 50,000. But, as the Ripon Society pointed out in its report on the South, Louisiana's registered illiterates—all 70,000 of them—could easily outvote the Republicans.

In 1971, James R. Satterfield, then the only Republican in the legislature, took aim at both the ideological emphasis and the personnel guiding the state GOP. "Sometimes I think the party looks at itself more as the Conservative party than the Republican party," Satterfield said. All nonconservative voters were being ignored, he asserted. Congressman Treen's political career began as a conservative firebrand, heading the Louisiana States Rights party in 1960 and urging voters to elect a slate of uncommitted Presidential electors. When Ben C. Toledano, another States Righter, ran for the U.S. Senate on the Republican ticket in 1972, he got only 19 percent of the vote, while President Nixon was sweeping the state with a 66 percent vote. An illustration of the GOP's lack of grass-roots strength was the fact that six of the eight Democratic congressional candidates were not even opposed in the banner Republican year of 1972.

Yet with a touch more flexibility, the Republicans might make real headway in Louisiana. Their principal strength is in the metropolitan areas, which have increased from 41 to 55 percent of the state population in the last 30 years.

Sentiment doubtless has a lot to do with Louisiana's Democratic allegiances. Over the years, for instance, there have been many battles to see which Presidential candidate would get the prized Democratic party symbol —the Rooster—over his slate of electors. According to political folklore, the Rooster is worth 100,000 votes. As Leander Perez explained in 1968, generations of French-speaking South Louisianans had been taught *tapez le coq* (pick the rooster)—without even looking to see whose name appeared below! In 1948, the Dixiecrats staged a coup in the Democratic state committee, getting the Rooster put above the electors for Strom Thurmond; Thurmond then proceeded to carry the state with ease. Since then, the regular Democrats have successfully barred a repeat of the larceny, though Humphrey in 1968 and McGovern in 1972 were accorded a donkey symbol instead of the prized Rooster. The professional Democrats, of course, know how little the party name really means. In the words of conservative Congressman Edward Hébert, in a *New Orleans Magazine* interview:

> I had a person come in and try to make me—try to persuade me or ask me to change my registration from Democrat to Republican. I said, "Why?" Neither party has any principle. They don't. . . . The outs are trying to get in and the ins are trying to stay in. There's no real, set, positive program of either party. . . . But we do need parties. And that amounts to this: the responsibility of housekeeping. Somebody's got to put the cat out and take the milk in. And it ends there.

Aficionados of the ethnic-regional oddities of Louisiana politics always look to see if an election has produced a definite cleavage between the fundamentalist north, which thinks and votes like most of the Deep South upcountry and pineywoods areas—and indeed was populated significantly by the overflow of settlers in Alabama and Mississippi—as opposed to the more Catholic and languid, Cajun- and Creole-dominated parishes of southern Louisiana, which bear such colorful names as LaFourche, Terrebonne, Calcasieu, and Plaquemines.

The geographic division actually has to be refined beyond a simple north-south cleavage. One division, used by the Public Affairs Research Council of Louisiana, splits the state four ways: north Louisiana (the entire upper half of the state), Acadiana (the bayou-dotted French Catholic parishes covering all of southwestern and south central Louisiana), the Florida parishes (so called because they were once part of West Florida, and were settled by Americans, not French), and finally the New Orleans area (which includes not only that ethnically variegated and worldly city but its vividly conservative outlying areas, including suburban Jefferson, St. Bernard, and Plaquemines Parish).

The December 1971 Democratic runoff primary for governor offered a clear-cut contest between the regions. Protestant state senator J. Bennett Johnston of northern Louisiana (who was subsequently elected to the U.S. Senate) faced Roman Catholic Congressman Edwin Edwards, who had grown up in a family of French-speaking sharecroppers and happily exploited the theme of "Cajun power" in his native Acadiana. By adding to his French base a coalition of urban, labor, and black voters, Edwards was able to eke out a narrow 50.2 percent victory. The regional pattern was this:

Region	*% for Edwards*	*% for Johnston*
Acadiana	68.0	32.0
Florida Parishes	39.9	60.1
New Orleans	49.2	50.3
North Louisiana	35.1	64.9

An especially heavy voter turnout for "one of its own" in Acadiana was vital to Edwards' victory—plus the fact that no clear-cut racial or ideological issues divided the two candidates. It was a different story in the bitter 1960 and 1964 governorship primaries, in which the segregationist-oriented candidates of northern Louisiana (Jimmie Davis in 1960, John J. McKeithen in 1964) piled up such overwhelming pluralities in their part of the state that they easily submerged the late deLesseps Morrison, who was the mayor of New Orleans for many years and considered a symbol of Catholic-Gallic, South Louisiana urbanism. The political genius of the Longs—Huey, his brother Earl, and their political surrogates in the years from 1928 to 1956—had been that they had submerged race and religion as cutting issues in Louisiana politics, establishing a firm base among both whites and blacks, Protestants and Catholics. McKeithen, a former Long legislative leader who was nonetheless scorned by some parts of the old Long camp, was able to turn the same trick as his mentors for a few years in the 1960s, pleasing all geographic regions and both races (with an alternating segregationist-moderate line) so well that he convinced the state's voters to change the constitution and let him run for a second term in 1964. He was an unpopular man by the end of his eight years in office, however.

A. J. Liebling relayed a delightful analysis of Louisiana's electoral patterns by his guide around the state, newspaperman Tom Sancton:

> [Louisiana is] the most complex state in the South. In just about every one of the others you have the same battle between the poor-to-middling farmers on the

poor lands—generally in the hills—that didn't justify an investment in slaves before the war, and the descendants of the rich planters on the rich lands, who held slaves by the dozen to the gross. . . . We had that same conflict, but in addition, we have a lot that are all our own. In other states it was just between the poor Anglo-Saxon Protestant whites and the rich Anglo-Saxon Protestant whites. But here we got poor French Catholic whites and poor Anglo-Saxon whites and rich French Catholic whites. Sometimes the Catholic French got together against the Anglo-Saxon Protestants and sometimes the rich of both faiths got together against the poor, or the poor against the rich.

And there's always been another problem in Louisiana that no other Southern state has. There are other large collections of people living close together in the South, but they are not big cities, just overgrown country towns. . . . They may have corruption, but not sophistication [like New Orleans has]. They lack the urban psychology, like ancient Athens, that is different, hostile, and superior, and that the countryman resents and distrusts. So you get a split along another line—you got not only poor rural French Catholic, rich rural white Protestant, rich rural French Catholic, and poor rural white Protestant, but poor urban Catholic not exclusively French, rich urban Catholic, poor urban Protestant (mostly Negro) and rich urban Protestant. Making out a ticket is tricky.

Liebling then asked Sancton how Huey Long had put all the bits and pieces together. The reply:

Huey got all the poor people over on one side. And there were a lot more of them. He made the poor redneck and the poor Frenchman and the poor Negro see that what they had in common was more important for voting purposes than the differences. The differences couldn't be changed by ballots.

The Depression helped, of course. [But] when people are living good again they can afford to fight over the unessentials.

In times past, those "unessentials" often revolved around religion-related questions—liquor sales, Sunday blue laws, or Roman Catholics running for office. During the early 1920s, for instance, the French-Catholic parishes began to drift toward the GOP; according to Kevin Phillips, the reason was their resentment over foreign policy differences President Wilson had had with France. But in 1928 the Catholics returned en masse to the Democratic column to register an overwhelming vote for their coreligionist, Alfred E. Smith. In 1960 the same French-dominated areas gave John F. Kennedy margins of 70 to 80 percent—while Kennedy was winning less than a quarter of the vote in northern Louisiana.

The other great "unessential," of course, was (and is) race. The fact that Louisiana politicians generally did not resort to "nigger-baiting" on a scale comparable to other Deep South states could not mask the fact that blacks were totally isolated from decision-making in Louisiana until the white primary was outlawed by the Supreme Court in 1944. In 1940 less than 0.5 percent of the state's blacks were registered, and in 1947, only 2 percent. In 1951 the Democratic State Central Committee belatedly dropped the requirement that a voter or candidate in party primaries "shall be a white person." The results were immediately obvious: in 1952 a quarter of the voting age blacks in Louisiana were registered, and they helped Adlai Stevenson carry the state that year. By 1956, black registration had edged up to 31 percent, and Negroes voted more Republican, helping President Eisenhower carry Louisiana. Yet there were still several black majority parishes where the whites had so intimidated their black brothers and sisters that not a single Negro was registered to vote.

Proportionately, the early Negro registration was twice as great in New Orleans and the French-Catholic parishes as it was in northern Louisiana—not because the French-Catholics were avid integrationists, but because the Catholic Church was actively expressing the ideal of the Negro's equality in society. As A. P. Tureaud pointed out, "in parts of southern Louisiana, you have a large number of Negro Catholics. There's a close association between a Negro Catholic and a white Catholic—they go to the same church, take communion together. Negro Catholics in such communities are often French-speaking. They're neighbors, they talk with each other, and they share the same economic level, more or less." In some areas of northern Louisiana, on the other hand, black voter registration could be effected only with the help of federal voting registrars in the 1960s. And to this day, one hears tales of plantation-based Negroes who fear social and economic repression if they dare to register and vote in that part of the state.

By the early 1970s, between 55 and 60 percent of the eligible blacks were registered in Louisiana, and the 1972 elections increased the number of black elected officials in the state from 79 to 119, including eight in the state house of representatives. (Previously there had been only one.) The first significant gubernatorial appointments of blacks came under McKeithen—McKeithen boasted, in fact, that he had appointed the first two black judges in the South.

By the early 1970s, memories were fast fading of the "hard-seg" days of the 1950s, when the legislature, spurred on by the (white) Citizens Council movement, had aided and abetted the purging of Negroes from voter registration rolls. Governor Davis, the late Hale Boggs told me, helped put through "the goddamnedest bunch of repressive tests on voting you could imagine—the whole idea was, 'if you're white, you're right.'" Also almost forgotten now is the 1960–61 series of five successive special sessions, which enacted an incredible array of bills designed to stem any and all forms of racial integration. The tone of the 1972 legislative session was set instead by Governor Edwards in his inaugural speech in which he said: "To the poor, the elderly, the unemployed, the thousands of black Louisianans who have not yet enjoyed the full bounty of the American dream, we extend not a palm with alms but the hand of friendship. We understand your plight. We shall lighten your burdens and open wide the doors of opportunity." Edwards subsequently appointed blacks to a number of important policy-making posts and in less than a year had increased the number of blacks in civil service by about 25 percent, even while the total number of state employees was going down.

The 1972 legislative session even had the grace to repeal the old Jim Crow laws, including most references to race in state statutes—and not a single legislator got up to give one of the crude racist speeches so popular a few years before.* In fact, the house chamber in Baton Rouge was the

* The repealed laws—which had already been declared unconstitutional—banned interracial marriage, dancing, or even interracial socializing, and required segregated seating on buses and trains, separate rest rooms for blacks and whites, separate water fountains and waiting rooms.

scene of a remarkable speech by Risley Claiborne (Pappy) Triche, a legislator from the south Louisiana bayou town of Napoleonville who had been Governor Jimmie Davis' floor leader in a marathon session 12 years before that tried to ward off federally ordered desegregation of the public schools. Now Triche was the chief floor leader for Governor Edwards, and he stood straight in a white seersucker suit to argue for two bills designed to protect blacks from discrimination in employment.

> I know [Triche said] what some of you think. I know what some of the people outside the halls of this house are going to think—"O, but listen to that segregationist. Isn't that the guy who offered all the segregation bills in 1960 and fought our public school system?"
>
> The only reply I can make to that, gentlemen, is that yes, that occurred. And at that time in the state of development of the history of our state we thought that we were correct. And we now find that we were wrong.

Triche said he had retired voluntarily from the legislature in 1968, planning never to return, but changed his mind after four years:

> The one thing that drove me back was that I did not want to leave my children with the legacy that their daddy was a bigot and a racist.
>
> I am not a bigot and a racist. I want my family and my citizens and my friends and my constituents and the citizenry of this state to grow out of racism and bigotry.
>
> Let us join hands with all the people of this state, black and white, regardless of race, creed, or color, for the advancement and betterment of our state and nation.

Triche, in his new incarnation, probably does not speak for a majority of white Louisianans. The voters, in fact, are more likely to support tacit racists and, on occasion, rabid segregationists. Most prominent of the latter is Democratic Congressman John R. Rarick, who sees a Communist plot behind every move for racial justice and was called by Michigan's black Congressman, Charles C. Diggs, "a leading racist in the Congress." Rarick has received John Birch Society support and—according to James H. Morrison, the moderate Congressman he ousted in 1966—once served as "Grand Cyclops" of the Ku Klux Klan chapter at St. Francisville, Louisiana.

There have, of course, been strong moderating influences in Louisiana. The U.S. Fifth Circuit Court of Appeals in New Orleans has been a bulwark in defending the rights of blacks in Louisiana and other Southern states during the crucial civil rights battles of recent years; as Pat Watters has written, the Fifth Circuit, under men like Elbert Tuttle and Louisiana's own John Minor Wisdom, "more than once salvaged the system of law, and American decency, from complete discredit in the eyes of Negro Southerners" and may have been "the most important court in the country except for the Supreme Court itself." But many of the district judges have done all in their power to preserve segregation of the races. A case in point is Judge Ben C. Dawkins, Jr., of Shreveport, who used every trick he could think of to slow down the pace of school integration and said in one hearing that if he could have his way, "I'd still be on *Plessy vs. Ferguson*, separate but equal."

Really significant school integration in Louisiana—like most other Southern states—had to wait for a decade and a half after the Supreme Court's 1954 decision. Since the late 1960s, federally mandated desegregation of the schools has rolled in like a great tidal wave in both rural and urban Louisiana. More than two-thirds of the state's students attended integrated schools by 1972, but there were still hundreds of schools 100 percent or almost all white or black. There were some cases in which integration was subverted by demotion and dismissal of black educators and the humiliation of black students.

In the biggest wave of court-ordered integration in the late '60s, some 40,000 white students (about 8 percent of total white enrollment) switched to private and parochial schools. But since then, there has been a steady shift back to the public schools, primarily because most Louisianans, especially in rural areas, cannot afford the cost of private schools. The Roman Catholic Church, which lost a golden opportunity to provide moral leadership when it failed to abolish segregation in its own schools during the 1961 school crisis in New Orleans, has integrated its schools slowly, often following the standard set by the state schools. The parochial schools have been in real danger of becoming havens for whites fleeing integrated public schools, but Archbishop Philip M. Hannan of New Orleans and Bishop Robert E. Tracy of Baton Rouge have tried to stop that from happening. The picture is complicated by the present-day financial pinch of the parochial schools; in 1970 Catholic lobbyists got the legislature to vote aid to parochial school teachers, but the bill was amended to aid teachers of segregated academies as well, and the state supreme court struck it down.

The election of more and more blacks to school boards * will help to eliminate racism in school administrations and classrooms alike—the only really insoluble problem being how to keep white children in schools which tip more than 50 percent black. Louisiana NAACP president Emmitt Douglas said in 1972 that "we still have a long way to go" in school integration, but that "I certainly feel that in the next decade most of our problems will be just about over."

Still, Louisiana blacks have little reason to believe their acceptance into the state's political life is more than grudging or partial. The Presidential election results illustrate the point rather neatly. Before the national Democratic party became identified with the civil rights cause, Louisiana had chalked up Democratic Presidential percentages like 93 percent in 1932 and 81 percent in 1944. But when Harry Truman spoke up for the Negro cause in 1948, Strom Thurmond's Dixiecrats swept the state. Kennedy won Louisiana in 1960 only because of his Roman Catholicism and because conservatives split between Nixon and an independent elector slate.

In 1964, as resentment boiled to a head over civil rights legislation backed by the national Democratic party, Barry Goldwater swept Louisiana with 57 percent of the vote. The French bayou and Gulf Coast parishes stayed fairly Democratic that year; the Republican edge was accounted for

* By 1973 there were 36 black school board members in Louisiana, part of an overall total of 127 black elected officials in the state.

almost entirely by northern Louisiana. But in 1968, south Louisiana, too, was voting against the national Democrats and for George Wallace. Kevin Phillips noted: "To French Louisiana, as well as the Georgia and Alabama upcountry, the national Democratic party has become the Negro party, and white voters looked elsewhere." Professor Perry Howard of Louisiana State University put it another way: "Push the 'race button' and the bell still rings."

The anti-Democratic trend in Presidential voting was reinforced in 1972, when Nixon swept every region of Louisiana with 60 to 70 percent of the vote. Even the city of New Orleans, where Humphrey had won narrowly in 1968, was in Nixon's column by '72. Acadiana was only a few percentage points less strongly for Nixon than northern Louisiana. McGovern, like Humphrey before him, could only make a strong race in areas of exceptionally high Negro registration. The isolation of Louisiana blacks was reflected in the fact that they gave McGovern 75 to 90 percent of their vote, compared to his statewide average of 29 percent.*

In non-Presidential elections, on the other hand, some of Louisiana's own regular Democratic politicians have managed to avoid disruptive race questions and focus on substantive issues like honesty in government. This was particularly true in the 1971–72 gubernatorial primaries and election, when the voters were hot for change after a long series of disclosures about graft, bribery, influence peddling and organized crime in their state. As attorney general, for instance, they elected William J. Guste, Jr., a liberal Catholic state senator from New Orleans who pledged to "raise the whole moral tone in state government" and to concentrate on consumer and environmental issues. Once in office, he proved to be an exceptionally aggressive law enforcement officer.

No less than 17 candidates entered the Democratic governorship primary, including a millionaire grocer, two blacks, two cousins of Huey Long, an oil company owner, the lieutenant governor, a *Life* magazine reporter who had written about Mafia ties to the governor's office, and (yet again) Jimmie Davis. Davis tried to exploit the race issue, coming down hard against busing of schoolchildren, but his past record came back to haunt and discredit him. When the smoke had cleared, the two men qualified for the runoff were young moderates who had campaigned as champions of reform —Edwin Edwards and J. Bennett Johnston. Both had appealed to the Negro vote, though Edwards got more of it. In the runoff, as we noted earlier, Edwards scored a narrow victory. He became the first governor in 28 years who did not hail from northern Louisiana, and the first Roman Catholic governor of the 20th century.

Edwards is a man of real intellectual capacity and potential, but like John McKeithen, he takes more joy in politics than in the nitty-gritty details of governing. All Louisiana governors seem to make the fatal error of

* One of the continuing anachronisms of Louisiana politics is that the names of all the Presidential electors are listed on the ballot, and a voter can "split" his ticket if he likes. The American party, which got only 4 percent of the vote statewide, had one elector named "McGowen." Voters in heavily black areas, apparently confusing his name with that of McGovern, gave him 8 to 20 percent of their vote.

executives: failing to hire outstanding staff. Instead, they tend to surround themselves with back-room politicians trying to fix things up for themselves.

McKeithen, for instance, must be listed as one of the tragic figures of modern Southern politics. He was a man of real charisma but also deviousness. I remember the day I interviewed him. I had laryngitis and could barely croak or whisper out five- or six-word questions. That didn't matter to Big John. With each hint of a question, he was off on flights of oratory, arms flailing in the air, extolling his own record. An astute observer of Louisiana politics later told me: "McKeithen could have been a much better governor than he was. He was too involved in trying to con people. He promised everybody everything, but when it finally came to delivering, he couldn't do it. He was the first to talk openly of really helping blacks, but he was afraid to go too far. He actually had aspirations to be Vice President in 1968. But he could never get past his political heritage. He learned how to lie from Earl Long, but Earl didn't teach him how to govern."

Yet for all the problems that remain, Louisiana politics have become a much more above-board, savory affair over the past several years. Issues are now much more important, and personalities less dominant than they used to be. The "ticket system" in the Democratic primary, in which gubernatorial nominees sometimes swept incompetents and thieves into office on their coattails, has passed away. And public awareness of candidates' records has increased dramatically. In the words of civic leader Edward Steimel: "People are more in control of their destinies—political, economic, and social—than they were 20 years ago."

Trials and Temptations of Louisiana Government

Louisiana labors under what may be the ultimate horror in overblown, obtuse state constitutions. Length alone tells much of the story. The Constitution of the United States and its 26 amendments, for instance, fits neatly into pamphlet form. But the Louisiana constitution, laden with more than 500 amendments, fills a tome of more than 800 pages. It was approved in 1921 but includes portions of the original constitution of 1812 plus parts of other constitutions written in 1879, 1898, and 1913. The document is filled with detail that should be in statutes, local charters, or administrative manuals; among the amendments recently proposed, for instance, was one "to authorize the Police Jury of Avoyelles Parish to reduce the number of justices of the peace in its Ward 9, from two to one." No wonder the Public Affairs Research Council of Louisiana (PAR) asserts that "local governments are hamstrung by constitutional provisions" and the constitution is "contradictory and incomprehensible even to judges and scholars." Margaret Dixon explained that "the constitution is so long because the people don't trust the legislature." But the people have tired of facing dozens of amendments on each election ballot; asked to vote on 53 amendments in 1970, for instance, they voted down all 53.

Among the fruits of a constitution gone amock is the total of state agencies in Louisiana: 263, the most of any state, and four times the national average. "No governor," PAR commented, "could sit astride this sprawling operation and administer it well. Rather, each agency tends to become an independent empire that runs itself." The governor sits on 26 boards and commissions, and has appointive power over 1,500 agency appointments. It is obviously impossible for him to know that many people with the diverse qualifications required, and to provide responsible leadership for them. The only advantage to him is political. As Southern reporter Nicholas Chriss of the Los Angeles *Times* commented, "the state structure drips with juicy patronage jobs, agencies are pyramided on top of other agencies, payrolls on top of payrolls." Until 1972, the state government used 1,113 bank accounts in a nightmarish bookkeeping system.

In contrast to the ideal of a state government with a minimum of elected officials who can be known to the voters and more easily held accountable for their actions, the Louisiana constitution requires the election of no less than 11 statewide officials, including a full complement of constitutional officers and even the custodian of voting machines. By district, voters must also decide who will sit on the board of education and the public utilities commission. Yet in relation to the legislature, the constitution permits and custom has sanctioned the passage of inordinate power into the hands of the governor. He dominates the selection of key senate and house floor leaders and committee chairmen, and actually appoints the members of the legislative budget committee who are charged with reviewing the executive budget he submits. Legislators often fear to buck the governor because of the local needs of their parishes; the attitude was described to me as "Why kill Santa Claus?"

The gubernatorial dominance was carried to its all-time high by Huey Long, but his brother Earl was no piker in whipping legislators into line. Earl had tote boards in his office, connected to the ones on the legislative floor with lights to show how members were voting. He also had loudspeakers in his office so he could hear what was being said in debate. When Earl was upset, he would burst into the house or senate floor during debate and read the riot act to anyone about to vote against him.

Over the years, the system was made all the worse by the custom of gubernatorial appointment of legislators to positions in the executive branch, another gross violation of the principle of separation of powers. In a 1968 report, the Louisiana Municipal Association said that "the powers of the legislative branch are so much under control and domination of the executive that it no longer deserves to be called a branch. It comes closer to being a twig and a badly bent one at that."

Edwin Edwards, McKeithen's successor, knows how to use the tools of patronage but has generally relied more on reason and persuasion in dealing with the legislature than did his predecessors. In his first year in office, Edwards began steps toward reorganization of the state government into a manageable number of departments, effected revision of the tax laws to eliminate several loopholes, and balanced the budget. And he made a major breakthrough by winning approval of a constitutional convention, which began its deliberations in January 1973.

By almost any standard one might name—from the professional qualification of its members to decorum—the Louisiana legislature has improved markedly in recent years. Reapportionment has helped to clean out some of the deadwood. A decade ago, senate districts ranged from 31,175 to 248,427 in population, and house districts from 6,909 to 120,205, thus preserving many a rotten borough. But now the federal courts have effectively killed malapportionment, so that today no district varies more than 2 percent from the average. When the legislators came up with a sleazy "protect incumbents" plan after the 1970 Census, a federal judge declared it invalid and asked Edward J. Steimel, executive director of PAR, to come up with a decent plan; the apportionment then ordered into effect eliminated multimember and overlapping districts, substantially increased the chances of blacks and Republicans to make gains, and resulted in an unprecedented turnover of membership in the 1971 election.

One change effected by the newly apportioned legislature was the barring of lobbyists from the floor of the house during sessions. I had visited Baton Rouge before that reform was effected and was shocked to see lobbyists—including representatives of labor, business, and even the redoubtable Leander Perez—leaning over the rails while votes were being taken to signal, cajole, and intimidate the legislators. Unauthorized persons sometimes pushed the legislators' vote buttons. Now the lobbyists are at least required to sit in the rear of the chamber.

A lot more reforms will be necessary before Louisiana has a decently run legislature, however. "Fiscal sessions," limited to 30 days every two years, are much too short to come to grips with the governor's budget. Legislators have no office beyond a three-by-two-foot desk on the chamber floor; their conference rooms are bars, restaurants, and hotel rooms. Committees float from place to place since they have no assigned rooms. There is no research staff. Overall, it is amazing that the Citizens Conference on State Legislatures gave Louisiana a rank as high as 33rd among the 50 states in the overall quality of its legislature.

Several well-heeled lobbies exert strong and continuing influence on the Louisiana legislators. Predictably enough in this major oil and gas state, the oil companies are particularly well represented. Each of the majors—Exxon, Chevron, Texaco, Gulf, Shell, Mobil—has its own man in Baton Rouge. The Mid-Continental Oil and Gas Association usually has three men lobbying for its membership. The gas pipeline interests are represented, as well as the closely allied Louisiana Chemical Association, representing 35 to 40 companies. There are also lobbyists from the forest industry, the rice industry, the Louisiana Manufacturers Association, the Farm Bureau, and organized labor.

The winds of reform never seem able to dispel the lingering aroma of corruption that surrounds government in Louisiana; as a well-informed Baton Rouge attorney said not long ago, "reform in Louisiana consists of turning out the fat hogs and letting the lean hogs in." A code of ethics adopted in the 1960s has disappointed its proponents, who privately agree with the late Margaret Dixon that it is "more loophole than reality," especially as it applies to elected officials. The reasons for Louisiana's ethics problems may lie in the unique fusion of Gallic and Anglo-Saxon cultures, or the general assumption, prevalent since the days of Bourbon rule, that "someone is making money off the state, and it might as well be me." Huey Long once called his legislature "the best legislature money can buy." Another former governor boasted, "When I took the oath of office, I didn't take no vows of poverty."

The standard form of corruption has been shakedown of state contractors, a milieu in which someone's palm needs to be crossed to do anything. But the corruption has taken many forms. When Jimmie Davis was governor, he gave his friends a charter for a tiny tin-roofed bank in Baker, Louisiana. John Corporon, then star reporter for WDSU-TV in New Orleans, revealed how Davis had shifted millions of dollars in state funds into the bank, so that its owners—who included Davis' administrative assistant, his chief financial backer, and his legal counsel—could invest the money elsewhere and draw enough principal to earn $200,000 a year. Earl Long told Corporon that when a trucker entered the state, he would be inspected at the state line, and if he wasn't cooperative, "you'd say he's overweight or these dimensions don't fit. If he's carrying eggs or vegetables," Long said, "he had to make an awfully fast decision."

In the late 1960s, *Life* magazine shook Louisiana with charges that Mafia influence was so great in the state that its politics and commerce were hoodlum-dominated. The center of *Life*'s exposés was an alleged "Mob chieftain," Carlos Marcello, who the magazine said was "the unchallenged giant of organized crime, and of the state itself."

After *Life*'s first story, in 1967, Governor McKeithen led a delegation of Louisianans to New York to confer with *Life*'s editors and writers on Mafia activity and returned home promising to use the evidence provided to "clean up our state and we think put some people in the penitentiary." But after the 1970 story, which implied that McKeithen was doing nothing to stop Mafia influence and had at least one top staff aide with some ties to Marcello, McKeithen decided he was the target of a vendetta and filed (but later dropped) a $10 million libel suit against the magazine.*

As for Marcello himself, he is a stocky, five-foot one-inch, fiercely authoritarian little man whom the Justice Department has sought for years to deport. By some accounts, the New Orleans "family" was organized by Sicilian immigrants in 1876 and thus has the distinction of being the first in America. Marcello, who has headed it since 1945, was called the most

* According to McKeithen, *Life* was after him because he spearheaded the investigations leading to indictment of some Baton Rouge Teamsters officials on racketeering charges. The Baton Rouge Teamsters were then headed by Edward G. Partin, who had been a nationally controversial figure since 1964 when he gave testimony that led to the conviction of Teamsters president James R. Hoffa for jury tampering. "Elements of the Justice Department were obligated by blood to protect him (Partin) from trouble because he had been responsible, they felt, in convicting Hoffa," McKeithen said in an interview. Therefore elements of the Justice Department "tried to get me in trouble" and were indirectly responsible for "the terrible smear placed on me by *Life* magazine. . . ."

powerfully entrenched Mafia chief in the United States by one federal investigator. Federal officials estimated his wealth in 1971 at $40 million, mostly in banks, real estate, motels, restaurants, and vending machines. Marcello has denied that he is a mob boss, a gambler, or anything illegal; he describes himself instead as a land-speculator, with a part-time job as a tomato salesman.

One of the clearest indications of continuing trouble in state government came in 1969 when the attorney general, Jack Gremillion, was indicted along with a state representative and three other men by a federal grand jury on charges of obtaining money and property by fraud and conspiracy. All had been involved with the Louisiana Loan & Thrift Corporation, organized in 1966 by Gremillion and others. The company took in some $2.6 million in deposits from 1,400 depositors. Gremillion wrote legal opinions which effectively insulated the company from S. E. C. regulation. He also received $10,000 in fees and got a $200,000 loan from the company—shortly before it went into receivership, leaving its depositors high and dry. Eventually Gremillion was acquitted on the fraud and conspiracy charges, but in 1971 he was convicted by a federal grand jury of having committed perjury when he denied having a financial interest in the loan company. The voters had had their fill of Gremillion and turned him out of office that year. Subsequently he was sentenced to three years in prison.

And by the time of the 1971 elections, several state education employees were also under indictment for accepting federal funds for jobs in which they allegedly did not work. One of the three state tax commissioners had retired abruptly after disclosure that he had collected an annual salary of $16,000 but never once in a year's time set foot in the commissioner's office. A legislative committee set up to investigate the influence of the Mafia in state government found that the treatment which the state revenue department had accorded various businesses and individuals associated with Carlos Marcello was "so noticeable and substantially improper as to create a suspicion of corrupt influence"—a remarkable decision by a commission which had first seemed more interested in discrediting *Life* investigative reporter David Chandler, who had first brought the Mafia allegations to public attention, than in getting at the root of the corruption he charged.

The reform wave of the early 1970s seemed to be one of the strongest in the state's modern history, but its durability was another question. Any Louisianan complacent about the moral tone would do well to recall the words of Henry Clay Warmouth, the Reconstruction-era governor, who said a century ago: "I don't pretend to be honest. . . . I only pretend to be as honest as anybody in politics. . . . Why, damn it, everybody is demoralized down here. Corruption is the fashion."

And it is not only the fashion in state government, but in an enduring and shocking way in local government. Exhibit A-1 must be the archaic, bizarre property tax assessment practices in the state's 64 parishes.

Under law, the parish assessors, all of whom are popularly elected, are supposed to assess all property at its fair market value, and then report the total assessment to the state tax commission, which should then set the millage rate based on instructions from the state legislature. The tax commission is mandated by the state constitution to determine in each parish the value of all assessed property in relation to actual value.

So much for theory. The fact of the matter is that assessments, compared to the true value of property, vary wildly from parish to parish and even more egregiously within each parish. In a study of 15 selected parishes, the Public Affairs Research Council found the variations in assessments of various pieces of property ranged from 2 to 21 percent of true value in suburban Jefferson Parish to an incredible 1 to 550 percent in rural Red River Parish. In Caddo Parish (Shreveport) the variation was 5 to 111 percent, in East Baton Rouge 6 to 66 percent. A typical example: in Calcasieu Parish, a $71,875 house was assessed at $4,800 while a $12,500 house was assessed at $6,050. In Caddo, a $10,000 and a $45,000 house were each assessed at $8,000. And between parishes, PAR found, average assessments varied more than four to one.

Since they are elected, the assessors curry political favor with voters by setting low assessments on their property—or punish people they do not like by setting high assessments on their property. Sometime they will hand a property-owner a pencil and let him set his own assessment. As a result, the assessor is often more powerful than all other parish politicians put together. Though elective, the assessor's job is often handed down from father to son. Challenging an incumbent assessor can be a risky business, because if one runs and loses, his penalty could well be sky-high taxes for life.

Obviously, the system invites wholesale skulduggery. Many assessors are surely greasing their own palms. And suspicious pressures must have been brought to bear on the state tax commission to persuade it brazenly to defy the constitutional requirement which says it must make an annual determination of the assessment ratio in each parish and see to it that all property is taxed equitably.

Like legislative malapportionment, such massive defiance of law by government itself invites intervention by the courts. In 1972 a favorable federal court ruling in a suit by New Orleans Mayor Moon Landrieu obliged the legislature to eliminate one of the most misused provisions in the state tax law—the provision requiring that the state government reimburse the parishes and school boards for the revenue they lost through the "homestead exemption" on the first $2,000 of assessed value of any owner-occupied home. The legislature substituted a form of state general revenue sharing, terminating the old system under which the parishes with the most egregiously low assessments—and thus the most homeowners paying no taxes, or virtually none, because of the homestead exemption—were actually subsidized by the taxpayers of Louisiana as a whole.

Then, early in 1973, the state supreme court upheld a suit filed by the state AFL-CIO to compel the state tax commission to comply with the state constitution by seeing to it that assessors placed a true value on all property. The court not only held that the state tax commission had to effect complete statewide property tax equalization by 1975, but it closed the door on any backdown by the legislature by saying the old practices violated both the Louisiana constitution and the equal protection clause of the U.S. Constitution.

PAR, CABL, and a Remarkable State AFL-CIO

Those who view industry and labor as eternally antagonistic, and would divide the forces influencing government into simplistic "white hat" and "black hat" groups, are in for a rude shock when they look at the Louisiana situation. For much of the postwar period, a remarkable industry-labor alliance has been at work in the state. It has strong "establishment" hallmarks, but on balance it has probably been as powerful a force for civic advancement and racial sanity as any in modern Louisiana or, for that matter, in any Southern state in our time.

The story goes back to 1951 and the bitter fight between the Longs and Standard Oil of New Jersey, a fight which indirectly provided the genesis of the Public Affairs Research Council. Cecil Morgan, a distinguished New Orleans lawyer who for years was counsel for Standard Oil and later became president of the National Municipal League, was the real founding genius of PAR, and explained to me how it happened:

> The newspapers had been the only group doing research on government, but the Longs always discredited them by calling them "those lying newspapers." I was a member of the Midcontinent Oil and Gas Association of which Charlton Lyons of Shreveport [who later became the first prominent Republican leader of modern Louisiana] was chairman.
>
> At some meetings, I said, "the oil companies can never present their case as oil companies and expect to have a hearing in the state legislature because it's a special interest that's speaking. We have to identify ourselves with the public interest to get anywhere. When we speak out alone we won't be recognized. We ought to find ways to organize a grassroots group that can be completely objective. It ought not to be dominated by any group—not even our group."
>
> I said we needed good citizens like Parrish Fuller, a respected man in the Long faction, to work with us in bringing an objective approach to the solution of Louisiana's problems. So we enlisted Fuller, and then I discussed with Charlton how we could go at the organizational job. We decided to have a meeting called by the presidents of four prominent private universities in the state. We needed to do a lot of groundwork and have support lined up. So I gave to Dan Spurlock, who was working under me at the Standard Oil plant in Baton Rouge, the job of going all over the state and quietly talking to leaders in both the Long and anti-Long factions.
>
> After we had gotten a hard core of leaders on both sides, in various walks of life—and that meant a real cross-section of farmers, laborers, big business, little business, Huey Longites, anti-Longites, all of them well represented—then Charlton Lyons went to see the presidents of the four universities, and they joined us in calling the organizational meeting in Alexandria.
>
> Now while all this was going on, I was directing and getting reports. And whenever it appeared that Standard Oil was having too much to do with it, I would say, "Dan, don't speak to a living soul. You can telephone Parrish Fuller and tell him to do something." That was OK, because he was on the other side.
>
> Eventually, the meeting was held with some 125 citizens present. I was in the hospital with ulcers and wasn't even present. But they organized under the charter and principles we had carefully worked out. They had to stay out of ac-

tivist politics. I refused to let my company contribute the largest amount, and put a definite ceiling on the amount it could give. I just operated on the sidelines. They took it over and made it run. It has been accepted because the studies it does are truly objective, and the facts it presents are accepted as facts by all factions.

PAR was distinguished from the start by the *quality* of the men and women involved in its efforts. The list included not only Cecil Morgan and Charlton Lyons, but men like Edgar Stern, Sr., the head of a prominent Jewish family in New Orleans which had made a fortune in investments and over the years was to exert as salutary and progressive an influence on Southern life as any family in the region's modern history. The Sterns were heavily involved in philanthropy, first through their Edgar Stern Family Fund in Louisiana and then its New York-based successor, the Stern Foundation. During the 1950s the Sterns made New Orleans television station WDSU into perhaps the most outstanding local station in the United States for investigative reporting and general public affairs programming. (The Sterns finally sold their New Orleans television holdings in 1972, about the time that Edgar Stern, Jr., who succeeded his father as manager of the family's Louisiana interests, moved to Colorado. Sad to report, the quality of television journalism on WDSU began to decline. But Edgar Stern, Sr.'s widow, the former Edith Rosenwald, heir to part of the Sears Roebuck fortune, continued to live in New Orleans, showing—despite her advanced age—a lively interest in vocational education and other civic projects.)

As one of its first staff members, and executive director from 1953 onwards, PAR selected Edward J. Steimel, an expert public affairs executive and fundraiser. Steimel has stepped gingerly through the quagmires of Louisiana politics to fulfill PAR's mission of being "a private nonprofit research organization devoted to improving Louisiana government and to correcting the state's basic political weaknesses through public enlightenment without political alignment." The organization has more than 5,000 members—business big and small, individuals, and for a decade now, the state AFL-CIO members contribute between $35 and $10,000 a year to support a large research staff and broad publications program. The long list of PAR interests has included constitutional revision, improvement of the legislature, quality education, ethics in government, reforming the state's horrendous tax assessment practices, crime prevention, economic growth, better campaigns and elections, and more enlightened race relations.

Despite Cecil Morgan's best efforts to give PAR a broad base, it was attacked in its early years—especially during the Earl Long administration—as a tool of the big industries, particularly oil. But the big business image has now faded almost completely, because PAR has bucked the special interests of some of its own members—and suffered periodic membership losses as a result. When it recommended that the state invest interest-free funds it had deposited in state banks, 30 banks withdrew in one fell swoop, and it took 13 years for the last banks to rejoin. Later, 60 insurance agencies resigned in a huff when PAR proposed a market system of establishing insurance rates, instead of guaranteed commissions. Whether by design or coincidence, PAR has never fought the oil interests, but Steimel believes the organization's general independence "has taken away the stigma of Standard Oil or any other major interest." Although the relationship has sometimes been strained, the state AFL-CIO has also been a PAR member since 1963. Some governors, McKeithen in particular, have attacked and ridiculed PAR for questioning the quality of their leadership of the state. But the organization's prestige got a great boost in the early 1970s, when Federal Judge Gordon E. West asked Steimel to be a special master to draw up the new legislative reapportionment plan. The entire PAR staff pitched in to draw the district lines, which were then sustained on appeal all the way to the U.S. Supreme Court.

A companion group to PAR, called the Council for a Better Louisiana (CABL), flourished during the 1960s and had a marked impact in effecting several reforms, including a code of ethics for the state government. At the time of CABL's formation, Governor Jimmie Davis and the legislature were on a racist binge that was plunging the state into economic and spiritual chaos. Moderate leaders wanted to create a direct lobbying organization, with political muscle, that could bring pressure to bear for reform on a broad array of issues.

Edgar Stern, Jr., called the meeting to form CABL in a room of the Royal Orleans Hotel. Several prominent business leaders were there, including Stern himself. PAR's Edward Steimel was in attendance, and later one of his staff men, Edward W. Stagg, became director of the new organization. CABL was required, Stern told me later, because Louisiana has no big home-based, civic-minded corporations that could exert moderating influence and "prevent the politicians from running wild." CABL's backers were primarily businessmen but also included clergy, leaders in education, and, very significantly, organized labor. The AFL-CIO agreed to participate on the condition that CABL would take no stands in direct opposition to its interests.

By the 1964 gubernatorial election, every candidate agreed to support CABL's goals on tax reform and other issues. McKeithen, elected governor that year, subsequently turned to CABL to help him in the race relations area and on its recommendation appointed a biracial human relations commission—one of the most important steps toward racial amity in the decade. Later on, Ed Stagg was actually lent to McKeithen and served for several months on his staff. In the view of many, however, Stagg eventually became too committed to McKeithen—one reason the AFL-CIO, which had sharp disagreements with McKeithen, eventually withdrew its support. CABL's influence has continued to decline in recent years, but PAR, even though it abjures regular lobbying, has been able to fill much of the gap through the quality of its reports and recommendations.

Our account turns now to organized labor and the man who may well deserve to be called the most skillful state labor leader in the United States: Victor Bussie, president of the Louisiana AFL-CIO. Bussie is a thoughtful and a kind man, but also a man with an iron will.

After graduating from high school in Shreveport in the late 1930s, Bussie spent years as a fireman in the city, rising to be president of the local firefighters union. In 1956, when the AFL and CIO merged, Bussie was elected president of the combined state council and immediately plunged into a fight to repeal a right-to-work law that had been put on the statute books two years earlier. With undercover help from the Longs, right-to-work was repealed within a few months, and to this day Louisiana is unique in the South in having no right-to-work law. "This is the only Southern state without any laws against labor," Bussie pointed out. "We have passed prevailing wage bills for all public construction, and bills prohibiting importing strikebreakers—laws usually approved only in the large industrial states. We have no laws prohibiting organization of public employees or strikes by them. Several neighboring states have many anti-union laws, and we have none. We can't say that we haven't been well treated."

That good treatment, however, is no accident. It starts with a broad program of election-time support—dollars and manpower—for candidates friendly to labor. "If a man in office has an acceptable voting record and runs for reelection, we support him regardless; it's an ironclad rule," Bussie said. Labor's enemies, of course, find themselves opposed by AFL-CIO backed opponents.

The second phase occurs when the legislature meets. Normally, the Baton Rouge staff consists of Bussie and four other full-time AFL-CIO state officials. But during legislative sessions, six additional lobbyists are brought to Baton Rouge—all but one or two loaned by member unions. The lobbying operation is a wonder to behold. All AFL-CIO lobbyists are under Bussie's personal direction—"no union sends anyone unless we ask for them." The labor men shun standard lobbying techniques like wining or dining of legislators. Instead, they succeed through meticulous attention to detail. When the legislature is in session, they meet every morning at 6 A.M. to review the situation in both chambers. "We keep up with every bill introduced," Bussie said. "We have an accurate committee voting record on labor, education, taxation, insurance rate legislation—anything that affects a workingman and woman. We're the only group that does it." The groups with which labor clashes the most frequently, Bussie said, were the Manufacturers Association and rice and forestry lobbyists. "We would be in a hell of a shape," Bussie said, "if they united and worked together as well as the AFL-CIO."

Under Bussie's leadership, however, labor picks no unnecessary fights with industry. "We have taken a responsible view and cooperated with business and industry wherever possible," Bussie said. Edgar Stern, Jr., described Bussie as "a strong-willed labor statesman," admiring his hard bargaining on getting the AFL-CIO to join CABL at its inception. Kenneth Gormin, a New Orleans public relations man with industrial clients, regards Bussie as a man of "intelligence, guts, and honesty, a tremendous force in Louisiana." Steimel of PAR called Bussie "fearless and immensely capable" and his labor lobby the most powerful in the state. PAR and Bussie have clashed on some issues, including the question of barring lobbyists from the legislative chamber floors. (Bussie positively loved to orchestrate his lobbying efforts in person on the senate and house floors, standing boldly at the rail to beckon and call his troops to put pressure on wavering legislators. Under the PAR-backed reforms, he is relegated with the other lobbyists to the back of the chamber.)

For the most part, however, the PAR-Bussie relationship has been a remarkable story of industry-labor cooperation. They have worked together closely on many issues, ranging from ethics and the legislative auditor to the AFL-CIO suit against the assessing practices of Louisiana, in which PAR's research director appeared as an expert witness to testify on Bussie's side. For several years, both Bussie and Steimel have served on the board of the Southwest Educational Research Laboratory, a federally funded group designed to upgrade black and Mexican-American education. The two men have also worked closely with the leadership of all-black Grambling College, in the heart of northern Louisiana's most hard-core segregationist territory. (Among Grambling's claims to fame is that it produces more professional football players than any other college in the United States.)

Bussie runs the Louisiana AFL-CIO in a democratic mode distinctly lacking in many state labor councils. He takes no role in the selection of the vice presidents who serve as his board of directors and supervise his activities. State AFL-CIO conventions are mainly information and public relations forums, to which the press and management representatives are invited. Speakers of state and national interest are brought in to talk on topics like tax equalization, sales taxes, or insurance. "We don't hesitate to bring in the worst anti-union individual you can find if it will enlighten the discussions," Bussie said.

Bussie's advanced stands on race-related issues have sometimes resulted in membership losses. The council fought closing of the schools in the big integration fight of the early 1960s, fought the proposal for unpledged electors that would have kept Kennedy off the ballot in 1960, and a sales tax to carry on the integration fight when Jimmie Davis was governor. The unpledged elector fight, in particular, was responsible for a loss of some 15,000 members in 1961. Bussie also went to Bogalusa in an unsuccessful effort to calm the racial wars there—a stand that cost the state council some 6,000 members. "We've tried to be consistent and fight for the things we should fight for," he said. "I've found that when you do that, even if people leave you, they come back eventually." His problem is that antiblack and anti-integration sentiment runs very high in some of his member unions. But they may forgive Bussie, in part, because his lobbyists have been successful in getting the legislature to approve the highest unemployment compensation benefits in the South, and workmen's compensation benefits among the highest in the region. Bussie has successfully persuaded his member unions to pay a monthly assessment of 45 cents a month for each of their 184,000 members, easily the highest figure of any state.

Overall, union membership has risen steadily in Louisiana over the past years—from 38,000 in 1939 to 136,000 in 1953, 160,000 in 1964, and 189,000 in 1972. But the percentage of the work force in unions has stabilized at 17 to 19 percent for about a decade now, a unionization rate that ranks only 35th nationally but quite high in relation to most of the Southern states.

Manufacturing wages are the highest among the Deep South states, chiefly because the state's industrial profile is weighted so heavily to plants that have a high investment per worker and use highly skilled people—industries like petrochemicals, paper, metals (especially aluminum), and electric generation.

The Ku Klux Klan and its friends have not taken kindly to Bussie's pro-integration stands, and tried—without apparent success—to intimidate him. "They burned so many crosses on my lawn in Shreveport," Bussie said, "that I finally just put up a little sign on the lawn, 'Burn all you want. Make sure they have the union label on them. I'm a union man.' They never burned another cross after that."

"And safe politicians," Bussie continued, "never get their homes bombed like I have." In 1967, when the issue of schools and segregation had reached one of its burning points, five sticks of dynamite were tossed at his Baton Rouge home from a moving car. The bomb landed near two automobiles parked outside, Bussie said. "If it had gone just three inches further, one of the autos would not have taken the principal force of the blast and it would have killed us. As it was, the explosion blew the windows out in the whole house. It moved furniture around. But it didn't hurt either my wife or me."

Just before the bombing, Bussie had urged the legislature to make an exhaustive investigation of the Klan because of 25 to 30 unresolved dynamitings in the Baton Rouge area. A self-identified member of the Klan later told New Orleans police that the bombings of Bussie's home and the home of a Negro school teacher in Port Allen had been planned by three other Klansmen in his home. But the authorities never chose to prosecute.

> The Klansmen and their cohorts [Bussie said] must have peculiar minds. I can't quite understand it. I've never owned a gun in my life, never threatened anybody. I've used force, but it was always to get people off of me. How they can decide they just want to go out to kill somebody they don't even know, and have no association with or anything else, I just don't understand.
>
> And it's amazing to me when you sit down and read about England and other countries—they just don't have anything like this. Why do we have it in this country? Death by violence in this country is a high rate, compared with almost any other country in the world. And we're supposed to be a Christian country.

When I asked Bussie if he saw any "light at the end of the tunnel" in Louisiana as far as race relations were concerned, he replied:

> I've been praying for it as long back as I can remember. And I look for signs and sometimes I know I see them and suddenly it breaks out again. It's inconceivable to me that the majority of the people of this state voted for Wallace in 1968, for instance. It can only be one thing—race relations.
>
> People say, "Oh no, that's not why I voted for Wallace. He just thinks like I do. He wants law and order." Well, that law and order they're talking about is to stop integration, that's all.
>
> Look at the people who are shouting for law and order in this part of the country. They're the Klansmen, the people who have created more violence than everyone else put together.
>
> They say they don't have anything against a "nigger," just as long as he stays

in his place. And of course they define what his place is. Well I think a Negro is entitled to have the same place in the sun that I have or anybody else.

Problems Galore

Louisiana is a poor state, but thanks in large part to the legacy of the Longs, it does not have a parsimonious, indifferent government. Measured against the income of the people, Louisiana makes a much greater effort than the average state to finance health, hospitals, welfare, and education. Its tax effort, including levies on corporations, is eighth highest in the U.S. in relation to income. The tax structure is much less dependent on the sales tax, and thus less onerous for lower income people, than that of most Southern states. Since the times of Huey Long, the oil companies have been forced to contribute heavily to the financing of the government. Presently they pay about a quarter of a billion dollars a year in severance taxes alone, at a rate almost double that of neighboring Texas. For years, various levies placed on oil and gas production represented as much as 40 percent of all state government revenues. The figure has dropped to about 30 percent since the late 1960s with the decline of taxable, on-shore production, but oil and gas still relieve individual taxpayers from personal taxes, as in no other state.

Louisiana's problem is that its government has been able to do only so much to relieve the grim economic situation of so many of its people. The poverty can be seen vividly in the backward towns and settlements of bayou Louisiana or in the hardscrabble parishes of the north. Federal government statistics confirm the point: while Louisiana's comparative economic situation has improved markedly over the years, the state still has far to go to reach the level of affluence of most of the nation.

Income levels are a case in point. Since 1929, the state's per capita income has risen from 59 to 78 percent of the national average—but in 1972 it still ranked only 45th among the 50 states. The 1970 Census found that 22 percent of Louisiana's families were living below the government-established poverty line. Only two states, Mississippi and Arkansas, had more poverty. According to a study by the federal Department of Housing and Urban Development, 28 percent of the 1.1 million housing units in the state are substandard.

Louisiana's million-plus black people—30 percent of the population—account for a lot of the poverty. (Only Mississippi and South Carolina have a higher proportion of blacks.) While the poverty level is 13 percent among Louisiana's whites, it is 47 percent among the state's blacks and soars as high as 73 percent among the Negroes of Tensas Parish, an old plantation area along the Mississippi River in northern Louisiana.

But illiteracy, the handmaiden of poverty, also afflicts Louisiana and works its ravages on whites as well as blacks. In Cajun country, until recent times, a fine living could be made from hunting, fishing, and shrimping. People didn't need to go to school, and they didn't. In 1960 there were more true illiterates in Louisiana—6.3 percent—than in any other state. By 1970, the figure had dropped to 3.9 percent but was still the highest in the country. The 1960s, one prominent Louisianan told me, was the first time the state had a school system worthy of the name. The literacy problem is still most acute in the French parishes, as these education levels (of people 25 years of age and over) indicate:

	No Schooling	*Less Than 5 Years (Functional Illiterates)*	*High School Graduates*
U.S. Average	2%	5%	52%
Louisiana Average	4	13	42
Selected French Parishes			
Acadia	12	26	28
Assumption	9	28	24
Evangeline	12	29	23
Vermillion	12	25	27

A sidelight on the low educational levels is that only 34 percent of the people in Louisiana read daily newspapers, compared to 63 percent in Massachusetts, for example, or 50 percent in Indiana. Uninformed people are likely to take little interest in government. Especially in the French parishes, vote buying is very prevalent, and people are often happy to let others vote for them. It is not unusual, for instance, for the head of a clan to take out absentee ballots for all the members of his family and to vote them as a bloc. "This is the way they think it should be done," one observer told me. "I don't know if you can classify it as immorality or if they really don't think it's immoral." But the ideal of well-informed, participatory democracy it is not.

Manipulation of the poor and unlettered has not deepened their poverty, however. The Longs, especially Earl, were responsible for instituting much higher welfare payments than the state's economic position would seem to justify, and for seeing that many of the poorer counties got major benefits from the program. By the early 1970s, Louisiana was expending, per capita of its population, close to $70 a year on welfare—the seventh highest level in the United States, even though the per capita income of Louisiana, as we have noted, ranked only 45th in the country. The percentage of the state's people receiving welfare was close to the highest in the U.S.—11 percent of all families and 17 percent of unrelated individuals, at least twice the national average. Since the days of the Longs, payments to old people have been especially high; for years they were the highest in the country, and they still rank 17th. (Payments tend to balloon around election time.) The average payments for dependent children, however, are much lower; they rank only 44th among the states.

Among those *not* eligible for welfare are the 5,000-odd workers, almost all black, who labor in the sugar cane fields that stretch like a great sea from the center of the state southeasterly toward New Orleans and the Gulf. The average sugar-cane worker earns only $2,750 a year to sustain a family of five children; he is "tied" to the sugar plantation in a morass of debt; he lives in a rundown shack, often so old that slaves may well have inhabited it once. The diets of his children are often so poor that at the age of 12 they have bodies like people 50 years old. On the average, sugar-cane workers have had two years of schooling; they are almost totally unprepared to break away and find decent work elsewhere. Under the Sugar Act of 1934, the sugar growers get handsome subsidies and price supports (about $500 million a year); the *quid pro quo* for that was that the growers were to pay "fair and reasonable" wage rates. But the wage rates are set by the U.S. Department of Agriculture, which seems to heed the planters and the planters alone. The wage presently paid is almost $2,000 below the federally established poverty level. There are no unions in the cane fields; an organizing effort in the 1950s failed as the planters accused the organizers of Communist leanings, got striking workers evicted and blacklisted, and then persuaded the state supreme court to issue an antistrike injunction.

Louisiana has struggled to reform its state prisons and mental hospitals, which used to be run like fiefdoms in which administrators got so much money from the state and pocketed anything they managed to save. In 1951, 31 inmates of the notorious Angola State Penitentiary sliced their heel tendons in a protest against brutality and overcrowding. That led to the recruitment of more competent administrators, construction of a new prison, and an end to flogging and sweat boxes. Many of the rehabilitation programs had been forgotten by the 1960s, but Governor McKeithen brought in more professionals to run both the prisons and the mental hospitals, even though sufficient money was still lacking for a number of basic reforms. In 1970 the state finally began to phase out the corruption-prone system of inmate guards at Angola.

"Education," in the words of PAR's Edward Steimel, "is the key to all our other problems in Louisiana," from the quality of state government to the economic prospects of the people. Of every 100 children who enter school, 45 drop out before graduation from high school; 40 go to college but half wash out the first year and only 13 end up with a degree.

The public schools, which were handicapped over the years by the dual system for blacks and whites and by pure neglect of the state's leadership, have improved dramatically in recent years—but still have far to go. Twice as many Louisiana boys failed Selective Service preinduction mental tests during the 1960s as the national average. One out of every five school-age youngsters is not even in school, still the worst attendance rate in the country, even though an extremely liberal school lunch program, the most broadly used of any state, has helped draw more young people to school and to improve nutritional standards.

Louisiana has been trying hard to come up to par with national school standards. Its per pupil expenditures are the highest in the South and not far behind the national average. Teacher salaries have climbed to a rank of 28th, ahead of all other Southern states except Virginia and Florida. Louisiana also does very respectably in terms of the money it raises for schools as a percent of personal income in the state. But many adjustments are still required, including better teacher training programs, expansion of kindergartens to all the state's school systems, and more innovative teaching methods and arrangements to accommodate the greater diversity in student bodies brought about by integration.

On the university level, Louisiana has long had quality private education, although some deterioration in the academic quality of the two most prestigious institutions, Tulane and Loyola, has been reported in recent years. (Notable exceptions to the decline are Tulane's excellent schools of law and medicine.) The system of public higher education is still fairly new. Louisiana State University was little more than a college until 1930, and it is sometimes more distinguished for its achievements in football than matters academic. LSU is nationally known, however, for its work in agriculture. Major development at the university was inaugurated in the 1930s; now there are four regional campuses in addition to the main one at Baton Rouge, as well as medical schools at New Orleans and Shreveport.

Louisiana has experienced an unfortunate proliferation of four-year colleges, some of which began as two-year institutions around the turn of the century. Any Louisiana town of any size tries to have its own college or university, both for income and prestige, and each then strives to become a complex university. Tuitions are low and there is a strong popular tradition of universal admission, but faculty salaries are well below national norms. Per capita expenditures for higher education rank only 35th in the country. The result, on the one hand, is a lack of distinguished departments and, on the other, a misguided system in which half the high school graduates who start college wash out after the first year and only a small number actually graduate with degrees.

A major recommendation of the Public Affairs Research Council is that the system be entirely reoriented to emphasize vocational-technical programs so that young people who leave the academic trail at any point can acquire the skills they need to be productively employed—and so that the state can expand its reservoir of skilled workers. An important element would be a "continuous progress program" of education that would be of special aid to often ill-prepared young black workers. PAR was the driving force behind a $54 million bond issue for building vocational and technical schools, approved by the legislature in 1973. A 1970 PAR survey of Louisiana industries had found that low labor skills were the chief disadvantage of doing business in the state.

In the meantime, a coordinating committee for higher education, set up in the late 1960s (also on PAR's recommendation) has been working on a plan for a more rational university-level program. One of the oddities it has to deal with is that LSU and its branches have their own board, appointed by the governor, while the other state colleges and universities, plus the entire public school system of the state, are under a popularly elected state board of education. The two boards engage in a scuffle for finances during legislative sessions, with politics rather than merit often deciding the appropriations.

The state's traditionally black colleges—Southern University at Baton Rouge and its New Orleans branch, and Grambling College in northern

Louisiana—have been wracked by protests and demonstrations, some of a violent character, in recent years. The problem, common to predominantly black institutions across the South, is that they have been, as slavery was described in its time, "a peculiar institution"—formed originally as an alternative to having blacks attend white universities, but never given adequate support. Louisiana's black colleges were consistently underfunded by the all-white elected state board of education through most of their history. A formula established by a coordinating council for higher education has given them a fairer shake since 1968 but does not compensate for past neglect. Moreover, the black colleges' administration is still generally in the hands of old-line Negro administrators who are beholden to the white establishment and rule their colleges with an iron hand, often regarding the students as mere immature juveniles.

For years, the youth in black Southern colleges have chafed under the poor curriculums, facilities, and equipment of their institutions. The civil rights movement of the 1960s gave them, for the first time, the organizing skills to do something about their predicament. Black students became activists in winning desegregation of public accommodations in their communities, and with the tactics they had learned in the civil rights movement, and the newborn self-confidence that came from it, they were suddenly in a position to challenge the system in the colleges. In 1969 Governor McKeithen felt obliged to call out the National Guard to put down student occupations of administration buildings at Southern's two campuses. In 1972 students at Southern again protested inadequate facilities and demanded a greater voice in school affairs, seizing buildings, staging mass marches, and boycotting classes to dramatize their case. At the New Orleans branch, the campus administrator was forced to resign before students occupying the administration building would give it up. A sympathy boycott, followed by a violent rampage, took place at Grambling. And then at Southern's Baton Rouge campus, which has 8,300 students and is the largest black university in the country, bloodshed occurred. Sheriff's deputies, called to quell an uprising by student militants, fired shots into a group of young blacks and killed two students.

The Louisiana violence led many blacks to suggest that black management and control of the black colleges, with adequate financing, was the best solution. But the fact was that black institutions could probably never expect to receive equal treatment from the white majorities holding the purse strings in the state legislature. One answer would be the solution sought by the civil rights enforcers of the federal Department of Health, Education and Welfare: the eventual amalgamation and integration of Louisiana's predominantly white and black universities.* Such amalgamation was actually ordered by a federal district court in 1973, prompting Governor Edwards to say he would accept a potentially crippling cutoff of federal education funds rather than "make a chocolate milk facility" out of the state's

* There are no legal bars left to entry by blacks into white colleges, and in fact several thousand are now enrolled. But most blacks cannot meet the standards because of their inadequate educational preparation.

universities. Logistically, integration would be relatively easy, because the three black institutions are physically close to white state universities or colleges. It would, of course, preclude one of the aims of the young demonstrators: total black control of black education. But the trade-off might be a very good one if young blacks could obtain quality education, comparable to that of their white peers, in the process.

Louisiana in Washington

The most powerful Louisianan alive today is doubtless the son of Huey, United States Senator Russell Billiu Long. The Senate Finance Committee, of which he is chairman and the dominating force, has jurisdiction over Americans' taxes, welfare, Social Security and Medicare, revenue sharing, foreign trade, and the national debt ceiling. Conservatives hold a majority of the seats on the committee, and liberals have made only slow progress in their effort to gain more of a foothold there.

There are Populist-liberal strands in Russell Long's character, reminiscent of his father, whom he regards as a "political Messiah . . . ahead of his time," "the greatest thing the good Lord ever put on the planet." Long has fought to facilitate government prosecution of the big drug companies for price-fixing, has tried to see to it that inventions made under government research contracts are not patented for private gain, and since the mid-1960s has battled to reform the financing of Presidential campaigns through a $1 citizen's tax form check-off that would make campaign funding a public affair.

Most of the time, though, the special interest side of Russell Long seems to dominate. There would seem to be a gross conflict of interest in his chairmanship of the tax-writing Finance Committee when, in his own words, "most of my income is from oil and gas"—the single American industry most dependent on federal tax policy. Needless to say, Long battles assiduously to preserve the oil depletion allowance. The fruits benefit him and his state alike. With less of a personal stake, Long also protects Louisiana interests by keeping a statutory requirement of a sugar quota that pegs U.S. sugar prices above world prices, with the federal government making up the difference. During the first Nixon Administration, Long was the member of Congress who did more than anyone else to defeat the Family Assistance Plan, which would have as much as *tripled* the income of many poverty-destitute rural Southerners. Long, however, had little interest in helping the working poor, and certainly not those already on welfare; instead he was concerned only with welfare chiseling being done by "brood mares." By denying FAP a chance, even on a pilot basis, when the Nixon administration was still willing to back it, Long may have set back the economic salvation of impoverished Southerners, black and white alike, for a long time.

Shipbuilders, on the other hand, bask in Long's favor. As chairman of the Commerce Committee's Merchant Marine Subcommittee, he has battled stoutly for a big fleet development and once said $1 billion for that purpose would be "a very small item." A major beneficiary of federal shipbuilding funds is New Orleans' Avondale Shipyards, the largest single employer in the state.*

Russell Long's power in Washington does have its limits. In 1965, when he succeeded Hubert Humphrey as Majority Whip in the Senate, Tom Wicker of the New York *Times* said Long was a "hot betting choice" to succeed Oklahoma's deceased Robert Kerr as "uncrowned king of the Senate." But in the succeeding years Long offended many of his fellow Senators, Northerners and Southerners alike, by his histrionics and obstructionist tactics in defending Connecticut's Senator Thomas Dodd against a censure resolution for misuse of campaign funds. The long, bitter fight over the Presidential election campaign fund act cost Long friends as well. In 1969 Long was defeated for reelection as Whip by Edward Kennedy of Massachusetts. A year later, a federal prosecutor in Baltimore wanted to indict him for bribery in connection with the contract for the House of Representatives' underground garage. Long called the allegations in the case a "cock and bull story," and the Justice Department overruled its own prosecutor. A remarriage has made Long more stable and sober, but the memory of his mercurial behavior has made it doubtful whether his colleagues will ever feel comfortable making him "king of the Senate"—uncrowned or not.

An untimely death in the election season of 1972 claimed one of the most able and broadspirited men Louisiana ever sent to Congress, Hale Boggs of New Orleans. Boggs was Majority Leader of the House of Representatives when the small plane in which he was riding disappeared in Alaska; if he had lived, he would probably have fulfilled, in the next years, his ambition to be Speaker of the House.

The capacity for growth was the leitmotif of Boggs' life. Born into a poor family on the Mississippi Gulf Coast, he got a college scholarship through a commencement speaker from Tulane who had heard Boggs, a forceful orator even then, give the valedictory address for his high school class. Boggs had known since the age of 14, when he read Blackstone, what he wanted to do in life: "to be a lawyer and a member of Congress." He started Tulane with $35 to his name, selling mail-order suits and distributing chewing gum samples to make his way. Boggs majored in journalism, worked as a part-time reporter for the New Orleans *States* (covering, among others, Huey Long when he came to town), and served on the staff of the Tulane student newspaper. A fellow staffer was Corinne Morrison Claiborne, a direct descendant of Louisiana's first governor. Later she became not only Boggs' wife, but his supporter and close adviser, helping him overcome many political and personal problems. One New Orleans friend of the family described "Lindy," as she is called, as "a woman of unimpeachable personal integrity, of true gentility and nobleness of spirit."[5] After Boggs' death, she was elected to fill his seat in Congress.

Boggs won a Phi Beta Kappa key at Tulane and shifted from journalism

* In 1970, the outspoken Navy contract specialist, Gordon Rule, accused Long and three other Louisiana Democrats—Senator Allen Ellender and Congressmen Hale Boggs and F. Edward Hébert—of using improper influence to win an award of $716 million for Avondale.

to law, leaving the campus with a law degree in 1937 to enter a political world still shaking from the political dealings and corrupt ways of the Long camp. Boggs and several other young lawyers set up a reform group, "the Peoples League," which fought corruption in New Orleans and in 1940 helped elect a prominent reform anti-Longite, Sam Jones, to the governorship. Later in 1940, Boggs was elected to Congress. Defeated two years later, he served in the Navy during the war and returned to Congress in 1947, where he would serve for the rest of his life. Years later, Boggs recalled:

> I was 26 when I came to Congress. Speaker Sam Rayburn had no family, no son, no children, and he more or less adopted me. He gave me a great sense of this institution. . . .
>
> Mr. Rayburn having done that for me, I find myself, as Majority Leader, spending more and more time with younger members of Congress. I spend a lot of time with them, talking to them, listening to them, keeping them interested. This is important, it is vital to the maintenance of the democratic process. It is a sense of continuity, one generation to another.
>
> Mr. Rayburn was a remarkable man, completely devoid of bigotry and prejudice, and yet in many ways he was still a small-town Texas politician. He and I were instrumental in putting [Lyndon] Johnson on the ticket with [John] Kennedy [in 1960]. At first Mr. Rayburn was against it, telling Johnson not to do it. But Mr. Rayburn had never been fond of Mr. Nixon, so I reminded him, "If you don't want Johnson to run, it means you elect Richard Nixon." Before the morning he had shifted and encouraged Johnson to run with Kennedy.

After the ticket was assembled, the task was to get the South to accept it, and Boggs showed his skills of persuasion as the Lady Bird Johnson campaign special rolled through Dixie that autumn. "On this great long train we had grits for breakfast!" he cried. There were loud cheers from the trainside crowds. "And we gonna have turnip greens and black-eyed peas for lunch," he roared. More cheers followed. "And after talkin' to a million Southerners we gonna have crawfish bisque, red beans and rice, and Creole gumbo for dinner," he concluded, to the delight of the Southern crowds.

The same politician who could ham it up that way was also an intellectual, a deeply devout Roman Catholic, and a man of introspective qualities. He was also a wheeling-dealing pork barrel Congressman for his district. He rose to the second-ranking position on the Ways and Means Committee, and in Senate-House conferences to iron out differences in tax bills, Boggs and Russell Long were able to get approval of all sorts of special interest provisions to benefit Louisiana, including New Orleans and its port. When New Orleans was seeking a professional football team and the National Football League was seeking antitrust immunity such as baseball enjoys, Boggs and Long were able to skirt the Judiciary Committee that was holding up the legislation and tack it onto the tax bill, and pass it. The New Orleans Saints were born. Since then the team has been a unifying force for New Orleans' polyglot population and, in the opinion of some, has helped to lessen racial tensions.

The 1960s brought trying times for Boggs, however. He became Majority Whip after Rayburn's death in 1962 and found himself supporting Great Society programs of his old friend, Lyndon Johnson—aid to education, medicare, housing, and the like—that were anathema to conservative Southerners. He served on the Warren Commission to investigate President Kennedy's assassination and was a member of the President's Committee on Violence. At home, there was a right-wing minority, rooted in Jefferson Parish, that opposed Boggs in what Rosemary James and Philip Moreton described in *New Orleans Magazine* as "an unyielding, withering wrath."

Boggs had always opposed civil rights legislation, but there was a moment of high drama in the House in 1965 when he strode to the lectern to speak for the Voting Rights Act of that year. In his booming voice, Boggs began:

> I wish I could stand here, as a man who loves my state, born and reared in the South, . . . and say there has not been discrimination. But unfortunately, it is not so. I shall support the bill because I believe the fundamental right to vote must be a part of the great experiment in human progress under freedom which is America.

Three years later, Boggs voted for the open-housing law, even though he was aware that "the vast majority of the people I represented" were against it. "Frankly, I voted on the question of right or wrong," he said later. Then he flew off to Chicago to serve—as Johnson had asked him to do—as chairman of the committee that wrote a very liberal platform in the midst of the stricken Democratic Convention. He returned home to Louisiana, exhausted, turning too often to liquor for solace, to face an irate district. He barely won reelection.

That would be the crucial election of his career, however, because of what it did for Boggs' own psyche. I vividly recall a lunch I had with him in the Majority Whip's office on Capitol Hill a few weeks after the election. "I'm over the big divide now," Boggs said. "I am a free man now. I can vote as I know right, and still survive." In the next year he would prove the point by providing the swing vote in Ways and Means to cut the oil depletion allowance from 27.5 to 22 percent—a lonely position indeed for any Louisiana Congressman. He also swung over to support of a direct vote of the people for President, abolishing the electoral college. In 1971 he was elected Majority Leader, proving he had finally dissuaded Northern Democrats from the idea that he was too much of a Southerner.

Even after Boggs became Majority Leader, shadows lay across his path. His behavior, on and off the House floor, seemed erratic to some. There was concern about his emotional stability when he told the House in a sometimes incoherent speech that the FBI had "bugged" his home and office, a charge for which he could offer no positive proof. Eyebrows were raised when word passed that a Baltimore contractor had remodeled the Boggs' white-columned Bethesda home at a price "substantially below cost," later seeking favors of Boggs. Some critics said Boggs' advertised independence was strictly limited by his role as an "inside man" for the AFL-CIO, that he went out of his way to do favors for clients of his lawyer son, and that he was not always straightforward in his dealings with other House members.

But while it would be foolish to call Boggs a saintly man, he did overcome many of his personal problems in his last years of life. His innate generosity was one of his greatest strengths. "There isn't a person, I don't care what his station in life is, who contacts me that I don't try to help in one way or another," Boggs said. "One reason they have never succeeded in defeating me, no matter how much they have spent, is the fact that we have always helped people."

It was in helping another that he lost his life, in fact. Unopposed for reelection in 1972, Boggs pledged to campaign for as many of his fellow Democrats in difficult races as he could. Weary from a grueling House session, he kept a promise to speak for Congressman Nick Begich of Alaska. Flying from Anchorage to Juneau on the last leg of the trip, the plane carrying Long and Begich simply disappeared in the Alaskan mists. A devoted search by military aircraft through the mountain ranges, glaciers, and icy seas of Prince William Sound—the most extensive search in aviation history—produced no trace of the lost plane.

Two months later, hundreds of national leaders and friends assembled for a moving memorial mass in the historic St. Louis Cathedral in New Orleans. Archbishop Philip Hannan stressed Boggs' civil rights record, saying, "He voted his conscience, however hard the consequences."

The elegy I liked best, however, was in a column by William S. White. White wrote that Boggs "stood as a truly effective human bridge between many competing qualities and interests. . . . He helped greatly to hold together the polyglot house of his party, as he did the House of Representatives itself. . . . As a man, he was big in body and large-spirited in action and motive. His faults were the genial faults of the warm-blooded and compassionate, the hospitable, the expansive—and the sensitive."

Boggs' passing did not leave Louisiana bereft of influence in the House. Seventy-two-year-old F. Edward Hébert remained chairman of one of the most powerful committees in Congress, House Armed Services. A strong conservative with an abysmal voting attendance record in the House, Hébert was a close political ally of the late Leander Perez, whose Plaquemines Parish is in his district. Like his predecessor as chairman of Armed Services, Mendel Rivers of South Carolina, Hébert is a superhawk and sees to it that the military forces get the fund authorizations they want. But he has not tried to load his own district down with military installations as Rivers did, and he has innovated to the extent of letting views other than those of the military be expressed before the committee.*

Another Louisiana septuagenarian, Otto E. Passman, has held extraordi-

* Hébert (pronounced "A-bear") made his first splash in public life as a crusading newspaper editor in the late 1930s, exposing gross corruption in the administration of a Huey Long heir, Governor Richard Leche. Leche eventually went to prison, and Hébert to Congress. The New Orleans papers treat Hébert with kid gloves, but not those in Washington. The Washington *Star and News* in 1972 gave details about Hébert's "lasting appreciation for the finer things in life." The paper said Hébert "rides around in a Cadillac and owns three homes. In each home is a complete, expensive wardrobe, so he never has to pack a bag. Since he first came to town, some of the nicest looking women in Washington have graced his offices. When the Rayburn House Office Building was under construction, he prowled around and found a place where the design would provide one office of extraordinary size. It is now the fanciest office on the Hill, complete with a foyer with fountain. Off his private office are two other rooms. One he calls the 'Adult Room.' It is a little bar decorated with seductive pictures of naked ladies and a street sign from Bourbon Street, which used to be in Hébert's district and was part of his beat as a reporter. The other is furnished with a television set, chairs and a couch. 'That's the Adultery Room,' Hébert chuckles."

nary power over the United States' foreign aid programs since he was made chairman of the Appropriations Foreign Operations Subcommittee in 1955. For the record, Passman has stated that the whole foreign aid program is conceptually wrong; in matter of fact, he has tended to cut economic assistance programs as much as he can but to support military aid. He had been an implacable foe of the Peace Corps. Passman has never hesitated to bully those he opposes, Presidents and dissident members of his subcommittee alike, and he is one of the most autocratic committee chairmen Congress has ever seen. His power on the Appropriations Committee has been trimmed considerably in recent years, however, and some members feel the old man has mellowed—and weakened.

When Passman appears on the House floor, resplendent in a white suit, he looks for all the world like central casting's conception of an affluent delta planter. There is no lassitude in Passman, though; the man is packed with extraordinary nervous energy. Elizabeth Drew once wrote that the "bumping and grinding" of his hips is "renowned in the House as 'Otto's Waltz,' " and Donald Riegle of Michigan commented that "Otto is the only man I know who wears out a suit from the inside."

Perhaps a more important man to watch in the next years is Joe D. Waggonner, Jr., the eloquent segregationist from Shreveport who some believe is becoming the most potent leader of the Southern conservative Democrats since the defeat of Howard Smith of Virginia. In 1973, in fact, Waggonner moved to organize a conservative counterpart to the left-of-center Democratic House Study Group. With a hard core of about 50 traditionally-minded Southerners, the group sought to offset the steadily declining power of Southern conservatives in House councils by coordinating their strategy and making appeals to moderate Democrats on specific votes. Waggonner has been an indefatigable foe of school busing, foreign aid, the poverty campaign, and environmental controls. He favors high military appropriations, farm subsidies without ceilings on what growers can receive, and tax breaks to stimulate business. He is now in his mid-fifties and —to the delight of Shreveport oil interests—Hale Boggs' successor on Ways and Means.

The Senate lost one of its patriarchs when Allen J. Ellender died in 1972, 81 years after his birth on a rundown plantation named Hard Scrabble in Terrebonne Parish. Ellender was a floor leader for Huey Long in the Louisiana legislature and helped save the Kingfish from impeachment. He was one of the last men to speak with Long before his assassination in 1935, and the next year succeeded him in the U.S. Senate—there to survive all his original peers because, as he put it, "I neither smoked nor drank and refrained from chasing women." Ellender did not refrain from good food, however. He frequently brewed up creole gumbo or shrimp jambalaya in his Capitol office and then invited colleagues or the press in to enjoy the feast.

A peppery little (five-foot, four-inch) individualist, Ellender abandoned Long-style Populism early in his Senate career. He was chairman of the Senate Agriculture Committee for 18 years and put his mark on every major farm bill from 1938 on. Perhaps more important for Louisiana, Ellender for years was chairman of the Appropriations Public Works Subcommittee. The position enabled him to funnel huge sums of money into projects for a coastal state historically plagued by floods and rising tides. Mainly through his efforts, Louisiana is now only one-eighth under water, whereas 20 years ago it was about one-fourth swamp. Ellender also took a great interest in river navigation and called himself "the daddy" of Louisiana's Tidewater Channel, opened in 1963, which enables ocean-going vessels to cut 40 miles off their customary winding Mississippi River route from New Orleans to the open sea. For the last year and a half of his life, Ellender was chairman of the full Appropriations Committee and President Pro Tempore of the Senate (third in line for the Presidency).

Ellender was campaigning for a seventh Senate term when he died, and the man who was opposing him—and then went on to win the seat—was a man half his age, J. Bennett Johnston. A self-styled "moderate Democrat," Johnston is a soft-spoken man with a wry sense of humor who ran a slick media campaign and radiates, in the words of one New Orleans newspaperman, "the air of class and style."

Matching Johnston's arrival on the Senate side, a moderate—perhaps even liberal—element was added to Louisiana's House delegation by the 1972 election of Gillis Long, one of the most able members of the famous clan. Long was immediately put on the House Rules Committee, where he was expected to play a distinctly national Democratic role by heeding the voice of Speaker Carl Albert on which bills should be cleared for floor action. Two other new Louisiana House members, including Lindy Boggs, were also expected to deviate from the state's old conservative pattern on Capitol Hill.

The Economy: Promise Partially Fulfilled

Given Louisiana's natural advantages, she ought to be one of the wealthiest states of the Union and certainly outshine her sister states of the South. Nature has blessed her with magnificent resources: oil and gas, sulphur and salt in fabulous quantities; fertile alluvial soils; forests that cover more than half her surface; great waterways and plentiful supplies of water for people and industries.

Louisiana has, indeed, exploited its resources; without them, she might be a poor Mississippi today. But, as we have noted earlier, the income levels of her people are far below the national average. Unemployment is chronically high, compared to the rest of the U.S. Not until the late 1960s did the number of manufacturing jobs reach the level of World War II; there is no other Southern state in which such sluggish growth has been recorded. The economic dynamism of neighboring Texas, of cities like Dallas and Houston, is simply not present in modern Louisiana. During the 1960s, big commercial developers in New Orleans were often obliged to go to Atlanta and Houston for their money because—in the words of a leading New Orleans attorney—"those cities have bankers who are more farsighted and progressive." One could well argue that more moderate growth is preferable to the kind of cultural mediocrity and wasteful practices that seem to be hallmarks of a boomtime economy. But the phenomenon of restrained growth in Louisiana must be noted. I would suggest it is due not just to the problems of education or racial division that we have discussed before, but to a lassitude, a let-well-enough-be attitude on the part of bankers and industrialists—perhaps some of the Mediterranean and the planter philosophy throwing a shadow all the way to the last third of the 20th century.

Some other reasons for Louisiana's slow economy have been the high number of people on welfare (and thus not in the economically productive part of society), poor quality education and vocational training, unstable politics, and, oddly enough, the wage structure of the petroleum industry. Oil, along with paper and metals, pays high wages by regional standards; the result has been to frighten away labor-intensive industries like garments, shoes, and textiles, which despite their low wages certainly can contribute to overall economic growth.

Shipping and oil are the two bulwarks of the state's economy; of these shipping was there first, and will remain longer, and we should start with it. Louisiana lies athwart the ocean end of America's most extensive river system, giving her ready access to all the ports of the Mississippi Valley and to the sea lanes and ports of the Caribbean and the Atlantic and, through the Panama Canal, the Pacific as well. There are literally thousands of miles of related waterways within her borders, including that inglorious ditch, the Gulf Intracoastal Canal, which runs from Florida to Texas and carries more tonnage than the Kiel or Panama canals.

By way of ports, one thinks first of New Orleans, the United States' second busiest (after New York). The port is Louisiana's economic aorta, its 18 miles of wharves handling immense quantities of iron, steel, coal, wheat, rice, soybeans, fish, bananas, rubber, plywood, oil, and chemicals. Through the port pass huge meat shipments from the Great Plains, tractors from Illinois, automobiles from Germany, Japan, England, and Detroit, tea from India, whisky from Scotland, and, from Brazil, about a fifth of all the coffee consumed in North America each year. Bale after bale of sisal is unloaded, because New Orleans is the rope-making capital of the United States. Hardly a commodity known to man, in fact, does not at some time pass across the New Orleans docks.

For a while in the 1960s, technological breakthroughs in world shipping—especially containerized ships and the advent of "LASH" ("lighter-aboard-ship") vessels, which pick up huge loaded barges and store them in cavernous holds—threatened the port's future. Another problem was advanced rot in 29 of the port's 88 public berths that date back to the early 1900s. There was no hope that the state-run Board of Commissioners of the Port of New Orleans, out of normal wharfage charges, could finance the needed improvements. But then, in 1969, the state of Louisiana came to the rescue with $31 million to start a 30-year, $400 million development plan. Many port facilities will be moved from the congested Mississippi River banks to an area near the junction of the city's Industrial Canal and the Gulf Seaway. Now new container terminals and LASH wharves are opening, and cargo is continuing to increase at a rate of 7.5 percent a year. The dollar value of waterborne trade, which topped the $1 billion mark in 1946 and $2 billion in 1965, passed $3 billion in 1970.

There are also deepwater ports at Baton Rouge—now seventh in tonnage in the country, chiefly because of oil and petrochemicals,—at Lake Charles (the nation's largest rice port), and at Morgan City.

Louisiana seems literally to float on a sea of oil and natural gas. There are, to be sure, some "dry" spots in the state, especially across its midsection. But between the huge reserves in northwestern Louisiana (centered around Shreveport), across almost all of southern Louisiana, and far out into the Gulf of Mexico, more oil and gas is produced than in any state save Texas. Oil output has risen rapidly in recent years, and by the start of the 1970s, the production and reserve totals of the state looked like this:

	Annual Production		*Proven Reserves*	
	La. Total	*Share of U.S.*	*La. Total*	*Share of U.S.**
Natural gas	7.8 trillion cubic feet	35.5%	83 trillion cubic feet	28.5%
Crude oil	948 million barrels	27.3	5.4 billion barrels	19.3

* Excluding Alaska.

In addition, Louisiana produces more sulphur than any other state—over 40 percent of the national total—and seemingly inexhaustible salt domes along the coast provide a quarter of the country's supply. The value of the state's mineral production will soon reach $6 billion a year.

All of this is a great boon for Louisiana, but in different ways than one might expect. The direct profits of the oil industry reach Louisiana only indirectly, because the largest producers—Texaco, Exxon, Standard of California, Shell, and Gulf—all have their headquarters outside the state, and their stockholders are spread to the seven winds. The number of Louisianans directly engaged in oil production and exploration has hovered around 50,000 in recent years, only 5 percent of the state's work force (albeit a very well paid 5 percent). But oil and gas production adds many jobs in a less direct way. More than 30,000 Louisiana workers are employed in the refining and petrochemical industries. Of the $9 billion invested in new plants in Louisiana since World War II, more than half has been in petrochemicals. The presence of natural gas has been of immense importance in this, since it provided both inexpensive power for the industries and was itself the basic raw material of many petrochemical operations.

A cloud has recently been cast over this growth and prosperity, however, by mounting shortages of natural gas. Seventy percent of the gas produced in Louisiana is being piped to other states (compared to only 50 percent 20 years ago). "We have been too generous with our gas, and now we are getting the short end of the stick," Governor Edwards said in 1973. "We built our entire economy around natural gas, and if we are robbed of it, we lose our chief inducement to industry." Some industries already in Louisiana might also be forced to suspend operations if gas becomes scarcer.

They had counted on gas and failed to build their plants with a capacity to burn alternative fuels, such as coal or oil.

Oil was first noted oozing to the ground in Louisiana in the early 1800s, and in 1812 a geologist observed an "island" on fire for at least three months—a harbinger of the senseless burning off of natural gas that would characterize the industry during the first decades of petroleum production, which began in 1902. The most spectacular change in the years since World War II has been the inauguration of offshore drilling on Louisiana's broad continental shelf in the Gulf of Mexico. The first offshore well was not brought in until 1947, but since then literally thousands of oil and gas wells have been drilled in the Gulf, providing an ever increasing share of the state's production. As the first acute shortages of natural gas hit the United States in the early 1970s, one oil executive described the Gulf as the "most important remaining province for gas exploration in the lower 48 states." (The Louisiana Gulf Coast may also be the site of an offshore "superport" able to accommodate the "superships" [deep-draft oceangoing tankers] which oilmen expect will supply the U.S. with vast quantities of Middle East oil as domestic petroleum production falls further behind demand in the next years. The superships are too big to go into U.S. Atlantic or Gulf ports, but they could unload offshore with the oil pumped to land through huge pipelines on the Gulf floor. The state of Louisiana has actively supported the superport concept as a way to save its oil and petrochemical industries.)

Sometime in the next century, when the last oil and gas wells in America sputter dry, the era of offshore drilling and the saga of the men who spent so much of their working lives on the weird looking platforms on the open seas may become part of America's economic history and folklore, like the era of the Yankee clippers, the gold rushes, or the early lumber camps of the upper Midwest. There are more than 6,000 offshore platforms now, producing 10 percent of the nation's oil, and more being added all the time. Welded together on land, they are towed to sea and stood upright by barge-based cranes, their legs embedded in anywhere from 10 to 150 feet of water. (They must be strong enough to withstand hurricane-frenzied waves as high as 50 feet.) On a clear day, one can get the impression of small cities springing up all across the watery horizon. The platforms become home for crews of 15 to 50 men, who work, eat, and sleep there on seven- or 14-day shifts, with equal time off in between. The work day is a grueling 12 hours long, laboring on the huge rigs that can drill holes thousands of feet down to draw up oil and gas from the primordial ooze of the Gulf. The unskilled—the roustabouts—are consigned to tasks like hoisting 100-pound sacks of chemical mud and dragging 300-pound sections of pipe. They earn $2.50 an hour, but a skilled driller can earn as much as $18,000 a year.

Leo Janos, of *Time*'s Houston bureau, reported after several days on one of the platforms that life there "resembles a cross between the Navy and a penal colony. . . . Roustabouts or technicians, all are effectively imprisoned on their tight little island. No alcohol, not even beer, is permitted on board. Fighting means immediate dismissal." He quoted James McAlister, 22, a Belfast-born roustabout who fled the religious wars of his homeland:

"At 6 in the morning, it's dark, wet, and cold. You begin sweeping the water from the deck that accumulates from the night's mists. The deck must be kept dry so that the men don't slip and fall. Everything is steel, so a fall can really do damage. Whatever you do, you get filthy. Your hands, your face, your shoes, trousers and shirt become smeared with grease, rust and mud chemicals. I never knew 14 days could take so long."

The threat of injury or violent death is always present. There are occasional blowouts in which several lives may be snuffed out in a moment, but more frequently men die in falls or when great sections of pipe fall and crush them. Veteran roustabouts often have fingers missing from accidents.

Who are these men, and why do they do it? The two prevailing cultures are Cajun and Mississippian, and some platforms offer alternate menus —rice, beans, and gumbo for the Cajuns, ham, greens, and potatoes for the Mississippians. Janos reported:

> The rural, Protestant faces of the Mississippi farmers, with grit-swollen bellies ballooning their overalls, contrast starkly with their darker, more sinewy colleagues, the Louisiana Cajuns, but they work together in harmony and satisfy their employers, the oilmen, who look for reliable, obedient labor, sufficiently motivated to do hard and dangerous work. The Catholic Cajuns of southwestern Louisiana and the Baptist backroad Mississippians are just hungry. Many of them are veteran oilfield workers, who for years worked oil patches across the Southwest, moving their families from job to job every few months in battered car trailers. Now, offshore, their families are anchored, their take-home pay the envy of their dirt farmer neighbors, as are their second cars, color TVs, Maytags, and freezers. At home, life is poor and hard. Offshore, it is harder still, but all they ask for in return is good pay, and no unions need apply.

Considering the number of wells drilled so far off the Louisiana coast (more than 20,000) it is amazing that up to the early 1970s, only five had ever "blown out," causing heavy pollution in the Gulf. The worst blowout on record occurred when a Chevron Oil Company well 30 miles offshore blew in 1970, spewing up to three-quarters of a million gallons of crude oil into the sea. Later it turned out that Chevron had been breaking the law by failing to install "storm chokes"—devices which stop oil flow in the event of fire, storm, or high winds—on many of its wells. The storm chokes cost only $800 a piece; Chevron was fined $1 million in federal court for its transgressions.

Most of the oil companies have "gotten religion" on the pollution problem in the last few years, and they have also given up the practice of throwing garbage and refuse into the Gulf waters; instead trash is picked up weekly and returned to the mainland. The water now sparkles around most of the platforms, and great schools of fish are attracted by plankton growing on the undersea pipes. The rules, however, are sometimes broken, and one can observe trails of junk or stray oil drums floating about. The most serious environmental hazard that the oil industry poses for the Gulf and for the rivers and marshes of Louisiana is the incessant barrage of minor oil leaks and spills. The reason, hard to detect or prevent by law, may be a faulty well, a routine transfer of oil, a small accident at sea, or deliberate dumping by tankers. No single incident is too serious in itself, but the cumulative effect can be devastating.

The future now looks brighter for the Mississippi River, which was in real danger, until the early 1970s, of becoming a "highway of pollution." Upstream, hundreds of communities were dumping untreated sewage into its waters. In the Baton Rouge-New Orleans area alone, the Environmental Protection Agency in 1970 found chemical, paper, and petrochemical plants dumping every kind of chemical contaminant, from arsenic, lead, and chromium to cyanides, mercury, and zinc, into Old Man River Among the chief offenders were the Ethyl Corporation at Baton Rouge and Kaiser Aluminum and Chemical Corporation near New Orleans. Some of the concentrations of heavy metals like lead or mercury, the EPA noted, "may endanger human life and the life of the aquatic biota." All of that was flowing into a river that provides the drinking water for half of Louisiana's people. Now, as a result of federally required sewage treatment plants and industrial antipollution equipment, the situation has begun to improve. The most serious remaining problems are illegal industrial dumping and the runoff of agricultural pesticides and fertilizers.

The direct tie between natural resource and industrial activity typified by oil-gas yields and the refining-petrochemical industries is typical of much of the Louisiana economy. The harvest from the state's vast forests (which have more than 150 varieties of trees) fuels many sawmills, pulp, and plywood mills. Sugar cane, which Louisiana raises in quantities second only to Hawaii, moves to the refineries. Cotton production has declined precipitously in recent times, but there is still enough to supply a goodly number of textile and apparel plants. Soybeans—successors to cotton as the state's top dollar crop—move to giant grain elevators and to margarine and cooking oil plants along the Mississippi River. Rice, which flourishes in southwestern Louisiana's coastal marshes, moves to cleaning and polishing plants. Livestock does not have the dollar volume of crops, but it is worth almost $300 million a year and sustains a healthy meatpacking industry. The hundreds of miles of coastline, bays, and bayous make possible a thriving fresh and saltwater commercial fishing industry, and Louisiana provides a major share of the national supply of shrimp, oysters, crabs, trout, redfish, flounder, red snapper, and—of course—more frogs' legs than any other state. Hurricanes and water pollution are serious threats, especially for the oystermen, but the annual fish catch has risen past $70 million in value each year, making possible a thriving cannery industry—and Louisiana's superb cuisine. In furs, Louisiana is second only to Alaska. From the traps set by Cajuns in the swamps of Southern Louisiana come millions of pelts of muskrat, raccoon, opossum, and nutria (a large fur-bearing rat). Occasionally—to the horror of the conservationists—limited "harvesting" of alligators is permitted in the bayous of southwestern Louisiana. (Alligators are on the federal list of "endangered species," but the state population of the ornery gators has risen to 250,000 —up from 175,000 a decade ago. Little of the processing into fancy handbags and shoes and wallets is done in the state, but one of the alligator men commented recently: "Have you ever seen a Louisiana governor walk around in anything but alligator shoes?") Our economic overview would be incomplete if we did not note that even the Spanish moss that drapes the cypresses and live oaks of the marshes brings in income: many Louisianans are employed in gathering and cutting the long moss for use in various kinds of upholstery.

Needless to say, tourism is a big and growing industry in Louisiana, and visitors are now spending close to $700 million a year in the state. On the other hand, Louisiana has not cashed in on the federal defense budget as heavily as states like Georgia, South Carolina, and Florida. There are some major installations, like Barksdale Air Force Base across the Red River from Shreveport, which is one of the oldest military installations in the country and is an important operational base for the Strategic Air Command. The state's congressional delegation was jubilant in 1968 when it finally got permanent status for Fort Polk, a huge infantry training base outside the little city of Leesville in west central Louisiana. In times of war (like the Vietnam conflict), Leesville booms; when peace comes, the town withers. The big Michoud Assembly plant at New Orleans was kept busy during the 1960s making Saturn rockets for America's trips to the moon, but employment there is now just a fraction of what it was. Louisiana will have a long way to go to equal the peak of $650 million in military prime contracts it achieved in 1967. Even in those years, Louisiana's defense-generated civilian employment, as a percentage of its whole economy, ranked behind 40 other states. Federally sponsored shipbuilding, an important factor in the New Orleans economy, has declined alarmingly since the mid-1960s.

One Louisiana industry is no more, but it deserves a footnote in American cultural history. I refer to Hadacol, the murky mixture of vitamins and minerals that was purveyed by one of the most flamboyant Louisiana politicians of all times, state senator Dudley J. LeBlanc of Abbeville. Back in the 1940s, no home medicine chest in the South was complete without its bottle of Hadacol. Bob Hope, Mickey Rooney, Chico Marx, George Burns, and Gracie Allen were recruited for a national caravan to advertise Hadacol. A hillbilly band, clowns, chorus girls, and two calliopes went along too. The ill-smelling, ill-tasting nostrum was promoted for the treatment of cancer, tuberculosis, heart trouble, diabetes, paralysis, gallstones, epilepsy, migraine headaches, blood diseases, stomach ulcers, rheumatism, arthritis, high (or low) blood pressure, cataracts, and the rundown feeling following colds. Perhaps the fact that Hadacol contained 12 percent alcohol had something to do with its popularity. Millions of dollars worth were sold before 1951, when the Federal Trade Commission stepped in, charging LeBlanc Corporation with "false, misleading, and deceptive advertising." The next day the company went bankrupt—but Dudley LeBlanc had already sold out his interest for $10 million.

Times were never really bad for LeBlanc, in fact. Born of sharecropper parents at Youngsville, Louisiana, in 1894, he was elected to his first office at 24, served in both houses of the legislature, sponsored old-age pensions, ran for governor in 1932 promising to put Huey Long in the penitentiary (a race he lost), became known locally as the "King of the Cajuns," and had close to 50 years in public office behind him when he finally died in 1971.

New Orleans: Character, Power, Landmarks

"This is a fantastically strange town," Mrs. Helen Mervis, a prominent civic leader, observed when we talked in New Orleans. "I love it: all the things that make it difficult to live in also make it easy to live in. There's a kind of ambivalence one has about it, because there is a great tolerance for everything, including corruption. That tolerance goes so far in many areas that it creates a kind of hedonistic environment. And never forget," she added, "that New Orleans is a Carnival City—everything revolves around Carnival."

Talking about New Orleans, one can suddenly be plunged into a discussion of anything from the amazing levees and pumps that keep the city from sinking into the ooze of deltaic Louisiana to defining the difference between New Orleans jazz and Dixieland jazz.* Constantly, there is the amazement that New Orleans is there at all. As Walker Percy wrote in a delightful article titled *New Orleans Mon Amour:*

> New Orleans is both intimately related to the South and yet in a real sense cut adrift not only from the South but from the rest of Louisiana. . . . One comes upon it, moreover, in the unlikeliest of places, by penetrating the depths of the Bible Belt, running the gauntlet of Klan territory, the pine barrens of south Mississippi, Bogalusa and the Florida parishes of Louisiana. Out and over a watery waste and there it is, a proper enough American city and yet within the next few hours the tourist is apt to see more nuns and naked women than he ever saw before.

Later on, Percy embroidered on the theme, saying that New Orleans had "the ideological flavor of a Latin enclave in a Southern Scotch-Irish mainland." Perhaps that is why New Orleans, despite its wealth and port location—which is to the South what New York is to the East—has never been a leader of its region.

Once there, the visitor has to be fascinated by the gumbo-melange of New Orleans society. People of French, of Spanish, of African, of Italian, of Irish, of German, of English ancestry—they are all there. It is a city, one Louisiana governor told me, that is "owned by the Catholics, enjoyed by the Negroes, and run by the Jews"—a gross exaggeration, of course, on all three

* According to jazz connoisseur Charles Suhor, New Orleans jazz is the original style of New Orleans' early musicians, characterized by a buoyant, uncluttered 2/4 or 4/4 rhythmic pulse, sensitive ensemble work, and relatively simple, nonvirtuoso solos. He defines Dixieland jazz as "a slick, smooth offspring of New Orleans jazz, with faster tempos, more 'schooled' instrumental tone and more and longer solos." To some critics, Dixieland is the white jazzman's diluted version of New Orleans jazz, which is thought to be exclusively black music. There have been two great revivals of New Orleans and Dixieland jazz, one in the late 1940s, another since the 1960s and centered in the city's two emporiums of jazz—Preservation Hall and Dixieland Hall. There are said to be only about 150 old-time musicians left in the city now, many in their sixties and seventies or older. But jazz is even taught in some classrooms, and there are some vital neighborhood troupes. Occasionally one can hear one of the authentic marching brass bands, renowned for their slow funeral dirges on the way to a graveside and then the soul-freeing refrains of jubilant music on the return. The late and incomparable Louis Armstrong, whose life began in New Orleans in 1900, made it abundantly clear that he had played too many New Orleans funerals to fear death.

counts, but not without a shred of truth. It is perhaps the only American city where Catholics are very much of the hierarchy and always have been. Of the Negroes, one must note that there are more there than ever before: they make up 45 percent of the city's population (593,471 in the last Census). Their heritage there runs from the fearful slave market of antebellum days to the wondrous invention of jazz and, in our time, newborn freedoms circumscribed by poverty and occasional terror.

There are only 15,000 Jews in all of Louisiana, but they play a very prominent role in the business and community organizations of New Orleans. "The reason," one of their number explained, "is that so many of the Christians who would ordinarily control the town have defected because they're too busy with Mardi Gras, and always have been." Raising money for culture or charity is extremely difficult in New Orleans, and one reason given is that the Christian elite expend too much of their spare cash on the floats and costumed balls of Mardi Gras. Again, it is left to the Jews, who are notoriously excluded from Mardi Gras activities, despite the fact that many of their families go back six or seven generations in New Orleans, to take the initiative.

There is much that can be said in favor of Mardi Gras. It is the epitome of what makes New Orleans one of the great fun cities of the world. Walker Percy has defended it as "an organic, viable folk festival, perhaps the only one in the United States." Carnival time begins on Twelfth Night, January 6, and ends on Shrove Tuesday, or Mardi Gras (literally Fat Tuesday), the day before Ash Wednesday and the season of penitence. Sixty-some "krewes" —private social groups or eating clubs—sponsor the parades and balls, and at its best the bacchanal on the streets is a kaleidoscope of colorful and boisterous sights and sounds, of the festive floats with their sequined and beplumed revelers lurching along. Half the float-riders and spectators are inebriated, and under cover of a costume mask, inhibitions are freed for innocent fanny-pinching or other amusements.

Things begin to get snooty in the private masked balls of the oldest and most socially prominent krewes—Comus (1857), Rex (1872), Momus (1872), and Proteus (1882). These presumably secret societies, almost exclusively male and white, dominate the city's social hierarchy. The greatest social compliment a member of New Orleans society can receive is to be made king or queen of one of the carnival societies. The elitist of the elite among the krewes is Comus, which rigorously excludes Jews, even as spectators, at its ball. (So, down to the present day, does the prestigious Boston Club, which is still what John Gunther called it—"a select distillation of the financial and social power" of New Orleans.) A half step below Comus is Rex, which was organized a century ago in the excitement of a New Orleans visit by Russian Grand Duke Alexis Romanoff Alexandrovitch. Rex is basically a businessmen's club, and does have some Jewish members. Its parades are the most extravagant of all.

Stockbroker Darwin Fenner, one of the two most powerful and socially prominent men of the city, is a member of Comus and once served as

Captain of Rex. A silverhaired man of impeccable manners, Fenner has been considered *the* civic leader of New Orleans, the man who can get things accomplished (as long as business interests are well protected). His interests have included Tulane, the Charity Hospital, CABL, and the Metropolitan Area Committee. In the midst of the 1960 turmoil over initial desegregation of New Orleans' schools, Fenner considered maintaining separate toilets for white and black first-graders the most important problem

Fenner's twin at the top of the social power structure has been Harry Kelleher, an attorney who is president of the Tulane board of administrators.* He was particularly successful in winning acceptance among Negro leaders in the city, and is also a leader in the area of medical education. His krewe is Rex.

For the most part, N … the white man's
Carnival celebrations, t… 85 black "social
and pleasure Mardi C… orate social peck-
ing orders. The mos… ure Club and its
offshoot, the Your… erold Doley, Sr.,
a member … are the Rex of
… ery, very highly
… y and we present

… o parade headed
… asure Club. Zulu
… aced with white
… lose his way, get
… civil rights revolu-
… and not only did
… u did not parade
… escort. But the
… at Zulu survived.
… , and stays firmly
… opefully forever,"
… ability to separate

… strom. Thousands
… traights—have be-
… ose without cash
… sleep during the
… handling and the
… lated, the streets
… id the local mer-
… as of 1970—later
… uck trumpeter Al

… tually synonomous. But
… oliticians. Leander Perez,

Hirt, a New Orleans fixture, while he was costumed as Santa Claus atop a parade float. The brick cut Hirt's mouth badly and nearly ended his musical career.

Now questions are being raised about the entire concept of Mardi Gras and its contribution to the total good of the city—culturally, economically, socially, philanthropically, and morally. The first public figure to speak out on the subject (an act of no little courage in New Orleans) was Peter Beer, a member of the city's commission council. Beer said Carnival does not have the benefits it should, saps energies that ought to be used for more creative undertakings, and detracts from the public morality through its exclusionary aspects in regard to Jews and blacks. Others have suggested that it does little good for the city's image when hotel owners gouge the more affluent Mardi Gras tourists by insisting on five-day stays at double rates.

The criticisms may force some changes in Mardi Gras in the next years. But it seems safe to wager that as long as there is a New Orleans, there will be Carnival.

Come Ash Wednesday, what else is there to New Orleans? Hale Boggs provided the answer: "The port is what accounts for New Orleans. It was one of the most unlikely spots on earth to build a city—literally on a swamp, mostly below sea level, with floods and hurricanes and every pestilence known to man. But the port did it; that's why President Jefferson effected the Louisiana Purchase. He wanted the Mississippi, the greatest river system on earth, to belong to the United States." Today it is estimated that the port supports 60 percent of New Orleans' economy. The first beneficiaries are the longshoremen, who earn close to six dollars an hour. They have segregated unions, both of them honestly run, which is one reason there is relatively little pilferage or waterfront violence. The bigger union is actually the black one, a neat reversal of usual Southern patterns; it is headed by an unusually able leader, Clarence ("Chink") Henry, described by one local reporter as "an inscrutable, pale beige version of the late Edward G. Robinson." * The longshoremen are only a small portion of the 50,000 people who earn their living through maritime-related industries.

As wet as New Orleans' location is, when the Frenchmen came up the river early in the 18th century to find a town site, it was probably the driest place they could locate. The city they founded, on a great crescent of the Mississippi, is almost an island. It is bounded on the south by the Mississippi, on the north by the waters of Lake Pontchartrain, a body of water half the size of Rhode Island and the prime swimming, fishing, and sailing grounds of New Orleans' people.† (The Mississippi, by contrast, is too swift, treacherous—and polluted—for recreation.)

New Orleans' famous cemeteries, with their aboveground crypts, are one byproduct of the city's watery location. In an aerial photograph, they

* Black longshoremen's secure position on the docks, like every other Negro right in the South, was hard won. The struggle began with strikes immediately after emancipation and continued through race-tinged clashes for decades afterwards.

† The South's most spectacular highway is the Lake Pontchartrain Causeway, which runs across open water for 23 miles. In the center section, a motorist has the sensation of being at sea, because he cannot see land. The causeway was opened in 1956, with a second parallel road in 1969.

resemble a neatly-laid out city; like cities, the cemeteries can accept successive waves of inhabitants because with each new burial, older bones can be pushed to the back of the vaults, spilling down a shaft. Next to cremation, it may be the most efficient burial system ever invented.

The jewel of the New Orleans milieu, of course, is the area of the original town laid out by the French—the *Vieux Carré*, or French Quarter. The Quarter's myriad attractions range from the marvelous architecture, including the decorative ironwork of French and Spanish design, to Bourbon Street's jazz and flesh locales, from Royal Street's choice shops and galleries to the landscaped oasis of Jackson Square. In the Quarter, one finds illustrious and venerable restaurants like Antoine's and Brennan's and Galatoire's, or if one likes, there is the lure of strong roast Louisiana coffee and hot fresh doughnuts at the French market by the levee. Hippies and other hangers-on have flooded the Quarter in unwelcome quantities in recent years (especially at Carnival time), but then again, one could ask where there is an interesting locale in America where that *hasn't* happened.

The *Vieux Carré* is packed with buildings of historic import; just at Jackson Square, for instance, one finds St. Louis Cathedral (which dates back to 1794), the Pontalba Buildings resplendent behind iron balconies from France, which are thought to be the oldest apartment buildings in America, and the Cabildo, headquarters of the Spanish administration of the city, where the formal transfer of the Louisiana Territory to the United States took place in 1803. Jackson Square was saved a horrible fate in the late 1960s, when the U.S. Department of Transportation, in a precedent-making decision, yielded to citizen pressures and denied federal funding for an elevated expressway along the Mississippi bank past the French Quarter. The superroad would have ruined Jackson Square's milieu and the view of ships coming down the Mississippi. Now the visitor to Jackson Square on a Saturday afternoon can hear one of the jazz concerts the city sponsors there weekly, or he or she can try the new walkway along the levee, which has a sign up saying "Moonwalk"—in honor of Mayor Moon Landrieu, who got the walk put there.

Landrieu is an avid preservationist who professes "a passionate love" for New Orleans. On a recent tour through the Quarter, Landrieu said: "We won't let anybody touch these buildings, except under strict control." The city, he added, has great difficulty finding the funds to restore and preserve some of its historic landmarks. He pointed to a rundown two-story building in which the Reconstruction state legislature first met after the Civil War, and to the oldest building in the Mississippi Valley, the Ursuline Convent, lamenting its decay. "Now do you think that because the city cannot afford to preserve or restore these buildings, we should just let them rot away?" Landrieu asked. "We can't do that. These are *national* treasures; they don't belong just to us. They are the historical property of the American people." But he said he would not use federal revenue sharing money for restoration, that there were too many other pressing projects for the benefit of New Orleans people alive today. (The voters rejected a proposed bond issue to raise money for buying and restoring some of the prime architectural examples, but Landrieu was able to grant tax breaks to property owners who restore historic structures.)

Simple restoration will not solve the French Quarter's problems. The hotel builders, for instance, have been replacing old landmarks in order to accommodate tourists coming to see the old landmarks. If they are high enough to be commercially feasible, new buildings may clash with the historic styles of the Quarter. Some new hotels, including a Holiday Inn that towers 18 stories over Royal Street, are a gross violation of the spirit of the area; others, including the five-storied new Royal Sonesta Hotel, with ample ironwork on its facade, or the new Vieux Carré Hotel, with gable roofs and alternating facades, have been quite successful.

The French Quarter by no means exhausts New Orleans' wonders. Even the normally prosaic *National Geographic* has caught the spirit of the city's ambience, writing of "warm air so soft it might have been washed in a rainbow; the rich odor of the wharves, seasoned with sugar, coffee, and bananas; the closeness of the blue sky, on which a majestic fleet of cumulus clouds runs before the gulf breeze; the worn look of weathered white clapboard houses, shaded by palm fronds, that stand on long avenues vanishing toward the horizon; terrain as flat as a figure in plane geometry." The Garden District, with its comfortable Greek Revival and Georgian style homes on spacious lawns, is a world apart from the French Quarter, where buildings crowd up on the sidewalk and one has to look for hidden courtyards to find greenery and peace. In antebellum days, the Garden District was known as "the American colony," in contrast to the Creole stronghold in the *Vieux Carré*. The once ubiquitous streetcar is an almost extinct species in the United States today, and in 1948 New Orleans put buses in place of the streetcar named Desire that Tennessee Williams had immortalized. But all is not lost; a single line of rickety old trolleys still runs down St. Charles Avenue, through the heart of the Garden District, almost a ghost of itself. The fare is like yesteryear: 15 cents.

Another echo of the past is the mournful steam whistle of the *Delta Queen*, America's last river packet, as she returns to New Orleans from her regular trips up the Mississippi. That grand old paddle-wheel palace had been consigned to oblivion by new laws prohibiting wood in large overnight steamers, and in the autumn of 1971 there was actually a sentimental farewell voyage. From St. Paul on downriver—past La Crosse, Prairie du Chien, Dubuque, Clinton, Davenport, Mark Twain's Hannibal, St. Louis, and Memphis—thousands had turned out to bid the *Delta Queen* farewell. At New Orleans, jazz bands blared and the ship's steam calliope belted out *Auld Lang Syne* as the ship docked for what was thought would be its last stop. But Congress, in its wisdom, granted a last-minute reprieve, and the *Delta Queen* steams on, bringing New Orleans a constant reminder that there are real *people* upstream, not just the constant flow of goods brought back on barges and freighters. (The real golden era of the steamboats was 1830 to 1860; then it was, as the WPA Guide reported, that "copious food and fine orchestras were featured on the floating palaces, whose passengers came from all walks of life—planters, pioneers, businessmen and their wives, as well as prostitutes and professional gamblers.")

All is not joy for New Orleans' traditionalists, however. Many of them are confounded by the obliteration of the city's old skyline by the generation of huge skyscrapers that started in the 1960s. A plethora of gargantuan office buildings and hotels were constructed or were on the drawing boards by the early '70s; the biggest so far is Shell Oil's 50-story tower. The 33-story International Trade Mart rose above the low-slung rooftops by the riverfront, a location that must have brought joy to its architect, Edward Durrell Stone, who loves dramatic settings for his buildings But the Trade Mart will not be alone by the river very long; in 1973 plans were announced for the New Orleans International Rivercenter, a $200 million cluster of high-rise apartments, office buildings, and a 1,200-room hotel, right beside it.

Iris Kelo, a respected correspondent for WDSU-TV, suggested to me that there was a strange symbolism in the two tragedies associated with the high-rise boom (which she said she deplores and hates) in the old city of New Orleans. First there was a high-rise office building fire in which several died, late in 1972; early the next year, there followed a murderous shooting spree from a lofty new Howard Johnson hotel by a young black named Mark Essex who was driven to apparent insanity through his hatred of whites. As the fire victims leaped to their death, multitudes watched from nearby buildings, and hundreds of thousands more on television film the same day. Again, by grace of the tube, practically the whole city watched the police's day-long sniper hunt. "These were real 20th-century tragedies, staged from those high-rises we are supposed to be so proud of. And they became part of the whole television culture we're living in," Miss Kelso said.

Shell's lofty new building bears a striking resemblance to One Shell Plaza in Houston, Texas, an unhappy analogy for a city that likes to think of itself as graceful and feminine. And now New Orleans has set out to *outdo* Houston—or any city on earth, for that matter—with a gigantic domed stadium called the Louisiana Superdome, built on 13 acres of what was city blight near the downtown business-hotel district and the French Quarter. The name superdome was conceived as a direct affront to Houston and its Astrodome; Mayor Moon Landrieu, an enthusiastic backer of the project, likes to boast to visitors that "we could fit that thing [the Astrodome] inside the Superdome with no sweat." It will, in fact, be the biggest indoor stadium in the world, 273 feet (27 stories) tall with a 680-foot diameter no other building anywhere can match. For regular football games, it will seat about 70,000 fans or, with portable chairs and standing room, over 80,000. What is more impressive are the Superdome's unique features: movable grandstands that can bring spectators closer to basketball, stage plays, rodeos, and concerts; giant color television screens suspended over the stands, that enable spectators to see the close-ups and instant replays so popular on home television, or sports and cultural events anywhere in the world, via closed circuit TV; theatrical lighting; and an immense convention capability. For a political meeting, the Superdome will hold 97,000 people.

The managers of the Superdome idea have hopes that both the Republican and Democratic National Conventions can be enticed there in 1976. Since Miami Beach has had its fill of the political conclaves, the chances are not bad.

Before the Superdome's construction could begin in 1971, the project had to clear five years of planning and delays, tight money markets, bond elections, escalating costs, and a plethora of hostile lawsuits. "Father of the Dome" status, according to *New Orleans Magazine*, goes to Governor McKeithen, whose influence on the state supreme court and "Sugar Daddy handling of the legislature [were] nothing short of pure political brilliance and expertise." McKeithen got through an enabling amendment to the state constitution in 1966, when the cost was to have been only $30 million, compared to a final price tag of $152 million. Landrieu, by contrast, was called "Mother of the Dome" for being a stalwart supporter from the inception of the idea, helping to write the enabling state legislation, and staking much of his political future on it. Along the way, opponents threw charges ranging from "swindle" to "boondoggle" at the stadium. But if growth and tourism are a good thing for New Orleans, the Superdome should be a great stimulant. A big tourist promotion effort for the city began under Landrieu, to get visitors from all over the country. The Superdome may have a particular unifying benefit for Louisiana, too, drawing to New Orleans thousands of rural Louisiana sports fans who now make the long trip over to the Astrodome in Houston.

A trusted New Orleans source told me: "The dome's cost has certainly skyrocketed. But the people responsible are not the kind to make it a political boondoggle. It will eventually become a productive entity. But it has a long road to go, and an awful lot of proving to do."

The Superdome would not be happening at all if some new entrepreneurial talent had not moved into New Orleans in the last few years, completely bypassing the old business-social elite that throttled growth there for so many decades. "In New Orleans," John Corporon, former news manager of WDSU-TV explained, "money counts. But it counts even more to be in a fine old family, even if it doesn't have much wealth left. If you have money *and* fine old family, then you're at the very top." During the 1960s, the New York-based Center for Urban Education interviewed several of the influentials of New Orleans and came up with the conclusion that the city had "a traditionalist nonmodernizing elite." Almost all had been born in New Orleans, most were from families there for 100 years, and some boasted their families had been in Louisiana for more than 250 years. When asked what attached them to New Orleans, the elites offered answers like this: "Ideal social atmosphere. Relaxed, pleasant living." "The way of life." "Pleasant and gracious." "Most wonderful atmosphere. Finest fishing in the world. Pace is good. Beautiful spring and fall." They also thought of themselves as a very Old South group: "My grandfather fought in the Confederate Army."

When the interviewer referred to Atlanta or Houston, the response was almost invariably one of disdain: "Who would want to live *there?*" The New Orleans' elite characterized cities like Dallas, Houston, and Atlanta as brash, money-grubbing, repugnant cities run by the *nouveau riche*, lacking in culture and civility, caught in the spirit of vulgar boosterism. They were not seen as really Southern cities at all.

But when it came to putting together the banks to buy $113 million worth of bonds to build the Superdome, the old New Orleans leaders were out to lunch. Instead, the job was done by James H. Jones, the aggressive 41-year-old president of New Orleans' National Bank of Commerce. Jones scoured the South for backing, getting especially warm support from Mills Lane's innovative Citizens & Southern National Bank of Atlanta. All the New Orleans banks helped—except Whitney National Bank, the city's largest. And where does Jimmy Jones come from? Dallas, Texas.

New Orleans: Light Years Advanced

New Orleans is a city of some hope today because its encrusted power structure has been end-runned. Jimmy Jones and young businessmen like him have done it on the economic front. The emergence of a potent political coalition—middle-to-upper class whites working with the city's big black population—has done it on the governmental front. To see how profound the change has been, one need only go back to 1960, the year of New Orleans' school integration crisis and one of the greatest "cop-outs" of a city's leaders in modern American history.*

In the autumn of 1960, the wall of solid school segregation remained unbreached, from Louisiana across the Deep South to South Carolina. But the handwriting was on the wall: at Little Rock, three years before, the federal government had made it clear that it would use its full force to require integration, and Judge J. Skelly Wright of the federal District Court in New Orleans had ordered the admittance of blacks to the schools in the city, starting with first-graders in the 1960-61 school year. His language was so crystal-clear that no rational person should have doubted the eventual outcome.

New Orleans, moreover, seemed the ideal place to break the Deep South's resistance to change. It was Catholic, it was tolerant, and its "salt and pepper" pattern of housing amounted to possibly the greatest degree of residential integration of any big American city, South or North. Quite peacefully, the city had already put Negroes on its police force and admitted them to its libraries, its places of recreation, and all the seats on its buses. And the resources for calm leadership into an era of integrated schools seemed to be there in an urbane, well educated elite and one of the most highly regarded "reform" mayors of the early postwar years, deLesseps Story Morrison.

Before Morrison, New Orleans had labored for a decade under the notoriously corrupt administration of Robert Maestri, a long-time ally of the Longs (who had installed him in office, the first time without benefit of

* For portions of the ensuing account, I am indebted to Morton Inger's *Politics and Reality in an American City: The New Orleans School Crisis of 1960,* a federally sponsored survey published in 1969 by the Center for Urban Education.

election). Maestri controlled the old Choctaw Club, New Orleans' equivalent of Tammany Hall, and was tied in with the city's organized gambling (run by Frank Costello of New York). He was considered unbeatable, but in 1946 middle-class reform elements in the city turned to "Chep" Morrison, just back from distinguished Army service and still in uniform, and asked him to run. Morrison was young (only 34), cut a handsome figure, and had good social credentials as a member of a 150-year-old Creole family. A group of dedicated female activists—dubbed "The Girls"—went to work for him and helped him win in a brief, whirlwind campaign.

Not long afterwards, *Time* featured Morrison in a cover story that called him "bouncing, talkative, tough and stubborn," a "symbol of the bright new day which has come to the city of charming ruins." The U.S. Junior Chamber of Commerce named him one of the "outstanding 10 young men" of 1947; another on that year's list was Congressman Richard M. Nixon. Morrison cracked down on gambling and prostitution, cleared slums, erected a new civic center, and set out to make New Orleans outstrip Miami as "the gateway to Latin America." The *Time* cover showed him with a dock pier and the ocean and South American flags in the background, and in fact he mastered Spanish and made many goodwill trips to Latin America. The International Trade Mart he helped to build was instrumental in propelling New Orleans from 16th to second place among U.S. ports. "His city leadership," Allan Sindler wrote in 1956, "comprised a blend of practical politics, liberalism, good government, and aggressive leadership."

Those who should know say Morrison never took a crooked dollar; his problems were more in the area of factional fighting and personal morality.* And in 1960, as the school crisis loomed, "Chep" Morrison had another problem: he wanted to make one more run for governor, and he feared being branded an integrationist if he did anything to facilitate school desegregation. As a result, he remained almost speechless while his city drifted toward catastrophe.

Morrison was not alone. Until the school crisis was full blown, not a single white moderate group in the city was willing to speak up for desegregation. The school board—a young "reform" group elected with the help of "The Girls"—blithely assumed that the day of integration would never arrive. The board took a survey of parents and found 82 percent favored closing the schools rather than accepting desegregation—and then asked Governor Davis to interpose the sovereignty of the state to prevent blacks from entering the white schools. Archbishop Joseph Francis Rummel, who had earlier pronounced racial segregation "morally wrong and sinful," was in poor health and had nothing to say. (The parochial schools would not be integrated until 1962, two years *after* the public schools blazed the way.)

When Judge Wright's orders finally convinced the school board that it

* Morrison, one veteran New Orleans reporter said, "had immense personal magnetism. But he was coldblooded, too; his wife either killed herself or died in an alcoholic stupor. He saw her deteriorating before his very eyes and did nothing. He was a great lover and slept with anything that wiggled. He had great leadership qualities and yet was so insensitive where his own family was concerned." Morrison resigned as mayor in 1961 to accept President Kennedy's appointment as Ambassador to the Organization of American States. His life ended three years later when the private plane in which he was riding crashed into a remote Mexican hillside.

would have to draw up a plan, the board president turned to the New Orleans elite—men like Fenner and Kelleher—for support. But he found that the *crème de la crème* would not meet with him unless the meeting were secret. One or two middle-level white groups called for moderation and keeping the schools open, but the elite said not a word until the worst crisis was past. The New Orleans *Times-Picayune* managed to take a fence-straddling position whenever it editorialized on the crisis. In Baton Rouge, Jimmie Davis steamrollered package after package of patently unconstitutional laws through special sessions. As soon as the bills passed, Judge Wright struck them down. In one crucial session at Baton Rouge, the house vote was 93–1 for suspending the rules to consider Davis' bills. The only state representative who dared vote "no" was Moon Landrieu.

When the school board got around to selecting which schools would first be desegregated, it made an error typical of apolitical reformist groups. It could have chosen schools in New Orleans' more affluent "uptown" district (west of Canal Street and the French Quarter), and in fact two PTAs in that area actually petitioned the school board to have black children sent to their schools. But instead, the board, using allegedly "objective" test data, decreed that the first integration would take place in the "downtown" area (east of the French Quarter), which is made up of the kind of poor working families most nervous about Negro advances. The schools chosen were actually in the Ninth Ward, adjacent to St. Bernard Parish, which was then under the control of Leander Perez.

As the four black children entered the schools, angry crowds—composed mainly of the wives of working-class and unemployed whites of the Ninth Ward and St. Bernard Parish—gathered and spat abuse at them. Equally vile treatment was reserved for the handful of white parents who did not withdraw their children from the schools. The employment of fathers was threatened, and four did lose their jobs. Volunteer drivers, according to the U.S. Commission on Civil Rights, "were threatened with death, arson, disfigurement." At that time, John Steinbeck was passing through New Orleans, gathering notes for *Travels with Charley*. Dressed in an old jacket and British navy cap so that no one would think he was a reporter, he watched the scene in front of one of the integrated schools:

> Sounds of sirens. Motorcycle cops. Then two big black cars filled with big men in blond felt hats pulled up in front of the school. The crowd seemed to hold its breath. Four big marshals got out of each car and from somewhere in the automobiles was extracted the littlest Negro girl you ever saw, dressed in shining starchy white, with new white shoes on feet so little they were almost round. Her face and legs were very black against the white.
>
> The big marshals took her on the curb and a jangle of jeering shrieks went up from behind the barricades. The little girl did not look at the howling crowd but from the side the whites of her eyes showed like those of a frightened fawn. . . . Slowly they climbed the steps and entered the school. . . .
>
> No newspaper had printed the words these women shouted. . . . But now I heard the words, bestial and filthy and degenerate. . . .

Some of the more printable threats reported later were "You little nigger, we'll get you and kill you," and "We're going to poison you until you choke to death." Sociologist Robert Coles later interviewed the woman who shouted the latter threat and described her as a person weary, very sad and frightened, and poor. Her education stopped at the eighth grade, she had many children and a drunkard husband, and she felt her life was cheated and impoverished. She feared and hated Negroes and felt that when the school integrated, Negroes would dispossess her children. Clearly, she was not demonstrating just to see her own face later on the television news.

Steinbeck also wrote:

> I knew New Orleans, I have over the years had many friends there, thoughtful, gentle people, with a tradition of kindness and courtesy. . . . I looked in the crowd for such faces of such people and they were not there. . . . I don't know where they were. Perhaps they felt as helpless as I did, but they left New Orleans misrepresented to the world. . . .
>
> The show was over and the river of us began to move away. . . . I was in New Orleans of the great restaurants. I know them all and most of them know me. And I could no more have gone to Galatoire's for an omelet and champagne than I could have danced on a grave. Even setting this down on paper has raised the weary, hopeless nausea in me again. . . .
>
> I bought a poor-boy sandwich and got out of town.

While all this was transpiring, New Orleans' top business and social elite remained mute. Mayor Morrison deplored violence and warned of what was being done to New Orleans' business image, but he never called for obedience to the federal law. Even the civic leaders who finally spoke out for open schools felt obliged to stress that they were *for* segregation. The Center for Urban Education observed in its report: "When a city is so permeated by fear that decent men cannot talk to their friends on the street, when businessmen are too frightened to speak for moderation, then the social fabric of a city is all but destroyed."

Only after a month of demonstrations did a group of business and professional men make the first public plea for an end to threats and violence and for support of the school board. Early in 1961, some 1,600 citizens attended a dinner to pay tribute to the board members for what they had done to preserve the schools. Harry Kelleher was the main speaker, praising the board for its "gallant" fight to resist desegregation, but saying "the public school system is worth preserving. . . . This country and the South cannot afford to go backward." With that show of support, the school board knew the worst of the crisis was past.

Since 1960, integration in New Orleans' schools has proceeded—but at the price of massive resegregation when black enrollments in individual schools top the 50 percent mark. In 1971–72, out of 135 schools in the system, 41 were totally black or white, and 42 others were 90 to 99.9 percent of one race. The system had 10,000 fewer white students than a decade before—and 20,000 more blacks, accounting for 70 percent of the total enrollment. The survival of the public school system in the 1970s is, in fact, just as much in question as it was in 1960. The superintendent has warned that the schools will keep on getting blacker, and that if the city does nothing to save its schools, it can look at Newark, New Jersey, and see where it will be in five years or so. Only radical action, it appears, can save the schools.

The most breathtaking proposal is that Roman Catholic Archbishop Hannan immediately close down the overwhelmingly white parochial school system in the city. A white majority would thus be restored—before it is too late. But will that happen? Instead of being one of the nation's most regressive cities, as it was in 1960, New Orleans would have to show leadership no other city has demonstrated. A local liberal said: "Nobody cares about the school system. There's violence in the school corridors, and policemen have to be assigned to keep order in the heavily black schools. It's not as dramatic as the women out shouting, but it's just as sad."

New Orleans' sense of helplessness in sustaining its schools is reflected in its quandary about how to deal with embittered groups like the Black Panthers or the notorious hotel sniper of January 1973. One of the ugliest incidents in the city's racial history occurred in 1970, when a group of Panthers occupied a house on Piety Street in a dirty, crime-ridden black housing project called Desire. The fact that Desire exists at all is a commentary on the city: it squats near the river, isolated by railroad tracks and canals, a home of sorts to more than 10,000 black people of whom 8,000 are under 21. A report to the mayor had described Desire as "an ideal incubator for crime, social disintegration, and disease," a place where children swim in sewers, garbage and trash pile up without collection, and drug traffic, muggings, and rape are so prevalent that families fear to leave their homes. The Panthers moved in, sandbagged their fortress, and terrorized the local merchants. Some nasty incidents prompted the New Orleans police to descend on Desire to restore order; what followed was a night of chaos, gunfire, and firebombs, at the end of which one black youth was dead and 21 other persons injured. But some of the injured young blacks claimed they had no connection with the Panthers and that the police had shot at them without provocation. A jury acquitted 12 Panthers accused of attempted murder of police.

The nervous overreaction of the police in the Desire incident was duplicated in the 1972 sniper incident. Of the whites murdered, one was the city's deputy police superintendent, Louis Sirgo, who had previously warned of the dangers the police faced in an era of black zealotry. But Sirgo had also tried to explain the reasons for black militancy, starting with the black's degraded status as "the invisible man" in society, the inner-city slums to which blacks are relegated, the crime-breeding conditions in revengist prisons, and society's ostrichlike attitude to all of this. "We must," Sirgo had said, "be prepared to deal with the greatest sin of American society, and that is the status of the Negro." Until then, he added, the police would be "kept busy putting out the fires which erupt in society."

Sirgo's point was that the police could not be expected to deal with a problem of that magnitude, and his death proved the point. His superior, Police Superintendent Clarence Giarrusso, has run a clean department but is an unsophisticated man. Where a race-crazed sniper was at work, Giarrusso saw a genuine, full-scale war between the races. Most white citizens of New Orleans had the same paranoiac reaction. And Giarrusso, instead of playing a waiting game, impulsively ordered his men into the line of fire, and Sirgo was one of those who paid with his life. Sirgo will doubtless not be the last decent and generous man to be sacrificed in the bitter aftermath of the segregation system which New Orleans' leaders once so proudly defended—and still have done so little really to end. And there is a question how much they really want to do. A survey of 644 community leaders, made in the early 1970s, showed that the majority favored change in nine specific areas (transportation and education, for instance) before a change in race relations. As a kind of atonement after the 1960 school crisis, some of the city's elite tried to ameliorate black-white tensions. Harry Kelleher, for instance, was involved in setting up a behind-the-scenes biracial community group, which eventually became public. But in the aggregate, all of what the traditional leadership has done smacks of too little, too late.

The black community of New Orleans has made some important advances, but not through white largesse. Instead, the black advance has been *self-generated*, and it has come about through that time-honored and most effective of all power tools, elective politics.

Until the 1960s, the black vote in New Orleans was rather small and narrowly based in the churches, without meaningful precinct organization. During the Morrison years, according to James Chubbuck, director of Loyola's Institute of Politics, New Orleans had a kind of "consensus politics." Blacks were thankful in those years to have a mayor who was at least not specifically anti-Negro. The 1960 racial disorder ended that era, and a year later Victor Schiro won the mayoralty with a strong segregationist appeal.

For the most part, New Orleans simply drifted through the '60s. Civic services deteriorated, the economy recovered only slowly from the shock of 1960, and the white exodus to the suburbs accelerated. Schiro had some political skills and did moderate in office, but he was best known for his ribbon-cutting and malapropisms. Nationally, the best known New Orleanian of the decade was the six-foot, seven-inch "Jolly Green Giant," District Attorney Jim Garrison. Garrison startled New Orleans and the country in 1967 with sensational claims about a hometown conspiracy that would solve the 1963 assassination of President Kennedy. He charged that Clay Shaw, a distinguished New Orleans businessman, had conspired with accused assassin Lee Harvey Oswald and others to kill the President. Eventually, Garrison's list of supposed conspirators included virtually the whole federal government. But it took a jury only an hour to find Shaw innocent. Garrison kept up his vendetta against Shaw until the federal courts stopped him. Though he was demonstrably unfit to hold office, the voters returned Garrison in 1970. Later he was indicted on federal charges of taking payoffs to protect pinball gambling operations—a favorite corruption in Louisiana. He was acquitted, and then sought reelection once again.

In the meantime, important things were happening with the black vote in New Orleans. For one thing, it almost doubled, from 36,000 to 66,000 during the decade. Secondly, some viable black political organizations appeared. Through grass-roots organizing, they began to mobilize the potential black vote in ghetto precincts. And they also harnessed the financial and organizing powers of the substantial black middle class, a bourgeoisie which had traditionally placed more value on personal economic advancement than politics. In the entire 20th century, not a single black had been elected to public office in New Orleans. But after those "decades of political serfdom," as Furnell Chatman wrote in *New Orleans Magazine*, three black candidates emerged victorious in 1967—two for the parish Democratic committee, and Ernest ("Dutch") Morial, an attractive young attorney, as state representative. The next year the white political establishment decided it was time to make a concession to the black community, and Dr. Mack Spears was elected in a citywide election to the parish school board. In 1971, Morial won a city judgeship, and single-member district reapportionment made it possible for blacks to elect five state representatives from the city.* Blacks were still vastly underrepresented at every level of government, but considering the fact they had started at ground zero in 1967, it was a heartening start.

At the same time, some young Negro leaders began to make an impact outside of politics. One was Norman Francis, a native of Lafayette, Louisiana, who had been the first Negro student integrated into Loyola's law school. In 1968, at the age of 38, he became president of Xavier University, a black college of some 1,200 students that had been founded and always run before by Catholic Creole nuns. A man quick of mind, with impressive vitality and resourcefulness, Francis proved a bridge between militant black youngsters, older Negroes, and the white community. He became the first Negro to serve on the New Orleans civil service commission and was then appointed to several more state and city boards.

In politics, the most dramatic change of all came in the 1969 mayor's election. As its leader, sluggish old New Orleans picked Moon Landrieu, an outspoken liberal and the man who had thought he was "gazing into my political grave" when he stood tall, but virtually alone, to cast the sole vote against Governor Davis' race-baiting bills in the 1960 school ruckus. Nor was Landrieu a member of the genteel old establishment, like "Chep" Morrison. His Catholic parents struggled to live off a neighborhood grocery store in the front of their home, and Landrieu still lives (with his wife and nine children) in a quite inelegant old New Orleans "double-shotgun" house in a middle-income, integrated part of town. He does not belong to the Boston Club, and his chances of ever being King of Carnival—even if such things interested him—are virtually nil.

Landrieu's election, however, was no accident. He came on the scene at the right moment, when New Orleans' leaders were becoming distressed about the decline of their city in the 1960s. He radiated sincerity about doing something to spark the economy, clean the streets, and improve municipal services, and he had the courage to say the city needed new taxes. And, for the first time, the black vote was big enough to decide a New Orleans

* One of these was Morial's successor, Dorothy Mae Taylor, one of the two women in the legislature. In 1972 she showed sufficient political skill to get herself appointed to the powerful budget committee of the house. Morial, in turn, advanced a notch by winning election to the state court of appeals from a district encompassing all of Orleans Parish.

election. In the crucial runoff primary, 90 percent of it went to Landrieu. He also won 40 percent of the white vote—principally from affluent, well-educated "uptown" areas along St. Charles Avenue and nearby Tulane and Loyola universities, and in the suburban-like Algiers section across the Mississippi River.

Landrieu's opponent, Jimmy Fitzmorris, was the only candidate (in either the first or runoff primaries) who refused to appeal directly for black votes. Fitzmorris did win an overwhelming vote in low-income, poorly educated white areas—Geroge Wallace country, as it were. A few years ago, he would probably have beaten Landrieu. But now the black vote is too big —about a third of the New Orleans total, and likely to grow more as the large reservoir of still unregistered Negroes is tapped. In the 1969 runoff, when they felt there was a white candidate who really cared about them, an amazing 80 percent of the city's registered blacks made it to the polls. And with their more affluent white allies, a voter segment no longer hung up on the race issue, New Orleans' blacks had forged a new coalition—a coalition which James Chubbuck has suggested "is likely to influence New Orleans politics throughout the 1970s," bringing, as in Atlanta, a far more liberal brand of politics and government.

Landrieu's victory over Fitzmorris was barely certified when he got the city council, of which he was still president, to enact an ordinance, long sought by New Orleans blacks, to prohibit discrimination in the city's public accommodations. As soon as he took office, he began to appoint blacks to boards and commissions at every level of government. He inserted bright young aides into virtually all the departments of the tradition-encrusted city government and was able, with several assists from the powerful Louisiana congressional delegation, to increase federal aid from $4 million to $40 million a year. A large portion of that went to programs of special benefit to the blacks and other poor. Landrieu also wrung concessions from the state legislature, proving, as one magazine reported, that a mayor politician who "can backslap, cajole and eat crawfish with the best of them" can "work miracles" for his city.

Perhaps most important, as Helen Mervis put it, Landrieu "gave a moral tone to the community that it had never had before. He gave the city new life and movement. He took some of the initiative away from the old power structure, and ironically, some of them are now in his camp and very strong supporters."

New Orleans continues to face the typical problems of big city governments. Landrieu's own description:

> In the last decade we lost 125,000 people—mostly white and affluent—moving out to the suburbs, and in their place, 90,000, mostly poor and black, moved in. We provide the transportation facilities, the parks, the zoo, the airport, the cultural facilities for a metropolitan area of 1.1 million [more than twice New Orleans' own population]. And we get nothing back from the suburbs. We don't even get the sales tax, because they have their own shopping centers. We don't have enough money even to put a coat of paint on our problems. We tax everything that moves, and everything that stands still, and if it moves, we tax it again.

As an example, Landrieu said, it would cost $125 million to fix up New Orleans' streets—"and I'm not talking about gold-lined streets, but just about bringing them up to a reasonable standard." A badly needed parish prison would cost $32 million. Some $100 million would be needed to build adequate housing in a single urban renewal area, where 70 percent of the units are substandard. Yet the best New Orleans can afford by way of a capital improvements budget is $5 million a year.

The magnitude of those problems led Landrieu to take a leading role in the Legislative Action Committee of the U.S. Conference of Mayors, a lobbying group that travels to Washington and cities all across the U.S. to press the big-city point of view. In 1972 the group chose Landrieu as its second chairman, succeeding New York's John Lindsay. The elevation came only after Landrieu's fellow mayors had been given a first-hand demonstration of his courage. The occasion was a 1971 audience the mayors had with Hale Boggs, then House Majority Leader, to lobby for federal revenue sharing. Lindsay had barely risen to speak when Boggs broke in abruptly to announce that revenue sharing was not on the Democratic leadership's list of priorities, that he would see that it not be put there, and that the matter would not be discussed further.* Lindsay, nonplussed, looked around the room in confusion. After an awkward moment, a Southern twang was heard from the back of the room. No exact record of what Moon Landrieu said is available, but it was essentially this: "Hale, I don't think you can leave it at that. Here we are, a group of primarily Democratic mayors, representing enormous constituencies, coming up here to talk to our majority leaders. And at the very least the Democratic leaders had better listen to the Democratic mayors, because I don't think you understand city problems. I give better time and treatment to the Black Panthers who come to my office than you've just given us. If we're not welcome to discuss revenue sharing here, then maybe Congressmen won't be welcome in the city halls of America." Boggs quickly backed down, a full hour's debate on revenue sharing ensued, and a year later the first general revenue sharing bill of U.S. history sailed through Congress.

Despite his support for revenue sharing, Landrieu sees serious problems if it is used as a reason to cut back—as the Nixon administration has sought to do—on earmarked federal aid programs, especially those that benefit the poor and the black. Revenue sharing received by the city, he points out, "all goes into one big pot, as the real estate tax, our sales tax, and every other revenue." New Orleans, until 1974, had an all-white city council and concentrated its budget expenditures in white neighborhoods. Experimental federal programs like model cities made it possible to "play catch-up" in the deprived communities of New Orleans. The federal guidelines also brought forth new community leadership by obliging the city to involve local poverty area residents in planning for their areas. But if federal revenue sharing

* Boggs' associates insist that he was particularly opposed to the type of revenue sharing originally proposed by the Nixon administration, which he felt lacked sufficient guidelines or accountability to Congress.

is used as a rationale to cut back on those programs, serious backsliding—with serious social repercussions—could well occur.

Landrieu's sensitive thinking on such problems had led many observers of the urban scene, by 1973, to rate him as one of the country's most outstanding mayors. James Chubbuck cited Landrieu's programmatic innovations and administrative skills and said he would "probably turn out to be New Orleans' best mayor of this century." The city's voters seemed to be agreeing when they reelected Landrieu in 1973 by an overwhelming margin. No serious candidate even entered the contest against him.

At the same time, the political climate, across the state as well as in New Orleans, has advanced light-years from the mood which prevailed at the time of the 1960 school crisis. Moon Landrieu expounds a highly unconventional view of the future of Louisiana politics. "The voting strength of blacks nationwide is now 10 to 12 percent," he said. "The state of Louisiana now has 21 percent black registration. It doesn't take much of a genius to recognize the fact that it's not going to take very long before the state of Louisiana is more liberal in its attitudes than the federal government."

Two more notes—one sentimental, the other hopeful—round up our New Orleans review.

The sentimental note is about the passing of the Choctaws, the old "Regular Democratic Organization" that reigned, as Iris Kelso has written, "when the ward leaders were the Cardinals in the Vatican of politics." Those were the days when "the caucus ruled the world," making and unmaking mayors and lesser luminaries, stealing votes, giving a widow a lottery shop in her kitchen, exchanging a bucket of coal or a bag of groceries for election-day loyalties, appeasing the destitute with $25-a-month city jobs. The Choctaws, who enjoyed state patronage even to the days of Earl Long, held forth in a club building filled with musty old wicker furniture and big round fat chairs, the walls adorned with pictures of old Indian chiefs and old mayors. From the '30s to the '50s, the press used to watch every subtle shift of power in the caucus, gathering outside the old club building while titanic battles raged behind closed blinds and windows. On one occasion, the old pols gleefully poured buckets of soapy water on eavesdropping reporters below. Thirty years ago, there was the occasion when Jim Comiskey, a fabled old caucus leader, knocked an acting mayor out cold at a meeting there. But more serious things went on: bargaining with candidates to get hundreds or thousands of dollars in exchange for endorsements.

The Choctaws never officially disbanded; some stirring of activity is still noted at election time. But 1972 was the year of the last real gasp. The lease on the old clubhouse was lost, and Jimmy Comiskey, "the last of the dinosaurs," passed away. "They had a grand requiem for him, and an era was over," Iris Kelso said. But, she asks,

> Who can say the old system was all bad?
>
> Today, patronage comes in the form of attorney fees, judgeship appointments, architects and appraisal fees, insurance policies, mineral rights. The fruits of politics today go to the big guys, not the sidewalk inspectors [and] sanitation depart-

ment deadheads, the little folks [who are now] increasingly alienated, suspicious of government.

By comparison to the days of Comiskey and comrades, the personal contact between politicians and their constituents today is forced, often shallow.

It's a little like comparing an old time Southern country wake to a funeral in a city cathedral packed with businessmen, eyeing their watches and wondering who'll get good old Charlie's accounts.

Who can say if it's better today than when the caucus ruled the world?

The hopeful note is that reform has come to the New Orleans *Times-Picayune,* which Walker Percy, with deadly accuracy, once depicted as "a fat, dull, mediocre newspaper which might as well be the house organ of its advertisers." Imbedded in the traditions of Mardi Gras, the paper kowtowed to New Orleans "society," refused to print Joe Louis' picture when he won the world heavyweight championship, and when Vietnam got hot, used to print white casualty pictures in front, black casualty pictures in back. The paper once had a rule against editorials on controversial subjects. Its editor for years was a beguiling Irishman named George Healy who never could quite shake off the segregationist attitude of his native Mississippi. The Newhouse chain bought the paper in the late 1950s and a while later installed a moderate, Ashton Phelps, as publisher. In 1972, Phelps finally fired George Healy. The sluggish old makeup has been revamped, and Fritz Harsdorff, the news editor, has hired some reporters who do real reporting, and he has printed their stories. Phelps' son, Ashton, Jr., a bright young man who used to work at Xavier University and for Hale Boggs, is now on the staff and has helped to further its new-found moderation on racial issues. In time, the new management may be able to break what I call "the San Francisco syndrome"—that exciting, storied cities have mediocre newspapers. Actually, the less prestigious evening *States-Item,* also Newhouse-owned, has been more progressive—and readable—for several years now. And *New Orleans,* the city magazine, is one of the best in the country.

From Suburbia Northward

Visitors to New Orleans are driven westward along Lake Pontchartrain's lovely city shoreline, enjoying the vista of parklands and sailing marinas and a pleasant middle-to-upper-class community.* Suddenly a canal appears, and a bridge, and the environment changes instantly to honky-tonk modern strip development, the world of Plantation Fried Chicken and Fun Arcade and Bonanza and Big Boy stands and garish gas stations. And the host, a New Orleans city leader, announces that the visitors have arrived in Jefferson Parish. Jefferson probably deserves to be called the most parasitic suburb in the entire United States.

"Here's a community with 350,000 people now—twice as big as Baton Rouge or Shreveport," the New Orleanian announces. "Would you believe

* These impressions were gathered by my *National Journal* colleagues, Timothy Clark and William Lilley.

that they don't have an auditorium in this parish? They don't have a golf course. They say they have some tennis courts and playgrounds, but just try and find them. There's no lakefront development—nothing. What you're looking at is all new construction. Imagine what it will look like 20 years from now. I should take you down the road through Jefferson to the airport. It's the ugliest in the world. It wins hands down."

The median family income in Jefferson, one discovers, is 37 percent higher than in New Orleans. But the parish's education system is horrendously overcrowded, its general government services poor, and for parks and playgrounds—well, New Orleans is close by. "But," says one's host, "they don't pay a cent of taxes to us. They don't want to pay no taxes and ain't going to pay no taxes. And what's worse, they don't pay any taxes out here either." Not surprisingly, it turns out that the colossus of power in Jefferson is Assessor Lawrence A. Chehardy, who has seen to it that no more than a handful of the residential properties—many of which go on the market for $35,000 to $45,000—are assessed for more than the homestead exemption level of $2,000. Unimproved property, a major share of which is in the hands of developers with political pull, is assessed at a value ratio only half that of improved property.

Before Chehardy became assessor in 1965, the real boss of Jefferson Parish was the sheriff—or, just as often, the Mafia. The parish used to have the biggest casinos outside of Las Vegas. Carlos Marcello still lives there. Jefferson has a fairly modern form of government now, but the hangover of a recent past lingers on. As one local sage put it, "an overgrown little police jury type of government, fightin', strugglin' for power, and always treatin' New Orleans as the enemy." One looks around and sees some nice enough residential subdivisions. But no land-use plan has ever been developed. The parish just grew up ugly. And it spread.

The big white noose around New Orleans swings from Jefferson (87 percent white) on the west and south to St. Bernard (95 percent white) on the east. St. Bernard, with about 55,000 people, has a fringe of conservative, beer-drinking white working families similar to their compatriots in adjacent "downtown" New Orleans, but basically it is still rural and Cajun. It melds, geographically and politically, into Plaquemines Parish (population 25,225), that spongy, hurricane-swept finger of swamp and marsh and bayou that extends a hundred miles from the New Orleans area down to the three ocean passes of the Mississippi.

"Timeless Plaquemines," one Louisianan has written of that strange parish, a place where "the land, the sea, the sky combine to create a feeling of remoteness." Practically, Plaquemines is also a place of immense wealth—rich from lush oil deposits and from sulphur taken from one of the world's largest cones of that mineral. And politically, America's closest approximation to a full-blown dictatorship was exercised there for 40 years by Leander H. Perez, the man who fought his state, his nation, the Navy, big corporations, and even his church in the cause of segregation of the races. Perez is dead now; a heart attack felled him 1969, and his funeral brought tears to the eyes of George Wallace and thousands of other mourners at final rites in the Catholic Church. Perez had once been excommunicated for telling the Archbishop of New Orleans to "go to hell" in a fight over integrating parochial schools in the parish.

Leander Perez's story has been told before in more detail than is possible here. One especially biting account was that of Robert Sherrill, in *Gothic Politics in the Deep South;* Sherrill said Perez had "gathered into one spirit all the money lust, moon-spawned hatred for the black man and Jew and foreigner, and painful paranoiac reaction to federalism, that have marked the Deep South for many years," and then "slopped them back upon the land."

Some revisionist history has been written about Perez, too, by Clint Bolton in *New Orleans Magazine.* Bolton wrote that Perez possessed "one of the most brilliant legal minds Louisiana has ever known" and in his lifetime "immeasurably improved the lot of the people" of Plaquemines and St. Bernard Parishes through roads and levees, ports and industry, and enough jobs to sink the unemployment rate to 1.78 percent. (Plaquemines people, incidentally, are primarily of French and Spanish origin, with a sprinkling of Italians, Irish, and other European strains, in addition to 25 percent of African descent.) Commercial fishing, river piloting, and muskrat trapping employ most of the working force not engaged somehow in the mineral industries. Perez also saw to it that Plaquemines had property taxes as low as any in the country; when tax rate equalization became a big issue statewide, it was already accomplished in Plaquemines.

Bolton, in his 1972 article, spoke kindly of the two men who continue the Perez dynasty: Leander, Jr., who succeeded his father as district attorney of Plaquemines and St. Bernard, and another son, Chalin O., who became president of the Plaquemines parish commission-council after his father. Chalin's control of Plaquemines is as complete as his daddy's ever was, but St. Bernard, which unfailingly danced to Leander, Sr.'s tune, is showing signs of independence and may one day cause Leander, Jr.'s defeat in the combined D. A. district of the two parishes.

The younger Perezes share their father's views on politics and race, but they do seem more approachable and reasonable in dialogue. They lack the verve and fire of their father, and things are no longer as terrifying as they were a few years past, when both civil rights workers and newsmen considered Plaquemines a "dangerous" place to visit. My friend David Baldwin, who was a reporter for the New Orleans *Item* 20 years ago and wrote a crackerjack series of articles on Perez and his doings, said he always felt obliged to carry a gun when he went into Plaquemines. "I was threatened all the time, by all sorts of people: by the guy who ran the ferry boat, by the deputy sheriff, by the guy who filled up the gas tank. They all knew what I was doing, because I was being watched by everybody. I've never been so scared in all my life." Baldwin tried, time and again, to get an interview with Leander himself; finally he reached Perez by phone to offer him a chance to reply to points raised in the articles. Instead of cooperating, Perez tried—unsuccessfully—to blackmail Baldwin into quashing the series.

Baldwin, of course, was only one of many to be threatened by Perez.

During the civil rights campaigns of the 1960s, Perez got the parish council to purchase an old fort from the War of 1812, half submerged in a swamp at the mouth of the Mississippi and infested with snakes and mosquitoes, for the incarceration of any "racial agitators" who might venture into Plaquemines. When the Navy tried to push nondiscrimination against Negro servicemen living in the parish, Perez looked a rear admiral in the eye and roared, "We say the hell with you (the U.S. Government). We'll take the initiative and declare you off limits."

Perez was honest about his racial feelings, as no credible politician would dare be today, and few were even in his time. "The Negro," he said once, "is inherently immoral. . . . I think it's the brain capacity. . . . There's only two kinds, bad ones are niggers and good ones are darkies. . . ." And during the school crisis in 1960: "Don't wait for your daughter to be raped by these Congolese. Don't wait until the burr-heads are forced into your schools. Do something about it now." The whites of Plaquemines did do all they could to keep the blacks out of the schools and out of the voting booths. But by the time Perez died, federal voting registrars and school desegregation orders of the courts had done their work. Black enfranchisement may have been one reason that Perez could get only 75 percent of the Plaquemines vote for Wallace in 1968. In 1952, when he favored Eisenhower over Stevenson, Ike got 93 percent of the vote in the parish, a level no other county in America reached. In 1964, Perez backed Goldwater, and the Arizonan got 86 percent of the vote in Plaquemines. Issues relating to oil (the tidelands dispute in the 1950s, oil depletion later on) contributed to these victories, but the fact was that Plaquemines on occasion reported more votes than there were voters in the parish. In 1972, when the Presidential election failed to produce much interest among the local blacks, Perez's heirs produced an 83 percent vote for Richard Nixon.

Perez, of course, was one of the granddaddies of the Dixiecrat, unpledged elector, and Wallaceite movements. Wallace's victory in Louisiana in 1968 was his last triumph, and Perez toasted the Wallace electors with orange wine when they gathered in Baton Rouge to cast their electoral votes.

Perez left behind more than a political fiefdom. An incessant lobbyist, he persuaded the legislature to pass an amendment that made it possible for the parish to claim the vast oil wealth within its borders. Tidelands oil enlarged the triumph. As the parish prospered, so did Perez—in part, Sherrill charged, through "coercive deals with Texas, Shell, Humble, Tidewater, Gulf and California oil companies, plus Freeport Sulphur." By the late 1930s, Perez was a millionaire; in his last years of life, some Louisiana politicians estimated his wealth at as much as $100 million. But he paid his taxes; several Presidents of the United States instructed the Internal Revenue Service to investigate him in hopes of finding irregularities, and all failed.

Hale Boggs, who once lost a governorship election when Perez smeared him as a Communist sympathizer, said late in 1968: "Leander won't be washed up until he gets to the cemetery." In a way, Boggs was right, but one wonders if the legacy is still not very much alive.

Seventy miles north of New Orleans lies the little city of Bogalusa (population 18,412), a town as spread out physically (one can hardly find its center) as it is concentrated economically (a Crown Zellerbach paper mill which employs 3,000). Bogalusa lies in the heavily wooded yellow pine belt, near the Mississippi border, and in the 1960s it became famous as the town of more race conflicts per capita than practically any other in America. Jack Nelson, the Los Angeles *Times*' skilled Southern correspondent, insisted that Bogalusa was "the meanest town in the South." He recalled that one night he, Gene Roberts of the New York *Times*, Richard Harkness of NBC, and several other reporters "had to call on the Ku Klux Klan to save us from a gang of non-Klan citizens from Bogalusa. We all agreed that when you've got to call on the Klan for protection, some kind of record in meanness is set." If Bogalusa was fearful for reporters, it was even more so for civil rights workers. Seven white Northerners entering the town on quite innocent business had reason for concern. A Jewish physician from New York told the story of how he went to Bogalusa to examine a federally supported, biracial health facility. After his day's work, he was having beers with black doctors and others from the hospital when the local police broke in and arrested him as an agent provocateur from the North. The good doctor was held incommunicado in the jail until 2 A.M., when he was suddenly set free. Stepping outside the jail, he saw rows of cars with Mississippi license tags, filled with hard-looking whites. "Oh, no," he cried, dashing back into the jail and slamming the cell door behind him—an act that very likely saved his life. The next day some heavily armed blacks helped him flee for the parish border.

Many Bogalusa Negroes were not so lucky, meeting death at the hands of the Klan and other bigots. The parish's first black deputy sheriff, for instance, was the victim of a terrorist slaying. Bombings were also commonplace. The big difference between Bogalusa and other race-crazed towns was that the local blacks responded. They formed the secret Deacons for Defense and Justice. The Deacons armed themselves, just like their Klan enemies, but when black or white civil rights workers were threatened, a chain telephone alarm system let them spring to instant action. The very existence of the Deacons probably accounted, at least in part, for the general subsidence of Klan activity in Bogalusa. In 1969 an amazingly peaceful integration of the city's schools was effected. Instances of unpleasant violence were reported in the schools later, but not the death-dealing kind of the mid-1960s.

Baton Rouge, Shreveport, et al.

When one travels to Baton Rouge and takes the elevator up to the top of the towering State Capitol, clashing views meet the eye. Directly below is a splendidly landscaped park and a lake, to the east pleasant residential areas, to the south the stingily laid out streets of the town's business district, and still further south, the LSU campus. Close by on the west, the Mississippi River flows by, vast and powerful. And with what is the Father of Waters adorned? An infested forest of oil storage tanks and stacks and distilling equipment, covering the ground northward almost as far as the eye can see, belching a continual haze of brown-black smoke into the skies. This is the beginning of the "petrochemical Gold Coast" that grew to full flower in the boom years of the late '50s and mid-'60s, concentrated at Baton Rouge and then downriver to New Orleans. Pollution controls are beginning to cut down the vilest smoke now—but a lot remains to be done.

The real fascination of Baton Rouge is the Capitol itself, the place where Huey Long met the assassin's bullet almost 40 years ago now. A. J. Liebling caught the spirit of the heroic statue of Huey that stands above his grave on the Capitol grounds: "The face, impudent, porcine and juvenile, is turned toward the building he put up—all 34 stories of it—in slightly more than a year, mostly with federal money. The bronze double-breasted jacket, tight over the plump belly, has already attained the dignity of a period costume, like Lincoln's frock coat." In bronze, Liebling said, Long looks like the waggish fellows "who used to fill our costlier speakeasies in the late '20s and early '30s." But there is some currency about that statue, too; it turns out that Russell Long posed for it. Inside the Capitol, in the corridor where Huey died, in the senate and house chambers and lobbyists' corners, the sense of *All the King's Men*, and the ghost of Earl, too, and all the sweat-soaked profundities of Louisiana politics, come rushing in.

As for the rest of Baton Rouge, it is a pretty prosaic place, a bit of a hick town. Social life centers on the half-dozen home games of the beloved Fighting Tigers of Louisiana State University. There are no good restaurants, at least none worthy of Louisiana's splendid culinary reputation. For years, factions of the power structure were at loggerheads and the downtown area rotted. Now that is changing, thanks largely to the voluble mayor of Baton Rouge and president of the East Baton Rouge Parish, Woodrow ("Woody") Dumas. Dumas holds both titles because the city and parish governments were combined in 1949. (Louisianans claim it was the country's first successful merger of city and county governments.) Dumas is as adept at glad-handing visiting schoolchildren as at getting Russell Long to expedite all sorts of federal aids. Now things downtown are picking up, with repaved streets, some flashy new high-rises, and construction of a long-delayed civic center.

Baton Rouge paid a heavy price for the big expansion of the petrochemical industry during the 1960s. As major oil and chemical corporations rushed in to build plants, labor shortages ensued and union racketeers perpetrated shakedowns of contractors on a scale rarely seen in America. Construction costs escalated unconscionably—the result, James Reichley reported in *Fortune*, of both public corruption and the willingness of national corporations to play the game of payoffs and kickbacks. Threats and violence, including beatings, marked the labor wars. In 1967 there was a shutdown of practically all major industrial construction around Baton Rouge. Governor McKeithen got the legislature to set up a blue-ribbon commission of inquiry, headed by Cecil Morgan. But Victor Bussie, in one of his less glorious moments, saw to it that the law included few real powers for the commission.

The situation corrected itself to a large degree because the corporations, alarmed about the news coverage out of Baton Rouge, curtailed their new construction there. A further damper in the petrochemical industry is now apparent because of shortages of natural gas.

The legacy of violence, however, lives on. In 1970 a bomb exploded in the senate chamber of the Capitol, splintering the lieutenant governor's dais and tearing marble slabs from the walls; later it turned out that a laborer whose union was striking a utility company set off the bomb to draw attention to the strikers' cause. Racial violence, too, rears its ugly head in Baton Rouge from time to time. We noted Klan bombings and the violence at Southern University earlier in this chapter. In 1972 several members of a Black Muslim faction moved into town, determined to force a showdown with the police. They got what they were looking for: a confrontation on a Baton Rouge street in which two blacks and two policemen died in a sudden spasm of gunfire. Police charged the Muslims had drawn weapons first (or had grabbed weapons from the police). Virtually all the fatalities were caused by the police's own .38-caliber revolvers and shotguns.

Race violence in Baton Rouge gets major national attention; what most outsiders don't know is that the prevailing powers decided in 1969 that it was time to let the blacks—who constitute 29 percent of the parish's 285,-167 people—have some voice in local government. Joe Delpit, a 28-year-old Negro, was elected to the city-parish council, and a substantial number of white votes helped in his election.

Due west and slightly south of Baton Rouge, in the heart of Acadiana, lie the prospering cities of Lafayette (population 68,908) and Lake Charles (77,998). The postwar years have been good ones for this area. An emphasis on the common French heritage has given cultural unity and helped to draw tourists. Wondrous to relate, French—either in purer form or a patois—remains the dominant language of Lafayette and many smaller towns. (Some 1.4 million Louisianans speak the language.) In fact, the government of Quebec, the center of French Canada, now has a permanent office in Lafayette, from which it encourages revival of the French language and trading with the Cajuns. And thousands of schoolchildren in the 22 Cajun counties of southern Louisiana are now being taught the purest French by young teachers dispatched by the government of France.

An interstate road ties the counties of Acadiana together, and gives it easy access to New Orleans or Houston. The growth of offshore drilling has shifted the emphasis of Louisiana's oil industry to this part of the state. Lafayette is the real center, but Lake Charles has benefited too, with a deepwater port and a petrochemical industry second only to the lower Mississippi's. The administrative end of the oil industry has brought in tens of thousands of outsiders. Collectively, the newcomers have corrected some of the Cajun's economic lassitude and propensity for civic corruption, without subjugating the brighter side of Cajun culture. Lake Charles, a starting place for wildfowl hunting in the marshes, freshwater and deep sea fishing, recently proved its modernity (and taste) by sealing off its main downtown street from vehicles. The new mall, with parks and fountains, is both an esthetic and economic success. The two cities have shucked off the old commission form of government in favor of strong mayor charters.

Things are much quieter in Alexandria (population 41,557), a sleepy old lumber town at the geographic center of Louisiana. Some more money for civic improvements has become available of late, but the city recently saw its mayor, George Bowden, go to prison for theft of city money and income tax violations.

The corruption issue also raised its head in Monroe (56,374), the trade center of northeastern Louisiana and one of the state's most attractive cities. Mayor W. L. ("Jack") Howard was indicted on numerous counts relating to allegedly shady land deals. Ironically, Howard was an outstanding mayor and did a lot to keep race relations cool and build a model civic center and government center.

Louisiana's second largest city is Shreveport (population 182,064), the center of a thriving metropolitan area of some 300,000 and a place where rigidly conservative voting for state and federal offices is combined with generally progressive, civic-minded city government. Shreveport lacks the Gallic flavor of southern Louisiana; instead it is predominantly white Protestant. There are minorities of Italian-, Greek-, and Mexican-descended peoples, plus a big black population that dates back to the days when thousands of slaves labored on the great cotton plantations along the Red River. Antebellum Shreveport was in fact one of the great cotton centers of the western world; as one account puts it, "the very streets and sidewalks were piled and cluttered with bales." Shreveport became the Confederate capital of Louisiana in 1863, and it was the last city in the Confederacy to fly the Stars and Bars.

Today King Cotton is but a ghost of his former self, and 20th-century Shreveport has made most of its money (and its millionaires) from the rich oil and gas fields of Caddo Parish and neighboring Bossier Parish (across the Red River). Now oil, like cotton before it, is starting a gradual decline because exploration and production have shifted so heavily to the Gulf Coast. Diversified industries have been taking up the slack in local employment—General Electric, for instance, or a single Western Electric plant which employs 5,000 people. Signifying its ties with neighboring states, Shreveport calls itself the center of the "Ark-La-Tex" trading area.

As cities go, Shreveport is one of the most attractive in the South. Unlike Baton Rouge, it never let its central business district go to pot, and a covey of striking office buildings and hotels have been added in the last dozen years. An impressive big convention center was opened in 1965, adjacent to a modern civic theater with murals that recall the city's colorful early history when founder Henry Miller Shreve first cleared the Red River for navigation. With its renowned Little Theatre, Shreveport Symphony, *et al.*, Shreveport probably makes a greater effort in the fine arts than any other Southern city its size. Many retired military personnel who served at Barksdale Air Force Base have chosen Shreveport as a retirement home. Pockets of slums remain, principally in the black parts of town; Tom Stagg, a local Republican leader, said, "We could work for 10 years on housing and not waste a single day." Many slum dwellers are reluctant to leave their old neighborhoods when renewal comes, but a modern city housing code is forcing demolition of buildings that are dilapidated or have inadequate sanitary facilities.

Residentially, Shreveport's shame is Cooper Road, a scabrous 99.9 percent black slum just outside the city border. More than half the 8,751 people in Cooper Road live below the poverty line, but Shreveport has turned a cold shoulder to suggestions that the area, now unincorporated, be annexed to the city so that it could reap the benefits of improved public services. By contrast, Shreveport's pride are neighborhoods like Pierremont and Springlake, where the elite hold forth.

The Republican party is stronger in Shreveport than any other place in Louisiana, but its foothold in local government remains tenuous. The local power structure corresponds closely to the men named by GOP leaders as the biggest Democratic donors—Rupert Campbell, who heads Shreveport's Pioneer Bank and Trust; J. C. Trahan, an independently wealthy oilman who is reportedly close to Governor Edwards; W. C. Rasberry, owner of Forest Park Cemetery (Shreveport's fashionable burying place) and other real estate holdings far and wide; J. Pat Beaird, retired head of AMF Beaird, Inc.; and Charles Roemer, a Bossier Parish plantation owner who has won some notoriety from the huge checks the federal government has given him for not planting his cotton lands. Roemer heads the state division of administration under Edwards. The power structure used to be loath to accept federal grants, but the town fathers are very happy now to get help, for instance, in building a $20 million sewage treatment plant which Washington insists on to stop the dumping of untreated sewage into the Red River.

Shreveport and surrounding Caddo Parish demonstrated their conservatism by giving Wallace and Nixon a combined 68 percent of their Presidential vote in 1968, and Nixon alone 77 percent in 1972. Whatever Democratic votes there are for President come almost entirely from blacks, who make up 37 percent of the parish population. School integration has triggered wholesale transfer of whites to private academies, including one opened in 1970 in a $1 million facility.

Nostalgia: a Postscript

After all is said and done with modern Louisiana, one lives still with a bittersweet nostalgia about this "strange sister" in the family of American states. Susan Fenwick grasped it a few years ago when she wrote in *New Orleans Magazine* of "the overwhelming feeling of longing for something we had." The omnipresent past comes to life, she suggested, when one visits Breaux Bridge and Opelousas, Dry Prong and Turkey Creek, Thibodaux and Pointe à la Hache—places far away from the urban rush, like the Cane River country, the meandering bayous of the lower parishes, the rolling hills of the Felicianas, the cotton fields of the Bayou Boeuf country.

What does one long for? One thing is a sense of those who came first —the thousands who "crossed the seas to the new France and left an imprint on the land that will last throughout an eternity. You find it in the curious accents and the treasured customs, but most of all, you find it in the people, those timeless, kind, warm-hearted people who say with their eyes and their smile—I am your friend. I am Louisiana."

This land, Ms. Fenwick wrote, "is full of lost stones, in its forests, its overgrown wilderness, its broken fragments of giant plantations with their family burial plots. Statesmen, doctors, lawyers, military men. Forgotten men who loved the land." Tombstones, broken and overgrown with the luxuriant vegetation, she found everywhere. One was of a man named Doyle, an Irishman who died in 1820. "A broken slab amid the dry leaves and pine cones," she wrote. "The end of a long journey to Louisiana. What did he do to help make Louisiana what it is? Who was he? A sturdy adventurer from an impoverished land? All we know is that the Doyles and the LeBlancs and the Waguespacks and the Cheramies and the hundreds of others, who would be foreigners today, gave this land its strength and beauty."

She spotted one of the thousands of unpainted ramshackle houses, complete with barking dog: "the sense of desperation that is not desperation, but an acceptance of what life has to offer, without poverty programs or strident political factions or organized selfishness."

Then there was a faded marker of a battle in which the Confederate forces had done themselves proud and a freshly painted, unpretentious country church where "the plain people gather in their best" and "faith in God still works." And finally, a deserted plantation manor with a skewed sign beside the front door: "Posted, Get Out, Stay Out." "Who were the men," the writer asked, "who built these homes, leaving shadows after them where their preemptors walk? Who were these men who carved out of a land with the labor of others a way of life that ended in a holocaust? . . . In this peaceful isolation there is nothing left but dreams of what might have been and thanks to God that it wasn't."

ARKANSAS

UP FROM PROVINCIALISM

Down through history, touched less by the ways of industrialized society than any of its neighbors, a place obdurately independent and hopelessly provincial, came the state of Arkansas. It was an island set apart, a civilization primitive and poor. "Whar's this road go to?", the *Arkansas Traveler* asked. "I've been livin' here fer years, 'n' I ain't seen it go no place," the squatter replied.

Then two men changed it all. The first was named Orval Faubus, an Ozark original. He made the name of Little Rock known around the world, not always positively. The second was Winthrop Rockefeller, reared in the drawing rooms of New York, hardened in the oil fields of Texas. He began to free Arkansas from its age-old poverty of body and of spirit.

This Arkansas, 53,104 square miles in size, is tucked away in the lower valley of the Mississippi just southeast of the center of the continent. The WPA Writers' Project of the 1930s defined it as "between the South of the piazza and the West of the pony." Its eastern border is the Mississippi River, opposite Tennessee and Mississippi; here is the flat, immensely fertile Delta country which is part and parcel of the Old South. Gazing at the fields across the distant, level horizon, the mind's eye can conjure up the past vision of blacks stooping under a hot sun to pick the cotton of the great landowners; these days, machines do the picking, cotton is being crowded by other crops, and while the region still has the most blacks of any in the state, thousands have left for the North. Southern Arkansas has low hills and swamp and also vast stands of pine supporting a prosperous timber industry. Some of the area is reminiscent of neighboring Oklahoma and Texas with great ranch spreads and oil wells. The Ouachita Mountains slice in about halfway up the western border; then in the northwest one comes on the ancient Ozarks, shared with Oklahoma and Missouri. These mountains are one of the few frontier places left within America, where the physical and cultural isolation has preserved the centuries-old life styles, including vestiges of Elizabethan speech and the ballads of the people's English and Scotch-Irish forebears. Spotted through the Ozarks are isolated hamlets where men still turn the soil with a horse or mule-drawn plow, though mostly now just for vegetable gardens or small truck patches, a quickly disappearing sight.

And through it all, bisecting Arkansas neatly from west to east, lies the valley of the Arkansas River, now made navigable thanks to federal largesse, so that Fort Smith, Little Rock, and Pine Bluff (the state's major population centers) have become true port cities. On the west, the river courses past high bluffs, then in the east it flows through the level Delta and into the Mississippi.

Professor Richard E. Yates of Hendrix College in Conway, Arkansas, has suggested that if one draws a diagonal line from the northeastern to the southwestern corner of the state, running through Little Rock, two distinct regions emerge, each with distinctive geographic, political, economic, and social characteristics. Southeast of the diagonal line is low-lying plantation Arkansas, where large land-ownings, some running into tens of thousands of acres, continue to dominate the economy. The conservative, states' rights political philosophy retains its greatest strength here, a clear reaction to the high Negro population (still over 50 percent in five Mississippi River counties in the 1960 Census). Down in the woodsy area adjoining Louisiana is Arkansas' strongest redneck and Klan territory.

North and west of Yates' diagonal line is territory mostly hilly and mountainous, and thus less amenable to large-scale agriculture, even though the plantation economy thrusts deep but narrow fingers into the interior. The farm economy centers around milk, poultry, fruit, and cattle; light industries have begun to settle here, and one finds two great national forests and vast stretches of pine and hardwoods. Living conditions are still so close to the frontier, especially in the Ozarks, that there are even a few log cabins still occupied, though most have fallen into decay and disuse. "This small-farmer, timbering and factory-employee population," Yates notes, "is largely white and native-born." With the exception of a few river counties, the Negro population is minimal—and almost zero in a handful of Ozark counties. The hill country was antisecessionist and Unionist and blamed the plantation east for the calamities of the Civil War. There was always a degree of Republicanism in western Arkansas, and since 1966 the region has in fact sent a Republican to the U.S. House. Western and hill Arkansas has been characterized as a region largely rural, individualist, loyal to family and soil, and given to "puritanic Protestantism."

The regional contrasts may be seen again in the ancestry of the people. The white plantation owners of eastern Arkansas came principally from Kentucky, Tennessee, and Mississippi, and this area has rarely sent progressives to Congress or the state legislature. Western and hill Arkansas, by contrast,

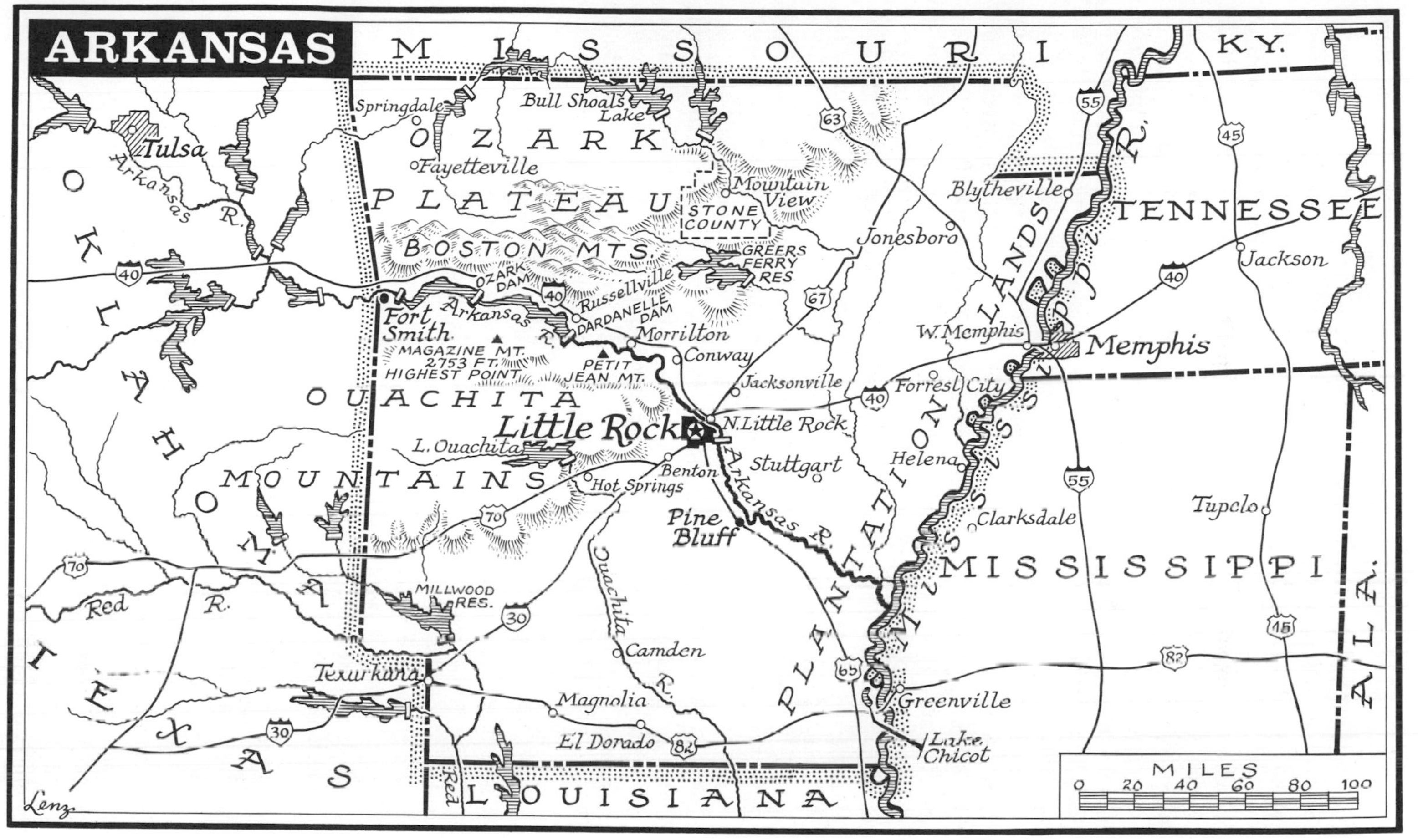
ARKANSAS
MISSOURI
KY.
TENNESSEE
MISSISSIPPI
ALA.
LOUISIANA
TEXAS
OKLAHOMA
OZARK PLATEAU
BOSTON MTS.
OUACHITA MOUNTAINS
MISSISSIPPI R.
LANDS
PLANTATION
Springdale
Bull Shoals Lake
Tulsa
Arkansas R.
Fayetteville
Mountain View
STONE COUNTY
GREERS FERRY RES
Jonesboro
Blytheville
Jackson
OZARK DAM
Russellville
DARDANELLE DAM
Fort Smith
Arkansas R.
Morrilton
Conway
MAGAZINE MT. 2753 FT. HIGHEST POINT
PETIT JEAN MT.
Jacksonville
W. Memphis
Memphis
Forrest City
N. Little Rock
Little Rock
L. Ouachita
Stuttgart
Helena
Benton
Hot Springs
Pine Bluff
Arkansas R.
Clarksdale
Tupelo
MILLWOOD RES.
Red R.
Ouachita R.
Camden
Texarkana
Magnolia
Greenville
El Dorado
Lake Chicot
Red
MILES
0 20 40 60 80 100
Lenz
40
55
45
63
67
65
70
30
82
15

was first settled by people from Missouri and mountainous areas of the South. The settler here, according to the WPA Writers' Project, "held a rifle under one arm, and from the creaking wagon peered a tired wife and a bevy of wide-eyed children. He built a dogtrot cabin, haggled the timber off a hillside, and plowed shallow furrows around the stumps in this 'miniature Appalachia.'" This is the home area of U.S. Senator J. W. Fulbright and also of former U.S. Representative Brooks Hays, the victim of a purge in 1958 after he had tried to mediate in the Little Rock school controversy. Orval Faubus is a native of the west, as well, but it should be remembered that he made his first start in politics as a populist and a moderate on the race issue, principles he had learned from a father who was once a Socialist.

Lying on the division line between the two great regions, and sharing some characteristics with both, are the capital city of Little Rock (1970 population 132,483) and its hefty neighbor, North Little Rock (60,040), an old railroad town. Another 94,666 people live in surrounding Pulaski County. Little Rock is not only the seat of government but the center of economic activity, home of the only two newspapers of statewide circulation and site of Arkansas' most widely heard radio and television stations. The *Arkansas Gazette* is a liberal queen among Southern newspapers, still reflecting the progressive attitudes which brought Orval Faubus' calumny down on its head after the 1957 school crisis at Central High. The *Gazette* is still "the Bible" in many parts of the Arkansan hinterland, despite its role as a whipping boy for demagogues. John N. Heiskell, the Pulitizer Prize-winning editor of the *Gazette* who remained active until shortly before his death at the age of 100 in 1972, said that a newspaper fails not when it loses subscriptions and advertising revenue (as it did for a while after the Little Rock school crisis) but when it ceases to be the conscience of its community. The rival *Arkansas Democrat*, more conservative, shares with the *Gazette* the luxury of home-town ownership, and these are two papers which have not resorted to the sometimes incestuous shared facilities and advertising approach.

Little Rock, in fact, was one of the pleasantest surprises among all American cities I visited in preparing to write these books. Expansive physically, it has a pleasing, low-keyed way about it. The downtown is undergoing good quality rebuilding as the banks compete to see who can build the highest. Both center city and some outlying areas were among the first urban renewal areas in the country; virtually every Negro area has gotten a face-lifting, and there is substantial public housing—of a physical and human quality scarcely known in northern cities. Very few real slums are left in town. No small part of this, of course, can be attributed to federal bureaucrats' desire to please the man who represents Little Rock in Congress, Chairman Wilbur Mills of the U.S. House Ways and Means Committee.

The dullest housing in Arkansas may well be the low-cost tract developments for middle-income whites that stretch endlessly to the south of Little Rock. In the city itself, there has been a succession of quite progressive municipal administrations and of late an opening up of governmental slots for blacks, including a first seat on the city council in 1969.

One more Little Rock image: for miles along the Arkansas River Palisades to the west of the city, beautiful homes command some of the loveliest river views in America.

Politically, Little Rock is in no position to dominate Arkansas. Pulaski County has doubled its share of the state population in the last 30 years but still accounts for only 15 percent of the statewide count (1,923,295 people in 1970). The only two large cities outside Pulaski County are Pine Bluff (population 57,489) in southeast Arkansas and Fort Smith (62,802) on the Arkansas River at the Oklahoma border. Between them, these two cities account for just 6 percent of the state population. Fort Smith advertises itself as "the gateway to the Ozarks" and has the most western flavor of any Arkansas city. Pine Bluff boasts a handsome modern civic center designed by native son Edward Durrell Stone; in recent years it has also elected one of the bitterest last-stand-against-integration school boards in the South. The Army's nearby Pine Bluff Arsenal produced and housed the nation's total supply of deadly antipersonnel biological warfare weapons from the 1940s until President Nixon ordered its destruction early in this decade. Now the $100 million biological facility has been turned over to the Food and Drug Administration to be the country's center for toxicological research, a life-giving rather than death-dealing enterprise.

Among lesser towns, the quiet Mississippi River city of Helena (population 21,422) has distinguished itself in recent years by becoming a musical center of some repute. In 1972 a $1 million auditorium was dedicated there, named for Miss Lily Peter, who is Arkansas' poet laureate, the owner-manager of an 8,000-acre cotton and soybean plantation on Big Cypress Bayou near Helena, and the person who raised the funds for the auditorium in the hopes it would ring with classical music for years to come. Miss Peters had personally spent as much as $45,000 to bring symphony orchestras (including the Philadelphia) to Arkansas, but the budgeting for the new auditorium already seemed assured. A bachelor farmer named Samuel Drake Warfield, who died in 1967, left behind a 28-year-old will giving almost all his estate (valued at more than $500,000) for annual musical concerts "to be held at Helena, Arkansas, and free to the inhabitants of that city regardless of race, creed, or color."

Such embellishments seem light-years away from the rusticity of "Arkie" country before World War II. Then families still came to town in horse-drawn wagons, roads were often seas of mud, and rural electricity was just starting to light the country homes. In 1940, 78 percent of the people lived on farms or in villages of less than 2,500 people. By 1970, the figure had dropped to 50 percent, but that still left Arkansas with one of the highest rural population shares among the 50 states.

Capsule History: 1541 to 1954

Arkansas was discovered by de Soto in his vain search for gold in 1541–42, first opened up to the French missionaries and traders in the 1660s, became a possession of the U.S. with the Louisiana Purchase in 1803, and broke off from Missouri to become a territory in its own right in 1819. That same year, the *Arkansas Gazette* began publication; two years later both the paper and the capital transferred from old Arkansas Post to Little Rock, where they have since remained.

A measure of adversity has surrounded Arkansas' development since the earliest years. When it was admitted to the Union as the 25th state in 1836, it had barely the minimum required 50,000 people, the light settlement due in no small measure to the immense, often impassable swamp that covered most of eastern Arkansas. (Not until the late 1800s did levees and drainage reclaim that land.) A quarter of a century after statehood, Arkansas was drawn into a Civil War which the great majority of its people would just as soon have ignored; though the state joined the Confederacy, it was said to have contributed thousands to Union armies as well. Fortunately, there were few major battles on Arkansas soil, and when the Union armies took Little Rock after Vicksburg, the operation was relatively bloodless. But Reconstruction came to Arkansas as surely as in every other state, embodied in a Northern Republican (or carpetbag) regime which came to power in 1868 and held sway into the next decade. Actually, the Reconstruction period, during which Negroes were enfranchised, the University of Arkansas founded, and the state's first system of free public education begun, was better in many respects than what was to follow—decades of control by conservative Bourbon Democrats, who proceeded to put the Negro back in "his place" and to let businesses off with low taxation and little regulation. At the same time, Arkansas' dependence on the single crop, cotton, became greater than ever before, and the demoralizing system of sharecropping entrapped great numbers of whites and blacks alike.

For three-quarters of a century, from the end of Reconstruction to the entry of rebellious young war veterans into Arkansas politics in the 1940s, Bourbon conservatism reigned supreme—with one exception. Riding a wave of small-farmer protest about taxes and their powerlessness, a colorful semi-demagogue named Jeff Davis opened up on "the high-collared roosters" and the "silk-stocking crowd" of Little Rock and actually won election as governor in 1900 and twice afterwards. Just what the Bourbons thought of old Jeff was summarized in a contemporary account by the *Helena World*, a conservative journal of the lowlands: "a carrot-headed, red-faced, loud-mouthed, strong-limbed, ox-driving mountaineer lawyer, and a friend of the fellow who brews forty-rod bug-juice back in the mountains." Political scientist V. O. Key, who dug up that delicious quote from some musty records, summarized Davis' achievements: "His war against the corporations, like those of his contemporaries in other states, ended in futility. The great upthrust of organized business killed off the loud but feeble agrarian protest."

Under the Bourbons, Arkansas stagnated. The white and black peasantry of the Delta lived under an almost feudal social structure and in dire poverty. The blacks were of course excluded from voting and of the whites, the *Arkansas Gazette* could report as late as 1948: "Plantation owners in the Delta counties usually control the votes of their many tenants, who cast their ballots in boxes set up in the owners' commissaries." The hillsmen were more independent but, if anything, poorer. Viewing the scene at the end of World War II, John Gunther identified the powers in Arkansas as the Delta plantation owners, the Baptist Church, timber interests, and the Arkansas Power & Light Company, the latter absentee-owned. Arkansas, rather than Tennessee, might have had a valley development in the 1930s, Gunther reported, but Senator Joe Robinson, a vassal of the power company, told President Roosevelt that the state was not interested.

Because the conservatives controlled Arkansas so completely, its politics clear into the 1940s were characterized by a fluid factionalism in which virtually no serious issues were discussed, with all attention centered instead—in V.O. Key's words—on "the petty argument and personal loyalty of the moment." It was just such a factional fight, between the followers of Carl Bailey, a rather moderately inclined governor in the late 1930s, and his successor, Homer Adkins, governor in the early 1940s, that led to the removal of J. W. Fulbright as president of the University of Arkansas by the Adkins-controlled trustees. Fulbright then ran in 1944 against Adkins for the U.S. Senate, and won. What was then seen primarily as a victory of the Bailey faction in local politics would turn out to have immense national importance when Fulbright 14 years later became chairman of the Senate Foreign Relations Committee.

Back in Arkansas, there were few thoughts of national prominence in the 1940s. The schools were among the nation's worst, and charges of election irregularity tantamount to direct fraud arose in election after election. "Arkansas' first problem," Key determined after talking with many informed citizens of the state, was "the establishment of the essential mechanisms of democratic government."

The first important politician who seemed willing to make a try was a young war veteran named Sid McMath who began in the gambling resort town of Hot Springs in 1946 by winning election as district prosecutor and breaking up a corrupt political machine which had held power there for a generation. McMath's "GI movement" went on to win a number of other offices and elect McMath himself as governor in 1948. There was hope that McMath would be a thoroughgoing reformer, and he did preside at a time of important changes—in 1950, for instance, the Arkansas Democratic party, under severe pressure from the federal courts, finally agreed to let Negroes register in the party and run as candidates in its primary. But McMath, who was hoping to run against conservative Sen. John McClellan in 1954, was tripped up by charges of highway department graft in his second term and was resoundingly defeated in 1952. Two years later he ran against McClellan anyway, giving the voters one of their few clear liberal-conservative choices in those years. McClellan won the primary, 164,905 to 127,941. Thus ended —it later turned out for good—the career of Arkansas' most promising liberal political leader of his generation.

Two years later, the remarkable era of Orval E. Faubus was ready to begin.

Orval Faubus from Greasy Creek

He came, as we noted earlier, not out of the "hard-seg" plantation lowlands of Arkansas but rather from a little place called Greasy Creek, near Huntsville in Madison County, up in the Ozark territory of northwestern Arkansas, first of seven children of Sam Faubus, a hardscrabble farmer who liked Eugene Debs, voted for Teddy Roosevelt, Robert LaFollette, and FDR's New Deal. The early Faubus record hardly suggested incipient greatness. There was a catch-as-catch-can education, including a short stint at a little-known college later accused of Communist connections, a spell out on the road as a seasonal migrant worker (making his way as far as Washington state, where he heard the arguments of the Wobblies), election back home as clerk of the circuit court, four years in World War II, return home and down payment on the local newspaper. But, as Robert Sherrill notes in an excellent essay on Faubus and his deeds,* "Faubus has the kind of stubbornness that serves impoverished, untutored hillbillies as the great evolutionary gene needed to pull them out of the mud and onto the sunlit shore of civilization."

Governor Sid McMath read some of Faubus' high-minded liberal editorials and brought him to Little Rock as his assistant, highway commissioner, and state highway director. Faubus rapidly made contacts, somehow avoided personal involvements with the highway scandals of the time, and when McMath was defeated, went back home to wait his time. The opportunity came in 1954 when Francis Cherry, the moderate Democrat who had upset McMath and then turned out to be in the hip pocket of Arkansas Power and Light, tried to run for a second term. Faubus jumped into the campaign and with a strong assist from McMath barely defeated Cherry in the runoff (tantamount to election in those days).

Faubus had not raised the race issue in his campaign, nor did he make statements on segregation for 13 months after taking office as governor; in fact, it is said that he had rather friendly personal feelings toward Negroes. What now seems quite apparent is that Faubus seized on the race issue as a way to perpetuate himself in power, to win more than the informal limit of two two-year terms to which governors had been held since the days of Jeff Davis. Immense power accrued to Faubus through long incumbency. Until a reform accomplished in 1971, real power lay in the hands of some 187 boards and commissions. Only continuous power of appointment over five or more years gave a governor real control over these multitudinous agencies, which regulated everything from highway contracts to banks, trucking tariffs to the university system. Once controlled, the boards were rich sources of patronage jobs, special favors, and indirectly, through those they regulate, the money needed for campaigns—and, as one hears it, for politicians' own pockets. A frequently asked question in Arkansas is how Faubus, a poor man when he

* "Orval Faubus: How to Create a Successful Disaster," in *Gothic Politics in the Deep South* (New York: Grossman Publishers, Inc., 1968).

became governor, and earning only $10,000 a year as the state's chief officer, was able to build a home valued somewhere between $100,000 and $200,000 the year he finally left office. Never a man to be cornered, Faubus has explained that his good fortune at the time came from his Scotch blood, which enabled him, he said, to husband his resources and use them wisely.

Faubus' close political friend was W. R. ("Witt") Stephens, chairman of the board and president of the Arkansas-Louisiana Gas Company, considered by some the power behind the throne in the Faubus years. Stephens is a tall, gruff, cigar-chomping man who was happy to tell a visitor what he thought of Orval Faubus:

> He was a great governor in my estimation. He was humble but a great salesman. He knew how to work with people. He had a complete knowledge of the state and its problems. He didn't fall out with people. He always took instead of giving advice. He was a born leader. He never sought to dominate. He could do more and be more places than anyone I ever saw. He went after industry energetically. The most important thing he did was the children's colony, a nationally recognized accomplishment. . . .

I wondered if I was being put on, but Stephens was open to a point about his relationship with Faubus. "The governor's office pays $10,000, so what happens when a man without a quarter comes in? It must have cost Winthrop Rockefeller a quarter to a half million a year to be governor. How in hell can one of our Democratic boys be governor when it costs that much? . . . Faubus got his support from people like me and a lot of other people who would chip in and pay the expense."

It is from other sources that one learns that the state Public Service Commission approved three yearly rate increases averaging $3.2 million in the 1950s, at the very time that two of the three commissioners and several PSC employees held Arkla stock. Arkla's officers, it was reported, were often on the boards of Arkansas' largest banks. The banks, in turn, held vast sums of state money which, at least until recently, was in absolutely interest-free accounts. Such arrangements are worth protecting. Stephens was said to be willing to put at least a little money on any serious statewide candidate. Rockefeller considered Stephens a charming, skilled, amoral business-politician who controlled much of the political process of the state through money and sheer skill. Seventeen of the 35 state senators in the late 1960s, Rockefeller said, were on Stephens' payrolls in one form or another (as public relations consultants, or attorneys on retainer, or some other device).* Once the state senate passed a bill to tax subsidiary corporations. The vote was almost unanimous, but that night Arkla's lobbyist threw a party and the next day the vote was reversed. Faubus' personal power over the legislature was, if anything, greater. Massive bond issues and other bills

* Stephens retired in 1965, turning over the presidency of Arkla to Sheffield Nelson, a 31-year-old vice president of sales for the company who did not seem the type to play the heavy in politics as Stephens had. In an interview when he stepped down, Stephens indicated a sensitivity and generosity few people had detected during his active years. He had lavish praise for Rockefeller as the man who turned Arkansas around on the race issue, and said he had always shared Rockefeller's abhorrence for capital punishment. A touching part of the old pro's confessions was that he had harbored secret ambitions all his life to be governor himself. In his retirement, Stephens said, he would devote his energies to setting up a two-year community college, concentrating on technical-vocational education, in his native Grant County. Stephens himself never got beyond the eighth grade in school, but he was accorded two honorary degrees.

legislators scarcely understood would be rushed through either the senate or house with the cry, "Governor's bill! Call the roll!"

But without a long tenure as governor, Faubus could have done little of this. As early as 1956, seeking a second term, he had begun to modify his approval of racial integration. But he was still no segregationist leader; indeed his chief primary opponent in 1956, a vituperative former state senator from southern Arkansas named Jim Johnson, accused Faubus of supinely submitting on the integration issue. Faubus brushed that challenge aside easily. But in August 1957 he is said to have called his staff together and announced he would make the third-term try the next year. His issue would be provided by Central High School in Little Rock, which was preparing—after two years of careful planning—to desegregate in accordance with the Supreme Court's *Brown* decision.

And so it was that Faubus warned before school opening that bloodshed and violence might result if "forcible integration" were carried out, and called out 270 Arkansas National Guardsmen and gave them orders to prevent the entry of the nine Negro students scheduled to integrate Central High. It was the only way, he said, "to restore or maintain order," and he spoke darkly of "caravans" of unruly whites on their way to Little Rock to cause trouble—a charge never since substantiated in any way. On September 3, as Harry Ashmore described it, "Little Rock arose to gaze upon the incredible spectacle of an empty high school surrounded by National Guard troops called out by Governor Faubus to protect life and property against a mob that never materialized."

Faubus had been adequately warned about the dangers of physically resisting orders of the federal courts—a step no governor had taken since the Civil War. Winthrop Rockefeller, then on good terms with Faubus as head of the state industrial development effort, had spent two and a half hours with the governor. "I reasoned with him, argued with him, almost pled with him" not to intervene and told him "the local situation was none of his business," Rockefeller said later. Rockefeller also insisted—though Faubus denied—that Faubus told him: "I'm sorry, but I'm already committed. I'm going to run for a third term, and if I don't do this, Jim Johnson and Bruce Bennett [two segregationist politicians] will tear me to shreds."

As it had to be, President Eisenhower federalized the Arkansas Guard, ordered in paratroopers, and insisted on implementation of the federal court order. At Central High, a band of nine Negro children, brave inheritors of a legacy of incredible hardship, marched through crowds of furious, swearing, shouting white supremacists. The school was integrated. But Arkansas' name was darkened across the land and across the seas.

The manufactured crisis at Little Rock would have other consequences. A modern-day example of white Southern mob resistance to integration had been set, and with it the model of gubernatorial posturing against the federal establishment—to be repeated at Ole Miss, the "schoolhouse door" at the University of Alabama, and a hundred other places in word if not in deed. (Always, these governors were threatening to "go to jail" if need be; of course, none of them ever did.) The second consequence of Little Rock was that everyone now knew that the federal government, pushed too far, would act. And finally, the crisis was the beginning of what has become in recent years one of the most successful ventures in school integration anywhere in America. One looks at Central High, a decade and a half after 1957, and sees a still handsome school, set in a wooded residential area, Negro and white children talking and playing sports and associating freely together. There have indeed been antagonisms between the races over the years, but student leaders of both races and the school administration (now also thoroughly integrated, with a black principal at Central High) have worked hard to correct them. What happened in 1957 was the first *desegregation;* what has happened over the years has been a gradual process of social *integration.* Black and white cultures—in musical tastes, for instance—remain distinct, but familiarity and mutual respect have built too. Central High's 2,000 students are now about equally divided between the races, and since 1970 substantial integration (made possible in part through busing) has come to the other Little Rock schools as well. The school system is perplexed by a slow but sure decline in its proportion of white students, but administrators are even more alarmed by the recent cutback in federal funds for programs that helped in the transitional years and must now be scaled down sharply or totally eliminated.

But to return to the 1950s, and the political situation in Arkansas then: Faubus' principal objective—to solidify himself as governor—was completely achieved by his demagoguery at Little Rock. Four times again, between 1958 and 1964, he would run for reelection, and each time he won by generally handsome margins—even against his former mentor, Sid McMath, in 1962. Had he harbored a strong desire for national power, or if he had reached his zenith of power a few years later, it might have been Faubus, not George Wallace, who emerged as the segregationist South's candidate for the Presidency.*

Finally, in 1966, Faubus decided to retire from the governorship—the year Winthrop Rockefeller was elected. In the next four years, Faubus (1) moved into and then out of that sumptuous home he had built for himself in Huntsville; (2) divorced his wife of many years' standing; (3) three weeks later married a divorcee 29 years his junior; (4) lived in a trailer while he published a handful of weekly newspapers; and (5) acted as president of Dogpatch USA, a private amusement park in the Ozarks which depicts Al Capp's famous characters. Then, in 1970, Faubus decided to run for governor again. Many thought the mere presence of the old wizard's name on the ballot would ensure him victory. It turned out not to be so. Faced with seven opponents, he was forced into a runoff with a clean-cut young "country lawyer," Dale Bumpers. Bumpers was an attractive opponent who could pick up every part of the anti-Faubus bloc that had built up over the years. There were Arkansas' racial moderates, who still regarded Faubus (who made the "reediculous idea" of school busing his major 1970 theme) as a dangerous demagogue. For many, the Faubus years as governor recalled 12 years of corrupt power

* Faubus was friendly to Wallace's 1968 Presidential candidacy and actually campaigned for Wallace in Arkansas.

politics. There were Democratic party loyalists who believed Faubus had crushed all efforts for new leadership within the party and left it a shambles when he relinquished the governorship.

But who was Bumpers? Outside his home area of Charleston, in the Ozarks, where he had been a businessman-lawyer-farmer and a Methodist Sunday school teacher for 18 years, he was little known when the campaign started. He presented himself as the sincere, concerned citizen, who would bring "a new day" in Arkansas and move the state into the '70s rather than back into the boss-controlled '60s. He refused to flail at opponents, saying repeatedly, "I'm not running against anybody. I'm running for governor." He was rarely too specific about issues. He proved to have one of those naturally magnetic personalities—some call it charisma—of which successful politicians are made. He conserved his television money and then used it all in the crucial two weeks before primary day. Some believed television made Bumpers, and it may have. After seeing Bumpers for the first time, one 60-year-old voter said: "He just looks like he's a cut above the kind we usually have running for governor."

In the runoff primary, Bumpers took 58 percent of the vote—apparently bringing the Faubus era, finally, to an end. Then in the general election he easily defeated incumbent Winthrop Rockefeller.

But we are getting ahead of our story, because Winthrop Rockefeller was probably more important to Arkansas, in the long sweep of its history, than all the Democratic politicians of the postwar era put together.

Winthrop Rockefeller: What a Yankee Transplant Did for Arkansas

"WR" entered the room, one of the many offices and conference places at his huge farm spread atop Petit Jean Mountain, a big man dressed in a single-piece green worksuit and the familiar monogrammed cowboy boots, still out of breath and sweating from an afternoon's work pruning trees. Without further ado, a long interview began, covering every topic from Orval Faubus to Arkansas' economic growth to two subjects that could turn Rockefeller on emotionally—penal reform and civil rights. He was governor when we talked but still one of the most candid sources I have encountered across the country.

And then there was a welcome invitation to cocktails and dinner, the first at one of the big, luxurious "guest houses" just outside the official Winrock Farm enclosure. We piled into WR's Cadillac, which had an appropriate headpiece of a big Santa Gertrudis steer mounted on the hood, and we sped toward the farm gate, and just as its white form loomed in front of the headlights, Rockefeller spoke into a radio, "This is number so-and-so coming through," and in the split second before impact a guard opened the gate by remote control. Even Rockefellers, it appears, need an occasional resort to dramatic effect. (If a stranger approached the gate, the guard post was alerted and a mysterious voice came out of a post saying, "May I help you?")

Later, there was dinner in the remodeled stone farmhouse, high on the bluff overlooking a broad curve of the Arkansas River. And every element of dinner in the handsome dining room, with wines and fine food and meticulously careful service, seemed perfect, yet WR was not troubled by the formalities, for he still wore the comfortable old green coverall. And after dinner, he took me for a tour of the lawn area between the house and the precipitous mountain edge, and we looked at the live oaks and other trees that had been carefully pruned (and in some cases moved completely) to preserve and frame the dramatic river vistas. The trees, Rockefeller said, were like friends to him, and while the planting and pruning may take years to get the effects one wants, "I come from a line of longevity, and we have patience." Winthrop, however, was not to share in that fabled Rockefeller longevity. He would die of cancer in February 1973, just two years after leaving the governorship.

The name Rockefeller, of course, stands for everything that Arkansas is not: Eastern, wealthy, cosmopolitan, liberal. Why did Rockefeller move there in the first place? The answer starts with his childhood, when he showed insecurity and shyness and somehow became the black sheep of that amazing generation of grandchildren of the great John D.—Abby, John, Nelson, Laurence, Winthrop, and David Rockefeller. Winthrop was the huskiest of his generation, six feet, three inches and 200 pounds by his early twenties. While his sister and brothers completed their education by the appointed formula, Winthrop dropped out of Yale during his third year, never to return. He was soon playing the rebel's role by getting work as a roustabout for Humble Oil in the Texas oilfields at 75 cents an hour. The world without family retinue or debutante parties or seashore summers or collegiate antics seemed to suit him well, and he got along well with the happy-go-luckies and the embittered dustbowl veterans in the oilfields. By the same token, after a few years living a more conventional young businessman's life back in New York, WR flourished again as a junior Army officer. A series of nerve-wracking amphibious landing operations in the Pacific, friends said, hardly fazed him. Then there was the fateful day in 1945 when Major Rockefeller found himself on a troopship just south of Okinawa. A kamikaze plane screamed out of the sky and fireballed onto the vessel, with a huge explosion and rapid, destructive fire. When the smoke cleared, 75 men were found dead, 200 wounded, and Rockefeller was the senior Army officer surviving. Though seriously burned himself, he took command until relief came a day later. In 1946 he was discharged from the Army, ready—at 34 years of age—to start a new career.

For the next seven years, that career proved vacuous indeed: the life of a New York playboy, more often photographed among nightclub champagne glasses than at any specific job. While his industrious sisters and brothers built families and began the Rockefellers' massive philanthropic push of the postwar years, Winthrop did the opposite, the indolent thing. Then, what had been a private irritation to the family became a monstrous public embarrassment when Rockefeller met and married blond "Bobo" Sears, a onetime model and bit actress who had been born the daughter of a Lithuanian coal miner in Pennsylvania. The marriage ended in a few months, shortly after birth of their son, Winthrop Paul. Bobo emerged with a staggering settlement of close to $6 million—the highest divorce settlement ever awarded to that date. Winthrop, whose ardor had already cooled by the wedding day, went through the whole excruciating experience in the knowledge that with a colder heart, he might have avoided the whole agony.

Winthrop was shaken seriously by the divorce proceedings; some of his friends describe him as "running from a hurt"—a personal affront, a scandal for his family to endure. Rockefeller now sought out his close wartime friend, Little Rock insurance man Frank Newell, and asked Newell to go into business with him in New York. But Newell turned the tables on Rockefeller, asking "Why don't you come to Arkansas?" For WR, whose love for the open spaces went back to his days on the Texas oilfields, the invitation was appealing. Newell checked out property that might be purchased in Arkansas, discovering a largely undeveloped site atop Petit Jean Mountain, 68 miles northwest of Little Rock. Rockefeller agreed to the purchase, and in June 1953 made his big move.

Winrock Farms grew to include several subdivisions operating a total of 50,000 acres. There were 17,000 acres devoted to Rockefeller's 6,000 head of Santa Gertrudis cattle (great mahogany beasts cross-bred from Shorthorns and Brahmans) and another 17,000 acres devoted to rice, soybeans, and grain. Another division of the farm was actually in west Texas. But the jewel was at Petit Jean Mountain. A minor army transformed the dusty mountain top—described by Rockefeller's farm manager, G. W. Adkisson, as "the sorriest land you ever saw"—into one of the fanciest farms ever inhabited by man. Here Rockefeller built roads, silos, and barns, an airfield (used by his four private planes, including a jet), a system to pump water up 850 feet to the stone-and-glass mansion atop the mountain and the nearby swimming pool, permanent guest and servant houses, a greenhouse, six artificial lakes, and even an antique car museum. Every year, some 150,000 tourists came to view the amazing complex.

Every painstaking detail of Winrock was carefully planned and supervised by Rockefeller himself. Friends say the man had an artistic bent, a love for design, that seemed to compensate for his distaste for books or reading in any form. One friend close to him told me: "I think if his name had been Perkins, he would have become an architect. But it's not in the tradition of the Rockefeller family to be a performer—a surgeon or a singer or an artist. You are in a family that has an enormous set of empires to administrate. There is a tradition of public service. You are not to abdicate."

Rockefeller's public service for Arkansas included major personal cash outlays—by his own estimate in 1970, more than $35 million since his arrival in the state. Rockefeller placed his expenditures, which he called investments, in these categories:

- "In excess" of $10 million at Winrock Farms and its Carlisle division.

■ "Well in excess" of $5 million for school, hospital, and educational programs and other philanthropic causes.
■ "In excess" of $10 million for activities like the Tower Building in Little Rock and Winrock Enterprises.
■ "Probably in excess" of $10 million for "good government"—a category under which Rockefeller included his four campaigns for governor, his contributions to the Republican effort in the state, and his role in encouraging industrial development.

The philanthropics were the first area Rockefeller got involved in in Arkansas. He contributed heavily to the magnificent new art center in Little Rock and stumped the state to raise the $1 million to build it; gave $1.25 million to construct a new public school in Morrilton (across the river from Petit Jean Mountain); donated $250,000 for college scholarships for outstanding Arkansas students; financed or contributed to numerous civic projects, especially in black communities; and made possible a number of mental health clinics.* An important figure in all this was Rockefeller's second wife, the former Jeannette Edris, whom he married in 1956 (but would finally divorce, after 15 often stormy years of relationship, just after leaving the governorship). Jeannette Rockefeller had a deep commitment and knowledge in the areas of mental health and retardation and also took a lively interest in the great Arkansas upswing in the arts that began in the 1950s. (When Rockefeller arrived, Little Rock had one museum, mausoleum-like in atmosphere and run on about $25,000 a year total budget. Now the city not only has its arts center, which has become a nucleus for everything from galleries to ballet, but many of the state's smaller cities—a cultural Sahara in times past—have begun to copy the model.)

Rockefeller's most important contribution, however, awaited the inauguration of Orval Faubus as governor in 1955. Faubus had decided to create an Arkansas Industrial Development Corporation and naturally wanted Rockefeller to head it. On an understanding of no political interference in the job, Rockefeller accepted, and from all accounts the men got along together quite well personally for several years.

Under Rockefeller's guidance, AIDC soon became the classiest state development authority in the country. It was the start of a veritable economic rebirth for Arkansas, which for decades had vied with Mississippi on various economic scales as the poorest place in all the U.S.A. Aside from sound business guidance, Rockefeller brought two unique assets: his name and an ability to recruit topnotch personnel from all over the U.S., occasionally dipping into his own pocket to supplement salaries (a policy he would later continue as governor).

Not every AIDC effort was what its sponsors hoped for; in fact many of the first plants were apparel factories that paid low wages, often recruiting only women workers. But gradually the effort gained sophistication, with light machinery and rubber factories and such major acquisitions as a $57 million International Paper plant at Pine Bluff, opened for business in 1958.

* Governor Francis Cherry commented not long after Rockefeller's arrival: "The people wish Winthrop Rockefeller had been quintuplets and that they all had come here."

By the time Rockefeller resigned his AIDC chairmanship to run for governor in 1964, more than 600 new industrial plants had been located in Arkansas, many built in rural areas that had subsisted before on farming alone. There were some 90,000 new jobs in Arkansas, with an annual payroll of $270 million, and Arkansas' per capita income spurted ahead 53 percent, much faster than the national or regional increase in the same years. Perhaps most significantly, young Arkansans began to lose the idea that the way to succeed was to buy a one-way ticket out of Arkansas. The state's population, which had been declining precipitously in the early 1950s, began to stabilize. The state emerged from the 1950s with a net loss of 6.5 percent, but with the momentum begun by the AIDC effort, the decade of the 1960s saw an actual gain of 7.7 percent—well below the national growth rate but still a vast improvement over the immediate past.

Rockefeller recalled a speech he gave in Faubus' stead before a group of New York industrialists in 1955. He had talked about his reaction to his new-found friends in Arkansas, the experiences of building Winrock, the men who would drive miles and miles in their pickups looking for work. "I told them it was a great state with tremendous potential, suffering from a mass inferiority complex," Rockefeller said. By the late 1960s, he felt, there had been "a whole about-face in people's attitudes here." But for some years, the change and growth were retarded by the very action Rockefeller tried so hard to prevent—Faubus' intervention in the Little Rock schools. "Not until 1963 or 1964 could we get new industries into Little Rock again," Rockefeller recalled.

By 1959, Rockefeller had seen enough of Faubus and the ways of Arkansas to decide that the state must have a two-party system. But in the Arkansas Republican party, he discovered a minuscule, patronage-geared organization that had never turned out a majority for a Republican Presidential candidate and not once in the 20th century elected a governor, a Senator, or a Representative. Rockefeller applied the typical family solution: an input of money (eventually millions) plus leadership. In 1961 he became Republican National Committeeman from Arkansas. By 1964, he was ready to take on Orval Faubus.

So that year the towns and hamlets of rustic Arkansas witnessed a scene unique in American politics: the urbane millionaire, globe-trotting businessman and patron of the arts touring the byways (accompanied by a hillbilly band or folk singers for the expected entertainment, of course) appealing for the votes of men in oldtime overalls and women in plain cotton dresses—some of the plainest people in all America.

No one was fooled into thinking Rockefeller was an Ozarks farmer. But there he went, the big hulk of a man, all the taller for his cowboy boots, striding down the main street of Smackover or Searcy, Thebes or Hoxie, a sweaty shirt on his back with sleeves rolled up, wearing the ever present broadbrimmed Western hat, a quarter-billionaire mixing with people lucky to earn $3,000 a year.

Rockefeller was warmly received wherever he went, but he was in a contest with a real master. Through the same crossroads of old plantation and hill country Arkansas came Orval Faubus. Faubus' entry into a town was much quieter; instead of coming with a Rockefeller-scale retinue he would sometimes arrive with but a single driver and begin circulating around the town square, evoking startled comments—"Why I declare, it's Orval Faubus!" And then a group would gather, and Faubus, with his winning grin and direct way, would begin his spiel. And if the place was along the Mississippi, the accent could thicken like molasses or, if in the hills, switch back into true hillbilly: "You know what they say about me. That when I came from the hills to Little Rock my cuffs were located somewhere north of my shoes. Now that's a smart-aleck way of sayin' my cuffs was too short and that I couldn't afford a $10 suit. They say I'm from Greasy Creek up in the hills —Yes, I'm a hillbilly and I ain't ashamed of it."

Back and forth the arguments went:

Rockefeller: Has Orval Faubus been here yet? Well, when he does he'll be over in the courthouse over there greasing his machine. . . . I want to lead my chosen people into a prosperous future. . . .

Faubus: Why, Rockefeller never had anything but a reputation as a playboy before he came to Arkansas. I gave him a chance to establish himself. I may have made a mistake. . . . This election will show if a poor boy can still beat a millionaire. . . . Why, his granddaddy was that oil magnate who raised the price of kerosene sold to the po' folks. . . . Yes, I tell you, if we owe the Rockefellers anything, we've been paying it a long time. . . .

Rockefeller: I would not permit the open flaunting of the law, as has been the case in Hot Springs with gambling and illegal sale of liquor. . . .

Faubus: Rockefeller has no right to bring up the so-called moral issue in gambling; why the Rockefellers own a hotel in San Juan, Puerto Rico, where gambling is carried on openly. . . .

Rockefeller: I believe that all people should have the right of equal opportunity [but that] we can make greater progress by voluntary action [than] through litigation and legislation. . . .

Faubus: Rockefeller is trying to change his spots on the racial issue. My position is well known. Rockefeller is an ardent civil rights advocate. . . . I'm the only candidate who you can count on to oppose immorality, atheism and forced racial integration. . . . The first time they [rights demonstrators] lay down in the streets [in Arkansas] to block the traffic of a legitimate business operation, they're going to get run over. And if no one else will do it, I'll get a truck and do it myself. [Author's note—all this before George Wallace ever thought of the line.]

Rockefeller: I am so shocked I am speechless.

Faubus was to win the 1964 election, even though Rockefeller's 43 percent of the vote was a high-water mark, up to then, for any 20th-century Republican. Two years later, when Faubus finally stepped down of his own accord, the Democrats ended up nominating Jim Johnson, founder of the White Citizens Councils in Arkansas and the very archsegregationist who had, some believe, spooked Faubus into his stand on Central High School nine years before. (Johnson, who learned a peculiar violence of language at the feet of another notorious Arkansan, Gerald L. K. Smith, showed his regard for Negroes by refusing to shake hands with any who stepped in his direction.)

The 1966 campaign was not without a share of humor. Frequently, Rockefeller lent his private planes to other Republican campaigners. One morning he lectured his staff on keeping track of where all the planes were, recalling "the Black Friday when I went out there (to the airstrip at Petit Jean) and found the planes were overcommitted—all signed away and I found I didn't have an airplane to my name." The remark passed without a smile on WR's lips; he apparently never stopped to think that none of his hearers had *ever* had an airplane to his name. Most of Rockefeller's campaigners were younger men and women, especially college students and graduates—a sort of "new politics" for Arkansas.

But if it was new politics, the old economies of Rockefeller oil lingered on. On one occasion, the great Rockefeller campaign bus rolled into a little Arkansas town, only to find it was almost out of gas. Precious time was spent circling around to find an Esso station; "grandfather's ghost" just wouldn't permit WR to fill up on Shell.

Johnson's image as an intemperate segregationist drove thousands of independents and moderate Democrats into Rockefeller's arms, and by this point the newly born GOP organization was showing some muscle. So it was that Arkansas elected its first Republican governor since 1873 by a margin of 49,037 votes—some 54 percent of the total cast. Marked sectional differences failed to show up in the vote, but Rockefeller did succeed in carrying the larger cities by substantial margins and in absolutely monopolizing the Negro vote. (The vote in some black precincts went his way by such margins as 445–39, 564–32, 245–2, 409–9, 185–1, and the like.) It was apparent to many that the black vote gave Rockefeller his margin of victory—ironically in the very year when Republican Barry Goldwater was proving to be such anathema to black voters, in Arkansas as across the country. Two years later, with another quite mediocre opponent, Rockefeller again ran strongest in the city areas and got a strong black vote that provided his margin for election. (By 1968, 67.5 percent of Arkansas' voting age Negroes were registered to vote, compared to a scant 37.7 percent just eight years before.)

Election as governor brought Rockefeller immense satisfaction. He had used the Rockefeller wealth, but he had done his own thing, in the time and place of his own choosing. One close acquaintance recalls a 1967 newspaper photo from a national governors' conference with the "two Rockefellers"—Governor Nelson of New York and Governor Winthrop of Arkansas—posing together. The friend recalls thinking to himself, "I wonder what effort it cost Winthrop to get that picture in the paper. I'm sure he feels a lot better now that he has Governor in front of his name." Ironically, the two Rockefellers shared the extremes in gubernatorial salaries across the U.S.—New York's the highest at $50,000 a year, Arkansas' the lowest at $10,000. It was just that neat.

Rockefeller turned in a highly creditable performance as governor, pointing the way, in field after field, to the first broad reform of Arkansas government in the 20th century. A department of administration was set up to coordinate disparate executive departments. The legislature was persuaded to pass the first meaningful minimum wage law in Arkansas history, to raise teachers' salaries, and to enact the Arkansas Freedom of Information Law, which required public bodies to allow public access to meetings. By executive order, Rockefeller created a code of ethics for government executives. That ancient hypocrisy, the law forbidding liquor by the drink in public establishments, was finally repealed. Machinery was set in motion to effect a rewriting of the museum piece 1874 constitution. (As an example, this noble document until 1968 had a provision limiting free public education to persons between 6 and 21, thus forbidding public kindergartens or free adult education.) Rockefeller ordered and got a complete shutdown of illegal gambling operations at Hot Springs. Unprecedented numbers of Negroes were appointed to important government jobs, together with the first black state troopers and the first blacks ever on local draft boards. Some, but not all, of Rockefeller's prison reform legislation was passed, and new industry continued to pour into Arkansas—at an average rate, Rockefeller claimed, of a new 50-worker plant every 36 hours.

It was the implacable hostility of the Democratic legislature, however, that proved to be Rockefeller's nemesis. There were only two Republican lawmakers in his first term and five in his second (out of a total membership of 35 senators and 100 representatives). Rockefeller wanted to effect a dramatic increase in state aid to education and expand services in many areas. But the legislature consistently refused to approve his program of tax reform and tax increases—proposals that would have boosted the state budget by as much as 50 percent, cut poor people's taxes, and exacted a much bigger bite from the more affluent. One of the most pressing needs, Rockefeller said, was higher salaries for government officials and university faculty, necessary if Arkansas was to pull itself out of its age-old slough of mediocrity in personnel and programs. The legislators, often representing impoverished towns, were either personally opposed or unwilling to take the political risk of approving what seemed to backwoods Arkansas like fancy and extravagant salaries. So it is, of course, that the pattern of poverty and second-rate government is perpetuated.

Rockefeller also came a cropper on the issue of appointments to boards and commissions. Two days before Faubus left office, the old master had nominated no less than 93 men to various state boards. Despite Rockefeller's protestations, the all-Democratic senate hurriedly confirmed the midnight appointments. Some of the appointees would have terms running to 1977. As for Rockefeller's appointments, they were often rejected by the Senate in a most cavalier fashion. This fate, for instance, awaited the first two Negroes he appointed to the state board of education. In four years as governor, in fact, Rockefeller was never to get the control of boards and commissions that means real control of Arkansas government.

It may be that WR never had a chance with the Democratic legislature, but on the other hand he did little personally to rectify the situation. Never was he willing to engage in the kind of cajoling and favor-swapping that most governors, especially those from the South, must engage in to get their programs approved. Privately, Rockefeller was contemptuous of the legislators, whom he described to me as shortsighted, petty men, the passers of frivolous resolutions, unwilling to face up to the state's gut problems. Less partisan observers say the decorum and quality of representation in the legislative halls has improved markedly in recent years. The Citizens Conference on State Legislatures in 1971 ranked Arkansas' only 46th among the nation's 50. The legislators took their bad rating to heart, however, and hired the Eagleton Institute of Politics at Rutgers University to make a detailed study of rules and procedures in both houses. By 1973, a significant number of reforms had been approved, including open meetings and clearer procedures for all committees, a reduction in the number of committees and making them identical in subject matter jurisdiction in both houses, broad authorization for committee work between sessions, program budgeting, and fuller staff.

Rockefeller's liaison problems were not limited to the legislature. He was often a strangely inaccessible figure, sometimes inexplicably absent from the seat of government, often ducking uncomfortable appointments, troubled by a drinking problem that became public knowledge—certainly not recommended habits for a minority party governor in a small, personal state. Among those who complained most bitterly were some of WR's earliest friends in Arkansas, who said that Rockefeller had become distant and remote. (When I heard that Rockefeller was dying of cancer, I sent him the first draft of this chapter, because I thought he would be interested in the assessment of his role in Arkansas history. When Rockefeller read the manuscript in the days immediately preceding his death, he was most hurt and upset by the thought that any of his friends thought he had turned his back on them. "If that's so," he said, "it's because those friends weren't facing forward. I had to go [for governor], and I went, and I wish they had come along, because I needed them.")

Outside of economic development, the two areas of Rockefeller's greatest impact in Arkansas were race relations and penal reform. "The day Arkansas changed," my friend Leroy Donald of the *Arkansas Gazette* observed, "was the day after Martin Luther King, Jr.'s assassination when Rockefeller stood on the capitol steps singing, 'We Shall Overcome.'" WR's joining the mourning Negroes that day (despite security warnings that rednecks or gambling interests might do him violence), and his consistent efforts to advance Negroes in state government, were not isolated events or purely designed to win votes. "You've got to remember the tradition of the Rockefeller family in race relations," Rockefeller told me, pointing out that the vast majority of Negroes over 35 in Arkansas with a college degree went to colleges assisted by Rockefeller family funds. "It's a tradition that has never wavered over four generations," Rockefeller insisted. At a time when many Southern Republicans were playing not-very-subtle racist politics, the Rockefeller stance stood out as a great exception and promise of another day in Southern politics. And a governor with that kind of attitude must have had a fundamental effect on the Arkansas psyche. At the memorial service after his death, the point was confirmed by William ("Sonny") Walker, the black man Rockefeller had nominated as Arkansas director of the federal Office of Economic Opportunity. "While Governor Rockefeller helped free the black man in Arkansas from the oppression of Jim Crow," Walker said, "he also helped free the white man of our state from the prison of his prejudice."

If one is to believe the almost unanimous judgment of criminologists and knowledgeable officials at the Justice Department, the conditions of brutality and bestiality at Arkansas' prison farms have been without compare in penal institutions across the United States. Across the 16,000 acres of the Cummins Prison Farm in southeast Arkansas, for instance, some 200 convicts stoop in vast cotton fields 12 hours a day, 5½ days a week—for zero pay. Conditions are not much better at the Tucker prison farm. Both places are virtual slave plantations in the 20th century and Arkansas' chosen way of inflicting a Calvinistic kind of retribution on its offenders while avoiding any cash outlay. Until a few years ago, the prison farms were indeed completely self-supporting, though the price for that was hiring only a handful of guards and leaving most of the control in the hands of armed "trusties"—men picked for meanness, often killers or armed robbers, ready to gun down the first man who might stray from the line in the fields. A 1966 report showed the Arkansas prisons were festering with "inmate abuse and official corruption including death, threats, shooting of prisoners, gratuitous beating with rubber hoses, blackjacks, brass knuckles, torture, stompings, lashings, kickings, sexual perversion and other forms of punishment."

Being the humanitarian man he was, Rockefeller was determined to effect reforms when he became governor, and indeed brought into Arkansas as his chief agent of reform a courageous reformer named Tom Murton, former assistant professor of criminology at Southern Illinois University. Murton effected a minor revolution in a single year. Instruments of torture were quickly banished.* Use of the hide, a 4½-pound leather strap that could break a man's ribs or slice his buttocks like a knife, was forbidden. Gun-toting trusties lost much of their power, and the free-world guard force was sharply increased. The extortions, rackets, and worst homosexual offenses were stopped. Then, in January 1968, men working under Murton's direction at the Cummins prison farm discovered three mutilated bodies in a mule pasture known as "Bodiesburg." Two were decapitated, and the skull of the third, by Murton's account, had been crushed to the size of a grapefruit. Critics, however, said Murton had merely stumbled on an old convict graveyard.

Thirty-eight days later, Murton was fired, Rockefeller and his prison board head explaining that he had been a "poor prison administrator." Rockefeller was later charged with a sell-out to powerful interests in Arkansas, or at least a fatal loss of nerve, in Murton's 1970 book, *Accomplices in Crime: The Arkansas Prison Scandal* (New York: Grove Press, 1970). Others tell me, however, that Murton developed something close to a messiah complex about his work at the prison, so that no one on the outside—legisla-

* The worst of these was the "Tucker telephone," components of which were an old-fashioned crank telephone, wiring, and a heavy-duty battery. James Bruton, superintendent until 1966, designed the device and used it in a horrifying way to communicate his displeasure to a prisoner. The man would be stripped, one wire attached to his penis and another to a wrist or ankle. When the crank was turned, he would be shocked nearly unconscious. Convicted in 1970 in federal court on charges of having violated prisoners' civil rights by administering cruel and unusual punishment, Bruton was sentenced to the maximum year's imprisonment under the Civil Rights Act of 1871. But the federal judge suspended the sentence, noting: "The court doesn't want to give you a death sentence, and quite frankly, Mr. Bruton, the chances of your surviving that year would not be good. One or more of these persons or their friends with whom you have dealt in the past as inmates of the Arkansas penitentiary would kill you."

ture, governor, his board, or the press—could deal with him on a rational basis. Those familiar with the prison farms insist that the Rockefeller years brought fundamental change, not only in the introduction of some vocational training, better foods, arts and hobbies, and the like, but in a fundamental recognition that prisoners are people, not animals. Nevertheless, a federal judge in 1970 found conditions on the two prison farms still so bad that confining inmates there was a violation of the Constitution's prohibition against cruel and unusual punishment. In a single summer month that year, Cummins recorded 19 stabbings, assaults, and attempted rapes. The legislature churlishly refused Rockefeller's pleas for a larger budget that could mean the start of more substantial rehabilitation programs.

Some more dollars became available when Bumpers took over the governorship and pushed ahead on the Rockefeller-initiated reforms. Bumpers picked a creditable commissioner of corrections, Terrell Don Hutto, a veteran of Texas penal administration. A maximum-security unit costing $500,000 was opened at Cummins, creating the first possibility of separating the most hardened criminals from the other inmates. But even then, a major scandal erupted in 1971 when a 17-year-old black, Willie Stewart, was subjected to unspeakable punishment during a one-day stay at Cummins—and died en route to the hospital. Stewart was brought to Cummins, like many other youthful first-time offenders, under the unique "one-day wonder program" designed to cure them, by seeing the horrors of prison life, of any future proclivity to crime. Well-intentioned enough, the program fell victim to the ancient brutalization of the Arkansas penal system.

I have often wondered about the thinking that preserves institutions like the Arkansas prison farms. In an interview with Waldo Frazier, executive vice president of the Arkansas Farm Bureau Federation, I think I got a clue:

> You don't send those bastards down there because it's a damned country club. You got all that unfavorable publicity for bringing in outside experts. That farm down there has been making its way for years and years, on some of the best land in Arkansas. Now production is way down.
>
> Some things need to be straightened out at the pen—in fact, so does everybody in there.

Rockefeller's personal popularity among the prison farm inmates remained quite high; like a bunch of schoolboys, they would call "Hi, Gov!" and "Hi, Rocky" when he went through. (WR recalled the day he toured the pen and saw a barber-convict giving another man a haircut. "Sorry I don't have time for a trim," Rockefeller said. "Don't worry about me," the man replied. "I got 15 years.")

When defeat came to Rockefeller in the 1970 governor's race, it was overwhelming. He received only 197,418 votes (32.4 percent of the total), compared to 375,648 for winning Democrat Dale Bumpers and 36,132 for a candidate of the hard-core segregationist American Independent Party. WR had always been an emotional man. Many recalled that on his inauguration day in 1967, he could barely stammer out words of thanks to his fellow Arkansans for the honor they did him. Now, in defeat, W R was crushed. For three days, he saw no one. He made no statement election night or the next day. Finally, he held the obligatory press conference, and there were tears in his eyes. Did he think he would lose that badly? "No, sir, I did not."

Not long after, Rockefeller said in an interview that "without reservation" he could have defeated any candidate except Bumpers. "I do not personally take my defeat as a condemnation of the achievements of my administration," Rockefeller said. The problem was Bumpers, whose faint Ozark drawl, a way with a funny story, a boyish grin, and the charm of youth were all more than a match for WR, the Arkansan "outsider" with a New York accent. Other factors included the feeling—reflected by the *Arkansas Gazette* and others—that divided government in Little Rock, blocking the passage of much-needed new revenue and spending bills, could not be resolved until a Democrat became governor (the legislature being so Democratic that a generation would be needed to shift it). The *Gazette*, which had backed Rockefeller in his first two campaigns when it found the Democratic party "still bogged down in a heritage of racism and scandal," also attacked WR for an "arrogance of spending" in his campaign, including saturation radio and television commercials, mass mailings of expensive brochures, repetitive telephone solicitations, and the use of "not one but two helicopters."

The irony was that without the Rockefeller interregnum, election of a racial moderate like Bumpers would probably have been impossible—an observation which Bumpers himself told me was correct in an interview shortly after he took office. Few could argue with WR's own parting view: that Arkansas, when he came, was "like a beautiful antebellum home, the doors and windows bolted, as though to deny the coming of Change; the curtains drawn in fear, somehow, of discovering what Change might bring with it. . . . But now the fresh winds of new and exciting change are blowing. . . . I am proud and happy to have been a part in helping to open the doors and windows, bolted too long, to allow those fresh winds to penetrate our homes, and yes, even our minds."

The prospects for the Arkansas Republican party were not as bright as those for the state as a whole. The party still lacked a foothold in local offices. There was a postelection meeting of the Republican state committee, when Rockefeller spoke for his own candidate for state party chairman, a moderate. Rockefeller cautioned his party against becoming "just another Republican party in another Southern state." But the Republicans went ahead and elected the conservative anyway. In 1972 they saw the fruits of their post-Rockefeller turn: while Nixon took Arkansas in a landslide, Bumpers beat his Republican opponent with more than 75 percent of the vote, and the GOP was reduced to one lonely seat in the state senate, one in the state house. Blacks, who had remained steadfast to Rockefeller through the 1970 election, were now giving only a fifth of their vote to the GOP gubernatorial candidate. But they awarded about half their vote to the Republican who opposed Senator McClellan—suggesting that even without Rockefeller money, the Republicans could win a major share of the black vote in some contested races, if they would only make the effort.

Just two weeks before his gubernatorial term expired in 1971, Rockefeller startled the state—and country—by commuting the sentences of all 15 men on death row in Arkansas, urging his fellow governors to follow suit. No other American governor had ever taken such a step. Many Arkansas legislators were furious over what seemed to them Rockefeller's parting outrage, and there was much talk about the victims of the sentenced men, and that Rockefeller had superseded the courts and juries that sentenced the 15 convicts (11 of whom were Negroes).

For Rockefeller, the explanation was quite clear:

> My position on capital punishment has been clear since long before I became governor. I am unalterably opposed to it and will remain so as long as I live. . . . Failing to take this action while it is in my power, I could not live with myself. . . .
>
> What earthly mortal has the omnipotence to say who among us shall live and who shall die? I do not. I cannot and will not turn my back on life-long Christian teachings and beliefs, merely to let history run out its course on a fallible and failing system of punitive justice.

The day WR commuted the sentences some 550 convicts sat in death rows across the country. "I yearn," Rockefeller said, "to see other chief executives throughout the nation follow [Arkansas'] suit so that as a people we may hasten the elimination of barbarism as a tool of American justice." None rushed to follow his example. But a spark had been lit, and that in the unlikeliest of states.

In the two years after his retirement, Rockefeller mellowed, reduced his drinking, and spent much time working among the trees and plants at Winrock. His divorce from Jeannette was announced—but it was not a rancorous one, and when Rockefeller fell ill in 1972, she would come to visit him several times. His son, Winthrop Paul, came to live at Winrock with his wife, and Rockefeller's first grandchild, Andrea Davison Rockefeller, was born in Arkansas in the summer of 1972. Rockefeller grew a splendid Hemingwayesque beard that marked him as the most liberated celebrity at the 1972 Republican National Convention in Miami Beach. "Very few people have urged me to get rid of it," he said, "and young people rather appreciate the fact that there is an established and mature man who had the fortitude to do something like this." (Rockefeller also said to his close friends: "You have to live with this beard to know the problems. Can you imagine, does it go outside the covers or underneath?")

The removal from public life was frustrating for Rockefeller; at one point he complained, "It's really damned foolishness for the taxpayers to train a man like me for four years for something, and then, poof!" Privately, Rockefeller gave much thought to programs that might vitalize rural regions and begin to relieve the population pressure on the megalapolitan population belts of the country. He was concerned that rural America, having failed to provide for the needs and aspirations of its own people, had in effect exported them to overcrowded urban regions, dehumanizing life for people at both ends. He was convinced that rational solutions to the problem were possible, and even considered building a new city in Arkansas. Even when he knew he faced death, Rockefeller's mind did not shut down; in fact, he took a briefcase of work with him when he entered the hospital for the last time.

In his will, Rockefeller created a charity trust—expected to have capitalization of several hundreds of millions of dollars—which he hoped would be used chiefly for Arkansas charities. But he did not restrict the trustees (who included his brother David), but rather asked in his will that they "be innovative and venturesome," and "not feel that they need be conservative in the use of principal."

When Winthrop died, the *Arkansas Gazette* received calls from scores of little people, asking in their thick Arkansas drawls, "Are we going to get to keep him here in Arkansas?" The answer was yes: Rockefeller's ashes were to be interred in a sanctuary near Winrock Farm. For so many years, Rockefeller had been trying to prove to his fellow Arkansans that he was really one of them. And now their concern, that he not be carried away for burial in some distant place like New York, was to be the final, conclusive proof that Winthrop Rockefeller was an outlander no more.

Arkansas in the '70s

Where are the "Arkies" headed in the post-Faubus, post-Rockefeller generation? Dale Bumpers, inaugurated as governor in January 1971, provided a key: "The future I envision must be shared by all Arkansans—old and young, black and white, rich and poor. . . . This administration will be one of concern, compassion, and reality. . . . We must not waste the new awakening of our people." The opinion of James Rachinc, a political scientist at Ouachita Baptist University quoted in *South Today*, is that "Dale Bumpers is the logical conclusion of a steady moderation of Arkansas voters during the 1960s." The political part of the equation, he said, is that "no extremist, right or left, can make it in a statewide race." The governmental part has been made easier, Leroy Donald told me, because "Bumpers has the personality, and the right party emblem, to carry out Rockefeller's program."

The correctness of those analyses was borne out quickly in 1971 when the legislature approved the Bumpers plan for reorganizing the state government—a plan based on a study financed by the Rockefeller Brothers Fund. A cabinet-style government was created, with some 60 boards and commissions and agencies put under 13 "superdepartments." Most were made directly responsible to the governor (the exceptions were highways, corrections, and licensing boards). Under Faubus, Donald pointed out, such a plan would never have passed for fear of how he might abuse its power. Under Rockefeller, it was impossible because a Democratic legislature would never give that much power to a Republican. With Bumpers in office, it sailed through in a few weeks.

Bumpers also proposed and got through a restructuring of the tax system to make it substantially more progressive. People on the lowest rung of the economic ladder were excused from income taxes altogether; the rate for upper-income people was raised from 5 percent (where it had been since 1932) to 7 percent, and Bumpers came within a vote in the state senate of setting the rate at 9 percent. Some of Bumpers' other priorities have included expanded health care for poor and rural areas, improvement in mental health facilities, and stepped-up programs in the fields of air and water pollution. During his first years in office, organized labor, forever loyal to the Democrats (despite Rockefeller's warmest blandishments), got its reward with a sweeping change in unemployment compensation benefits, which were raised to a scale considered close to the country's most generous.*

Still, by most economic indicators, Arkansas has a long, long way to go to become equal to or competitive with the other states. Her per capita income has recently ranked 49th among the 50 states, about 73 percent of the national average—though this in itself represents a huge advance over three decades before, when the Arkansas income figure was only 42 percent of the national average. In direct defense-generated civilian employment, so important to many southeastern states, Arkansas ranks far below most states. Its labor force has more blue-collar and fewer white-collar workers, proportionately, than almost any other in the U.S. In 1971 the average family on welfare got payments ranked only 45th among the states. More families live below the poverty line—22.8 percent in the 1970 Census—than in any state except Mississippi. The number of physicians and nurses per capita rank 50th, and there is a distressing lack of medical care available outside of the Little Rock area, which alone has 40 percent of the state's physicians. State and local taxes per person in Arkansas in 1970 were $252, rock bottom among the states. The rate went up some after Bumpers' $22 million tax package passed in 1971, but the fact is that Arkansas, if it were willing to tax at average rates for state governments around the country, could still raise its annual income by more than $150 million, the bulk of it from personal and corporate income taxes.

Education is one way Arkansas could start to make itself a better society. The 1970 Census found that Arkansas had fewer college graduates (3.7 percent of the adult population) than any other state, and that almost 10 percent of the state's people were functional illiterates (less than five years of schooling). Yet to this day, per capita expenditures for education in Arkansas rank 50th among the 50 states. Schoolteachers are still notoriously poorly paid, and in 1961 4,000 of them were angry enough to march *en masse* on Little Rock in protest. The financial squeeze in education has also been acute at the University of Arkansas, which has its main campus (with about 10,000 students) in scenic Ozark territory at Fayetteville and medical and other graduate schools in Little Rock. The U of A library is reportedly bad enough to risk loss of accreditation. But the Razorback football team is known across the country, and the coach earns three times as much as the governor.

The temptation when one deals with a state like Arkansas is to forget the interstate comparative statistical game (because it is so depressing)

* Arkansas unions, long hampered by the state's right-to-work law, had organized only 18 percent of the nonfarm work force by 1970 (ranking 33rd among the states). The Arkansas AFL-CIO has exceptionally strong leadership under its president, Bill Becker, however, and may be expected to grow.

and to concentrate instead on relative improvement of internal conditions. "If your population is stable, and your income and educational levels are getting better," one state legislator asked me, "so what if other states get further ahead? At least our way of life is progressing." Perhaps he has a point, though one wonders—as Rockefeller did—how Arkansas government can possibly attract adequate personnel if it pays several grades below almost all other states, or if attractive jobs are so limited that the state ends up (as Arkansas does) producing an absolute surplus of college graduates in most fields. It exports, for instance, 70 to 80 percent of its engineers.

So the state must look to its private sector for major new growth. Part of the problem there, Winthrop Rockefeller said, was the mental set in the multitudinous small towns and cities of Arkansas, where he saw thinking still mired at the turn of the century. Often, he said, a few affluent merchants and farmers were still against new industry, because of the competition it would bring. Rockefeller said he agreed with the old Arkansas saying: "There's nothing wrong with this town that about five good funerals won't take care of." But he saw a lot of bright young people coming along in the late '60s and early '70s. And the young chamber of commerce types, he noted, had begun to look beyond the beauty pageants to come to grips with basic problems.

Changes in farming and new industry, in fact, present brand new problems and possibilities for Arkansas. "Through Arkansas' first 100 years," business-farm editor Leland Duvall of the *Arkansas Gazette* said, "we ravaged our topsoil and ruined our forests and silted our lakes, until those resources began to be endangered. We were a supplier of raw materials; economically, we were a colony, selling a lot of raw cotton, unfinished lumber, and the like. It was only 35 years ago that we began to reforest our timber lands and to conserve and improve our soil." Only through the New Deal's farm programs were many conservation steps introduced, and among plantation owners of the Delta, opposition to F. D. R. and his programs was extreme.

As it became possible to farm scientifically, with machinery and chemicals rather than by hand, the nature of Arkansas farming shifted. Cotton virtually disappeared from the hill counties, where it was once important, and even on the Mississippi lowlands it had to compete with soybeans, rice, and other crops. Chickens and beef replaced cotton along the Arkansas River, and in fact Arkansas is now a big chicken state, second only to Georgia in the number of broilers it sells. In a fairly typical recent year, Arkansas farmers sold $229 million worth of soybeans, $151 million in broilers, $109 million in rice, $89 million in eggs, $31 million in turkeys, $98 million in cattle and calves, and $85 million in cotton. Some planters' profit margin comes from underpaid labor. Even though formalized sharecropping has ended, there are many Delta planters who live in relative affluence while 10 or 15 tenant farmer families live on the place in shotgun housing, windows replaced by old sackcloth, incomes at rock bottom. (There are a few enlightened planters who provide sound housing for their tenants and even share profits with them—a hopeful sign for the future. And at spots along the Mississippi, black and white farmers are building ponds to raise a new crop that promises fine per acre yields: catfish, sold fresh and frozen, popular at big fish fries and for Memphis restaurant sales.)

Another vital shift was in the labor force, as more and more people were forced off the farms by mechanization. During the 1940s and 1950s, Arkansas simply exported its excess labor—to California, Detroit, Chicago. The state suffered a staggering net migration outflow of 417,000 people in the '40s, 433,000 people in the '50s. There were almost 200,000 farms in Arkansas at the end of World War II but only 60,000 by the end of the 1960s. Yet in the '60s, Arkansas experienced the fastest rate of growth in manufacturing employment of any Southern state. As a result, the net migration drain was reduced to 74,000 people in that decade. And in 10 years, the number of young people between 20 and 24 years of age jumped by 43 percent. Suddenly, they saw a future in Arkansas.

The economic revival had begun with the AIDC effort in the late 1950s and state legislation letting cities or counties sell tax-free bonds for construction of factories. The first result was a plethora of small plants, making textiles, apparel, and shoes in low-wage rural Arkansas. Then came more wood products and paper factories (using raw materials from Arkansas' thriving lumber industry—fourth largest among the states), chemicals (based in part on Arkansas' quite modest natural gas and petroleum production), metals and machinery. Arkansas supplies 96 percent of the nation's domestic bauxite (the ore from which aluminum is made) and has had several aluminum plants ever since World War II.

Now Arkansas is receiving a vital, latter-day stimulus through the Arkansas River navigation project. With formal completion in 1972, the river became navigable all the way from the Mississippi to Tulsa, Oklahoma. The $1.3 billion project, assailed in earlier years as the "biggest pork barrel in history," provides cheap water transportation for Arkansas rice and soybeans moving to distant ports and goods moving in the other direction: Caribbean bauxite for the aluminum plants near Little Rock, for instance, or steel from anywhere in the Mississippi Valley or abroad. In a single weekend of early 1973, two foreign car agencies opened in Little Rock, stocked with autos shipped directly by sea. Factories are springing up in cities all along the river's course through Arkansas.

AIDC chairman Dan Roebuck acknowledged in 1972 that "one of the big attractions Arkansas offers besides abundant natural resources and availability of land is an hourly wage scale that is about 70 percent of the U.S. average for manufacturing." * Some plants doubtless still come to take advantage of those low wages—only in North Carolina, in fact, do workers earn less. But other factors are now becoming equally important for prospective industries, including improved worker training and convenient locations in medium-sized cities.

It was Rockefeller, the first big promoter of industry for Arkansas who

* Roebuck told *Business Week* that Arkansas labor scales compare favorably with countries like West Germany, an important factor for companies fighting competition from imports. And now any relatively advanced industry knows that it can go into Arkansas, pay substantially less in wages than it would in the industrialized North, but still be welcome because its pay scales are over the local average.

spoke what was then near-heresy in 1967 by suggesting that "the South should become increasingly selective in the types of manufacturing it develops." Then, in 1970, WR warned his fellow Southern governors at a meeting in Biloxi, Mississippi: "The danger, in playing economic catch-up, is that we could adopt false definitions of progress. The ultimate cost of such a course—we are reminded by grim evidence to the North, East, and West—would be disruption of the Southland's priceless natural environment. . . . It should be clear to us by now that man cannot, in the name of progress, destroy nature without slowly destroying himself." For Arkansas, with its pulp mills and plans for petrochemicals and other heavy industries along the barge-served Arkansas, the warning was apt. The state has, at least by regional standards, rather well developed air and water pollution control programs, which were inaugrated under Rockefeller.

Arkansas may soon face an energy crisis of potentially grave dimensions because of the growing shortages of natural gas. The availability of gas has been a major inducement to bring new industries into the state, but the fact is that all of it has to be imported from outside. The chairman of the public service commission has noted that Arkansas "jumped straight from a wood and kerosene era to the use of natural gas without fooling around much with coal and fuel oil like other parts of the country." Now the power companies in Arkansas rely almost exclusively on gas to fuel their generators, and the Arkansas Louisiana Gas Company is building a 300-mile gas pipeline to Texas and Oklahoma. But when the natural gas runs out there, as it will in a few years, what will happen then?

People have long been saying in Arkansas that "one tourist is better than two bales of cotton—and he's easier to pick." The problem is that most of the picking has been done in that one grand old resort town, Hot Springs. (Hot Springs may have lost gambling under the Rockefeller regime, but at least he saw to it that liquor by the drink would at last be legal there. Other attractions are therapeutic thermal baths, the horse races, golf, antique shops, and, as the cynics say, wheelchair races.)

The present wave of serious tourist development is in the Ozark Highlands, centered around the man-made lakes there. Already some large summer home and retirement home communities are being built there, and the wave of retirees has helped to stem the population outflow from the area.

As Arkansas' economic climate slowly improved, so did its racial. In 1970 there were 357,225 Negroes living in Arkansas—125,353 less than in 1940. During the same period the Negro share of Arkansas' total population declined from 25 to 19 percent. But there were signs that the great northward migrations (with Chicago a favored destination point) were beginning to slacken, with many of the smart young blacks determined to make a go of it in Arkansas rather than accept expatriation to the northern slums.

Arkansas still had pockets of extreme racial tension, the worst being a 50-mile stretch of rich cotton and soybean lands in the Delta lands across the Mississippi River from Memphis. Many of the little towns there were left virtually untouched by the civil rights movement of the 1960s, with older style black leaders—mostly clergymen and businessmen—continuing to speak for other blacks in a way that rarely offended the white power structures. But around the end of the '60s, a number of tough, articulate young blacks who had left home for military service or college training returned home and began to organize in a militant way. In 1969 the town of Forrest City exploded in the worst racial confrontation in Arkansas since Little Rock in 1957. The scene of angry black boycotts, incensed white mobs, gunfire, and arson was repeated early in the '70s in nearby Marianna and Madison. The prototype young black leader was Olly Neal, Jr., the 30-year-old leader of a controversial medical center at Marianna, financed by the U.S. Office of Economic Opportunity. The New York *Times*' veteran Southern reporter, Roy Reed, called Neal "a younger version" of Mississippi's Charles Evers: "He is big and blunt and believes that only political power will improve the lot of poor blacks. Like Evers, he is open-faced and straightforward. He does not lower his eyes when talking to white men."

The white power structure at Marianna, used to holding blacks in subservient positions, worked hard—but unsuccessfully—to get Governor Bumpers to veto OEO money for the clinic. Bumpers responded by pointing out that poor people made up 74 percent of the 18,000 population of Lee County (where Marianna is located), that blacks are 80 percent of the poor, and that the black infant mortality rate there was 53 per 1,000, compared to 12 per 1,000 for whites. Bumpers said he was "not about to" cut off the funds "when rural health care is one of the main parts of my program."

As in other Southern states, black elected officials are increasing and will make an increasing difference in the next few years. Before 1972, Arkansas had not elected a black state legislator in this century. Now there are three in the house, one in the senate. Arkansas blacks held 139 other elective jobs by 1973. There were eight mayors, 46 aldermen or city councilmen, 49 school board members and the like. In most sections, Arkansas does not manifest the teeth-clenched resistance to Negro advances apparent in states like Mississippi and Alabama. Blacks are now freely accepted as part of the voting pool, their support is a prize in statewide elections, and school desegregation has moved forward rapidly. All of this comes not many years past the day in 1959 when the Arkansas legislature voted to prohibit any state agency from hiring a member of the National Association for the Advancement of Colored People—on the grounds the organization was "Communist-controlled." Only six members of the legislature had had the courage to vote against the bill.

Still, a deep streak of traditional Southern conservatism, strongly rural in flavor, remains in Arkansas. In the elections of 1970, it was rural voters who were responsible for the defeat, by a vote of 301,195 to 223,334, of the proposed new constitution which Rockefeller and other good-government types had enthusiastically endorsed. The rustics were said to fear the new charter would do everything from increasing their taxes to restricting their private arsenals. The old constitution, which now remains in effect, has been depicted as giving "great power to local political satraps, many of whom, over the years, have grown hidebound, corrupt, and unbelievably insular."

In Presidential voting, Arkansas has shown the same conservative tendencies as its Deep South neighbors in recent years, but by somewhat lesser margins. In 1968 Wallace carried the state, but his 39 percent vote there was much less than he received in Alabama, Mississippi, or Louisiana. Nixon's 69 percent in 1972 was impressive enough, but again not quite as high as he received in some other Deep South states. Arkansas had refused to go for Thurmond in 1948 or for Goldwater in 1964; in fact, more than a century elapsed between its two Republican Presidential years (1868 and 1972). Whenever the black-white issue subsides as an issue in Presidential elections, Arkansas may well be the first Deep South state to return to the Democrats.

Through the 1968 elections, the Democratic party seemed to remain in the control of the Faubus organization. That year's Democratic gubernatorial nominee, Marion Crank, was actually a public relations employee of Ark-La Gas's Witt Stephens. But Crank, after his defeat, decided that the time had come to extend an olive branch to the young, the reformers, the black and city people within the party—those whose defections had twice elected Rockefeller. As Democratic state chairman, he designated a 30-year-old, Charles Matthews. Matthews began to draw the alienated factions into the party, simultaneously courting the old-line county machines by telling a sheriff or judge or whoever was in control that if the Democrats failed to pull together, WR and the Republicans would have all their jobs in a few years. To a remarkable degree—as Bumpers' two big election victories indicated—the strategy was successful. Today the only major Republican officeholder in the state is Congressman John Paul Hammerschmidt, a conservative who first won election from western-northwestern Arkansas with the help of WR's coattails in 1966 and has since built a solid political base for himself.

From time immemorial, Arkansas was plagued by odoriferous election-day manipulation. Some of the worst practices were done away with in 1964, when a public-spirited citizen, Dr. H. D. Luck, organized a broad coalition of labor unions, Negroes, League of Women Voters and American Association of University Women to support an initiative proposal to amend the state constitution. The successful amendment (1) abolished the poll tax—long a source of discrimination against blacks, and (2) established a model voter registration law. But, as Richard E. Yates has written, "much more than a new registration system . . . is required to clean up the conduct of Arkansas primaries and elections." Yates notes there are many laws on the books to stop corrupt practices, but says "they are disobeyed whenever disobedience promises to produce an electoral victory. . . . Revelations of law-breaking in this field provoke more public amusement than public indignation." Specifically, he notes that voting booths required by statute are frequently omitted, endangering a secret vote; that unauthorized persons often help with the vote count; that highly suspicious numbers of absentee ballots are frequently issued, and that "the cruder forms of vote-buying, false tallying, ballot box stuffing, and the destruction of ballots are not so uncommon as to provoke astonishment, especially in the 'machine counties.' . . . On one occasion, it was reported, ballots were dropped through a crack in the floor; another story, not lightly to be believed, relates how an election clerk disposed of some unwanted ballots by eating them."

The raising and spending of campaign money is another dark island of Arkansas politics, one where not even the dim light of a state disclosure law penetrates. Apparently the major contributors include highway and other contractors doing business with the state, sources close to banks interested in interest-free deposits, the gas interests and officials and employees of state government (the latter especially when an incumbent is running for reelection). Yates reports occasional discrepancies between the amounts raised and spent for campaigns, and that politicians occasionally run for office with the hope of picking up a comfortable surplus for personal use.

But still, the light of "democracy" burns bright. A candidate who is unwilling to tour through the most minuscule towns of rural Arkansas may find himself marked down as a city slicker, or just an indifferent man, and suffer accordingly on election day.

A Right-wing Diversion

Professional right-wing political movements have flourished for years in isolated spots around Arkansas, though generally outside the mainstream of normal conservative politics in the state. Harding College, a fundamentalist church school located in the wooded Ozark hills at Searcy, Arkansas, has been the country's leading producer of radical right propaganda for most of the postwar era. The guiding spirit at Harding College since the mid-1930s has been George S. Benson, now in his early seventies. Benson was president of Harding for years and then switched over to head an innocuously named front, the National Education Program, working out of headquarters on the campus. NEP seeks to awaken America to the perils facing the free enterprise system, to show how Negro rights movements are manipulated by international Communism, and, since the late 1960s, how the antiwar movements in the U.S. are the "Communist Enemy's second front."

Dudley Lynch, a church newsman who has made careful studies of Benson, describes him as "a veteran of hundreds of hard-sell evangelistic revivals" who "still prays in public with arms lofted. His speeches, which he delivered at the rate of 200 a year at the height of his career, are lean, blunt, propagandistic, . . . a block-letter blend of quasi-Hamiltonian democracy, undiluted 19th-century capitalism, and an agrarian, rural theology that acknowledges no flaws and tolerates few divisions in the interest of justice or equality." A 1954 poll by the *Arkansas Democrat* in Little Rock brought Benson the "Arkansan of the year award." But if his philosophies were today widely accepted in the state, many of its most prominent public men would never have been elected to office.

In another Ozarks town, Eureka Springs, the great American demagogue of the 1930s, Gerald L. K. Smith, has retired to start a number of "Sacred Projects" in his twilight years. These include a snow-white, seven-story graven image of Christ on a hilltop, Smith's Christ Only Art Gallery, and a Passion Play à la Oberammergau which blames the Jews for the death of Jesus. Once an associate of Huey P. Long and the right-wing Detroit priest

Charles E. Coughlin, Smith was described by H. L. Mencken as "the gutsiest and goriest, the deadliest and damndest orator ever heard on this or any other earth—the champion boob bumper of all epochs." Smith returned to his native Arkansas in 1965, planning to one day be buried at the foot of the Christ image. In the meantime, he has continued to write for "The Cross and the Flag," organ of the Los Angeles-based Christian Nationalist Crusade he founded. At first it seemed Smith would separate the hate business from his activities in Arkansas, declaring that "strong opinions and deep convictions shall not be introduced into the Sacred Projects at Eureka Springs." The fading old resort town gave him a seemingly unanimous welcome, as his statue and play drew visitors by the thousands. But a plucky local dress shop owner, Mrs. Georgia Ziffzer, organized opposition to Smith and to a federal grant of $181,500 to build a road past the statue and passion play amphitheater. Mrs. Ziffzer said she feared that townspeople "eventually will be so charged with bigotry and racism that people who otherwise would like to come here for a restful vacation, giving them a chance to turn back the clock so to speak in a place that so far has retained much of its turn-of-the-century charm—those people will no longer come."

Rounding out the right-wing picture, it may be reported that Texarkana, a farm town that sprawls across the Texas-Arkansas border (21,682 people in Arkansas, 30,497 in Texas), won distinction in the late 1960s as headquarters of Freedom Inc., a group formed to fight for freedom of choice plans and thus avert widespread integration of schools. Texarkana was one of hundreds of towns that had to be omitted from my travels if this book was ever to be assembled, but I cannot resist quoting from a 1969 report in *Time:*

> Texarkana . . . serves assorted crooks as a distribution center for stolen cars and appliances. Now the city boasts a new source of notoriety: 17 of Texarkana's 24 sq. mi., including some of the better sections, are infested with sleek, fat rats. According to U.S. Interior Department investigators, the town harbors about 900,000 of the rodents. . . . With their 11 internal parasites and 18 kinds of fleas, they expose people to rat bite fever, murine typhus, bubonic plague and other diseases. . . . Many of the people of Texarkana are technologically unemployed farmhands who have no concept of sanitation. They persist in tossing their garbage out the back door without remembering that rats, not hogs, are there to eat it. . . . People here just don't give a damn," sighs W. T. Westbrook, [a local] sanitation director. . . . "Even if we had strict sanitation laws, it's doubtful that people would obey them," he says. "People around here are not accustomed to obeying laws."

There, it seems, is a problem that Freedom Inc., the National Education Program, and the Sacred Projects might really sink their teeth into.

Fulbright, McClellan, Mills, et al.

Arkansas has made a great mark in Washington by electing smart men to Congress and keeping them forever. Each of its Senators head major committees—J. W. Fulbright the Foreign Relations Committee, John Mc-

Clellan the Appropriations Committee. Wilbur Mills is head of House Ways and Means; Oren Harris (until he retired to become a federal judge) was in charge of House Interstate and Foreign Commerce; E. C. Gathings was a senior man on Agriculture, and James W. Trimble on the powerful House Rules Committee.

Brooks Hays is the only prominent man whom Arkansas refused, in modern times, to keep in Congress through his prime years. Hays was defeated in 1958, after 16 years of House service, through a scurrilous last-minute campaign in which even some election judges and clerks handed out and used stickers for his archsegregationist write-in opponent in the general election (a now forgotten ophthalmologist named Dale Alford). The anti-Hays campaign was inspired by Orval Faubus, who was angered that Hays had gotten him to a negotiating table with Eisenhower during the Little Rock school controversy.

As anyone who knows him will testify, Hays is one of the most delightful raconteurs of the modern South, as well as being a Christian gentleman of the highest integrity (he was once president of the Southern Baptist Convention) and a man who has grown with his times. Despite his seemingly heroic stand for reason during the school controversy, he admits he "had not always been so brave" and actually signed, with some reservations, the Southern Manifesto of the 1950s. ("I was known then as a States' Rights liberal. It's hard for 'moderns' to know there even were such things," Hays said in an interview.) Now he scarcely regrets his defeat, looking back to 1957–58 as "the one time in my life I took an unshakable position because I thought it was right. . . . I gained greatly in publicizing my position: conformity to the law and obeying the court." Hays later became an official of the TVA, second in command of the Community Relations Service of the Justice Department, and a lecturer and guest professor at several universities.

The most often asked and never satisfactorily answered question about Arkansas politics is why such a provincial state can tolerate such an urbane and even intellectually arrogant man as Fulbright in the U.S. Senate. Part of the answer may simply be pork barrel—Fulbright sharing with others on the delegation credit for such plums as the $1.2 billion Arkansas River navigation project, a big B-58 Strategic Air Command base, missile installations, and half a dozen enviable federal hydroelectric projects. A second explanation is that no matter how daring his oratory on subjects like the Vietnam war, Fulbright has voted (1) against virtually every civil rights measure before Congress during his tenure and (2) for maintaining the tax privileges of the oil and gas industry. I asked an influential leader of the Arkansas gas industry about his support of Fulbright, and he related what he had told Fulbright before the 1968 campaign: "Senator, I'm gunna help you financially and be for you. Because the people of Arkansas have very few luxuries. And you're a luxury to us. We're just gunna keep you." * There may even be a

* In that election, Fulbright brushed aside ex-Arkansas Supreme Court Justice Jim Johnson in the first primary, only a few voters apparently responding to the charge that his foreign policy stands aided the Communist cause. He got 59.1 percent of the vote against a wealthy Delta planter in the general election, carrying every region of the state and also the Negro vote with comfortable margins. Fulbright dwelt heavily on his seniority in Congress, pork barrel projects, and his success in opening up foreign markets for the state's farm products.

perverse hillbilly pleasure in electing a man of Fulbright's unusual qualities. "You get up in New York in those fancy clubs and when you talk about Fulbright and you say Arkansas they kind of shudder," the same gas official said. Another point may be that Fulbright's Arkansas image is not quite what it is in Washington. There are still people in Arkansas, for instance, who remember him as the star ball-carrier, passer, and kicker on the University of Arkansas football team who threw a perfect 20-yard touchdown pass and kicked a 40-yard field goal to beat Southern Methodist in a great Homecoming Game in 1922.

Fulbright's independence, it has been written, came in large measure from his mother, fiery columnist and publisher of the Fayetteville *Northwest Arkansas Times*, who pushed Fulbright's appointment as president of the University of Arkansas at a very youthful 34 years of age. "It was Roberta's training," one of Fulbright's old friends told a magazine writer some years ago, "that made Bill as honest as the day is long and as independent as a hog on ice." His early warnings of the limits and dangers of applied American military power already have a prophetic ring about them. His crusade against the Vietnam war stemmed from a deep sense of guilt for having urged the Senate to pass the Gulf of Tonkin resolution in 1964. Yet few Arkansas Negro leaders lightly forgive Fulbright his civil rights voting record, his total silence at the time of the Little Rock school controversy, and what he said in his 1944 Senate race: "I am not for Negro participation in our primary elections, and I do not approve of social equality." In a switch from his old voting patterns, Fulbright voted in 1970 against Nixon's nomination of G. Harrold Carswell to the Supreme Court. Now—perhaps—he was in trouble from the other side. Martha Mitchell, a native Arkansan and wife of then U.S. Attorney General John N. Mitchell, telephoned the *Arkansas Gazette* with a blunt demand: "I want you to crucify Fulbright and that's that."

John McClellan, Arkansas' other (and senior) Senator, wields immense power in Washington as head of the Senate Appropriations Committee. He succeeded to that post in 1972, following the death of Allen Ellender of Louisiana. Now in his late seventies, McClellan has been in the Senate since 1943. He has gotten his share of publicity over the years by leading investigations that looked into abuses by labor bosses, the backers of the ill-fated TFX military fighter plane, and alleged instigators of the big city riots of the 1960s. Before McClellan took over Appropriations, he had been chairman of the Government Operations Committee for many years. Some of his best remembered investigations came in the 1950s, when he chose as chief counsel of his Senate Permanent Investigations Subcommittee none other than Robert F. Kennedy. The Teamsters were their most illustrious target, and the investigation set in motion the chain of events leading to Jimmy Hoffa's conviction and jailing.

McClellan has said that he "never resented" being called a conservative, because he "did not become a Senator to transfer the United States into a socialistic, paternalistic state." He is a major opponent of expanded federal budgets, except when projects for his state (like the Arkansas River navigation channel) are proposed. He has worked assiduously, and even staged investigatory hearings, to protect the interests of the First National Bank of Little Rock, of which he is a board member and major stockholder.* McClellan has authored major crime legislation and holds the U.S. Supreme Court chiefly responsible for what he perceives as a wave of crime, violence, and organized guerrilla warfare in the U.S. unprecedented since the Civil War. He is a drawling Southern Baptist who would probably be as much at home representing Mississippi or Alabama as his native Arkansas.

McClellan barely escaped defeat in the 1972 Democratic primary at the hands of David Pryor, a 37-year-old Congressman from McClellan's home town of Camden. Age-versus-youth, Congressional seniority, McClellan's big business ties, and Pryor's support from organized labor all figured in the campaign. While McClellan pointed to the heavy advantages of his seniority, Pryor said McClellan had used his Senate power just to represent "the big corporations, the influential wealthy, the arrogant rich, and the upper crust." McClellan, in an amazingly vigorous campaign for a man of his age, retaliated by proving that large national unions were backing Pryor—just part of a plot, McClellan said, of his old labor boss enemies "to buy a Senate seat from Arkansas." McClellan ended up the victor, but by a margin of only 4 percent.

Pryor may be heard from again, and his three House terms, during which he became a prominent advocate of America's often unheard and unheeded 20 million old people, deserve notice. Pryor became upset by what he heard were conditions in the country's 24,000 nursing homes, many of which make handsome profits with help of the $2 billion in federal assistance pumped into them each year. So he began to moonlight as a volunteer in Washington area nursing homes. His technique was simply to knock on nursing home doors, identify himself as David Pryor (but not as a Congressmen) and ask if he could spend some of his time helping the old folks.

After months of shaving shaky old men and writing letters for distressed old women, Pryor disclosed abominable conditions in the nursing homes. From across the country, thousands of letters poured into his office. Some told of outstanding facilities and kindly staffs. But many were plaintive cries for help, citing conditions of poor food and sometimes near-starvation diets, uncleanliness beyond description, petty thievery, cruelty, and overcharges. Pryor failed in his attempt to get a special House committee on the aged set up, but he had dramatized—as few other men in the largely anonymous ranks of the U.S. House are able to do—a national problem of serious dimensions.

One of the half dozen most influential men in the United States for the past several years has been Congressman Wilbur Daigh Mills from Kensett, a little town of 1,444 people located where the Ozark foothills meet the Delta. The reasons for Mills' power are twofold. First, the House of Repre-

* McClellan's bank holdings and related hearings of his subcommittee are discussed fully in *The Case Against Congress,* by Drew Pearson and Jack Anderson (New York: Simon & Schuster, 1968), pp. 195–196. I remember being shocked a few years ago when the First National Bank of Little Rock ran an advertisement in the local press, just before election time, featuring a picture of McClellan and carrying a glowing description of his sagacity and contribution to the bank as a director.

sentatives originates, according to specific provision in the Constitution, all tax legislation; the committee from which it must come is Mills' Ways and Means Committee. Second, Mills is as masterful a legislative craftsman as the U.S. has known in modern times. Part of this is based on his expertise; he has, for instance, a grasp of the tax code unmatched by any other member of Congress and can cite section after section almost by heart. He is also the chief Capitol Hill expert on trade legislation, on welfare, and on Social Security—all matters that fall under the purview of his committee. Mills' mastery of these subjects has been achieved by heroic dedication to his work. He seldom reads anything not related to his committee's work, lives extremely modestly, shuns the Washington cocktail party, and has rarely taken a vacation. Until 1971, he had never traveled outside the United States. He runs his committee by letting everyone talk and debate to their heart's content and then slowly forming a consensus; since an initial reversal in early 1958, when the House rejected a bill from his committee, he has seen to it that he never again loses a major bill on the floor.

The criticism based on this approach follows almost naturally: by being "an expert in followmanship," submitting to endless delays to get a fail-proof bill, Mills fails to get through the basic reforms and changes in the American tax system which most economists say are desperately needed, and which Mills himself had dreamed for years of effecting. A related criticism is that he worries too much about reaction in his Arkansas district, when the fact is he has had no opposition there for years and is so popular he could take practically any stand he liked.

Those criticisms, and the personality of Wilbur Mills himself, flow out of his own youth in backwoods Kensett, where his father slowly built himself up from country store clerk to owning a cotton gin and running the local bank. Mills attended Hendrix College in Arkansas and Harvard Law School, and after four years as a youthful county judge he won election to Congress in 1938. The late Sam Rayburn made a spot for him on Ways and Means in 1943, and 15 years later, through the inexorable workings of seniority, Mills became chairman. Flamboyance is outside Mills' ken; his demeanor has frequently been likened to that of the small-town banker his father was, and he glories in the patient, slow-moving, harmonious ways of the House. When he made a bid for the 1972 Democratic Presidential nomination, he was obviously outside his element and began to make ill-advised policy decisions in his committee. It was also in 1972 that Mills, who is normally very jealous of the prerogatives of the House, pushed through a bill (later killed in the Senate) to let the President cut any appropriations he liked to hold the national budget to a set figure. It would have been one of the most serious abrogations of congressional authority in history; Mills was believed to have done it because of his concern about runaway budget figures, but many of his House colleagues were chagrined. And he may now have passed the zenith of his strength because of House reforms enhancing the power of the Speaker and the Democratic Caucus at the expense of the once all-powerful committee chairmen. The Caucus, for instance, has undermined the closed rule, which obliged the House to vote simply yes or no on bills coming out of Ways and Means, without a possibility of floor amendment. In the future, it will only take a majority of the caucus to direct that revenue bills be opened to multiple amendment. And Mills' capacity to work out compromises within his committee has been undermined by increasing ideological divisions, exacerbated by the growing watchdog function of consumer-minded groups.

At home in Arkansas, Mills has rarely if ever exerted substantial influence, though he has great reserve power. He has worked closely with state administrations, which see him as an unofficial state ambassador in Washington. He must bear some responsibility for the Faubus era, which he condoned and never opposed.

A shadow was thrown over Mills' future in 1973 when he said that unless pain from a degenerated spinal disc improved, he might retire from Congress at the end of 1974.

The Ballads of Stone County

One thing about Arkansas is happily not changing, and that by one of the most simply conceived but farsighted plans of our times: to preserve in the exquisite, wild country of Stone County, close by the primeval Ozarks National Forest, a strain of music and folk culture which has been handed down to this generation, almost untouched, from a distant earlier time. The first settlers came up the White River, a tributary of the Mississippi, early in the 19th century, from Tennessee and Kentucky, bringing with them their native music and instruments, such as the mountain dulcimer and the autoharp. From generation to generation, the ballads were handed down. And as the 20th century and mass culture gathered momentum, Stone County remained a kind of hidden crevasse in which the Anglo-Saxon culture of old lived on, the people stoically enduring the crop failures and howling winters and sicknesses and early deaths that had always been their lot, and nurturing a hope of heaven when all would be righted, and singing ballads about it all.

The center of interest is Mountain View, where the road "drops down" into a village of 1,866 souls. In 1963 some Mountain Viewers cast about for ways to start some local business that would draw federal money for a new water system and better schools. Up to then, the area had absolutely no industry beyond salad bowls and wood carving, and there were no more than a dozen people in Mountain View earning as much as $10,000 a year. So the idea evolved: why not make an industry of ourselves? Why not have a large folk art festival, with music, and try to draw thousands of visitors? The idea caught on quickly, with first and continuing support from Jimmy Driftwood, who lived on a Stone County farm and was known to thousands for his *Battle of New Orleans* in the late 1950s. Hundreds of Stone Countians became involved, and the spring of 1963 there were 20,000 visitors on hand for the first big festival, and by the end of the decade almost twice that number were coming for a big weekend each spring with such singing luminaries as Driftwood, Bookmiller Shannon, Bobby Blair, Seth Mize, and Grandma Rainbow offering their talents.

And from the festival grew the idea of a folk cultural center. Wilbur Mills became interested, the Ozark Folk Cultural Center Commission was formed, and the Economic Development Administration granted $3.9 million, some 80 percent of the cost. The Center, opened in 1973, includes an amphitheater to seat 1,200 and a marketplace for folk arts and crafts.

So Mountain View will have its year-round industry, and its people perhaps more of the comforts of the modern world. But there will still be that one great festival weekend each spring, when the thousands of campfires around Mountain View might convince a nighttime visitor that Coxey's Army had re-encamped. The flower children are there, and older folks too. The attraction? Here at last is a place in America with roots that run true and deep. Here is a place where the plastic civilization is still held at bay, a longed-for remnant of our America when it was younger, and purer, and simpler.

MISSISSIPPI

HOPE AT LAST

THE LONG WINTER OF Mississippi's discontent is ending, and some of its black and moderate white leaders, who endured the bitter years, are rubbing their eyes in disbelief.

Lt. Gov. William Winter, one of the most progressive white politicians, has observed: "Compared to where we were in the mid-1960s, we've come a thousand light-years."

Wilson F. Minor, veteran Mississippi correspondent for the New Orleans *Times-Picayune*, has said: "The monolith of segregation and bitter-end resistance has crumbled and a new kind of society is arising." (Minor should know whereof he speaks. As Robert L. T. Smith, a longtime NAACP leader in Mississippi, said of Minor and Jerry W. DeLaughter, former Jackson correspondent for the Memphis *Commercial-Appeal*: "They stood up back yonder when it was dangerous to tell the whole truth. They're courageous men.")

Charles Evers, the Democratic National Committeeman, mayor of Fayette, and one of the most articulate black leaders in America, described for me the change since the day in 1963 when his brother Medgar, head of the Mississippi NAACP, was ambushed and killed by a white racist:

> Mississippi has done a complete about-face. It's not as safe as we hope it to be, but as far as the idea of being against a person just because he's black, that's just about faded.
>
> Ten years ago—when Medgar was killed—there was not a single black elected

official in the entire state. And now we have the third highest number of black elected officials in the country.

When Medgar was alive, we couldn't get a drink of water, we couldn't get a hamburger, other than in some black place—"nigger joint," they used to call them. And now we can go anywhere we got the money and buy 'em without a problem. I can walk into any restaurant with my secretary, who happens to be white, and I doubt if they'd even look around. If we'd even been caught near a white restaurant in the early 1960s, there probably would have been a lynching or burning.

On the economic front, many blacks who were down at the welfare level 10 years ago are now living in the $8,000–$10,000–$12,000 a year bracket. Much of it is poverty program and other federally funded programs. But we're there.

At this time 10 years ago, there wasn't a single school in Mississippi integrated. Now I don't know of a school here that doesn't have blacks and whites in it.

There are some of the things we've done. It's been a lot of work, a lot of suffering, and we have a long ways to go yet.

The most important thing: black folks ain't scared anymore. And white people begin to realize that they got to live with us. And they aren't as mean as they used to be. They're mean, but not as mean as they used to be.

There were a lot of whites in the crowd, in fact, when 9,000 people gathered at the state fairgrounds in Jackson in 1973 to commemorate the tenth anniversary of Medgar Evers' death. Governor William L. Waller made the occasion official by issuing a proclamation declaring the Medgar Evers memorial festival day.

William Winter agreed that there was still racial prejudice in Mississippi, but that "as far as its coloring every element of life as it did so long, that's no longer the case." When I asked him why, he replied: "The basic common sense of the people came to be asserted."

He might have added that the cumulative weight of federal laws and civil rights enforcement, a weight the likes of which the national government had not brought to bear on one of the states in this century, created the climate in which the flower of reason and decency could bloom. To the old adage, that laws cannot create morality—or at least provide a milieu in which fruitful change can occur—the Mississippi experience gives the lie, clearly and decisively.

In all that transpired, no small role was played by the armies of freedom riders and civil rights activists, the liberal lawyers and poverty workers and assorted do-gooders who poured into Mississippi in the 1960s. Working for and with the long downtrodden blacks of Mississippi, they meddled in the prototype of the closed society. They were deeply and bitterly resented, and some paid with their lives. But in the end, they overcame.*

So it is that today the national media no longer flood Mississippi with reporters and television crews to record the most dramatic story of racial confrontation of 20th-century America. To quote Bill Minor again: "Now that Mississippi has settled down to accept integration of the races in schools, jobs, public accommodations, businesses, voting, and other areas without resorting to the bomb, the torch, or the lynch gang, it is no longer regarded

* James W. Silver wrote in *Mississippi: The Closed Society* that "the chief function of civil rights workers of whatever description has been to offer their bodies and their minds as catalysts in the creation of a nationwide public opinion that, in turn, would demand action in Washington, a mission in which they have been eminently successful."

as the quaintest society in the nation." Mississippi recedes into the shadows of national attention, to nurture its wounds and heal its scars and grasp for a new identity. "We're in the process of learning," Charles Evers said. "White folks don't know black people, and black folks don't know white people. But many of us are now beginning to realize we got to begin to know each other."

But, one asks, can the bitter legacy be laid to rest so easily? Some distinguished Mississippians think the answer is clearly "no." Hodding Carter III, editor of the Greenville *Delta Democrat-Times*, whose late father fought a long and lonely battle for moderation, said it was true that the racial tone of the state had changed and that "the grudging acceptance of what has occurred is pretty much complete. But if you write that given a little help from Washington, we wouldn't revert pretty damn fast, you'd be wrong. The medicine (of integration) is being taken, but a great number of people still think it's medicine."

While Mississippi today is obeying the federal law, it is not yet fully prepared to take the thousands of voluntary steps, public and private, which must come if it is to be, as some of its sons and daughters hope, the vanguard of a truly biracial society. Until those steps come, Mississippi's whites and blacks will be unable to escape their common damnation: a standard of living, of culture, of health, and of political participation far below the norm in modern America, and usually flat 50th among the 50 states. No other state has such a low per capita income (only 67 percent of the national average). None has so many poor people (35 percent). None has such a large share of substandard housing. Only one other (Arkansas) has such low teacher salaries. None has so few newspaper readers. None has so few physicians proportionate to the population. None has such a high infant mortality rate. And few are so high in illiteracy, so low in educational attainment, so high in murder rates, or so low in the share of citizens who take part in elections.

Forty years ago, H. L. Mencken did a series for the *American Mercury* rating all the states in terms of their wealth and culture, their health and civic affairs. Mississippi ranked last then. It still ranks last today.

The primordial Mississippian cared not what Mencken or any of us outsiders concluded; for him there was satisfaction in the business of living in an undisturbed, inward-directed society. The late William Faulkner of Oxford, Mississippi, said of that Mississippian and his milieu: "Loving all of it even while he had to hate some of it because . . . you don't love because; you love despite; not for the virtues, but despite the faults."

Yet our venture here is sociological, not romantic, and it has to be said that a lack of diversity has been one reason that Mississippi failed to generate the interior forces that might have led to constructive social change. An isolated society, by its very nature, repels outsiders. The 1970 Census showed that only 14 percent of Mississippi's population had been born in another state; in 1940 the figure had been 9 percent—the lowest "mobility factor" of any American state. Mississippi's lack of cities—the classic breeding ground of new thought and social change in human society

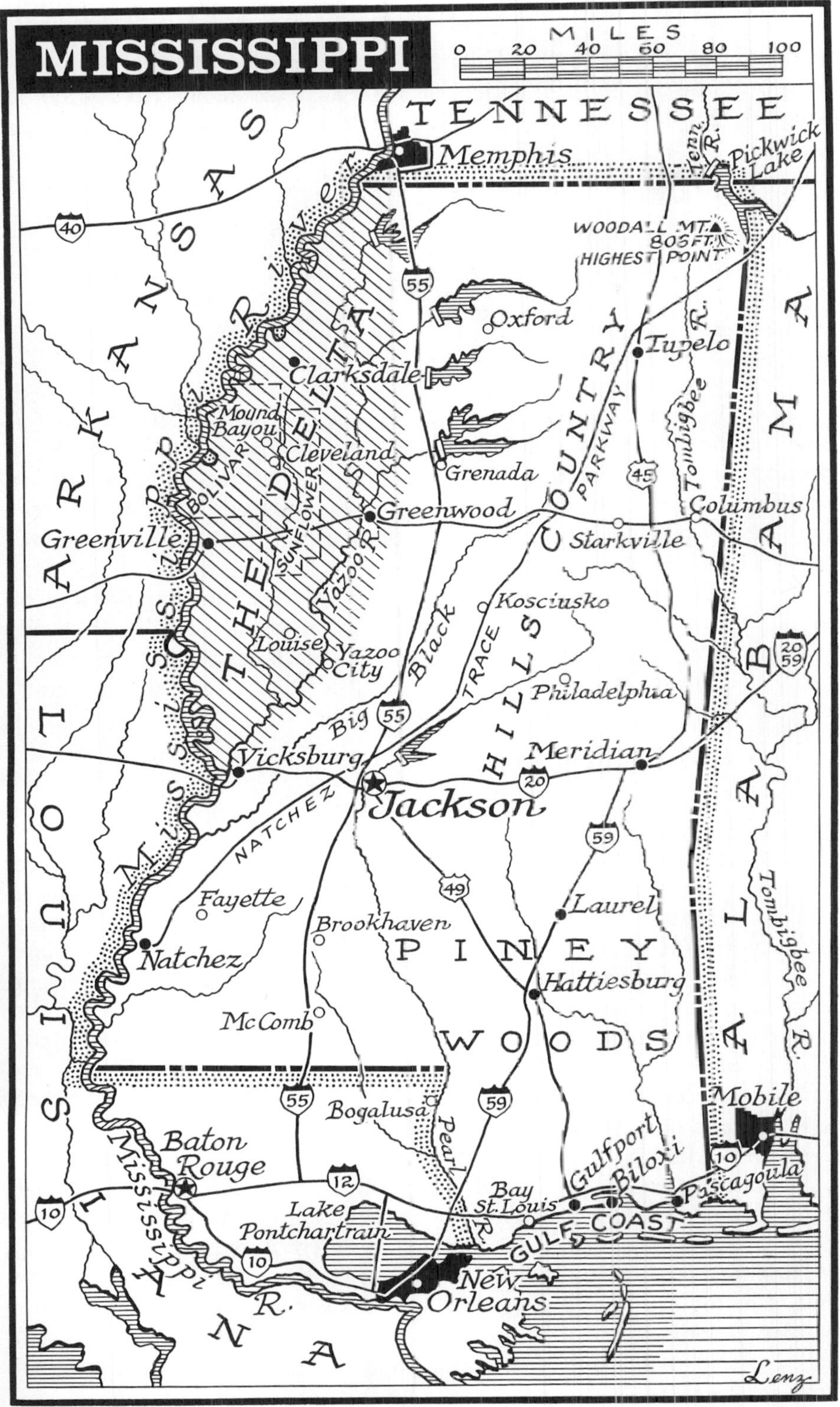
MISSISSIPPI
MILES
0 20 40 60 80 100
TENNESSEE
ARKANSAS
LOUISIANA
ALABAMA
Memphis
Pickwick Lake
Tenn. R.
WOODALL MT. 806 FT. HIGHEST POINT
Oxford
Tupelo
Clarksdale
Mound Bayou
Cleveland
BOLIVAR
SUNFLOWER
Grenada
Greenwood
Greenville
Starkville
Columbus
Tombigbee R.
THE DELTA
HILLS COUNTRY
NATCHEZ TRACE PARKWAY
Yazoo R.
Mississippi River
Kosciusko
Louise
Yazoo City
Black
Big
Philadelphia
Vicksburg
Meridian
Jackson
Fayette
Natchez
Brookhaven
Laurel
PINEY WOODS
Hattiesburg
McComb
Bogalusa
Pearl R.
Mobile
Baton Rouge
Gulfport
Biloxi
Pascagoula
Bay St. Louis
Lake Pontchartrain
GULF COAST
New Orleans
Mississippi R.
40
55
45
20
20 59
59
49
12
10
Lenz

—also contributed to the insularity. The percentage of Mississippi's people living on farms and in little villages of less than 2,500 people has constantly exceeded that in every other Southern state and the United States as a whole:

	Percentage Rural	
Year	*Mississippi*	*United States*
1860	97.4%	80.2%
1900	92.3	60.4
1940	80.2	43.5
1960	62.3	30.1
1970	55.5	26.5

A study in the *Journal of Politics,* by John L. Sullivan, ranked all the states in the degree of diversity within them in the 1960s—in levels of education, income, and occupation, in regard to the proportion of first- or second-generation immigrants from abroad, and in regard to differing religions. Mississippi turned out to be the least diverse, the most homogeneous state of all the 50 on the scale.

But what Sullivan did not include, and what one finds at the root of Mississippi's problems, no matter what statistical strand he takes in hand, is the matter of race. That conflict of white and black has plagued Mississippi through every year of its history, has diminished the lives of both the races, and still remains to be fully resolved in our time.

Seeds of the Legacy

The white man's domination of his black brother—first as chattel, then as sharecropper in an overwhelmingly rural society—has been the leitmotif of Mississippi history. For two-thirds of the state's history, starting in antebellum years and running clear up to the 1930s, there were actually more Negroes than whites in Mississippi. In 1860 the population was 55 percent black—and slave. And today, while sharply reduced by outmigration, the black population share (36.8 percent) is the highest of any American state.

The transcendent event of Mississippi history was the Civil War. As a result of that conflict, the white plantation owners lost ownership of 437,000 slaves, whose value was more than $218 million. Yet most of that was quite new wealth when it was lost, and the fact is that Mississippi did not have many years to "enjoy" the antebellum existence it would later romanticize beyond belief. It was a rough-hewn, raw frontier society with only 40,000 people in 1810, and when it became a state seven years later, two-thirds of its land area was still in Indian hands. But in those antebellum years the price of cotton was high, the price of land was low, and through fast-moving speculation and settlement the pattern was set for the exploitive and closed society which would cripple human development in the state for more than a century to follow.

Mississippi was second only to South Carolina in seceding from the

Union, and one of its United States Senators, Jefferson Davis, became president of the Confederacy. The human toll of the war was immense; Mississippi sent 78,000 men into the fight—more than its total male population between the ages of 18 and 45—but only 28,000 of them returned. In his book *The Past that Would Not Die*, Walter Lord provided a graphic picture of the devastation in which Mississippi lay when the war ended.* Jackson, Meridian, and other cities lay in ashes and "Mississippi seemed but a forest of chimneys." Most of the cotton was confiscated as Confederate property; a third of the farm animals were carried off; land values crashed. Nearly everyone's personal wealth was wiped out. Before the war, Mississippi had been the country's fifth wealthiest state; afterwards it was last (and still is today).

The Mississippi story for the remainder of the century closely paralleled that of its sister Southern states: an original period of pure anarchy after Appomattox; then imposition of the infamous Black Code in an effort to re-enslave the black man in fact if not in law; the angry reaction of Congress in nullifying the Confederate-dominated state government and imposing Reconstruction rule under which Negroes controlled much of the political structure; the recapture of the government by white Bourbons in 1875, accompanied by the refusal of a strife-weary national government to intervene, and finally, around 1890, the imposition of the Jim Crow laws and the almost total disenfranchisement of the black man.

The uniqueness of the Mississippi story in those years was the ferocity with which these things took place, the lack of moderate voices, the uninhibited violence, and the utter and abject poverty which endured for decade after decade. When the war ended, hundreds of thousands of freedmen roamed the state, thinking that emancipation meant they need work no more, eating off the federal troops—almost all of whom were Negroes after August 1865. Before the war it had been illegal to teach slaves how to read or write; now 95 percent of them were illiterate, and few had any idea of citizenship or responsibility. The badly outnumbered whites recoiled in horror at the prospect of Negro equality. As Walter Lord noted:

> To the ordinary Mississippian political equality automatically led to social equality, which in turn automatically led to race-mixing. It was inevitable—and unthinkable. To a people brought up to believe that Negroes were genetically inferior—after all, that was why they were slaves—the mere hint of "mongrelization" was appalling. And all the more so in view of the homage paid white Southern womanhood. It was she who had sacrificed so much, whose purity, in fact, carried on the whole system. She was everything.
>
> Of course there were other factors too. Cotton planters didn't want their field hands getting out of line; the redneck farmers worried about Negroes taking their bread. Yet these were areas where something might be worked out; but there could be no compromise—not an inch—on anything that might open the door to race-mixing. Emancipation made absolutely no difference. "A monkey with his tail off," explained the Natchez *Courier*, "is a monkey still."

So it was no surprise when the Jackson *Daily News* announced in November 1865: "We must keep the ex-slave in a position of inferiority. We must

* I am indebted to Lord for much of the background in the ensuing account.

pass such laws as will make him *feel* his inferiority." William Faulkner echoed the same thing years later when he had the Mississippian say: "We got to make him a nigger first. He's got to admit he's a nigger."

Mississippi led the South with the first of the Black Codes. The state's law forbade that any Negro vote, or keep firearms, or "make insulting gestures," and stipulated that any Negro over 18 who had no job could be declared a vagrant, fined $50, and turned over to any "master or mistress" who would pay the fine for him. The black man would be chattel again.

Reconstruction ended the Black Code, and for a few heady years Negroes rose to more political prominence in Mississippi than in any other state. More than half the electorate was Negro. In the legislature, there were 64 Negroes and 24 carpetbaggers. Two Negroes were sent to the United States Senate to represent Mississippi, and one to the U.S. House. The lieutenant governor and several other statewide officeholders were blacks. And the Reconstruction governor was a former Union officer. Corruption and incompetence marked the Reconstruction rule, but the Reconstruction government did all it could for the people (given the destitution of the state), laying the groundwork, for example, of public education. Many of the Negro legislators were well-educated clergymen, and the carpetbaggers, Southern myth notwithstanding, were often solid Middle Westerners who had come to farm, not to loot. Reconstruction was brief—from 1867 to 1875—but decisive for future Mississippi politics, since it offered "proof" to the state's whites that Negroes and Republicans were either fools or knaves.

The white Democrats broke Reconstruction by sheer intimidation of white Republicans and Negroes—gunfire at political rallies, threats to blacks who voted Republican that they would lose their jobs, ostracism for nonconforming whites. The cotton-owning Democratic gentry took control of Mississippi government again, and for a few years "good" Negroes were allowed considerable leeway—access to public accommodations, voting, holding minor offices, and the like.

So even at that point, some half-reasonable *modus vivendi* might have been maintained between the two races if it had not been for Mississippi's seemingly unbreakable, wretched poverty. High tariffs and discriminatory freight rates stifled all efforts at economic recovery. The government in Washington came forward with no 19th-century Marshall Plan; in fact, between 1865 and 1875 the federal government spent $21 million on public works in Massachusetts and New York but only a paltry $185,000 in Mississippi and Arkansas. Per capita wealth was only 26 percent of what it was in the Northern states. The Mississippi state government economized brutally, perpetuating illiteracy by spending only $2 a head on schoolchildren (compared to $20 in Massachusetts). "Whether holding out in some paint-peeled mansion or hanging on in the squalor of a dogtrot cabin," Lord wrote, "most Mississippians knew only the bitterest poverty."

As the economic situation continued to fester, white Mississippians could never dispel from their minds the specter of the majority blacks rising up to gain power, perhaps through federal intervention. The landed gentry controlled state politics in part through the controlled black vote they commanded in the old plantation lowlands, but the cost of that control—one or two dollars a vote—was a burden to them and could not offset their fear of a black political revolt. And the Reconstruction-era constitution, still in effect, was a continuing offense to the whites' sense of pride and "Southern rightness." So a constitutional convention was called in 1890 to legalize the methods of all-white, Democratic party control. It was at that convention that Judge J. J. Chrisman made an oft-quoted speech that defined the farmers' problem quite specifically:

> It is no secret that there has not been a full vote or a fair count in Mississippi since 1875—that we have been preserving the ascendancy of the white people by revolutionary methods. . . . We have been stuffing the ballot boxes, committing perjury, and here and there . . . carrying the election by fraud and violence until the whole machinery for the elections is about to rot down.

In view of the 15th Amendment, which specifically guaranteed Negroes the right to vote, the 1890 constitution-writers had a ticklish problem in disenfranchising the blacks without incurring the wrath of the federal courts. They accomplished their purpose first by imposing a poll tax as a prerequisite for voting, on the theory that it would prove a much greater barrier for impoverished blacks than for whites. Then they increased residency requirements for voting to two years in the state and one year in the election district, reasoning that blacks were less likely to keep long residence anywhere. Finally, they required that all voters had to read any section of the state constitution, or understand it when read to them, and then be able to interpret its meaning. The sole judge of whether an applicant had passed or not was the registrar, inevitably a white person. Thus most unqualified whites could pass, and blacks, no matter how exalted their education, could be rejected.

The 1890 constitution, Sen. Theodore Bilbo could boast half a century later, was a document "that damn few white men and no niggers at all can explain." But it was so successful in disenfranchising black people—legally and permanently—that the "Mississippi Plan," as it came to be known, was rapidly adopted by most of the other Southern states.

At the same time, innumerable Jim Crow laws were put on the Mississippi statute books: eventually they applied to every kind of public accommodation, transportation, and even cemeteries. The caste system had become enshrined in law and would remain that way until the 1960s. When Mississippi adopted a direct primary in 1902, the law was predictably written so that whites only could participate. To shake hands with a Negro, to call him "Mr." or "Mrs.," was to break the code. And when the black man refused to act in total deference to whites, he was in danger of being killed. According to statistics compiled by the Tuskegee Institute, 538 Negroes were lynched in Mississippi between 1883 and 1959. A sixth of all the lynchings in America in those years occurred in Mississippi; in no other state was the figure so high.

White supremacy was so thoroughly entrenched by the 1890 constitution that the Negro no longer counted in Mississippi politics, except as an oratorical whipping boy, and other divisions could come to the fore. The essential conflict was between the Delta and the Hills, or as it has frequently been put, between the planters and the "rednecks." The planters were concentrated in the rich alluvial Delta plain that stretches along two-thirds of the state's western border beside the Mississippi River; essentially conservative and devoted to agricultural and corporate interests, they were Mississippi's version of an aristocracy, and while they subjugated and exploited the black man, they professed abhorrence of the overt violence of the rednecks. (Their protestations had to be taken with a grain of salt. There were many lynchings in the Delta, for instance.) The Hills, encompassing most of the remainder of Mississippi, were less fertile and peopled by hardscrabble farmers of minimal literacy who hoped that state government—through decent public roads, free textbooks, and the like—could do something to alleviate their miserable lot. They were influenced to an extent by the Populist movement which bloomed in the 1890s, but the Mississippi version of Populism added vitriolic anti-Negro harangues to the standard fare of anticorporationism and resentment against the banks and vested interests.

One of the great aristocratic families of the South was the Percys of Washington County, in the heart of the Delta. Leroy Percy represented Mississippi for several years in the U.S. Senate, only to see his reputation finally torn to shreds by the epitome of redneckism, Theodore G. Bilbo. Years later Percy's son, William Alexander Percy, would describe his impression of an audience of Hillsmen to which his father spoke. The statement is a classic expression of Bourbon prejudice against lower-class whites, yet very worth recording:

> I looked over the ill-dressed, surly audience, unintelligent and slinking, and heard him appeal to them for fair treatment of the Negro and explain to them the tariff and the Panama tolls situation. I studied them as they milled about. They were the sort of people that lynch Negroes, that mistake hoodlumism for wit, and cunning for intelligence, that attend revivals and fight and fornicate in the bushes afterwards. They were undiluted Anglo-Saxons. They were the sovereign voter.

The first man to break up the closed circle of planter leadership was the "Great White Chief" of the Hillsmen, James K. Vardaman. A classic Southern populist-demagogue, Vardaman burst on the scene in 1903, campaigning for governor in a large lumber wagon drawn by eight white oxen. He was for the common man, against the corporations, for better schools in the Hills, for which the Delta would pay. And he appealed to race hatreds with cynicism and ugly rhetoric. The Negro, he said, was a "veneered savage" who, "like the mule, has neither pride of ancestry nor hope of posterity." "Why squander money on his education," Vardaman said, "when the only effect is to spoil a good field hand and make an insolent cook? . . . the way to control the nigger is to whip him when he does not obey without it."

Vardaman won the governorship, inaugurating an era of moderate reform including county agricultural schools for whites, a state normal college, regulation of child labor, and the like. The semiprogressive strain continued even when he went off to succeed Percy in the U.S. Senate, but all the while more Jim Crow laws were being added to the statute books.

Bilbo succeeded Vardaman as Mississippi's prime demagogue, serving twice as governor (1916–20, and 1928–32) and as U.S. Senator from 1934 until his death in 1947. As governor, he did put through some reforms in the field of education, and in the 1930s he voted for New Deal programs—TVA, REA, and anything he thought would help the marginal white farmers of the South. But, in character, Bilbo deserves his reputation as one of the most reprehensible men ever to appear in American politics. In 1910 he came within a single vote of being expelled from the state senate after making a false claim that he had accepted a bribe in voting on the U.S. Senate seat at issue between Percy and Vardaman. His colleagues did pass a resolution pronouncing him "unfit to sit with honest, upright men in a respectable legislative body." Just before his death in 1947, a U.S. Senate Committee found that "Senator Bilbo improperly used his high office as a United States Senator for his personal dealings with war contractors."

William Alexander Percy described Bilbo as

> a pert little monster, glib and shameless, with that sort of cunning common to criminals which passes for intelligence. The people loved him. They loved him not because they were deceived by him, but because they understood him thoroughly; they said of him proudly, "He's a slick little bastard." He was one of them and he had risen from obscurity to the fame of glittering infamy—it was as if they themselves had crashed the headlines.

The same "he may be a bastard but he's our bastard" reasoning, incidentally, is not unique to Mississippi; it was said to be a reason that the people of Harlem tolerated Adam Clayton Powell during his later and more corrupt years, or why the people of southern Illinois tolerated and were proud of their Democratic secretary of state, Paul Powell, one of the biggest thieves ever to be involved in state government.

But Bilbo's oratory—filled with obscenities and Biblical references learned during his early days as a Baptist preacher—set him apart. Once he described an opponent as "a cross between a hyena and a mongrel . . . begotten in a nigger graveyard at midnight, suckled by a sow, and educated by a fool." (Bilbo got a pistol whipping in return for that sally.) On another occasion he called on "every red-blooded American to get out and see that no nigger votes." Today a bronze statue of Bilbo stands in the rotunda of the State Capitol at Jackson. When I looked at it, several adjectives flitted through my mind—"short, stocky, arrogant, reckless." But the overall impression could be boiled down to one word—"uncouth."

Part of Mississippi lore, in fact, is a story going back to the days when Bilbo was governor and a paternity suit was filed against one of the state officials by a country girl who had been working as a secretary in the State Capitol. There was a suggestion that Bilbo himself may have partaken of the young lady's pleasures, and he was sought as a character witness in the trial. Bilbo used every stratagem he could think of to avoid a subpoena, but the process servers finally cornered him on his farm one day and chased him through the house to the barn, where the governor was cornered standing behind a heifer calf. There he was handed the subpoena as photographers ignited their flashbulbs. A Jackson paper wrote an editorial about "the shame of Mississippi," extending its sympathies to the misused country girl, to the lovely Mrs. Bilbo who had suffered such indignities over the years, and particularly to the heifer calf. Bilbo held a council of war with his advisers on how to handle the situation, at which he finally exclaimed, "O well, never yet beat a man for public office to get himself a piece of ass."

An even more rabid racist—as if that were possible—was Bilbo's contemporary, Mississippi Congressman John Rankin. Palmer Weber, a former Southern labor organizer, told me: "If a black man got on the elevator with Rankin, the blood would come up in his face. I saw it actually happen myself, in the House Office Building elevator. He couldn't stand the sight." On the day that Estes Kefauver, then a Congressman from Chattanooga, voted for the federal anti-poll tax bill, John Rankin ran across the House floor and jumped on Kefauver's back like a little dog, shouting, "Traitor! Traitor! Traitor!"

Under the spell of blatant racism and demagoguery, furiously resistant to new ideas or change, tied to a slowly declining one-crop economy, Mississippi continued to stagnate through the first half of this century. The 1920s brought the revival of the Ku Klux Klan, the boll weevil, and disastrous floods. The 1930s brought the Great Depression, tumbling cotton prices, and Negro wages sinking to ten cents an hour. Some industries began to appear in the 1940s, helped along by World War II and a new set of laws passed to help industry, but even in 1950, 43 percent of the people still made their living from farming. Jackson, the closest thing to a major city that might serve as a catalyst for growth, had only 4.5 percent of the state population in 1950. For every person moving into Mississippi, 10 were leaving, and some counties had fewer people than they had in 1900, or even 1840. The outflow of black Mississippians—many riding the Jim Crow cars of the Illinois Central line straight north to Chicago—had begun as a trickle around the time of World War I. By the 1940s, it had reached a mighty flood: in that single decade, 326,000 black people left Mississippi. But whites were leaving, too: 108,000 in the same decade, for instance. Three-quarters of the college graduates saw no future in Mississippi and departed.

The School Decision and Its Afterburn

Surveying the Mississippi scene of 1950, Walter Lord noted a peculiar air of isolation in the state. No major Presidential candidate had been there since Henry Clay. The only bookstore in Jackson was run by the Baptist Church and sold religious titles only; at Oxford, the state's supposed center of learning, there was not a single regular bookstore.

> The tendency to conform [Lord wrote] was enormous. Far more than elsewhere, men wore the same necktie (dark), drove the same cars (cream colored), lived for the same football games (Ole Miss-LSU), and above all belonged to the same party (Democratic). . . .
>
> The more postwar America changed, the more Mississippi retreated into its own self-contained little world. Bypassed by the march of events, the state saw little connection between itself and all the strange new things going on—the UN, Marshall Plan, NATO, welfare measures at home. All that meant only more cen-

tralized government, and the people were in no mood for that—states' rights were the very heart of the South's solution to the race problem. . . .

The state officially observed Confederate Memorial Day, Lee's and Jefferson Davis' birthday—while studiously ignoring Lincoln and the national Memorial Day. . . . Confederate flags hung from porches all over the state; and in case anyone ever needed reminding, there was always the reproachful gaze of the noble stone soldier who stood atop the Confederate monument in every courthouse square . . .

Lord God of hosts,
Be with us yet,
Lest we forget,
Lest we forget.

So ran the lovingly carved inscription on the monument at Kosciusko. . . . The inscription went on to promise that "the South will live forever in the glory of your world."

But Mississippi's days in its Confederate time capsule were numbered. Step by step, the brave and brash lawyers of the NAACP in New York and Washington had been winning cases against segregated universities in the border South. Now, in 1950, they decided that the time had come for a frontal attack on the public school system, on the doctrine of "separate but equal" that had been used to keep the races separate since the end of the 19th century. Plaintiffs from four states were found—understandably, not from Mississippi; one shudders to think what would have happened if a Mississippi black had dared to put his name on that suit. But in no state would the decision in *Brown et al v. Board of Education of Topeka,* finally handed down on May 17, 1954, have such a momentous impact. The impact would be delayed for years, but its reverberations would change every aspect of the closed society.

Consider, for instance, Mississippi schools. Some grim figures explain what "separate but equal" had meant there. In 1950 the rigidly segregated system was spending a low $78.70 a year for each white pupil. It was spending $23.83, *less than a third as much,* for each Negro pupil. The salaries of white teachers averaged $1,865 a year, those of Negro teachers only $918. And the average Negro class had 31 percent more children in it. Actually, Mississippi was trying by 1954 to equalize its exenditures between the two races in order to stave off an unfavorable court decision. But the historic pattern was indisputable. In 1945 Negro schoolteachers had averaged only $398 a year in pay, compared to $1,108 for whites. Over most of the earlier decades, most black children in the state had been educated in one- and two-teacher sheds and cabins and old churches, often without desks; in 1930, the vast majority of Negro schoolteachers had not even finished high school.

Mississippi's reaction to the *Brown* decision was predictable and swift. "A black day of tragedy," the Jackson *Clarion-Ledger* said. For if applied, Mississippi knew, the decision would be a blow to the solar plexus of the segregated society. According to the state's ancient folklore, race mixing in the classroom would lead to interracial marriage, and mongrelization of the races, and a destruction of the supreme white race. Mississippi Circuit Court

Judge (and later State Supreme Court Justice) Tom P. Brady rushed into print with a book entitled *Black Monday*—the designation Mississippi politicians quickly applied to the day of the Supreme Court's decision. In the forward march of civilization, Judge Brady wrote, "the negroid man, like the modern lizard, evolved not." By contrast, he continued, "The loveliest and purest of God's creatures, the nearest thing to an angelic being that treads this terrestial ball is a well-bred, cultured Southern white woman or her blue-eyed, golden-haired little girl."

At Indianola, in the Delta black belt, the first Citizens Council was organized in the summer of 1954, and by the next year the movement had ballooned to some 60,000 members, all Mississippi community leaders intent on preventing any Negro inroads into "the Southern way of life." The Citizens Councils professed to oppose any type of violence and screened their membership to exclude those "with the Ku Klux Klan mentality." But they were immensely powerful because they included the most respected and influential people in each community—bankers, planters, merchants, and politicians. It was a coterie that could apply frightful pressure on dissenters, whether white or black, in the enclosed, isolated Mississippi society. In some communities, Negroes who instituted desegregation suits or petitioned for school integration or even registered to vote suddenly found themselves out of work, thanks to the action of Council members. And not long after that, a string of shootings of black voting registration workers began. The murders were not traced back to Council members; indeed there were no convictions, and even if a Council member had been guilty in a case, the structure of the Councils was so loose that it might have been his personal, irresponsible act. Yet by their very presence and rhetoric, the Councils created a climate in which racial murder could be tolerated still longer in Mississippi.

Some 15 years after the birth of the Citizens Councils, their long-term leader, William Simmons, explained in an interview in his ultramodern Jackson office that the Councils still had 80,000 hard-core active members spread across the South and a handful of locations in the northern states. At one time or another, he said, 350,000 people had belonged. But it was clear that the Councils were no longer the force they had been in the 1950s and early 1960s, when no Mississippi politician in his right mind would have dared to cross them. Instead, they were reduced to organizing private schools as desegregation finally got underway.* Simmons remained as he appeared to reporters in the 1950s—urbane, sweetly reasonable in his own way, but unbending in his advocacy of "separate development" of the races. (He prefers that term, borrowed from South Africa, to "segregation.") Simmons' office had the pictures of two politicians on the wall: one autographed by George Wallace, the other of Ian Smith of Rhodesia. Simmons said that even avowed integrationists would soon see the error of their ways "through bitter experience—physical fear, crime, and the schools turning into blackboard jungles." He said he favored resegregation of schools and public accommodations and would bar the government from forcing integration. But

* Until the federal courts declared the practice unconstitutional, the state government actually subsidized the segregation academies to the tune of $185 to $240 a year per child.

while he stressed the theme of "freedom," he favored giving the government the power to *stop* integration.

In the atmosphere of the 1950s and early 1960s, the Councils were no laughing matter. Their message played on Mississippian prejudice: that "the racial revolution seeking to wreck America's entire social system" was part of a "hideous" scheme, cooked up in the Soviet Union, "to mongrelize the races." Senator James Eastland, a close friend of the Councils, carried the message to the Senate floor in 1955:

> Will the South obey this decision of the Supreme Court [the *Brown* decision]? Who is obligated morally or legally to obey a decision whose authorities rest not upon the law but upon the writings and teachings of pro-communist agitators and people who have a long record of affiliations with anti-American causes and with agitators who are part and parcel of the communist conspiracy to destroy our country?

Mississippi, Eastland said, would simply "not abide by or obey" the decision. The Supreme Court had said the schools must be desegregated with "all deliberate speed"; Mississippi interpreted that to mean "never," and mountains of laws were put on the books to reinforce segregation. One law—a so-called interposition resolution—declared that Mississippi was "sovereign," had never delegated to the federal government any power over its schools, and thus was exempt from the "unconstitutional" decision of the Supreme Court. Another tried to cripple civil rights organizations by making it literally a crime to institute a desegregation suit in the state courts. There was a law abolishing common law marriages; the rationale behind that was that many Negro children were illegitimate and thus could be barred from the public schools on moral grounds. Yet another law, almost laughable in retrospect (and it was indeed vetoed by the governor) would have put any federal official in jail for five years if he tried to integrate schools, buses, or public facilities in Mississippi.

The legislature also established a State Sovereignty Commission to plan strategy for circumventing the integration decision. Several years later, it turned out that the Sovereignty Commission was channeling big chunks of money to the Citizens Councils. Before the practice was stopped, almost $200,000 of taxpayers' money had flowed to the white-collar bigots.

Moderate Mississippians drew back in fright in the face of the ugly mood of the '50s, and scarcely a voice was raised in defense of editor Hodding Carter when he wrote an article for *Look* warning of the Citizens Councils—"A Wave of Terror Threatens the South." The Mississippi house publicly censured Carter for "selling out the state for Yankee gold."

Only the once complacent blacks of Mississippi provided a major obstacle to the state's plans for resistance. Governor Hugh White in 1954 called together what he thought would be a group of "safe" Negroes to endorse his program of "separate but equal facilities." But the vote in the meeting went against him, 89 to 1. Almost all the Negroes on whom White had counted for support got up to oppose him. The climax came when the Reverend H. H. Humes, a known friend of the white man, said to his white hosts: "Gentlemen, you all should not be mad at us. Those were nine *white* men that rendered that decision. Not one colored man had anything to do with it. The real trouble is that you have given us schools too long in which we could study the earth through the floor and the stars through the roof."

Governor White's reaction to the Negroes' meeting was a classic. He asked the legislature (which quickly complied) to pass a constitutional amendment authorizing abolition of the state's public schools if necessary to preserve segregation. The Negroes had made the step necessary, White said, because they refused to pledge themselves to voluntary segregation—and now must suffer the responsibility for their action!

From interposition to abolition of the schools, the Mississippi resistance laws were patently unconstitutional and eventually either found so by the federal courts or allowed to atrophy. But still, scarcely anyone in Mississippi could imagine school integration actually occurring *there*, of all places in America. Contemplating the possibility in 1957, Governor J. P. Coleman—one of the least extreme Mississippi politicians of the period—said, "Not in 50 years, certainly not in my lifetime."

And for a while, it looked as if he might be right. Not until 1964 would the federal courts actually force the first trickle of black entrances into Mississippi's lily-white public schools, and not until 1969 were Negroes in various quantities attending schools with whites, mostly under "freedom of choice" plans, in 145 of the state's 148 school districts. Yet even then five-sixths of the black schoolchildren were still in all-black schools.

The final legal blow came in October 1969 when the Supreme Court in *Alexander vs. Holmes*—a case initially brought by Beatrice Alexander in Holmes County, Mississippi—ruled that " 'all deliberate speed' for desegregation is no longer constitutionally permissible. . . . Every school district must terminate dual school systems at once and . . . operate now and hereafter only unitary schools." Complete desegregation of the schools went into effect in January 1970. Several thousand whites panicked and "went rushing," as W. F. Minor described it, "into makeshift 'instant' private schools which proliferated across the landscape, in creek-bank Baptist churches, long abandoned school buildings, empty factories and in private homes." But by 1973, only 40,000 children—7 percent of the statewide total—were in the segregation academies, and some children were filtering back into the public school system. Children of both races were working together openly in classrooms, in sports, and in extracurricular activities. They were learning the falsehoods of many of the racial stereotypes taught by their parents. Lewis Perdue, a Northern journalist who returned to survey the scene in his native Mississippi late in 1972, observed that "the gains of freedom and civil rights wrought by federal action have provided room for the seeds of a Populist society to germinate within the youth of the state." The segregation academies—especially numerous around Jackson, under sponsorship of the Citizens Councils, and in the heavily black Delta counties—were serving an ironic purpose. Many school officials said they had siphoned off most of the troublemakers from the public schools.

But if Mississippi had overcome the integration barrier as well as—or perhaps better than—any other American state, its educational standards were still a gnawing problem. On the American College Test (ACT), Mississippi students in 1972 still had the lowest score in the country—16.3, compared to the national average of 19.9. The ACT scores showed black students scoring less than half as well as whites—a deficiency it might take years to correct. White teachers placed in integrated classrooms had discovered, at least in the first year of unitary schools, that there were some black high school seniors who could not even read their diplomas. And the vestiges of the integration battle lingered on. In 1973 the legislature was still unwilling to reenact the compulsory school attendance law it had repealed in its fit of segregationist fervor in 1956. As a result, only 50 to 60 percent of Mississippi's school-age children were actually graduating from high school. Nor was the legislature willing, despite a startling (although short-lived) $150 million surplus in 1973, to enact a public school kindergarten program that would provide the most dramatic upgrading for poor black youngsters—and perhaps replace, with the withdrawal of federal support apparent in the early '70s, the vibrant Mississippi Head Start program that had given tens of thousands of the state's young children their first brush with a wider world, their first chance to develop their personalities, and often the first nutritionally adequate or balanced meals of their lives. But official Mississippi had fought Head Start at every turn, and continued its heartlessness.

On the other hand, the 1973 legislature did grant major increases in teachers' salaries. That move discredited the almost universal prediction of earlier years—that when complete integration came, the segregationists would cut way back on state expenditures for education. But today in Mississippi, the commitment to public education is as great, or perhaps greater, than ever before. The long-term benefits—for whites, and especially for the blacks so shortchanged in the classroom over past Mississippi history—are sure to be enormous. It may be no exaggeration to say that within a few years, adequate education could provide a milieu in which the character of this most backward of all states might be transformed.

By 1959, Mississippi was so immersed in its latter-day segregationist fury that the two candidates who made the runoff for governor were both from the Hill country, and both were Citizens Council members—Ross Barnett and Carroll Gartin, who was then lieutenant governor. But Barnett, who had begun life as the youngest of an impoverished Confederate veteran's 10 children, was the more extreme of the two on race—and won easily. The inner coterie of the Citizens Council in Jackson, including Simmons and the city editor of the *Clarion-Ledger*, Gene Wirth, were his chief backers. Barnett's campaign song was entitled "Roll with Ross" and included the words: "He's for segregation one hundred percent. He's not a mod'rate like some other gent." A kindly man in many ways, Barnett differed from men like Vardaman and Bilbo, whose racism always seemed to include some cynicism. Barnett really believed in segregation. And though he had built a $100,000-a-year law practice for himself, his mental acumen was not of the highest. Jackson newsmen tell the story—which they admit may be apocryphal—of the morning after one of the 1960 Kennedy-Nixon debates, when people were coming in in droves to bid for jobs in Barnett's administration. An aide entered to say: "Governor, what do you think we ought to do about Quemoy and Matsu?" To which Barnett supposedly replied: "Well, put 'em over in the Game and Fish Commission." Robert Sherrill called Barnett "a peat-bog mentality" and recalled how he was confounded when a prison trusty ran away while on an errand for the governor. Barnett exclaimed: "If you can't trust a trusty, who can you trust?"

Barnett's big crisis came in the fall of 1962, when the impatient federal courts told the University of Mississippi at Oxford ("Ole Miss") to stop its stalling and enroll Negro applicant James Meredith. Barnett had promised to "rot in jail" before permitting a single black to enter a white school, and he let Mississippi—egged on by the Citizens Councils and the vituperative Jackson newspapers—work itself into an emotional froth over Meredith's prospective admission. There was an Ole Miss versus Kentucky football game in Jackson that weekend that embodied it all—Ole Miss students displaying the world's largest Confederate flag, "Go Mississippi" flashed in huge letters on the score screen, and then the 46,000 students and friends calling in unison: "We want Ross! We want Ross!" Barnett moved from his box to a microphone on the floodlit field, raising his fist to shout in a hoarse voice: "I love Mississippi. I love her people. I honor her customs." The crowd went delirious with pleasure; in that last moment before the wall of segregation began its fall, the concepts of Mississippi and white supremacy and embattled resistance were all one, and the crowd was like the Southern boy of whom Faulkner had once written, for whom "not once but whenever he wants it, there is the instant when it's still not two o'clock on that July afternoon in 1863, the brigades are in position behind the rail fence, the guns are laid and ready in the woods . . . and it's all in the balance, it hasn't happened yet."

The next afternoon it did happen: with Ross Barnett's full knowledge—he had, after all, been found in contempt of court by the Fifth Circuit, and faced a $10,000-a-day fine if he failed to cleanse himself. Federal agents whisked James Meredith onto the Ole Miss campus and to a tightly guarded dormitory. That night, there was a pitched battle between 400 federal marshals and a screaming mob of 2,500 students and segregationist sympathizers from all over the state and the South before the Ole Miss Lyceum; inside were Deputy Attorney General Nicholas deB. Katzenbach and other federal officials, receiving moment-by-moment instructions from the command post set up in the White House in Washington that night, but still unable to prevent the violence. Obscenities and then bricks, sticks, and burning missiles poured in on the beleaguered marshals, who responded with tear gas; sporadic gunfire broke out; two people were killed; the Mississippi National Guard was federalized and called in, and finally regular Army troops arrived to raise the siege and end the long night of fighting.

Early Monday morning, Meredith was officially registered and started classes; protected by federal officers, he would remain until his graduation on a peaceful, sunlit morning of August 1963 that was a world apart from the night of Mississippi's Last Stand.

Now, more than a decade later, Ole Miss has about 300 black undergraduate and law students out of an enrollment of 8,000.* Burnice Morris, editor of the black student newspaper at the university, said in 1972 that most of the black students had been "routinely" admitted. "The biggest reason you don't have more blacks is that this place still seems like a planter's school—you know, the rich white kids—so blacks don't apply." Some may, indeed, be thrown off by the Stars and Bars flying over the campus, or the symbolism of roads like Rebel and Confederacy Drives. A conservative board of trustees has not made things easier for blacks there, and it was 1970 before black students began to demonstrate for black studies and black faculty. The varsity football team was finally integrated in 1972,† and in spring 1973 the first black fraternity opened—a significant development on the socially conscious campus. Edwin Meek, director of public information for the university, said he had three blacks on his staff. "Ten years ago," he noted, "I would have been in jeopardy if I had even been seen talking with blacks." At the start of the '70s, *Newsweek*'s Joe B. Cumming, Jr. visited the campus and reported some of the first real dialogues between the races. In one sociology class, a white girl flared at the blacks: "If you don't like it here, why don't you leave and go up North?" Every black in the class wanted to answer, and the reply—which says a world about blacks' present attitude in Mississippi—came from one coed: "This is my state as much as yours. And as much my university. And I have as much right to get things changed the way I want as you have to get them changed the way you want."

No one who visits the Ole Miss campus fails to be impressed by the pleasant, sedate setting; as Joe Cumming put it: "Hurrying to classes among the white-columned buildings, students seemed as unchanged as the seasons: the boys in sweaters and open collars, self-possessed, milk-healthy; the girls, in miniskirts and knitted vests, as exquisite as blossoms." But pretty as its milieu may be, Ole Miss faces the same problem of all small-town universities that are located far from metropolitan centers—extreme difficulty in attracting and holding top-grade faculty. Speaking (for obvious reasons) off the record, a high state official described Ole Miss as "a third-rate college." The logical thing would be for it to be in Jackson, he said. The law school's accreditation is in jeopardy, for example, because of its poor library. The university administration headed off a move to shift the law school to Jackson, but it may one day regret the decision. Moves were reported in 1973 to start up a private law school in Jackson. It could well outpace Ole Miss's in a few years because of all the resources—the state supreme court, the big law offices, the libraries—at hand in the capital.

* For a period in the '60s, the Ole Miss Law School was actively recruiting poor blacks and whites—the idea of then Dean Joshua Morse, a native born white Mississippian who ironically had been appointed by Ross Barnett. Morse also showed real courage by bringing speakers like Robert Kennedy to Ole Miss. He later left for a post at Florida State University, but the young Mississippi blacks who got a law degree by virtue of his initiative will be playing a role in the state's public life for years to come.

† Mississippi State University was well ahead of Ole Miss in recruiting top black athletes. In 1970, in fact, there was an amazing contest between coaches Paul ("Bear") Bryant of the University of Alabama and Charles Shira of Mississippi State to obtain the services of an all-American high school student from Gulfport, Mississippi. The black youngster, Melvin Barkum, finally picked Mississippi State. In the 1972–73 school year, another black football star, Frank Dowsing, was elected "Mr. MSU." The comment of one native Mississippian: "That's damn near impossible to believe."

A postscript about James Meredith himself: A loner always, he has spent the years since the Ole Miss crisis in such assorted activities as getting a law degree from Columbia, staging his voters' march through Mississippi, trying unsuccessfully to raise $1 million for an educational fund in his own name, withdrawing at the last moment from a congressional race in Harlem, and running unsuccessfully for Republican nominations for governor and U.S. Senator in Mississippi. In 1972 he told Wayne King of the New York *Times:* "For years I was involved in extending freedom for black people. . . . Now I don't see any value in that. The only thing I'm interested in is fighting for the whole thing, for total freedom. I don't think there is ever going to be any freedom for the black man as long as he is submerged in the white structure."

If those words frighten white Mississippians, they might be more comforted by Meredith's reasons for living in Jackson, in a mostly white neighborhood. Jackson, he said recently, "doesn't have the general fear of being in the streets like New York. New York has more muggings, robbery, and unconnected murders." And in Mississippi, he said, his three boys "can go outside without fear and even without someone guarding them every minute."

The Vital Decade

The integration of schools and universities was only part of the revolutionary change that overtook Mississippi in the 1960s. That decade, at this writing, is not long past. But it is already clear that it was the time of Mississippi's *real* Reconstruction, unquestionably the most important decade of this century. Charles Evers recalls that while he and his brother Medgar began their civil rights activities in 1947, "until the '60s we were just scratching the surface and making folks mad. The real breakthrough came in the '60s."

Mississippi's first taste of what was to come was supplied in the late spring of 1961, when the Freedom Riders organized by the Congress on Racial Equality (CORE) came into Mississippi. They were promptly jailed when they reached Jackson, but soon the college students and teachers and young ministers were staging marches all over Mississippi. The price was high: 24 documented cases of beatings, clubbings, and shootings in that one year. But Mississippi's own blacks were slowly awakening.

The Ole Miss crisis of 1962 was to have an immense effect, because the simple white folks would never again quite believe their leaders when they said "never" to desegregation; in addition, news of Ross Barnett's secret dealings with Attorney General Robert Kennedy prior to the Ole Miss debacle began to breed doubt in people's minds about their state leadership.

But the prejudices would be slow in dying. In June 1963 came the cowardly sniper murder of Medgar Evers, who led the Mississippi NAACP—then and still today the most influential black organization in the state. (A salesman and Marine veteran from the Delta named Byron de la Beckwith was charged with the murder and vigorously prosecuted by now Governor William Waller, who was then a district attorney. Both trials ended with hung juries.*) When President Kennedy was assassinated, there was cheering in some of the schools (the white ones, of course). Cruelty and sadism were noted among some police, and indeed the "peacekeeping forces" were often the most lawless element in the community. Walter Lord noted that "no group did more to bolster the spirit of resistance than Mississippi's collection of tough, fiercely independent sheriffs, deputies, and town cops. . . . There were dozens of communities where beet-faced deputies, bulging with holsters and cartridge belts, happily wallowed in defiance"—forever railing, of course, against "outside interference" in Mississippi's affairs.

Decent white Mississippians might have been shocked by the excesses of their police, the continuing trail of intimidation and violence condoned or practiced by the authorities, but they knew little of it. Most of the state's newspapers were propaganda sheets for the closed society. The few newspaper editors who dissented pursued a dangerous course. One of them, Oliver Emmerich in McComb, tells the story of how he was approached one day on the street by a man he had never met before. The man asked Emmerich a question about his relations with Northern newspapermen and then, without warning, smashed the 68-year-old Emmerich in the face, knocking him to the sidewalk.

If that was the fate that awaited the intrepid white moderate, the lot of blacks who sought to assert their rights was immeasurably worse. In December 1962, Mrs. Fannie Lou Hamer, the wife of a Mississippi sharecropper, was thrown off the plantation (where she kept the books for the boss man) because she tried to register to vote. At Winona the next June, she was one of several civil rights voters who were arrested and severely beaten with blackjacks by state officials. There had been hundreds of instances like it, but Mrs. Hamer's was to be aired dramatically on national television the next summer when she was one of the blacks trying to gain seats as members of the Mississippi Freedom Democratic Party delegation at the Democratic National Convention. As Pat Watters and Reese Cleghorn observed in *Climbing Jacob's Ladder: The Arrival of Negroes in Southern Politics*, Mrs. Hamer's story "encompassed many of the recurrent themes of the rights movement in the South; police-state repression; beatings; sadism; involvement of the state police; clinical detachment of FBI men in their dealings with the victims, but good-faith cooperation with local police who obviously were suppressing constitutional rights; the deep religious faith of many of the Negroes in the most desperate circumstances, and, finally, their growing despair."

In the midst of that despair, President Johnson signed the monumental Civil Rights Act of 1964 into law. Its broad-ranging provisions for fair employment and free access to public accommodations, and the powers it gave the Justice Department to enforce equal rights, would have an immense impact in Mississippi. At the very moment the law went into effect, large

* Beckwith had the audacity to run for lieutenant governor in the 1967 primary, invariably introducing himself as "the man they say killed Medgar Evers." But he only got 5 percent of the vote, finishing fifth among six candidates in the primary.

numbers of Northern college students—most of them white—were arriving in Mississippi to participate in the "Freedom Summer" of 1964. Their contribution was to be a momentous one, for as James Silver wrote, "The one affront that Mississippi's caste system could least tolerate and survive was the presence of more than a thousand whites living with and working amiably alongside Negro families."

The Freedom Summer visitors were recruited by the Council of Federated Organizations (COFO), whose major components were CORE (Congress on Racial Equality) and SNCC (Student Nonviolent Coordinating Committee)—with the ever-vital backing of the NAACP and its Legal Defense and Education Fund. The students paid their own way, lived with black Mississippi families, helped with voter registration, established black community centers, and set up schools for illiterates. They knew the dangers when they came to Mississippi, and some paid the highest price. In Longdale, a little community near Philadelphia, Mississippi, a Negro church was burned. Three young COFO workers—one of them black, two white—went to investigate, were arrested, released, and then abducted and murdered. Today the church is rebuilt, and this plaque is attached to its wall:

OUT OF ONE BLOOD GOD HATH MADE ALL MEN
To the Memory of
MICHAEL SCHWERNER
JAMES CHANEY
ANDREW GOODMAN

> Whose concern for others, and more particularly those of this community, led to their early martyrdom. Their death quickened men's consciences and more firmly established justice, liberty and brotherhood in our land.

These would be the only fatalities among students who came for the "long, hot summer" of 1964, but the toll of lesser incidents that year was staggering—countless cross burnings, bullets fired into automobiles and homes, and police harassments. Altogether, there were 80 beatings, 35 churches burned, 30 homes dynamited, 35 shooting incidents, and more than 1,000 arrests.

It was too much for the rest of the country to continue to accept with equanimity. Up to 1964, the FBI had played a light role in Mississippi racial disturbances, usually just dispatching observer agents from Memphis or New Orleans. But now, after an on-the-spot look by former CIA chief Allen Dulles, the FBI opened one of its largest bureaus in the country in Jackson, stepped up investigations that fingered many criminals, and undertook a broad campaign of public education concerning the respect for law.

And despite the barbarity of its response to the Freedom Summer, Mississippi was on the brink of a fantastic change in customs and mores. Three days after the 1964 Civil Rights Act was signed, several black leaders registered without incident at the Heidelburg Hotel in Jackson. It was an historic day in Mississippi. Quickly, the color line was broken in hotels, restaurants, theaters, parks, and public places across Mississippi. The easiest compliance was in the cities, the longest holdouts in the countryside. Not that blacks always got a cordial welcome. Five years later, an acquaintance of mine discovered this sign on the counter of Henry Kouthman's Phillips 66 Cafe near Bay St. Louis, Mississippi, not far from New Orleans:

ALL PROCEEDS DERIVED FROM SALES TO NIGGERS
WILL BE DONATED TO THE KU KLUX KLAN

That same spring, in the shoddy little delta town of Arcola, I stopped for lunch at a cafe (which turned out to be incredibly dirty and dark) where there were separate entrances, the signs worn but still legible: WHITE and COLORED. No one in Arcola dared break the line. Yet these are exceptions; in the vast majority of public accommodations, blacks are accepted and even treated these days to the traditional friendliness—"Y'all come back now, hear?"—once accorded whites only. The corpse twitches now and then, but for all practical purposes Jim Crow is dead.

Early in 1965 Mississippi's leading industrialists, concerned over financial troubles within the state and threats of boycotts in other states of goods made in Mississippi, broke with the Citizens Councils and began to speak out against racial lawlessness. Two large and prestigious business groups, the Mississippi Manufacturers Association and the Mississippi Economic Council (MEC), urged their members to comply with the equal job opportunity provisions of the 1964 law. "We realize now that the Civil Rights Act is the law of the land and that we have lost the battle," said Owen Cooper, president of the MEC. The sheriff's association also issued a formal statement of praise of obedience to law, and so did the bar association and the association of country supervisors. The Klan and other never-say-die racists continued sporadic bombings and assassinations, but without the umbrella of official protection that they had enjoyed before. As the Citizens Councils lost their grip on Mississippi public opinion, previously silent voices of moderation began to be heard. Among these were a group of women who called themselves Mississippians for Public Education and began a spirited campaign to keep the public schools open. Paul B. Johnson, Jr., who had been elected governor in 1963 after campaigning up and down the state joking about what NAACP stands for ("niggers, alligators, apes, coons, possums"), began to act more moderately. (But Johnson, who as lieutenant governor had helped Barnett try to stop integration at Ole Miss in 1963, would never publicly condemn segregation. Johnson's way of being a moderate governor, Hodding Carter III noted, was "to keep his mouth shut.")

The last barrier to fall was disenfranchisement of the Mississippi black. In the racist-extremist reaction to the Supreme Court's *Brown* decision, the legislature and voters in 1954 had approved a constitutional amendment adding a literacy requirement for voting (in addition to the old requirement that a prospective voter be able to interpret any section of the state constitution). But the new amendment contained a clause waiving the new reading requirement for anyone who had qualified to vote before its passage; the effect was to continue illiterate whites on the rolls but to bar previously registered illiterates, most of whom were Negroes. Even literate Negroes took their lives in their hands if they tried to register in some areas of Mississippi. The Rev.

George W. Lee, president of the Belzoni NAACP, in 1954 led more than 100 blacks to register in his county. When racists subsequently demanded that Lee and the other Negroes remove their names from the voter rolls, Lee refused; a short time later, he was slain.

Another Mississippi law of the 1950s required that any new registrant have his name printed in the local newspaper for two weeks—a gruesome intimidation for a black worried about his job or rented home. In the fearful atmosphere of those times, the number of registered blacks stood at only 22,000 in the mid 1950s, and only 8,000 had paid their poll taxes and were actually eligible to vote. In the 31 Mississippi counties with a black majority in 1958, no Negroes at all were registered in six, and less than 1 percent in 13 others. Statewide, only 3.89 percent of the voting age blacks were registered. By 1962, the number of registered blacks had risen slightly but still represented only 5.3 percent of the potential—compared, for instance, to 13.4 percent in Alabama, which was otherwise the nation's most repressive state for black voting, or 26.8 percent in the old Confederate states as a whole.

Workers funded by the Southern Regional Council's Voter Education Project and other civil rights workers repeatedly risked their lives in an effort to register Mississippi blacks in the early 1960s, but their results were almost negligible. Local officials subjected them to repeated false arrests; police dogs were used to intimidate blacks trying to enroll for voting; and blacks still feared for their jobs. In 1963 the civil rights workers staged mock voting by Mississippi blacks with Aaron Henry their candidate for governor on a "Freedom Party" ticket. One of the people who thought up the plan was Allard K. Lowenstein, who was later instrumental in recruiting for the Freedom Summer and in 1968 would be the principal instigator of the movement to oust President Johnson from office. Another was Robert Moses of SNCC, an almost legendary black registration worker of the early 1960s whom Theodore White described as "a sweet and luminous person," "a confessional revolutionary, the most difficult for government to handle." Before he finished his five-year stint in Mississippi, Moses had been beaten bloody, put in solitary confinement, and seen many of his vote-seeking Negroes killed by the Klan. Eventually, he turned bitterly antiwhite, but not before he had laid the groundwork for the revolution of black votes to come. In 1963 some 90,000 blacks took part in the mock election he and Lowenstein organized —a mute testimony to the suppressed desire of blacks to participate in the democratic process.

The Voting Rights Act of 1965 brought federal examiners into Mississippi, and finally Negroes began to register in large numbers. But, even then, there was a heavy price to pay. Six months after the law was signed by President Johnson, Vernon Dahmer, an NAACP leader in Hattiesburg, spoke on the local radio as the chairman of a new black registration campaign. Before dawn the next morning, his home and grocery store were firebombed. Grievously burned, Dahmer staggered from his flaming home and fired shotgun blasts at a fleeing car. On his deathbed, Dahmer said: "I've been trying to get people to register to vote. People who don't vote are deadbeats on the state. . . . What happened to us can happen to anyone, white or black."

In the summer of 1966, Mississippi was again astir with a vivid confrontation. James Meredith made his famous walk into the state to dramatize and defy the pall of fear so many Negroes still felt there; after he was wounded by a shotgun blast from a white man, Dr. Martin Luther King and some of the militant apostles of the new "black power" concept, including Stokely Carmichael, came too. A massacre at the hands of white extremists seemed possible, and indeed the marchers were mauled by whites armed with rocks and clubs at infamous Philadelphia. But Governor Johnson, anxious about the state's image, reluctantly provided protection by the state police, and bloodshed was avoided. The miles of march through the murderous Delta heat brought some concrete dividends: registration of at least 4,000 new Negro voters and an opportunity for an estimated 10,000 rural Mississippi blacks to participate in a civil rights demonstration for the first time in their lives.

Since the mid-'60s, the effort of the black leadership has been to encourage the black masses to take full advantage of the right to vote for which so many of their brothers and sisters died in past years. The effort has been immensely complicated by the frightfully low educational levels of so many Mississippi Negroes—the 1970 Census found, in fact, that 28 percent of the adult blacks in the state were functional illiterates, and only 26 percent had ever made it as far as high school. And what was called a high school education, a well-informed Mississippian said, may have produced for most blacks the functional equivalent of a third-grade education.

Low political interest is the inevitable fruit of poor (or nonexistent) education, but in a few rural counties where the vestiges of the plantation system linger on there remains another distinct factor: fear. The poorest black turnouts have been in counties where blacks are most directly dependent on whites for their livelihood. As a white attorney in Wilkinson County (68 percent black) told a visiting political scientist in 1970, "Those fellers from the Justice Department thought they were so smart when they gave the vote to these illiterate darkies. What those smart fellers didn't realize is that we can still get at these darkies a whole lot of subtle ways."

In some counties, voter registrars inform plantation owners when their black residents register, and even in recent years some blacks have been summarily evicted when that happened. In others, blacks are allowed to register, but their vote is still white-controlled. An example is Tallahatchie County in the Delta, notorious as the place where a black youngster from Chicago named Emmett Till was lynched in the 1950s because he supposedly "wolf whistled" at the wife of a white man in a rural store one day. A majority of the voters are blacks in Tallahatchie, but no black candidate has yet been elected. Eugene Carter, a black candidate for the state legislature in 1971, explained to the Washington *Post*'s Robert Maynard: "These plantation owners tell their workers that they have a way of knowing how they voted. These are the poorest and most unsophisticated people in America. They only average $600 a year. They believe the boss can tell, so they vote as they are told." Carter estimated that the "fear factor" accounted for 10 to 15 percent of the county vote.

Such phenomena give support to the conclusion of the U.S. Civil Rights Commission that the last barriers to full black participation in Southern politics can be overcome "only by eliminating the economic dependence of Southern Negroes upon white landlords, white employers, and white sources of credit—dependence which deters Negroes from voting freely and seeking political office." White Mississippi is still, in fact, accused of many stratagems to limit black voting, ranging from isolated instances of raw violence to requirements for mass registration of voters after counties have been reapportioned. Lawyers working for civil rights groups charged that the Justice Department, after its initial intervention in the wake of the 1965 Voting Rights Act, became grossly negligent in guarding the right of blacks to vote in Mississippi.

Yet even Charles Evers, who has been highly vocal in protesting white-perpetrated election irregularities in the state, acknowledges that actual voter intimidation "is pretty much isolated to a few areas now." The real problem, he said, "is that black people, particularly in the rural areas, don't know the value of voting. Where many of them are not afraid of voting, they still haven't accepted the responsibility they have now that's part of freedom." Evers insists the problem is understandable: "You can't expect to eliminate within 10 years the disinterest of people who have been enslaved and in bondage and denied and deprived for 300 or 400 years. We are overcoming it, but change comes slow."

For his part, Evers has attended hundreds of black voting rallies, traveled from one end of the state to the other, and even undertook a hopeless 1971 race for governor to help awaken the black voter—the kind, he said, who couldn't believe, even long after he became mayor of Fayette, that there was really a black man in authority there.

My mind goes back to an early spring evening at the end of the 1960s, when it was already fashionable to say that "the movement"—the civil rights effort of the '60s—was ended, and Evers was on hand to address a black peoples' voter meeting at the Bethel AME Church at Brookhaven, Mississippi. The people gathered were plain, simple folk, dressed in their Sunday best (but telltale work shoes), and the church, whitewashed and clean-scrubbed, was a little island of pride. An aura of religious revival filled the room as the minister prayed for protection of a black man running for alderman. A choir of four lanky youths, led by a big, genial lady in a bright red dress, sang that indomitable *We Shall Overcome* to hand-clapping accompaniment. The yoke of fear in Mississippi had already been broken; indeed a *black* policeman had helped me find the church—in the same town where Lamar Smith, a black man trying to get Negroes to register, had been gunned down on the courthouse lawn in 1955, where the White Knights of the Ku Klux Klan had flourished in the mid-1960's, and where two Head Start centers had been burned to the ground in 1967. And then Evers speaking:

> The white man is clever. He takes care of himself, because he is informed, and he has *his* alderman.
>
> And what about us?

Where we live (in town) is where the dust begins. [Congregation responds: Right!]

Where we live is where the streetlights end. [Right!]

Where we live is where the sewers end. [Right!]

Where we live is where the sidewalks end. [Right!]

Where we live is where the police protection ends. [Right!]

The men who put the sewers and sidewalks down are the aldermen and mayors. Remember who you're voting for!

You can pray all you want. But it won't do you any good unless you get out and work for what you need. You got to be in charge of something, not just praying and hoping.

That year, Evers was making his first race for mayor of Fayette, and he took a moment to tell the Brookhaven Negroes what it would be like after he won:

When we're elected whites won't have to be afraid to come through Fayette—that they'll be charged outlandish amounts for speeding, or be beaten by black policemen. They'll be treated absolutely straight, just like blacks. We ain't gonna have no police brutality. We're not gonna be hate-monger creatures.

Don't preach hate. Don't kill. Just stop 'em for doing it to us. Look him in the eye and say, "No, white man, this ain't your country—it's *our* country. This ain't your town—it's *our* town. We're gonna share it."

The Voting Rights Act of 1965 invalidated in a single stroke the mountains of restrictions Mississippi had put on the right to register and vote, and sent federal examiners into the state to make sure blacks could really enjoy the voting rights guaranteed them. And the years of exhortation, of organizing, of cajoling the black man to vote by Evers and his friends would have their effect too. From its base point of 28,500 in 1964, black registration increased almost sevenfold to 190,000 in 1967 and to 264,000 in 1968. By 1971–72, it had leveled off at about 270,000. That represented 59 percent of the Negro voting-age population—meaning that there were still 184,000 unregistered blacks in the state. The whites, by contrast, had reached a 70 percent registration rate, compared to 41 percent back in 1960, when they had no reason to be concerned about black ballot box incursions.

But the new black vote was important enough, because it represented 25 to 28 percent of the total electorate. The white politicians, who knew how to count, soon accommodated themselves to it.

The black vote impact was partially felt in the transitional gubernatorial election of 1967, when an ingrained segregationist, John Bell Williams, won the governorship. Williams, however, toned down his segregationist rhetoric, concentrating instead on his longtime devotion to conservatism and claiming persecution at the hands of the national Democrats who had stripped him of his congressional seniority after he backed Barry Goldwater for President in 1964. But while the redneck-conservative coalition elected Williams, 45.5 percent of the runoff vote went to William Winter, an outstanding moderate-conservative. City voters and blacks were Winter's strongest backers. Two fire-eating white supremacists tried for the governorship that year—country radio singer Jimmy Swan (a self-styled disciple of the late Theodore Bilbo) and

Ross Barnett. Barnett by then was discredited because his "stand in the schoolhouse door" at Ole Miss had proven so futile and because his administration had been marked by inefficiency and corruption. Neither he nor Swan made the runoff. That was the same year that Robert G. Clark, a Holmes County schoolteacher with a master's degree from Michigan State University, won election as Mississippi's first black legislator of the 20th century.

In the local elections of 1969, the black political movement gathered momentum as Evers won election as mayor of Fayette, ousting a 74-year-old white incumbent who had been unopposed for 18 years. A total of 155 Negroes sought office in 52 towns and cities, and 18 were elected. The results might not have seemed impressive numerically, but each represented a major breakthrough in Mississippi. Just as important, the black vote became the decisive factor in determining the outcome of races between whites all across the state. White candidates began to appear in black churches and civic clubs, campaigning for votes—a spectacle unthinkable before the Voting Rights Act became law.

The 1971 elections would suggest the extent—and limitations—of Mississippi's political-racial progress in the 1960s. It was clear that most of the voters were disappointed with the administration of outgoing Governor John Bell Williams and its racist politics image. The traditional segregationists, including Jimmy Swan, were eliminated in the first gubernatorial primary. The two runoff candidates opposed school busing but generally ran "more-moderate-than-thou" campaigns. Jackson attorney William Waller, the eventual winner, ran political advertisements saying he had "not tried to pit black against white, rich against poor, young against old." He said that Mississippi was "in transition from the typical Old South party politics to where we're running on the issues." His opponent, Lt. Gov. Charles Sullivan, promised that blacks "will be able to live in dignity in my Mississippi." Like Waller, Sullivan pledged to promote fair employment and to appoint blacks to state boards. With both candidates appealing to them, blacks split their votes, though a majority appeared to vote for Waller over Sullivan. The decisive factor in Waller's victory, however, was his success in depicting Sullivan as the candidate of the Jackson banks, the corporations, and the big state news papers—Mississippi's "establishment." Waller, by contrast, called himself a "redneck" and appeared as something of a modern-day Populist. The fact that he came from the Hills country, and Sullivan from the Delta, helped to reinforce the image. Charles Fortenberry and F. Glenn Abney later noted in *The Changing Politics of the South* that the runoff voting patterns "showed signs of a return to the economic and social cleavages prevalent before the 1950s"—Hills versus Delta, the more privileged people versus the plain people. What was different now was that many blacks were lined up with the Hills people in voting for the "populist" candidate—the very coalition of the dispossessed that the framers of the 1890 constitution had feared the most.

Neither Waller nor Sullivan was considered as moderate or progressive (one dares not say "liberal," a taboo word in Mississippi) as William Winter, the man who lost to Williams in the 1967 gubernatorial primary. Winter considered running for governor again in 1971 but decided the risk was too high and went for lieutenant governor instead—winning against a conservative opponent with about 60 percent of the vote. "Frankly, I didn't realize the state had changed as much as it had when I made my decision to run for lieutenant governor," Winter told me subsequently. He is likely to try again for governor in the future, but some of his close friends fear a tragedy may be in the making. They view him as a man of high integrity and ability but perhaps unelectable as governor because he is "too liberal for the white folks and too conservative and establishment for the blacks and liberals."

Charles Evers ran for governor in 1971 as an independent opposing Waller in the general election, an act that garnered a lot more publicity than it did votes. He never really expected to win; the campaign was waged rather to get blacks to the polls and spearhead the effort of 284 blacks who were running for offices ranging from the state legislature to school boards, sheriff's offices, and county supervisor slots. On the surface, the outcome was a distinct disappointment for the blacks. Evers got only 22 percent of the vote, well under the 28 percent that blacks represented of the total registration. Fearful of the black effort, white voters turned out in unpredecented numbers. Even in counties where whites were outnumbered, the blacks generally failed to take control. Civil rights leaders Aaron Henry and Fannie Lou Hamer were defeated in the races they made, and Robert Clark barely won reelection to the legislature.

After the election, the blacks charged gross election irregularities—intimidation of voters, exclusion of poll watchers from the balloting places, and physical violence—especially in the counties where a black takeover seemed possible. The Delta Ministry of the National Council of Churches issued a postelection report in which the irregularities, including out-and-out cheating by white elections officials, were confirmed. The election was actually "stolen" in at least eight races, the Ministry said. But the main point of the report was that Mississippi blacks had not yet mastered basic political techniques, including voter education, sound candidate selection, and get-out-the-vote activities on election day. The fruits of past political illiteracy were all too clear in some counties where as many as 44 percent of the black voters who cast their ballots for Evers failed to vote for local black officeseekers. In addition, 5 to 20 percent of the Evers voters crossed over to vote for white over black candidates—often in response to intensive appeals made to them by the white politicians. The white sheriff in heavily black Holmes County won, for instance, by doing an about-face from the old Southern stereotype. "He's terrific," Representative Clark acknowledged. "He treats everybody like a man. If he comes to your house with a search warrant, he's polite, and if he has to arrest you, he apologizes for it."

As it was, 51 blacks were elected in 1971, more than doubling the previous total. But if the blacks had been better organized and the election conducted more fairly, the Delta Ministry said, 52 more blacks could have been elected, with black takeover of four additional counties. The conclusion was that in the future, blacks would have to rely less on personality politics and more on tough, grass-roots political activity. Some black critics said Evers had gone on an "ego trip," forgetting that the only realistic purpose of his race had been to help local black organizations. Evers disagreed with that, saying the basic reason he had run had been to coax black people out of the apathy and fear they had lived in so long. "It's sorta like bringing a newborn child into the world," he said.

A year and a half later, when I asked him what his race had accomplished, Evers replied:

> The main thing was that it put into the mind of white people and blacks the idea that a black man can run for state office and he can get close to 200,000 votes and he can talk about issues.
>
> Many of the things we talked about have been used by the present governor [Waller]. We talked about the correcting of Parchman, the state penitentiary. We talked about easing taxes. We talked about involving whites and blacks in government. We talked about black highway patrolmen.
>
> We're getting a few of all those things. We have blacks in state government. We have black highway patrolmen—only three, but that's three more than we had three years ago. We have $6 million for rehabilitating the Parchman Penitentiary. We're gettiing rid of the old trusty system up there which I've fought over the years.* The fact is that we were able to talk about issues, and not color, and to expose what the leaders of our state had been doing, covering up and doing wrong. This in itself was a victory.

Evers' own governance of little Fayette (population 1,725—76 percent Negro) in southwestern Mississippi is an example of what it can mean when —as he puts it—"Negroes can get together and control and rule something in America." Even before he was elected, Evers had opened the Medgar Evers Shopping Center on the edge of town, including a supermarket and other stores and services, a cafe, and a lounge. Then, during his first four years in office, Fayette was able to open a comprehensive health program clinic visited by 75 to 100 persons a day. It is staffed by four physicians and four nurses —of which there were none in Fayette before. Three industries were brought in—an ITT plant making circuit controllers, a commercial chemical, and a concrete mixing plant. An amount of federally subsidized housing was built. And work began on a $400,000 multipurpose center building, to include a day care center, a dental clinic, a cafeteria, a library, sewing instruction room, and counseling services.

Echoing his campaign promise of four years before, Evers boasted that we "haven't had a case of police brutality yet. We allow no guns in this town. We allow no profane language on our streets. We allow no name calling. If you come down here and call me a nigger, I'll arrest you for disturbing the nigger's peace. If I call you a honkey, I'll be arrested for disturbing the honkey's peace."

Evers' public image suffered a reverse in 1971 when he published, on the

* Evers may have been a trifle over-optimistic about the prospects for ending the armed trusty system and effecting real reforms at the Mississippi State Penitentiary at Parchman, in the Delta's Sunflower County. Over the years, trusties have beaten, shot at, and wounded dozens of prisoners and killed several outright. There have been many stories of men forced to drink castor oil, of women prisoners stripped naked, and of molestation. In 1972 a federal judge ordered the state to begin dismantling the trusty system. A blue-ribbon committee appointed by Governor Waller also recommended abolishing the long-time farming operation (on its 21,000 acres of land) that the prison had used to make a profit for the state of Mississippi.

Despite its reputation for brutality and violence, the 1,900-inmate Parchman Penitentiary did lead the nation in permitting conjugal visits by wives (and common-law wives) twice a month. The goal was to cut down on homosexuality at the prison.

eve of his campaign announcement, his autobiography—*Evers*—including some sensational revelations about his past. In the Philippines during World War II, when he was in the Army, Evers said he had supplied GIs in Manila with prostitutes. In Chicago, right after the war, he had run both prostitution and policy rackets. And back home in Mississippi, where he ran a funeral parlor, he had tried his hand at bootlegging whiskey while the state was still officially "dry." Though the statute of limitations had long since run out on all these offenses, Evers said, "I want the people to know that I told them first."

Evers also alienated many rank-and-file blacks and "loyal" Democrats by supporting Republican Nelson Rockefeller for reelection as governor of New York in 1970 and by bitterly denouncing George McGovern and saying kind things about Richard Nixon during the 1972 campaign. The conduct was especially frowned on because he held the post of Democratic National Committeeman.

But Hodding Carter III said that "no matter what Charles' problems may be, no matter what revelations may be made, the fact is he's still the only black in Mississippi who can draw a big crowd anywhere he goes to speak, who will command the great attention of blacks and the media. He has an unbelievable charisma."

Evers was also the first legitimate folk hero Mississippi blacks had had (or been allowed to have) in living memory. From his broken grammar and troubled past to his flashes of insight and lack of hatred and dogged determination, he best embodied what the 1960s wrought in black Mississippi. But after 1971 the black political leadership in the state had become so factionalized that his role as leader and spokesman in future years was in some doubt.

Democrats vs. Democrats vs. Republicans

If moderation has become acceptable in Mississippi state politics of late, it is much harder to argue that the same has happened in Mississippi's approach to Presidential elections or in its congressional delegation. The state has cast astronomical percentages for the most conservative Presidential candidates—or, to be more accurate, those who seemed to be the most against the black man. In Congress, James O. Eastland symbolizes the sentiment of the Magnolia State.

Mississippi's long-term, automatic allegiance to the national Democratic party ended in 1948, when Mississippi's own Governor Fielding Wright ran for Vice President on the States Rights ticket headed by Strom Thurmond. The state vote was 87.2 percent for Thurmond and Wright—the Dixiecrats' highest percentage anywhere. In the 1952 and 1956 Eisenhower-Stevenson elections, Mississippi gave about 60 percent of its vote to Stevenson—partly out of vestigial party loyalty, perhaps, and in part because neither national candidate was to its taste. But in 1960, when there was a Dixiecrat-like unpledged elector slate available, it carried Mississippi.

White Mississippi's fury over the pro-Negro bent of the national Democrats in the early '60s was apparent in the Johnson-Goldwater contest, when the Arizonan got a thumping 87 percent of the Mississippi vote, his highest percentage in any state. ("It would not have mattered," Walker Percy wrote, "if Senator Goldwater had advocated the collectivization of the plantations and open saloons in Jackson; he voted against the Civil Rights Bill and that was that.") In 1968 George Wallace reflected the Mississippi mood perfectly and got 63.5 percent of the vote. Only his native Alabama was for Wallace by a greater percentage. Nixon that year got only 13.5 percent in Mississippi —a narrow base of the country club set and some business leaders. Humphrey received 23 percent, an almost exclusively black vote which would prove to be virtually identical to Evers' 1971 support.

Finally, in 1972, Nixon defeated McGovern in Mississippi with 78 percent of the vote—a lopsided 505,125 to 126,782. Again, it was the biggest percentage for the more conservative candidate in any state, and again, the only appreciable number of votes the liberal received was from blacks. But Mississippi was actually closer to the national vote for the winner (17 points off) than it had been for years. In 1964, for instance, the difference had been 49 points, and in 1968 it had been 30 points. "Our mainstream," Bill Minor noted, "has moved to the national mainstream in a lot of ways. What I'm worried about is that the national mainstream is coming toward ours." Significantly, 1972 was the first time since 1944 that Mississippi voted for the same Presidential candidate who carried the country as a whole.

Mississippi's estrangement from the ideologic mainstream of the national Democratic party has created an acute and still unresolved problem for its own regular Democratic party. Until the 1960s, the cleavage was unimportant because the national party never looked behind the façade of state parties that called themselves Democratic. National conventions rarely questioned credentials, and there certainly was no challenge in Congress, where Southern Democrats (including several of Mississippi's own) held exalted positions through the workings of the seniority system.

In effect, the lily-white Mississippi Democratic party spoke not only for white Mississippi but for the state's blacks, whose population count swelled its representation in Congress and at Democratic National Conventions. It was a morally indefensible position, and with the organization of the Mississippi Freedom Democratic Party in 1964—the same people who staged the mock election for Aaron Henry the year before—it came under legal challenge as well. The Freedom Democrats sent an integrated full delegation to the Democratic Convention in Atlantic City that summer, and there was the emotional moment which I referred to earlier when Fannie Lou Hamer—giving her address as Ruleville, Sunflower County, Mississippi, "the home of Senator James O. Eastland"—recited the brutalities to which she had been subjected in her attempts to register and get other blacks to register to vote. Aaron Henry and Robert Moses testified as well. The national Democratic party recognized full well the immensity of the moral challenge it faced, and President Johnson designated no less a figure than Hubert Humphrey to spearhead the effort for an acceptable compromise. The solution, though rejected by some of the Freedom Democrats themselves, represented a momentous breakthrough. The regular white delegation would be seated, but only those persons on it who would pledge allegiance to the national Democratic ticket (and only four members of the regular delegation were willing to do that); two Freedom Democrats would be allowed to sit as delegates at large with full votes; and, most vital of all, at all succeeding Democratic conventions, no delegations would be seated from states where the party process deprived citizens of the right to vote by reason of their race or color.

The convention quickly accepted that compromise, which would lay the groundwork for the entire Democratic reform movement of the late 1960s and early 1970s—the most fundamental challenge to closed caucus, unit rule, unrepresentative party operations in the 20th century. In 1968 the Freedom Democrats formed a coalition with the state's moderate Young Democrats organization, the state NAACP leadership, and organized labor and sent a delegation to Chicago which easily won recognition as *the* Democratic party of Mississippi. The regular Mississippi Democrats had added some token blacks to their delegation, but it was obvious that the systematic exclusion of legitimate black representation had continued, and the convention denied them any seats.

So, since 1968, there have been two distinct Democratic parties in Mississippi. Each has its strengths and weaknesses. The Loyalist Democrats (as they have come to be called), headed by Charles Evers as National Committeeman and Aaron Henry as state chairman, are the legal Democratic party of the state in the eyes of the Democratic conventions and the Democratic National Committee. The regular Democrats, on the other hand, continue to control the normal Democratic party machinery within Mississippi, are the party of the governor and other statewide officials, and are the party of the Democrats on the congressional delegation.

Both factions have problems, and each has something the other wants. The Loyalist Democrats' weakness lies in the thinness of their white support. Only a few whites—figures like Hodding Carter III, Patricia Derien (the wife of a wealthy Jackson physician), and J. Wesley Watkins (a Greenville attorney)—have participated. The choice of Henry and Evers for the two key leadership posts gave the party an overwhelmingly NAACP-civil rights image. At the state and local level, they have felt obliged to run their candidates as independents in the general election, because they feel hopelessly outnumbered by whites in the regular party, and they allege discrimination and intimidation when they deal with the regulars. Yet their very presence is a threat to the regular Democrats—not only because they receive the official call to Democratic National Conventions but because they might one day succeed in their repeated efforts to have seniority privileges revoked for Mississippi's white Democratic Congressmen, on the grounds that the regulars do not support national Democratic nominees. Loss of seniority would be a body blow to the regular Mississippi Democrats.

Moreover, the Republicans have been gaining strength in Mississippi congressional elections, and in 1972 one of their nominees won because an independent black associated with the Loyalist Democrats drained off enough normally Democratic votes to cost the Democrats the election. If that pattern were repeated frequently in the future, there would one day be no regular Democrats left in Congress to accumulate seniority and wield power in Washington.

The Loyalist Democrats' problem, as one of their friends put it, is that they are "a name in search of a massive following." Their high water mark will probably always be 25 to 28 percent of the electorate—basically all black. They were formed as a party to have a national connection, but without a Democratic administration in Washington to sustain them and help them grow, they are bound to atrophy. Moreover, attrition is sure to take place as white leaders like Governor Waller bring more and more blacks into state government and the regular party, and blacks no longer feel as alienated as they once did from the official system. Hodding Carter III said the Loyalists had already succeeded in accomplishing their two most important goals: forcing the regular party to open itself to black participation, and assuring that no delegation can go to a Democratic National Convention without adequate black representation.

Before the 1972 Democratic National Convention, efforts were made to effect a rapproachement between the two sides. The Loyalists demanded equal representation on the local and state Democratic committees, arguing that they deserved that break (beyond their actual numerical strength) because their supporters had proved their loyalty to national Democratic candidates while the regulars had consistently supported third-party or conservative candidates in Presidential elections. Aaron Henry said he would be willing to step down as state chairman in a 50-50 split arrangement. But Waller and the regulars were unwilling to concede the Loyalists anything beyond one-third representation, and that only in a limited number of counties. So the Loyalists were again seated as the legal Mississippi delegation at the national convention.

The rationale for compromise will become increasingly strong, however, so that a settlement is quite possible before the 1976 Democratic National Convention. Governor Waller or his successor could in effect resolve the whole issue by getting the legislature to enact a truly democratic primary law for the election of national convention delegates and local and state party officials. If the law included enough single-member districts so that a substantial number of blacks could be elected—like the system carefully maneuvered by Democratic Chairman Robert Vance in Alabama—then there would be a compelling case for the credentials committee at the next Democratic National Convention to accept the delegation elected in the primary. Evers said he would be open to that kind of a settlement, but with a big "if"—"if you first guarantee fair elections." The fascinating element in the situation is that those fair elections, and the absence of intimidation, would be necessary for acceptance of any delegation at the national convention. Thus for the first time since Reconstruction, it would be in the fundamental self-interest of the white-dominated regular Democratic party to guarantee elections without a trace of coercion or repression.

Mississippi's Republican party became a negligible factor in Mississippi politics after the 1870s. It was run by blacks and was the epitome of the "post office Republican party" of the South, a vestigial organization that sometimes reaped patronage benefits when Republicans were in control in Washington. President Herbert Hoover, after his election in 1928, tried to encourage Southern white Republicanism, and from 1929 to 1960 there was an embittered struggle between two Mississippi GOP factions—the older Negro-run "Black and Tans" and the "Lily Whites." The Black and Tans won consistently until the 1950s, when the Lily Whites won recognition of the national party. In 1960 the Black and Tans gave up the ghost, and without the slogan, the Mississippi GOP has in fact been lily-white ever since. For the most part it has been ultraconservative too, a position exemplified by Wirt Yerger, the party chairman from 1957 to 1966, who drove both Negroes and disaffected Democrats away from the party. The party's most spectacular victories—in the 1964 and 1972 Presidential elections—were based almost exclusively on antiblack sentiment and won the GOP few permanent converts.

The Republicans' first major gubernatorial candidate of the century was Jackson businessman Rubel Phillips, who ran first in 1963 and got 38 percent of the vote against Democrat Paul Johnson. Johnson was running a bitterly racist campaign, and Phillips got substantial support from some of the moderates and liberals who had backed Johnson's losing primary opponent, former Governor J. P. Coleman. Since then, Fortenberry and Abney noted, support for GOP state nominees has correlated closely with support of defeated Democratic primary candidates, "suggesting that at least some of the votes do not necessarily represent enthusiasm for the Republican cause as much as they represent antagonism toward the Democratic nominee."

Rubel Phillips ran for governor again in 1967 and got only 30 percent against John Bell Williams. But he did take a courageous stand on the racial issue, for which history should grant him a nod:

> The influence of race upon the thoughts and actions of Mississippians [Phillips said] is so dominant that it is utterly unrealistic to expect any significant progress in such vital fields as education, economic development, and federal-state relations until we have brought the race issue out into the open and begun—at least begun—to deal with it effectively. . . .
>
> As long as they remain in Mississippi, the Negro and the white are bound together—even though they may live separate lives, in separate communities. They are bound together so closely that neither can rise significantly without lifting the other.

Up to now, the Mississippi Republicans have made their most significant gains on the coattails of popular GOP Presidential candidates. In 1964 they elected their first Congressman of the century in the midst of the Goldwater Mississippi landslide; if they had nominated congressional candidates in more than that single district, they might have done even better. In 1972 they set out not to repeat the mistake and nominated candidates in three of the state's five districts. Two of them won—Trent Lott, a new GOP convert who had been an aide to retiring Democratic Representative William Colmer, and Thad Cochran, a Jackson lawyer. Both were in their thirties, and

Cochran in particular was considered a moderate by Mississippi standards. He even got a measure of black votes in his race against conservative Democrat Ellis Bodron, a blind state senator from Vicksburg and one of the powers in Mississippi politics.

The future will tell whether those gains were coattail accidents or more firmly based. In 1966 Republican Congressman Prentiss Walker, the man who had won with Goldwater's assist, challenged no less a figure than Senator James O. Eastland. A chicken farmer by profession, Walker had first won notice as chairman of the 1960 unpledged elector slate in Mississippi. Walker demonstrated his limited political acumen by trying to suggest that Eastland had merely been pretending for 25 years that he was a real conservative. (I have always been amused by the image conjured up by Walker's charge that Eastland, unbeknown to the good people of Mississippi, "hobnobs and prances" with the Kennedy political clan in Washington.) The argument that Walker was the truer Mississippian simply didn't wash; as state AFL-CIO chief Claude Ramsey pointed out, Walker was trying to "outsegregate" Eastland and "this, of course, was impossible. You just don't outsegregate Jim Eastland." Not only did Eastland win again with two-thirds of the vote, but the Republicans lost all four congressional districts in which they ran candidates.

Ironically, the Republicans today are in much the same position as the old Black and Tans—they can control the patronage, but they can't, except under exceptional circumstances, get a significant vote. They have occasionally elected mayors in cities like Columbus and Hattiesburg, but their representation at the local level is generally minuscule. After years of effort, and despite the benefit of Nixon coattails in 1972, all they could elect were two members of the 52-man Mississippi senate and two of 121 members in the house. Their state chairman of the last several years, Clarke Reed of Greenville, is one of the ablest political operatives in the country, but even he has acknowledged the major hurdles the Republicans face, including the necessity of getting a huge majority of the white vote in any election if Mississippi's blacks continue to vote overwhelmingly Democratic. The Ripon Society observed that it was "a tribute to Reed's great personal charm that with as little as the Mississippi GOP has to show for results," he nevertheless became chairman of the Southern state Republican chairmen and a voice to be listened to in the Nixon Administration.

Were it not for Mississippi's century-long Democratic voting habits, the Republicans would have a much better chance. Their basic conservatism should have as strong an appeal in Mississippi as anywhere in the South, and a growing middle-class, urban society gives them increasing opportunities. But that building process is so slow that they have sometimes dreamed of having Mississippi's conservative Democrats come over to them *en masse*. John Bell Williams publicly flirted with that idea while he was governor in the late 1960s. The possibility of party-switching was (and is) dimmed by the fact that Mississippi's veteran Senators and Congressmen would give up centuries of accumulated seniority if they switched parties. Moreover, those very Senators and Congressmen are essential to legislative success for a Republican administration in Washington, so that there is national pressure not to cross them.

An example was the 1972 Senate election, when Eastland's seat was up again. Eastland had given staunch defense to former Attorney General John N. Mitchell during hearings on the nomination of Richard Kleindienst to succeed him, had backed the President's appointments of Clement Haynsworth and G. Harrold Carswell for the Supreme Court, and had voted a conservative line much to the President's liking. Small wonder then that the President let it be known through his press secretary that he would be happy to see Eastland reelected, and that he and Eastland had "great respect for one another."

Before the Republican primary, however, Reed had prevailed on Gilbert Carmichael, a Meridian businessman and toiler in state GOP circles for a dozen years, to run for the Senate nomination. James Meredith had filed for the same nomination, and Reed was afraid that with Meredith on the ticket, the Republicans' chances of picking up U.S. House seats would be destroyed. The problem was that Carmichael, once nominated, refused to roll over and play dead. He accused Eastland of absenteeism and of representing chiefly plantation owners and other millionaires. When Vice President Agnew visited Jackson during the campaign, he managed to invoke the names of Henry Clay, Andrew Jackson, Jefferson Davis, and the three GOP House candidates —but never mentioned Carmichael. In fact, Carmichael was kept off the platform from which Agnew spoke. Carmichael was not amused, and he angrily accused Eastland's supporters and Mississippian Fred LaRue, a high executive of the Nixon reelection committee, of running "a bogus Republican party." * Eastland did win again, but with only 58 percent of the popular vote—the closest he had ever come in a general election. The possibility remained open that the Republicans, with a united effort, might have defeated him.

Carmichael made an overt bid for the black vote and in fact got just under half of it, compared to the minuscule percentage accorded Phillips when he made his lonely pro-integration campaign in 1967. The results suggest a growing flexibility among Mississippi blacks that the Republicans, with smarter tactics, might exploit more often.

The recent increases in two-party competition and black voting have had one impact—to increase dramatically the number of Mississippians who bother to vote in Presidential elections. Back in 1920, the Presidential turnout of voting-age Mississippians was an infinitesimal 9.4 percent. By 1960, the figure was still only 25.3 percent—another one of those indexes in which Mississippi ranked last among all the states. But by 1968, the turnout was up to 53.1 percent, and in 1972 still fairly high (in comparison with the dismal past) at 46.0 percent. Yet the figure was still the lowest in the Union.

* LaRue, it later turned out, had been up to his ears in the effort to cover up the Nixon campaign's sponsorship of the Watergate burglary. He had first made his mark as a big Goldwater supporter in 1964, and before the 1972 campaign he had an office in the Nixon White House, carrying out mysterious duties.

Seniority's Sons

Mississippi may be 50th in many comparisons between the states, but in modern times it has rarely been second to any in Congressional seniority. In 1972 the average seniority of Mississippi's Senators and Representatives was 22.4 years—more than any other state. Yet if seniority and the attendant committee chairmanships amount to unique congressional power, one can ask why Mississippi is still America's poorest state. The answer, of course, is that Mississippi's power in Congress has been used more to fight civil rights and social welfare proposals than to improve the lot of poor people and backward areas. Again, the strands—and the tragedy—of the Mississippi story can be traced back to the race issue.

It is almost too neat: the senior Democrat in the Senate, now President Pro Tempore and for years chairman of the Judiciary Committee, is a man whose very name long ago became synonomous with the fight to preserve racial segregation: James O. Eastland. He has been a member of the Senate since 1942. He is the owner of a 5,400-acre plantation in Sunflower County in the Delta, where hundreds of black field hands used to work in the cotton fields for as little as 30 cents an hour. Today no more than 50 or 60 families are left, and only half that number are really needed to perform the functions of modern, mechanized cotton planting. Eastland's plantation blacks live in miserable little houses that could best be called shacks, and all but a handful of them are desperately poor. But Eastland does not throw the unneeded people off the land, perhaps out of *noblesse oblige*, or perhaps, as his administrative assistant for farming said in the late 1960s, because eviction would merely consign them "to the ghetto in Chicago or Washington."

But, however paternalistic Eastland may be toward individual blacks, his attitude toward them as full citizens has varied little since 1947, when he said: "The mental level of these people renders them incapable of suffrage."

Each year, the Eastland plantation produces $500,000 or more worth of cotton and other crops. His protagonists frequently point out that while he opposes a "free dole" from the federal government to Mississippi's poor, he accepts huge sums for not growing cotton. In 1970, over Eastland's opposition, Congress passed a law limiting federal farm subsidies to $50,000 for any recipient in any year. But Eastland's cotton subsidies dropped only $3,000 from the $163,000 level of 1970, because Eastland was able to take advantage of a loophole in the Agriculture Department regulations permitting individual partners in a partnership to receive the maximum payments. Early in 1971, Eastland dissolved Eastland Plantation, Inc., replacing it with a partnership of six entities in which he, his wife, and four children were the partners.

Sunflower County is one of the poorest in America. The 1970 Census found that 72 percent of its black people and 17 percent of its white people were living in poverty. Between welfare, Head Start programs, OEO neighborhood health centers, welfare, and school lunch programs, the federal government disbursed $3 million in Sunflower County in 1971. (Eastland had opposed enactment of most of those programs.) In the same year, cotton planters in the county received almost $12 million in direct payments from the Department of Agriculture.

James Eastland is not a raw, crude character like Theodore Bilbo, whose supporter and protegé he once was in the Mississippi legislature. I recall visiting his office one afternoon to pick up some routine information when I was first reporting in Washington, and being ushered into Eastland's personal office at 5 P.M. to share in the bourbon and branch water. The talk was all about the elevation of the courthouse in Sunflower County and similar bucolic themes, and Eastland was as pleasant a host as one could imagine. He is round-faced and bespectacled, has a ruddy complexion, and walks with a slight hunch that belies his six-foot height. He has used his Judiciary Committee chairmanship to kill civil rights bills whenever he could—127, he claimed at one point in the 1960s—and to expedite or stall confirmation of Presidential appointees, depending on their philosophy. In 1961 he held up for a year the appointment of Circuit Court of Appeals nominee Thurgood Marshall, who later became the first black Justice of the Supreme Court. Finally Eastland let the Marshall appointment go through when the Kennedy administration agreed to appoint Harold Cox, Eastland's college roommate, to the federal bench. (According to Robert Sherrill, Cox later called defendants "chimpanzees" and "niggers" from the bench.) Yet in the last several years, liberal colleagues on Eastland's Judiciary Committee have said that he conducts committee business fairly and respects the prerogatives of other Senators, even when he disagrees with them. And some Mississippi state officials say that Eastland has helped them—always behind the scenes—on programs that would help impoverished blacks.

Eastland's power to kill civil rights legislation was seriously undermined in the late 1950s and early 1960s when the Senate leadership put House-passed rights bills directly on the calendar or placed tight time-limits on Judiciary Committee consideration—the latter a device that Eastland assailed as "legislative lynching." But in the run-of-the-mill business of the Senate, his power is still enormous. The Judiciary Committee handles 60 percent of all legislation in the Senate, including private bills and measures in the fields of crime, gun control, civil rights, the courts, patents, immigration, penitentiaries, antitrust, and proposed constitutional amendments. Close to a third of all Senate committee funds are channeled to Judiciary, and the *National Journal* noted Eastland's "ability to pry funds for his committee and its subcommittees from the Senate Committee on Rules and Administration." As if that were not enough, Eastland is also second-ranking on the Senate Agriculture Committee, a panel which handles, among other things, the farm subsidy programs so important to him personally. His critics see a clear conflict of interest in that role.

Back in Mississippi, the basis of Eastland's strength is his reputation as a friend of the cotton farmer and foe of racial integration. Geography has something to do with it too, however. He was born almost 70 years ago in the Delta, but he spent most of his youthful years in the Hills town of Forest, Mississippi, before returning to the Delta. Robert Sherrill wrote: "The impoverished rednecks do not normally trust Delta moneyed men. Eastland has the best of both worlds: born among the rich and reared among the rednecks, he carries both blocs."

To read their voting records, Eastland and his Mississippi colleague, Senator John C. Stennis, might as well be the Bobsey Twins. They agree almost 100 percent of the time. Both are fiscal conservatives, opposed to social welfare programs, against civil rights, for tax breaks for business, and for high levels of military expenditures.

John Stennis, however, has a very different public image. Quiet and introspective by nature, he is considered the very epitome of Southern gentility, of decorum and dignity and unimpeached integrity. In 1954 he was the first Democrat to urge on the Senate floor that Senator Joseph McCarthy be censured. He headed the 1967 investigation of alleged misuse of funds by Connecticut's Thomas Dodd, a task he said he found distasteful but one in which he said he was motivated by his love of the Senate as an institution.

Over most of his career, Stennis was not a household God in Mississippi. He was too scholarly and aloof; he never shouted the loudest, as Eastland did, about the abominations of race mixing. Writer James Batten quoted Stennis as saying that when he ran for Bilbo's seat in 1947, he was pressured to engage in some of the traditional racial demogoguery. "Some of my advisers thought if I didn't make an anti-Negro statement I might not be elected. But I wouldn't do it, and I never have." Since the mid-1960s, however, Stennis has sought out opportunities to assail programs like the Head Starts and to be a Southern spokesman on legislation affecting school integration. The Mississippi rednecks know just where he stands. The state's black leaders think they know too. In 1969, after many high Nixon administration officials attended a testimonial dinner in Jackson in Stennis' honor, Aaron Henry complained:

> There they were, lionizing a man who has voted against every issue of progress for the state. He's voted against the war on poverty, federal aid to education, Medicare, Medicaid, the minimum wage. . . .
>
> The difference between Eastland and Stennis is that Stennis is a segregationist, Northern-style. He uses subtlety. Eastland would say, point-blank, "Get the hell out of here, I ain't going to serve you because you're black." Stennis would say, "You don't have a reservation." But either way, you still haven't eaten. One is shrewd and sophisticated in promulgating segregation, the other is blatant—and maybe more honest.

Stennis' primary Senate interest has been in the military. In 1961 he succeeded Lyndon Johnson as chairman of the Preparedness Subcommittee. In 1969 he succeeded Richard Russell as chairman of the Armed Services Committee. He soon found himself leading the fight for the Nixon administration's antiballistic missile (ABM) program in the midst of the first Senate revolt against major new weapons systems and continued high defense outlays in the face of mounting domestic needs. Stennis won the ABM fight and ably represented the Pentagon-administration side in the military authorization fights of the succeeding years. A strong defense was Stennis' constant—and perhaps overriding—concern. In a 1966 speech he said: "Great Society programs with the billions they are gulping down should be relegated to the rear. . . . They should be secondary to the [Vietnam] war."

Stennis is not the prototypal military pork-barreler; in fact, his personal sense of honor would stop him from putting pressure on the Pentagon to spend more money in Mississippi. There are still only four military installations and three defense contractors in the state. But the Pentagon money-allocators, perhaps noting on which side their bread was buttered, sharply increased their outlays in Mississippi during the 1960s and early 1970s.

Early in 1973, Stennis was shot and seriously wounded by three street hoodlums in a robbery outside his Washington home. It was a senseless, shocking attack, and leaders of both parties and races expressed deep regret and sympathy. Yet there were ironies in the situation. The shooting was done with a cheap handgun, but the year before Stennis had voted against a handgun control bill. And the young blacks who perpetrated the attack were in a sense symbolic of the legacy of ignorance and lawlessness that had its roots in the racial and economic practices of the South and the Northern migration of a perennially dispossessed people. One looked in vain in Stennis' record for a single vote or stand aimed at alleviating the root causes of those problems.

The glare of national attention on Senate goliaths like Eastland and Stennis has diverted public notice from some of the most powerful Mississippians of all—its committee and subcommittee chairmen in the House. No man in Congress, for instance, has exerted more influence over the years on federal farm policy—a vital factor in heavily rural Mississippi—than Jamie L. Whitten, chairman of the Appropriations Subcommittee on Agriculture. Whitten has been called "the permanent Secretary of Agriculture," a man with more influence over the gargantuan Agriculture Department than Presidents or Agriculture Secretaries, who come and go while he remains. As one of the 13 Appropriations subcommittee chairmen—sometimes known as the "College of Cardinals"—Whitten not only reviews and decides on, line by line, $7 billion each year in federal appropriations for agriculture, but also, since 1971, funds for virtually all government agencies responsible for environmental control and consumer protection.

Jamie Whitten's institutional power is augmented by studious application to the details of the programs and departments his agency funds. He is also a man with an outgoing personality and a verbal virtuosity that baffles opponents and charms the home folks. Dr. Spencer Smith, lobbyist for the Citizens Committee on Natural Resources, traveled through Whitten's district—an amalgamation of north Mississippi Hills and Delta counties—and later described the experience to researchers for Ralph Nader's Congress Project as "absolutely incredible." Smith said Whitten would walk into the drugstore in a town of 1,800, sit in one of the wire-backed chairs, order a "sody," and start to kibitz with the townsfolk. To get more of an audience, Whitten would go out the door, throw his arms in the air, and "let out a bull-like cry that sounds like 'Jamie's here!'" Cars would stop in the middle of the road and people gather round. Whitten had instant recall of the names of countless people in each town, and would be quick "to compliment Miss Mae on winning the prune award at the county fair and Judy Jones on winning the Audubon contest on the male mocking bird." He even had good rapport with the Negroes he met, so that he could go "right into the kitchen at some of the grubbiest black homes and eat a piece of rhubarb pie." Whitten had enough strong black contacts, Smith reported, so that if militants went into his district, "they'd be lucky to come back with their heads."

For an outsider, it is hard to believe that Whitten really represents the interests of blacks in Mississippi or anywhere. He showed his sentiments in the 1950s by warning that the Supreme Court's school decision had started America "on the downhill road to integration and amalgamation and ruin." Later, he voted against all the civil rights acts. He opposed the poverty program at every turn and voted against Medicare, the family assistance plan, and child care for the working poor. He was a strong, early opponent of the food stamp program.

Reporter Nick Kotz, in his 1969 book *Let Them Eat Promises* asserted that in the 1940s Whitten killed an Agriculture Department study that sought to anticipate the social and economic problems of Negro GI's returning to the feudal cotton South. Thus rebuffed when it looked at social issues, the Department increasingly focused its attention on planters and their crops and failed to develop policies that might have ameliorated conditions for poor field hands and stopped so many of them from being thrown off the land and forced into the big cities. Kotz also said Whitten had killed the Johnson administration's Rural Community Development Service, an effort by Agriculture Secretary Orville Freeman to coordinate programs for the rural poor. Dr. Jean Mayer, nutrition professor at Harvard and chairman of the White House Conference on Food, Nutrition and Health, alleged that Whitten "fought practically every single financial measure directed at allaying malnutrition among the poor." One year in the 1960s, a study showed that $23.5 million was pouring into Whitten's district for agricultural payments to big producers—those receiving $5,000 a year or more from the federal government, a group representing about three-tenths of one percent of the district population. But the food relief programs for the 59 percent of the district's people living in poverty totaled less than a fifth as much—$4 million.

Whitten's own point of view is that overgenerous food and welfare programs destroy the incentive for poor people to work. As for the nutrition issue, he once laid that to rest by saying: "All welfare families want is cola and candy."

Yet the fact is that while Whitten has fought hard to preserve high subsidies for planters in his district, the lot of poor people there is one of the most miserable in the nation. In 1970 their median family income was $2,847, compared with the $9,433 median of all families in the United States. Not far from Whitten's own neat frame home in Tallahatchie County, Negroes live in shacks without toilets, running water, electricity, or adequate food. Nick Kotz wrote:

Jamie Whitten truly believes in his own fairness, his idea of good works, and the imagined affection he receives from Negroes back home. . . . He has anesthetized his soul to the human misery and indignity only a few yards from his own home and has refused to believe that the responsibility for that indignity lies on his white shoulders. His belief in the basic laziness, indifference, and unworthiness of the black poor is as strong as his belief in the virtue of a way of life that for three centuries has denied these same black poor any avenues of pursuing ambition, self-respect, or a better future for their children.

Whitten has been defended against such attacks, even by Congressmen who disagree with him on the issues; one of these was Colorado Democrat Frank Evans, a liberal who told the *Wall Street Journal* in 1971 that "criticism of Jamie Whitten by some liberals has gone beyond the realm of propriety and accuracy." Whitten is considered one of the fairer subcommittee chairmen. His defenders point out that he finally accepted the idea of food stamps and let their annual appropriations level rise to more than $1 billion in the early 1970s, and that he beefed up funding and staffing for the Food and Drug Administration and the Environmental Protection Administration—without a word of credit from the Northern liberal press. (Some believe he may have taken a moderate position on those issues to avoid liberal attacks on farm appropriations.) Whitten was taken to task in the public prints for having accepted help from the pesticide industry when he was seeking a publisher for his 1965 book *That We May Live*, a rejoinder to Rachel Carson's *Silent Spring*. But Whitten had a point in defending farmers' use of pesticides—at least in reasonable quantities; without those protections, he said, "the health danger would greatly increase, and malaria would be back with us, and many, many other things."

In 1973 Whitten had 32 years of congressional service behind him—but he was still only 63 years old. He was, as his friends like to say, "only a heartbeat away" from chairmanship of the full Appropriations Committee, headed by 73-year-old George Mahon of Texas.

Another Mississippian whom the seniority system elevated to immense national power was William M. Colmer, a member of the House for 40 years and chairman of the Rules Committee for six years before his retirement—at the age of 82—in 1973. Colmer did not preside over the Rules Committee, which controls the flow of legislation to the House floor, with the unfettered power enjoyed by his ally and predecessor, Virginia's Howard W. Smith. Speaker Sam Rayburn had been able to enlarge the committee in 1961 to break the wall of conservative control that had killed so much progressive legislation in the 1950s. But Colmer was able to bottle up liberal bills on many occasions; among these were a consumer protection bill and a measure —which he called "vicious"—to give the federal government broad power to enforce nondiscrimination in employment. When Colmer announced he would step down, the New York *Times* (obviously no friend of his viewpoints) editorialized: "The Mississippian's retirement should stimulate a reconsideration of the Rules Committee's powers. It might even raise once more the question of whether mere aging can do for Congressmen what it does for cheese and wine."

Governing Mississippi

Given Mississippi's other problem, it would be surprising to find that its state government was a citadel of progressivism. Rather, it was a citadel of hypocrisy for decades as it maintained a statewide "dry" law while it collected an open black market tax on the booze that netted as much as $4.5 million in a single year. Repeatedly, the fundamentalists and the *sub rosa* liquor lobby got together to defeat referenda for repeal of prohibition, in effect since 1908. Paul Johnson was the first governor who had the courage to back repeal, saying it was "high time" to talk honestly about "whiskey, prohibition, black market taxes, payola, and all the other many-colored hues that make up Mississippi's aurora borealis of prohibition." The liquor had always flowed freely on the Gulf Coast and Natchez-Vicksburg-Greenville-Delta areas, but Johnson said "a 15-year-old child can take a $5 bill and buy whiskey in practically any county." A sheriff's raid on a well-oiled country club party in Jackson, where Governor Johnson himself was present, was one of the last straws. Repeal came in 1966 by the legislature without a referendum.

The liquor story, however colorful, misses the point of Mississippi's deep-seated conservatism—what V. O. Key called "the Delta mind." It has been expressed time and again, perhaps best a few years ago when the late Walter Sillers, perennial speaker of the Mississippi House, opposed progressive taxes to support public education. "After all," Sillers declared, "the people who have the children should pay the tax, and you know the favored few don't have children."

The mood and temper of Mississippi government is beginning to change now. Governor Waller, despite some poor judgments in administration and actions that offended blacks, is the most progressive executive the state has had in modern times. The senate and house are changing too. State AFL-CIO president Claude Ramsay, long a lonely exponent of racial moderation and liberal government policies, told me in 1973, "We have the best legislature in my lifetime." Organized labor's political impact has long been considered minimal because of low membership—the rate of unionization, depressed in part by right-to-work, ranks only 47th among the states. But in 1971, Ramsay claimed, "we were able to help elect a majority of the legislature." The new legislature showed its appreciation by boosting workmen's compensation from $40 a week (the lowest figure in the country) to $56 with an escalation to $63 a week. It was a startling development in a state where the dominant lobbies have long been the Mississippi Economic Council (the state's chamber of commerce), the Mississippi Manufacturers Association, the Mississippi Medical Association, and the Farm Bureau.

William Winter, who had been a state legislator in the early 1950s and then returned to the legislative halls to preside over the senate after his 1971 election as lieutenant governor, said he was amazed by the change in temperament. In the old days, he said, the legislators had been preoccupied with fighting the federal government over the integration issue. The new agenda, by contrast, centered on implementing programs that involved a good deal of federal participation. "It's a bread-and-butter situation now," he said. Reapportionment had helped to change the mood, Winter thought, but the participation of Negroes in elections might have been more vital. "Remember," he said, "that many legislators are here by virtue of the fact they got more black votes than somebody else did."

The change in the legislative mood is vital, because the legislature has long been the vital center of decision-making in Mississippi government—never the subservient body that its counterparts in states like Louisiana and Georgia were for so many years. The Citizens Conference on State Legislatures rated Mississippi's legislature relatively high in independence but very low in its information sources, accountability, and capacity to act in an efficient manner. But marked improvements have been made on all those fronts, including a shift to annual sessions, reduction of the absurdly high number of standing committees (which had been the most numerous of any legislature in the country), authorization of committee work between sessions and a legislative services office, and passage of a campaign spending reporting law. "Mississippi's legislature," W. F. Minor reported, "can no longer be described as perhaps the slowest-moving, most undisciplined legislature in the country."

Even if the legislature, by Mississippi standards, has taken a long step forward, it would still rank as one of the most conservative on a national scale. The rejection of public kindergartens and compulsory school education, to which I referred earlier, are cases in point. Another is the deeply regressive tax system which the ruling circles have impressed on Mississippi over the past several decades. In 1932, Mississippi became the first state to enact a retail sales tax. Today the rate is 5 percent, and it is the most all-inclusive in the nation, extending even to medicine, groceries, and yes—even to food stamps! A sales tax is inherently regressive, but in a poor state like Mississippi, where so many people must expend every dollar of their meager incomes on the essentials of life, the burden is extreme. The Old Guard fiscal leadership in the legislature, according to Bill Minor, resists any change in the sales tax—"a vestige of the philosophy that the sales tax is the 'one tax which blacks pay.' "

Seventy-seven percent of Mississippi's tax revenues come from general and selective sales taxes—the highest proportion of any Southern state except Florida (which keeps its sales taxes up to collect from the tourists) and one of the four highest in the country. In 1971, for example, Mississippi collected $398 million through general and selective sales taxes, compared to only $66 million from personal and corporate income taxes. The Mississippi personal income tax has a generous personal exemption that relieves practically all poor families from paying it, but the rate is low and virtually ungraduated so that its burden is also light on "the favored few" whose interests powerful Mississippi legislators have been so anxious to protect.

It is worth recording that in 1971 Mississippi's state and local governments collected an average of $593 per person in taxes. That figure ranked only 37th among the states. But when the Mississippi taxes were measured against personal income, the state's ranking on a scale of comparative tax effort was 15th from the top in the country. Thus in relation to their wealth, Mississippians pay quite heavy taxes, even if the dollars produced are far below the national norm.

Andrew Carr, a Delta planter of unusually liberal views, put his finger on another unique element of the state's fiscal situation when he said: "Mississippi is a welfare state, dependent on the federal dole at all levels." The figures support Carr's conclusion. In 1971 the federal government collected $1.2 billion in taxes in Mississippi. But it spent almost twice as much—$2.3 billion, to be exact—in the state. Federal outlays in Mississippi were close to $1,100 for every man, woman, and child living there, a momentous factor in a state where per capita income was only $2,766. Federal grants represent 45 percent of state and local government revenues in Mississippi—easily the highest in the country. And the formula is not likely to be reversed soon. When federal revenue sharing went into effect, Mississippi got more per capita than any other state in the Union.

Military, veterans, highways, education, and agricultural programs make up the lion's share of federal expenditures in Mississippi, but the most controversial items are those in the social welfare field, simply because they pose a challenge to old power relationships and the traditional ways of handling poor blacks and whites within Mississippi society. Starting in the mid-1960s, millions of federal dollars began to flow into Mississippi for Head Start, legal services, community health, and community action programs. Often the once mute poor people sat on the boards of the new programs and controlled their course. In effect, the programs were on-the-job training courses in how government works—a potentially serious challenge to the existing political power structure of a tightly controlled state. The hostile reaction of conservative and segregationist leaders like Governor John Bell Williams, who objected both to the substance and mode of operation of the various poverty programs, was predictable enough—and simply overridden by Washington.

It was another matter altogether, however, when the "moderate" William Waller became governor in 1972 and began to veto several multimillion-dollar grants to community health services, as well as the Mississippi Neighborhood Legal Services Program. Waller's point did not seem to be that the programs were bad in principle, but rather that they were being poorly run and that he, as govenor of the state, should be able to appoint their boards, set their guidelines, and in effect control them. Waller also developed a plan for hundreds of government-run day-care centers around the state, which would in effect replace the community-run Head Start programs. "Waller wants to control every federal buck he can coming into the state," Hodding Carter III said, reflecting a widely held viewpoint. "Power is his first motive." Carter said Waller had begun with the black-controlled projects because they were politically weaker than older programs run by influential whites.

In 1973 the picture began to change again as the Nixon administration moved to dismantle the Office of Economic Opportunity and reduce federal grant-in-aid programs for social services. Waller was among the several governors who protested the reductions, saying that poor rural states like Mississippi, which have less of the population and more of the problems, would suffer the most. (Mississippi's attitude toward federal assistance has changed radically since several years ago, when a veteran Delta legislator said that he would favor outright refusal of *all* federal money in exchange for real "sovereignty"—at a time when federal funds amounted to seven times the amount of the state's general fund budget. But in the '60s, even John Bell Williams set up a federal-state programs office to seek federal money and appointed David Bowen, a Harvard- and Oxford-trained "liberal," to head it. The ability to snare federal funds is now a major talking point of moderate candidates in Mississippi. It was an issue Bowen used, for instance, to win election to Congress in 1972.)

The threatened reductions of federal assistance for socially advanced programs threw an especially long shadow over Mississippi. The 816,000 black people of the state still had only one of their race in the legislature, and precious few county posts in their control, and not very many white allies to turn to. Yet as gloomy as that picture seemed, the rapidity of political change and the potential power of the black vote seemed to assure that a turning back of the clock a decade or more, to a time when Mississippi's blacks and other poor were treated as nonpersons with nonproblems, would be impossible. Governor Waller himself gave the best reason when he noted that "in addition to some 170,000 blacks who are classified in the poverty area in Mississippi, there are approximately 160,000 whites who fall into the same category.* It is no longer a black or white problem, but an underprivileged problem." It is also, he might have noted, a potentially powerful political coalition in the reconstructed Mississippi of the '70s.

Mississippi Economy: From Cotton to Computers

Up through the 1930s, Mississippi was like one great cotton plantation. The ownership, to be sure, was split into many thousand pieces, but the cotton mentality was all-pervasive and stifling. Fearful of competition for labor, the Delta legislators—acting in concert with Populist leaders who feared Wall Street—at one point even passed a law forbidding the location within Mississippi of any industry with more than $1 million in capitalization. That statute was repealed after World War I, but in the Great Depression it was obvious that Mississippi had come to the end of the line with its old way of doing things. Cotton agriculture was becoming more concentrated and more productive, but it was using less and less labor to produce. Starting in the '30s, and then with increasing speed, the tractor began to replace the old picture of the tenant farmer encouraging a balky mule to pull a broken-down plow through the cotton fields. The clanking mechanical pickers arrived on the scene after World War II, each one throwing scores of untrained, unlettered field hands onto a labor market where virtually no other opportunities

* Waller's poverty figures were much lower than those reported by the Census for Mississippi in 1970: 520,746 blacks and 242,628 whites, representing 65 and 18 percent of their respective populations.

awaited them. Mississippi simply had no industrial base on which it could build. And its agricultural support economy lay in ruins, because as the dirt farmers left the fields, the infrastructure of stores and suppliers that had serviced them lost its principal reason for being.

"Our state," editor Oliver Emmerich of McComb told me, "was like an underdeveloped Latin country." Except for cotton, about the only resource Mississippi had had was its great timber stands. But outside industries had swept the state clean of pine, leaving scarcely enough trees behind to provide seeds for natural regrowth. Vast cutover lands and sediment-clogged streams were the legacy of that rape. "And our politicians spent their time attacking Wall Street and industry," Emmerich said. "How did that help the poor farmers in the fields?"

The year 1936 was to prove an historic one for Mississippi, for it was then that the legislature authorized the state's first industrial recruitment program. "Reflecting the long agrarian history of the state," historian Thomas D. Clark wrote, "the new law paid its respects to the past and courted the future in its title, 'Balance Agriculture With Industry.'" His account continued:

> Mississippi went on an advertising spree to attract industry. Signs along main railroads proclaimed the glories of local communities, with the hope that they would catch the eyes of business executives as they raced by in Pullman cars. National magazines carried advertisements, and news stories described the glories of Mississippi's industrial future.

The "BAWI" program was to prove a resounding success. One can see it today in the landscape dotted with light manufacturing plants. And figures prove the point. In 1939 the value added by manufacturing in Mississippi was $73 million; today the figure is over $2 billion a year. In 1940 manufacturing employment was only 59,000; today it is close to 200,000. In 1966, for the first time, there were more Mississippians working in factories than on the land—proof that agriculture had indeed been "balanced" with industry. And thousands more make their living in services, trade, finance, and government, as a result of the industrialization.

BAWI notwithstanding, Mississippi has suffered a staggering loss of people in the past three decades. In the 1940s and again in the 1950s, Mississippi lost almost 435,000 people; in the 1960s, the figure was 269,000.* But one can only imagine what would have happened if there had been no BAWI. Mississippi might look like a semideserted colony today, inhabited only by plantation owners, their few remaining field hands, and perhaps the support personnel for the tourist industry along the Gulf Coast.

Despite the achievements, Mississippi paid a price for the BAWI program. The tendency was to grab any factory one could get, no questions asked, if the result would be a smokestack for a job-hungry town. One of the first plants snared was an Armstrong Rubber and Tire facility in Natchez,

* These figures represent net migration—the changes in a state's population after births and deaths are deducted. Over the 30-year period (1940 to 1970) the state lost 928,000 black and 208,000 white people through outmigration. But the natural increase—births over deaths—was enough to hold the total population fairly constant over the entire period. The 1970 statewide total was 2,216,912.

which quickly added a new aroma to that historic old city. The unsubtle advertising pitch was for "willing and able labor," so that most of the plants that came were low-skill, low-wage outfits, many fleeing the pressures of Northern labor unions and minimum wage laws in other states. Garment and hosiery plants, paying rock-bottom wages to largely female work forces, came in special abundance. (Other factory types included furniture, paper, glass, light bulbs, tools, wood and metal gadgets, and the like.) BAWI plants sometimes seemed anxious to bow to the local mores on race, making off-the-record agreements to hire only whites or predominantly white labor forces. Local tax rolls were shortchanged by agreements, sanctioned by state law, to waive *all* local property taxes for 10 years for a new industry. Local bond issues were used to finance the entire cost of industrial buildings. There were some cases in which unscrupulous operators befuddled the locals by moving in only long enough to enjoy the tax free period in taxpayer-supported buildings, then disappearing from the scene.

Over the years, however, those kinds of abuses have diminished. Cheap labor may still be an inducement for some industries, but they know they are moving into a new kind of climate now. A 1972 advertisement in *Fortune* even featured these words beside a smiling picture of Bill Waller: "We're undergoing a sociological as well as an industrial revolution and we welcome you to come down and view it, firsthand." A few years ago, "sociological . . . revolution" would have been fightin' words in Mississippi.

One problem with BAWI was that the more low-wage industries were acquired, the more a low-wage level in the state was perpetuated. For years, little seemed to be done to get heavy or technologically advanced industries. Waller said in the 1960s, before he became governor "We've been busy giving away ten-year exemptions to shirt factories, when we should have been out working with General Motors for a tank factory."

By the mid-1960s, the state's Agricultural and Industrial Board, which oversees the BAWI program, had approved close to 600 bond issues amounting to well over a quarter billion dollars—almost all in the low-wage field. Then came what the state's leaders saw as a magnificent opportunity to break into the big time by snaring a highly automated and advanced "shipyard of the future" for the Ingalls Shipbuilding Corporation, a subsidiary of Litton Industries, at Pascagoula. Litton envisaged great opportunities in military and commercial shipbuilding in the '70s and '80s, and was considering an alternative location at Tampa, Florida. But Governor Johnson and the state's economic leaders wanted the facility and its promised 12,000 jobs for Mississippi. And they agreed to Litton's stiff terms: that Mississippi float, on its own faith and credit, a tax-exempt $130 million bond issue under BAWI to finance the shipyard. Litton would pay off the state over a 30-year period, under a lease-purchase arrangement, at interest of only 5 percent. Its own investment cost would be only $3 million (for basic design).

Ellis Gardner, then head of Litton's Pascagoula operations, later described how Governor Johnson and the Mississippi political establishment prostrated themselves at the feet of the big California-based conglomerate:

In July 1967 I went to the governor's office. The Democratic governor and state primaries were about to start. There were seven candidates for governor and many for lieutenant governor. We knew they'd be at each others' throats for three months and that nothing would be sacred from political debate.

The governor had every single candidate for governor and lieutenant governor there. He put a tape recorder on the table and said, "Gentlemen, I have a matter of utmost urgency to discuss with you. I want to introduce Mr. Ellis Gardner, senior vice president of Litton Industries, who wants to tell you about something."

We had charts there to show what would happen to our shipyard employment if we did not go ahead, and what would happen if we did go ahead. I told them the project was dependent on a special session of the legislature to enact the necessary tax-exempt bonds. And it was also contingent on our convincing our labor unions to enter into an unprecedented five-year contract.

I said, "We will drop this whole subject like a hot potato, right now, unless we have your assurances, gentlemen, that this matter will not be made a political football in the coming campaign." The tape recorder was whirring away and each man got up and identified himself by name and said, "I will keep this out of politics." The result: not once during that year's election campaign did the bond issue become a political issue. The issue passed the legislature with only one or two dissenting votes—and as someone observed, "The incidence of psychiatric cases is higher than that."

And the unions, one by one, accepted the five-year contract. We got labor stability unheard of in this industry.

The reader may make his own judgment on whether it was so wonderful to isolate a decision of such magnitude for Mississippi from political debate, or really much debate at all. The fact was that if Litton failed to secure contracts for the installation, the taxpayers of Mississippi, a not very affluent lot, would be left holding the bag.

As it turned out, Gardner and the other Litton executives—including president Roy Ash, who later became director of the federal Office of Management and Budget—were not quite the managerial geniuses the bedazzled politicans thought them to be. It was true that Litton's design experts did tour the world's shipyards and return to design a highly mechanized facility modeled after yards in Germany, Sweden, and Japan. The idea was to apply principles of mass production—somewhat akin to auto assembly lines—to shipbuilding. It was a sound concept, but Litton's problem was that it was trying to build and perfect its modern West Bank shipyard at the very moment that it faced stiff production deadlines on two big Navy contracts it landed—$2.2 billion for 30 high-speed destroyers, and $1.2 billion for nine helicopter assault ships. Most of the people in charge were experienced mainly in the aerospace industry but had a lot to learn about shipbuilding. Workers with new crafts and skills were required, but Litton had difficulty finding them or in training new workers (a result, perhaps, of Mississippi's inadequate educational-technical base). The labor turnover was excessively high, and sometimes components for ships built under the new system did not fit together—a proof that computers, or at least their programmers, can be quite fallible. The Defense Department Audit Agency discovered that Litton had collected an extra $7 million for Navy work that was in fact done on commercial ships. The helicopter assault ship work ran into such construction delays and gross cost overruns that the Navy actually canceled its order for four of the nine ships originally ordered. By 1972, Litton was involved in an imbroglio with the Navy over hundreds of millions of dollars in claims, counterclaims, and penalties. Before it finally straightened out its management situation in 1972, the Litton facility at Pascagoula had gone through three presidents, five financial vice presidents, five operations vice presidents, six program managers for the assault ships, and four quality control directors in three years. Ellis Gardner had been one of the first to go.

Many of those problems were irrelevant, however, for the state of Mississippi, which could count fairly surely on its gamble with Litton finally paying off. Employment at the shipyard by 1973 was up to 18,000, above initial expectations. The Navy-forced contract cutbacks actually stabilized the situation in the shipyard, which had overcommitted itself quite seriously. There was a dollar volume of contracts remaining that promised prosperity for several years. And as far as Litton's big potential losses from its disputes with the Navy were concerned, Wisconsin Congressman Les Aspin, one of the conglomerate's strongest critics, wrote late in 1972: "Despite the cost overrun [and] delays, . . . the big fix is in. As long as Roy Ash—so recently departed from Litton Industries and on his own assertion a 'five-figure' contributor to Mr. Nixon's reelection campaign—occupies a pivotal White House post, it is inconceivable that Litton will not be bailed out."

One of the most encouraging present-day signs for the Mississippi economy is that the state is no longer concentrating its efforts on the traditional BAWI-type low-wage industries, or even waiting for another plum like the Pascagoula shipyard to drop in its lap. Instead, Mississippi is taking a number of steps which cumulatively should have important impact in the next decades. Some were alluded to earlier in this chapter—the improved racial climate, for one, and the emergence of quality elementary and secondary schooling for the first time in Mississippi history. The median school attainment level of Mississippi adults increased two full years in the 1960s. Vocational and technical training, provided through the junior colleges and geared to teaching specific skills for specific industries, gained momentum very rapidly. Adults completing manpower and training programs in Mississippi were able to increase their incomes by an average of 52 percent, proving the possibilities of vastly improved utilization of the state's human resources.

As Mississippi's once abundant supply of unskilled labor began to diminish, the state's leaders felt they could shift their sights from the raw numbers of new jobs to the quality of those jobs. The door was not closed to new apparel plants, but state research efforts began to turn to getting industries offering higher pay, demanding higher skills, and utilizing higher technology.

Symbolic of this development was the creation, in 1964, of the Mississippi Research and Development Center, based on a recommendation of the Stanford Research Institute after a study of the state's needs. Governor Johnson sponsored the R & D Center and got the legislature to create it. The idea was to maximize Mississippi's economic potential by coordinating through the Center all applied research relating to economic development.

The R & D Center was placed under the Mississippi-wide Board of Trustees for Institutions of Higher Learning, but it was made independent of the individual institutions so that it could operate with relative autonomy.

The R & D Center was a leap into modern research and systems analysis amazing to see in the most economically backward of all American states. The man chosen as its director was also an untypical Mississippi choice: Kenneth Wagner, an Iowa native with a doctorate in sociology from the University of North Carolina who had headed the industrial development division of Georgia Tech for several years. Wagner was paid a salary well above that of the governor, a fact that would cause considerable grumbling in the legislature, where he and his center became a storm center as he continually reasserted his independence, sometimes in an abrasive way. "But what Wagner lacked in political tact," William Winter said, he made up for in ability to put together a good staff and do some first-class research and development work. It's obviously paid off for us." Interviewed in the sleek new buildings complex built for the R & D Center and Mississippi Universities in Jackson, Wagner stated his own approach this way:

> We're applying a systems approach—a total approach to economic development that considers every factor, from natural resources under the ground to human resources on top. We help existing plants to expand and potential new ones to get started. We're also developing economic blueprints for the 10 planning and development districts into which the state has been divided. We try to show which areas are best for which kind of industry, so that they'll pitch for the right kind of firms and not waste their time on wild goose chases. And our interest is not only in manufacturing, but the whole employment spectrum, including wholesale and retail trade, service industries, and jobs in tourism. This requires an understanding of production economics—shipping costs, labor costs, power costs, water and sewer systems, transportation resources, and the potential productivity of the local work force. We provide the planning and development districts with goals, with an overall scheme of what they can and should do, and how to get from here to there. They pick it up then at the local level with some technical assistance from us. And they can interface with the local government units—with which they can deal better politically.
>
> We're also involved in information services for industry and government, in technical support to state, regional and local development agencies, and in providing computer services for state government and universities.

Not every program the R & D Center has tried has been a smashing success. Despite multimillion-dollar funding from the federal government and the Ford Foundation, a big systems approach project in the Delta, designed to increase job opportunities, especially for underpriviledged blacks, had to be abandoned when the outside funding ran out. Some critics felt Wagner and his agency had been better as showmen naming the potentials than as producers of concrete results. There may have been a parallel to the overpromise, underdeliver syndrome at the Pascagoula shipyard, where a systems approach was also in vogue.

Wagner, however, has remained undaunted, forever proposing new plans for Mississippi. In 1973 he was waiting for funding to move ahead with a so-called "Delta food project," aimed at reorienting that rich soil area to a new technology food industry that could furnish 25 to 30 percent of the nation's foodstuffs. Beef production and feedlots would be emphasized, a wide variety of crops and vegetables introduced, and an effort made within a few years to move to entire menu manufacturing. It was the only way, Wagner said, that he could see the Delta producing enough jobs to stop the outmigration and put people to work.

Wagner's ideas of a diversified, highly productive Mississippi agriculture are not as visionary as they seem. The historic Southern pattern—small farms, sharecroppers and tenants, and cotton-cotton-cotton—has been upset all across the region. But nowhere has the change been as breathtaking as in Mississippi. A few figures tell the story:

■ In 1950 there were a *quarter of a million* farms in Mississippi, averaging 82 acres in size. By the end of the 1960s, there were only 70,000 farms, and they averaged about 225 acres. And more than half the harvested cropland was on 2,800 big, prosperous farms with more than 1,000 acres of land.

■ In 1950, 459,000 people worked on Mississippi farms; by 1972, that figure was barely 100,000, and half of those considered some other employment their primary occupation. Sharecropping all but disappeared by the time of the Korean War, and only a few thousand tenant farmers are left today.*

■ Cotton acreage, 2.2 million acres in 1945, is now barely half that amount. Soybeans have come on fast in the last several years, their growth spurred by soaring prices since the late '60s. There are now more acres planted in soybeans than in cotton—in Mississippi!

■ Mississippi's sales of cattle, chickens, and other livestock went up from $29 million in 1940 to more than $500 million a year in the early 1970s. The farmers' livestock income now exceeds what they get from cotton and all other field crops combined. Except for Kentucky, Mississippi now has more cattle on its farms than any other state east of the Mississippi River. And it is one of the country's largest poultry producers.

In the midst of all these changes, farm income has risen sharply. The figure was $138 million in 1940, $600 million in 1960, and is about $1 billion a year now. And the future could scarcely be brighter. Delta planter Andrew Carr put it this way: "The world needs more foodstuffs, and the country needs increased exports to offset its dollar trade imbalance. Acreages will be opened up, we will have more freedom to plant, subsidies will be eliminated, and exports will be encouraged in crops like soybeans, rice, and wheat. Even if prices are lower, we can make a profit on volume. It gives incentive and opportunity for the smart manager—but not for the dumb old farmer."

All of this also provides a golden opportunity for new jobs and capital in food processing, already a growing business in Mississippi. Plants can be developed for the many industrial processes for soybeans. Canning, freezing, and other processing of fruits and vegetables and meats can grow apace. In the words of William Cox of the Federal Reserve Bank of Atlanta, "Fifty years from now, we may find that Mississippi has come full circle back to

* The difference between a tenant and a sharecropper was this: a sharecropper provided his labor to chop and pick cotton, with the landowner supplying him with a mule, a plow, and a place to live, and sharing the final crop. A tenant leased farmland and generally owned all his equipment. The prevalent pattern now is for farmhands to live on plantations, renting their homes from the owners and receiving hourly wages.

agriculture—a new, more sophisticated agriculture—as a primary economic base."

If one adds fiber to the food equation, the same phenomenon can be seen in the lumber and wood products industry. In the view of state leaders like Robert Hearin, chairman of the board of Jackson's First National Bank, the most important industrial expansion in recent years has been in paper and plywood mills. Technological breakthroughs have made it possible to make plywood out of pine, thus competing with the West Coast in plywood. Particulate board (à la Masonite at Laurel) has helped the state to participate in the national housing boom. Mississippi is now able to process much of its tree harvest within the state, rather than shipping out the raw timber for processing elsewhere. This has encouraged a steady growth in tree farming, which began rather tentatively back in the 1930s. Many big paper companies own forest lands in Mississippi and work on a massive scale, reseeding pine from airplanes after killing oak and other unwanted growth. But farmers benefit too, since they can sell timber from their lands. As marginal farms have closed down, especially in the Hills regions, some 70,000 acres a year have returned from row crops or pasture to forest. And it takes only 14 or 15 years for pines to grow to maturity in Mississippi's warm, moist climate. Some 55 percent of the state's land area is now in forests, and in the last half of the 1960s there were capital expenditures of more than $300 million in the wood products industry in Mississippi. A single St. Regis paper plant at Monticello cost $130 million. Presently, close to 50,000 Mississippians work in lumbering and wood products, and the industry's products have an annual value of well over half a billion dollars. Workers in the paper mills earn well over the state average for factory jobs.

Dr. Frank Rose, president of the L. Q. C. Lamar Society, recalls that when he grew up in the Depression-poor Mississippi of the 1930s, every desperate farmer's dream was that oil might be found on his property and that all his troubles would be over. But it was 1939 when the first successful oil wells were drilled (following up on gas finds a decade earlier). Today more than $200 million a year is realized from oil and gas production in Mississippi, but the figure is paltry compared to neighboring Louisiana. There are several refineries, but only a few thousand workers make their livelihood from the industry.

More than oil, Mississippi's most important natural resource is an abundance of water—vital for recreation, for industry, and for low-cost shipping. In 1972 work was begun on the $500 million Tennessee-Tombigbee Waterway, which will provide northeastern Mississippi with a water route to the Tennessee River Valley on the north and the Gulf of Mexico (via Mobile) on the South. Mississippi has its share of water pollution problems but has done better than its Southeastern neighbors in getting industries to control their emissions.

The R & D Center believes there are enough growth factors in the Mississippi economy to permit the state to reach the per capita income level of the rest of the country by the year 2000. Others are less optimistic, pointing out that while Mississippi's per capita income has climbed from 50 to 67 percent of the national average in the last two decades, the dollar gap has actually widened—from $1,011 in 1960, for instance, to $1,372 in 1971. U.S. Department of Commerce experts prophesy that it will be 1990 before Mississippi even reaches 75 percent of the national per capita income level. Crude regressions run at the Federal Reserve Bank of Atlanta suggest equality may not be reached until the year 2100!

A Whiff of Urbanism: Jackson . . .

We turn now to the towns and regions, and the nascent phenomenon of Mississippi urbanism. But first, a recollection of how it was "before." Faulkner wrote:

> In the beginning it was virgin—on the west, along the Big River, the alluvial swamps threaded by black, almost motionless bayous and impenetrable with cane and buckvine and cypress and ash and oak and gum;

—there Faulkner was talking of what is today the drained, flat Delta, safe behind its levees—

> to the east, the hardwood ridges and the prairies where the Appalachian Mountains died and buffalo grazed; to the south, the pine barrens and the moss-hung live oaks and the greater swamps, less of earth than water and lurking with alligators and water moccasins, where Louisiana in its time would begin.

Many years would pass between the first white man's incursions on that land and the emergence of notable urban centers. Even in 1900, Vicksburg and Meridian could boast only 14,000 inhabitants, and Natchez 12,000; Jackson, the present metropolis, was a village of 7,800. A million and a half people lived in Mississippi, but one had to look to the land to find them.

Now that is changing. The Census cartographers devised a map showing counties that gained population between 1940 and 1970 (all in blue) and those that lost (in red). Mississippi is a great splotch of red except for three areas: the Jackson region, the Gulf Coast, and a northeastern pocket around the little cities of Columbus and Tupelo.

When John Gunther passed through Jackson a quarter of a century ago, he saw "a curious town" with "a handful of impeccably shining skyscrapers, rising straight out of a muck of Negro hovels and poor-white slums." The legislature had designated the location as a state capital in 1821, but it had taken Jackson a long time to reach its 75,000 population level in World War II. And not until recent years has it reached the size (city population 153,968, metropolitan area 258,906) to make it a really important urban center, a place with the substantial pool of skilled labor and cultural-educational amenities and financial institutions that major high-wage industries pick for their major installations.

Jackson today is one of the most attractive cities of the South—green, open, and pleasant, a surprise to outsiders who expect a city that would match Mississippi's olden image. In a beauty contest with Baton Rouge or Montgomery, the capitals of its neighbors, Jackson would win hands down. It does have defects—for one thing, remnants of the slums Gunther saw, places now filled with a constant influx of impoverished, ill-educated Delta Negroes. In 1969 the NAACP held its national convention in Jackson, and Charles Evers, fearful that the delegates would be bedazzled by the cleanliness and gleaming new offices of center Jackson, warned them that "Mississippi is not all peaches and cream, despite what you have seen." To prove the point, he took them to see the shanties and junked garbage and open sewer of Town Creek, a black ghetto embarrassingly close to the rococo State Capitol. Jackson also suffers from a number of marginal, honky-tonk neon arteries. But because it is so new, Jackson also has quantities of suburban developments of decent enough style and eye-pleasing greenery.

Jackson banker Robert Hearin likes to call his city "a little Atlanta," and he points to growing wholesale facilities and a jet airport as his evidence. The analogy is probably right if one puts the emphasis on "little." Jackson has two interstates, while Atlanta has five; Atlanta's airport activity is many times that of Jackson; the aggressiveness of Atlanta's bankers is not matched in Jackson, and private capital is still in relatively short supply. (There are a significant number of people in Jackson and other Mississippi cites with huge personal fortunes, but gettng them to gamble some of it on Mississippi enterprises, rather than exporting it to New York or Texas or California, has been a slow, arduous process.) Jackson's convention facilities, however, have mushroomed in the last few years, and a merchandise mart has been built that should provide a convenient marketing center for apparel and furniture plants scattered across the state.

Jackson does not have a very happy history in race relations. For years the racist fulminations of the Jackson *Clarion-Ledger* and *Daily News* poisoned the atmosphere; the city was a fountainhead of Citizens Council strength; and in 1963 the city fathers closed down the public swimming pools rather than bow to the integration order of a federal court. (The pools are still closed and a decade later appear beyond rehabilitation, with 8-inch pine trees growing through their bottoms.)

It is true that Jackson bankers led the way in Mississippi employment integration by hiring Negro tellers and clerks in the 1960s, and that some local firms, including MPI Industries (a large woodworking plant), took an early role in black hirings. In 1969, the segregationist hold on City Hall was broken with the election as mayor of Russell Davis, a native of Maryland who broke with precedent by promising "to work with the responsible Negro leadership of this community." Davis' administration became the first to put blacks in appointive city policymaking jobs.

Racial tensions were exacerbated in 1970 following the nationally publicized killings of two young blacks and wounding of 12 others during a student demonstration at the all-black Jackson State College. Both Mississippi highway patrolmen and Jackson police took part in the indiscriminate firing of some 200 rounds of ammunition at a crowd in front of a women's dormitory, responding to the threat of an apparently nonexistent sniper. Governor Williams, who had let the state police get out of control in countless racial incidents, sought to shift 100 percent of the blame onto the students. Davis, by contrast, went on local television to say that "the facts, regardless of what they show, will record a dark day in the history of this city." Then he agreed to the request of the Mississippi NAACP to appoint a biracial investigating committee. The committee submitted a report roundly critical of the Mississippi Highway Patrol. Davis also fired the city's inept police chief and replaced him with a professional who forbade his men to use derogatory words like "nigger" in dealing with black citizens.*

Just 16 months after the tragedy at Jackson State, television viewers around the nation heard Walter Cronkite—in the midst of reports of dynamited school buses in Pontiac, Michigan, and angry protests by Chinese mothers over school busing in San Francisco—praise Jackson schools on the evening news as the nation's model for peaceful integration. An intriguing confluence of events had made it possible for Cronkite to render that amazing—and correct—judgment.

Eight years before, the NAACP Legal Defense Fund had begun a long string of successful desegregation suits against the Jackson school board. Piecemeal integration had resulted, but the Jackson schools by 1971 faced a dire emergency. Thousands of white students had taken refuge in private academies, so that a system once 60 percent white had become 67 percent black. The courts were beginning to order broad-scaled busing, but Jackson faced the danger of the city's white voting majority cutting off tax support to the schools.

In the meantime, Jackson since the mid-1960s had encountered an alarming downturn in economic growth. The city's influential chamber of commerce had turned to the Mississippi Research and Development Center to draw up a comprehensive plan for industrial recruitment and general economic improvement plan. In 1970 that effort was beginning to bear fruit with negotiations by Allis-Chalmers, the heavy equipment manufacturer, to bring in a divisional headquarters and open a plant with at least 1,000 workers. The operation would include a research group, with important R & D benefits for the entire Jackson area. But Allis-Chalmers president David Scott, in a meeting with the most influential local business leaders, said: "You have some problems with your image you will have to face up to. I'm not about to ask 50 people [his divisional management group] to come down here from Wisconsin to Mississippi unless you can get the school situation stabilized—unless you can get the schools out of court and come up with a plan for upgrading them."

The message to the power structure could hardly have been clearer. A biracial chamber of commerce task force on education, organized at the suggestion of the R & D Center, recommended numerous improvements in the

* The President's Commission on Campus Unrest, appointed by President Nixon after the Kent State and Jackson State killings and disturbances across the country at the time of the Cambodian invasion, later issued a report saying that the 28-second police fusillade at Jackson had been "clearly unwarranted." The committee criticized the black students for heaping "vile verbal abuse" on the police but pointed also to the white policemen's "racial animosity" toward blacks and their "confidence . . . that if they fire weapons during a black campus disturbance they will face neither stern departmental discipline nor criminal prosecution or conviction."

A shocking record exists of what Inspector Lloyd Jones, commander of the highway patrolmen at the scene, radioed to his headquarters. It is filled with references to wounds received by "nigger males" and "nigger gals" and a jocular announcement that "we got two students 10-7 here." In radio code, 10-7 means "out of service"; it was Jones' way of reporting that two young men lay dead before him.

local schools and sparked a coalition of 19 civic and community organizations to keep whites in the public schools. Kenneth Wagner of the R & D Center became a key figure in the negotiations between the civic-business groups, the school board, and the NAACP lawyers. He came up with the central idea that finally broke the impasse: educational parks that would be accessible to both races. While only for fifth- and sixth-graders, the parks represented a "creative learning concept" and an incentive for white families to keep their children in the public schools, even though almost a third of them would have to be bused to achieve thorough integration for all grades. In return for these concessions, the NAACP Legal Defense Fund agreed not to reopen the Jackson case in court for at least three years. The advocates of the plan claim it has achieved the most unitary school system in the United States.

The school breakthrough and generally improved race relations proved to be a great spur for economic growth. Not only did the Allis-Chalmers plan move forward, but largely as a result of the groundwork laid by the R & D Center, since the late 1960s, a total of 3,300 new manufacturing jobs in Jackson were announced in 1972—an all-time record and more than the preceding 15 years combined. Wagner said he expected the boom to continue for several years.

Scott of Allis-Chalmers set another interesting condition on coming to Jackson: that a master's degree in engineering be offered at the University Center there, so that his technical people and executives could take advantage of it. As a result, the university system agreed to authorize the first master's degrees at off-campus locations—a move stoutly but vainly resisted by the individual campus administrators, who rightly feared that many people would prefer earning their degrees in Jackson or other urban centers to setting up residence in such isolated campus towns as Starkville (the very name of which says a lot), Hattiesburg, or Oxford. The pressures are likely to increase to make Jackson a center for graduate education, simply because the city will be where the real action is in Mississippi.

Jackson is already, and has been for some time, the center of Mississippi's recognized business-media power structure. Robert Hearin, board chairman of the city's First National Bank, was the central figure in the 1960s and still has great reserve power, though his interests shifted to out-of-state financial operations in the early '70s. Major influence is wielded by Warren Hood, vice president of the Masonite Corporation and a man who has strong contacts to the Nixon administration, and Edward Brunini, a Jackson attorney and savvy behind-the-scenes operator. Brunini's influence is something of a surprise, since he is the brother of the Roman Catholic bishop in one of the most Protestant (and Baptist, at that) of all American states. Then there is Hearin's competitor, Pat McMullan, Jr., president of Jackson's Deposit Guaranty National Bank. Finally, one must mention the brothers Hederman—Bob, Henry, and Zach, and cousin Tom. Tom is the most powerful of all, since he controls about half the family inheritance. The Hedermans have controlled the Jackson *Clarion-Ledger*, Mississippi's largest morning daily, since the turn of the century, and Mississippi's largest afternoon daily, the Jackson *Daily News*, since the 1950s. The *Daily News* had been an archcompetitor before its purchase. But it was no less racist. It said of William Faulkner when he won the Nobel Prize for literature: "He is a propagandist of degradation and properly belongs to the privy school of literature."

The Hedermans are abstemious Baptists, fundamentalist and self-righteous and hard-core segregationist. Their empire extends from Jackson's only newspapers to two weeklies, a third large daily in Hattiesburg, part ownership in television and radio stations, a printing company that does a lot of business for the state of Mississippi, and business properties all around Mississippi, including a large share of downtown Jackson. In a sense, the Hedermans *are* the power structure. They had close ties to Governors Barnett, Johnson, and Williams, who appointed all of them to important state government boards. They are closely allied politically with Senator Eastland, whose father grew up in the same county (Scott County) and was a close friend of the Hedermans.

The establishment's power is said to be somewhat diminished these days because they bet on the wrong horse—Sullivan—in the 1971 governorship election and got a Populist-style adversary—Waller—instead. The "colonel's fund," which Robert Hearin used to see was regularly replenished for the sometimes very personal benefit of past governors, has disappeared.* Waller has attacked the big banks, tangling with them over issues like maximum interest rates on small loans. He also removed all but one of the Hedermans from state boards.

The establishment has not always spoken with a single voice. Hearin, for instance, helped to steer Governor Johnson onto a course of quiescence on the race issue, making it easier for the state to comply with the 1964 Civil Rights Act. But if Hearin wanted to reduce race tensions (a shift from his own earlier segregationist beliefs), he was certainly receiving no help from the Hederman's newspapers, whose editorials and slanting of the news contributed mightily to the fanaticism of the times. As James Silver wrote of the Jackson papers in 1963, "Negro crime and immorality in the North, Negro complicity in Communism, even Negro support for Barnett are given the headlines every day. Shotgun blasts fired into a Negro home become a NAACP plot, the assassination of Medgar Evers is turned into a sacrificial offering to rekindle racial unrest, Mississippi is victimized by hate peddlers jealous of the state's economic progress. . . . The Fifth Circuit Court becomes 'the nine judicial baboons in New Orleans'; . . . and Tougaloo College, a center of integrationist activity, rechristened 'Cancer College.'" One of the prize headlines of all those years accompanied the arrest of Byron de la Beckwith, scion of an old Delta family born on the Pacific Coast but resident in Mississippi for 38 years: "CALIFORNIAN IS CHARGED WITH MURDER OF MEDGAR EVERS."

The same tone continued in the Jackson papers throughout the '60s. The Head Start program, for instance, was said to be, "as all federal programs are now designed, . . . one of the most subtle mediums for instilling the acceptance of racial integration and ultimate mongrelization ever perpetrated in this country." Edwin Williams of the Delta *Democrat-Times* analyzed the cover-

* The custom was for governors to appoint honorary staff members with the rank of colonel on their staffs. Those so honored were expected to open their pocketbooks for the fund. Reporters thought the money was behind the big spending habits of some of the governors and their wives. There were unsubstantiated rumors that one governor benefited by some $300,000.

age of the Jackson State killings in 1970 and found that the *Ledger's* first three days of coverage included 73 inches of coverage from the police, another 47 from Governor Williams, and only 16 inches altogether from students, on-the-scene newsmen, NAACP officials, and college faculty and officials. The papers still had no black newsmen and no rapport with any black leaders (however moderate). Blacks were nonpersons on the society pages, and most black news was relegated to a special page in papers carrier-delivered to Negro homes but not to be seen in editions available in white neighborhoods.

Since 1970, there has been definite improvement. Deliberate slanting of the news has diminished, and Jacksonites rubbed their eyes when they saw the first picture of a black bride in the wedding section. Tom and Henry Hederman even put their names on full-page newspaper ads supporting Jackson's public schools and their busing plans. The editorial pages, however, often fall back to viewing civil rights as a Communist plot, and the *Clarion-Ledger* continues to run the column of Tom Ethridge, a throwback to the racial invective of the '60s. One wonders how many people in Mississippi detected the irony when Vice President Agnew visited Jackson in 1971 to deliver a speech in which he exhorted "the great majority of thoughtful Americans" to reject the "editorial doublethink" of the "Seaboard Media."

A revolution of sorts in Jackson (and American) television began very quietly in March 1964 when 25 men and women filtered into a home on one of Jackson's residential streets to compile a meticulous, minute-by minute record of the picture and sound of commercial television offerings in the city from 7 A.M. to 1 A.M. the next morning for one full week. They were volunteers for the New York-based office of communication of the United Church of Christ, and they were setting out to test the thesis that the local television stations were not serving blacks, who make up 45 percent of the viewing audience.

A month later, the United Church of Christ, along with Aaron Henry, president of the state NAACP, and the Rev. Robert L. T. Smith, representing Jackson's black community, filed a petition with the Federal Communications Commission asking it to deny license renewal to two Jackson stations. Later the case was narrowed to WLBT-TV alone, which was accused of permitting racial slurs to be spoken on the air, of excluding black community news, and of blacking out civil rights news reports from the NBC network. The FCC, forever solicitous of existing station ownerships, refused to take the WLBT license away from Lamar Life Broadcasting Company, which is mainly owned by Texas millionaires Clint and John D. Murchison with Jackson's Robert Hearin as board chairman. But Warren Burger, then a federal Court of Appeals judge, overruled the FCC shortly before he became Chief Justice. And in 1971 the FCC turned over interim operation of the station to Communications Improvements, Inc., an integrated nonprofit Jackson-based citizens group headed by Kenneth L. Dean, then director of the Mississippi Council on Human Relations. The group promised to use WLBT's profits (about $500,000 a year) to finance the development of educational television in the state and to fill staff vacancies with blacks until a black employment level of 40 percent was reached.

The new WLBT-TV became a new and unique voice in Mississippi. Under general manager Bill Dilday, a black who was formerly personnel manager for WHDH-TV in Boston, public affairs programming was stepped up, broadcast editorials critical of Mississippi's political leadership have been aired, and programs like "Soul" and "Black Journal," never before seen in the state, suddenly had an outlet. Despite a rapid influx of black personnel with little prior television experience, the station outstripped its two competitors in ratings and revenue. Jackson, Mississippi, had suddenly outpaced every other U.S. city in equality and exposure for black people on the public airways. The durability of the reforms was brought into question in 1973, however, when the FCC tentatively picked Dixie National Broadcasting for the permanent WLBT license. Everett Parker, the chief of the office of communication of the United Church of Christ, the man who had sparked the first legal challenge to Jackson's white television monopoly, complained that Dixie National's commitment to black staff and programming was so light that a takeover by that firm "would represent a dramatic reversion to the past." He promised further court action to stop it.

. . . And the Gulf Coast

Mississippi's 70-mile Gulf Coast—literally a "strip city" between New Orleans and Mobile—is growing even faster than the Jackson area. Between them, the coastal cities of Gulfport, Biloxi, Pascagoula, and their satellites and immediate hinterland had 239,944 people in 1970—an 88 percent increase since 1950.*

The Gulf Coast has always been a place set aside from the rest of Mississippi—heavily interladen with French Catholics à la Southern Louisiana, less hung up on the race problem because it has had fewer Negroes (only 16 percent by latest count), oriented to tourism and fishing and port life, and a place where a traveler could always get a drink in a bone-dry state. "People from the dry counties," managing editor Clinton Blackwell of the Gulfport *Daily Herald* said, "would come and imbibe and then curse us as a den of iniquity."

For more than a century, the coast was a favored summer playground of Old South gentility—and, in winter, a favorite vacation spot of Midwesterners. The outlanders built stately gulf-front mansions, circled with moss-covered oaks and magnolia trees, and also provided a clientele for luxurious resort hotels like the Edgewater Gulf, where all rooms faced the sea and black tie dress was *de rigueur* for dinner each evening.

All of that began to change with World War II and its aftermath. A new industrial flavor was supplied by the shipbuilding industry at Pascagoula and new refineries and petrochemical plants. Large banana terminals and other port facilities were transferred from New Orleans. Veterans hospitals and big military bases provided substantial local employment. And at one

* The 1970 populations of the major Gulf Coast cities were: Biloxi 48,486, Gulfport 40,791, and Pascagoula 27,264.

point in the 1960s, 4,000 people were employed at a $250 million NASA test center for moon rockets in Hancock County, close to New Orleans.

The postwar era brought a tourist boom of a new character. Much of the coast became a neoned strip of motels and boisterous nightclubs. Especially in Biloxi, gambling was wide open for intermittent periods; occasionally the state stepped in to clean out the slot machines and dice and roulette and blackjack games, but when Jackson's control relaxed, they always reappeared.* The old summer mansions and hotels became relics of another age, and in 1971 even the Edgewater Gulf came down to make place for a Sears Roebuck store and parking lot.

On the 17th of August, 1969, Hurricane Camille—described by some as the most powerful hurricane in American history—roared ashore from the Gulf of Mexico. It brought winds of up to 200 miles an hour and tides of 35 feet, cutting a path of destruction in which 144 people met their death and more than $1 billion of property damage was inflicted. Gulfport, Biloxi, and Pass Christian seemed to lie in ruins, with doubtful future prospects. Some of the old Victorian mansions emerged as frontless, roofless shells. When the owner of Woodrow Wilson's summer White House saw its ruin, she suffered a heart attack and died. Camille, New York *Times* reporter James T. Wooten noted, "played no favorites. Plush resort inns where affluent whites came to play were flattened along with the squalid shacks where Negroes lived on welfare. And the shrimpers, predominantly of Slavic and French-Canadian origins, were destroyed."

But, like a phoenix rising from the ashes, the Gulf Coast rebounded with incredible rapidity. Part of the recovery was due to relief funds—$82 million from the federal government, $13 million from the Red Cross, $10 million (belatedly) from the state government. Equally important, recovery came because the essential health of the region—its tourism and shipping—gave impetus to businessmen to apply their skills and resources for a new period of growth and expansion.

A symbol of the recovery was the day in June 1970 when a long line of shrimp boats at Biloxi steamed by a Roman Catholic priest in white vestments as he blessed them in an ancient mariners' ritual. The return of the shrimpers to the sea was accompanied by dancing in the streets to a Dixieland band and the consumption of gallons of beer on the ships and white sand beaches. It was the old, relaxed Gulf spirit reasserting itself in a state where its free ways have rarely been appreciated. An interesting sign of that had been the composition of the emergency council Governor Williams had set up to coordinate state and federal relief efforts after the hurricane. It had included several members of the Jackson business establishment but only three people from the Gulf area and not a single woman or black person. But strong objections came from a coalition of social action-civil rights groups including state representative Robert Clark and Biloxi physician Gilbert Mason, a prominent local black. The Economic Development Administration held up federal aid until Williams expanded the emergency council

* The go-go clubs that accompanied all this remained, but things are no longer as raucous as the mid-'60s, when Biloxi had a topless, bottomless cabaret where stark naked girls greeted men at the door.

to include four blacks (including Dr. Mason), one woman, and one elderly person.

Gulf area blacks, according to Mason, had continued to face severe discrimination up to the time of Camille, even if public rhetoric was less extreme than in other areas of Mississippi. But in 1973, Mason said that "the racial climate has certainly improved, and even if some subtle forms of racism remain, on the whole we have built toward mutual respect since the hurricane, because we met segregation and discrimination head-on, and through the agony of facing it—and Camille—we have overcome."

Mason is symbolic of the small but growing black middle class in Mississippi, breaking out now from the traditional base in teaching and the ministry to white-collar jobs in banking, insurance, and the professions. But it remains a fragile base. Even in urban areas, where twice as many blacks are earning decent incomes as in the rural areas, only 8 percent of the families earn as much as $10,000 a year, and only 15 percent more than $8,000. As for the professions, black attorneys remain a rarity and there are less than 50 Negro physicians and 10 Negro dentists in the entire state.

Despite its growth and recovery from Camille, the Gulf area faces difficult physical and planning problems. As W. F. Minor reported in 1973 to the Southern Growth Policies Board, "there are too few places to live, transportation systems are inadequate, and municipal expansion is severely restricted." Pascagoula, for instance, has an alarming housing shortage and a street and highway system that is a relic of yesteryear. The city is hemmed in by marshland on two sides and large land tracts on the north and east held by wealthy landowners. Biloxi is restricted by water to the south and east and the sprawling Keesler Air Force base to the north. The transportation problem may be relieved some by construction of Interstate 10, some 10 miles inland from the coast. The highway could open the way for inland development and possibly breed bedroom cities for people who work in New Orleans. (A new city of 35,000 to 40,000 has been proposed in Hancock County, near New Orleans.) But no overall planning is underway. A Gulf regional district to coordinate future growth was proposed by the emergency council after Camille and authorized by the legislature, but only one major city (Biloxi) voted to join it, so that the idea remained in limbo.

So the Gulf Coast rushes pell-mell toward a fate William Winter says Mississippi should avoid at all costs: "becoming just a plastic imitation of some other place that's grown up without any planning or direction."

Small Cities and Miscellanea

After Jackson, the Gulf Coast, and the Memphis bedroom suburbs in its northwest corner, Mississippi has few population concentrations that would be considered very urban elsewhere in the United States. There are a number of towns worth noting because they are centers of their respective geographic regions. Meridian (population 45,083), in the dirt-poor Hills country of east-central Mississippi, is the largest of all but not growing. It makes most of its money from the region's cattle and timber, plus a sprinkling of industries. Columbus (25,795), noted for its antebellum homes, and fast-growing Tupelo (20,471) are centers of northeastern Mississippi; Tupelo in particular has broken away from hardscrabble small farms and ruined land to capitalize on TVA power and mount an impressive bootstrap campaign of industrial expansion. The chief cities of the big Piney Woods section of southern and southeastern Mississippi are Hattiesburg (38,277) and Laurel (24,145). Some of these little cities have made interesting contributions to American culture. Tupelo, for instance, was the birthplace of Elvis Presley. Laurel, on the other hand, was the native city of Leontyne Price. The cost of her musical instruction was defrayed by one of the old white families, a member of which was present when she made her debut at the Metropolitan Opera in New York. (Also of note: film director Fred Coe was born in Alligator, Mississippi, and actress Stella Stevens came from Hot Coffee!)

Laurel is in Jones County, a cussedly independent spot that refused to fight on either side in the Civil War. Laurel itself did not exist until 1882, when a railway was built through the vast south Mississppi forest and a lumber camp sprang up to serve the needs of a new lumber mill beside the tracks. Big lumber companies followed, and within 40 years Laurel had shipped more yellow pine lumber than any other city in the world. But the theory of "cut out and get out" extended from the woods to the mills, and the slabs and sawdust of the virgin forest were burned without regard to their potential value. In the 1920's the late William Mason was in Laurel extracting turpentine from pine stumps and discovered the process of using steam to explode wood fibers like puffed wheat and then recompressing them into a wallboard. The Masonite Corporation's Laurel plant is now the largest of its kind in the world. At nighttime (when I visited there) the atmosphere is ghostlike as one walks through banks of steam to watch the huge cookers, rollers, and presses creating the construction board from a mountain of wood chips shoved by tractors into the plant.

The Masonite plant workers were organized in 1939, and years of strained management-labor relations ensued, including a bitter strike in the 1940s. The situation was complicated in 1964 when Sam H. Bowers, grandson of a former Congressman, formed the nation's most notorious branch of the Ku Klux Klan—the White Knights—at Laurel. Bowers himself was charged with numerous terrorist attacks, including the fatal bombing of Vernon Dahmer's home and a role in the infamous killing of the three civil rights workers at Philadelphia, Mississippi. Many White Knights Klansmen were employed by Masonite and members of the local of the International Woodworkers of America there. Yet the union also included a number of black Masonite workers. In 1967 Masonite determined to automate and reduce its labor force, and the Laurel plant workers went on strike. There were ugly confrontations outside the plant gates, one of Masonite's Wackenhut guards was killed, the railroad tracks and a waterline were blown up and many beatings reported. Klansmen were considered perpetrators of most of the violence, and Masonite broke the strike by firing all its workers, hiring hundreds of college students on an interim basis, and then using the issue of Klan involvement to get its black workers to return. The settlement was actually made by the international union, which imposed a trusteeship on its Laurel local.

While the 1967 strike was in progress, organizers of the Southern Conference Educational Fund, a Louisville-based militant civil rights organization with predominantly white leadership, sent its workers into the Laurel area to try to bring black and white workers together. The result was formation of the Gulf Coast Pulpwood Association, which flabbergasted official Mississippi by uniting a "bunch of niggers and white trash" together in a common cause. The organizing work went slowly until 1971, when some 200 impoverished timber truckers—independent suppliers of pulpwood who rarely earn more than $3,000 a year—went on strike when Masonite changed its measurement system so that the truckers were paid several dollars less for each load of pine they delivered. Soon the strike had spread to dozens of woodyards across southern Mississippi, and the new union led the effort. As the strike dragged on for 12 weeks, many of the workers became desperate for food for their families. Relief was arranged by Charles Evers, who got Washington to issue food stamps and arranged NAACP emergency funds for the men—including some who were once Klansmen or Klan sympathizers. Eighty-four whites were so grateful that they actually joined the NAACP.* With chapters all across southern Mississippi and Alabama, the Gulf Coast Pulpwood Association represented a unique interracial alliance of the Southern poor—a development of potentially momentous importance for the future of the region.

The Mississippi redoubt of an encapsulated Old South is Natchez (19,704), on the Mississippi's banks in the southwestern part of the state. Natchez's golden era was in the decades before the Civil War, when the great fortunes were made from the buying and exporting of cotton, and thousands of slaves lived on vast plantations. In these days of brutal superhighways, one road anyone with a love for the land and history will enjoy is the Natchez Trace Parkway, a quiet, two-lane road that the U.S. Park Service has built in recent years along the Trace—Old French for "a line of footprints"—linking Natchez with Nashville. Before the age of the steamboat, it was easy enough for men from Kentucky and other regions of the then western frontier to float their farm products downriver to Natchez and New Orleans. But sailing or rowing upstream was too laborious, and by 1800 a thousand a year were walking the Trace to Nashville on their return trips. And until the 1820s and the era of the steamboat, the Natchez Trace was one of the great frontier roads of the American Republic. Later it fell into disuse, only to be "restored" in modern times. (Its route across Mississippi is shown on the map on page 165.)

There is new oil and manufacturing money in Natchez these days, but the upper crust remains the families who made their fortunes in antebellum days. Many of them live in exquisitely preserved mansions with romantic names like D'Evereux, Rosalie, Monteigne, Mount Repose, Dunleith, and

* In Evers' gubernatorial race, much of the small white vote he got came from this rural southeastern woodworking area.

Green Leaves. The tourist folders, however, omit mention of the half of the city's population which is black, much of it quartered in shacks reminiscent of the less pleasant aspects of antebellum society. A celebrated civil rights demonstration against Natchez's segregationist establishment in 1965 resulted in the detention of more than 100 demonstrators at the state penitentiary at Parchman, where they were later subjected, according to a federal judge, "to subhuman treatment which beggars justification and taxes credulity." *

Despite its port and oil wells and industries like Armstrong Rubber, International Paper, and Johns Manville, Natchez actually lost population in the 1960s. So did its upstream neighbor, Vicksburg (25,478), another place where the hand of history lies heavy. The fall of this "Gibralter of the Confederacy" on July 4, 1863, sealed the doom of the Southern cause, and Vicksburg has lived in the tortured glory of the war ever since. Like Natchez, Vicksburg has a port, oil, and many new industries; major employment is also provided by the U.S. Water Experiment Station, and the city has been headquarters of the Mississippi River Commission since 1930. The city is home base of multimillionaire Francis L. Cappaert, the self-made chairman of Guerdon Industries who logs 5,000 miles a week in his private jet keeping track of industrial and land investments all over the country. Cappaert makes and invests most of his money outside Mississippi, but *Fortune* did quote him as saying that the satisfaction of seeing barley grow on his Nevada desert property was the same he felt "the day we finished putting up clean, pretty houses where we tore down those rotting slums in Vicksburg."

Another 90 miles upstream is Greenville (39,648), an old port and cotton processing center which used to suffer from severe floods. One in 1927 kept the city under water for 70 days. Finally, in the 1930s, the Mississippi was forced seven miles westward by new levees, though there is still an outlet to the main channel which keeps the harbor open.

But more of Greenville anon. It is the leading city of the Delta, and now it is time to conclude our story with that region that holds, in this writer's mind, more fascination than any other region of Mississippi, or perhaps the entire United States.

The Delta: A Phantasmagoria

The classic social definition of Mississippi's Delta is that it "begins in the lobby of the Peabody Hotel in Memphis and ends on Catfish Row in Vicksburg"—a line penned by native writer David Cohn, a foremost interpreter of Delta society. The semantic definition of the Delta has to do not with the delta at the river's mouth but rather with the shape of the Greek letter. Which brings us to a topographic-geologic definition: the Mississippi-Yazoo Delta is a flat alluvial plain of incredibly rich black earth—its depth as great as 35 feet—that was laid down through countless eons by the inun-

* The treatment included forcing the prisoners to strip naked, forcing them to take laxatives and submit to blood tests against their will, and holding them in the notorious maximum security area—though they were only accused of a misdemeanor (under a statute later found unconstitutional).

dations of the Mississippi River. Its greatest length is 200 miles, its greatest width 85 miles. Today the Mississippi's floods are held back by powerful levees constructed and improved over the past century.

The Delta has to be seen to be believed. It is as level as the mind could imagine, its wide flat fields, steaming with fertility, stretching on in seeming infinity. There are occasional plantation houses of the grand Southern style, contraposed to squat shack towns where the field hands live today. Until a few years ago, the fields were dotted too with little unpainted gray wood shacks; now because of mechanization most have been bulldozed away, or torn down, or stand deserted as reminders of a culture past.

Nowhere in America do the life styles of the privileged and the less fortunate contrast so vividly. Modern Delta farming has its vicissitudes. In spring 1973, for instance, the Mississippi reached its highest level of this century, and while the major levees along the river held, hundreds of thousands of acres were covered by backwater flooding from the Yazoo River and other streams that empty into the Mississippi. Even in more "normal" times untimely rains can ruin a crop. National and world markets vary, and federal farm subsidies spell the difference between loss and profit on the cotton lands. But essentially a Delta planter with a modicum of intelligence and any substantial amount of acreage has it made. Farming cotton and soybeans together, he should be able to clear $25,000 to $30,000 a year on a 1,000-acre holding. The values of land have doubled in the last dozen years to as much as $600 an acre, and multi-thousand-acre farms are not uncommon. Contrary to popular belief, the Delta aristocracy has few antebellum roots; the region after all was a flood plain until the levees came, and much of the virgin hardwood cover was not cleared until after the Civil War. There are some planter families, like the Percys, whose Delta roots go back five or six generations; others are descended from some smart foreman a generation or two back who got hold of a piece of land and scratched his way to affluence.

And a good life those planter families lead. They give lavish parties at home or the country club, charter air-conditioned buses to take their friends to the football games in Memphis, jet off to New York for Broadway shows, or to Europe, or to places in the sun for long winter sojourns. Even those of less flamboyant tastes lead a very good life. Roy Reed of the New York *Times*, one of the most sensitive interpreters of the modern South, caught the spirit in a 1972 interview with the family of farmer Sterling W. Owen, who farms, with his two brothers, 5,400 acres of cotton and soybeans in the Delta's Tunica County:

> "Our life style is the same as people who live in the city," Sterling's wife, Bankie, said. She was referring to affluent city people. She sat in her large brick air-conditioned house, eating lunch in a splendidly furnished dining room, looking out on a lush lawn shaded by magnolia and pecan trees.
>
> Just out of sight behind her mother-in-law's big white house was a tennis court equipped with lights. Sterling and his friends often play there at night after working 11 to 12 hours.
>
> Tennis is not the only "urban" pastime for these Mississippi Delta farmers. Sterling and Bankie ride bicycles. Their house is well supplied with books and records. His taste in music ranges from country to classical.

Sterling was graduated in 1963 from Vanderbilt University. He studied economics, on the advice of his late father, but he was fascinated by the humanities. His greatest joy was philosophy. . . . As he drives his air-conditioned pickup from one hot, flat field to another, he turns over in his mind a book that he would like to write, a history of Tunica County. His great-grandfather settled here more than 100 years ago to farm and practice medicine. . . .

Sterling with his tennis and books is probably not as untypical a Delta farmer as an outsider might think. Many of the younger farmers here think of themselves as businessmen who happen to live in the country.

Politically, the planters are a conservative lot—but, as we noted earlier in the chapter, rarely given to the Vardaman or Bilbo brand of racist extremism. The height of Delta moderation and cosmopolitanism is reached in Greenville. The U.S. Commission on Civil Rights noted with some wonder that in the mid-1960s, when officially condoned lawlessness gripped most of Mississippi, the leaders of Greenville insisted on scrupulous and even-handed application of the law and saw to it that their city, unlike any other in the state, arrested and prosecuted the cross-burners of the Ku Klux Klan.

Hodding Carter III, successor to his late Pulitzer Prize-winning father as editor of the *Delta Democrat-Times,* had this to say about his home town: "Greenville has a more open society than the rest of Mississippi. Financially, our paper couldn't have survived in any other city of the state." Over the years the Carters got their share of threats for their willingness to print the news straight and advocate racial harmony. But, said Carter, "we've never had a shot fired, never had anything bombed; I've never been beaten up, nor my father. I don't know why, except that the old man always talked as if he carried a big stick, and that may have discouraged people." The Klansmen and their ilk may also have known that the Greenville police would have been hot after them if they dared an attack.

(Not all Mississippi editors were so fortunate. As an example, Hazel Brannon Smith, Pulitzer Prize-winning editor of the *Advertiser,* on the border of the Delta, learned the fury of the local Citizens Council when she had the temerity to depict the Supreme Court's 1954 school decision as legally and morally correct. The Council set up an effective boycott of her advertising space; a cross was burned in her yard; and the offices of a newspaper she owned were burned. Only in the early '70s did the boycott begin to ease.)

So many writers have made Greenville their home—the list is a long one, including the Carters, the Percys (William Alexander and Walker), Shelby Foote, and novelist Ellen Douglas—that the city has sometimes been called the Concord of the South. The rest of Mississippi has had its share of illustrious literary figures—Faulkner, of course, and Willie Morris (whose writings have made his native Yazoo City familiar to many), playwright Tennessee Williams, and the novelists Eudora Welty and Richard Wright. But Greenville is the only place where so many have congregated, and that must say something for the city—and, by transference, for Delta society as a whole. This was the region, for instance, that sent the only Mississippi moderate in many a decade, Frank L. Smith of Greenwood, to the U.S. House for five terms. A man of exceptional principle, Smith had been ready to vote for expanding the House Rules Committee in 1961 if his vote were crucial, even though he knew he would probably be signing his political death warrant. As it was, he lost his seat anyway the next year after redistricting put him in with Jamie Whitten—a defeat that was the work, Walker Percy said, "of peckerwoods, superpatriots, and the Citizens Councils." President Kennedy subsequently appointed Smith as a director of the Tennessee Valley Authority, a mark of recognition accorded few Mississippians in the poisoned atmosphere of the '60s.

Cheek by jowl with the planters and the plainer white folk of the Delta live the Negroes—60 percent of the area's population. David Cohn wrote almost 40 years ago:

> The Negro's identification with the life of the Delta is fundamental and complete. . . . It was he who brought order out of a primeval wilderness, felling the trees, digging the ditches and draining the swamps. The vast rampart on the levees upon whose existence the life of the Delta depends sprang from the sweat and brawn of the Negro. Wherever one looks in this land, whatever one sees that is the work of man, was erected by the toiling, straining bodies of the blacks.

The Delta Negro has little to show for those generations of toil. His average family income is an appalling $2,413. One finds him (and her and the little ones) at the wrong end of whitey's town, or in a rural hamlet, in some teetering shotgun shack, the walls plastered with old magazines and newspapers and occasional sheet rock, without running water, dependent on an outside privy. Just a lucky few live in pleasant brick homes with insulation and adequate plumbing and modern conveniences—houses built for them by white planters who put a high value on their services as tractor operators or mechanics, and have some human regard for them. Andrew Carr's 4,000-acre plantation near Clarksdale is one such example, but its rarity is underscored by the fact that Carr pays his workers $1.50 to $2.00 an hour—well above the prevailing $1.30, the minimum wage level. Carr told me he had few maintenance problems with his workers' houses—"disproving," he said, "the myth that Negroes will destroy good property."

The bitter fact is that for most Delta blacks, there are simply no farm jobs available anymore. The mechanical cotton pickers and chemical herbicides have drawn down the curtain on the historic sight of thousands of black hoe hands in spring and summer and the rows of men, women, and children moving through the fields at picking time in the fall. The going wage for casual farm labor had been only three dollars *a day*. The introduction of the minimum wage for farm hands in the '60s ended that, and severe cutbacks on cotton allotments contributed further to the drastic reduction in Delta farm employment. Between 1960 and 1971, the number of full-time farmers and farm workers dropped from 81,000 to 39,000, and the number of seasonal workers from 31,000 to 9,000. Even the remaining seasonal workers left did little work; in 1960, they put in 1,200,000 man days, in 1971 only 22,000.

Consider what happened to the Delta's largest plantation, the Delta and Pine Land Company, one of the world's largest cotton seed-breeding concerns. In past times, the plantation cultivated 16,000 acres of cotton using some 5,000 workers, including 1,200 tenant families. In 1972–73, total acreage was up to 24,000, but only 10,000 of it was in cotton. The plantation had diversified to 5,000 acres of soybeans, 1,000 of rice, 1,200 for feed crops, and 5,300 in pasture (for a cattle herd of 3,700). About 500 field workers still lived on the plantation, but the average monthly employment was only 300. Mechanization had filled the labor gap, as the plantation relied on 140 tractors, nine combines, and 38 mechanical cotton pickers. Pesticide control, Delta and Pine president W. John Daniel said, was done mostly by airplanes on a contract basis.

Where did the displaced blacks go? Some stayed on the land, living on Mississippi's lowest-in-the-nation welfare dole. Some drifted into Mississippi's cities and towns, where they were almost as likely to remain unemployed. But most went North, on that famous Illinois Central line to Chicago. Hodding Carter III tells of a friend who rode the line from New Orleans to Chicago and later remarked, "I felt like Simon Legree driving the slaves before him."

The northward flow appears to have dropped off some in recent years. One reason may be that the official state and local policy is no longer to *force* black outmigration. Another is that a number of young blacks are rejecting the psychology of the '60s, when even the word "plantation" seemed to conjure up images of slave days. Many of the blacks who went North have returned to visit, passing the word that the big cities are not the pot of gold at the end of the rainbow they had expected. They denigrate farming less, so that many intelligent young black Mississippians are choosing to remain on the farms and trying to improve their skills in handling complicated equipment so that they can earn decent wages.

But those jobs will be relatively few, and one wonders what will happen to the thousands upon thousands with no work, no skills, no prospects. Driving through the Delta on a late winter day, I made a random stop at a hamlet called Louise and wrote in my notebook: "A prime rural slum, largely black, the Negroes living in ramshackle, dilapidated little shacks on unpaved streets. Debris everywhere: discarded furniture, old auto parts, tires, tin cans. Livestock rambling everywhere." Later I discovered a report by Anthony Dunbar, who spent seven weeks in that plantation community. Some excerpts:

> The health of the people of Louise is incredibly poor. The community is ridden with sickness, disease, and chronic illness. . . . Barely a household is free of a case of high blood pressure, which shows itself in the swollen ankles of the women, results in a weakened heart, fainting spells, [and] "nervous breakdown." . . . Diabetes is a common disease. Cases of tuberculosis and amoebic dysentery are not hard to find. Many children have a variety of internal parasites. . . .
>
> Many women in Louise eat corn starch when they are pregnant. Some keep up the habit and continue to eat as much as they can get after childbirth as a means of filling themselves up. The same is true of baking soda. And the same is true of clay. . . . Sometimes you can see a woman at work in the fields after a mealtime pick a piece of dirt off the ground and pop it into her mouth.

Is Louise unique? Not if one is to believe the report of six eminent physicians dispatched by the Field Foundation to examine health conditions in several counties in the Delta and other parts of Mississippi in 1967. Later they told a Senate committee what they had seen, and their report was published by the Southern Regional Council. They found prevalent, chronic malnutrition, hookworm and severe kidney ailments, untreated skin infections and ulcerations, wasting of muscles, weakened bone structure, enlarged hearts, edematous legs, and in some cases the presence of abdominal endema (so called "swollen" or "bloated" belly), and as a consequence, fatigue, exhaustion, and weakness—the telltale signs, in other words, of incipient starvation. The living conditions explained why:

> We saw homes without running water, without electricity, without screens, in which children drink contaminated water and live with germ-bearing mosquitoes and flies everywhere around. We saw homes with children who are lucky to eat one meal a day—and that one inadequate so far as vitamins, minerals, or protein is concerned. We saw children who don't get to drink milk, don't get to eat fruit, green vegetables, or meat. They live on starches—grits, bread, flavored water. Their parents may be declared ineligible for commodities, ineligible for the food stamp program, even though they have literally nothing. We saw children fed communally—that is, by neighbors who give scraps of food to children whose own parents have nothing to give them. Not only are these children receiving no food from the government, they are also getting no medical attention whatsoever. They are out of sight and ignored. They are living under such primitive conditions that we found it hard to believe we were examining American children of the Twentieth Century.

Official Mississippi simply could not bear the indictment. Governor Johnson scoffed at reports of malnutrition, saying of the alleged victims: "Most of 'em I've seen are so fat they shine!" Senators Eastland and Stennis called the physicians' report a "libel" of Mississippi, and even the normally moderate William Winter (then running for governor) felt compelled to call the report "a smear typical of the way our enemies try to lie and paint a distorted picture about our state." When the physicians turned to Agriculture Secretary Orville Freeman for help, he expressed sympathy but said the man they would have to reckon with was Jamie Whitten, who controlled USDA funds. Since then Whitten has relented some on the subject of food stamp availability, and the school lunch program has also expanded. But the legacy of ignorance and unsanitary living conditions and virtually nonexistent medical care for indigents lingers on. Even in 1972, only half the 767,000 Mississippians living below the poverty line were receiving federal food stamps or surplus agricultural commodities.

It takes a stranger driving through the Delta only an hour or two to see the human misery, and one wonders how the sophisticated planters view it all. "Many local wealthy people live on the incredible fiction that they don't have poverty all around them," Hodding Carter said. "It's an elaborate edifice you have to maintain if you want to live with yourself." A few have broken that mental fix; one was Clarksdale planter Oscar Carr, a past president of the Delta Council (an agricultural lobbying group) and brother of Andrew Carr, whom we quoted previously. Carr later departed the Delta—temporarily, he said—to head the office of development of the national Episcopal Church. He said that his revelation had come as he returned home from a trip of some 12,000 miles to eight European countries. "I saw more poverty between

Memphis and Clarksdale than I had in all of Europe, and my eyes were opened. Before, I guess, the shanties and little Negro children urinating from the porches had just blended into the landscape."

The problems involved in assuring decent living conditions and education and health care for the Delta's 190,000 black people stagger the imagination. The least one can say is that before the 1960s the problem was a hidden national shame. Since then, it has become known, and, with many false starts, the arduous work of lasting change has begun. After the Freedom Summer of 1964, most of the out-of-state civil rights activists disappeared from the scene. But "deep in the morass of broken Negro hopes," as one writer put it, there remained a handful of young activists sent South by the National Council of Churches to act as spiritual advisers in that famous 1964 summer. They formed the Delta Ministry, a permanent Christian ministry with headquarters in Greenville. The goal: to help blacks with their problems of illiteracy and to teach new skills to people who had never known any livelihood except hoeing and chopping cotton. The Delta Ministry initiated Mississippi's first Head Start programs,* began an audacious cooperative colony called Freedom City, and pressed for federal funds to alleviate hunger. Early in the 1970s, the Ministry changed its board structure to lessen reliance on churches and advance the poor and advocacy groups from Mississippi to a controlling position. Cutbacks in budget inevitably resulted, but the organization remained about the only broad-scaled social action agency working with Mississippi's blacks.

In the northern Delta lies Mound Bayou, a virtually all-black town founded by former slaves in 1887—ironically, on land that once belonged to Jefferson Davis, President of the Confederacy. Black power reigned in Mound Bayou when it was an impossible dream in the rest of Mississippi, but the town and its hinterland were all too typical of the grinding poverty of Mississippi black life. Then, in the late 1960s and early '70s, Mound Bayou (population 2,134) became the center of experimentation in delivering health care to poor black people.

A thousand miles away, Dr. Jack Geiger of the Tufts University School of Medicine had determined to do something about the health plight of Delta blacks, and he picked Mound Bayou as the location of a Tufts Delta Health Center. The location was appropriate because Boliver County, where Mound Bayou is located, is one of the poorest in America, and because the all-black community would provide insulation from potential harassment by Mississippi whites. Grants were obtained from the Office of Economic Opportunity, and medical specialists—white and black—were dispatched to the Delta to inaugurate a humanly touching and socially revolutionary chapter in American health care.

* In human terms, perhaps the most heartening sight of the '60s was the arrival of the Head Starts. I came across one near Anguilla, in the Delta: the True Light Head Start Center, just a row of jerry-built wooden structures alongside a stinky drainage ditch in the midst of the cotton fields. What was happening there was exciting, though: little three- to five-year-olds, enjoying all the games and picture books one would see in any American town; the shy teachers (probably with skimpy education themselves, but so enthusiastic about their work); and the news that the children got not only breakfast there, but a midday "dinner" of beef, turnip greens, potato salad, cornbread, and milk. Perhaps Head Start was pedagogically unproven, as some critics said, or a subterranean way to provide federal jobs for untrained black women, as its enemies asserted. But there was love there that day at the True Light Head Start Center, and hope.

For many patients, the visit to the Tufts Delta Health Center was the first contact of their lives with any kind of medical care. It was *help at last* for people in desperate need. The doctor teams, on the other hand, quickly realized that many of the health problems brought to their door—sore throats, intestinal ailments, rat bites—were only the surface manifestation of a deeper problem. The real health enemy was malnutrition, aggravated by life in broken-windowed shacks infested by rats and roaches and by often contaminated drinking water from shallow wells.* So the health center's main purpose, as Dr. Geiger put it, was to act as a catalyst for extensive social and political change, with health care the point of entry into the poverty cycle. Under John Hatch, an energetic black community health services director, the center began "garden clubs" to encourage families to grow vegetables on their own small plots. But in the little towns people were crowded together almost as closely as in city ghettos, and when backyards weren't crowded with junk, the cotton fields reached practically to the shack doors. So a full-scale "North Bolivar County Farm Cooperative" was started on several hundred acres of leased land, and hundreds of families began to earn all or most of their food supply by working on the farm. OEO grants of $250 a house made it possible to install sanitary vault privies and assure sanitary water supplies. Ten community health care and civic improvement associations were started, providing services like hot lunch programs for the elderly.

Late in 1968, the Tufts Delta Health Center moved into a gleaming new clinic on land carved from a cottonfield, financed with $800,000 from the OEO. Patients from a broad geographic area came in in a steady stream, some in buses, others in car pools organized by the community health associations. Close to 200 physicians, nurses, social workers, physical therapists, and sanitarians awaited them in the cheerfully decorated center. But there was a method in the bustle, because whichever member of a family came in, he would be seen by the same medical team. It was really a medical systems approach, in which every relevant factor—from home interpersonal relationships to sanitation and nutrition to specific health problems—could be treated.

Despite the Tufts Center's high black staff involvement and effort to involve poor black families in planning for their own health programs, criticism came from some militant blacks who called the clinic and its outreach "Tufts' own plantation" in Mississippi. There was also the delicate problem of relationships with the nearby Mound Bayou Community Hospital, a more conventional health facility begun 30 years before by a black fraternal organization and staffed by the Meharry Medical College of Nashville. The new "black establishment" created by the Delta Ministry began to play a major role in both institutions, and Tufts finally pulled out—as gracefully as it could—leaving the field to the Mississippi blacks, backed up with continuing OEO grants. Those grants, however, became a point of controversy between Governor Waller (who charged mismanagement and misuse of funds) and the blacks (who said Waller was just trying to get control of a very lucrative feder-

* In one of those deteriorating shacks, Geiger said, it was common to see a two-month-old boy who weighed less than when he was born and suffered from infectious diarrhea, dehydration, malnutrition, and anemia. He would drink contaminated water and in his first week of life would have eaten his own excrement. By the time he was three, he would be mentally retarded.

ally funded program). And as the OEO itself was threatened with dismemberment, and the community hospital lost its license because of overcrowding and other physical inadequacies, the future of the brave experiment at Mound Bayou hung very much in the balance.

The irony was that the whole package system of health care delivery developed at Mound Bayou would almost certainly be part of whatever health care answer the whole United States decided on in the 1970s. For once, a Mississippi program could be a model for the nation. Yet could it be that a concept crystalized in the Mississippi Delta would help others but not its own, who need the help the most?

ALABAMA

THE "CRADLE" GETS ROCKED

ALABAMA, whose capital city was the "Cradle of the Confederacy," could not have been expected to welcome the civil rights revolution of our time. The state had, to be sure, nurtured a number of progressive leaders over the years, and it was the home of one of the boldest defenders of constitutional rights ever to sit on the United States Supreme Court, Justice Hugo L. Black. It was in Alabama that Martin Luther King, Jr., and Ralph David Abernathy, and Andrew J. Young had all had their first churches. (All three, interestingly, married girls from a single Alabama county—Perry.) It was events in Alabama that would trigger the second American Reconstruction—the Reconstruction of the 1960s.

But official Alabama had been dead set against all that. The Stars and Bars still flew over the gleaming white State Capitol at Montgomery, with the United States flag relegated to a shorter flagpole on the grounds. (Some Alabamians said it was a mistake to read too much symbolism into that, since the Confederate States had been organized in the building, making it a kind of historic shrine. However, the government of present-day—not Confederate—Alabama was being administered from the building.) The words "White Supremacy—For the Right" adorned the ruling Democratic party's symbol on election day ballots. From their bitter reaction to the Montgomery bus boycott, to Bull Connor's police dogs in Birmingham, to the nightsticks and whips beating down on the bodies of the rights marchers by the bridge in Selma, white Alabamians showed their abhorrence for the changes sweeping the South and the nation. Most men and women of moderation sealed their mouths; some fled the state.

Even in the late 1960s, as other Southern states began to readjust themselves to the new realities, Alabama seemed to remain hopelessly obdurate. "Here, as in no other state," Pat Watters of the Southern Regional Council wrote in *The South and the Nation*, "large numbers of young whites, high school age and over, still spouted unquestioningly the old catechisms of racism and Southern aristocracy. Before 1964 Mississippi had been more totalitarian, but in the late 1960s Alabama was the last bastion of Southern totalitarianism and it was not incapable of spreading its influence across the South—or the nation."

That national influence, of course, was the work of a single man—the dominant figure of modern Alabama politics, and one of the most skilled politicians to emerge on the American scene in modern times—George Corley Wallace.

Even as Watters' book was published in 1970, however, some vital changes were taking place in Alabama. Cumulatively, they meant that Alabama in the '70s would not be the island of reaction that many outsiders took it to be. And most of them were occurring despite George Wallace, and often in the face of his determined resistance. To wit:

■ The surge of Klan-inspired terrorism which sullied Alabama's public life through the 1950s and much of the 1960s was clearly receding. As Ray Jenkins of the *Alabama Journal* (Montgomery) wrote, "At some point in the 1960s, Alabama turned its back on the use of the club and the pistol, the bomb and the torch, as weapons for resisting social change."

■ Jim Crow died a long overdue death. The process may be said to have begun on December 1, 1955, the day Mrs. Rosa Parks refused to relinquish her seat to a white man and move to the back of a Montgomery bus. Official Alabama fought the change tooth and nail, yet by the end of the 1960s and the start of '70s, Alabama's public schools and universities were finally integrated. Restaurants and hotels and theaters had given up their discriminatory practices. Black clerks were newly visible in banks and stores. The chambers of commerce had opened their rolls to black businessmen. Only in suburban housing did segregation continue—or even worsen.

■ Blacks began to register and vote in massive numbers. In 1960 only 14 percent of Alabama's black people of voting age had been registered to vote; by 1970, 64 percent were registered. By 1973, Negroes held 144 elective positions in Alabama, compared to zero in 1960. They controlled cities like Tuskegee and Prichard and rural Greene County in the Black Belt, and they were making inroads elsewhere. Their vote had become a major factor in state elections.

■ In tough, violent Birmingham—once nicknamed "Bombingham" for its response to Negro advances—race relations improved so dramatically that *Look* magazine bestowed an All-American City award in its last year of publication.

■ The breezes of independent political thought began to waft through a state where as recently as 1969 a Birmingham attorney had told me, "Around here, if you raise your head and say George Wallace is wrong, the next minute

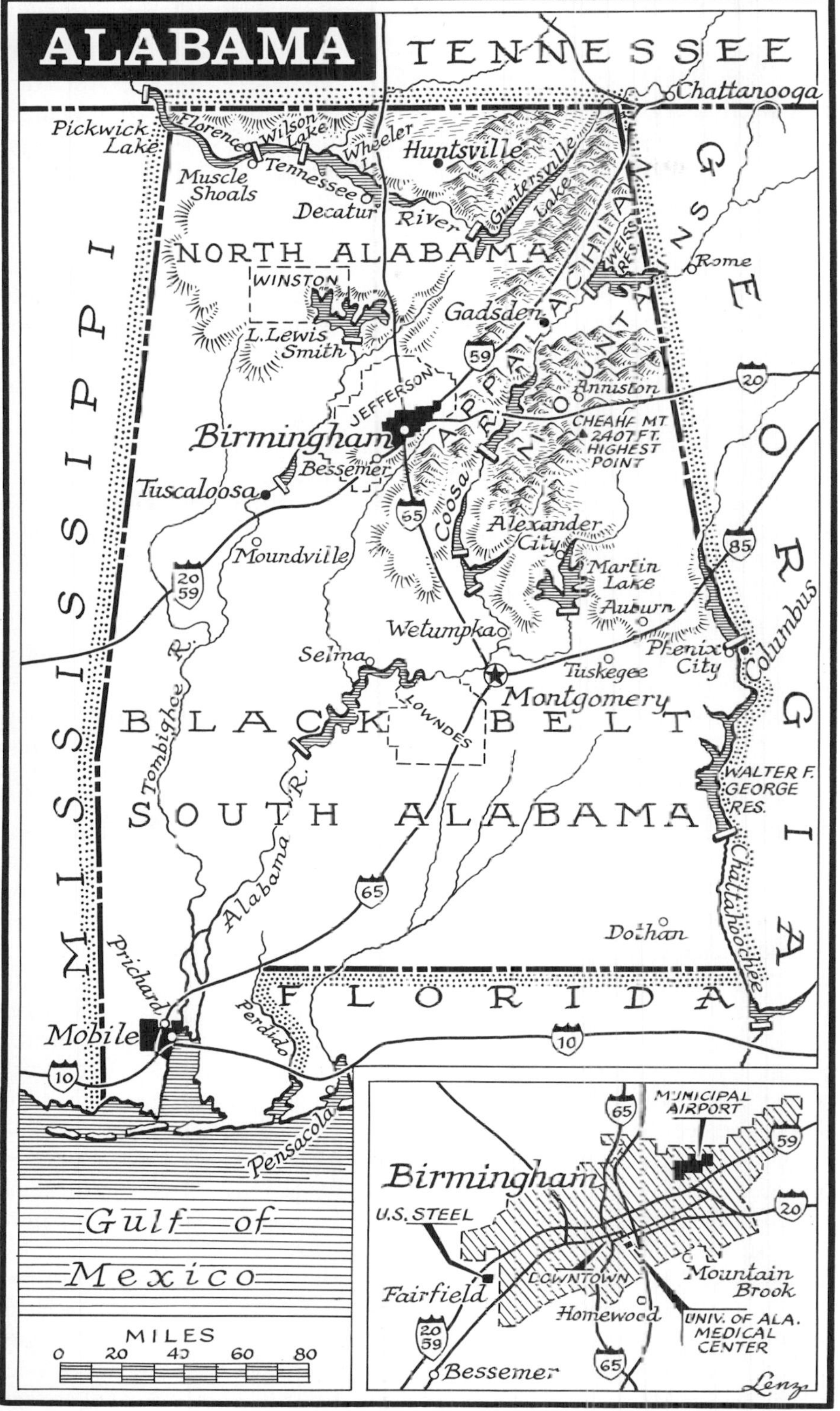
ALABAMA
TENNESSEE
Chattanooga
Pickwick Lake
Florence
Wilson Lake
Wheeler L.
Huntsville
Guntersville Lake
Muscle Shoals
Tennessee
Decatur
River
GEORGIA
NORTH ALABAMA
WINSTON
Rome
WEISS RES.
APPALACHIAN MOUNTAINS
Gadsden
L. Lewis Smith
59
20
JEFFERSON
Anniston
Birmingham
CHEAHA MT. 2407 FT. HIGHEST POINT
Bessemer
Tuscaloosa
Coosa R.
65
Alexander City
85
Moundville
20
59
Martin Lake
Auburn
Columbus
Wetumpka
Phenix City
Selma
Tuskegee
Montgomery
MISSISSIPPI
Tombigbee R.
BLACK BELT
LOWNDES
WALTER F. GEORGE RES.
SOUTH ALABAMA
Alabama R.
Chattahoochee
65
Dothan
Prichard
FLORIDA
Perdido
Mobile
10
10
Pensacola
Gulf of Mexico
MILES
0 20 40 60 80
MUNICIPAL AIRPORT
65
59
Birmingham
20
U.S. STEEL
DOWNTOWN
Mountain Brook
Fairfield
Homewood
UNIV. OF ALA. MEDICAL CENTER
20
59
65
Bessemer
Lenz

it's kind of hard to breathe." It was only a year later that more than 1,000 students at the University of Alabama's main campus at Tuscaloosa—an institution described by one observer as "a bastion of idolized athletics and lionized coaches, pretty coeds, fervent fraternity men, and racism"—held a candlelight vigil in protest against the invasion of Cambodia and the killings at Kent State.

▪ The Democratic party's rooster symbol was finally shorn of its "White Supremacy" slogan by the state party committee in 1966. At that same meeting, Birmingham attorney Robert S. Vance was made state Democratic chairman, and he immediately set to work bringing the long rebellious state party into line with the national party. He arranged for blacks to win positions on the delegations to both the 1968 and 1972 Democratic National Conventions, thus saving Alabama the ignominy of national party disaffiliation which was inflicted on neighboring Mississippi. Responding to national party reform rules, the Alabama Democrats in 1970 reorganized themselves so that the urban counties, not the lightly populated rural areas, would control the state committee in future years. For the first time in the party's history, blacks were brought onto the state committee. The States Rights-Wallace faction, which had manipulated the party machinery so that it had been *impossible* for Alabamians to vote for Harry Truman for President in 1948, or Lyndon Johnson in 1964, appeared to be relegated to a permanent minority position.

▪ Appalled by Wallaceite dictation and the power of the old courthouse gangs, young people of a moderate bent became active in Alabama politics. In 1970 they helped to elect a *legitimate* Populist, 29-year-old Bill Baxley, as state attorney general. Baxley befriended blacks, cracked down on Birmingham's industrial polluters, fought official corruption, and battled for consumer interests.

▪ Federally ordered reapportionment of the state legislature broke the decades-old grip of the conservative Black Belt politicians on both the senate and house. Urban interests began to be heard, and exceptionally strong air- and water-pollution control bills were passed. A court-ordered second-stage reapportionment plan, scheduled to go into effect in 1974, promised to multiply several times over the representation of blacks and Republicans in the legislative halls at Montgomery. (In 1973 there were still only two blacks and two Republicans in the entire legislature.) The new blood seemed to promise fundamental change in a legislative body the Citizens Conference on State Legislatures had ranked 50th among all the states in its ability to act in an independent, functional, and representative manner.

▪ Although the federal courts, rather than Alabama's own leaders, were responsible for the major part of sociopolitical change in the state, the Alabama supreme court was also changing. Howell Heflin, an outstanding lawyer from northern Alabama, was prevailed upon to run for chief justice and defeated former Governor John Patterson in the 1970 primary. For years, the court had been in the total control of old men, segregationist on race matters and conservative on economics, many of them incompetent or inactive or both. Cases used to stagnate for five to seven years before decisions were reached. Under Heflin, the docket was made current and a remarkable job was done of streamlining the entire Alabama court system (including the removal of incompetent circuit judges).

▪ The federal judiciary was moving well beyond reapportionment and pure race matters in the pressures it applied to Alabama. Awaiting full implementation in the '70s were decisions that would force the state to equalize its scandalously unequal tax assessments and to upgrade sharply the facilities and treatment made available to the patients in its mental hospitals. There was no state in the country in which the federal courts were intruding themselves so deeply into the basic governmental process—but perhaps none in which their interference was more justified, because of the inaction and reaction of state government. "We holler about the federal courts having too much power," Attorney General Baxley said. "But if you have states' rights, you also have to have states' responsibilities. The state refused to face up to its responsibilities time and again. We abdicated our power."

The lion's share of the vital federal court decisions was the work of a single federal district judge in Montgomery, Frank M. Johnson, Jr. Ironically, Johnson was a Republican in a state where Republicans have traditionally counted for naught—and not a Republican of the latter-day "Southern strategy" type, but a racially tolerant son of Winston County, the "free state" of Winston in northern Alabama, which seceded from Alabama during the Civil War and has been Republican ever since.

When President Eisenhower appointed Frank Johnson to the bench in 1955, he was 37, the youngest federal judge in the nation. Three years later, Johnson clashed with an obscure state judge who threatened to jail any federal agent who came into his jurisdiction to examine voter registration records under the 1957 civil rights act. The state judge was George C. Wallace; the winner of the confrontation was Frank Johnson. Ironically, the two men had been law school classmates and friends at the University of Alabama in the 1940s.

Just a partial list of Johnson's decisions confirms his central role in recent Alabama—and American—history. It was he who extended for the first time the principle of the 1954 school decision to a nonschool area—the Montgomery bus system, thus ending the Rev. Martin Luther King, Jr.'s boycott and speeding the desegregation of all public facilities. It was a Johnson order which gave black Alabamians, and their Northern allies, the right to march from Selma to Montgomery and to seek and finally gain the right to vote. Johnson was the judge who presided over the trial of the three Ku Klux Klansmen convicted by an all-white jury under the civil rights statutes in the murder of Viola Liuzzo. He issued landmark decisions affirming the rights of students to express their views and to hear the views of others in campus appearances. He was a member of the three-judge courts which abolished the Alabama poll tax, handed down the epic decision in *Lee v. Macon* (the nation's first statewide school desegregation order), and ruled in *Reynolds v. Sims* that Alabama had to reapportion its legislature immediately in the mid-1960s, adopt one-man, one-vote districting, and then move to the momentous new single-district plan due to go into effect in 1974. In each of these cases, Johnson was a coauthor of the majority decision (often with Circuit Court Judge Richard T. Rives, a Truman appointee). Singly, Johnson also ordered Alabama state agencies receiving federal funds to put an end to their traditional patterns of job discrimination, and that the lily-white state police force must be integrated up to a 25 percent black membership.* He for the first time applied the 14th Amendment's equal protection clause to the rights of women, striking down an Alabama statute which barred them from jury service. The mental health and tax equalization decisions were Johnson's too. He also ordered Alabama to desegregate its jails and make adequate medical treatment available to inmates. A lesser known but important Johnson decision established for the first time in the United States that when citizens went to court to secure their constitutional rights against a state, and where willful state neglect of citizens' rights was proven, then the state must pay fees for "private attorneys general"—the civil rights lawyers who fought the cases in court. The Supreme Court affirmed that decision in 1972.

An intense, trim man known for running a taut courtroom and handing down thoroughly researched and scrupulously fair decisions, Johnson was the kind of Southern judge President Nixon, had he been seeking a brilliant and courageous jurist, could have appointed to the Supreme Court. Charles Morgan, Jr., director of the Southern and later the Washington office of the American Civil Liberties Union, said Johnson was "the best judge in America—bar none." In Alabama, Johnson was a lightning rod for segregationists' protests, suffered innumerable threats, and saw his mother's house bombed. "But it will take more than buffalo dust in the eyes of a federal judge to stop proper decisions from this court," Johnson said in an interview. He had been the effective catalyst for change in Alabama, making decision after decision that shaped the fundamental course of a racially paralyzed state government. He always gave the state ample time to fulfill its constitutional responsibilities, but when it failed to do so, then he shaped remedies. He was a bridge to the era of more responsible Alabama leaders emerging in the 1970s, and while George Wallace got the headlines from coast to coast, Frank Johnson really had the last word in Alabama.

But what, the reader may ask, of George Wallace's real impact in Alabama? Has he stood for more than the losing cause of segregation, typified by his vainglorious stand in the schoolhouse door? Today even moderates in Alabama say that the answer to that question is yes—that Wallace, in Alabama as across the country, has been a symbol of many of the gripes and frustrations of ordinary people and a legitimate warning light about government that is too distant from everyday needs and problems.

Harry Brandt Ayers, editor-publisher of the Anniston *Star*, described the problem in terms of his own medium-sized Alabama city. The chamber of

* As a result of Johnson's rulings, blacks by 1972 were actually better off in state government jobs in Alabama than in federal government white-collar employment in the state. They held 7.2 percent of the state white-collar jobs, but only 3 percent of the federal. The Southern Poverty Law Center, headed by Georgian Julian Bond but with headquarters in Montgomery, filed a suit to end the federal discrimination, charging that blacks made up only 4.2 percent of the Justice Department's Alabama employees, held only two of the 901 rural mail carrier positions, and were entirely closed out of Selective Service System and FBI employment in the state.

commerce types, Ayers said, represent 1 percent of the population but about 80 percent of the wealth. He described them as organized, funded, a group with a strong sense of goals and missions and an ability to draw the attention of the community to their agenda. Then there is the black community, which in the past decade has developed a similar mechanism. It represents 34 percent of the people in Anniston (and 26 percent statewide)—"an organized and articulate body that can attract attention to their cause."

That leaves what Ayers calls "the other 65 percent—who are 100 percent of the resistance." Some of their resistance is still on the racial front, Ayers said, "but there is a whole host of other problems which cumulatively are much stronger than racism." The examples are somewhat mundane but quite real. The state highway department takes away a traffic light in one of the blue-collar communities, and there is a serious accident, but it seems almost impossible to get the bureaucracy to react so that the light is reinstalled. Likewise, despite the sanitary hazard of a drainage ditch in a blue-collar suburb, the local residents feel that "nobody's listening to them and they don't have the ability to make anyone listen." Ayers described the feelings of a typical member of the 65 percent this way: "Nobody seems to understand the conditions of my life. Hell, I know I'm the majority in this country. I built it with my hands. The only person who understands me is George Wallace, who knows what I mean when I say I'd like to punch one of those bureaucrats or chamber of commerce types, or one of those blacks I see in the paper or on TV, on the nose. Everybody's getting something but me."

The exacerbation of those feelings, and particularly the racial element within them, has been Alabama's contribution—through George Wallace—to American political life since the late 1960s. What is less known is that at least two Alabama communities—notorious old Birmingham, and more recently Ayers' own Anniston—have begun to form a solution that could also be a model for other Southern states and the rest of the nation.

The Birmingham story marks a phenomenal departure from 1963, described by Jerome Cooper, a labor attorney in that city (and the first law clerk to Hugo Black) as "the dog and hose year—when Birmingham was seen as a big mining camp with Bull Connor yelling his head off. The bombs were flying. Our parks were closed. Our schools were segregated and threatened by mobs. Our baseball team was out of business." In those unhappy days, the seeds of the first ongoing communication between leaders of the races were planted in Birmingham. Operation New Birmingham, formed in 1963, concerned itself primarily with the physical development of the city, but it did include a biracial membership that would have been unthinkable only a few short months before. And in 1969 Operation New Birmingham gave birth to a Community Affairs Committee, designed particularly to deal with the social area by bringing leaders in government, industry, unions, and the black community into *weekly* meetings where problems could be thrashed out and solutions found. If one attends one of those meetings, he will find the Rev. James Edward Gardner, who was parade marshal of Martin Luther King, Jr.'s 1963 demonstrations in Birmingham, sitting next to a white merchant against whose store he led a boycott in those days. "It's give and take. They fight sometimes, they agree other times," one observer said. "But at least they're talking now."

The newer Anniston equivalent, initiated by Ayers, is called "COUL" (Committee on Unified Leadership), a group which meets each month, together with a Community Action Committee that gets together for a 7:30 A.M. breakfast each Tuesday. The membership list is impressive enough: the head of the local labor council, leaders of middle-income blue-collar suburbs, several black representatives (and not just the one or two preachers who had always been out front), the city manager, the Anniston area's state senator and representatives, the superintendent of schools, the police chief, a real estate developer, the newspaper publisher (Ayers himself), and military representatives from big bases nearby. But the organization, Ayers noted, "is totally private, without government sanction. All the meetings are on an off-the-record basis. You get the gripes and all the problems aired in a fairly open but controlled setting. And you have the ability to deal with some of the negative questions." There have been concrete results—including getting that traffic light put back in place in the blue-collar area. "I think," Ayers said, "it's the best and most positive way to preempt the Wallace appeal and get at the problems which people have and which he evokes."

The vast majority of Alabama communities still have no official counterpart to Operation New Birmingham or Anniston's "COUL." But if the idea spreads, and if statewide politicians begin to learn the language of the people without resorting to racist demagoguery, then George Wallace, in a way he never imagined, may have helped to create a better society in his own home state and a model for the rest of the country in the 1970s and beyond.

Alabama's Political Roots

Alabamians of moderate persuasion bristle at the implication that their state has always been—and thus, perforce, is sure to remain—a citadel of monolithic Southern reaction, in which the mores of a slaveholding society adapt automatically to modern-day racism. Back in the 1930s, 1940s, and 1950s, Bill Baxley pointed out, Alabama was sending outstanding progressive legislators like Hugo Black and Lister Hill to the U.S. Congress—while in neighboring Georgia Richard B. Russell and Herman Talmadge typified the dominant conservative ideology, and in Mississippi the vote went for men like Theodore G. Bilbo and James Eastland. "George Wallace," Baxley said, "changed all that because he was such a superpersonality. But he is a once-in-a-hundred-years phenomenon, with a uniquely personal following that can't be transferred to another person or some other cause." When Wallace finally retires, Baxley added, "you'll find that Alabama will revert to being what it was before —probably the most liberal state in the Deep South."

Only time will tell whether Baxley's prognostication is correct. But a dip into the history suggests that his thesis has much to recommend it. The roots of an interesting duality in Alabaman life styles and attitudes were apparent in the first waves of Anglo-Saxon settlement in the late 18th and early 19th centuries, which ended centuries of Indian culture and a long but light period of Spanish and French settlement (the latter finally terminated when the Spanish commander at Mobile withdrew in the face of U.S. arms in 1813)

The American pioneers who flooded into the territory were of two rather distinct types. Into southern Alabama came settlers from Georgia and South Carolina, establishing a cotton plantation economy with large slaveholdings and a distinctly conservative political orientation. The heart of the old cotton kingdom was the Black Belt, a 13,000-square-mile strip of sticky black soil that spanned south-central Alabama. The Black Belt was largely responsible for Alabama's ability to produce nearly a quarter of the nation's cotton production by the years before the Civil War. In 1820 there had been only 41,879 Negro slaves in Alabama; by 1860, through natural increase and a continued flood of human chattels entering through the port of Mobile, the figure had swollen to 435,080—45 percent of the state's population. The great bulk of the slaves were on plantations of the Black Belt and other portions of southern Alabama. While the plantation owners led lives of legendary opulence, marked by fox-hunting and lavish balls, the blacks lived in what one English lady visiting a plantation near Montgomery in 1835 described as "small, dingy, untidy houses . . . something between a haunt of monkeys and a dwelling of human beings. . . . The animal deportment of the grown-up, the brutish chagrins and enjoyments of the old, were all loathsome." The fate of runaways could be branding, mutilation, or even execution.

The hillier area of northern Alabama, territory less suited for large plantations, received more settlers from North Carolina and Virginia and other areas of the upper South—yeomen who had been displaced by the slave economy of their home states and were following the Appalachian paths to a more promising frontier. The life that awaited them in Alabama was not exactly idyllic; as Ray Jenkins noted in a review of the state's early history, "the common white farmer lived in degradation not far above that of the ever-growing number of slaves." Tracts for cultivation were laboriously carved out from the forests; housing was in rough log cabins; malnutrition was common; clothing was usually of deerskin, and shoes, especially for children, were a rare luxury. The planter class looked down on these common whites as "hillbillies" or "dirt-eaters" or "po' white trash." D. R. Hundley, a planter of the era, described the class as "lank, lean, angular, and bony, with . . . sallow complexion, awkward manners, and a natural stupidity or dullness of the intellect that surpasses belief."

There was, however, a natural intelligence in the hillsmen that let many of them see that their interests and those of the plantation owners were not exactly the same. And a division of the "two Alabamas" was apparent as early as the constitutional convention which met in Huntsville in 1819, just before Alabama was admitted to the Union. The division was confirmed in the Presidential elections of 1824 and 1828, when the small farmers of northern Alabama went almost unanimously for Andrew Jackson for President, while the planters of the Black Belt and south Alabama, deeply suspicious of Jackson's ideas of popular and progressive democracy, were more inclined to John

Quincy Adams and Henry Clay. Northern Alabama became a bastion of Jacksonian Democracy; southern Alabama evolved into a big Whig stronghold.

Because slaveholders never numbered more than a quarter of the Alabama population—and large plantation owners far less—the Democrats, with their base in northern Alabama, won most of the elections in the years immediately after statehood. But gradually the slaveholders, through their wealth and superior political skills, gained the upper hand. In 1846 the state capital was moved from Tuscaloosa, in middle Alabama, to Montgomery, near the heart of the Black Belt. There had once been considerable abolitionist sentiment in the state, but as the economy became more and more dependent on slave labor and the cotton trade, and as slave rebellions spread, sentiment for secession mounted. One of the fieriest national advocates of slavery, Southern rights, and finally secession was Alabama's William Loundes Yancey.

The Jacksonian soldiers who returned to the hill country remained loyal to Jackson and knew he had been for national rights against John C. Calhoun. So when the idea of secession was raised, they and their sons reasoned that Old Andy wouldn't have liked the idea, and they resisted as long as they could. In 1860, when delegates were elected to a convention to decide on secession, northern Alabama (except for one county appropriately named Calhoun) voted uniformly for antisecession delegates, while southern Alabama chose almost all prosecession delegates. The strength of pro-Union sentiment was still so strong that when a secessionist was elected chairman of the convention, it was by a narrow vote of 53 to 46—the highest level of opposition to secession in any Deep South state. The secessionists carried the day, however, and the Confederate States of America was organized in the halls of the Alabama Capitol at Montgomery in February 1861. But when the Confederates tried to go into northern Alabama to conscript the hillsmen, those sturdy farmers and hunters drove them out with their squirrel rifles. Winston County and its neighbors contributed at least two regiments to the Union Army, and the citizens of Winston held a mass meeting at a tavern and voted to secede from Alabama.* But the state's majority decision was overwhelmingly for the Confederacy, and for more than a century Alabama would continue to pay a heavy price.

The history of the state in the years after the Civil War closely resembled that of its sister states of the South: slow recovery from physical devastation (the wartime property losses, including the value of slaves, was estimated at $500,000,000); the black codes which sought to reinslave the Negro, congressionally imposed Reconstruction (marked both by abuses and unusually progressive reforms); and after 1874 the return to power of the wealthy landholding whites—the Whigs of yesterday, become Democrats out of necessity, and popularly known as the Bourbons. One of the tools the Bourbons used to regain power was the Ku Klux Klan, which had been orga-

* Winston, a rural county of rough hill country and red dirt, timberlands, and poultry farms, embraced the Republican party after the Civil War and has continued as a GOP stronghold in the heart of Democratic Dixie ever since. It has only voted once for a Democratic Presidential candidate —1,006 to 1,005 for Roosevelt over Hoover in 1932. The overwhelming Republican majorities have been somewhat reduced in recent years, however.

nized just across the Tennessee border in 1866 and waged a campaign of violence and intimidation against carpetbaggers, scalawags, and, of course, the Negro. The Black Belt Bourbons also appealed to North Alabama for help in their campaign to overthrow Republican (and black) rule: this editorial, for instance, appeared in the Montgomery *Advertiser* in November 1874:

> South Alabama raises her manacled hands in mute appeal to the mountain counties. The chains on the wrists of her sons and the midnight shrieks of her women sound continuously in their ears. She lifts up her eyes, being tormented, and begs piteously for relief from bondage. Is there a white man in North Alabama so lost to all his finer feelings of human nature to slight her appeal?

North Alabama responded with help, but in time would have reason to regret its generosity. The Bourbons ruled as rank agrarian reactionaries, installing many conservative ex-Confederate officers in high government positions, cutting taxes needed for developing the state's primitive school system, and repudiating Reconstruction-era state debts so that the state was considered a poor credit risk and industrial expansion was discouraged. And, to top it all off, they manipulated and controlled the vote of their former slaves, at the expense of the white yeomen of northern Alabama. The vast majority of plain farmers lived in poverty and were exploited either as sharecroppers or by unscrupulous merchants who took liens on their crops in exchange for all the food and supplies they needed.

Alabama was thus ripe territory for late 19th-century Populism, which had its roots in the Farmers Alliance and the debtor-oriented Greenbackers of the 1880s. The Populist movement of Alabama crested in the 1890s as leaders like Reuben F. Kolb demanded controls over banks and railroads, laws to regulate the crop lien system, relaxed monetary policies, and abolition of the notorious system by which the state of Alabama leased convicts to work for private mines, mills, and farms. Kolb ran for governor first as a Democrat and then under the banner of a new "Jeffersonian Democratic party," losing by narrow margins in 1892 and 1894. Again, Alabama's sectionalism appeared as the Populist-inclined counties of Northern Alabama, together with their poor white farmer allies in the Wiregrass section of southeastern Alabama, lined up against the Black Belt. Kolb was defeated each time he ran but only by a few thousand votes; there seems little doubt that the Black Belters used outright fraud, and their controlled black vote, to defeat him. In 1894, Kolb lost to a one-armed Confederate general named William C. Oates, who later confessed: "I told them to go to it, boys, count them out. We had to do it. . . . We could not help ourselves."

Kolb and the other Populists, along with their colleagues like Tom Watson in Georgia, had initially appealed for black votes in the hope of building a general coalition of the dispossessed of both races. But the Black Belt's cynical use of Negro votes to "count out" the opposition disillusioned them, and they became convinced that honest elections could never be held as long as blacks were allowed to vote. At the same time, Black Belt leaders concluded that they had reached the end of the road in winning elections by fraud, and as they watched the rise of the great unwashed in the Populist period, they decided that both blacks and the white rabble should be disenfranchised.

They also noted that the "white" counties were prepared to stuff ballot boxes as the Bourbons had been doing.

A general meeting of the minds was thus reached in a 1901 constitutional convention, which adopted what Alabama historian Malcolm C. McMillan has called "the most restrictive and complicated suffrage article ever adopted by any state." To vote, a person had to (1) be 21 years old—and male; (2) never have been convicted of 30-some crimes, which began with wife-beating; (3) prove his literacy by interpreting a section of the U.S. Constitution—or, alternatively, be a property holder; and (4) pay a $1.50 yearly poll tax—which if unpaid over a period of time, would be due cumulatively, so that a delinquent taxpayer might have to ante up as much as $36 to cast a ballot. Both the blacks and a huge proportion of the whites were illiterates at the time, but the whites were given an extra chance by the notorious "fighting grandfather clause" which said that any male could register if one of his ancestors had fought in any American war—including, of course, the Confederate side in the Civil War.*

If disenfranchisement was the objective of the 1901 constitution, it did its work well. In 1900, 78,311 Negroes had been registered in 14 Black Belt Counties; three years later the total was only 1,081. Many whites decided the poll tax was too onerous, and popular participation in elections plunged to abysmally low levels. Even in the 1920–46 period, only 19.2 percent of the adult population would take part in the Democratic primaries for governor; it was 1970 before the participation rate finally crept above 50 percent. Alabama's turnout rate for Presidential elections ranked 46th in the nation in 1968 (even when George Wallace was running), and 47th in 1972.

The 1901 constitution also tried to close the door on progressive reforms by putting a severe limitation on taxes, adding a debt limit, and forbidding the state to engage in internal improvements. About the best one could say for the constitution was that it earmarked some of the very low property taxes, and proceeds from the poll tax, for education. But proposals to give taxing power to local school districts or to allocate a fixed percentage of state revenues for education were rejected. The reason was that Black Belters, who generally sent their own children to private academies, shared none of northern Alabama's interest in public education. At the time, the average amount spent each *year* on a public school child in Alabama was 50 cents, compared to $2.84 in the country as a whole. Almost a quarter of the whites and four-fifths of the Negroes were illiterate.

One of the most lasting effects of the 1901 constitution was its apportionment plan for the legislature, which was weighted heavily in favor of the Black Belt. With power handed over to them, the Black Belt counties would refuse for more than six decades to carry out the decennial reapportionment mandated in the constitution. As the population shifted increasingly toward

* The grandfather clause lasted only until 1915, when it was invalidated by the U.S. Supreme Court in an Oklahoma case. A 1954 constitutional amendment stripped the poll tax of most of its retroactivity after a campaign led by such women's organizations as the League of Women Voters and the American Association of University Women. They found that the poll tax had held down the registration level of white housewives in the state to a mere 20 percent. The poll tax was finally invalidated in the 1960s—in a decision by Judge Frank Johnson. Most of the other voting restrictions were consigned to oblivion by the Voting Rights Act of 1965.

urban areas and northern Alabama, the situation became more and more egregious. In the late '50s, the 2,057 white voters of Lowndes County in the Black Belt (where the 81-percent majority blacks were 100 percent disenfranchised) had the same voting power (one seat) in the state senate as 130,000 registered voters in Jefferson County (Birmingham). The disparities in the state house of representatives were almost as gross. Until the federal courts finally blew the whistle in the mid-'60s, the Black Belt and allied counties of southern Alabama held an effective veto power over every progressive impulse in state government.

Alabama did not have, at least, the county unit system for picking governors that prevailed in next-door Georgia. As early as 1896, Democratic governors of a liberal bent were elected from time to time. In 1902, when the Negro had been safely disenfranchised, Alabama felt it feasible to nominate officials in primary elections, instead of state party conventions dominated by the courthouse rings. Thus the way was further opened to the election of progressive governors. And several made great strides forward, the general intransigence of the legislature notwithstanding.

One was Braxton Bragg Comer (1907–11), a progressively inclined Birmingham industrialist who regulated railroads, enacted the first conservation laws, and did so much for the schools and universities that he came to be known as "Alabama's education governor." Another was Thomas E. Kilby (1919–23), an Anniston businessman who pioneered in penal reform and established Alabama's first state board of education. The dominant figure of the '20s and '30s was the dynamic "Little Colonel" Bibb Graves. During his first administration (1927–31) Graves got the convict lease system abolished once and for all; later he led the state in a little New Deal of his own (1935–39), making immense strides in developing the schools and building roads to get rural Alabama out of the mud. Alabama enacted its first sales tax under Graves, most of the revenue going to schools. One of the small band of old-time liberal leaders in Alabama told me: "Old Bibb Graves was a fantastic guy—a Kluxer and he always had tobacco juice running down the side of his jaw. He was an honor graduate of Yale Law School. He was in the best Populist tradition, and he did a lot for the state in New Deal days. He knew how to shake the plum tree in Washington and was really concerned for the people."

For robust showmanship and deep-gut Populism, no Alabama politician in living memory has bested James E. Folsom. He was called "Big Jim" with good reason—he was six feet, eight inches tall, weighed 245 pounds, and wore a size 16 shoe. He deserved the appellation of "Kissin' Jim," too, because when he burst onto the statewide political scene in the '40s, he did indeed scatter kisses along the campaign trail and made no bones about his appreciation of the fairer sex. ("If my political enemies," Folsom once said, "think they can catch ol' Big Jim by gettin' some pretty young thing, puttin' a nice dress on her, and reelin' her by in front of Big Jim—if they think they can catch ol' Jim that way, they're right. . . . They're gonna catch Jim every time.") Folsom also lightened Alabama campaigning by adding a string band —the "Strawberry Pickers"—to his campaign entourage, offering the folks at the rural branch heads, where his real strength lay, a welcome diet of country, Western, and gospel songs.*

Charles Morgan, Jr., remembers, as a boy, listening to Folsom's appeal to the rural folk in '46. "He told them how their state government was run by the industrial interests of Birmingham and the North and East, and the Black Belt plantation owners. In the classic Populist tradition of the South. he waged political war against the rich city folk. Folsom spoke of the dreams of the little man, of the worker and the farmer, and they listened. He told them he remembered lying in bed in the morning at sun-up on his family's farm, when the dew was on the ground, and breathing that 'clean, fresh, green breeze that comes across the fields.' When he got to Montgomery, Folsom said, he was going to be that 'clean, fresh, green breeze' blowing."

"Ol' Big Jim" was not to be taken lightly, because he understood instinctively what V. O. Key observed—that "Alabamians retain a sort of frontier independence, with an inclination to defend liberty and to bait the interests." Folsom later said he had been "the first and last governor the little man, the young people, and the blacks ever had in Alabama." He had been raised in the poor Wiregrass area and moved to northern Alabama in 1940, thus gaining what Key called the "friends and neighbors" support of the two areas that had stood together against secession and the Black Belt planters and for the Populist cause. Folsom never stopped battling for reapportionment of the legislature; he was for repealing the poll tax; he wanted pensions for the old folks; he fought for (and got) state funding to pave thousands of miles of farm-to-market roads; and he won higher pay for teachers on the theory that "We don't want our children penalized for being born in Alabama." His earthy vocabulary made him anathema to proper city people, and the big interests and big circulation newspapers were unanimously against him. But, as political scientist Donald Strong of the University of Alabama noted, "the very qualities that repelled the country-club set convinced those lower on the economic pyramid that 'old Jim' was indeed one of their own."

For his time, Folson was remarkably advanced on race relations. "I could never get excited about our colored brothers," he said once. "They've been here 300 years and I estimate they'll be here another 300 years or more. I'm not going to get my ulcers in an uproar. I find them to be good citizens. If they had been making a living for me like they have for the Black Belt, I'd be proud of them instead of kicking them and cussing them all the time." One of the first things Folsom did as governor was to take the hoods off the Ku Klax Klansmen by pushing through a law making it illegal to wear a mask on the state highways; the KKK's power was greatly diminished as a result. In those years, it was still customary that when a Negro was accused of rape, he was on his way to the electric chair. But during Folsom's terms as governor (1947–51, 1955–59), he regularly commuted their sentences. In a moving Christmas message to the state's people in 1949, Folsom said of the Negroes:

* The fiddle and guitar—often the most expensive Nashville talent from the Grand Ole Opry—are now *de rigueur* for big-time Alabama candidacies. Other campaign embellishments include mammoth barbecues and fish fries which may draw as many as 10,000 people.

Are they getting adequate medical care to rid them of hookworm, rickets, and social disease? Are they provided with sufficient professional training to produce their own doctors, professors, lawyers, clergymen, scientists?

As long as the Negroes are held down by deprivation and lack of opportunity, the other people will be held down alongside them. Let's start talking fellowship and brotherly love and doing unto others. And let's do more than talk about it—let's start living it.

Eventually, the race issue precipitated Folsom's downfall because his attitudes were too tolerant to match Alabama's tense and angry mood after the 1954 Supreme Court school desegregation decision. When the legislature in 1955 declared the decision "null, void, and of no effect" in Alabama, Folsom termed the resolution "hogwash" and likened it to "an old hound dog bayin' at the moon." Constitutionally, he was right; politically, it was not a tenable position. Nor did the voters appreciate Folsom's gesture in inviting Adam Clayton Powell, Jr., into the governor's mansion for a cocktail, or the accumulation of scandals caused by the coterie of small-time crooks who surrounded him. Alcoholism was another factor. In 1946 Folsom had said: "The only thing that's better for breakfast than beer is whiskey." In 1962 he proved he meant it when he went on television the night before the gubernatorial primary gloriously drunk, unable even to remember the names of his children when he tried to introduce them. (Folsom claims he was drugged by someone —not drunk.)

George Wallace won that 1962 election and set the tone for Alabama in the '60s. Folsom has since tried several comebacks but has been repelled each time. He is a discredited man, perhaps the greatest living tragedy of modern Southern politics. With Folsom's fall, the causes the old roué believed in also went into eclipse, awaiting rebirth on another, more promising dawn.

George Wallace: Compulsive Campaigner

The thorny issues of state government are really of little interest to George Wallace. Campaigning is much more to his taste than governing. I had always sensed it from afar, but the impression was driven home in a long interview I had with him in 1971. Questions about the specifics of state government he answered laconically, almost by rote. But when the subject turned to politics, the fire of the old Wallace was there. We were sitting in adjoining chairs in a hotel suite, and it was soon apparent that Wallace's form of communication was as much physical as verbal (though he is no piker in the latter category). With the less controversial questions, he used the technique of calm persuasion, often reaching over to rub the interviewer's knee as he spoke. But when he suspected skepticism in the interviewer, there would be the finger jabbing at one's chest and Wallace all pugnacious, the black eyes jutting out assertively.

My mind went back to those raucous rallies of the 1968 campaign, half revival, half political meeting, and Wallace warming up the plain folks—those steelworkers and beauticians and cab drivers decked out in red, white and blue

—with his rhetoric about pseudo-intellectual government and long-haired students, bussin' and lenient judges, welfare loafers and the fate that awaited any anarchist "scum" "who lies down in front of our car when we get to be President." (The line that always brought down the house, reflecting the quintessential violence of the Wallace appeal: "It'll be the *last* car he'll ever lie down in front of.") Rare was the speech in which Wallace said much about what he would really do about the problems of government. I watched one big rally in Baltimore and a couple of smaller events, but it was soon apparent—as Spiro Agnew said of the slums that year—that "when you've seen one, you've seen 'em all."

What was important for and about Wallace was his touch with "the folks." Marshall Frady in his 1968 book, *Wallace,* said that contact was

> almost sensuous, almost mystic. They are his only reality. He feels that without them he is nothing, and with them he is everything and cannot be intimidated. . . . Behind his indefatigable scrambling, his ferocious concentration, his inexhaustible ambition, there seems to lurk a secret, desperate suspicion that facing him, aside from and beyond his political existence, is nothingness—an empty, terrible white blank. It's as if, when the time finally arrives for him to cease to be a politician, he will simply cease to be.

And that indeed was the specter that faced Wallace in the months of operations and incessant pain after the attempt on his life, and the reason that Wallace watchers were sure that as long as there was any strength and breath left in George Wallace, he would assiduously court "the folks" in any campaign at hand. Long before Wallace's injuries, the late Grover C. Hall, Jr., editor of the Montgomery *Advertiser,* noted that "When there's no campaign in sight, he gets to looking wan and sickly." Ray Jenkins has described Wallace as a "compulsive campaigner":

> For proof of Wallace's insatiable yearning to hear the roar of the crowd, one need only look at his political track record:
>
> —In 1958, he made his first race for governor, and lost.
>
> —In 1960, he did not run for any office, and [until 1972] his associates would refer to that period as the low point in his life.
>
> —In 1962, he ran for governor, and won.
>
> —In 1964, he ran in Presidential primaries in Maryland, Wisconsin, and Indiana. His respectable showing brought him into serious national attention for the first time, and he almost certainly would have mounted some kind of third party campaign if the Republicans had not undercut him by nominating a Southern hero, Barry Goldwater.
>
> —In 1966, he ran his wife, Lurleen, for governor, and won.
>
> —In 1968, he made his first national campaign for President.
>
> —In 1970, despite a seemingly ironclad public and private pledge to Governor Albert Brewer that he would not run, he entered the race and won.
>
> —In 1972, he ran in numerous Presidential primaries as a Democrat and might well have undertaken another campaign under the banner of his American Independent party, if he had not suffered almost-fatal wounds at the hands of a would-be assassin.
>
> That adds up to seven races in 14 years—a record unmatched by anyone except Congressmen, who regard biennial elections as a Constitutional curse.

And there seemed to be little doubt that if his health permitted—and it seemed to be improving markedly in 1973—Wallace would run again for governor in 1974 and probably for President once more in 1976.

Wallace did not invent third-party, independent elector style Presidential politics in Alabama or the South. As early as 1948 the Alabama Democratic party, angered by President Truman's civil rights stance, had preempted the Democratic elector slate for Strom Thurmond's Dixiecrat party. With their choice limited to their fellow Southerner and Thomas E. Dewey, Alabamians gave 80 percent of their vote to Thurmond. In 1960 there was fierce competition between Alabama states righters and loyalist Alabama Democrats for control of the Democratic elector slate. The Democratic voters actually chose their electors in a primary election, nominating six unpledged (states rights) electors and five loyalists. This incongruous crew was able to run together under the Democratic column in the November election, because Alabama, unlike all other states, does not list the names of the actual candidates for President on its ballot—only the names of the electors. The Democratic electors carried the day with 57 percent of the vote, but the arguments among election aficionados continue to this day over whether the voters thought they were voting for John Kennedy or for the unpledged electors (who ended up casting votes for Harry Flood Byrd in the electoral college).*

George Wallace was not part of the Dixiecrat movement in its early years. He came from a poor cotton-chopping county, Barbour, in southeastern Alabama, where Negroes were a majority and segregation was accepted as a way of life. At the 1948 Democratic National Convention as an alternate delegate, he fought the strong civil rights platform plank backed by Hubert Humphrey and the other liberals, but when it passed, he refused to join the half of the Alabama delegation that walked out in protest. He was a lieutenant of Jim Folsom in the legislature and introduced progressive-type legislation to build trade schools and let towns issue municipal bonds to attract industry.

When he made his first race for governor in 1958, however, Wallace suffered a jolting defeat at the hands of John Patterson, the first postwar Democratic governor to make the race issue his chief talking point. Patterson was so extreme in his denunciations of the Supreme Court and the black cause and so happy about the support he got from the Ku Klux Klan that Wallace seemed like a real racial moderate in comparison and even got the endorsement of the state NAACP. After that election, Wallace reportedly said that Patterson "outniggered me, and I'll never be outniggered again." † In 1962, Wallace was the most rabid segregationist in the field, learning how to evoke crowd passions by lines in which he called Frank Johnson "a low-down, car-

* I developed a theory, shortly after the 1960 election, that in computing the national popular vote for President, the only proper way to count the Alabama vote was to divide the vote for the highest-polling Democratic elector there (324,040) by the way the Democratic elector slate itself was constituted—six-elevenths for Harry Byrd, five-elevenths for Kennedy. My Democratic friends did not appreciate the exercise, because it erased the 118,559-vote national popular vote lead for Kennedy which the wire services had compiled by erroneously crediting Kennedy with the entire Democratic elector vote in Alabama. In fact, my six-elevenths, five-elevenths formula actually showed Nixon the national popular vote leader over Kennedy by a margin of some 58,000 votes. See Peirce, *The People's President* (New York: Simon & Schuster, 1968), pages 102–104, 348–349.

† Other versions quoted Wallace as saying he would not be "outsegged." Wallace denies having said it either way.

petbaggin', scalawaggin', integratin', pool-mixin', race-mixin' liar." He promised to stand in the schoolhouse door to stop segregation, and white Alabamians, educated by Patterson to worry about black children actually entering their schools, responded to his appeal. Wallace (and liquor) polished off his old mentor, Jim Folsom, in the first primary and Ryan deGraffenried, a moderate state senator from Tuscaloosa, in the runoff.

It was in his January 1963 inaugural address that Wallace issued his clarion call for "segregation forever" in the Anglo-Southland: "In the name of the greatest people that have ever trod this earth, I draw the line in the dust and toss the gauntlet before the feet of tyranny, and I say: Segregation now —segregation tomorrow—segregation forever."

Only six months later, Wallace was to make his promised schoolhouse door stand, trying to bar two blacks from being enrolled at the University of Alabama at Tuscaloosa. His own National Guard was quickly federalized by President Kennedy, and the students registered a few hours later. It may have looked like a Wallace defeat, but, as Frady noted, Wallace had played masterfully on Southern psychology—showing, in proper Confederate style, "an unvanquished and intransigent spirit in the face of utter, desolate defeat." Only four years later, 300 black students were attending the university without incident. And just a few months after Wallace's stand at Tuscaloosa, the first black children were enrolled in white Alabama schools, even though Wallace at one point sent state troopers to encircle a Tuskegee school and prevent desegregation.

I often wonder about the true feelings of staff aides to politicians who fight the rear guard actions of history. *South* magazine provided a clue in a 1971 interview with John Peter Kohn, Jr., a former Wallace appointee to the Alabama supreme court and longtime Wallace confidant who helped to write the governor's "segregation forever" speech and the statement Wallace made before yielding to federal authority at Tuscaloosa. Kohn made no bones about the fact that he had urged Wallace (if he needed any urging) to run a "racist" campaign in 1962. "I am not a racist, neither do I feel is George Wallace," Kohn said. "But I had enough Jesuit training as a young man to believe that on occasion the ends justify the means. I am not proud of my participation in a racist type campaign, but at the time I felt it was justified." By the time of his interview, Kohn had soured on most politicians, saying he found them "putrid, bilious, megalomaniac." But there were some exceptions to Kohn's condemnation of public figures from Alabama: Judge Frank M. Johnson—"He is my idea of what a judge should be. It is a city disgrace the way Montgomery has treated him." Justice Hugo Black—"He is the greatest judge who ever sat on the bench. He has taken the Constitution of the United States and wrapped it around the poor, the weak, and the humble. He has made it a cloak of protection for the unfortunate."

The scenario at Tuscaloosa had been carried on national television, and with increasing out-of-state forays, Wallace soon became a national figure. The temptation to run in the 1964 Presidential primaries was impossible to resist, and he might well have run on a third-party ticket if Barry Goldwater, newly revered in Dixie for his vote against the Civil Rights Act, had not been the GOP nominee. Goldwater swept Alabama with 70 percent of the vote; his only opposition was a group of Democratic electors pledged to nobody.

"Wallace's brief flash on the national scene clearly established him," Ray Jenkins wrote, "as the first Southern politician since Huey Long of Louisiana to assemble a national following." To white Alabamians, who had seen one of their own frighten the national Democratic establishment, it was a heady experience, and Wallace's popularity soared. But it was not quite great enough, despite every principled and unprincipled pressure Wallace could bring to bear, to get the legislature to approve an amendment to the state constitution which would have permitted him to run again for governor in 1966.* There was a dramatic moment during senate debate when Kenneth Hammond, a former football player from a northern Alabama mountain village called Valley Head, threw the issue into ugly relief. Wallace, he said, was "one of the greatest political manipulators this century has known." Wallace, he said, was using the Hitlerian tactic of setting race against race, and had in mind "a dictatorship which would make Huey P. Long look like a piker."

Running Lurleen for governor—a decision made only after the popular deGraffenried died in a plane crash while campaigning—neatly solved Wallace's problem, because it enabled him to remain governor in all but signature. She beat nine opponents, including two former governors, without a runoff—a clear sign that Alabamians wanted Wallace to run for the Presidency in 1968. Lurleen, until her death from cancer in May 1968, was essentially a ceremonial governor. She was a shy woman, who had previously had little interest in politics, but she did make her mark by starting a program of regional mental health centers after being shocked by the conditions she saw in one of Alabama's infamously deprived mental institutions

We have alluded already to the tenor of Wallace's 1968 third-party campaign, in which he developed a whole panoply of little people's emotional issues—underlain, of course, by the race issue. The success of his workers and lawyers in getting his name on the ballot in all 50 states was one of the organizational miracles of recent-day politics. As small campaign contributions cascaded in from all over the country, and his standing in the early autumn national polls surged over 20 percent, it became clear that Wallace's challenge was far more serious than Thurmond's 20 years before. But the herculean efforts which organized labor expended to cut down his blue-collar vote, and people's awareness that he really had no chance of election, would sharply diminish his actual vote in the North. Wallace's Southernism worked strongly for him and against him. He played strongly on the region's lingering sense of inferiority, telling Southerners they were tired of being looked down upon and repeating a sure-applause line: "Folks down here in Alabama are just as refined and cultured as folks anywhere!" † But the provinciality doubt-

* An amendment authorizing two successive terms was finally approved in 1970.

† Another Wallace home-state pitch that told a lot was this "Those liberal newsmen look down on you as bigoted redneck hillbillies, crackers, and peckerwoods who can't even cross the street. Now I'm on those big shows, *Meet the Press* and *Issues and Answers,* folks are used to that now, you know. They used to be right rude and crude 'cause I was just a redneck, and one of them once asked me if I didn't act like I thought I was the smartest man in the country. I told him I wasn't the smartest man in the country, but I sure am the smartest man on this program."

less hurt him in the North. When the election returns were in, Wallace had carried only five states, and all in the Deep South—Alabama itself, Mississippi, Louisiana, Georgia, and Arkansas. It was not much different from 1948, when Thurmond had won three of those states—Alabama, Mississippi, and Louisiana—and his own South Carolina. Ironically, South Carolina was denied Wallace in 1968 because Thurmond went all-out for Richard Nixon.

Opinions differ on whether Wallace ever believed he had a chance to win in 1968, but in addition to the build-up it gave him for future runs, he counted it a solid success. "I think my movement defeated Hubert Humphrey, which was something the majority of the people of my region wanted done," Wallace told me. "My running took away enough labor vote from Humphrey in California, in Ohio, in Illinois, in New Jersey and Missouri, so that those states went for Nixon." (Independent analysts think Wallace hurt Nixon much more than Humphrey, especially in the South, but the interesting point is his own analysis.) Wallace also thought he had changed the whole tone of the campaign, especially on issues like "law and order and tax exemptions for the multirich such as foundations and otherwise. Before it was over it sounded as if both national parties' speeches were written in Clayton, Alabama."

Wallace's 1968 campaign probably marked the high-water point of Southern-based third-party politics in the 20th century, and one of those tantalizing historical "ifs" is what would have happened if Nixon had received a few less electoral votes, so that he would have lacked a majority and George Wallace would have held the power to choose the next President through his 46 electors. That eventuality was barely averted—and would have come to pass if 53,034 strategically placed Nixon votes in three close states (New Jersey, Missouri, and New Hampshire) had gone to Humphrey instead. A shift of 111,674 votes in California alone—1.5 percent of the total cast in that state—would have had the same result.

When I asked Wallace how he would have handled the situation, he first made it very clear that he would have instructed his electors how they should vote in the electoral college, which convenes in mid-December, and would never have permitted the choice of a President to remain unresolved there so that, under the Constitution, the House of Representatives would have chosen the following January. "Why," he said, "would I want to lose control of the matter by throwing the election into the House where we would have no control whatsoever? No, the matter would have been settled in the electoral college." And his own electors, Wallace said, "were pledged to go along with me in the matter, and they would have gone with me."

How would he have instructed his electors? "The chances are the votes probably would have gone to Mr. Nixon, because we were violently opposed to Mr. Humphrey's philosophy and ideology." Would he have demanded concessions, in advance, from Nixon? "We would probably have asked Mr. Nixon to reiterate some of his campaign statements he'd already made . . . just to restate what he had already said in substance: 'I want to work for world peace, I want tax reduction, tax reform. I want the neighborhood school concept protected. I'm in substance for freedom of choice in the public school system and against busing. . . .'" Wallace on other occasions talked of a "solemn covenant" to stop foreign aid to Communist nations and left-leaning neutrals, of a revamping of the U.S. Supreme Court, and a halt to federal civil rights enforcement. In other words, Wallace might well have forced on Nixon the same kind of a "hands-off" attitude toward the South that Rutherford B. Hayes had agreed to in 1876 in exchange for the electoral votes he needed to be elected President. The South's price then had been termination of the first Reconstruction, a decision that would be followed by three-quarters of a century of impingement of black people's rights in the South. The net of Wallace's demands would have been to end the "second" Reconstruction—the civil rights advances of the 1960s.

In 1970 George Wallace was back on the stump, trying to oust Governor Albert Brewer, a slender, urbane north Alabamian who had bucked the sentiment of his native Tennessee Valley to become a loyal Wallace confederate and legislative ally from 1958 onwards. Brewer was no Populist or special defender of black people's interests; essentially he was the favorite of the more prosperous urban whites, the big business and chamber of commerce crowds. Wallace needed to eliminate Brewer for a simple reason—he stood in the way of Wallace's return to the governorship, and Wallace said he needed that base to keep his national "movement" alive. (It was fear of a revived Wallace Presidential effort, in fact, that impelled the Nixon political coterie—as evidence during the 1973 Senate Watergate hearings revealed—to pump as much as $400,000 in secret money into Brewer's campaign.)

Traveling the Alabama campaign trails before the first primary, the *National Observer*'s James R. Dickenson reported: "Early spring in Alabama is as delicate as wisteria in the rain and as gentle as falling in love, but George Wallace is having none of this. He is dishing out his politics the way many of his fellow Alabamians like their whiskey and religion—as hot and raw as white lightnin' and as primitive as Baptist fundamentalism."

In the first primary, Wallace muted his old racist appeals and concentrated on promises to the small farmer and worker and attacks on the big interests, utilities, and intellectuals. But it was not enough: Brewer actually ran ahead, though falling just short of a majority. Threatened with political extinction, Wallace reverted to rank racism in the runoff. His talking point was the big black vote which had gone for Brewer in the first primary. Privately, Wallace told folks: "If I don't win, them niggers are going to control this state."

In the end, Wallace won the nomination—but by a margin of less than 34,000 votes out of more than a million cast. A Brewer aide summed it up pretty well for a visiting reporter (R. W. Apple, Jr., of the New York *Times*): "When you boil it down, it was the rednecks versus the niggers and the Jaycees. Even in 1970, there are still more of them than us."

Wallace moved quickly to erase the racist image of his campaign. His 1971 inaugural address had none of the fiery defiance of the 1963 "segregation forever" version; in fact, he even included a line saying that "Alabama belongs to all of us—black and white, young and old, rich and poor alike." When I asked him shortly thereafter about his 1963 stand, Wallace replied that he believed then that segregation was the best system. "But now segregation is dead. It's outlawed, and it won't be again," he said. He even permitted (through the house speaker he controlled) the appointment of two black legislators to key committee posts when the legislature convened in 1971. Two years later, Wallace was making news by crowning a black beauty queen and getting a hand from an assemblage of black mayors. Those overjoyed about a "new" Wallace did well, however, to remember this advertisement, which he had countenanced using as recently as his 1970 campaign:

IF YOU WANT TO SAVE
ALABAMA AS WE KNOW ALABAMA
REMEMBER!
THE BLOC VOTE (NEGROES AND THEIR
WHITE FRIENDS) NEARLY NOMINATED
GOV. BREWER ON MAY 5TH. THIS
BLACK AND WHITE
SOCIAL-POLITICAL ALLIANCE
MUST NOT DOMINATE
THE PEOPLE OF ALABAMA!
THIS SPOTTED ALLIANCE MUST BE DEFEATED!
THIS MAY BE YOUR LAST CHANCE.
VOTE RIGHT—
VOTE WALLACE

Just before his inaugural, Wallace married for a second time. His new bride was Mrs. Cornelia Ellis Snively, a poised and attractive 31-year-old divorcée who happened to be a niece of Jim Folsom—and a smart politician in her own right. By the time of the 1972 Presidential campaign, Cornelia had been able to get Wallace a bit more fashionably dressed and to improve his television style. Wallace made another change: he decided to run in 1972 as a Democrat, forsaking the foundering American Independent party he had established four years before. (The AIP failed to make a respectable showing in any contest without Wallace as its candidate, a proof of the enduring futility of third-party politics in the United States.)

A desire for political "respectability," or the fun of running in so many primaries, or perhaps even a serious belief he could win the nomination, may have convinced Wallace to run as a Democrat in 1972. His Georgian friend, Lester Maddox, claims credit for Wallace's decision: *

> I told George and Mrs. Wallace, "Look, if you run as an independent, the Democratic officeholders don't have to respond to their constituents. If you do run as a Democrat, they have to squirm. As an independent, you have no chance of becoming President of the United States. As a Democrat, your chances are almost nil, but not so much so as running as an independent." I also told him that as an independent he'd continue to be downplayed by the news media, but as a major contender in the Democratic party, he'd be in a prominent position.
>
> "If you run as an independent," I told Wallace, "I'll run as a Democrat. Because we're not going to let it go by default."

* An alternative theory is that Wallace abandoned the idea of a third-party race as part of a deal in which the Nixon administration dropped a grand jury investigation of campaign funds which involved Wallace's brother, Gerald. Wallace denied the existence of any deal.

In December [1971] he finally came around. When he was in the hospital after the shooting, Mrs. Wallace especially thanked me for talking him into running as a Democrat.

Lester Maddox's own Presidential track record (he made an abortive, almost comical run for the 1968 nomination) would not recommend him as a big-time strategist, and to many old Southern political hands it is inconceivable that Wallace would ever listen very seriously to Maddox. Nevertheless, it was sound strategy for Wallace to campaign as a Democrat. He plunged into 15 primary battles, and in his first big one, Florida, coined *the* political slogan of 1972: "Send Them a Message." Millions of voters were upset with the power elites that sent their sons off to fight unwinnable wars, raised their taxes, meddled with their neighborhood schools, and never seemed to listen to plain folks. Wallace hit pay dirt on the tax issue ("We're sick and tired of the average citizen being taxed to death while those multibillionaires like the Rockefellers and the Fords and the Mellons go without paying taxes"), and most particularly on busing ("This busin' business is the most callous, asinine thing I ever heard of, the whim of some social schemer in Washington who messed up the schools there and then moved out to Virginia or Maryland"). He whipped Humphrey and Edmund Muskie and Henry Jackson and the whole pack of Democratic hopefuls in Florida, giving the Democratic establishment a shaking up it would not recover from all year long. After that he went on to win five more primaries, two of them—Maryland and Michigan—in the North. He placed second in six others—generally a strong second. His only serious miscalculation was that he did not read the fine print on the Democratic party reform rules, so that he failed to train his staff to get his share of delegates in nonprimary states If he had, he might have been a major power to contend with at the Miami Beach Convention.

Fear rode with Wallace wherever he went on his campaign forays—a scarcely controllable fear of flying and, above all, a fear of assassination. A large bulletproof rostrum was carried around and used almost everywhere he spoke. And it was unusual when he decided, after a speech at a Laurel, Maryland, shopping center on May 15, 1972, to mix with the crowd after he had spoken. In Frederick he had been hit by a brick; at College Park, students hit him with popsicles. He told a friend: "Somebody's going to get killed before this primary is over, and I hope it's not me." And in that crowd at Laurel, the most feared happened. A "loner" named Arthur Bremer was in the crowd—it was later discovered he had been shadowing Wallace—and he fired a volley of pistol shots at the governor. Wallace fell, one bullet penetrating his spine. He was to recover but would be confined to a wheelchair, possibly for the rest of his life.

Assassins had felled other prominent Americans in the years before—John Kennedy in 1963, Robert Kennedy and Martin Luther King, Jr., in 1968 (all men, incidentally, who played important roles in the Alabama civil rights story). But there was a difference between those assassinations and the attempt on Wallace's life. A man who had known Wallace since his earliest days in politics observed: "The Kennedys and King may have been lightning rods for violence, but Wallace was unlike them in that his words actually encouraged it. He was really a magnet for violence—a small, physical man, a former boxer, always on the balls of his feet and always evoking the most brutish emotions. Remember that his words—a stage or two removed, to be sure, but still his words—were behind case after case of elemental violence inflicted on black people and other dissenters in Alabama."

Marshall Frady put it another way:

> In a sense, Wallace is common to us all. That, finally, is his darkest portent. There is something primordially exciting and enthralling about him, and there still seems to be just enough of the wolf pack in most of us to be stirred by it and to answer to it. As long as we are creatures hung halfway between the mud and the stars, figures like Wallace can be said to pose the great dark original threat.

By a stranger quirk of fate, Wallace's brush with death—coinciding with some of his greatest primary triumphs—gave him the respectability he had yearned for so long. The President and would-be Presidents and party chairmen came to his bedside. Fourteen months later, even Edward M. Kennedy came to Alabama to present a "spirit of America" award to Wallace. But Wallace made it clear that he had changed none of his old beliefs. In autumn 1972, he urged the people of his state to support "Alabama Democrats"—a backhand way of saying it was OK to go ahead and vote for Nixon-Agnew (which 72 percent of them proceeded to do). He said he was interested in the Democratic party's future, but only if it would get back to "the middle ground"—as he defined it. If the Democrats thought they were dealing with a sincerely reconstructed George Wallace, they were wrong.

George Wallace: Populist or Not?

> I'm a Populist. Look what I did for the folks in Alabama. My administration built 29 trade schools and 18 junior colleges located in every geographic area of the state. Busing is free to them, and they afford many lower- and middle-income families their first chance to send their children to college or to trade schools. All the time the federal government was stepping in through HEW and court orders written by HEW—the beginning of what had become chaos in many school systems in the country. But I felt youth should be afforded the opportunity. I'm very proud of the system. It's probably the only one of its kind in the government.
>
> We got free textbooks for all public school children in the state. We made the banks pay interest on state deposits. We're opposing any rate increases for public utilities because we feel they've been underregulated.
>
> You want to know about borrowing in my administration? Sure, we did it. We borrowed a lot for roads, for school buildings, for junior colleges, for docks—and I tell you the big parks program begun under my wife's administration will be one of the finest in the South when it's completed. Building capital outlay improvements on borrowed money in your own state to enhance your own wealth and productivity is one thing, but borrowing money to build these same harbors and roads and bridges in Yugoslavia or Cuba or China—that's different, because that money's gone.
>
> —Governor Wallace, in interview with the author

Evaluating George Wallace's record as the leading force of Alabama government since the early '60s reminds one of the old joke about the man who was asked how his wife was, and queried back, "Compared to what?"

Compared to the abysmal condition of public education in Alabama a dozen years ago, impressive advances have been made during the Wallace years; compared to its sister states, Alabama still ranks a mediocre 34th in per capita expenditures for higher education and a dreary 50th in outlays for elementary and secondary schools. Wallace helped to encourage major advances in medical education, but in the most recent count there were still only 89 physicians for each 100,000 people in Alabama, a ranking of 47th among the states. Wallace and especially his first wife, Lurleen, began programs to pull Alabama out of the Middle Ages in its mental health programs, but conditions were still so abysmal in the early '70s that Judge Frank Johnson found patients were being deprived of their constitutional rights and ordered 70 improvements to be made, including an immediate increase of staff psychiatrists at the mental hospitals from four to 42.

Compared to the rest of the country, the state under Wallace spent just under the average amount per capita on highways. But it was a big deal for Alabama, because the state's low yield from regular taxes obliged Wallace to ask for more than $600 million in bonds to provide the state share of mostly federally financed highways. If "pave now, pay later" is a Populist doctrine, Wallace is a master of it; one $100 million highway bond issue in his first term had a feature delaying any payment at all on principal for several years. It also carried a "balloon" note in its final year (1984), when $22 million in outstanding principal will be due. By 1971, when Wallace made yet another request for what opponents called "political road building in Alabama," they were able to cut almost in half the amount he requested.

On the labor front, Wallace's claim to be a friend of the blue-collar worker was vitiated by the fact that Alabama had some of the lowest levels of workmen's compensation and unemployment insurance in the whole country. Stung by union attacks in the 1968 campaign, Wallace in 1971 did upgrade workmen's compensation benefits to make them comparable with other Southern states. But the Alabama level was still below the rest of the country, right-to-work was still on the Alabama statute books, and there was still no state minimum wage law.

Wallace claimed credit for $3 billion in new industrial development during his first term and Lurleen's—a somewhat inflated figure, according to federal government figures. It was true that 87,100 new manufacturing jobs were added in Alabama between 1962 and 1970. That was a 35 percent increase, impressive in comparison to the national gain of 19 percent but actually a point below the aggregate gain in the other Deep South states. Between 1962 and 1970, average hourly wages of Alabama production workers rose from $2.06 to $2.86. But the gap between the Alabaman and national wage figures, which had been 33 cents an hour in 1962, had widened to 50 cents in 1970.

In 1971 the Wallace administration was able to boast about passage of some of the strongest air and water pollution bills in the country. But the new laws were more the work of Attorney General Baxley—and general public pressure, including that mounted by the Birmingham *News*—than Wallace. The tough air pollution bill did not get Wallace's endorsement until he had been embarrassed by disclosure that his executive secretary had met secretly with some of the leading polluters and agreed to weakening amendments. The legislature reacted by passing an undiluted bill, which Wallace signed. But Wallace then delayed appointing the pollution control commission called for in the bill until six weeks beyond the statutory deadline. (Many pressing state problems were postponed when Wallace was out of the state campaigning for President, and then during the long recuperation from his near-fatal injuries in 1972.)

Finally, one must look at Wallace's record on taxation, the one area in which he had the clearest chance to prove his Populist oratory by making the burden light for Alabama's medium- and low-income people, his chief supporters. In one sense he succeeded, because Alabama collected less taxes per capita (or in relation to personal income) than any state except Arkansas. The price of that, of course, was seriously below-par state services. And the way the tax was distributed was to the benefit of the Big Mules, not Wallace's little folks. The state sales tax—applicable even to groceries—was increased from 3 to 4 percent.* Localities can add another 2 or 3 percent, so that the sales tax total is as high as 7 percent in some parts of the state. Several other taxes that fall heavily on low-income people were enacted or increased during the Wallace years. In fact, general and selective sales taxes added up to 70 percent of state tax revenues—one of the highest shares among all states.

On the other hand, personal and corporate income taxes, though raised under Wallace, had a 5 percent lid and accounted for a very small share of state revenue. Wallace yielded to the proposal of corporations that their tax level be written into the state constitution, thus making later increases extremely difficult. Property taxes were kept at the lowest level in the country, a point Wallace made much of when he campaigned in the North. But he made no effort to correct the grossly inequitable assessments which favored, among others, big land-holding corporations which were assessed as little as 17 cents an acre on their timberlands—less than the cost of fire protection. Some major land holdings, Baxley told me, were not even on the tax rolls. There were many laws, he said, giving industries exemptions from paying taxes. Wallace's Populist oratory notwithstanding, he took little interest in reform in these areas. To the contrary, Alabama newspapers carried frequent reports of questionable ties between Wallace administration officials and corporations doing business with the state.

Thus, by the record, Wallace's claim to being a Populist is open to serious challenge. When one puts that issue aside and asks simply if Alabama, under his leadership, mustered the concentration of talent and resources it would need to make a quantum jump past Deep South averages

* Wallace sought assiduously to shift the blame for tax increases to the legislature. Former University of Alabama president Frank Rose tells the story of how the sales tax got increased to pay for expanded educational programs: "Wallace called me into his office one day and said, 'If you want that money you're calling for publicly for education, you're going to have to get it out of the legislature. I promised the people that I wouldn't increase the sales tax.' I replied: 'Well, there's no way I can get it out of the legislature unless I have the support of your floor leaders.' And Wallace said: 'Well, you can have them. But I'm going to make a lot of noise about the sales tax going up.' I responded, 'I don't care how much noise you make about it, just as long as we get the money.' So Wallace made his noise, but he did deliver his floor leaders, and the tax went up, and the education money was approved."

toward national averages in anything from education to income to tax equity, the answer is clearly "no."

In fact, whatever progress Alabama *has* made in recent years has been due in large part to the largesse of the federal government and the pointy-headed bureaucrats Wallace loved to assail. That conclusion was driven home mercilessly in a 1966 editorial which Ray Jenkins wrote for the *Alabama Journal:*

Don't Make the "Outlaws" Mad

In almost the same breath with his promise to give counties their share of the "taxpayers' money," Gov. Wallace, a master of ambiguity, allowed that if he (pardon, Lurleen) is elected, there will be no cooperation with those "outlaws" in Washington. There would be, he suggested, if one of several of his opponents should win, thus giving aid and comfort to the "socialist, beatnik crowd running this government."

The fact is that Wallace, while making a showing of telling the federal government where to get off, has cooperated pretty well with the outlaws. No more evidence is needed of that fact than that the state gets back just a bit under $3 for every $1 sent to Washington.

Without the millions in federal aid pouring into Alabama, Gov. Wallace's school, road and other programs would have been virtually impossible. We're subsidized not only in what the federal government pays directly for but in the money this frees for other state expenditures. In cussing Washington, Wallace sounds like one of those pipsqueak foreign ingrates who take U.S. dollars and berate the benefactor.

If the outlaws—the Robin Hoods who collect from the rich states and distribute to the poorer according to need—should withdraw federal support from Alabama, grass would grow in every street in every city, village, and hamlet.

The Governor knows this. He knows that Alabama's economy is as heavily dependent on federal grants, assistance in hundreds of forms, payrolls and expenditures as it once was on cotton.

So may we enter a plea in Alabama's behalf to the Northern press Wallace dearly loves to paste—please don't print that "outlaw" quote in Washington, fellows. They might get the idea we're severing fiscal relations and, with the favorable gold balance we have, we want to keep every one of those integrating, carpetbagging, scalawagging dollars we can get our hooks on. (Right, George?)

Saints and Sinners: Alabamians in Washington

George Wallace may have failed to get a lease on the White House, but his political era did have a profound impact on Alabama's delegation to Capitol Hill. At the start of the 1960s, Alabama's nine-man contingent was neatly balanced between four loyalist and generally progressive Democrats from the northern part of the state, four standard Southern conservatives from the South, and a swing man in Birmingham. By the start of the '70s, all of the progressives save one—Robert Jones of the Tennessee Valley area of northernmost Alabama—had been eliminated, their seats taken by more conservative men, some of whom had been floor leaders for Wallace in the legislature. Among the casualties were Carl Elliott, who had authored the first student loan legislation in Congress, Kenneth Roberts, who preceded Ralph Nader by several years in investigating automobile safety standards, and Albert Rains, one of Congress' most outstanding legislators in the housing field.*

Three Goldwater-sweep Republicans sat on the delegation, where there had been none in 1960; all three voted a straight conservative line, though there were differences of tone between them. William L. Dickinson, for instance, placed himself in the ranks of lesser demagogues through never-proven charges of free sex and other wild behavior during the 1965 voting rights march from Selma to Montgomery. John Buchanan of Birmingham, by contrast, once assailed the Ku Klux Klan and insisted that political conservatism was not racist or reactionary. Jack Edwards of Mobile maintained such good personal relations with blacks that many voted for him over his Wallace-style opponents, even though his voting record gave minorities little to cheer about.

On the Senate side, John J. Sparkman, first elected in 1946, easily survived all the elections of the period. He could take credit for virtually all of the housing legislation passed by Congress in the postwar period, and his record on public works and spending legislation generally was more liberal than that of his Southern colleagues. Sparkman's home city is Huntsville, known as "the town that John Built" for all the wealth introduced by federal military and space installations and the TVA. Sparkman opposed the Dixiecrat movement in 1948 and was Adlai Stevenson's Vice Presidential running mate in 1952, but over the years his voting record drifted to the right, and he defended himself against Alabama's Negrophobia by voting against every civil rights bill of his times. He showed his consummate political skills by maintaining good relationships with Lyndon Johnson and nonaggression with George Wallace. When he was up for reelection in 1966, President Johnson told him: "Just let me know what you want, John. I'll be for you, or *agin* you, whichever will do the most good." In that same campaign, Wallace told Sparkman he preferred that they not appear together since Wallace would be attacking federal spending programs while Sparkman would—and should—defend them. Sparkman told an interviewer that while his relations with Wallace were correct and even friendly, they were not "comrades in arms."

Sparkman rose to be chairman of the Senate Banking and Currency Committee and the second-ranking Democrat on the Foreign Relations Committee. In 1972 he was challenged by Republican Winton Blount, a self-made millionaire contractor whose firm built much of the NASA Cape Kennedy complex.† Sparkman again confounded his critics by displaying a personal letter from President Nixon praising him for "a demonstration of courage and statemanship" for helping the administration on two key foreign affairs

* A less serious loss was that of Mobile's Frank Boykin, a flamboyant big man who garnished his political career with the catchwords, "Everything's made for love." Boykin spent 28 years in the U.S. House, demonstrating a proclivity for long speeches, absolute conservatism, and sponsorship of very little legislation. He was a Southerner of the grand style, given to mammoth breakfasts (ham, eggs, hot cakes, grits, fruit, and coffee). In 1949 he invited 1,000 people to a party for Speaker Sam Rayburn, providing them with a feast of salmon, elk, venison, bear steaks, turkey, antelope, and opossum. He lost his seat in 1962 when he placed last in a field of nine starters in a statewide primary for eight congressional seats. A year later a federal jury convicted him of receiving $250,000 from Maryland savings and loan interests to intercede with the Justice Department to halt prosecution of one of their executives. President Johnson showed some Southern generosity by pardoning Boykin in 1965, however. He died in 1969.

† Sparkman had won the Democratic nomination over six opponents, the strongest of whom was State Auditor Melba Till Allen, a consumer-oriented political newcomer.

votes, including a proposed Vietnam war fund cutoff. The letter seriously undercut Blount's efforts to identify Sparkman as a spiritual bedfellow of George McGovern. Sparkman also received large sums of money from national business and labor circles worried about the prospective advance of Wisconsin's Senator William Proxmire to the Banking and Currency chairmanship, should Sparkman lose. "To a lot of bankers, home builders, and other moneyed interests affected by Banking Committee decisions," the *Wall Street Journal* reported, "Proxmire is a dirty word." AFL-CIO construction unions were also opposed to the independent Proxmire. The Washington *Star* reported in spring 1972 that a legal loophole in the campaign spending laws was being used to channel a rich tide of dollars to the Sparkman campaign without identifying the donors. Housing and banking interests were reported to be the big givers.

Lister Hill, who retired in 1968 after 45 years in the Congress, probably did more for the average Alabamian than any other man—Hugo Black perhaps excepted—the state ever sent to Washington. Hill's father was a distinguished surgeon—the first American successfully to suture the human heart—and health legislation became Lister Hill's consuming interest over his long congressional career. The Hill-Burton Act, passed in 1946, helped to build more than 9,500 general hospitals, public health centers, and other medical facilities across the country. Over 300 of the facilities were in Alabama, and more than half the general hospitals made possible by the act were in the rural South, which needed them more desperately than any other region. (Hill-Burton had been the first program that ever accepted need as the basis for allocation of federal funds between the states.) Anyone familiar with the dismal health history of the old South must appreciate the momentous nature of Hill's contribution. As he put it himself, "before we got those hospitals built here in Alabama, if someone had appendicitis, he might have been driven in a horse and buggy or old surrey or old Model T Ford over a rough muddy road to a local town to wait for a train to come through that could carry him—probably with a change of trains along the way—to one of the few big cities for his operation."

Hill was chairman of the Senate Labor and Public Welfare Committee from 1955 onwards—a position which permitted him, with heavy backing from the medical lobby, to pass scores of health bills. He was also chairman of the Appropriations subcommittee with jurisdiction over health, hospital, and medical programs. When he took over that subcommittee in 1955, he recalled in an interview, federal health appropriations totaled \$81 million; in 1968, his last year, the total was \$1.5 billion. In his earlier years, Hill had worked with George Norris in establishing the TVA. Forerunner legislation had been vetoed by Presidents Coolidge and Hoover, but when President Roosevelt took office in March 1933, he invited Norris and Hill to the White House to discuss a bill, and the TVA authorization law was passed within two months. TVA was to rescue northernmost Alabama from its ancient poverty and make it into the most prosperous region of Alabama. Yet, oddly enough, Lister Hill was the only one of Alabama's progressive legislators of recent years to come from southern Alabama.

Hill's act would be a hard one to follow, and the Alabama voters apparently decided not even to try. The man they elected to his seat, James B. Allen, had distinguished himself chiefly as a rote follower (he had been lieutenant governor of George Wallace). A signal of how far Alabama politics had sunk was that Allen won nomination chiefly by lambasting his opponent, Congressman Armistead Selden, as a member of "that Washington crowd." It was true Selden had served 16 years in Congress, but his conservative-segregationist credentials were impeccable. But in an era when many Alabama officeholders have been caught with their hand in the till, Allen deserves high marks for personal integrity. He edified the voters by publishing a detailed report of his net worth (about $100,000)—a step his colleague John Sparkman, for one, has consistently refused to take. Allen also learned the ropes of Senate parliamentary tactics—a skill he put to work in 1973, even in the wake of the Watergate revelations, to filibuster to death a bill for federal financing of Presidential campaigns.

One sad effect of the last several years has been to diminish the number of Alabama Congressmen of real *quality*. Aside from the work of two holdovers from earlier times—Sparkman, with his contribution in housing, and Robert Jones, a battler for TVA, rural housing, public power, and public works in general—no members of the delegation have shown much excellence or promise of excellence. A possible exception would be Jack Edwards, an exceptionally hard-working Congressman who won a position in the GOP House leadership structure. But one looks in vain for a figure of the stature of Oscar W. Underwood, the Birmingham Congressman and later Senator who was an outstanding contender for the Democratic Presidential nomination in 1912 and 1924, authored the first significant tariff reduction since the Civil War, and fought for President Wilson's programs. No Alabamian today seems likely to offer a piece of legislation as vitally important in controlling industrial monopolies as the Clayton Anti-Trust Act, authored by Alabama's Congressman Henry D. Clayton early in this century. It is unlikely that the State's present crew in Washington will do anything for the small farmer comparable to the contribution of the Bankheads—House Speaker William B. and Senator John H. Bankhead.*

And one wonders when—or if—Alabama will ever again produce a figure of the stature of Hugo Lafayette Black. Born in 1886 on a north Alabama farm—he was the youngest of eight children of a farmer of Scotch-Irish descent—Black exhibited from early manhood the best of the Southern Populists' concern for the problems of ordinary men and women. He was once a member of the Ku Klux Klan—the "thing to do" for aspiring young politicians in the 1920s and a point of acute personal embarrassment to him later. But he won attention as a hard-working labor attorney and a fighter for downtrodden people, including blacks. As a Senator to the left of President Roosevelt in the 1930s, he battled for FDR's New Deal programs and

* W. J. Cash wrote in *The Mind of the South* that while neither of the Bankheads "could be accused of being Leftist in their proper sympathies, . . . both [showed] a better grasp of the case of the tenant and sharecropper than almost any other Southern politician, and both exhibited a consistently wider understanding and sympathy for the masses in general than was usual in their Southern colleagues." Will Bankhead's daughter was none other than the illustrious actress, Tallulah Bankhead.

was the sponsor of the bill that became the Fair Labor Standards Act. Roosevelt appointed him to the Supreme Court in 1937, where he would sit for 34 years—a longer period of service than that of any other Justice except John Marshall and Stephen J. Field. For years he found himself in a minority on the court on issues like free speech, legislative apportionment, and the right of defendants to counsel. But eventually the majority turned in his direction, and no other Supreme Court Justice lived to see so many of his dissents become law.

Yet, as Anthony Lewis wrote when Black retired, it was his qualities as much as his particular views that made him a remarkable figure in American public life. "There was a serene simplicity in him that baffled sophistication, a power that seemed to be drawn from the earth. He was an elemental force." His absolutist faith in the Bill of Rights, and above all the First Amendment and its guarantee of free speech, another commentator noted, "resembled a fundamentalist preacher's interpretation of the Bible" and enabled him to make "some of the stunning breakthroughs in the history of the battle over free expression." The framers of the Constitution, Black once said, knew the risks they were taking in denying the right of government to place any limits on the subjects people could investigate and discuss. Free speech, they recognized, could lead to change and even revolution. But free speech, the framers also recognized, "is always the deadliest enemy of tyranny." Black thus believed he was one with the framers in believing "that the ultimate happiness and security of a nation lies in its ability to explore, to change, to grow and ceaselessly adapt itself to new knowledge born of inquiry free from any kind of governmental control over the mind and spirit of man. Loyalty comes from love of good government, not fear of a bad one."

In Alabama, many viewed Black as a pariah, a traitor to the white Southern cause. Through most of the 1950s and 1960s, he was never invited back to Alabama to address any group—a bitter exile that did not end until the last years of his life, when various lawyers' groups invited him back for appearances. There was a climactic dinner sponsored by the state bar association in Birmingham, when 500 Alabama lawyers raised their glasses in tribute to the old man. It must have been an immensely gratifying moment for Black, for those who knew him well said he never lost any feeling of kinship for and loyalty to the Southern soil that nurtured him.

One of the Alabamians who went to Washington and provided a vital national service was Clifford Durr, who as a member of the Federal Communications Commission fought in the 1940s to reserve television channels for public educational use. Later Durr and his wife, Virginia Foster Durr, returned to Alabama and fought a lonely battle for persons attacked for disloyalty during the McCarthy period, and for Negro rights. Durr believes that only three Alabama politicians in his lifetime really tried to do something for the political education of the state's people—Bibb Graves, Jim Folsom, and most particularly Hugo Black. As a Senator, Durr noted, Black was always touring the state, even when he was safe politically, trying to educate the people to the political realities of the world.*

* Mrs. Durr, it should be noted, was Hugo Black's sister-in-law.

Hill and Sparkman, Durr said, had been good Senators. "But neither provided any moral leadership or political education *in Alabama*." He noted that after the Supreme Court school desegregation decision (of which Black was one author), Hill and Sparkman did nothing to urge Alabamians to obey the law of the land. So the field was left to the extremists. "The Hills and Sparkmans all said when they were asked to help on moderating the race issue, 'I have to preserve my effectiveness.' My God, we've been stockpiling effectiveness down here. Just wait until all that effectiveness is unleashed. It's going to be like unleashing Chiang Kai-shek." If Hugo Black had not gone to the Supreme Court, Durr said, he might have been the Southern political leader to provide leadership and save the region from its racial agonies of the '50s and '60s.

People and Economy of a Blue-Collar State

Attorney Sam Earle Hobbs of Selma tells the story of one William Mitford White, who died in a Selma rest home in the 1960s at the age of 94, after being *non compos mentis* for several years. Hobbs represented the bank which was White's guardian, and since the old man died without writing a will, Hobbs had to trace his heirs—all offspring of White's seven brothers and sisters. "The whole family had started out from Grove Hill in nearby Clarke County," Hobbs said. "But seeing where these people fanned out to is a comment on our society. My dragnet letters found the heirs—White's nieces and nephews, great- and great-great nieces and nephews—in every corner of America, from Alabama to New York, Florida to Texas, Ohio to California."

But if many Alabamians have found their homes in far-flung parts of the United States, not many people from other states have seen fit to settle in Alabama. Those who have come have helped to leaven the state's inbred society, but they are really quite few in number. In 1940 the Census found that less than 10 percent of the people living in Alabama had been born elsewhere. By 1970, the figure had crept up to 15 percent, but this still represented one of the lowest levels of fresh blood in any American state. (Only Mississippi, in fact, had a lower percentage of "outlanders.")

The overall population of Alabama has inched forward over the past 30 years, but only because natural increase has balanced a massive tide of out-migration. During the period, the state lost 949,000 people—650,000 Negroes and 290,000 whites—through migration. In 1940 the state had 2,832,961 people, of whom 34.7 percent were Negroes; in 1970 it had 3,444,165 people, and the Negro share had dropped to 26.2 percent. But there were only three other states—Mississippi, Louisiana, and South Carolina—which had a higher percentage of blacks.

Change in agriculture precipitated—and made necessary—a transformation of the Alabama economy, which in turn caused a rapid shift in population patterns in the years following World War II. Since antebellum days, Alabama had had a one-crop economy in cotton, and in the 1930s it was hard to imagine that it would ever change. Cotton dominated agricultural life from the Gulf to the Tennessee Valley and reached its crescendo in the Black Belt where, as Ray Jenkins noted, the traveler in late summer would see mile after mile of fleecy cotton fields, a physical impression "like snow in August." But if Alabama embodied and romanticized cotton, as the very essence of its Dixiehood, it was ignoring the life of the sharecroppers and tenant farmers who tilled the fields—in a condition not far removed from serfdom. In the early 1930s the late A. B. Moore, in his authoritative history of Alabama, described what farm life was like:

> Even in normal times the margin of economic security is so small as to make life uncomfortable for many thousands of farm homes. The lot of the Negroes is particularly deplorable. Large numbers of them are half-fed and half-clothed, and their homes are hovels of filth. Thousands of white families, located principally in the hill counties, are living under conditions almost as bad. From any road one may see dilapidated old cabins of poor whites, ramshackled farm buildings, a few scrawny specimens of livestock, and large families of pale-faced and unkempt children. These are unmistakable evidences of a shabby life. Upon the streets of the towns on Saturdays the simple and perhaps tattered and dirty habiliments, the hollow eyes and stolid and unshaven faces, and the shambling walk of many farm men tell the same story. In the demeanor of these men of toil and poverty and depressed spirits one sees much that is suggestive of the Roman slave. . . .
>
> The dynamic forces in society during the last forty years have scarcely touched them. They possess little either of this world's goods or knowledge. . . . They are content to think old thoughts, to speak the old tongue, to worship at old altars, and to make their music out of old tunes upon old fiddles and of songs sung by fathers.

Today the cotton culture has almost vanished—the victim of the boll weevil, unreliable weather, sharply fluctuating prices, and competition from the huge, irrigated farms of Texas and California. One sees some reminders of the old life: a tired, gray shack abandoned by a sharecropper of yesteryear and, on rare occasions, the anomaly of a lonely farmer still coaxing his mule to turn a fresh furrow.* By 1969, only 563,000 acres of Alabama farmland were planted in cotton—compared to 3,500,000 acres in 1930. Relatively few of the remaining cotton acres were in the Black Belt, where the flat meadows had been transformed into grazing lands for beef and dairy cattle. The center of Alabama's cotton production had actually been transferred to the limestone valley of the Tennessee River in northern Alabama. Soybeans were the big new crop—tripled in acreage between 1964 and 1969 alone. But Alabama is no longer a crop state, predominantly; in recent years livestock has accounted for up to three-quarters of farmers' cash receipts, the highest proportion in the Deep South. And rather than cattle, it is egg and poultry production, concentrated in northern Alabama, that has brought in the most dollars. Poultry production was relatively insignificant in Alabama 20 years ago, but today it is valued at close to $300 million a year, a third of the state's entire farm income.†

* In 1940 there had been some 300,000 mules on Alabama farms; by the 1960s, there were so few that the Census gave up counting them. In the same years, the number of tractors rose from less than 8,000 to 75,000.

† Not all is well with the chicken business, however. Until 20 years ago, it was highly fragmented, with hatcheries, feed producers, and the actual growers operating independently. Then large feed companies like Pillsbury and Ralston-Purina, plus some big local firms, discovered they could cut

The 1940s and '50s were the decades of the most profound economic change in Alabama—not only the years when the basis of agriculture was transformed, but the years when the essential transition from the soil to urban life for the majority of the state's people took place. "King Cotton," former University of Alabama president Frank Rose said, "had been dead for 25 years, but the people of Alabama were just finding out that they couldn't make a living on a 100-acre farm." But find out most of them did, leaving the farms by the hundreds of thousands. In 1940, 70 percent of the state's people lived in rural areas; 20 years later, the population balance had been turned around and 55 percent of them lived in urban areas, the vast majority in a handful of metropolitan areas.

The number of farms slipped from 232,000 on the eve of Pearl Harbor to 72,000 in 1969, and of those still in business, only 13,000 were economically viable units registering sales of $10,000 a year or more. Farming had become a complex big business in which the successful operator needed sophisticated training, substantial acreage, and enough capital to make major investments in machinery and fertilizers. Along with tractors, mechanical cotton pickers appeared, throwing field hands out of work by the thousands. Federal farm policies discouraged planting and favored the big operators. So it was that the marginal "dirt farmer"—and there were thousands in his circumstances—simply had no future on the land. The tragedy of one Negro tenant farmer, in the Black Belt's impoverished Sumter County, was told in this letter, reprinted in *New South:*

Charlie White
Route 2, Box 80
Panola, Alabama

November 25, 1966

Charlie:

This letter is to advise you that the land which you have been renting from me for the past several years will no longer be available to you for rent. I have rented this land to .... Paper Company, and they are going to grow timber on the lands.

This is to give you notice that you will not be able to have the acreage formerly cultivated by you, for the years 1967 and thereafter, and you can make arrangements to get acreage elsewhere.

If you wish to live in the house which you have occupied, you can continue to do so for a monthly rental of $15. The first rent payment will be due on or before the 5th day of January, 1967.

Under my contract with the paper company, you will not be able to have a garden or any cultivable land, or have any pasture or run any livestock, nor will you be able to cut any wood from the woods.

This is to advise you that if you do not wish to rent the house, then you must

---

out the middlemen in the system and maximize their profits by contracting out the raising of chicks to small farmers. The chickens belong to the companies from the first peep to the last squeak, and the small chicken farmer—like the sharecropper of old—found himself being told how much to raise, being provided with his raw materials, having his books kept for him, and then being told how much he would be paid. When the chicken market turned sour early in the '70s, many Alabama chicken raisers turned to the militant National Farm Organization and staged a strike against the big companies, demanding higher pay and more independence. When an NFO organizer spoke to a group of white Alabama chicken raisers in Cullman and told them they were the "last slaves to be freed in the South," one farmer stood up and shouted: "Ya'll better hurry up. They already done freed the mules!"

immediately make your arrangements to vacate the property before January 1, 1967, when the .... Paper Company will take charge of the property.

Yours very truly,
Mrs. Deborah Calhoun

New South commented:

It was one month before Christmas when Charlie, thus addressed by the first name like a child to make certain there could be no confusion between him and a man meriting Christian consideration, received this classic letter. Charlie White was given five weeks in dead of winter to decide where he would go, what he would do to live now that he had no land, how his family would eat.

If Charlie was old, he might stay on in abject poverty; if young enough, he would migrate to one of Alabama's cities in search of work. There he would find fierce competition for the only kind of job for which he was suited—unskilled labor. A white farmer in the same quandary would be preferred and possibly succeed in the big Alabama town. But for the black man, hopelessness would probably soon ensue and he would be likely to give up in despair, joining the throngs of other blacks headed for Chicago, Detroit, St. Louis, or Omaha.

As agricultural employment faded, Alabama tried hard to take up the slack with new factories. A state planning and industrial development board was set up in 1955 under Governor Folsom, and Alabama went the route of publicly subsidized industrial-development bond financing, perhaps more heavily than any other state. By the end of the 1960s, low-paying garment factories were employing about 44,000 people in the state; as the Birmingham *News* commented, "stick a needle into each town on a map of Alabama where a garment plant is located and the state would look like a porcupine." About the same number of people were employed in textile plants, concentrated in the Piedmont region of east and central Alabama. A sign of the times was the fact that Alabama, once the heart of the "land of cotton," was actually *importing* substantial amounts of raw cotton to process into cloth.

The state's biggest industry was metal production, centered in the steel mills of Birmingham and Gadsden and the aluminum industry that benefited from cheap power along the Tennessee Valley. But total employment in metals—just under 50,000 in 1970—was not much greater than it had been at the end of World War II. Employment in mining had declined precipitously with the advent of mechanization and the decision of U.S. Steel to close its Alabama iron ore mines and import the mineral from Venezuela instead. But north central Alabama was producing more than $300 million worth of bituminous coal each year, and the area still had the vastest coal deposits of the South—an important resource in steelmaking and increasingly in electricity generation. In the early 1970s, work was nearing completion on the TVA's Browns Ferry Nuclear Plant on the Tennessee, the world's largest nuclear power facility.

Alabama was registering major employment advances through new sawmills and paper plants (which depended on the state's ample water resources and millions of acres of land in commercial forestry), in chemical industries (mostly along the Tennessee River), in transportation equipment (largely railroad cars at Bessemer and shipbuilding at Mobile), and in food processing. The result of all this was to raise the value of new manufactured goods in Alabama to more than $4 billion a year—compared to $246 million in 1939, $1 billion in 1950, and $2 billion in 1960. The state came to have the fourth highest percentage of blue-collar workers of any state. Alabama also gained thousands of new workers in government (federal, state, and local) and in retailing and service industries. But the percentage of Alabamians working in white-collar jobs was one of the lowest in the country.

Back in 1940, the per capita income of Alabamians had been only 47 percent of the national average—the telltale sign of a backward, agrarian economy. By 1971, the Alabama figure was up to 74 percent of the U.S. average—a gain only explained by the surge in industrialization. But the state's per capita income was more than $1,000 behind the rest of the country and ranked only 48th among the states. Adding more needle plants or sawmills or mobile home factories in rural areas was obviously not going to solve the problem of giving Alabamians a standard of living comparable to that of the country as a whole. Economists speculated that all but a small share of the unskilled labor set loose by the collapse of traditional agriculture had already been soaked up, and that a sharp shift in emphasis to attracting higher-wage, high-technology industries was in order.

The politicians were beginning to get that message. Attorney General Baxley said: "We can't just take any old industry that wants to come and pay substandard wages and pollute the waters and the air and act like they're doing us a favor. We have to attract quality industry, and we have to go out and actively seek it."

Some Alabamians believe that the state's economic salvation lies in improved transportation facilities. There are already more than 1,000 miles of navigable rivers, and commerce is especially heavy along the Tennessee River, which has attracted more than $1.5 billion in heavy industry since the birth of TVA. The Warrior-Tombigbee waterway, which runs 463 miles from Birmingham to Mobile, carries millions of tons of barge traffic each year and is one of the busiest in the Southeast. In 1972 work finally began on the long-debated Tennessee-Tombigbee canal which will link up the river network of central and southern Alabama with the Tennessee River. The canal could make Mobile a port to rival New Orleans, because it will have a direct link with the Tennessee, the Ohio, and the great inland waterways of mid-America.

Time, too, will correct the road transportation of some of the major metropolitan regions. The rural counties were powerful enough in the legislature to get the interstate highways built through their areas first, and as a result Birmingham, for example did not have its interstates completed by the early '70s. This was one reason it failed to become a regional exchange place of goods and services—and people—in any way comparable to Atlanta. Alabama needs that kind of input, rather than one blue-collar factory after another, if it is ever going to be more than a workshop for big companies whose headquarters and wealth are outside the state. The economic pattern has its political ramifications too. "If there had been major home-grown industrial leaders," James Free of the Birmingham *News* said, "they might at least have tried to lay down the law to Wallace."

Cityscape: Huntsville and the North

The "metropolitanization" of Alabama—the process in which the population weight shifted heavily from rural areas to big cities and their environs—was essentially a phenomenon of the 1940s and 1950s. By 1960, 51.7 percent of the people lived in metropolitan areas, and in the succeeding decade the figure increased less than a percentage point.

During the 1960s, in fact, four of Alabama's six largest cities—Birmingham, Mobile, Montgomery, and Gadsden—actually lost population (although their suburbs gained slightly). Tuscaloosa, largely through the vitality of the University of Alabama, made a small gain. Only Huntsville spurted forward. Stimulated by TVA, federal installations, and new industries, and in the wake of annexation of some of its booming suburbs, Huntsville grew to 137,802 people—almost twice as large as it was in 1960, and ten times greater than in 1940.

Huntsville has to be counted one of the luckiest towns in America. It has always had a splendid setting on the side of a sharply curving valley, with a jagged horizon of mountains to the east. But in 1940 it was just a sleepy old mill village and cotton distribution center, with rock-bottom levels of income and education. There were a few smokestacks in town, but as the WPA Guide noted, Huntsville's industry—except for large cotton mills—was limited to "broom, mop, and mattress factories." The Depression had hit hard, and in 1938 there were still bread and soup lines.

Then, on July 3, 1941, banner headlines in the Huntsville *Times* proclaimed: "Huntsville Gets Chemical War Plant; Cost Over $40,000,000." A picture of a very-much-younger-looking John Sparkman graced the front page, with the caption: "DISTRICT GETS PLUM. Rep. John Sparkman, above, played a major role in the selection of Huntsville as the site of the new chemical warfare plant."

And quite a plum it was. The Redstone Arsenal, quite literally carved out of cotton fields and pastures, was quickly constructed and started manufacturing poison gases and ordnance for gas weapons. Employment, drawn principally from the neighboring countryside, reached a peak of 19,000 during the war. The work was hazardous, and there were many accidents, but Redstone was the price of economic prosperity that would draw north central Alabama out of the outhouse and the mule and wagon era.

When peace came, the bubble burst, and employment plummeted to 200. In 1949 big signs were posted, "HUNTSVILLE ARSENAL FOR SALE." Just before the ax fell, however, the Army decided to take over the facility and use it for its beginning efforts in rocket missilery. The man who convinced the Army Chief of Staff to make that decision was Major General Holger Toftoy—the man who had brought Dr. Wernher von Braun and his band of some 125 German rocket scientists to the United States at the end of the World War II. Von Braun and his team went to work, developing the first generation of missiles for the Army. As early as 1953, he proposed sending an earth satellite into orbit—but failed to get the permission or support he sought. That situation, of course, changed instantaneously when the space age opened with the Soviet launch of Sputnik I in October 1957. Washington pushed the panic button, and von Braun happily responded; in fact, he had a Jupiter C rocket in his warehouse, made on bootleg time, that was close to readiness for a low earth orbit mission. Only 84 days after he was given the green light, von Braun and his team were able to place the United States' Explorer I satellite into orbit from Cape Canaveral.

In 1958 the National Aeronautics and Space Administration was formed, and the next year President Eisenhower decided to transfer von Braun and his operation to the aegis of NASA. The Marshall Space Flight Center was born at Huntsville, with von Braun as its director. Thus Huntsville, which had begun with a military base, ended up with NASA's largest space research and development facility. It was there that the major development work was done on the Saturn, the huge rocket whose flawless performance would carry the first men to the moon in 1969. In the meantime, the Redstone Arsenal continued as the Army's most important missile facility. Huntsville throbbed with activity from the dual installations, which eventually accounted for 27,000 workers and an annual payroll of about $350 million a year. Some 12,000 were on the Army payroll, 6,000 on NASA's, and at one time as many as 13,000 on the payrolls of directly related contractors. "It was like ascending stairs—everything just got better and better for Huntsville," public affairs director David Harris of the Redstone Arsenal commented.

Fear came to the valley in 1970 when von Braun, the local hero and savior, finally left for a NASA post in Washington. But NASA employment, with post-Apollo space missions and vehicles to develop, was not due to dip below 5,000 until 1974, and the work force at the Redstone Arsenal—which continued as headquarters of the U.S. Army Missile Command, and since the late '60s of the Safeguard (ABM) System Command—was still 11,000 in 1973.

Some of the big NASA subcontractors reduced their payrolls in Huntsville in the late '60s and early '70s, but the major ones—firms like Boeing, IBM, Brown Engineering, Northrup, and Hayes Aircraft—all continued to maintain a presence, and most diversified their product lines. Since the mid-1950s, Maj. Gen. John B. Medaris (commander of the Army Ballistic Missile Command) and other Army and then NASA officials had been urging Huntsville to diversify, to avoid the perils of being a one-industry town. The local civic leadership worked hard to do just that, attracting firms like Dunlop Tire, PPG Industries, Barber-Coleman, and Automatic Electric. A massive Research Park was begun, with a University of Alabama research institute on its edge. A nonprofit group, the University of Alabama Foundation, bought up prime industrial land for industrial use and when firms seeking a location came to town they could be shown the available locations, be given an immediate land price, and be told their taxes—without any bickering with local property owners.

But there were other qualities that made Huntsville attractive. James G. Haney, manager of the PPG Industries aircraft windshield manufacturing plant, commented in 1970: "Huntsville had everything we were looking for. It was completely integrated. It had an excellent school system, and the city, though not large, had a cosmopolitan atmosphere. You have people here from all over the world, and each adds to the city's qualities." (One scratches one's head in wonder at that kind of comment about an old Alabama town; it reminded me of the line about another Southern city: "When you're in Atlanta, you can forget you're in Georgia." By contrast, one could say, "When you're in Birmingham or Montgomery, you *never* forget you're in Alabama.")

The peculiar Huntsville atmosphere was not just the result of the accident of heavy federal investment. While Huntsville may have been an impoverished town before the feds came, it was also a place with a rich legacy of independence, and tolerance, and quality in its leading families. The constitutional convention preceding statehood had been held there in 1819, and the town was briefly the capital of Alabama. There were (and still are) many stately old homes set far back on shaded lawns, homes of a native aristocracy that produced six governors of Alabama and a United States Supreme Court Justice (John McKinley). Leroy Simms, publisher of the Huntsville *Times,* took me and my traveling companion (Bruce Biossat, the national columnist) to visit the home of Mrs. Martha Richardson, a prominent civic leader. The house had been built in pure Greek Revival style by Thomas Fearn, a revered pioneer physician who had been Andrew Jackson's surgeon during the Creek-Indian War. And it stayed in the Fearn family's hands for seven generations until the Richardson family acquired it in 1964.*

Simms noted that Huntsville's "otherness" in Alabama went back to 1840, when James G. Birney of the city was the Abolitionist candidate for President. ("We may have run him out of town on a rail—but he was from here!" Simms commented.) In the 1850s the Huntsville *Times* had warned that if Alabama seceded from the Union, northern Alabama would secede from Alabama. Only Winston County was to go that far, but the undercurrent of pro-Union, antislavery sentiment remained strong—made easier, of course, because Huntsville never had a very heavy Negro population. During the 1960s some grim warnings from NASA officials were necessary to make Huntsville stop its lingering Jim Crow practices. But the day after Wallace had stood in the schoolhouse door in Tuscaloosa, a young black man drove his own car up to the University of Alabama branch in Huntsville, walked in, and registered himself—with no objections. When Wallace sent in his patrolmen to block elementary school integration, some angry white Huntsville parents marched their children right past the troopers and into their classrooms. A community relations council was begun in 1960, and the integration of public facilities and accommodations had been largely accomplished

* Not all of the notable old structures have survived. Huntsville allowed its historic Cotton Row on the courthouse square to be razed as the downtown area boomed with high-rise buildings and a gleaming new City Hall.

before the Civil Rights Act of 1964 forced the rest of Alabama to take that step.

Some of the racial progress took place grudgingly, and unfortunately few Negroes were able to qualify for high-level technical jobs for NASA or the Redstone Arsenal. The 1970 Census found that while the median family income of Huntsville families was $11,654, the highest of any Alabama city and $4,388 ahead of the state average, black families in Huntsville had a median income of only $5,202, only $1,118 above the miserably low statewide black average. For some Negroes there is real hope, however, thanks to the quality of the Huntsville schools in recent years. Simms told the story of his maid's family as an example. The husband had been injured years ago and was blind. But three of their children were college graduates, and one son had gone to Yale on a National Merit Award scholarship.

The civic leaders of Huntsville are still drawn largely from the old aristocracy, with a strong injection of young men of the space-age technical world who have been elected to the city council. On the whole they are a pretty independent lot, though I had a strange experience with a city councilman named Joe Peters, who worked for the Boeing Company. Peters agreed that he would see me, but I was told an outright lie by one of the city fathers—that Peters had unexpectedly been called out of town. It sounded suspicious to me, and when I tracked Peters down, he admitted he had been told by his Boeing superiors not to talk with an outside reporter—even in his capacity as a city official.

The availability of great blocks of cheap electric power from the TVA triggered the first choice of Huntsville for the Redstone Arsenal and has also been responsible for making north Alabama the prime area of the state for new industries in recent decades. Several cities along the Tennessee River reflect the growth. Decatur, a few miles west of Huntsville, has grown from 16,604 souls in 1940 to 38,044 in the most recent Census; among its factories today are Chemstrand, 3M, Goodyear, Amoco, and Fruehauf, plus one of the nation's largest poultry feed mills. (A lot of attitudes had to be changed in Decatur, which was a dying town before TVA came on the scene. When David Lilienthal, TVA's early director, visited Decatur, he was welcomed by the city fathers, according to one Southern history, "in about the same spirit their antebellum forefathers would have entertained William Lloyd Garrison." To question TVA and public power in Decatur today, of course, would be like assailing the Holy Grail.) Another Tennessee River city, Florence, grew from 15,043 people in 1940 to 34,031 in 1970. Its salvation has been Wilson Dam, built as part of the World War I Muscle Shoals project, which has helped Florence and its environs attract plants like Ford, Union Carbide, and aluminum-producing Reynolds Metals. Muscle Shoals, interestingly, was designated as TVA headquarters in the original TVA authorization law, but temporary headquarters were set up in Knoxville, and the transfer has never been made.

Outside of the thriving Tennessee Valley and the metropolitan areas, it is hard to find many Alabama cities that have improved economically as well as the Southern average or shown major spurts in population in recent years. One exception is Dothan, just above the Florida border in southeastern Alabama. Long a marketing center for the local farmers. Dothan got a first breath of prosperity during World War II, when an Army airfield opened nearby. But since 1946, an average of two new industries a year have been added, the schools have been upgraded until they are among the best in Alabama, and even some high-brow culture (a civic ballet and concert association, and a little theater group) has been added. The population more than doubled in three decades, to 36,733 in 1970.

The picture is more static in the heavily industrialized city of Gadsden (1970 population 53,928), which is second only to Birmingham as an iron and steel center. Having filled up with plants like Republic Steel and Goodyear Tire, Gadsden and its suburbs simply stopped growing about a decade ago. Gadsden's physical image—of belching factories and a high proportion of mobile homes—may repel newcomers. It is a highly unionized city and lies within the Alabama "liberal belt" which encompasses the territory north of Birmingham.

We will return to Birmingham in a separate section, but a further word might be said about Anniston, whose blue-collar culture was touched on in the introduction to this chapter. Anniston lies in the twilight zone between northern and southern Alabama, and its economic roots go back both to cotton growing and steelmaking that began in 1863 with a blast furnace to supply the Confederate army. After the war, a former Confederate munitions manufacturer, Samuel Noble, and a retired Union general, Daniel Tyler, pooled their resources to turn Anniston into a model industrial center of the "New South". Indeed Atlanta's Henry Grady was on hand to present Anniston's new mayor with the keys to the newly incorporated town. The city became an unusually wealthy one for Alabama, with much of the industrial wealth from iron pipe manufacturing, chemicals, and textiles kept at home rather than being taken elsewhere by absentee owners.

But if Anniston believed itself a model of a South made more tolerant by industrialization, the myth was effectively shattered in 1961 when a screaming mob of whites attacked and burned a Freedom Riders bus near the town. Only by good fortune was an actual lynching averted. Through the '60s, Anniston's leaders—some out of conviction, others for purely pragmatic reasons—went to work to create communication between the races there. Well ahead of Birmingham, a community relations service was set up. Jim Crow practices in parks and libraries and restaurants were ended peacefully, and the 1965 Voting Rights Act broke the dam on Negro vote registration, which increased fivefold during the decade. When I visited there in 1969, the established Negro leaders (all of whom were ministers) spoke with pleasure of "something unique in Anniston—the fact that we've been able to talk to the leaders of the white community." They were still dissatisfied enough in that year to be staging a boycott of white stores in a demand for better jobs for members of their race (who make up 34 percent of the city's 31,533 people). More recently, the weekly meetings of representatives of all segments of the Anniston community have gone a long way toward making communication—and actual changes—even easier. The Anniston *Star* and its editor H. Brandt Ayers have been catalysts in much of the productive change, first by providing aggressive issue-oriented coverage of community news, and secondly by encouraging communications between blacks, blue-collar workers, and the pragmatic, modestly progressive business leadership of the city.

Despite Anniston's job opportunities, however, the "good life" is still elusive for many poor blacks and whites there. Anniston has some lovely residential sections but also blocks of ugly old company shacks still inhabited by people in desperate poverty. Many have left the city to seek greener pastures elsewhere, though the county (as opposed to the city) population grew slightly in the 1960s and the President's Growth Commission has placed Anniston in the center of a growing urban belt stretching from Greenville, South Carolina, to Meridian, Mississippi.

Notes on Montgomery, Mobile, and the University Towns

The Montgomery Chamber of Commerce will tell you that the city, which registered a population of 133,386 in the 1970 Census, is "the largest cattle market south of the Ohio River and east of Fort Worth," a center of the cotton trade and food processing, and the biggest spot in the U.S.A. for Victorian furniture reproductions. But government employment is what really occupies the town and gives it its *raison d'être*—the sprawling state government offices and the Air University at nearby Maxwell Field. The State Capitol on Goat Hill exudes a Confederate spirit, but for our time it is the events of the 1950s, not those of the 1860s, which are the most vital. For in the Montgomery bus boycott Southern blacks won their first significant direct-action victory of this century over the hardened ways of a segregationist society. It was a telephone call to a youthful pastor, the Rev. Martin Luther King, Jr., on the evening of December 1, 1955—just hours after Mrs. Rosa Parks had been arrested for refusing to give up her bus seat to whites—that would initiate the set of events leading King to national and historic importance, the Nobel Peace Prize, and ultimate martyrdom.

The story of how Mrs. Parks defied the white bus driver's command—"Niggers move back"—and all that followed in those tumultuous days of the 1950s is a familiar one, but some details merit retelling. While King would soon become the leader of what would quickly become "The Movement," it was E. D. Nixon, a leader of the Brotherhood of Sleeping Car Porters and one of the founders of both the Montgomery and Alabama NAACP branches, who first proposed the boycott, who made that first telephone call to King, and proposed King—freshly arrived in Montgomery as pastor of the Dexter Avenue Baptist church—as the leader of the boycott effort. It was the white attorney, Clifford Durr, recently returned to Alabama after years of distinguished service in Washington, who immediately saw the possibility of challenging the constitutionality of the Alabama segregation law in federal court, thus winning (as ultimately came to pass) a Supreme Court ruling striking a heavy blow against Jim Crow. And one of the black pastors contacted by Nixon on the first day was Ralph David Abernathy, who would participate the next year, after the Montgomery victory, in formation of the Southern Christian Leadership Conference.

King's eloquence became legend from the first days of planning the boycott; in fact, it was only two hours after he accepted the responsibility that the 27-year-old pastor addressed a packed meeting at the Holt Street Baptist Church, stating the classic case for nonviolent protest: "We are tired. Tired of being segregated and humiliated. . . . If you will protest courageously, and yet with dignity and Christian love, future historians will say, 'There lived a great people—a black people—who injected new meaning and dignity into the veins of civilization.' " One elderly woman there that evening later remembers feeling that she "saw angels standing all around him when he finished, and they were lifting him up on their wings!"

The black leaders hoped to have a boycott that was 60 percent effective, but in the predawn darkness of the first day King and his wife, Coretta, stood by a stop on one of the predominantly Negro runs and saw that the buses, usually filled with black domestic workers on their way to make breakfast in white kitchens, were absolutely empty. For a year, through official harassments, arrests, bombings, and court cases, the boycott went on, in an amazing show of black community solidarity. Clifford and Virginia Durr recalled how each white woman would say, "Why, my Susie is completely different. She has nothing to do with that boycott." But each Wednesday night, Susie would be down "whooping it up for Martin Luther King, shouting and saying Amen." Queried by whites, blacks would say: "We just stay off that bus and leave that boycott alone."

One can forget the depths of humiliation that Montgomery blacks had been suffering. Every element of the city's life was brutally segregated, but the buses were the most offensive. The drivers (all white) forced Negroes to suffer epithets like "black ape," "black cow," and "dirty nigger." Blacks often had to get in the front door and pay their fare, then get off the bus and enter by the rear door. "The game," Janet Stevens wrote in *The Montgomery Bus Boycott,* "was to wait until a black passenger got outside, slam the two doors, and drive off, leaving him standing on the curb without his dime."

Even after integrated buses began to roll down the streets of the Confederacy's first capital in December 1956, Montgomery was wracked by last-gasp violence on the part of the white haters—bullets fired at buses, assaults on Negro passengers, and, in a single night, the bombing of six homes and churches. But the cooler heads in the white community eventually took control. In 1961 the Freedom Riders were attacked in Montgomery by a white mob, and Attorney General Robert Kennedy found it necessary to send in 600 U.S. marshals to maintain order. Since then, the city has been remarkably free of racial violence. Today it is a relatively well integrated, peaceful city.

In recent years, the town's two newspapers, the *Alabama Journal* and

Montgomery *Advertiser*, have been biting critics of the Wallace regime—surprisingly independent because since the late '60s they have been outside-owned (Multimedia), a pattern that often leads to dollar-and-cents-first journalism. Editor-publisher Harold E. Martin, who won a Pulitzer Prize in 1970 for exposing a questionable drug-testing program in the state prisons, is Wallace's most prominent newspaper critic in Alabama. Martin's predecessor, the late Grover C. Hall, Jr., was a friend of George Wallace but did question many of Wallace's policies. In the 1920s, Hall's father, a crusading editor of the *Advertiser*, had won a Pulitzer Prize for his editorial attacks on the Ku Klux Klan.

Montgomery is a rather provincial city, but the same cannot be said of Mobile (1970 population 190,026), which some Alabamians view as "a little state in itself." The city is located on Mobile Bay, 31 miles from the Gulf of Mexico, and it was actually the white man's first settlement, begun by the French in 1711 when Indians still held all the interior. Catholic influence remains strong in Mobile, and it was there that the first Mardi Gras festival in the United States was celebrated. Like New Orleans, there are "mystic societies" which hold annual balls climaxing just before Ash Wednesday. The deviation from the inward-looking ways of the Southern interior is underscored by the subtropical climate and the coming and going of ships from all countries of the world. Port activity has shown a brisk increase in recent decades and is complemented by major shipbuilding activity and broadly diversified industries—pulp and paper products (International Paper, Scott Paper, and others), steel fabrication, chemicals and petrochemicals, and food processing.

Mobile has traditionally been run by an oligarchy of businessmen, newspaper publishers, and the old aristocratic element—all quite conservative in their politics and policies. One aberration was Joseph Langan, a liberal Democrat and the dominant municipal figure for 20 years before his defeat in 1969. As mayor, Langan ran a clean, businesslike city administration and knew how to tap Washington for funds. He was finally turned out by a candidate who made an overt racist appeal. Simultaneously, Mobile's reputation as a city of racial moderation—it was hiring black policemen when Bull Connor was still using the dogs—began to deteriorate. Virtually nothing had been done to achieve school integration, and when the federal courts stepped in with a stiff busing plan, there were serious confrontations and disorders in the schools. Black power factions were accused of responsibility for a rash of firebombings. The city issued orders to its police to shoot arsonists on sight.

Three university towns have experienced interesting growth since World War II—Tuscaloosa (65,773 in 1970), Auburn (22,767), and Tuskegee (11,028). The University of Alabama was founded in 1831, when Tuscaloosa was a foundering frontier town, and the two grew together—but with plenty of tragedies, ranging from burning by Union troops during the Civil War to the trauma over admitting and then excluding Autherine Lucy in 1956, when hundreds of students rioted, burning a cross on campus and shouting "Keep Bama white—to hell with Autherine" in a march through the normally placid downtown streets.* But the university, and especially its law school, had shown its mettle over the years by graduating men who became the top political leaders of Alabama, and several in neighboring states as well.

Eighteen months after the Lucy incident one of the South's outstanding postwar educators, Dr. Frank A. Rose, became president of the university. Backed up by an independent (self-perpetuating) board of trustees, Rose defied the vilest verbal abuse and innumerable threats by the Ku Klux Klan and its ilk to build the university into an oasis of academic freedom and independent thought in Alabama. Through symposia and meetings of local and statewide groups, the university, in Rose's words, "emerged as a center for integration in the state." (Wallace maintained outwardly cordial relations with Rose but provoked his legislators to make attacks on Rose and try to force his resignation.) When Rose took over his post, the total state budget for the University of Alabama system had been $6 million a year; the figure multiplied rapidly during the '60s, and more than $100 million in federal money was attracted in the last half of the decade. By the time Rose departed in 1969, the number of Ph.D. programs at the university had been increased from six to 26.

Tuscaloosa is such a pleasant city that it is easy to forget that it lies next door to classic Black Belt counties like Greene and Hale, and some of the grimmest poverty in America. The city is the home of Robert M. Shelton, Jr., Imperial Wizard of the United Klans of America. Like his hero, George Wallace, Shelton has traveled a lot to the North in recent years, claiming new wellsprings of support there. Tuscaloosa is also headquarters of the Selma Inter-Religious Project, which was begun as a one-man interfaith ministry by an Episcopal priest, Francis Walter, after the murder of Jonathan Daniels in 1965. Supported initially by the churches and Jewish groups that had marched in Selma, the organization later became a nonprofit corporation governed by a board of black and white Alabamians—an evolution something akin to that of the Delta Ministry in Mississippi. The Selma Project's focus remained the Black Belt people "who once shook the nation under Martin Luther King"; its activities include a hand-craft cooperative called the "Freedom Quilting Bee," farm cooperatives, legal defense of Negroes in trouble, and assistance for the black elected officials of Greene County.

Within commuting distance of Tuscaloosa is Moundville, a sleepy little Black Belt town where a sign advertising "Tackle-Minnows-Crickckets [*sic*]-Red Worms-Ice" graces the gas station in the middle of the village. Victor Poole, the thoughtful young president of the Bank of Moundville, told me he was a Wallace man—Wallace actually appointed him to the state board of education—but that he'd learned in the service that "integration is not so bad." "It lifted a burden from our conscience to know black folks can go to our schools," Poole said. "But, by God, we're not going to do it because the government tells us to." Lurleen Wallace, he pointed out, "was a local

* Miss Lucy was rescued from a classroom building by state troopers and subsequently expelled by the trustees after she accused the university of complicity in the demonstrations. It was not until 1963 that the first Negroes, Vivian Malone and James Hood, and David McGlathery at the Huntsville campus, became regular students (in the wake of George Wallace's unsuccessful defiance).

girl—she grew up down in the woods not far from here." As the local banker, Poole is an expert in agricultural economics. Cotton used to be the only crop; now it is soybeans, and out-of-state interests from Missouri and elsewhere—often father and son combinations—have come in to farm and to stay. They work so hard, Poole said, "that it's a shock to lazy white Southerners. But some local white farmers are going into soybeans now too."

There are two industries in Moundville—the Cracker Asphalt Company, run by a man from Chicago, and K-Way Manufacturing Company, a needle plant that hires both white and black women. Both plants were built with heavy local industrial bonding help. Just outside of Moundville are the prehistoric Indian burial mounds that gave the town its name. On one of the mounds the Crucifixion is reenacted at an Easter sunrise service each year, attended by up to 10,000 people from all over the South.

Auburn University, in the town of the same name, has grown from a humble agricultural and mechanical college begun under the Morrill Act in Reconstruction times to be the largest university in Alabama (13,000 students). Its specialties are in fields like veterinary medicine and pharmacy, and its agricultural experimentation station has been a boon to the more advanced Alabama farmers.

The famed Booker T. Washington started Tuskegee Institute back in 1881 "in a dilapidated shanty near the colored Methodist Church, with the church itself a sort of assembly room." And so successful was he in attracting support, including that of Northern philanthropists, that when he died the institution had more than 100 buildings. It was also Washington who brought George Washington Carver, the illustrious black chemist, to Tuskegee. The institution became a beacon of black education and also of black pride, years before the civil rights revolution of the '60s. William G. Carleton, a Northerner who had lived in the South many years, recalled a trip to Tuskegee shortly after World War II. Some of the student leaders took him on a sort of sentimental pilgrimage to the bleak old cotton patch and shanty where Washington had started his efforts. But Carleton noted that the students "kept their history and sentiment in one compartment and their contemporary politics in another." Booker Washington's doctrine had been that Southern Negroes should be initially content with the trades and mostly manual labor if it meant gradual progress and peace with whites. But as the students returned to the modern campus and passed the impressive statue which shows Washington lifting the blindfold from the eyes of a kneeling Negro, one of them commented: "We don't think too much of Booker today. We feel that he is not lifting that blindfold; instead, we think he is lowering it, pressing it more tightly over the Negro's eyes."

The Tuskegee Institute helped to develop a black intelligentsia and middle class that would make the city of Tuskegee the nerve center of black politics in Alabama. Up to the 1950s—when blacks represented 84 percent of the Macon County population but only 28 percent of the registered voters—gross discrimination was used to keep Negroes from enrolling to vote. But black leadership, centered in the Institute, forced more and more black registration until blacks made up a majority of the registered voters in 1964. In 1957 the Alabama legislature made a blatant attempt to stop a black takeover in Tuskegee proper by gerrymandering the city boundaries to exclude most of the blacks. Dr. Charles Gomillion, of the Institute staff, filed suit in federal court and won the landmark case of *Gomillion v. Lightfoot*, in which the U.S. Supreme Court ruled that political redistricting designed to reduce Negro electoral participation was a violation of the 15th Amendment. Gomillion counseled against vindictiveness when blacks became a voting majority, and in 1964 and 1968 the biracial slates backed by the black Macon County Democratic Club, which he headed, were victorious. But by the early 1970s, with a three-to-one voting advantage, blacks were no longer in a mood to compromise with the whites, and all-black slates were being elected. Lucius Amerson, elected initially in 1968, won fame as the first black sheriff in the South. Tuskegee was the home of the first two blacks in the Alabama legislature. And in 1972 the town elected a black mayor, 30-year-old Johnny Ford.

In an intriguing piece of television journalism, CBS News in 1973 portrayed the Tuskegee situation with a flashback to 1957, when blacks had begun a four-year boycott of white-owned shops and John Patterson, as state attorney general, had raided the headquarters of the boycott and won a court order banning the NAACP from operating in Alabama. State senator Sam Englehardt of Macon County had been asked then what might happen in the unlikely event of a black administration in Tuskegge "If you had a Negro mayor in Tuskegee," Englehardt had said, "it'd be utter chaos. . . . You can't imagine the resentment that white people would have."

Immediately after the Englehardt clip, the CBS program shifted to Johnny Ford's white wife, the former Tas Rainer, whose now deceased father belonged to the Citizens Council. Her mother, Mrs. Ford said, had been alive when she became engaged to Johnny Ford, and initially "it was a frightening experience to her. But then she began to know him and . . . she really just fell in love with him. . . . She really loved him as a person." Ford commented that it had also been quite a shock for his black working-class family when he married a white girl, but "they've certainly come to love her and she's a part of the family."

From his birth in a shack in Tuskegee, Johnny Ford grew up as a model young boy, went to college in Tennessee, and then took a job with the Boy Scouts in New York and worked in Robert Kennedy's 1968 Presidential campaign and to help reelect Mayor John Lindsay in 1969. Then he returned to Tuskegee, anxious not only to win as a mayor but to put out lines so he could get both state and federal aid for the city. He backed President Nixon for reelection in 1972 and even formed a political alliance of sorts with George Wallace. "Are you George Wallace's house black?" CBS asked Ford. His reply (an echo of Booker Washington): "If they're looking for a favorite fellow to give some extra money for his people, I'll certainly take it. . . . It's business with me—no emotion. . . . What you must do is penetrate the system and, once within the system, learn how it works. And then work it well. Don't turn Uncle Tom, but work it well. Take that same system, redirect those resources so that same system which has kept you down so long can be used to raise your people up."

On the same October 1972 day that Johnny Ford took office, another young black leader and veteran of Robert Kennedy's campaign, A. J. (Jay) Cooper, was sworn in as mayor of Prichard, a blue-collar and poverty-plagued suburb of Mobile. Cooper had also gone north for his education (Notre Dame and New York University Law School), returning in 1969 to be a civil rights lawyer in Alabama. His campaign was much more difficult than Ford's, because blacks make up only a scant majority (52 percent) of Prichard's 41,578 population. Negro candidates had run for office several times before, always unsuccessfully. Cooper won by a phenomenal registration and get-out-the-vote effort among blacks, plus an appeal to whites to end the lackluster and fiscally bankrupt administration of the incumbent mayor. Just enough whites defected to permit him to win by a 540-vote margin out of more than 10,000 cast in the runoff. "I brought in black buddies from all over" for help, Cooper said; he also phoned friends all over the country to raise much of his $22,000 campaign fund. The victory was all the more amazing because Prichard was known as a town with high race tensions, where the Ku Klux Klan still maintained a downtown meeting hall and Governor Wallace used to speak every Labor Day.

Birmingham: In Metamorphosis

Birmingham—Alabama's greatest city, the "Pittsburgh of the South"—was spawned in the free-wheeling capitalistic years that followed the Civil War, when the lords of industry made and lost vast fortunes in a twinkling and workingmen were pawns and serfs in their surge to power. One of the early "Birmingham Barons" observed that the coal and iron and limestone beds of the region—the ingredients needed for the manufacture of steel—were "intended by nature to feed some great creature." The symbol of it all came to be the largest iron figure ever cast, a 55-foot-high statue of Vulcan, the Roman deity of fire and metal, which was erected atop Red Mountain, overlooking Birmingham and the Jones Valley. Vulcan is depicted with hammer and anvil, the tools of the mighty blacksmith who had forged the spears with which gods and demigods of classical times made war.

Birmingham had none of the softer features of the Old South. It was a hard society of the survival of the fittest, in which money and power overshadowed all else. Few voices were raised in protest when the Tennessee Iron and Coal Company bought up most of the independent furnaces and in turn sold out to U.S. Steel. From that merger, a United States Senate committee charged, U.S. Steel derived "control of the open-hearth output of steel rails, the ultimate control of the iron supply of the country, the practical monopoly of the iron and steel trade of the South, and the elimination of a strong and growing competition."

If the lords of steel had few qualms about gobbling each other up and suppressing competition, they had even less about contracting for convict labor and using the arms of the state to smash fledgling labor unions. "Birmingham," Charles Morgan, Jr., wrote, "was a crucible of all the forces that breed violence: poor and impoverished whites and Negroes; an economy controlled in the North; a political and economic system based on the blood and sweat of workers whose lives were made up of fists and knives, guns and dynamite, Saturday-night whiskey, and chits at the company store." Birmingham fell into the racial phobia of the rest of Alabama, and industry tried to play off one race against the other. City ordinances forbade integrated gatherings, and many of the Steelworkers' meetings were broken up by the police, the members arrested for meeting in joint groups. The United Mine Workers—whose numbers would eventually drop sharply with mechanization of the coal mines and importation of Venezuelan iron ore—had the same experience. But mining left one legacy: familiarity with dynamite. It had been a tool in the mines; in the 1960s it would be used against homes and churches.

Clear down to the 1960s, Birmingham lacked much of a natural aristocracy or leadership group with humanitarian values. Many of the leading families were only three generations out of the coal mines, and the rough edges were only starting to wear off. Society was essentially divided between the quite rich—the steel executives and their associates living "over the mountain" in Mountain Brook, one of the snazziest suburbs of America—and the poor and blue-collar classes in Birmingham proper and grim old industry satellites like Bessemer and Ensley. One looked in vain for a very large white-collar middle class or for much culture or university life or independence of thought.

Instead, Birmingham indulged in unbridled economic boosterism—exemplified by the prediction of the Birmingham *News* that the 1907 takeover by U.S. Steel would "make the Birmingham district the largest steel and manufacturing center in the universe." That prediction was not to come true, although the Birmingham metropolitan area by 1970 had 739,274 people and remained the leading steelmaking center of the South. The area might have grown even more rapidly in the first half of the century if U.S. Steel, until the early 1950s, had not tried consciously to keep out other industries that might compete with it for labor. The executive secretary of the chamber of commerce, which U.S. Steel dominated through those years, had the job of fending off new industry. That ended when the wages of miners and steelworkers came to be established by nationally negotiated contracts.

By the first years of the 1950s, Birmingham had reason to believe its years of violence were behind it. The strife over unionization had been completed in the '20s and '30s, and despite the rigid racial segregation of the city's life, some interracial meetings were held to deal with race problems, and an attempt—albeit unsuccessful—was made to put Negroes on the police force. But after the Supreme Court's 1954 and 1955 school desegregation decisions, racism and violence erupted again in virulent forms. Between 1956 and 1961, 20 violent acts were reported in the city, including racially motivated bombings and beatings and one castration. In 1957 the voters replaced police commissioner Robert Lindbergh, a moderate on race problems, with Eugene ("Bull") Connor. When the U.S. Commission on Civil Rights conducted a field study in spring 1961 regarding violence and the administration of justice in the city, three out of four persons interviewed insisted on complete anonymity. The field report stated: "The very reluctance of these persons to be quoted is the clearest documentation of the climate of fear and the conspiracy of silence that exist in Birmingham." On Mother's Day that year, a Freedom Rider bus rolled into Birmingham, to be met at the Trailways station by a gang of white toughs who assaulted the riders—plus local news and television reporters—in a bloody fashion. The bus station was close to police headquarters, but Bull Connor's men did not arrive until the violence was done. There was strong reason to believe Connor had kept them away so that the gang could do its job.

Two springs later came the tumultuous events of what blacks would later call "the Year of Birmingham." John Egerton later summed them up well in his book, *A Mind to Stay Here:*

> Birmingham, 1963. Steel and smoke and white supremacy. George Wallace and Al Lingo, Bull Connor and Jamie Moore, Arthur Hanes and Albert Boutwell. Police dogs and fire hoses and cattle prods. Tear gas and armored cars and fire bombs. Thousands of arrests. Martin Luther King and Ralph David Abernathy and Fred Shuttlesworth and Arthur Shores and A. G. Gaston and Orzelle Billingsley and Andrew Young and James Bevel and Dick Gregory and scores of others, lesser known but no less courageous. Wallace saying he would "not be a party to any . . . meeting to compromise on issues of segregation," and white terrorists taking their cue from that defiant attitude to establish their own deadly brand of "law and order." King writing his "Letter From Birmingham City Jail," a document which makes a good companion piece to the letter Paul wrote to the Ephesians where he was a "prisoner for the Lord," nineteen centuries ago. President John F. Kennedy, Attorney-General Robert F. Kennedy, mediators, negotiators, federal troops, federalized national guardsmen. An explosion in the Sixteenth Street Baptist Church, killing four little girls. Riots, more bombings, more killing of Negroes by whites.

The day after the frightful bombing of the Sixteenth Street Baptist Church, Charles Morgan, Jr., then a 33-year-old attorney in the city, addressed the Young Men's Business Club of Birmingham:

> Those four little girls were human beings. They had lived their fourteen years in a leaderless city; a city where no one accepts responsibility, where everyone wants to blame somebody else. . . .
>
> Birmingham is a city in which the major industry, operating from Pittsburgh, never tried to solve the problem. It is a city where four little Negro girls can be born into a second-class school system, live a segregated life, ghettoed in their own little neighborhoods, restricted to Negro churches, destined to ride in Negro ambulances to Negro wards of hospitals or to a Negro cemetery. Local papers, on their front and editorial pages, call for order and then exclude their names from obituary columns.
>
> And who is really guilty? Each of us. Each citizen who has not consciously attempted to bring about peaceful compliance with the decisions of the Supreme Court of the United States, each citizen who has ever said "they ought to kill that nigger," every citizen who votes for the candidate with the bloody flag; every citizen and every school board member and schoolteacher and principal and business-

man and judge and lawyer who has corrupted the minds of our youth; every person in this community who has in any way contributed during the past several years to the popularity of hatred is at least as guilty, or more so, than the demented fool who threw that bomb.

Morgan concluded by saying: "Birmingham is not a dying city. It is dead." And when he had finished, one member rose to move that the club admit one Negro. But the motion died for lack of a second. Not long after, Morgan moved to Atlanta, there to carry on for the American Civil Liberties Union many of the legal battles that would change the South in the following few years.

Birmingham's business leaders had known long before 1963—when events made their city known as the "Johannesburg of America"—that the cancer of racism was eroding the viability of their city. As early as 1957, William P. Engel, former chairman of the committee trying to attract new industries to Birmingham, had warned that the city was losing potential plants because of the "hoodlumism" and Klan activity in the city. Birmingham leaders protested violently—but admitted they had received an eye-opening jolt—when Harrison Salisbury of the New York *Times* reported in April 1960 from Birmingham: "Every channel of communication, every medium of mutual interest, every reasoned approach, every inch of middle ground has been fragmented by the emotional dynamite of racism." *

Business leaders had plenty of excuses for not speaking out openly for racial harmony. They feared bombings or other reprisals if they were publicly identified as advocates or even negotiators in a process that could lead to desegregation. Another defense, offered by board chairman Roger Blough of U.S. Steel when his corporation was criticized for not having done more, was that the company had instituted a nondiscriminatory hiring policy in its Birmingham mills, and that the use of its economic clout to force changes in the city would be "repugnant" and "quite beyond what a corporation should do." Critics said that was a novel philosophy to be expressed by a corporation that had never hesitated to pressure governments in its drive for broader profits or favorable "operating" conditions. "Steel," Morgan said, "has extracted great wealth from the soil and sweat of Birmingham. Can it now leave it a carcass to grapple alone and meaninglessly with America's most powerful enemies—bigotry and hatred?"

The web of responsibility, Morgan said, started with the local business leadership and extended to the corporate board rooms and executive offices of the Northern firms that controlled so much of Birmingham's economic activity. The local corporate leaders, he said, had felt secure in their homes "over the mountain" and had blocked efforts in the 1950s to accomplish annexation of their communities to the city of Birmingham. The city was thus denied both their financial support (through taxes) and the moderating influence of upper-class, educated persons. One of the city's business leaders was quoted as saying in 1963, "We can't negotiate for the city on voting rights and social problems, because 90 percent of us don't even live here." Morgan said all that was a cop-out, and that so-called "moderate" business

* A Bessemer grand jury indicted Salisbury on 42 counts of criminal libel for his pains.

leaders, North and South, could not escape the onus of blame. He identified them as "Yale and Harvard men, the upper-middle-class oriented, respected people. They are more concerned with golf, family, cocktails at the club, money and respectability. Their lives are the antithesis of controversy."

Bull Connor in 1961 had been elected to a new term as police commissioner that would run to 1965, and both the Birmingham *News* and (more belatedly) the *Post-Herald* were evidencing disenchantment with the autocratic, unresponsive tone of the city commission form of government he symbolized.* In 1962—even while George Wallace was becoming governor of Alabama—a group of attorneys belonging to that same Young Men's Business Club startled the city's older leaders by getting enough petitions, and then votes in a special referendum, to throw out the three commissioners and shift Birmingham to a mayor-council form. Part of the motivation was to get Connor out of office, and it worked: in a special April 1963 election to pick the new mayor, Connor was defeated. But Connor refused to move out of his office or give up his police commissioner powers, and the affair was being argued out in court at the very moment that Martin Luther King and his allies launched their mass demonstrations to break down Birmingham's high walls of segregation.

Frenetic negotiations in the midst of the Negroes' mass demonstrations finally led to agreement by some business leaders (who were initially petrified at the thought that their names would be made public) that lunch counters, rest rooms, and drinking fountains in a few downtown department stores would be desegregated. The personal intervention of Burke Marshall, head of the U.S. Justice Department's Civil Rights Division, helped ease the way to the agreement. And in May, when the courts upheld the new government and ordered Connor's ouster, the Negroes finally felt they had a city government with which they could deal.

Despite their pleasure in seeing Connor ousted, Birmingham's Negroes chafed under the administration of the new mayor, Albert Boutwell, who tended to appoint committees which studied problems to death and even left water fountains plainly marked "white" and "colored" outside his City Hall office suite. But they took hope in the moderate tone of the new city council and especially one fair-minded member, businessman George G. Seibels. In 1967, with major black support, Seibels was elected mayor, pledging racial harmony in the city. More than any other white person, he deserves credit for turning Birmingham into a more humanly decent city. Seibels shares two characteristics with Judge Frank Johnson: both are Republicans (although Seibels has played down his party ties in Birmingham's nonpartisan elections), and both have taken long strides toward changing, for the better, the life of black people. But after that, the similarity ends. Johnson's roots reach back into north Alabama history, while Seibels was born in California and raised in Virginia. Johnson is cool, intellectual, almost haughty. Seibels is emotional, forceful, given to flights of evangelistic oratory. Johnson is tall and thin, while Seibels is short and chunkily built and has gray hair and

* The *Post-Herald* in later years has moved ahead of the *News* as a voice for progressivism, in the view of some observers. The *Post-Herald* is owned by Scripps Howard, the *News* by Newhouse.

blue eyes and an overall appearance highly reminiscent of another evangelistic politician, George Romney. A couple of heart attacks have slowed Seibels down recently, but Bruce Biossat and I still laugh over the afternoon in 1969 when we spent two hours listening to Seibels' nonstop proclamations of the glories of the new, tolerant Birmingham. When we finally extricated ourselves and had pushed the elevator button in the hallway, the glass doors of the mayor's office burst open and George Seibels came charging out, calling to us to wait a minute so he could give us a copy of his Fourth of July speech.

Some critics said Seibels lacked administrative skills or the ability to delegate authority well, but he did give Birmingham real grass-roots government. He walked the streets in the early morning hours (starting practically at daylight), looking for problems like open sewers and abandoned houses, and then kept maps with the sore spots pinpointed by location. As an example, he said, "I found a half block of abandoned refrigerators and stoves, infested with rats and mosquitoes in the summertime. I got those things off that damned block and cleaned up. When I do things like this, the people can *see* the progress." Seibels also spearheaded a HUD-supported project to refurbish the rundown streets and houses of the city's north side, got "dawn to dusk" vest-pocket parks located throughout the city, supported award-winning youth recreation programs, and gave businessmen his hard sell on opening jobs to the hard-core unemployed.

In 1971 Seibels won reelection by a wide margin over a conservative opponent. And Birmingham showed its growing toleration by electing civil rights attorney Arthur Shores, whose home had been bombed in 1963, to the city council in 1967. In 1971 a second black, Dr. Richard Arrington, director of the Alabama Center for Higher Education, was elected to the council. In a special legislative election in spring 1973, Jefferson County voters sent Chris McNair, a professional black photographer, to represent them in the state house. Ten years before, McNair's only daughter, Denise, had been one of the children killed in the bombing of the Sixteenth Street Church. (McNair showed an amazing lack of bitterness after his daughter's tragic death and was in fact a member of the civic team which made Birmingham's "pitch" to be an All-American City. A very different reaction was that of another Birmingham native, Angela Davis, who had been a friend of McNair's daughter and the three other girls who were killed. Miss Davis in later years cited the death of her friends as one of the factors that propelled her toward radical ideology.)

The victories of blacks in Birmingham politics were due in large part to the city's big Negro population. Blacks made up 42 percent of the city's people in the 1970 Census, and there have been predictions of a future black majority in the city. White support and thousands of white votes have also abetted the black electoral breakthroughs, however. Blacks now sit on practically every policy-making board in the area, including two on the Birmingham board of education. And as a result of designation by the city council, a black judge now presides over the court where Bull Connor's victims used to be tried.

Of all the problems the new city government faced, the elimination of police brutality was the hardest to crack. The first Negroes were added to the force in 1965, but a "Bull Connor mentality" held on, especially in the person of the police chief, Jamie Moore, who resisted Seibels' assiduous efforts to modernize the department and refused to issue clear instructions against addressing Negroes as "nigger" or "boy." The situation came to a head in 1969, after two Negro women had been senselessly beaten by police officers. An angry group of 21 blacks, the most prominent people in the Negro community, then went before the city council and mayor with a 14-point declaration demanding justice for blacks.

Two important results came from the confrontation. The first was that Seibels' hand in dealing with the police was immensely strengthened, and after his reelection he was able to get rid of Chief Moore. Police brutality has dropped off sharply since. The Rev. James Edward Gardner, the long-time president of the Alabama Christian Movement for Human Rights and one of the complaining black leaders in 1969, put it this way: "Mayor Seibels has complete authority now, and he doesn't cut any corners. If an officer's caught in an act of brutality, he's suspended or he's fired. When the police find out there's a man in office who's not going to tolerate it, they change their attitude. These officers now are much nicer, because they know they can't get away with it at City Hall."

The second result was that Birmingham's business leadership for the first time committed itself openly and deeply to resolving the human relations problems of the city. The impetus came out of Operation New Birmingham (ONB), and the vehicle was the Community Affairs Council (CAC), to which we referred briefly in the introductory pages of this chapter. Since its inception in 1969, CAC has grown from 27 members to 60. But its balance—approximately one third from the white community (both business and labor), one third from the black community, and one third from government—has been maintained. Vincent Townsend, Sr., vice president and assistant to the publisher of the Birmingham *News* and a driving force behind Operation New Birmingham, said the whole idea of CAC was to get a wide representation of people who could speak for their organizations and make decisions for them, meeting regularly and behind closed doors. The secrecy, he acknowledged, was "anathema to the press" and put him in a difficult position as a newspaper executive. "But it discouraged people from making long speeches and enabled us to get down to the gut issues." The regularity of weekly meetings, he said, has also been an important feature, because problems are not just allowed to blow away. The CAC was well equipped to deal with the police brutality issue, since its membership included not only a broad range of black community leaders, but also the mayor, the chief of police, and the county sheriff. "They are all there to talk about it directly, right away," Townsend said.*

The biracial nature of CAC was underscored by the fact that it had

* Other participants include representatives of the chamber of commerce and leading businesses, the county commissioners, most of the larger banks, the Fraternal Order of Police, the Steelworkers and Hod Carriers, the local OEO director, and several factions of the black community.

cochairmen—one white, one black. The first white cochairman was W. C. Bauer, president of South Central Bell Telephone Company, and the first black cochairman was Dr. Lucius Pitts, president of Miles College. As it matured, CAC began to deal with problems well beyond the police issue. Housing, employment, public works, and education were all treated, with special subcommittees set up to handle each. Neighborhood planning staffs were organized to get the input of people from all over Jefferson County, both blacks and whites. When hungry blacks in Bessemer were unable to get a county food stamp distribution point set up near them, CAC intervened to get the job done and then proceeded to persuade the local governments to start mobile food stamp offices covering the entire county. Computer specialists were brought in to develop food stamp authorization cards, and food stamp sales rose from a few hundred thousand dollars a month to over $1 million.

No one would claim in the early '70s that the millennium had arrived for blacks of Birmingham. It had been years since violence erupted on the streets. But in 1969 it took a federal court order to force the Elmwood Cemetery to allow the burial there of a neighborhood youngster, Bill Henry Terry, Jr., a 20-year-old Negro Army private who had died fighting for his country in Vietnam. A few months later, tears welled up in the eyes of 11-year-old Twilda Bryant when she and her mother were told they could not join the First Baptist Church because they were Negroes. (The pastor, Dr. J. Herbert Gilmore, Jr., looked out at his lily-white congregation and said: "I will not be a pastor of a racist church." He and 300 followers then formed a new congregation dedicated to an interracial ministry—the very first integrated Southern Baptist Church in Alabama.) Despite the school desegregation that began in 1965, there were still many schools practically all-black or all-white. And in 1970 the Justice Department filed suit against U.S. Steel and the United Steelworkers of America locals at the Fairfield Works outside of Birmingham, charging—despite the fair employment gains that both the company and the union boasted of—that there was still serious discrimination against blacks in the mills, in violation of the Civil Rights Act of 1964. The suit ended in victory when a federal judge ordered the company and the union to scrap old seniority rules and institute a new system that would equalize job opportunities for members of both races.

To match black frustrations, there were indeed breakthroughs. Miles College had risen from the ditch of disaccreditation to become a thriving center of black education with the distinguished former dean of Harvard College, John U. Monro, on its faculty. The University of Alabama at Birmingham Medical Center was providing dramatically improved health care, and thousands of semiskilled and skilled jobs for black people. There was even a stab at black self-determination in Roosevelt City, the all-black suburb of 3,600 souls incorporated in the '60s under the leadership of civil rights leader Orzell Billingsley (who greeted me by saying, "I hope you didn't come here to talk about civil rights and all that—what I want to know is, 'Where's the money?' ").

The black advances were not enough, especially for a newer, somewhat more aggressive class of emerging black leaders, who were no longer content with the victories won by such past Brimingham civil rights heroes as the Rev. Fred L. Shuttlesworth, organizer of the Alabama affiliate of the SCLC. But the Rev. James Gardner, who was one of Martin Luther King, Jr.'s men in the city, ticked off the gains—blacks given job opportunities in the utilities, in the department stores, in the city government, in the police force—and was telling the younger Negroes, "If you have something else, let me know and we'll go out and have a march. The fact is that almost all the things we fought for have come to pass." Gardner sang a different song in the early '60s, when he said: "We have nothing to lose but our lives," or as recently as 1969, when he said continued black demonstrations were necessary "to keep the establishment moving."

Two quotes helped to sum up the Birmingham human relations story in 1973. Vincent Townsend: "Not all those who don't like black people have gone away, but at least they don't control the community anymore." Charles Morgan: "Birmingham changed because the law changed and the people had to obey. That was more basic than Operation New Birmingham and all the rest."

On the physical side, no one was holding his breath in hopes that Birmingham would become the garden spot of the South. But improvements were being made. U.S. Steel and the other big factories, including the American Cast Iron Pipe Company, were in the midst of a far-reaching air pollution control program, which might eventually clear the thick banks of smog from the mills that covered the city some days. One could not say that the clean-up was exactly voluntary. U.S. Steel, for example, had not installed a single precipitator or other pollution-control device in Birmingham before 1972—and, in its typically secretive manner, was refusing to say when it would do so. But in 1971 the gray and red and black and brown smoke billowing out of the stacks at U.S. Steel and its sister industries became trapped in a long temperature inversion that sent the Birmingham air particulate counts soaring and posed serious dangers to public health. After U.S. Steel and some other firms spurned the requests of the U.S. Environmental Protection Agency that they reduce their emissions voluntarily during the crisis, the government went to court in a first major test of the Clean Air Act of 1970 and forced them to do so. Then the tough new Alabama air pollution law went into effect, and Attorney General Bill Baxley sued 13 of the largest Birmingham polluters under the nuisance doctrine of common law. Not long after, U.S. Steel announced it would install precipitators "to eliminate the smoke and particulate matter" that spewed from the 12 open-hearth furnaces of its Fairfield plant. Later it improved further on that plan by closing the open-hearth furnaces altogether, installing advanced basic oxygen process furnaces in their place. The result by late 1973 was a 99 percent reduction in the volume of emissions from the open-hearth units. The other big companies were also installing pollution control devices or new nonpolluting equipment. Birmingham would be a less grimy city in future years, but it still had no plan to deal with its pollution from autos and other sources. Nor, one might add, did it have any plan for mass transit to relieve its perennial traffic snares, or much hope of annexing the 35 independent municipalities that surrounded it.

Birmingham up to the late 1960s had all the appearances—save for one or two newer buildings—of the 1920s. And the railroad lines ran like an ugly gash, 16 tracks wide, directly through the middle of the city. But change was on the way, made possible by the improved racial climate and the the efforts of Operation New Birmingham (which had been founded in 1963 as an outgrowth of the old Birmingham Downtown Improvement Association). ONB was able to negotiate with the Birmingham League of Architects for 5,000 free hours of the architects' time to develop a design for progress for the inner city. The plan was completed and presented to the city at a big luncheon in 1965. "This was the beginning," Vincent Townsend said in the language civic boosters like to use for such things, "the beginning of the big dream and the big push." And one has to be impressed with what was planned, and then executed, to save Birmingham's heart from urban rot. One element was a six-square-block, $58 million civic center, including a music hall, theater, large exhibition hall, and coliseum. Another was a huge regional postal facility, filled with automated and computerized equipment ahead of what any other U.S. city had. These developments helped Birmingham to snag Southern Bell Telephone's six-state headquarters, in a brand new 30-story building. Another bank and gas building of the same size was completed in the early 1970s. And mall-type treatment with redstone street furnishings—the whole called "Birmingham Green"—was begun on several downtown blocks.*

One can dismiss all those physical improvements, however, as minimal steps to save an old heavy-industry city—and a pale shadow of what has already transpired in Atlanta, New Orleans, and Miami. The single factor likely to make Birmingham a city of some distinction in the future is the massive $100 million complex of the University of Alabama at Birmingham. It began in 1945 when the Alabama medical school, then a "mediocre two-year college," was moved from Tuscaloosa to Birmingham and expanded to four years. Not long afterwards, Dr. Joseph F. Volker arrived from Tufts University to set up a dental school. And from then on, the complex simply grew and grew. Volker and his colleagues were able to draw renowned heart specialists from all over the country, creating one of the leading cardiovascular centers of the world. Experts in cancer, diabetes, obstetrics, and other fields followed in a kind of "critical mass" advanced by unusual interdepartmental and interdisciplinary cooperation.

By the 1960s, the medical school covered 15 square blocks that used to be a wretched slum in the heart of Birmingham. But it was only a beginning.

* The Birmingham rooters also list airport modernization and expansion on their list of great things for the city. I prefer to skip those details (all cities seem to be getting new airports these days) and quote a remark Charles Morgan made to Justice William Douglas when he arrived with the jurist at the Birmingham Airport in 1970, en route to a speaking engagement. Morgan asked Douglas to pause before entering the terminal and gave him a rundown on the local sights: "Over there you can see the Alabama National Guard, which was headquarters for the general and others who commanded the Bay of Pigs Operation. Over there you can see Hanes International Corporation, where A. J. Hanes, formerly with the FBI, and later the lawyer for James Earl Ray, used to be the chief of plant security. . . . And over there is the Aeromarine Supply Co., where the gun was purchased that James Earl Ray used to kill Martin Luther King, Jr. Which is one hell of a view, unparalleled in the rest of the country."

In 1966 the University of Alabama at Birmingham was formally established—one of the few places where a university has sprung from a medical school, rather than the reverse. And then a 45-square-block expansion program was announced, made possible with federal urban renewal assistance. (In fact, about three-quarters of the whole has been financed by the federal government.) University College, consisting of the institution's faculties of arts and sciences, business, education, and engineering, moved into the new facilities of a large "west campus" dedicated in 1973.

With Volker as its president, UA-Birmingham as a whole had grown to well over 7,000 students and 5,500 employees by the early '70s. And it was growing fast—scheduled to outstrip U.S. Steel as the largest employer of the Birmingham area by the mid-1970s and by the mid-'80s to have nearly 50,000 persons as students or employees. The benefits to the Birmingham community were widespread. Several hundred academic figures were drawn to the city, tens of thousands of poor people were given medical care each year, and many professional and technical jobs were made available to both blacks and whites. University officials noted with some pleasure that the institution was already giving some white-collar balance to Birmingham's traditional blue-collar majorities and was beginning to stem the historic brain drain from Alabama. Dr. Keith Blayney, administrator of the university's hospitals, told a reporter that "able faculty and students don't have to flee to the North anymore—including the bright Negro kids for whom we could not compete before."

There is little reason to believe these expectations will not be fulfilled. And if they are, "big, bad, terrible Birmingham" will have an entirely new reputation in times to come.

Alabama Futures

When one asks if Alabama life will be different in the 1970s and '80s from the familiar patterns of the past half century, the answer has to be "yes." With rising levels of education, both vocational and on the university level, there will be inducements for more forward-looking projects like the university center in Birmingham. The industrial affluence of the Tennessee Valley is likely to appear in central and southern Alabama as well, as industries discover a more literate and better-trained work force and the possibilities of foreign trade through the port of Mobile become more fully recognized. The more open public life that has already come to the big cities will begin to permeate the smaller cities and rural areas of the state.

Important changes will come on the political front too. There are several reasons, but the cardinal ones are these: the blacks now have the vote, and reapportionment has broken the back of Black Belt control in state government. The continuing trend toward urbanization and industrialization, and away from an agrarian economy, complement the trend. The overall results for the 1970s are likely to be: an end to overtly racist politics, election of more blacks and Republicans to office, a greater role for organized labor, and a return to old Populist issues combined with new issues like consumerism and the environment. As George Wallace's role fades, the historic division between north Alabama progressivism and south Alabama conservatism may reappear. But the picture will be more complicated than it used to be, because black votes will offset, at least in part, the conservatism of south Alabama, and both blacks and Republicans will be playing a larger role in the urban areas, which by virtue of the population shifts will become more and more important in legislative and statewide elections.

When Judge Johnson and his colleagues reapportioned the state house in 1965, for instance, they effected traumatic changes by putting several Black Belt counties, which had had their own representatives, in multicounty districts and then drastically increasing representation for the urban areas. Jefferson County (Birmingham), which had had only seven representatives since 1901, suddenly had 20. Under threat of court action, the legislature screwed up enough courage to reapportion the state senate itself. Jefferson County, which had had only one senator, gained six more; there was also increased representation for the Mobile, Montgomery, and Huntsville areas. The results of the new legislative makeup were quickly apparent as the cities began to get a fairer share of state revenues.

The mid-'60s reapportionment, however, left intact the Alabama custom of electing all the legislators from large urban counties at large. The result in the metropolitan areas was to drown black and Republican votes in a sea of white Democratic votes. (Republicans, holding no primaries, participated in the Democratic primaries, so that those elected were primarily conservatives.) Because it cost so much to run county-wide, poor whites were also underrepresented. In Jefferson County, for instance, 20 of the 27 senators and representatives came from extremely high-income sections. Not a single black and only one Republican was among them. The members of the Birmingham delegation, one legislator said, "squabble a lot among themselves, but when you get down to the voting, they hew the chamber of commerce line."

Acting on behalf of a group of Alabama blacks, the American Civil Liberties Union (whose Southern director had entered the original Alabama reapportionment case, *Reynolds v. Sims*) went back to Judge Johnson's court. The court ordered the legislature to rectify the situation in a new reapportionment plan, but when the legislators failed to devise a satisfactory scheme, the court ordered into effect a radically different plan devised by Dr. David Valinsky, chairman of the department of statistics at the Bernard M. Baruch College of the City University of New York. (One has to note the irony—the shift in a few short years from frozen Black Belt control to a reapportionment plan devised by a professor from New York City.) The Valinsky plan shattered Alabama custom by disregarding county lines, using U.S. Census enumeration districts, a very small unit of population, as its building blocks. The final districts had a population variation of less than 2 percent, and the sensible decision was made to make each three house districts (105 in all) coterminous with one senate district (35 in all).

Under the new plan, blacks expected to elect at least 15 to 20 legislators (compared to the two they elected in 1970). The Republicans, also mired at a level of two representatives (one from Mobile, one from Huntsville), expected to elect 10 with even a minimum effort. Under the new plan, a progressive legislator close to the Wallace administration was quoted as saying, "we will have a meaningful dialogue between diverse groups who have never even talked to one another in the past." The *Alabama Journal* editorialized: "The 'Big Mules' are going to get chased off Goat Hill for good."

The quality of the legislature began to improve after reapportionment. ("It was so bad, it just *had* to improve," one of my Alabama friends said.) The jury is still out on whether a changed membership will correct three age-old problems of the legislature—subservience to the governor of the moment, inefficiency, and horrendous decorum. Since the turn of the century, the governor has been able to use promises and threats to get legislators to pick "his man" as house speaker, and with rare exceptions he has dictated the makeup of major committees in both chambers. In recent years, the senate has grown somewhat more independent, but the subservience of the house continues. In the early '70s, when the Citizens Conference on State Legislatures made its highly embarrassing report on Alabama, an interim committee on legislative moderation came up with 68 recommendations for self-improvement. But under pressure from Wallace, virtually all the major proposals, and especially those that would have given the legislature a greater measure of independence from the executive branch, were voted down. (Veteran legislators grumbled that they needed no advice from outsiders like the CCSL, and suggested that since the Ford Foundation had financed the study in part, it was automatically suspect.)

Even physically, the legislative halls leave a lot to be desired. They were the shoddiest I have seen anywhere in the United States. The only "new" thing in the Capitol building was a pale white marble bust of Lurleen Wallace smiling vacantly in the center of the entrance hallway.

Since the early 1970s, some significant reforms have been effected in the legislative halls. Outsiders—including lobbyists—are no longer allowed on the house and senate floors during debates. Barefoot boys no longer pass up and down the aisles selling peanuts, and legislators are less frequently seen relieving the monotony with nips of hard liquor. And there is less of the knavery and horseplay of the past. (It was not too many years ago, for instance, that one house speaker created a committee with no members, to which handy graveyard he assigned bills he wanted to kill. On another occasion, a legislator was tricked into signing a bill that would have abolished his own county.)

A constitutional reform commission was also at work, creating a new draft that would reduce some of the immense power advantage of the governor over the legislative branch. That imbalance had been made all the worse by the 1970 succession amendment permitting two successive terms for a governor, giving him all the more time, through appointments and the like, to get a stranglehold on state government. The new constitution drafters, headed by a respected probate judge, Conrad Fowler of Shelby County, recommended annual legislative sessions, annual pay for legislators, and a "fail-proof" system to save the legislators from their periodic stalemates on reapportionment. In other areas, a unified judicial system and steps toward reducing the number of statewide elective offices were proposed. The antiquated 1901 constitution had been amended 327 times since its adoption.

In recent decades, the Farm Bureau Federation has been the strongest lobby in the legislature. It controlled about 40 percent of the members until reapportionment, and even after that, Wallace gave the rural legislators the most powerful committee chairmanships. Other lobbies with unusual clout include the utilities, the highway interests, and the Associated Industries of Alabama (a local version of the National Association of Manufacturers). The Alabama League of Municipalities represents urban districts but lacks the strength or imagination to force through much legislation opposed by the rural interests.

One of the Farm Bureau's major interests has been to shape any reform of the Alabama property tax classification system so that rural landowners would get a special break. Reduced in legislative power, the bureau nonetheless showed its political prowess in 1970 by electing its candidate, Jere Beasley, as lieutenant governor (and thus presiding officer of the senate). Beasley bears a striking physical—and political—resemblance to George Wallace. He has Wallace's boxer's build, with dark eyes and brows, and like Wallace, he has had warm relationships with the Ku Klux Klan, has denounced the big-city dailies, and chastized the federal courts for their desegregation rulings. He comes from the same county as Wallace, has scrambled in Wallace-like style to aggrandize power to himself (thus clashing with the master on several occasions), and is a likely future gubernatorial candidate.

The property tax muddle remains one of Alabama's greatest scandals. If the state taxed property at a rate approximating the national average, it could collect almost $300 million more each year for its state and local governments—and perhaps do something more effective about the crying lack of social services in Alabama. The average family on welfare, for instance, is expected to subsist on $55 a month, or $13 for each child—less than a third of what would be required for adequate food, shelter, and clothing. In 1971 the state contrived rules to force 33,000 families off AFDC welfare. One reason may be that AFDC families are mostly black; by contrast, old-age assistance recipients, a predominantly white (and voting) group, are treated better.

Sheer inefficiency plagues the Alabama executive department almost as seriously as it does the legislature. A total of 140 agencies, bureaus, boards, and commissions report directly to the governor. There were reports in 1973 that Wallace, in order to bolster his front for another governorship race, might implement the recommendation of a study committee that suggested reorganizing the state government into five major areas, affording better control by the governor and savings of some $45 million a year.

Alabama's utilities and their rate increases were lambasted by Wallace—and Beasley, his unofficial running mate—in the 1970 campaign, but it remained for Attorney General Baxley to do something about the composition of the popularly elected public service commission, which regulates the rates. Eugene ("Bull") Connor, of Birmingham fame, had been president of the commission and was seeking reelection in 1972. (The great white supremacist had suffered a stroke and was being pushed about in a wheelchair by a black man.) In the first primary, Connor ran 65,000 votes ahead of his closest competitor. Then, a few days before the runoff, Baxley held a press conference to advise his 3.5 million "clients" that in the eight "disgraceful" years Connor had been on the commission, he had done more to raise their utility bills than anyone else. Baxley said Connor was a "tool of the big utilities," and that the hearings held before the commission were "a farce, a fraud, and a charade," because the utility lawyers simply wrote the orders raising rates. "I'll be durned," Baxley said later, "if the people didn't reverse themselves and defeat Connor by a heavy margin." Baxley said it was the accomplishment he was the produest of. (Ten months after his defeat, Connor died.)

As Alabama politics "open up" in the 1970s, a crucial question will be the capacity of the groups previously on the "outs"—Negroes, labor, and Republicans—to take advantage of their new opportunities.

Except, perhaps, for Mississippi, Alabama offered more intransigent resistance to black suffrage than any other state. After the Supreme Court outlawed the white primary in 1944, the state tried to revive the part of the 1901 constitution requiring all would-be voters not only to read and write any article of the U.S. Constitution but also to interpret it for local boards of registrars (which themselves had no training in constitutional law). Almost invariably, whites passed the test while blacks failed. Unimpressed by that obvious fraud, the federal courts disallowed it in 1949, and from that point until 1965 the chief weapon to exclude blacks was a long, complex registration application form. Registrars would usually disallow black people's forms and approve those by white persons. As Donald Strong noted, "the effect of the questionnaire was to disenfranchise Negroes, not illiterates."

Threats and violence, as well as economic reprisals were also used to prevent blacks from voting, and by the early 1960s there were still only 66,000 registered in the entire state. There were two Black Belt counties (Lowndes and Wilcox) where more than 80 percent of the population was black, but not a single black person was registered. In Birmingham, only 10 percent of the voting-age blacks were registered, the lowest level of any major city in the South.

In 1965 Martin Luther King, Jr., decided to focus voting rights demonstrations in Selma, a proud old town in the heart of the Black Belt. Dallas County, of which Selma was the county seat, provided a crystal-clear example of the reasons for black disenfranchisement. Negroes made up 58 percent of the county and represented 51 percent of the voting-age population. But when the Selma campaign began, there were 9,542 white registrants and only 335 Negroes. By law, registration took place only two days a month. An applicant had to fill in more than 50 blanks, write by dictation part of the Constitution, answer four questions on the governmental process, read four passages from the Constitution and answer four questions on them, and sign a loyalty oath to the United States and to Alabama. In the previous two years, the applications of only 12 percent of the 795 Negroes who sought to register had been accepted. Justice Department federal court suits were delayed by Mobile Federal District Judge Daniel H. Thomas, who seemed as opposed to equal rights as Montgomery's Frank M. Johnson was in favor of them.

The Selma demonstrations began with modest marches on the courthouse to demand that the registration office open daily until all Negroes who wanted to vote were registered. As word spread across the country, many whites joined the Negroes, including clergymen of all faiths. Sheriff James G. Clark responded with mass arrests and drove the captured demonstrators on long forced marches during which cattle prods were used to keep them moving. When King organized a march to Montgomery, 45 miles distant, to present grievances to Governor Wallace, Wallace forbade the march. The demonstrators began their walk in defiance of his order, but as they marched over the Edmund Pettus Bridge at Selma, the state troopers set upon them with tear gas and clubs and whips, severely injuring 40. Two weeks later the march finally took place after Judge Johnson, into whose Montgomery federal district the marchers were headed, forbade Wallace to interfere. Twenty-five thousand strong, their numbers swelled by supporters from all over America, the demonstrators walked into the heart of Montgomery—and into American history—on the 25th of March.

The Selma demonstrations took three lives—Jimmie Lee Jackson, a young black demonstrator killed by a police officer; the Rev. James J. Reeb, a white Unitarian minister from Boston who was clubbed by whites on the streets of Selma and died of skull fractures; and Mrs. Viola Liuzzo of Detroit, a white woman murdered by Ku Klux Klansmen as she drove at night along Highway 80, the road through the Black Belt which connects Selma and Montgomery. Klansman Collie Leroy Wilkins was accused of murdering Mrs. Liuzzo and acquitted by an all-white Lowndes County jury whose foreman said: "If Mrs. Liuzzo hadn't been down here where she had no business, doing something she shouldn't have been doing, she wouldn't have been killed." That foreman, Lewis H. McCurdy, was not the type one would call a "redneck"—rather he was a wealthy owner of one of the great plantation farms bordering Highway 80, an Auburn graduate and World War II intelligence captain. He liked to talk paternalistically of "my niggers." Later Wilkins was convicted in Judge Johnson's courtroom of conspiracy to violate the civil rights laws and was sent to prison for 10 years. It was also in Lowndes County, some five months after the march, that Jonathan Daniels, a young seminary student from New Hampshire sent to Alabama by the Episcopal Society for Cultural and Racial Unity, was shot to death while helping with Negro voter registration. A local white deputy sheriff was acquitted of murder charges by an all-white jury.

(Driving Highway 80 a few years later, I found the typical pattern was still that of a little town like Benton—population 115. There were a couple of big, pretentious white folks' houses with large brick fences and then dozens of unpainted shanties with scores of ill-clad black kids swarming about them. In the fields, cotton had given way to soybeans and vast herds of Hereford and Angus cattle. Selma—a much uglier place than I had anticipated—was still trying hard to shake off the ghosts of 1965. One did learn that everyday relations between blacks and whites had improved immensely. Sheriff Clark had been defeated, blacks were voting, and whites even shook hands with blacks on the streets, an unthinkable act a few years before.)

The violence at Selma concerned and outraged the nation. President Johnson appeared before Congress to urge approval of the most sweeping voting rights legislation of the century, ending his presentation with those familiar words, *We Shall Overcome.* Congress quickly passed a bill even broader in some respects than the one the President had proposed. In states and counties where less than half the voting-age adults had voted for President the year before, all literacy tests and similar voter qualification devices were suspended, and the Attorney General was authorized to send in federal voting examiners to make sure that Negroes were actually allowed to register.

The effect in Alabama was swift and momentous. Before the act, 93,000 Negroes had been registered to vote; by the last year of the decade, almost 300,000 were registered, and they represented more than a fifth of the entire state voting pool. Blacks began to win offices in some of the 10 Black Belt counties where they were in the majority and could outvote the whites by sheer weight of numbers. By 1969, instances of actual intimidation of would-be black voters had dwindled to an almost insignificant level, and as we will note later, there were a few white Alabama cities where blacks were actually winning election with the help of whites. In Lowndes County, the juries were integrated, a black sheriff and county clerk were installed in office, and there was a white judge friendly to blacks. The percentage of Negroes registered in Selma and Dallas County was higher than in Harlem.

In most areas, however, blacks faced frustrations in getting their vote to the point where it would reflect their population strength. The onrush of black registrations—to 55 percent of the black voting-age population by the early '70s—was exceeded by an increase of the white level to 78 percent. Black registration levels were held back by deficient voter education and time-ingrained attitudes of civic indifference or deference to whites. Often blacks running for office as Democrats would lead in the first primary but then be defeated by a diehard white majority in the runoffs. Alabama lacked a viable two-party system, or even a clear-cut factional split in the Democratic party that would permit blacks to bargain between the two sides for support.

An example of the perils a moderate Democrat faced, even in the late 1960s, was the fate of Tom Radney, a young state senator who supported Edward M. Kennedy at the 1968 Democratic National Convention and as a result received such hideous threats against his family that he felt obliged to withdraw, temporarily, from politics. I had heard of Radney's story, and a year after the convention I visited him in his law office at Alexander City, 60 miles northeast of Montgomery. Radney pointed out that he was no newcomer to the South, that his Alabama ancestry went back 140 years, and that his great-grandfather had fought for the Confederacy. He had been elected to the state senate in 1966—with substantial black support—and opposed the Wallaces on a number of issues, including the Wallace effort to cut off all state appropriations for Tuskegee Institute. Radney described what had happened to him the year before:

> I was a member of the regular Alabama Democratic delegation to Chicago. We had fought for the Democratic party in this state when it had been tough to fight, and we had wrestled the party machinery from George Wallace.
>
> After I came out for Kennedy at Chicago, a telegram arrived: "Roses are red, violets are blue, two Kennedys are dead, and so are you." It was signed, "The Concerned Citizens of Alabama."
>
> Our maid telephoned and suggested we'd better come home. When we did, I discovered my law partner had closed the office because of abusive telephone calls. The calls followed at our house during the night—what a traitor I was to the state, that my little girl wouldn't be found at her kindergarten class when I picked her up the next day. I'd pick up the phone at 3 A.M. and a voice would say that when I cranked up the car in the morning, I'd be blown to bits. At night I'd take out my gun, look under the bed, search the closets, and then lock the bedroom door.
>
> We have a cabin on a lake about 10 miles away and they knocked holes in my boat and the windows out of the cabin. At our house, they ripped out a name-post in cement in the middle of the night. I'd get in my car and stop at a service station and they'd say, "You nigger-loving son of a bitch, we ain't gonna sell you no gas."
>
> The abuse kept up for about 10 days, and it all got to be a little too much, and I finally said, "If you'll leave me alone, I won't bother you—I'll just get out when my term is over. I'll just quit."
>
> Only then did the threats stop. It had all worried me so much. I'm not a crusader at all. I've never attacked George Wallace—he's a good friend of mine. I just wished he would come into the Democratic party. And I believe the state needs a new spirit. I'm just as Southern, and love the mint juleps and magnolia trees as much as anybody, but I know that can't be anymore, and that we need to move forward without a racist attitude.

As much as Radney might have considered George Wallace his "friend," the fact was—as Radney himself pointed out—that the "roses are red" telegram had been sent to him by a lawyer from his home town who was Wallace's campaign manager in eastern Alabama. It was probably true, as Radney's wife Madoline observed, that Radney was just "10 years ahead of his time." (In 1970 he returned to the political wars in a bid for lieutenant governor, placing third in a field of several candidates.) But with such events fresh in its political experience, Alabama will probably not be immune to reverting to the politics of repression for some time to come.

In the 1970 gubernatorial primary, the bugaboo of the black "bloc vote" was raised by George Wallace. But, as some others point out, it is essentially a phony issue, because whites, when a black candidate or even a racial moderate is on the ballot, often vote just as much as a bloc against that candidate. Where a black bloc vote does appear, it is usually the creation of bigoted white politicians. Bill Baxley commented: "If you have two white candidates, and both of them try to do the right thing, it's been shown in city after city of this state that both candidates will have friends in the black community and there won't be any bloc vote. The bloc vote appears when you have somebody that's run and kicked 'em and tried to keep 'em down every way possible. Then certainly blacks are not going to vote for that candidate. They're only human."

One reaction of blacks to the hostility they felt in the Democratic party was to go the third-party route. An early manifestation of that was the Lowndes County Freedom Organization, otherwise known as the "Black Panther" party. By 1968, the black third party was organized statewide as the National Democratic Party of Alabama (NDPA), headed by a Huntsville dentist, Dr. John Cashin. It was under the NDPA's banner, in 1969 and 1970 elections, that poverty-stricken Greene County, in the Black Belt, became the first black-ruled county since Reconstruction.* The NDPA's major thrust was local rather than statewide, and while the vast majority of its support came from blacks, some whites were included in party office. The NDPA was backed by civil rights groups like SCLC on the theory that since there was no runoff in Alabama general elections, the blacks might win by plurality vote in the general election, rather than being eliminated as customarily happened in Democratic primaries. Also, the often illiterate black voters could vote a straight party ticket under the party's eagle emblem in the general election. That limited the influence of white election officials, who often helped blacks with their ballots in primaries.

The NDPA had hopes of becoming the nationally recognized Democratic party in Alabama, like the predominantly black loyalist faction in Mississippi. State Democratic chairman Robert Vance, however, easily outmaneuvered the NDPA by proving to the national party that he was making a serious (and successful) effort to include black people in the regular party.† On a statewide basis, the NDPA failed to get much support. Some of Cashin's supporters thought he had made a good showing when he ran against Wallace for governor in the 1970 general election and got 125,491 votes (15 percent). In 1972, however, another NDPA candidate, John LeFlore, ran for the U.S. Senate and got only 31,421 votes (3 percent). That election, Vance said, "sounded the death knell for the NDPA. They just lost their credibility. The NDPA candidates for the Senate and Congress just got the stew beat out of 'em—in *black areas*, where their only base is."

Whether Vance is right or not, an ironic fact about the NDPA is that its mere presence made it easier for Vance to put blacks on the state committee and make other approaches to the black community without undercutting his own white support. In historic perspective, the NDPA may appear as a helpful bridge to the day when blacks would get a fairer shake in the Democratic party, not only in organizational matters but in primaries

* The victory in Greene County, which is 75 percent black, did not come easily. In 1968, the white probate judge left the NDPA slate off the ballot in defiance of a federal court order. But ACLU lawyer Charles Morgan, Jr., pressed the case for the NDPA, and Negroes swept a court-ordered special election the following year. The Southern Christian Leadership Conference and other civil rights groups had made Greene County a focus for their rural Alabama organizing activities since the mid-'60s.

† The only time the NDPA caused Vance any serious trouble was in the spring 1972 primary election to pick delegates to the Democratic National Convention. Vance wanted blacks properly elected from a number of districts, so that his delegation to Miami Beach would have enough black faces to insure its being seated. But the NDPA deliberately caused the defeat of two black delegate candidates by telling its followers to shun the Democratic primary.

as well. For while the NDPA attracted a following of fairly militant blacks, the better long-term prospects probably lay with groups like the Alabama Democratic Conference, a group of loyalist black Democrats which showed considerable strength in organizing the black vote in contested primaries.

More than 200,000 Alabama workers are unionized, the highest rate of organization (just over 20 percent of the work force) of any Deep South state. Under leaders like Barney Weeks, the Alabama AFL-CIO president, and Howard Strevel, the Steelworkers chief in the state, the unions dared to take a moderate stand on the race issue when Alabama as a whole was tied up in the tightest racism. Jerome Cooper, a Birmingham attorney with labor clients, said that "the CIO and the Mineworkers began desegregation, putting people of different colors together within the same plants, when the churches, the chambers of commerce, the bar association, the medical association, and the schools didn't let whites and Negroes in together." Despite the resistance of some racist locals, the unions remain in the forefront on race relations today, sponsoring many workshops to improve relations and trying to advance blacks to better positions in the factories. The unions' past history on the race issue is not entirely clean, however. In the 1930s, for instance, the Steelworkers' locals insisted on separate lines of promotion for white and black workers. Negroes were generally given low-paying jobs with little opportunity for promotion. Not until the federal government threatened a cut-off of government contracts in the early 1960s were the lines of promotion merged.

The Steelworkers (Birmingham, Gadsden, and other cities) are the biggest union today, followed by electrical, communications, and mine workers. New organizing efforts in recent years have been the most successful among clothing workers, and the unions' next priority is organization of state, city, and county employees.

None of the past victories came easily, a factor that may explain the relative liberalism of the state's union leaders. For 60 years after the Civil War, Alabama leased out its prison convicts to private industries in a system that Julia Tutwiler, a social reformer of the 1890s, said was one "that combines all the evils of slavery without one of its ameliorating features." Thousands of convicts—mostly blacks but some whites—were put to work in the iron ore mines at Birmingham, laboring 10 or 11 hours a day at dangerous work. This was the way that the Tennessee Coal and Iron Company (later bought out by U.S. Steel) got its start in Alabama. Prisoners were originally leased by the local sheriffs, and when the sheriff ran short of prisoners, he would get a decoy to go out and start a crap game in the woods. The decoy would let the sheriff know where the game would be, and the sheriff would raid the game, turn the decoy loose, and make all the rest prisoners. Finally the state took over the system, making substantial profits for itself out of the leasing. The early union organizing efforts among coal and steel workers were easily thwarted by having the state send in more convict labor, so that strikes would pose no threat to production—or profits. The system was finally ended in the late 1920s, and one of the men instrumental in its final demise was

Hugo Black. As a lawyer in Birmingham from 1909 until the '20s, Black represented many convicts (or families of convicts) who had been killed or injured in the mines.

With convict leasing finally abolished, the unions were at last able—despite fierce company resistance and some pitched battles—to organize most iron ore and steel workers in Alabama in the 1930s. Some owners were so violently opposed to unionization that they sold out rather than accept it. One of these was the DeBardeleben family, which had owned the Alabama Fuel and Iron Company, which operated several coal mines in St. Clair County, near Birmingham. According to a 1942 report by a National Labor Relations Board investigator, the company had resisted unionization with every weapon known to an anti-union employer, including the use of hired thugs, labor spies, mine guards armed with machine guns, dynamite in mining approaches to its property (both on public and company roads), gunfire as a means of greeting organizers, and prostitution of the ballot in the county. Company-paid deputies were used to intimidate voters and mark their ballots, thus assuring the continuation in office of county officers who were in accord with the company's anti-union policy.

Organization of smaller factories, especially textile plants, was less successful than coal and iron. Weeks recited case after case in which plant owners, often in collusion with local and state authorities, used the baldest methods of intimidation to prevent unionization in rural and small-city Alabama. He said the work of civil rights activists in the '60s was actually a boon to labor organizing in rural areas, where local blacks had previously "been scared to death." The local power structures, he said, "got their hands burned" in many of the civil rights cases that went to court, "and this made it possible then for our organizers to go in."

Up to the 1970s, organized labor's effective work in elections had been largely confined to local races in heavily organized cities like Birmingham, Gadsden, and Mobile. Weeks pointed out that the AFL-CIO had been the only statewide organization publicly to back President Johnson against Barry Goldwater in 1964, but many unionists obviously disregarded their leaders' advice as Goldwater carried Alabama in a landslide. By the early '70s, however, as the racial fog lifted in Alabama, organized labor was becoming more and more of a factor in statewide elections. "Barney Weeks," Baxley said, "held out when it was tough to do so, and now he's getting a lot of help."

From a "good government" point of view, it is obvious that Alabama could well use a strong Republican party. The Alabama Republicans themselves crystalized the issue in their 1970 platform, which said: "The need for the competitive and constructive thrust of a two-party system in Alabama is readily apparent. The scandal and failure of the legislature is an indictment of the present 'clubhouse' system of government. Republicans in state government would provide a much needed 'watchdog' and offer constructive alternative programs." The GOP's problem is that up to the present time, most Alabama voters have shown a marked indifference to those issues. When they have voted Republican—for Goldwater in 1964 and Nixon in 1972—it has been because of their rejection of modern-day trends in the national

Democratic party. James E. Jacobson of the Birmingham *News* summed it up well in 1970 when he said that "the Alabama Republican party is still very much an actor in search of a role."

Tagged as the party of Reconstruction, the Republicans had gone into a long decline after 1874. Democratic nominations were "tantamount to election," and the Republicans existed chiefly to pick up scraps of federal patronage when their party controlled the White House. Some Republicanism held on in the northern hill counties, but Alabama lacked the large number of such counties found in eastern Tennessee or western North Carolina. The only Presidential election in decades in which they ran reasonably well was 1928, and that was not their own doing but the result of Senator "Cotton Tom" Heflin's warnings to rural Alabamians that if Al Smith won "the Pope will sail up Mobile Bay in a submarine."

The glimmerings of a real GOP revival were apparent in the 1950s and 1960, when Eisenhower and Nixon almost carried the metropolitan areas where high-income voters, in particular, evidenced a class interest in voting Republican. Then, in 1962, a young attorney, John Grenier, only recently arrived in Alabama from New Orleans, was elected state chairman and proceeded, very rapidly, to build a powerful state organization. The Democrats, by contrast, had never had an organization as such, simply because none seemed necessary. Grenier persuaded a Gadsden oil dealer, James D. Martin, to run against veteran Senator Lister Hill in 1962, and Martin astounded Alabama politicans by sweeping the Black Belt and other bedrock Democratic areas to come within 6,845 votes of defeating Hill. Hill had been in Washington for a long time, and while he had voted against civil rights bills, his association with the national Democrats who were forcing Negro rights advances on the South made him vulnerable to Martin's conservative segregationist appeal. Hill was saved from defeat by the support he got in less racially tense northern Alabama.

The Alabama GOP was transforming itself from a progressive or moderate party, based in the hills country, to a bulwark of segregationist support, based in the Black Belt and some cities. This was symbolized by Barry Goldwater's overwhelming victory in Alabama in 1964. Grenier helped engineer that nomination and won a share of notoriety when he moved into Republican national headquarters in Washington and took Abraham Lincoln's picture down from the wall. On Goldwater's coattails, five Republican Congressmen were elected from Alabama that year. One of them was James Martin, who two years later became the Republicans' first serious gubernatorial nominee of this century. But Martin had not counted on Lurleen Wallace's candidacy, and he got only 31 percent of the vote. "No one doubted," Donald Strong noted, "that Martin was an Alabama segregationist, but it is hard for a rich man's segregationist to defeat a poor man's segregationist."

The Republicans have since been able to hold onto three of the five congressional seats they won in their 1964 breakthrough, but otherwise their pickings have been slim. In the 1968 Presidential race, when Alabamians had the alternative of voting for their own George Wallace, Nixon ran third in the state with a minuscule 14 percent of the vote. The state did go heavily for Nixon over McGovern in 1972, but the senatorial candidacy of Winton M. Blount of Mobile, Nixon's former Postmaster General, backfired badly. Blount ended up with a scant 33 percent of the vote against Senator John Sparkman. One reason was that Sparkman and the Democratic Congressmen—some of whom had not even come home to campaign in 1964—had taken the Republicans seriously and worked hard to maintain their traditional support.

Democratic chairman Vance admits that much of the stigma has been removed from voting Republican in Alabama, but he said that the GOP had really failed to capitalize on its big opportunities in the 1960s and will now have to count on a slow erosion of Democratic strength, not any big breakthroughs. He noted that when the Republicans held their first statewide primary in 1972, only 53,000 people voted in it. "They're really just a country club party," Vance said. "They don't want to deal with what they consider to be the riff-raff. Blount's campaign was symptomatic of the whole difficulty the GOP has. His big deal was to let the people know what a big-shot he was. He could carry the Mountain Brook Country Club and the suburbs of Birmingham nine-to-one, but he just couldn't sell much out in the steel mills."

Objectively, there is no reason the Alabama Republicans should not be able to do a lot better for themselves in the next several years. They have already won the mayoralties in several cities, will automatically pick up seats when the urban counties are subdistricted for legislative elections, and have their greatest relative support in the fastest-growing areas of Alabama—its cities and suburbs. The party, however, suffers from internal divisions which have hampered its growth. Republicans like Martin, for instance, have not hesitated to reach out for John Birch Society support, and they see their future in "out-segging" the Democrats in an appeal to whites of the Black Belt and other ultraconservatives. It is a possibly fruitful course if Alabama remains hung up on the race issue through the '70s—though always subject to being undercut if Wallace-type Democrats win their party's primaries. If Populist and consumer issues become dominant in Alabama, it could be a disastrous strategy. The growing black vote in the Black Belt also makes it tactically questionable. In the Sparkman-Blount race, for instance, the GOP's weakest showing in any region of the state was in the Black Belt.

An alternative strategy is offered by a small group of progressive Republicans, who up to now have been a minority in their own party. They counsel a moderate course on matters affecting race and the economy and say the party should concentrate especially on good government issues, which may become increasingly viable as the educational level rises in Alabama. Birmingham Mayor George Seibels is one Republican who advocates that strategy; another is state representative Bert Nettles, a young Mobile attorney and a director of the Alabama chapter of the L. Q. C. Lamar Society. Nettles would like to see the Republicans do for Alabama what the party, under the late Gov. Winthrop Rockefeller, did for Arkansas. The emphasis, he believes, should be on youth, ending Democratic courthouse domination, and appealing for some share of the Negro vote. Without a sizable proportion of the black vote, Nettles said, "we can't win consistently."

Nettles believes the best chance for GOP advances in the '70s lies in combining city support with the vote from traditional Republican bases in the mountain counties. If the Republicans follow his advice, they will probably build slowly but solidly in the state; if they stick with a segregationist appeal, they may score some dramatic upsets when the Democrats are in disarray, but they will face a dismal long-term future.

The same choice between racism and reason faces the regular Democrats, George Wallace, and in fact all of Alabama's people in the 1970s. Out of the tumult of the past several years has come the opportunity for Alabama to cast off its historic hang-ups and emphasize, as Bill Baxley suggested, the legitimate progressive politics that are also part of its heritage. If he really cares for national power, George Wallace—even if unreconstructed in his heart—might do that too, as his welcome for Teddy Kennedy in 1973 suggested. The changing economy and city life have opened fresh possibilities, and the coalitions between people and power structures in Birmingham and Anniston might spread to all corners of the state. Ethics in government may improve too, if the legislature does not repeal the exceedingly tough conflict-of-interest and financial disclosure law for public officials which it approved in 1973. So there now seems to be a good chance that Alabamians may tuck their battered Confederate cradle into the attic, cast off some of their more malodorous public practices of times past, and start to create some new traditions, more relevant to this century than to the last.

GEORGIA

EMPIRE STATE OF THE SOUTH

"LET'S GET OFF TOBACCO ROAD," Georgia's Governor Ellis Arnall declared at the end of World War II. Georgia has done just that. The postwar gains of the entire South, as it has striven to make economic gains that it took the rest of the nation a century to achieve, have been impressive. In Georgia, they have been nothing short of phenomenal.

At the end of World War II, Georgia had a work force of about one million people, and one out of three of them worked on a farm. The value of manufactured goods in the state was only $500 million a year when Arnall said it was time to get off Tobacco Road; today the annual output is close to $6 *billion*. In terms of value added, the giants are textiles and apparel, wood products (69 percent of the Georgia land area is covered by forests), transportation equipment, chemicals, and food processing. Up in the Appalachian foothills of northern Georgia, two-thirds of America's production of tufted carpets—a major growth industry of recent years—is produced. Textile mills boom in central Georgia, paper mills and mobile home factories are humming in south Georgia, and refined old Savannah prospers on planes and paper. Not once in the past decade has the Georgia unemployment rate been as high as that of the country as a whole.

Georgia has less than a third as many farms as it did a generation ago, but they are producing more than ever: $1.2 billion worth a year in the early 1970s, more than any southeastern state except Florida. Cotton now represents only 3 percent of farm income, and the state dropped the slogan

"Peach State" from its auto tags in 1971—appropriately so, because California and South Carolina now produce more of that furry fruit. A better slogan these days, though it is unlikely to make it onto the license plates, would be "Chicken State"; Georgia leads the 50 states in poultry production.* The other big farm moneymakers are peanuts (again, more than any other state), cattle, and hogs. Average income per farm went up 55 percent between 1964 and 1969 alone. It all seems like a far cry from conditions earlier in this century, when—as John Gunther put it—"farmers in the North got silos, hybrid corn, and mechanization; those in the south got pellegra, hookworm, and malaria."

Then there is the $2 billion that the federal military establishment pumps into Georgia each year—about half for the 15 military bases located there, about half for defense contractors who employed, at last count, some 77,000 workers. (Only five other states—California, Texas, New York, Pennsylvania, and Virginia—get more Defense Department dollars.) And tourism: people coming to visit metropolitan Georgia, or to see places like Stone Mountain, Jekyll Island, Warm Springs—or just on their way to Florida—drop off some $250 million each year.

Expanding industry, agriculture, and tourism are not unique to Georgia, however. Nor are they the only reason that Georgia's per capita income, which was only 50 percent of the national average back in 1929, and 68 percent in 1950, is now up to 86 percent of the U.S. figure—and still climbing. (The per capita income would be much higher already if Georgia industries, capitalizing on a very low rate of unionization, paid their workers better than 79 percent of the national average weekly wage. Only 16 percent of the nonfarm labor force is unionized—42nd ranking among the states.)

The real reason for Georgia's modern rise and regional preeminence—and the reason an old sobriquet, Empire State of the South, fits better than ever—can be summed up in one word: Atlanta. Here is one of the most vibrant cities of the latter 20th century, at once a symbol and the heartbeat of the new Southern economy.

Ever since the Civil War, of course, Atlanta has been a key city of the Southeast, simply because its strategic location made it the major distribution point for the region's agrarian economy. But in the present day, according to Philip Hammer, one of the South's leading economists, Atlanta's position is based on more than its location (though that is still vital). "It is based rather," according to Hammer, "upon a new set of essential functions in an increasingly complex industrial structure—the 'central work' functions of business, industry, finance and government that cannot be duplicated anywhere else. No other city in the region occupies or duplicates Atlanta's role as the spark plug, catalyst, generator, service center, financier, clearing house, trading point, policy maker and pace setter for the region's new economy."

* Thousands of Georgia farmers deserted the cotton patch for the chicken house when they found that the boll weevil and mechanization made cotton raising uneconomic, especially on limited acreages. The moderate Georgia climate favors year-round production of chickens with only a minimum investment for shelter—a strong attraction for farmers on small family-sized units with managerial skills. And though the South is not a strong feed-grain-producing area, the development of cheap water transportation along the Tennessee Valley and large-scale railroad transport facilities helped to overcome cost disadvantages of importing feed grains from the Midwest.

He might have added that no other Southern city comes close to Atlanta as a center of intellectual ferment, black leadership, and the civil rights movement. Singly, no one of these factors might mean too much; taken together, they effect a kind of critical mass that makes Atlanta the premier city of the South and a force to be reckoned with nationally. Atlanta *Constitution* editor Reg Murphy suggested that Atlanta today has something of the glitter and sophistication that F. Scott Fitzgerald saw in the New York of the 1920s. Like New York, some Southerners sense a brittle, frightening quality in the new Atlanta—yet are drawn irresistibly to it.

No matter what measure one draws from the statistical handbag, Atlanta's preeminence is illustrated. The rail lines of the South still converge there, but so do the interstate routes and the air routes; in fact, there is only one busier airport in the entire United States, Chicago's O'Hare. There was an old joke in railroading days about Southerners agreeing that whether they went to heaven or hell, they would have to pass through Atlanta; now it has been revamped with a new punch line in which a Southerner, asked whether he will go "down" or "up" after death, replies: "I don't know, but whichever way it is, I know I'll have to change planes in Atlanta." On this side of the Great Divide, all Southern capitalists turn now to Atlanta for money; its banks are indeed among the most aggressive in the entire United States, and it is no longer necessary to run to New York for big financing. Atlantans like to point out that 440 of the 500 biggest industrial firms on *Fortune*'s list have offices in Atlanta. The city is also the nerve center of federal government offices in the South. Retailing, professional services, light manufacturing, and construction have all boomed in postwar Atlanta. The downtown skyline has been entirely remade in the past years, and will be remade again in the next decades. In the 1960s, the tax base of the central business district doubled; it is expected to grow half again as big before 1980.

All of this advance in America's modern-day "Cinderella city" is now taken for granted by many. But it was not automatically predictable a few years ago. The biggest praise that John Gunther could work up for Atlanta's economy was to note that "its pace is almost as quick as, say, that of Rochester or Akron." George Sessions Perry wrote up Atlanta in a 1945 *Saturday Evening Post* article and said its chief claims to fame were (1) the "now defunct" Ku Klux Klan, (2) Coca-Cola, (3) grand-slamming Bobby Jones, and (4) Margaret Mitchell's *Gone with the Wind*. Atlanta, Perry said, "is a hot-bread, boiled-greens, fried-chicken-and-cream-gravy town," and "her downtown business district is less attractive than Birmingham's."

Gunther and Perry could not have known, of course, that architect-developers like John Portman would build some of America's most architecturally adventuresome buildings in postwar Atlanta, that the city was about to produce two generations of remarkable economic hustlers, and that the traveler of later years would even find some spots of fine international cuisine there. Nor could they have dreamed that future visitors would discover Yankees on Peachtree Street, Negroes in City Hall, hippies in the parks, and a social scene one reporter called "the sauciest, swingingest" in America with

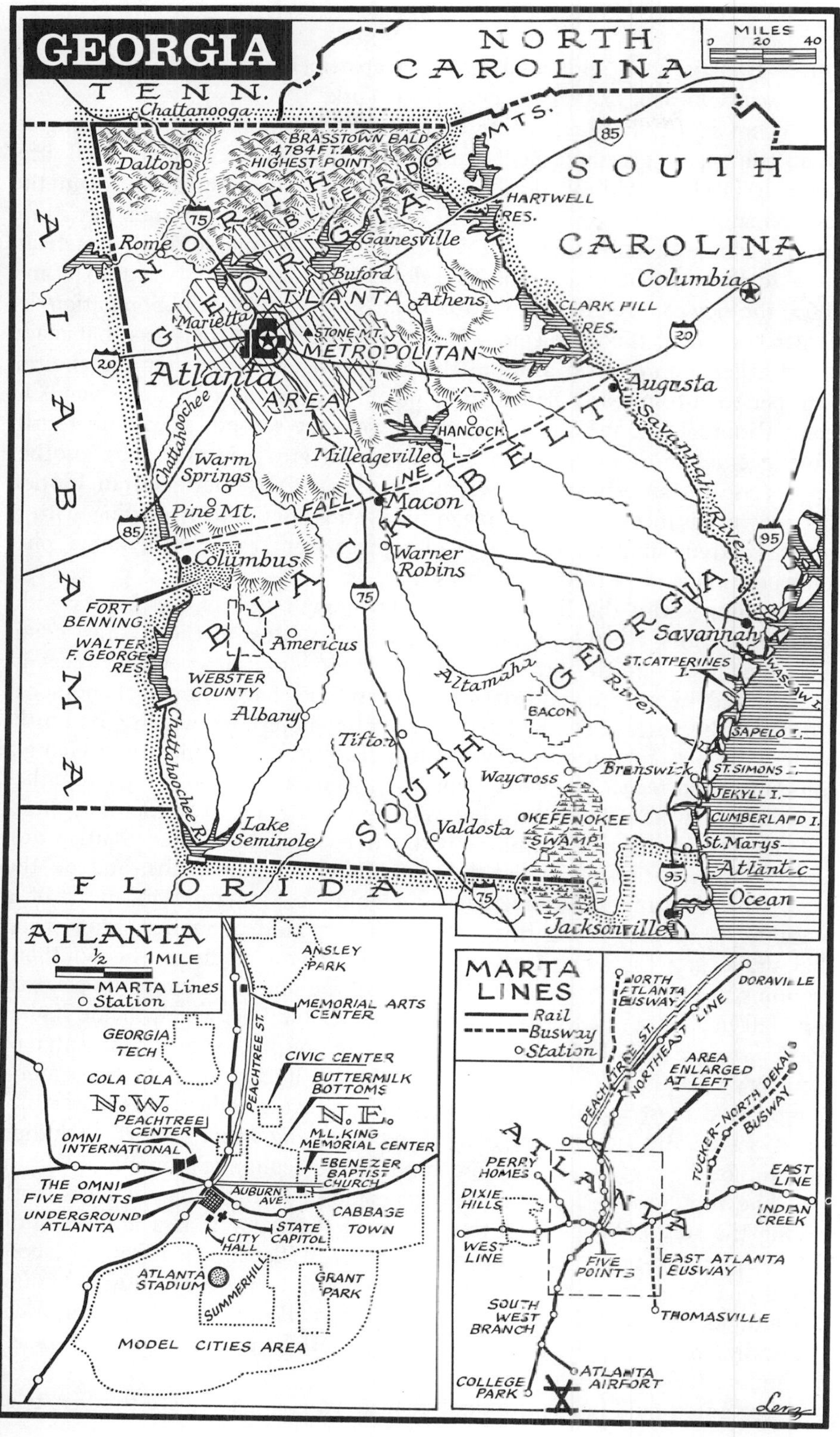
GEORGIA
NORTH CAROLINA
MILES
0 20 40
TENN.
Chattanooga
BRASSTOWN BALD 4784 FT. HIGHEST POINT
BLUE RIDGE MTS.
85
SOUTH CAROLINA
Dalton
75
NORTH GEORGIA
HARTWELL RES.
Rome
Gainesville
Buford
Columbia
ATLANTA
Athens
CLARK HILL RES.
Marietta
STONE MT.
METROPOLITAN
20
20
Atlanta
AREA
Augusta
Chattahoochee
HANCOCK
Savannah River
Warm Springs
Milledgeville
FALL LINE
Pine Mt.
Macon
BLACK BELT
85
95
Columbus
Warner Robins
FORT BENNING
75
WALTER F. GEORGE RES.
Americus
Savannah
WEBSTER COUNTY
Altamaha River
ST. CATHERINES I.
WASSAW I.
BACON
Albany
SOUTH GEORGIA
SAPELO I.
Chattahoochee R.
Tifton
Waycross
Brunswick
ST. SIMONS I.
JEKYLL I.
CUMBERLAND I.
Lake Seminole
Valdosta
OKEFENOKEE SWAMP
St. Marys
95
Atlantic Ocean
FLORIDA
75
Jacksonville
ALABAMA
ATLANTA
0 ½ 1 MILE
MARTA Lines
Station
ANSLEY PARK
MEMORIAL ARTS CENTER
GEORGIA TECH
PEACHTREE ST.
CIVIC CENTER
COLA COLA
BUTTERMILK BOTTOMS
N.W.
N.E.
PEACHTREE CENTER
OMNI INTERNATIONAL
M.L. KING MEMORIAL CENTER
EBENEZER BAPTIST CHURCH
THE OMNI
FIVE POINTS
AUBURN AVE.
UNDERGROUND ATLANTA
STATE CAPITOL
CABBAGE TOWN
CITY HALL
ATLANTA STADIUM
SUMMERHILL
GRANT PARK
MODEL CITIES AREA
MARTA LINES
Rail
Busway
Station
NORTH ATLANTA BUSWAY
PEACHTREE ST.
NORTHEAST LINE
DORAVILLE
AREA ENLARGED AT LEFT
TUCKER-NORTH DEKALB BUSWAY
ATLANTA
PERRY HOMES
DIXIE HILLS
EAST LINE
INDIAN CREEK
WEST LINE
FIVE POINTS
EAST ATLANTA BUSWAY
SOUTH WEST BRANCH
THOMASVILLE
ATLANTA AIRPORT
COLLEGE PARK
Lenz

"more grooving guys, girls, and grass per apartment than Los Angeles, San Francisco, Chicago, or perhaps even New York."

There are, to be sure, plenty of warts on Atlanta's body civic, ranging from crime and gruesome traffic problems to a school system tilted irretrievably black by white flight. We will return to all of them later. But the fact remains that by any commonly accepted standard, Atlanta has "progressed" mightily and made itself one of the most desirable of all American cities to live in. Consider population alone, for instance. Between 1940 and 1960, the five-county Atlanta metropolitan area increased in population by 82 percent, about the same gain—Philip Hammer noted then—as that made by all other metropolitan areas in the Southeast combined. During the 20-year period, he noted, Atlanta had "pulled sharply away" from New Orleans, Birmingham, and Memphis, which were the second, third, and fourth ranking cities in 1940. Since 1960, the Atlanta area has grown by another 43 percent (to an estimated 1,450,000 in 1973). Only metropolitan Florida has shown advances of greater magnitude, and there one is dealing with a growth pattern imposed by hoards of retirees from the North, not a phenomenon indigenous to the South as a region.

Atlanta is also the linchpin of a vital growth line of the New South, which runs along the foothills of the Blue Ridge. Most of the Georgia counties immediately north and south of Interstates 85 and 20, which meet in Atlanta and bisect the state on an east-west line, have shown phenomenal growth in the postwar era. So have the counties along I-75, which goes northwesterly from Atlanta toward Chattanooga. Practically the only other Georgia counties which registered strong population gains after World War II either contained or were next door to big military installations. On the east, Georgia's new growth corridor connects with the bustling North and South Carolina Piedmont cities of Charlotte, Spartanburg, and Greenville, and on the west, with Alabama's Birmingham. It would be premature to speak of a megalopolis forming along this line, but it is a kind of metropolitan string that draws growth to itself and promises to be the focus of the Southern economy in the decades to come. In Georgia, the line has thoroughly eclipsed the "fall line" cities of Macon, Augusta, and Columbus, which divide higher north Georgia and the broad coastal plain of south Georgia. The water of Georgia's rivers begins to drop rapidly at the fall line, so that the cities along it prospered most in the early decades of the textile industry, as water provided power. But now power is more portable and other factors, including the skills of the work force, are more important to economic growth.

The 1970 Census found 4,589,575 people in Georgia, a ranking of 16th among the states. About 30 percent were in the Atlanta area and an additional 24 percent in five other metropolitan areas (Savannah, Albany, Macon, Columbus, Augusta, and suburban Chattanooga, Tennessee), plus the counties around the medium-sized cities of Athens, Rome, and Valdosta. Economically and culturally, these cities and suburbs are "where the action is" in modern Georgia.

But one should not forget rural-small town Georgia, where the life styles and attitudes of the Old South hold on more tenaciously Forty-six percent of the state's people still live in these areas, which one observer has in fact summed up as "static Georgia" as opposed to "dynamic Georgia" of the larger cities and suburbs. Politically, rural Georgia divides into three regions: north Georgia, an Appalachian territory with few blacks; the black belt, which cuts across central and southwestern Georgia, including territory both above and below the fall line and many counties with a black majority; and finally south Georgia, where whites form a heavier majority than in the black belt.

We will have more to say about the cities and rural stretches later on, but first it is time to see what has been happening in the public life of Georgia.

Politics: Constancy and Upheaval

The years since 1960 have brought a simply incredible change in Georgia politics. A state that had *never* failed to go Democratic for President has twice voted Republican and once for George Wallace. The county unit system, Georgia's "rotten borough system in excelsis," has been discarded as a way of nominating statewide officials. Malapportionment in the legislature has also fallen in the face of federal court orders. Negroes have begun to vote in massive numbers, not only in the cities but also in the black belt and south Georgia. Even Senator Herman Talmadge, the son of arch-segregationist "Old Gene" (Eugene) Talmadge of red galluses fame, the same Herman Talmadge who campaigned as a racist in his early years and once warned there were not enough troops in the country to force Georgia whites to go to school with Negroes, now looks for black votes.

Yet for all the change, much of the basic schism that rent Georgia for a century remains. On the one side there is rural, "wool-hat" Georgia, the "pore white trash," as it used to be called. "The lower status whites," the University of Georgia's Numan Bartley wrote in an illuminating little book called *From Thurmond to Wallace*, "are simply Georgia's most politically conservative people. Racist in social attitudes, fundamentalist in religion, provincial in outlook, [they] have tended to place their reliance upon tradition and folk custom." These folk were the defenders of the county unit system and white supremacy; they ruled the rural counties of the black belt and south Georgia when those counties ruled Georgia. When Ole Gene lived, they were cruelly exploited by the Talmadge philosophy of "Keep 'em poor, keep 'em honest"; today the politics of destitution has softened, but in the voting booth, lower-class whites are still likely to let race prejudice edge out their basic economic interests.

The other side of the ancient schism were the most affluent whites of Atlanta and some of the other major cities. Theirs was a *genteel* conservatism that abhorred Talmadge-like rabblerousing; on the question of race, the more affluent whites never looked for integration, but they did have a feeling of *noblesse oblige* toward Negroes, and they were not rabid white supremacists. And in fact, after the white primary was overthrown by federal court order in 1946 and some Negroes (especially in the cities) began to vote, the affluent whites and the blacks often voted together—a strange coalition of the richest and the poorest against the rural and working-class whites.

The last few years have brought some changes in the geographic strengths of both coalitions. Many of the wool hats have moved to the cities and poorer suburbs, bringing their old attitudes with them. The townsmen of north Georgia, who were quite lukewarm about old-brand Talmadgeism, have begun to vote more like the other rural conservatives. And the growing black vote, Bartley noted, has tempered, but not basically altered, the conservative domination of politics in the black belt.

At the same time, many of the affluent whites have moved to comfortable suburbs as the cities have become blacker. Quite a few of them have become Republicans. Theirs is a politics of businesslike progressivism: repelled by a Lester Maddox, for instance, but strong for a Richard Nixon.

The only dependably liberal voters of Georgia are its blacks: because they want to erase the vestiges of segregation, and because they want more government social welfare programs.

One of the anomalies of modern politics was how long this very conservative state remained Democratic in Presidential voting—and then, when the change came, how complete it was. This line of figures, showing the Democratic share of the vote for President, tells the story:

1932	*1936*	*1940*	*1944*	*1948*	*1952*	*1956*	*1960*	*1964*	*1968*	*1972*
92%	87%	85%	82%	61%	70%	66%	63%	46%	27%	25%

Party loyalty, pure and simple, has to have been the reason that the Democrats won so easily and so long. Even in 1948, when Strom Thurmond from neighboring South Carolina was running for President on the States Rights ticket and appealing to the regional-race sentiments dear to many Georgians' hearts, he got only 20 percent of the state vote. Democrat John Kennedy swept Georgia with one of the biggest votes he got in any state, even though Georgia is 98 percent Protestant (with Baptists dominating)—presumably inhospitable ground for a Roman Catholic candidate. Breakdowns of the Presidential vote through 1960 showed rural and small-town Georgia, including the black belt, giving about three-quarters of its vote to the Democrat.

But as Numan Bartley noted, "the tendency for Georgia's most conservative voters in state politics to be the most liberal voters in national politics was a political absurdity that could not forever endure." The straw that broke the camel's back was the support the Kennedy-Johnson administration gave to the civil rights movement of the 1960s. In 1964, Barry Goldwater became the first Republican ever to carry Georgia, and he did it by sweeping the south and central Georgia lowlands, the bastions of white supremacy. Goldwater also won most of the urban counties. But he lost in Atlanta, where blacks—who had amazingly given 58 percent of their vote to the GOP ticket in 1960—switched heavily to the Democrats. Many Georgia whites still voted Democratic in 1964, but the new thrust in Presidential voting—black voters supporting national Democratic candidates, white voters rejecting the Democratic party—was clearly established. In 1968 and 1972, the vote for Humphrey and McGovern coincided very closely with the percentage of black voters. In 1972, Nixon took Georgia in a 75 percent landslide. The sharp setbacks for the Democratic candidates reflected the anger of Georgia Democrats about the way the national party was being run. In 1968, the Democratic National Convention in Chicago insisted that the regular Georgia delegation —handpicked by Governor Maddox under the extremely undemocratic delegate selection process always employed in Georgia—would have to share their votes with a biracial group headed by state representative Julian Bond. The regular delegation walked out in protest. In 1972, Georgia Democrats conformed to the party's new reform rules and chose their delegates by state convention after democratically constituted Congressional district caucuses. But the party regulars were asleep at the switch when the grass roots caucuses were held—and often packed—by liberal students, labor, and blacks.*

If the national Democrats continue to nominate candidates most Georgians view as ultraliberal, and if the national Republican party remains subtly racist, as it has been since 1964, the GOP advantage in Presidential elections may endure for years to come. But the Republicans would be foolhardy if they thought their advantage rested on any affinity for the Grand Old Party. In 1968, when Georgians had the alternative of George Wallace, they gave him three votes to every two for Richard Nixon. The reason for Wallace's big lead had been spelled out by Roy V. Harris, Wallace's Georgia campaign manager: "When you get down to it, there's . . . only one issue, and you spell it n-i-g-g-e-r."

Georgia's voting in state and local elections—as opposed to those for President—is a much more complex matter and requires a flashback to earlier times to make the present real. V. O. Key depicted Georgia politics in the 1930s and '40s as being under the "rule of the rustics," a hegemony that had its roots in rural revolt against the Northern financiers and Georgia big-city interests who had tried to build an industrialized "New South," championed by Atlanta editor Henry Grady, in the years after the Civil War. The "New South" movement, however, ignored the interests of Georgia's plain dirt farmers, making a political counterattack inevitable.

The first of the rustic leaders was Thomas E. Watson, the son of a once wealthy slaveholding family made destitute by the Civil War. My friend Tom Watson Brown, an Atlanta attorney who is one of his descendants, claims that Watson was "the only true Georgia intellectual from the Civil War to now." Watson won his fame as a criminal lawyer, developed gut instincts for rebellion and reform, and entered politics as an agrarian reformer. He served terms in the legislature and Congress, inveighed against the railroads and banks and high interest rates, and first proposed the idea of rural free delivery of mail. Georgia's ruling Bourbon Democrats used gerrymandering and fraud to oust Watson from office, and he twice ran for President as candidate

* It is safe to say that if there had been an open primary in the state, Wallace would have swept it. Starting in 1976, in fact, Georgia will have a Presidential preference primary, scheduled right after New Hampshire's and Florida's in the third week of March.

of the Populist Party. Disillusioned by his defeats, Watson began to hurl invective at Catholics, Negroes, Jews, and Socialists, and became a champion of the Ku Klux Klan. The white primary was one of his monuments; he saw it as a way to prevent the selling and manipulation of Negro votes by the Bourbons. Another monument was the county unit system, which Watson thought would curb what he regarded as the corrupt influence of big-city politicians and also prevent the kind of chicanery that had deprived him of his seat in Congress.

The county unit system, used extralegally by the Georgia Democratic party for several years and then frozen into law in 1917, gave the state a miniaturized version of the electoral college, in this case for use in nominating governors and other statewide officials and members of Congress. Each county was given a certain number of votes, generally reflecting its number of seats in the state house of representatives. The candidate who got a plurality in the county won its unit votes; a majority of unit votes nominated. As long as Georgia was predominantly rural, the system was reasonably related to the popular vote. But the growth of the cities and suburbs made it, in the words of political scientist Joseph L. Bernd, "an increasingly grotesque caricature of a democratic representational system." It exacerbated rural-urban tensions by rewarding the politician who appealed to every rural fear and prejudice. Corruption appeared, too, as the bosses or "courthouse crowds" of the little counties manipulated vote totals. Editor Ralph McGill of the Atlanta *Constitution* once charged that 60 of the state's 159 counties were for sale to the highest bidder. The dice were so loaded in favor of the rural areas that many popular-vote winners were denied Democratic nominations —which were then tantamount to election. The ultimate disparity was reached in 1960, when the 556,326 people then living in Fulton County (Atlanta) had the same unit vote strength as those of three small rural counties with 6,980 inhabitants among them—a disparity of almost 100–1.

The greatest beneficiary of the county unit system was Georgia's prime 20th-century demagogue, Eugene Talmadge. He was so effective in galvanizing support of the rustics that he won four terms as governor, and there was only one year between 1926 and 1946 when he was not a candidate for some office in the Democratic primary. Georgia politics in those years divided fairly simply into pro-Talmadge and anti-Talmadge groups. Old Gene often boasted that he did not want to carry a county with a streetcar, and he once pastured a cow on the lawn of the governor's mansion because Mrs. Talmadge was dissatisfied with the milk being delivered to her door in big, slick Atlanta. Talmadge also appealed to the "forgotten" rural white voters by defending segregation and lambasting the corporations. But, as Key noted, "Talmadge, like many professed champions of the forgotten man, in the showdown turned up on the side of the fellows who did the forgetting." He fought New Deal social welfare programs, because he resented federal control over the programs in Georgia. He was for a balanced budget, a low tax rate, and minimal regulation of private enterprise. Thus while the rustics gave him his votes, Talmadge often got his financial support from Atlanta bankers and corporation executives who learned that he was "safe."

Occasionally, Talmadge or his candidate would be defeated. One rebel who succeeded most spectacularly was Ellis Arnall, who had been a Talmadge loyalist as a young state legislator but then rose up to win the governorship as the anti-Talmadge candidate in 1942. Arnall made historic strides in modernizing the climate of Georgia, including a leadership role in ending the poll tax and lowering the voting age to 18.

Old Gene celebrated his Last Hurrah in 1946 in a campaign that stressed white supremacy and won him a victory based on unit votes—even though the moderate candidate backed by Arnall actually got more popular votes. But Talmadge died before inauguration day, and there ensued Georgia's famous "two governors" controversy, a battle vividly described in Gunther's *Inside U.S.A.* Herman Talmadge, then a young man of 33 anxious to don his daddy's mantle, lost out in his effort to be declared the governor, but he returned two years later to win a clear-cut victory of both unit and popular votes, and stayed on as governor until 1955. Talmadge-backed candidates, including S. Ernest Vandiver, a moderate, and Marvin Griffin, a prominent segregationist-spoils politician, held the governorship until the early 1960s. Men friendly enough to him have held the office since.

Herman Talmadge, unlike his father, used the governorship to make Georgia into a modern, progressive state. He imposed a statewide 3 percent sales tax and used the money to spend more on education ($452 million) than had been spent in all the years since the start of the state's public school system in 1871 ($408 million). New industries were attracted, some 13,000 miles of new roads helped to get Georgia "out of the mud," and he presided over big advances in mental health and agricultural research. But while he proved his prowess as an executive, Talmadge never lost sight of the race issue as a way to ensure his political future. He experimented with a registration system designed to prevent 80 percent of Georgia's blacks from voting, abandoning it only when it appeared the educational requirements for voting would disenfranchise more "wool hats" than blacks. He tried to reinstate the poll tax to frustrate Negro bloc-voting, and in 1952 almost succeeded in having the unit vote system extended to cover general elections as well as primaries. "The Atlanta bloc vote crowd," he warned, "wants to run Georgia with the Negro vote, which would cancel out the combined will of every other county in the state. The entire principle of segregation is tied closely to the county unit system. A governor who owed his election solely to the bloc vote would not raise his hand to keep Negroes out of white schools and colleges."

As time went on, Talmadge cut back on overt rabblerousing and learned to use television. "I use a calm, deliberate, rational, reasonable approach on TV," he said in the mid-1950s. "The viewer sitting in the quiet comfort of his home is not subject to the emotional hysteria of the stump." (One wonders if Old Gene could ever have made that transformation, though like Herman, he was a college-educated man and put on a lot of his rustic airs just to please the rabble.) What remained constant from one Talmadge era to the next was the dependence on the infrastructure of courthouse bosses, sheriffs, county commissioners, and tax assessors in the multitudinous counties of the state. Herman Talmadge has an amazing memory and once estimated he knew 30,000 voters on a first-name basis. The "Talmadge machine" remains remarkably powerful in Georgia, even though the intervention of the federal courts and Congress have struck down so many of the pillars on which Talmadgeism was thought to rest—the county unit system, legislative malapportionment, and the disenfranchisement of blacks.

The opening shot against Georgia's *ancien régime* was fired by the U.S. Supreme Court on March 26, 1962, in its momentous decision in the Tennessee apportionment case, *Baker v. Carr*. By declaring that citizens of a state denied equal protection of the laws could seek and find redress in the courts, even in areas once declared "political" and thus beyond the reach of judicial relief, the Justices cut away in a single stroke the rationale used over the years to deny court review of Georgia's county unit vote system. On the very day that the *Baker* decision was handed down, a new challenge to the county unit vote scheme was filed in Atlanta. And only two months later, the federal court there declared that Georgia must henceforth nominate candidates on a direct vote basis. A year later the Supreme Court would uphold that decision (*Gray v. Sanders*). In the 8–1 decision, written by Justice William O. Douglas, the Court laid down an historic principle, much more specific than the *Baker* opinion:

> The concept of "we the people" under the Constitution visualizes no preferred class of voters but equality among those who meet the basic qualifications. The concept of political equality from the Declaration of Independence to Lincoln's Gettysburg Address, to the 15th, 17th and 19th Amendments can mean only one thing—one person, one vote.

The slogan "one man, one vote," adapted from the *Gray* opinion, soon became the rallying cry of forces backing straight population-based apportionment in all state legislatures. Georgia's own legislative districts, which had been so skewed to rural dominance that just over a fifth of the state's voters could elect a majority in both the state senate and house, was forced to the "one man, one vote" principle by the mid-1960s.

In 1962, the demise of the county unit vote made it possible for Georgia voters, for the first time since 1908, to nominate a governor on a direct vote basis. The choice was between former Governor Marvin Griffin, a rowdy white supremacist who seemed to embody all the values of the past, and Carl E. Sanders, a young state senator who symbolized the businesslike moderation of a new day in Georgia. There was also an ethics issue because Griffin, as the state's chief executive from 1955 to 1959, had proven himself a typical spoils politician who let his henchmen dip freely into the public treasury. With city votes counting as much as country votes, Sanders launched a media-type campaign geared much more strongly to urban areas than any in recent history. The reform impetus of that year was so strong that his 58-percent vote would even have given him victory under the old system, because so many rural areas (especially in north Georgia) could not stomach Griffin.

The growth of black voting in Georgia started earlier, and was more gradual, than in states like Mississippi or Alabama, where Negro voting was almost totally repressed before the Voting Rights Act of 1965 opened the floodgates. By the same token, while the late 1950s and early '60s brought sporadic racial outbursts to Georgia—some beatings, church bombings, even killings—they lacked the magnitude of violence in Alabama or Mississippi. "One important reason," reporter Jack Nelson said, was that "Georgia left the segregation-at-all-costs road" to those other states. It was not that white Georgians liked the civil rights movement a bit more than Alabamians or Mississippians. But Georgia had, perhaps, a touch more old South gentility. It had an aspiring national city whose leaders were determined to shake the Georgia cracker image. And it had two governors, elected at strategic moments in time, who were under obligation to many of their supporters to practice moderation. The corruption issue, rather than the race issue, helped both win elections—Ernest Vandiver in 1958, at the end of four odoriferous years under Griffin, and Sanders four years after that. Vandiver had used the slogan that "no, not one" Negro would enter Georgia's white schools, but desegregation began while he was in office. Faced in 1961 with the stern choice of closing the University of Georgia or permitting at least token integration there, Vandiver opted for the token integration. Unless Georgia faced up to some integration, he told the legislature, the issue, "like a cancerous growth will devour progress—consuming all in its path—pitting friend against friend—demoralizing all that is good—stifling the economic growth of the state." *

In 1940, only 2 percent of Georgia's voting age blacks had been registered to vote, but the figure was up to 20 percent a year after the white primary was struck down in 1946. During the late '40s and early '50s the forces of white supremacy used violence, intimidation, and purges of voting rolls to hold down black voting. It was 1960 before the black enrollment figure even approached 30 percent, and even then most of it was in the cities and larger towns. But in 1962–64, there was a sharp increase to 44 percent. Then, with federal legislation to back it up, black registration began to roll in rural areas as well. By 1968 the statewide figure was 56 percent, and in 1972 it was 64 percent. The arrival of blacks as a major political factor helped to stimulate increased white enrollment; actually three times more white than black voters were added during the 1960s. But that did not prevent blacks from electing their first state senator, Leroy Johnson of Atlanta, in 1962; in the wake of federally ordered reapportionment, they elected another 10 black legislators by 1966, and 16 in 1972. Today, forced segregation at political rallies in Georgia is virtually unknown, and most serious candidates for office treat blacks with respect.

Any talk of black peoples' political advance in Georgia has to be tempered by the phenomenon of Lester Maddox, the feisty little politician who first won high visibility brandishing ax handles—and, on one occasion, even a pistol—to scare away unwanted black customers from his flourishing Pickrick chicken restaurant in Atlanta in the early 1960s. Maddox's election as governor in 1967 confounded not only Georgia's blacks—Martin Luther

* Charlayne Hunter, the harassed and worried looking girl who was one of the first two blacks to integrate the University of Georgia, said she did it because she wanted to study journalism, and no black college in Georgia then had a school of journalism. In 1972, she was named the first Harlem bureau chief of the New York *Times*.

King, Jr., said it made him "ashamed to be a Georgian"—but also moderate white leaders like Atlanta's Mayor Ivan Allen, Jr., who said when Maddox won: "The seal of the great State of Georgia lies tarnished." But Maddox is more than a crude racist, as the title of Bruce Galphin's charming book about the 1966 election, *The Riddle of Lester Maddox*, would suggest. Note carefully Maddox's answer when I asked him in 1972 if he still considered himself a segregationist:

> Yes, sir. Every person, black and white, who has enough racial pride and integrity and love for his own and other races and wants to preserve them is a segregationist. Those who force racial integration on others are the real racists. . . . Forced segregation is cruel and criminal and wrong. But so is forced integration.

And how did Maddox apply his segregationist beliefs to his administration as governor? His reply:

> The people who came to the mansion, or to my office—it didn't make any difference to me whether they were black or white. I was their governor. I conducted myself in a way that had nothing to do with race. I told department heads to hire people on their merits only, and there were more black appointments than under all other governors in the history of the state.

Maddox's willingness to appoint blacks to draft boards and state jobs was acknowledged by Leroy Johnson, a Negro state senator from Atlanta. But Maddox made all his black appointments without consulting the black community, Johnson said, and muddied the waters with his incessant rhetoric against school desegregation—urging school boards, in effect, to disobey the law. "Maddox is like a Jersey cow," Johnson said. "He gives a good bucket of milk and then kicks it over."

Any moderate side to Lester Maddox was well hidden when he ran for governor. He was seen as the high priest of segregation, a fundamentalist in religion, a champion of the free enterprise system and the sanctity of private property, and a fervent believer in honesty in government. He had minimal campaign financing and scarcely any formal organization. White Georgians were alarmed by freedom riders and civil rights marchers and big city riots and the laws for the benefit of blacks pouring out of Washington, and Maddox was the perfect lightning rod for their frustrations.

Good breaks, however, had a lot to do with Maddox's election. Former Governor Vandiver had been planning to run, but his announcement speech turned into a declaration of noncandidacy when he suffered a "minor" heart attack on his way to Atlanta to throw his hat in the ring. The party regulars were stunned, and Senator Talmadge, in one of the few political boners of a long career, even indicated he might come home to run. But he decided to stay in Washington, and in a six-way first primary race, Maddox got 24 percent. That was enough to put Maddox in the runoff against Ellis Arnall, returning to the political wars after a 20-year hiatus. Arnall had once been a giant killer—in 1942 he had defeated Eugene Talmadge for governor, the only man ever to do that. But in 1966, Arnall ran an unbelievably anachronistic campaign. He pitched his campaign against the bad guys who precipitated the Depression, but time had made his message irrelevant. So had the methods of campaigning. On television, Arnall showed a balding head and dark visage and came across as blustery and arrogant. As Galphin put it, "The oratorical style that wowed 'em when he beat 'ol Gene Talmadge sounded like a parody on TV." And where Arnall thought he was up-to-date, in calling for racial moderation, Atlanta style, he was out of step with plain Georgia people. Maddox won by 54 percent, sweeping the rural areas and carrying the nonaffluent white city precints.

It was not enough for Maddox to win the primary. In that fall of 1966, he faced the first serious Republican gubernatorial opponent of modern times, Howard H. ("Bo") Callaway, scion of the Callaway Gardens family that had made its fortune in textiles. A former Democrat, Callaway switched to the GOP in 1964 and rode into a U.S. House seat on Barry Goldwater's coattails. In Congress, Callaway established the reputation of being the most conservative Representative from his state—"a feat of no mean magnitude," Numan Bartley commented, "considering the ideological orientation of the Georgia congressional delegation." Callaway launched a lavish but inefficient campaign; his plan was to castigate Arnall, who he thought would be his opponent, as a left-winger. But when Maddox won the Democratic nomination, Callaway's plan to ride into office on Goldwater's formula—winning both racist-rural Georgia and the increasingly Republican big cities—was thrown awry. Callaway was able to get the city vote, but the rustics' hearts belonged to Maddox.* Callaway, in fact, showed as much rigidity in campaign planning as he did in ideology. He refused to meet with Democratic liberals or give Negroes, who abhorred Maddox, the least reason to vote for him. Several white and black liberals organized a write-in campaign for Arnall. When the returns were in, Callaway led by 3,039 votes out of almost a million cast. But the Arnall write-in vote of about 50,000 deprived him of an absolute majority, and the Georgia constitution required an absolute majority for election, with the legislature electing the governor if there was none.† The federal courts refused to intervene, and the heavily Democratic legislature proceeded to elect Maddox with dispatch if not enthusiasm.

Maddox would have liked to run for reelection as governor in 1970, but the state constitution forbade him from succeeding himself, and he settled for the lieutenant governorship instead. Carl Sanders had been the winter book favorite to win in 1970. He had a creditable reputation from his earlier term as governor, ample financing, and the backing of "establishment" leaders like Atlanta banker Mills Lane and state highway director Jim L. Gillis.‡

* Maddox also got help from the county courthouse Democrats, who were quietly urged to back him by Senator Talmadge.

† This troublesome provision has since been amended to require a runoff election between the top two candidates if neither receives a majority.

‡ Gillis's career was a classic story of a politician who wheeled and dealed and survived as a force to be reckoned with in his state for more than 30 years. The political boss of rural Treutlen County in central Georgia, he backed President Roosevelt in his unsuccessful effort to purge Senator Walter F. George in 1938. As a reward, FDR called him to Warm Springs and gave him control of all the federal money and patronage in Georgia until World War II. Gillis managed four governors' campaigns, including Eugene Talmadge's last, and helped Herman Talmadge get elected to the Senate. He helped Lester Maddox win election in the legislature and later told Margaret Shannon of the Atlanta papers, "I ran Mr. Maddox's business for him." He was state highway director under Herman Talmadge, Vandiver, Sanders, and Maddox, and boasted in an interview I had with him that "we built the best road system in the United States." One of his aides said: "Mr. Jim gives the politicians the regular roads they're entitled to, and makes them think he's doing a favor for them." Gillis presided over construction of most of the interstate highway system in Georgia, but his real love was the farm-

But, as two of Sanders' campaign aides later wrote, his 1970 campaign was too cool and lofty; he refused to use the race issue or even show much sympathy for the middle- and lower-class whites who had taken the brunt of the social and economic changes of the '60s; he insisted on flying in jet aircraft, wearing electric-blue suits, and living in a luxurious Atlanta townhouse; and he ended up projecting the image of a rich, slick, arrogant politician. Average voters often commented: "Carl Sanders is too good for us." Jim Gillis's son had a telling comment on the school integration issue, which Sanders ignored in his campaign: "The school thing is like a funeral. The family knows you can't bring the body [a segregated system] back to life, but they want you there holding their hands."

The man who beat Sanders was state senator Jimmy Carter, a wealthy south Georgia peanut planter in his mid-forties who made 1,800 speeches and met 600,000 Georgians in the process of four years of campaigning. While Sanders spent his time meeting businessmen and other community influentials, Carter was more often seen on the factory shift lines at five o'clock in the morning and again at midnight. Carter did not resort to the red hot oratory of a George Wallace, but he did let the people know his sympathies by criticizing school busing and racial balances and "the establishment"—of which he said Sanders was the ultimate candidate. In Carter's own eyes, he is a kind of mild-mannered modern Populist in the mode of Governors West of South Carolina and Askew of Florida, or former Governor Scott of North Carolina. In his grass-roots campaign, he tried to get across the idea that he wanted to speak for "the formerly silent people who are not economic or political or social leaders." The wealthy, Carter noted, are not as affected by the things the state does—in schools, welfare, prisons, or highways—as the less affluent. "Maddox feels this too," Carter said in an interview; "he comes from a poor background, and though my family has been in Georgia for 220 years, I was the first one who ever finished high school." Carter is a tall, prematurely graying, soft-spoken man with a toothy smile a bit like that of the Kennedys; apparently the voters accepted him as a fresh face, a man just enough like themselves to deserve election. He beat Sanders with 59 percent of the runoff primary vote and in the general election defeated Republican Hal Suit, an Atlanta television personality, with the same percentage.

The essentially conservative Democratic orientation of Georgia was proven in 1972, when Sam Nunn, a bespectacled 34-year-old great-nephew of the late House veteran Carl Vinson, won in the face of the Nixon landslide. Nunn first defeated David H. Gambrell, a wealthy Carter backer and political moderate whom the governor had appointed to fill the Senate seat vacated by the death of the late Richard B. Russell. Then he triumphed in the general election against Republican Congressman Fletcher Thompson of Atlanta, an archconservative who had deluged Georgia with his denunciation of school busing, Jane Fonda's antiwar statements in Hanoi, and the "liberal" Atlanta

to-market, personal-type roads that are the mother's milk of rural politics. His two sons have been in politics, too—one as president of the county commissioners association, another as a major leader of the state senate. Despite his support of Sanders, Jim Gillis had no taste for big-city ways. "The people in the state, whatever the Atlanta papers are for, they're against," he said.

newspapers. Nunn, like Maddox and Carter before him, managed to get close to the little people by commiserating with them over "forced busing" and "welfare loafers"—issues akin to Thompson's. But he had an immense advantage in being a card-carrying Democrat. Senator Talmadge entered the fray on Nunn's behalf, warning that if Republicans took control of the Senate, Southern Democrats would lose their committee chairmanships—and Talmadge himself would no longer be chairman of the Agriculture Committee. Talmadge got the courthouse crews to work for Nunn, and Maddox arranged an endorsement of him by George Wallace. The Nixon landslide failed to harm Democrats running for the Senate and other offices because the legislature, in the wake of Goldwater's 1964 victory, had separated the Presidential ticket from all other candidates. And blacks gave Nunn more than 80 percent of their vote, because they thought Thompson would be an even worse alternative. Nunn won by 94,000 votes—about 54 percent. But without the overwhelming support of blacks, who number 450,000 or 22 percent of the Georgia registration total, he would doubtless have lost.

It is worth noting that an unvarnished, fire-and-brimstone segregationist, Savannah attorney J. B. Stoner, came to grief in his runs for statewide office in 1970 and 1972. Stoner had at one time represented James Earl Ray, the convicted slayer of Martin Luther King, Jr., and said he hated "niggers, Jews, mongrels" and liberals of any stripe. In 1970 he assailed Jimmy Carter in particular as "a nigger lover of the worst sort." After some of Stoner's anti-Semitic remarks, Maddox walked off the platform and refused to appear with him. In one of his races (for governor), Stoner got 2.2 percent of the Democratic primary vote; in another (for Senator), he got 5.7 percent.

What is the moral of all this for an aspiring Georgia Democrat? Probably something like this: One must have a common touch, and relate to the country folk and lower-class whites in the cities too. Being (or at least appearing) slick and wealthy is dangerous. Some Wallaceite lines about the evils of welfare and school busing are a good idea. One dare not be (as Ellis Arnall was) an avowedly enthusiastic "national Democrat." By the same token, a candidacy pitched to Atlanta is inadvisable; the three biggest counties there (Cobb, DeKalb, and Fulton) represent less than a third of the statewide vote, and voters across Georgia have most frequently turned down candidates associated with the big city.* But averting blatant racism and keeping some lines out to the black community are advisable, especially in a general election. Then it is that a Republican might get you if you don't watch out.

Offering advice to a Republican is a shade more difficult, because no Georgia Republican, unless one wants to count Callaway in 1966, has won a statewide election in this century. Part of the problem is a weak base. Although the party is well financed and efficiently organized in urban areas, and has actually won major elections in cities like Macon, Columbus, and Savannah, it remains pitifully weak in the town and rural counties, where a

* These included Arnall in 1966, Sanders in 1970, and Gambrell in 1972—plus Republicans Suit in 1970 and Thompson in 1972. The three big Atlanta-area counties cast 24.4 percent of the statewide vote in 1960, and 30.5 percent in 1972.

kind of stigma is still attached to Republicanism. The Republicans' own state chairman, Bob Shaw of Atlanta, defined the dilemma when he said that many Georgians "see Republicans as people from the North, carpetbaggers who burn Atlanta, march to the sea, pillage crops, harm the women, represent big money interests, and bring on depressions. Yet this could not be farther from the truth." In 1970 there was a hotly contested GOP governorship primary between Suit and James L. Bentley, an ex-Talmadgeite comptroller general who had switched to the Republican party in a fanfare of publicity in 1968. But the total Republican primary vote exceeded 1,000 in only 13 counties; there were 99 counties with fewer than 100 Republican votes, and one county, Quitman, recorded exactly one GOP vote. There is no registration by party in Georgia, so almost everyone votes in the Democratic primary, where the fun is; building up GOP loyalty under those circumstances is not easy.

The other Republican problem relates to what might be called the soul of the party of Lincoln or, more practically, how to get a share of the big, growing black vote in Georgia. Until the early 1960s, the Georgia Republicans took a moderate line on race matters and even had Negro chairmen in a number of counties. Their leader was Robert Snodgrass of Atlanta, a man who had been a classmate of Thomas Dewey at the University of Michigan and wanted to build a party with black as well as white support. Eisenhower in 1956, and Nixon in his 1960 incarnation, received many Negro votes to back up the large contingents of urban, affluent whites who were moving toward the GOP.

But it was in Atlanta in 1961 that Barry Goldwater made his famous formulation of a lily-white Southern strategy: "We're not going to get the Negro vote as a bloc in 1964 or 1968, and we ought to go hunting where the ducks are." By the spring of 1964, Snodgrass' moderate leadership in Georgia was purged by the Goldwater movement. Two archconservatives, Joe Tribble and Roscoe Pickett, were picked to be the new Republican state chairman and national committeemen. Negroes and their white allies were literally read out of the party at that spring's Republican state convention. The immediate payoff, as we noted earlier, was Goldwater's historic victory in Georgia, in which the GOP traded off its black vote for the support of hundreds of thousands of conservative rural people who had never voted Republican before in their lives.

Since then, the Georgia GOP has tried to build a majority out of affluent city dwellers and suburbanites, who like its economic conservatism, and country and city whites, who see the new GOP as the new party of the white man. Compared to where they were before, the Republicans have made noteworthy gains; but if they hope to become an equal of the Democrats, they have a long way to go. Until 1964, they had no seat whatever on the 10-man U.S. House delegation; since then they have had one or two seats in each Congress. Before the 1964 election, Republicans held five of the 260-odd seats in the Georgia General Assembly; by 1968 that figure had risen to 32, and in 1972 it was up to 37. But that still represented only 16 percent of the total seats.

There now seems little doubt that the Republicans can hold, for the foreseeable future, big margins in several major urban counties. In 1970, for instance, Suit carried Fulton County (Atlanta) with 56 percent of the vote, and neighboring DeKalb, which is heavily white and upper-class Republican, by a margin of 2–1. But unless the Republicans can break the hold of the Talmadgeites and other conservative Democrats on the rural vote, or find a genuine way to attract many Negroes back into the party, their prospects in Georgia may remain bleak for years to come. The Republicans' problem is that they are trying to be like the Bourbon Democrats of old, offering the people a dish of negativisms covered by racist gravy. But this is an era in which the voters—be they blacks looking for social welfare programs, or country whites who like Talmadge's rural development programs and Maddox's mental health and penal reforms—simply expect more of their government.

It may have been a hopeful sign when the Republicans, at their 1973 convention, elected the first black man to their party's executive committee in modern times and also approved a platform calling for strong environmental protection, consumer protection, and tax reform laws. But at the same time they refused to endorse a statewide kindergarten program. Many Georgians still associate the GOP with the "rich" landowner image of "Bo" Callaway, whom President Nixon appointed Secretary of the Army.

Governing Georgia

Georgia's state government has advanced by leaps and bounds since World War II—but still has a lot of improving to do.

Two examples, reorganization of the executive department and the state constitution, illustrate the dichotomy. When Jimmy Carter took office in 1971, Georgia had a confusing welter of 253 separate boards, agencies, and commissions that cried out for streamlining and more businesslike management procedures. Not since 1931, when Richard Russell was governor, had a thorough reorganization been effected. Carter made it his number one priority, and while his administration was still on its honeymoon he got the legislature—over the bitter opposition of Lt. Gov. Lester Maddox—to approve a bill giving the governor authority to reorganize the state government from stem to stern. The final plan was to go into effect barring a quick veto by both the senate and house.

To write the reorganization plan, in what Carter called "the most thorough and complete study ever conducted of a state government," some 100 bright young executives were recruited from private life and the state government itself. Half the $200,000 cost, ironically, was supplied by a federal government grant. And 45 of the reorganization whiz kids were lent by Georgia businesses and industries (Coca-Cola, Sears, Delta Airlines, the utilities, and so on), firms which continued to pay their salaries while they worked for the state government. The reorganization team went to work with enthusiasm and a sense of purpose, its efforts aided by the national accounting and management consultant firm, Arthur Andersen and Company. That firm made available its national partner for state government reorganization, George Kaiser, who had worked previously on a model plan in Wisconsin.

The reorganization scheme was completed in less than a year and the legislature let almost all of it become law. Functions were consolidated into 22 budgeted state agencies, each agency's own table of organization was made more rational, and increased central control was established over electronic data processing, purchasing, printing, personnel recruitment, and the investment of state funds. State planning and budgeting, long thought to be incompatible, were combined into a single office. A new department of natural resources combined, except for forestry, the disparate agencies working in that field; likewise the agencies dealing with physical and mental health, welfare, vocational rehabilitation and the like were put under the umbrella of a single department of human resources.

In the long run, Carter expected the reorganization plan to save at least $50 million a year and make Georgia government far more efficient than it had been in the past.

On the other hand, Georgia has been unable to redo its 1954 constitution, a document that looked quite modern when Ellis Arnall got it enacted but has proven, in practice, to be an incredible mishmash of provisions that belong in a constitution and those that belong in statutes. About 700 amendments, good and bad alike, have been added to it, and they keep on coming. Governor Sanders tried to get a new document written, but his effort aborted, and Carter put constitutional reform on the back burner in order to get reorganization approved. A Georgia governor has little chance to get more than one major program approved, since he uses up his political credits in his first legislative sessions and is then a lame duck because of the one-term limitation.

For decades, Georgia governors exercised an inordinate amount of power vis-à-vis the state legislature. A precedent was set in the 1930s when Eugene Talmadge, as governor, seized control of the state coffers when the legislature adjourned in a huff without providing a budget. Old Gene declared a state of emergency, took over the treasury—first under martial law—and got his coup legitimized by the courts. From then on, the legislature seemed like a puppet of the governor. In 1951 Herman Talmadge put through Georgia's first sales tax and, as two Georgia newsmen later noted, "dispensed millions of the new tax dollars from his hip pocket, allowing the legislators little or no control over the money they helped raise." Successors like Marvin Griffin used their free-wheeling fiscal powers to club enemies and reward friends. But the irate legislators began in 1962 to pass laws reasserting their power over the state purse strings. By the time Lester Maddox was governor, his discretionary budget was only $2 million—less than one of his predecessors could spend on the fieldhouse at the University of Georgia.

Another cornerstone of gubernatorial dominance was the custom by which each new governor designated the speaker of the house. The house speaker appoints all committees and usually can make or break any bill before the legislature. As long as he was strictly the governor's man, a really independent legislature was impossible. In fact, there was a "hot line" telephone to the governor's office behind the speaker's podium, through which the executive's instructions could be instantly relayed. But that system was broken in 1967 because of the unusual circumstances of the disputed Maddox-Callaway election. There simply *wasn't* any governor to handpick the speaker, and the legislators caucused and decided on their own man for the post. That was the year the legislature picked the governor, instead of the governor picking the speaker. George L. Smith II of rural Emmanuel County, elected speaker, has stayed in the post since, exercising calm, strong leadership. He must be considered the real architect of the newly powerful and independent legislature.

Governor Maddox lacked the skill to control Smith, even if he had wanted to; in fact Maddox had little grasp of the legislative process, and a very limited ability to wheel and deal. "Legislation," Maddox said, "was *way* down the list" of his concerns as governor "because we've got more laws now than we know what to do with." His real concern, Maddox said, was to assert the ancient principle that "government belongs to the people" and "to put honesty and efficiency and morality into state government." In his own eyes, Maddox most certainly accomplished that. "We were able," he said, "to have more people visit in the governor's office and mansion—black and white, rich and poor, young and old, weak and strong, rural and urban—than in the rest of the 20th century." That meant, Maddox said, while people "normally just see the outside of government, we insisted on them seeing the inside too." How much they learned from their walkthroughs of the governor's office or mansion might, of course, be doubted. The reason may be that Maddox *himself* was often in the dark as to what was happening in state government; for the most part the agencies and departments ran themselves, without inquiry from Maddox; as editor Jack Spalding of the Atlanta *Journal* once said, "Lester Maddox has successfully demonstrated that Georgia does not need a governor." As a politician, however, Maddox demonstrated continued mastery, balancing his ultraconservative rhetoric with some progressive programs and turning his legislative defeats into psychological victories for the "little man." He remained what he had been at the start—a supersalesman but not an administrator.

Governor Carter told me he had campaigned for a strong, independent governor *and* a strong, independent legislature—"so now we have both." His audacious reorganization scheme was clearly a gubernatorial victory of immense proportions, but in other areas the legislators have exercised their own will and judgment, regardless of his wishes.

One thing is clear: the Georgia legislature is unlikely soon again to tolerate the gubernatorial dominance that began with the Talmadges or to let governors pick its leaders. The rise of legislative power has come at a fortuitous time—when the legislature, for the first time in its history, has acquired the leadership and quality of membership necessary for sound and progressive governing. The Citizens Conference on State Legislatures in 1971 gave Georgia an ignominious rating of 45th among the states on tests of its ability "to perform in a functional, accountable, informed, independent, and representative manner." * But, in fact, Georgia political writer Robert Coram noted in 1972, the Georgia legislature in recent years "has striven valiantly to upgrade itself, to become more professional, more deserving of public approbation and confidence."

Reapportionment, forced on Georgia by the federal courts during the 1960s, has been a powerful catalyst for change. Before, Georgia had one of the most egregious malapportionments in the country. The smallest senate district in 1961 had 13,050 people, the largest 556,326. House districts ranged from 1,876 to 185,422 in population, and the rural grip on both houses was absolute. But after reapportionment, the heavily urbanized areas went from 6 to 57 seats in the house and from 1 to 21 seats in the senate. The average age dropped from 51 to 35 years; in the house the number of college-educated members rose from 69 to 85. Blacks went from 1 seat to 11, Republicans from 2 to 23. Before reapportionment, the legislature generally gave urban areas the back of its hand; the problems that got official attention and treatment then were often those of the cotton or peanut or peach farmers—a classic example of the use of a public forum to echo private problems. Today that picture is radically changed. Urban problems—municipal revenues and taxes, local government powers, the regulation of business and labor—get talked about, and often something is tried to solve them.

When the first wave of urban legislators arrived in the statehouse, they lacked cohesion or leadership, and many retired after a term or two to make money in their private businesses. Now more of them are sticking, some outstanding leaders are appearing among them, and they are succeeding in passing major bills like the authorization of the quite powerful Atlanta Regional Commission. The leadership of the legislature is still heavily in the downstate area, but even it is becoming more sophisticated about statewide, and urban, problems. The improvement is most notable in the house, under George Smith's leadership. Although they lack adequate staff, the house members now study bills in more depth, the quality of debate has improved, and less legislation is killed capriciously to prove independence from the administration. By contrast, the senate, presided over by lieutenant governor Lester Maddox in the 1971–74 period, lacks quality leadership and tends to be the graveyard of much excellently conceived legislation. Among the progressive bills killed there in recent years were measures for land use control, annexation of a part of northern Fulton County by Atlanta, consumer protection, and protection of the Chattahoochee River from ecologically insensitive developers. "Maddox's negative psychosis is not rural," one veteran observer said. "It's just noncontemporary."

The arrival of Negro members in the 1960s was a real shock for many rural legislators, especially those from black belt and south Georgia. Leroy

* Specifically, the conference said Georgia should have annual sessions of at least 90 days (in place of the restrictive 40–45 day limits presently imposed by the state constitution); reduce the size of its house, now fourth largest in the U.S. to no more than 100 members (presently there are 180, down from a previous high of 205); increase legislative salaries; reduce its unwieldy number of committees and exercise control over its multitudinous interim committees; provide a decent amount of office space for legislators; and end the power of the lieutenant governor to appoint committee chairmen and members in the senate.

Johnson, the first black legislator of the century, recalled his experiences in his first session (1963):

> Many of the white senators thought all hell would break loose, that the seats would crumble, the ceiling would fall because a Negro was seated. Some of them just stared and looked at me. People were reluctant to befriend me as a senator. At just about the end of the first session, one of the rural legislators walked up to me just as we were walking out of the cloakroom and said, "Senator, you probably know I've never spoken to you since the session started. I want to shake your hand and say I respect you as a senator. I'm from south Georgia and I believe in segregation. But I've watched you during this whole session and you've conducted your business and I just want you to know that I respect you as an individual." Well, I thought it took a great deal of guts for him to do that; truly during the whole session he had not spoken one word to me.

During that same session, Johnson said, he and a fellow senator of Lebanese extraction from Fulton County "decided that on this particular day we would integrate the Senate cafeteria, where no Negro had ever eaten before." As the two men started toward the cafeteria, Johnson's white colleague stopped group after group of Senators and said, "Senators, Leroy and I are having lunch, come on and have lunch with us." And each one would reply, "Well, no thanks, I'm not hungry." That sequence was repeated three or four times until the two men reached the cafeteria door, when yet another white senator refused to join them, saying he "wasn't eating that day." Johnson's colleague then turned to him and said, "Leroy, you're the greatest thing since Metrecal."

As time wore on, Johnson said, it became common for him to eat lunch and socialize with many senators. A key turning point of his legislative career occurred in the education committee, where he first served. At one committee meeting, the author of a bill was trying to get it cleared for the floor. The issue was deadlocked, 7–7, when Johnson arrived late. "As I walked in, senators jumped over and asked me to vote with them," Johnson said. "Some were men who had refused to speak with me before. But they saw a vote, not a Negro, walking through the door. I said I had two bills pending I wanted to get out of committee. It was the ancient *quid pro quo* of legislative politics. I made my deal, and then my vote got the stalled bill out of committee. Since then, I've been able to get my own bills through."

Johnson said there were both advantages and disadvantages to being one of the few black senators. An advantage was that he was the president of the Georgia Association of Citizens' Democratic Clubs, a veteran black political organization with chapters in more than 100 counties. When bills vital to black interests came up, Johnson could contact Negro club members in cities like Macon, Augusta, Savannah, and Albany, where the black vote makes the difference, and get them to contact their legislators immediately. One bill that passed after that kind of pressure—pressure some senators said they didn't appreciate—was a teacher tenure measure to protect black teachers who were being fired summarily by local superintendents when they backed integration efforts. The pressures on a black legislator, Johnson said, can come from many sides and be hard to accommodate at one time:

As a black man, I represent blacks from all over Georgia. From south or middle Georgia, blacks would write me as *their* senator. But I'm elected from Atlanta, and have a special responsibility there.

Then there's the problem of militants snapping at your heels. Your position in the black community has to take on a veneer of militancy. But at the same time, in the senate, you have to be willing to negotiate, to compromise, in order to be effective.

The last gasp of virulent racism in the Georgia legislature occurred in 1966 when the house, by a vote of 184 to 12, barred Julian Bond from taking his seat because he had endorsed a rather headstrong antiwar statement by the Student Nonviolent Coordinating Committee (SNCC). The pacifism of Bond's statement was alleged to undermine the Selective Service Act and thus aid enemies of the United States. But there was little likelihood that such a *cause célèbre* would have been made of the affair if Bond had not been a black man. The U.S. Supreme Court ruled that Bond's First Amendment rights had been violated, and he was seated.

Six years later, in the same Georgia house that had tried to bar Julian Bond, a bill was debated that would prohibit public school board members from sitting on the boards of private schools. This was the legislative way of dealing with mounting instances of use of public school property by the so-called segregation academies. A few years before, it would have been political suicide for a white legislator, especially from rural Georgia, to support such a bill. But now Tom Murphy, a conservative legislator who had been Maddox's floor leader, rose to support the measure. It was time to take a stand on "the moral issue" posed by the threat to public education in Georgia, Murphy said. The bill passed overwhelmingly.

Today the Georgia legislature has a strong black caucus. Julian Bond was the man who organized it, and he calls the caucus his "most significant contribution." Jimmy Carter's 1971 inaugural address showed how far the race-related rhetoric of Georgia had come: "I say to you quite frankly that the time for racial discrimination is over. Our people have already made this major and difficult decision," Carter said. "No poor, rural, weak, or black person should ever have to bear the additional burden of being deprived of the opportunity for an education, a job, or simple justice." The musical accompaniment to the inauguration was also a clue to a new day in Georgia. It included the U.S. Navy Band playing *Dixie*, and the all-black choir from Morris Brown College in Atlanta singing the *Battle Hymn of the Republic*.

Even after 1972, when Jimmy Carter decided it was politically wise to assail "massive school busing" and to cotton up to George Wallace, the basic commitment of his inaugural remained. Black employment in state government more than doubled in his first two years in office, and blacks were appointed to a number of important second-tier administrative positions. Early policy board appointments of blacks included pardons and parole, public safety (with supervision of police), and real estate. The latter appointment facilitated the first open-housing regulations in Georgia's history. Carter promised that by the end of his term there would be black representation on *all* policymaking boards of state government. It may still be years until blacks are represented in relation to their share of the state population (25.9 percent), but the break with centuries of consciously discriminatory practice is striking.

Despite Georgia's economic advances, its per capita outlays for local schools, for higher education, for highways, and for welfare have continued to lag well below the national averages. No program has been more controversial than welfare; when a team of Atlanta *Constitution* reporters crisscrossed Georgia in the fall of 1972, they found that "overwhelmingly, welfare is the one issue that sticks in the craw of Georgia voters." A milk truck driver in Manchester said, "I see all these people on welfare sitting on their porch with their feet on the banister while I'm out working and sweating for a living. I just don't like it." A Savannah businessman offered the typical prescription: "I say put the niggers to work." The statistics show that the number of people receiving welfare has risen rapidly in the last years (until a leveling off in 1972). But the recipients are overwhelmingly dependent children, and the welfare rolls contain a substantial portion of whites. Under Georgia law, it is actually impossible for a working-age man to receive welfare unless he is blind or totally disabled. The maximum aid to families with dependent children is $154 a month, and the average in 1970 was only $101, compared to a nationwide figure of $187.

Lester Maddox's most famous appointment may have been that of William Burson as state welfare director. Burson, a 40-year-old ex-Talmadge and Sanders aide, became a crusader in his job, confronting rebellious county commissioners with facts about the poor and initiating suits to prevent Congress from putting a freeze on welfare payments to children whose fathers are not in their homes. Helpless children would suffer even more than they suffered already, Burson warned. "While it is true that starvation is a very effective and very permanent cure for illegitimacy, it is not one that I believe any responsible or sensitive citizen will advocate or support." Burson also declared a "war on hunger" with the goal of establishing surplus commodity or food stamp programs in all Georgia counties. When some banks refused to redeem food stamps bought in local groceries, Burson said he was "sickened" to see bankers, "who are protected in their wealth by the guarantees of our federal government, take advantage of their positions of power by trying to promote their prejudices." "The real truth," Burson said, is "exploitation of cheap labor, . . . politics, . . . and the unspoken decision to put no stumbling block in the pathway of rural-to-urban migration."

Some of Maddox's supporters waxed apoplectic over Burson and his policies. But Maddox—himself capable of demagoguery about the welfare issue—stuck with his appointee. "Burson is a man of talent, abilities, and compassion," Maddox told me later. "You wouldn't want a person directing that department who's against helping folks." Burson, interestingly, was able to run for and win election as state treasurer in 1970, though he did badly when he tried for the U.S. Senate in 1972.

By the time Carter became governor, the climate had changed sufficiently so that his welfare director, Thomas Parham, could abstain from browbeating recalcitrant county leaders. Instead, he concentrated on getting local churches, chambers of commerce, and county commissions to set up a variety of federally assisted programs—day care, job training, and job placement—to help poor people break the welfare dependency syndrome. Many local leaders took real political risks to start up the new programs, only to see the ground cut out from beneath them when the Nixon administration began to impound funds for their type of project. (The national administration's impoundments and budget cuts enraged Carter, as they did many other governors. Carter assailed federal revenue sharing as "a cruel hoax," saying that after Georgia, "with great fanfare," was given $36.6 million a year of shared funds, it immediately lost $57 million under two titles of the Social Security Act and faced a direct loss of $174 million under President Nixon's fiscal year 1974 budget. "The poor," Carter said, "are being robbed to pay for the revenue sharing fund.")

A new degree of professionalism was apparent in Georgia state government in the early 1970s. In addition to his reorganization effort, for instance, Carter boasted about the "zero-based" budgeting he inaugurated and called it "the best budget system in the nation." He explained:

> We take the state government and divide it up into 11,000 small pieces or functions. And we let the person responsible for carrying out that function analyze his own job on a one-sheet form. He says what his duties are, how many people he has working for him now, and in the past, and expects in the future, and how he could perform his job better, and how well he could perform at various levels of budgeting—beginning with a 15 percent reduction. We then take all those "decision packages," as we call them, put them together with each department head's knowledge, and let him arrange them in an order of priority, balancing old programs with new proposals. He then submits them to me in a private conference. Later on we determine how far down each list of priorities we can go, and then we submit the whole as a package to the General Assembly. It's the only way I know that you can control a bureaucracy.

The Georgia state budget has almost quadrupled in the past decade—from an annual rate of $465 million in 1963–64 to $1.1 billion in 1970–71 (Maddox's last budget) to $1.7 billion for 1973–74.* But the increases are only now beginning to chip away at the accumulated social neglect of the state's history. Public education is the best example of the problem. Until recent times, the ruling circles of Georgia viewed education as a social refinement for the few, while farm families resisted full school years because children were needed in the fields. It was 1937 before a seven-month school year was required, along with free textbooks. A nine-month school year had to wait until 1949. One-teacher schools, most of which were black, were not replaced until the late 1950s. There was no provision for adult basic education until 1965.

Some grim figures show the fruits of all this. In 1960 the Census found

* The rapid budget increases make it difficult to say just how Georgia's tax effort to meet its problems compares with the other states. At the start of the 1970s, Georgia's combined state and local taxes amounted, on a per capita basis, to $312 a year. That was less than all but eight other states, and only 73 percent of the U.S. average. The lion's share of Georgia state government income is from the inherently regressive sales tax, but the rate has been held at 3 percent—just where Herman Talmadge pegged it in 1951. There are corporate and progressive personal income taxes that account for just over a quarter of the state's tax collections.

that 4.5 percent of adult Georgians were totally illiterate—one of the highest rates in the country. A decade later, there were still hundreds of thousands of Georgians who had not gone beyond the fifth grade in school and thus could be classified as functional illiterates, totally unfit for a modern industrial economy. In the late 1960s, 28 percent of Georgia's young men were failing Selective Service mental tests, more than twice the national rate. The high school dropout rate was the worst of all 50 states. The median education level ranked 45th among the states.

As the 1970s began, Georgia was doing fairly well, compared to the rest of the country, in vocational-technical training, in school lunch programs, and in school building. But teacher salaries still ranked only 38th in the country, the prevailing notion among some legislators being that as long as Georgia paid more than Alabama and Mississippi, it was doing all right. Per pupil expenditures were 39th—only 76 percent of the national average. The high-school dropout rate was exceptionally high. And there were no public kindergartens, so that each September thousands of children started first grade unequipped for the world of words and ideas and learning that confronted them.

Georgia has an outstanding state superintendent of schools, Jack P. Nix, who has been calling for years for sharply increased expenditures to give the state an adequate educational system. But it took some words in Jimmy Carter's inaugural address to throw the issue into sharp relief:

> Our people are our most precious possession. We cannot afford to waste the talents and abilities given by God to one single Georgian. Every adult illiterate, every school dropout, and every untrained child is an indictment of us all. Our state pays a terrible and continuing human and financial price for these failures. It is time to end this waste. If Switzerland and Israel and other people can eliminate illiteracy, then so can we.

Carter made kindergartens and other aspects of preschool training one of the priorities of his administration. In 1972 he persuaded the legislature to approve the so-called early childhood development program, which would rely heavily on federal funds to provide kindergartens, day-care centers, and job training and placement for mothers supporting families. The plan passed despite mutterings by Maddox that it was a Communist plot to take kids away from their parents on the model of Chinese communes. Then the federal government eliminated the program, so that Carter had to go back to the legislature with a plan to phase in kindergartens and training for three-to-four-year-olds on a gradual basis over five years. (He did get a $7 million plan for handicapped preschoolers authorized in 1973.) That year he proposed state expenditures of $600 million for local schools—an increase of $118 million in a single year. The state government already financed close to 60 percent of local school costs, one of the highest state support levels in the country.

In postsecondary education, Georgia has long been, and remains, much stronger in vocational training than in the refinements of higher learning. The state university system has an enrollment of just over 100,000, but the percentage of the state's young people enrolled there and in private institutions is among the lowest of all the states. The prestige and salary levels for faculty tend to be well below national norms. The University of Georgia, at Athens, is an adequate but undistinguished institution traditionally known as the place for future Georgia leaders to get their educations. But despite embellishments like Dean Rusk as a professor of international law, the university's most outstanding department is still agriculture. The academic level of Georgia Tech, in Atlanta, is substantially higher. Atlanta is also the site of the fast-growing Georgia State University in Atlanta, which started out as a branch of Georgia Tech's evening school and operated out of a garage for several years. Now it has 18,000 students (almost as many as Athens), is still working on a big construction program, and has the most integrated, politically active student body in the state. Black students who pick Georgia State are likely to get a much better education than those at all-black colleges within the system, some of which have abysmally poor standards. Georgia has recently doubled its number of junior colleges, now specializing more in vocational training, to 14. But there is no master plan for higher education.

Among private universities, the most distinguished are Emory in Atlanta (known especially for its schools of medicine and law) and the various colleges of the black-operated Atlanta University Center.

Mental health is another field in which Georgia was long derelict, and is now trying to make amends. The modern reform movement began after an Atlanta newspaperman exposed the almost animal-like existence of patients at the big Central State Hospital at Milledgeville, which at that time was a typical custodial insane asylum. A comprehensive plan to substitute treatment for the warehousing of the mentally ill was approved in 1963, a plan that set a long-range goal of 33 all-purpose community mental health centers and five regional mental health hospitals. Some of those facilities were built—enough so that Central State's population sank from 12,300 patients in 1960 to 7,600 in 1972. But many communities failed to cooperate in constructing local treatment centers, and much of the 1963 program bogged down in bureaucratic red tape and mismanagement. Dr. Melvin Kaufman, a mental health expert at Georgia State University, said in 1972 that "Georgia still has a long way to go before its mental health program can be considered adequate."

The same might be said of Georgia's penal system. Ellis Arnall ameliorated the vicious chain gang system that made Georgia a national symbol of prison brutality, but real change has been slow in coming. The modern-day variation of the chain gangs are the public work camps in 50 counties, where prisoners are still used as chattel—to maintain and work on county roads, to clean up courthouses and local state patrol barracks. In past years, the work camps were a source of political power for county commissioners who used inmate labor to do favors for political supporters. That practice has been forbidden, but the counties still want their free labor, and they form a base of opposition to penal reform. In Tattnall County, where close to 3,000 inmates share the convict culture of the Georgia State Prison, the prison is the mainstay of the local economy.

Governor Maddox took a keen interest in prison reform and boasted that his administration "released 3,100 people on early release—a bigger scale than ever before tried in the United States." During the time they would have been in prison, Maddox said, less than 3 percent got into trouble. "I got them to sign pledges on how they would conduct themselves. The plan succeeded because someone trusted them for the first time. One black said, 'I've never had a second chance before. In fact, I've never had a first chance. Even if that man's Lester Maddox, I'm not going to let him down.' "

The Maddox philosophy—which even the most sophisticated penologist would have difficulty arguing with—is that "being confined and taken out of society is quite a bit of punishment. Being punished after you've been confined is wrong." Maddox did his best to improve health care, clothing, and food for inmates, and said as he left office, "I brought a new day in penal operations in this state." But he admitted "we've still got a long way to go." He was not able, for instance, to do much to break up the clique of guards and inmates who run the State Prison much like a pre-Civil War plantation. Carter put Ellis MacDougall, former South Carolina and Connecticut prison director, in charge of the system, and a number of progressive reforms were slowly instituted.

Part of any thoroughgoing reform will have to be a complete revamping of Georgia's court system too. Judge Robert H. Hall, a judge of the state court of appeals and former professor of law at Emory University, defined the problem when he wrote * that the system of criminal justice in Georgia was "a failure":

> To be adequate, justice—which includes punishment—must be swift and sure. Today it is neither. . . .
>
> Georgia has an archaic, decentralized system of crime detection for its 159 counties and many municipalities. What is needed is a computerized, central criminal and statistical information center which should include a state fingerprint system.
>
> The criminal has the advantage of a localized, fragmented and autonomous system of prosecution. The local prosecutor is completely independent of the state attorney general.
>
> The criminal will face an unorganized court structure in Georgia that is substantially the same as that in existence more than a century ago. Its structure is so complex, chaotic and gargantuan that it is difficult to even diagram it on a chart. . . .
>
> There is no way even to catalog our ignorance. We are one of only 15 states in the country which have no court administrator. We need to establish a simple court structure and then organize it into a unified system of courts. . . .

Another basic reform, Judge Hall said, would be to enact a "merit plan" for selection of judges in place of Georgia's present system of popular election. Legislators and governors rightfully reflect the views of a political party and a constituency, he noted. But "a judge should not."

Finally, a word about consumer interests and the men who hold the most power in Georgia public life today. Georgia is like many other states in that the various regulatory bodies of state government, as well as legislative

* In an article for the Atlanta *Journal and Constitution Magazine*, May 5, 1971

committees, have often been under the control (direct or indirect) of men from the very industries they are supposed to regulate. But there are some bright exceptions. By 1970, the Georgia water quality control board was cracking down on polluters from the mountains to the sea and was viewed by experts as the best agency of its kind in the South and one of the best in the nation. The staid old public service commission, which controls public utilities, was shaken up when a stormy south Georgia politician named Bobby Pafford in 1970 won election as one of its members. Pafford began to champion consumer over utility interests and demanded that the commission's deliberations be made open to the public. The simple consumer-versus-utility battle may well be overshadowed in the next years, however, by the problem of how to allocate the electric power rate increases that will stem from the country's mounting energy crisis. Herbert Wiltsee, director of the southern office of the Council of State Governments, said that in Georgia, as in other states, "the allocation of power cost increases will be a key question." The society as a whole will have to decide if it wants to continue power rate incentives for big users, thus spurring economic development at the expense of the homeowner, or whether it wants to protect the small consumer by making industries and other large users bear the cost of added energy bills, a course that could dampen the fires of industrial expansion.

I conducted an informal poll among a number of well-informed Georgia observers and came up with a list of the most powerful men in the state in the early 1970s. Several politicians were named, including predictable choices like George L. Smith II, Jimmy Carter, Herman Talmadge, and Lester Maddox; among blacks, Leroy Johnson was considered the most influential politico until 1973, when Maynard Jackson won election as Atlanta's first black mayor and thus became the most prominent Negro elected official of the entire South. The business and industrial names included Mills Lane, who recently stepped down as head of Citizens and Southern Bank and moved back to his home town of Savannah; Robert Woodruff of Coca-Cola; John Portman, the architect-developer; J. B. Fuqua, the head of Fuqua Industries, the Atlanta-based conglomerate, and an associate of Carl Sanders; Thomas Beebe of Delta Airlines; and John Sibley, the retired chairman of the Trust Company of Georgia, who is now in his late eighties but "still a good man to have on your side." In the foundation field, the most power is held by Boisfeullet Jones, the operating head of the Woodruff Foundations, which disperse millions from the Coca-Cola fortune.

A listing of the most powerful groups in Georgia, my sources said, would have to start with the Atlanta business group and to a lesser degree the commercial elite of Columbus, Savannah, and Macon. The most powerful lobby in the legislature these days is probably the education bloc, led by Jack Nix. The rural county commissioners are still a power to be reckoned with, especially in elections, but bigger clout now rests with the Georgia Municipal Association.

Georgians in Washington

Georgia has sent some giants to the U.S. Senate in this century—men like Walter F. George, who served from 1922 to 1956, and Richard Brevard Russell, who had already completed a term as an outstanding reform governor of his state before he went to the Senate in 1933, there to serve until his death in 1971. Thomas Watson might have achieved similar status if death had not taken him in 1922, a year after he entered the Senate. Even today, Georgia need make no apologies for the legislative competence of Herman Talmadge (1957–).

On the House side, there have been fewer standouts, the most notable exception being Carl Vinson, who served the half century from 1915 to 1965 (an all-time record for members of the House) and made his mark as chairman of the Armed Services Committee and "father of the modern Navy." But for the most part, Georgia Representatives have followed the success formula spelled out by a Washington correspondent of the Atlanta *Journal-Constitution:* "Keep your mouth shut and vote right, which is conservative, patriotic, and as white as possible." One Georgia House member who did gain a measure of national notice was Phil M. Landrum, when he coauthored the Landrum-Griffin Labor Reform Act in the late 1950s. But Landrum has been little heard from since, except in his leadership of the unofficial House Committee on Textiles. The non-Southern press viewed Atlanta's liberal Charles Weltner (1963–67) with special approval—and with good reason, for it took immense courage for him to break with his regional colleagues and vote for the 1964 civil rights bill. But there were doubts about Weltner's judgment when, as a matter of conscience, he resigned as a candidate for reelection in 1966 rather than honor a standard-type party loyalty oath which he found bound him to vote for Lester Maddox for governor. A young black of exceptional talents, Andrew Young, now represents much of the territory that elected Charles Weltner.

Walter George was one of the Senators who withstood President Roosevelt's purge of conservatives in 1938; in fact he was actually seated on the platform at Barnesville, Georgia, when FDR threw the gauntlet to him. Always the gentleman, George replied simply: "I accept your challenge in this campaign." When George first went to the Senate, Robert Sherrill noted in *Gothic Politics in the Deep South,* he had the support of the Ku Klux Klan and "trailed (they thought) the unbreakable reins of Georgia business and utility interests. . . . However, George was not a man to stay tied. He remained conservative, but he became magnanimous." He opposed the Wagner Housing Act and FDR's proposal to enlarge the Supreme Court, but he voted for a number of the New Deal alphabet agencies, including TVA, and for Social Security. George became engrossed in the issue of world peace and abandoned the chairmanship of the Finance Committee for Foreign Relations, where he became a tower of strength for a bipartisan foreign policy during the early years of the Eisenhower Administration—often in opposition to the isolationist irreconcilables of the President's own party. But he had lost his touch, both with redneck Georgia and with its business interests. Herman Talmadge, hungering for a Senate seat, easily forced him aside before the 1956 primaries.

In the introduction to this book, I wrote of the personal tragedy of Richard Russell, one of the greatest Georgian—and Southern—Senators of all time, a man who might well have been President if he had not been so much the embodiment of his own region and its racial mores. Fortunately, not all of Russell's energy was devoted to the losing cause of segregation. In the 1930s he was an enthusiastic New Dealer, helping to pass the act creating the Rural Electrification Administration, authoring the first nationwide school lunch program, and playing a key role in creating the Farmers Home Administration. Then, as chairman of the Armed Services Committee over many years (where he was a member, he once boasted, "longer than all the Secretaries of the Defense Department put together"), he spoke the voice of the Senate on national security affairs. No one seemed to mind much if he also used that post (with Carl Vinson's help) to load Georgia with military bases. One of Russell's brightest hours was his fair, wise chairmanship over the hearings on General Douglas MacArthur's dismissal in the early 1950s. He long influenced national priorities as second-ranking Democrat (and, after Carl Hayden's retirement in 1969, as chairman) of the Appropriations Committee. And in retrospect, the power of his personality still shines brightly. LBJ's Senate aide Harry McPherson, a thoroughgoing liberal on the civil rights issue, wrote that Russell's "quick mind and unfeigned courtliness won him deep respect of people who had little sympathy for his conservative views. . . . Often I found myself offering counsel to him, seeking to forward his purposes, because his character and professionalism were magnetic to me."

In the reshuffling of Senate committee posts that followed the deaths of Russell and other Senate patriarchs in the early 1970s, Herman Talmadge emerged as chairman of the Agriculture Committee, second to Russell Long on Finance, and second ranking on Veterans' Affairs. He is also a member of the influential Democratic Policy Committee, and his colleagues have a high regard for his intelligence and legislative craftsmanship. That attitude was one reason Talmadge was selected to sit on the Senate Watergate Committee in 1973, a position in which he distinguished himself. But Talmadge is not about to contract a case of Potomac Fever. He returns to Georgia almost every weekend and makes about 170 speeches there each year. Several times each week he speaks to Georgia high school students and civic organizations by amplified telephone (courtesy of Southern Bell Telephone Company). And he never refuses a telephone call from a Georgian.

That attention to the home folks, plus Talmadge's ideoligical flexibility and ability to learn, probably mean he can stay in the Senate for the rest of his life. A close associate, quoted in Ralph Nader's congressional study, said that Talmadge was a "bellwether for Southern politicians" and "a master at keeping his feet on the shifting sands of time." In 1966, Talmadge appeared before the predominantly black Hungry Club of Atlanta to say that if he were governor again, he would appoint Negroes to high office in Georgia. "In future races," Talmadge said, "all candidates are going to solicit the votes of all Georgia citizens." This was the same man, one correspondent noted, who had been the featured speaker at a birthday barbecue in honor of Samuel Green, grand dragon of the Ku Klux Klan, in Atlanta in 1946—an occasion on which he inveighed against "the danger of allowing some 300,000 ignorant Negroes to vote, particularly if they can be controlled by a shrewder race," and when he asked, "Why should Negroes butt in and tell white people who should be elected in a white primary?" Somehow, Talmadge always lands on his feet. At the Hungry Club in 1966, a questioner said that five or six years before, he would not have spoken there—and why had he changed? "Five or six years ago," Talmadge replied, "you didn't invite me." The audience broke into appreciative laughter.

Talmadge has also given up on setting the rural countryside against the city. In 1968 this erstwhile champion of the county unit system said: "Our cities touch the lives of every one of us, every day. Their problems are our problems."

This is not to suggest that Herman Talmadge has become "a liberal." He may have switched from hawk to dove on the Vietnam war in the late 1960s, but he has yet to vote against a defense appropriation or new weapons system. He may have taken a real interest in the problems of hunger in rural Georgia—a problem that hits blacks the most severely—but he has never voted for a civil rights bill, and he opposed an income maintenance plan to replace the present welfare system. The ultraconservative Americans for Constitutional Action says he votes "right" about two-thirds of the time. And lest anyone think Talmadge has become too citified by his years in Washington, he rises at the crack of dawn each day for a two-and-a-half-mile run, keeps a Confederate flag by his desk, chews tobacco, and has an old-fashioned spittoon two feet from his chair as he works.

As he moves into his sixties, in firm control of the Senate Agriculture Committee, Talmadge could make his greatest positive contribution in development plans for rural America. He appointed Hubert Humphrey chairman of a subcommittee to look into ways to revitalize small-town regions of the nation, despite rumblings from some Georgians who view Humphrey as a liberal-leftist. Talmadge's interest in federal programs to benefit the rural areas was likely to put him on a collision course with the Nixon administration's budget-cutters—and might have a political fallout, too, by suggesting to Georgians that the new Republican party was not necessarily their friend.

Atlanta: Spirit, Money, Architecture

"Bumptious, fractious, energetic, upstart: Atlanta was that always," *Atlanta Magazine* wrote about the city's rather brief 125-year history. It all started in the 1830s, when the Georgia legislature decided to build a rail line connecting the sea with the opening American interior—a line along the southern end of the Appalachians that could rival the Mohawk Valley of New York, or Harper's Ferry and the Cumberland Gap. The line would go inland from Augusta (on the Savannah River) to a terminus with a line going northwesterly to Chattanooga, where there would be barge connections on the Tennessee River to the Ohio and thence to the Mississippi. The place in the forest where Atlanta now stands was chosen as the terminus; indeed "Terminus" was the first name of the hardscrabble settlement of the first railroad workers.

Ten years later, a New York teacher visiting Atlanta wrote in his journal that "the people here bow and shake hands with everybody they meet, as there are so many coming in all the time that they cannot remember with whom they are acquainted." A little of the same remains today, as young people from Richmond to New Orleans pour into Atlanta, national corporations move their people in and out, and the kaleidoscope of contact that makes an urban center vital revolves before one's very eyes. The constant flow of people in and out of Atlanta made it from the start a more urbane and tolerant place than most of the South but also a touch more predatory; in antebellum days the city was known for its "pushy people" (a phrase from *Gone with the Wind*). Margaret Mitchell also wrote of Atlanta: "It's brash and I like it."

No genteel, familied aristocracy ever ruled in Atlanta; from the start it was the business entrepreneurs, the men who could attract capital, who held the highest status. The monied group, and its sons and sons' sons, became the Establishment and directed the political life too. But they never became a "closed corporation." "Where in the world but in Atlanta," Mills Lane asked me, "could a guy come to town as a regional vice president for Sears Roebuck, and in the first week he gets to be a member of every important club in the town? Within 50 days he's a director of the First National Bank of Atlanta. Where but in Atlanta could a man come to take over the managership of the gas company and in two years be president of the chamber of commerce? We're a mixture of tradition and constant new blood. We're not really Southern." Mills Lane ought to know; his home town is Savannah, where an encrusted aristocracy has ruled for about 200 years now.

It is interesting to note that Lane framed Atlanta's openness entirely in terms of opportunities for men. Margaret Mitchell and the femininity of its name notwithstanding, Atlanta has always been a man's, not a woman's, town. There are some notable exceptions—Patricia LaHatte, promotion manager of the Atlanta Newspapers, Inc.; 29-year-old Bonnie Reeve, president of Peachtree Center Models; Marie Dodd, board member and promotion manager of Ivan Allen Co.; Grace Hamilton, the first black woman elected to the state legislature; Ruth Kent, whose "Today in Georgia" program has been broadcast by WSB-TV for 20 years; Celestine Sibley, author and columnist with the Atlanta *Constitution;* and Helen Bullard, a key City Hall adviser during Ivan Allen, Jr.'s mayoralty and possibly Atlanta's shrewdest political and campaign strategist. Women are particularly active in advertising, philanthropy, and the arts. But while Jews and Negroes have now been admitted to the Commerce Club, inner sanctum of the power structure, it will probably be a long time before women make it to full membership.

The success story of modern Atlanta is all the more appealing because the city, like its region, was really in a state of depression from the day Sherman burned Atlanta on his march to the sea in 1864 until the start of World War II. Not until the 1940s did Georgia property tax assessments, for instance, return to the levels they had had on the eve of the Civil War. Atlanta did reestablish itself as a transportation center after Sherman, and Yankee capital played a role in minor industrial growth in fields like textiles and woolen shops. ("The Yankees burned Atlanta. We made them come back and rebuild it," one Atlanta mayor said.) But before World War II, Coca-Cola was the *only* pool of indigenous capital. Not that Atlantans were not trying through all 75 years of depression. Henry Woodfin Grady came to Atlanta from Rome shortly after the Civil War and as editor of the *Constitution* preached his doctrine of a New South where diversified industries would cast off the shackles of a one-crop economy. Before his early death, in 1889, Grady sparked the first two of three big Atlanta expositions designed to underscore the city's modernity. The Cotton States and International Exposition of 1895 brought in visitors from all over America, but the most important one may have been a 20-year-old typewriter salesman from Dalton, Ivan Allen, Sr. In 1925 Allen would launch the first "Forward Atlanta" program to proclaim the city's advantages in location, climate, labor supply, and natural resources. Even *Atlanta Magazine*, published by the chamber of commerce, admits that "the antiunion and ethnic thrust" of Forward Atlanta's advertisements are jolting to view today. But the campaign did help to create 762 new businesses with 20,000 jobs in the space of four years.

In one sense, Atlanta's snail-like progress in the 75 years after Appomattox may have been its blessing in disguise. "Because this was a transportation and distribution center, but never became a manufacturing center," Mills Lane pointed out, "we avoided the overcrowding, the smokestacks, the tenements of a Pittsburgh." The physical location was then and remains one of Atlanta's greatest assets. Not only did it become a gateway to the West, but the flow of trade and migration down the eastern flank of the Appalachians from the central Atlantic states led naturally to the city. And since Atlanta's altitude is higher than that of any large American cities except Denver and Phoenix, it has one of the more salubrious climates in the Southern states (little of the oppressive mugginess of the coastal plains, for instance, but a location far enough south to enjoy relatively mild winters).

One of the seeds of future prosperity was planted in the 1930s when William B. Hartsfield, a young attorney and alderman who had flown with the barnstormers in the early days of aviation, set out to make Atlanta the chief regional airport of the New York-to-Miami lighted air route. As Hartsfield later told the story, a rather low-ranking federal aviation official had been to Birmingham and had been well treated. Birmingham lay at the tip of the mountains, and since mountain-top beacons were being used to mark the mail routes, the selection would normally have gone to that city. But when the official arrived in Atlanta, he received a gala reception. He was met by civic leaders, taken downtown with a flashy police escort, and given a big dinner with the city's business leaders. "We greeted him just out of everything," Hartsfield said. Atlanta won the designation, and out of that came its role as the air center of the modern South. Hartsfield was elected mayor in 1937 and served continuously (except for a brief hiatus) until 1961. Though not a businessman, he forged the close business-political alliance that would characterize postwar Atlanta.

Despite its growth in the first postwar years, Atlanta was suffering a net loss of jobs in the late 1950s, and the second Forward Atlanta program was born. Its inventor was Ivan Allen, Jr., an inveterate Atlanta booster like his father. But there was more than boosterism to the second Forward Atlanta; Allen insisted that while the city sang its own praises, it would have to add expressways and mass transit, build a stadium, and preserve its public schools in the new era of integration. Taking the new Forward Atlanta program, which he had formulated as president of the chamber of commerce in 1960, Allen ran for mayor and won election as Hartsfield's successor in 1961.

What happened to metropolitan Atlanta in the 1960s was scarcely credible. A *quarter million* new jobs were created (for a new total of more than 600,000). The movers and shakers and entrepreneurs and hustling bankers transformed the formerly humdrum business center of Atlanta into a shimmering, high-rise vision of the New South. They also went underground to develop the nightclubs, restaurants, and shops of Underground Atlanta—filling resuscitated old brick and stone buildings where the Western & Atlantic Railroad had had its terminus in the downtown part of the city. Around the turn of the century, the streets of the Terminus area were raised a story over the tracks to ease traffic, and until the late '60s the Victorian store fronts below remained intact but empty. Then two young bachelors, Steve Fuller and Jack Patterson, began restoration (eventually expected to cost $10 million), creating one of the liveliest nighttime entertainment areas in America.

During the 1960s, the chamber of commerce counted up 247 new office buildings and 353 warehouses around Atlanta. The number of housing units expanded by 52 percent. Per capita income went up 80 percent. Retail sales rose by 97 percent, bank clearings by 133 percent, and the number of hotel rooms by 211 percent. Ivan Allen, when I spoke with him in 1969, acknowledged that the concomitant national prosperity had helped a great deal in the growth. But he agreed with the business leaders who exulted: "This has been Atlanta's decade."

Aggressive banking had a lot to do with that, and the chief catalyst was Mills Lane, who made Citizens and Southern National Bank of Georgia into one of the nation's most innovative and competitive consumer banks. There was a lot of pure razzmatazz to Lane's leadership; he always wore (and gave away to friends) bright neckties with a shining sun, cotton bales, and his slogan, "It's a wonderful world." "No community is better than its banks," Lane said. "I think banking is fun." He was one of the most accessible big bankers of the land, with his office right off the main lobby of the C & S central office, instead of upstairs with the other executives. Visitors were always welcome. C & S formed a holding company which in turn controlled eight affiliated banks and bought 5 percent interest, and thus a big voice, in more than 30 smalltown banks all over Georgia. C & S led the way with bank credit cards in Atlanta, and outdid its incredulous competitors by letting people borrow money on the cards. Lane had been president of C & S since 1946, but he capitalized on the 1960s—in a kind of synergism between his own ebullience and that of Atlanta as a whole—to expand C & S until its deposits ($1.4 billion) were almost as large as those of its two largest competitors (Trust Company of Georgia and First National Bank of Atlanta) combined.

By the end of the 1960s, Atlanta was not only the leading money market of the South, but competitive with almost any other in the country. The total capital funds of Atlanta banks, which had been $20 million in 1935 and $147 million in 1960, were $448 million by the early 1970s. Deposits, $200 million in 1935 and $1.6 billion in 1960, rose to $4.4 billion by 1972. In the 1920s, Georgia financier Ernest Woodruff had been obliged to go to New York to borrow the $25 million he needed to buy Coca-Cola; in 1970, the Atlanta banks headed a syndicate that loaned Delta Air Lines $220 million. "This time," a local finance writer noted, "the Atlanta banks called the cadence and New York, Chicago, and San Francisco joined the march." Late in 1973 the 1970 loan was topped by another arranged by C & S for Delta—this time for $300 million, the largest loan ever closed in the Southeast.

Before 1971, when Mills Lane retired as president of C & S, some had thought one of the bank's fiftyish executives would succeed him. Not so. Lane's handpicked successor was 35-year-old Richard L. Kattel, a New York native who had started out as a C & S trainee in 1958 and worked up through the ranks. A whole new team of bright young executives was installed with Kattel. *Atlanta Magazine* said everybody considered Kattel the "greatest thing since sliced bread"—a big, attractive, outgoing man who seemed to be destiny's darling. Lane was asked if Kattel could really be such a paragon. "You're goddamn right," was the answer. "He has the confidence of bankers, security analysts, and the goodwill of everybody in this bank . . . If half the people in the country are under 25, then people in business have to understand them. I don't understand people under 25. Dick Kattel does."

The start of the 1970s brought a dip in the Atlanta area economy that gave the local business types some concern. Part of the reason was the national recession and a drop in employment at auto assembly plants, but the biggest single factor was a swift drop in the job rolls of Georgia's largest private-sector employer, the Lockheed-Georgia Company in suburban Marietta. Boom and bust had been the pattern at the Marietta plant, located at Dobbins Air Force Base, ever since Bell Aircraft, its wartime operator, shut down operations after V-J Day. Some 30,000 employees were out of work overnight. Then, when the Korean War broke out, the Air Force asked Lockheed to reopen the plant to revamp B-29s and build the B-47, first of the big jet bombers, and later the C-130 prop-jet cargo plane. Employment rose to 20,000 by 1956, but by 1961 it was down to 10,000—only to pick up again in an instant when Lockheed got the contract to build the C-141 and then, in 1965, the gigantic C-5A, a plane with a tail as high as a skyscraper, a length that would barely fit onto a football field, a fuselage as big as the Holland Tunnel.

Lockheed employment was so important to Georgia because the company paid salaries far above the Southern average, or indeed most other places in the United States. Visiting the plant in 1969, I watched men pouring out of every hole of the monstrous fuselages when the coffee break whistle blew, a bit like ants escaping from a hill. Many were blacks holding complex machinists' jobs; a cross-section of both races told how their fathers had been dirt farmers or mill hands or truck drivers from counties all over the South. Robert Carter, from nearby Cartersville, Georgia, whose father was a pea farmer, said he had worked for Lockheed for 16 years, rising to the highly skilled post of tank sealer. As we talked on top of one of the high C-5A wing assemblies, Carter said: "I may not be far from home, but I've come a long ways."

Then, in 1969–70, the C-5A bubble burst.* Wheels and motors began to fall off, innumerable landing gear failures were reported, and cracks were detected in the wings. *Newsweek* dubbed the big plane "the Edsel of the airways." And the mismanagement that had led to mechanical failures turned out to be fiscal too; cost overruns were estimated at a staggering $2 billion. From a peak of 32,892 in August 1969, the employment rolls at Marietta dipped well below 10,000 in 1973, when the last of the problematic C-5A's was delivered. The amazing thing was that the Atlanta economy, after the first shock, absorbed the laid-off workers without any difficulty. Starting in mid-1971, total Atlanta and statewide employment, especially in manufacturing, began to rise again, and no one saw any reason for the advance to slacken any time in the 1970s.

Where do all the jobs come from? There is no easy answer, because the Atlanta area economy is so widely diversified today. Its role as regional headquarters for major corporations continues to grow, along with federal government payrolls. And according to the chamber of commerce, metropolitan Atlanta now has more than 300 companies with a net worth of $1 million or more. And while some of the success stories are familiar national stories, others are little known outside the Atlanta area. Everybody has heard of Coca-Cola, for instance, but how many people know about National Service Industries, which was started in 1919 by a wounded Atlanta doughboy named Isadore Weinstein to provide hospital linens and today is a widely diversified company with 20,000 employees, 2,500 of them in Atlanta, and annual sales of about $400 million? Or the auto supply company, Genuine Parts, which Atlanta's Carlyle Fraser started in 1928 with six employees, a company that now has 6,000 employees and annual sales of $340 million, the biggest auto parts company in the world? And unless one has visited Atlanta, is he likely to know about that fabulous department store, Rich's, which never questions a customer about returned merchandise but still has annual sales of $230 million and no less than 10,000 employees?

The Coca-Cola story, of course, is so fascinating that it merits telling and retelling. The world's most popular soft drink was invented by a pharmacist and Confederate veteran named John S. Pemberton, who had been born in Knoxville, Georgia, in 1833—before there was an Atlanta. Pemberton delighted in mixing up patent medicines to relieve distresses of the liver or what-

* Details of the C-5A fiasco, and the Pentagon's complicity, may be found in A. Ernest Fitzgerald's *The High Priests of Waste* (New York: Norton, 1972).

ever else ailed people, and he originally thought of Coca-Cola as a cure for hangovers. In 1886 he made the first batch of Coke in a three-legged iron pot in his Atlanta back yard. Ownership soon passed to another local pharmacist named Asa Griggs Candler, one of those eccentric early capitalists (akin to Henry Ford). Candler paid only $2,300 for his interest in Coca-Cola; when he finally sold out in 1916 to become mayor of Atlanta, he was worth $50 million. Robert Woodruff, who became president in 1932, made the beverage an international as well as a national phenomenon. He has been estimated in recent years to have a net worth of more than $100 million. In philanthropy, or just about any field he cares to touch, Robert Woodruff remains *the* power behind the scenes in Atlanta. But he rarely surfaces publicly.

Coca-Cola is not an especially large employer in Atlanta; at last count it had less than 1,400 employees there. A huge portion of the company's business is done through its franchises (to which it sells syrup); there are now 1,800 bottling plants in 135 countries, but the company owns only 22 of them. Nevertheless, it grosses close to $2 billion a year and has been a literal money tree for many Atlantans and franchises across the world. Under J. Paul Austin, who took over operating control of the company in 1960, Coca-Cola began a modest program of acquisitions. One was Minute Maid, the producer of frozen orange juice. For a company so anxious about its image that a bosomy girl has never graced a Coke ad, the shock must have been great when a 1969 NBC-TV documentary revealed miserable conditions among the migrant citrus pickers in Minute Maid's Florida orchards. As it turned out in later Congressional hearings, Coca-Cola's top management had already been apprised of the destitution among its Florida workers and had begun corrective steps. But the unfavorable publicity spurred progress toward full-time employment for the citrus workers, most of whom are black. They were organized by César Chávez's United Farm Workers and began to acquire a sense of dignity and self-worth they had not known before. Housing was upgraded sharply and each worker was assured a guaranteed annual income of $6,500, compared to $2,200 for pickers in the rest of Florida. Some of the other Florida growers, without a global image to protect, were reportedly furious over Coke's newly magnanimous policy.

One of the biggest Atlanta-based corporations today is Delta Airlines, which started out as a crop-dusting service four decades ago and now has 22,000 employees (9,500 of them in Atlanta) and annual sales of three-quarters of a billion dollars. Delta is literally the air lifeline of the South and has recently expanded its operations as far afield as New England (after buying Northeast Airlines) and California. The secret of its success is hard-headed management and an intense team spirit among its workers that makes it possible to keep Delta planes in the air an extraordinarily high percentage of the time—and thus to rack up top profits in the air industry. Atlantans, I discovered, take a personal pride in Delta's service record and success. As Mills Lane would say, "Where in the world but Atlanta could you make that statement about an airline?"

A new generation of big-time entrepreneurs sprang to view in the Atlanta of the 1960s. Among them is J. B. Fuqua, a Virginia farm boy now in his mid-fifties who got rich pioneering television in the South and today owns a leisure-time conglomerate that had sales of $430 million in 1972. Fuqua's personal fortune is about $50 million. "Atlanta and Birmingham were about equal 25 years ago," Fuqua told an interviewer for *Forbes* recently. "But over the years Atlanta boomed, while Birmingham stayed about like it was. Why? Because Atlanta had leadership. Birmingham didn't." Fuqua invested heavily in Atlanta real estate but never spent a dollar in Birmingham; today he owns several low-rise buildings at Five Points, Atlanta's Times Square, an area zoned for high-rise development. A still younger Atlanta capitalist is A. J. Land, who could claim by 1972, when he was 34, credit for building some 4,000 apartments around the city, half of them for the single and young marrieds set. His next project is to be a $75 million complex with a shopping mall, office building, and 35-story Hilton Hotel. Any list would have to include Thomas G. Cousins, now in his early forties, whom *Atlanta Magazine* describes as "the analytical dynamo and spawner of corporations who has become a major economic force in Metro Atlanta in the past dozen years." Some people scoffed when Cousins, in 1965, bought the air rights over 70 acres of defunct railway yards in a blighted part of the city. But since then, a 17,000-seat coliseum has been constructed there—and, to ensure tenants, Cousins bought the St. Louis Hawks basketball team and brought it to Atlanta and started his own National Hockey League team, the Atlanta Flames. For the same site, Cousins plans an awesome $65 million recreation-office-exhibition "megastructure" called Omni International, plus $500 million in other construction.

But when the history of Atlanta's growth era is written, the central role will go not to a man who started as a real estate developer or financier, but rather to an architect: John C. Portman, Jr. The fact that Portman has a very practical business sense, and owns anywhere from 15 to 60 percent of the buildings he has designed, does not detract from the fact that his architectural inventiveness has set the tone and topped the skyline of the new Atlanta. By the early 1970s, many considered him the leading architect-developer of the United States.

An Atlanta native, Portman graduated from Georgia Tech in 1950, worked for three years for the local branch of a New York architectural firm, and then went into business for himself. His biggest project of the early years was the Merchandise Mart on Peachtree Street—the wholesaling nerve center of the Southeast, two million square feet in size, second only to Chicago's Merchandise Mart. Portman is president of the stock corporation that owns and operates the Atlanta Mart. Since the late 1950s, he has had a partner in all his projects, Trammell Crow of Dallas. It is probably fortuitous for their relationship that Crow is a promoter but not an architect.

Portman described his professional career during an interview in his 21st-story Peachtree Center office, a room filled with multicolored crystals and flooded with light from windows on three sides:

> The idea of the Peachtree Center began to form in 1959. As we built the Mart, I kept looking at the one- and two-story buildings all around us and thought to myself: "We can't just allow anything to happen there." So we started acquir-

ing property around us. The coordinate unit concept was not yet formed, but in the early 1960s I went to Brasilia for its dedication, and I began to think in terms of building an entire city. Then I made a trip to Sweden and visited two of their satellite cities and a downtown development in Stockholm. I saw how they separated people from automobiles, how you could just cross footbridges to get to shops and schools. I began to think in terms of putting man on foot, to free him from the mechanical monster.

Other men with that kind of vision might have approached the city's business or political leadership, but Portman and Crow operated independently, trying to prove that each step-by-step addition to what they now called the Peachtree Center would have to justify itself as a business matter. "We're not building things to sell," Portman said. "We don't take rapid depreciation. We're trying to build sound, solid developments of lasting value." Financing was obtained from financial giants like Metropolitan Life and Connecticut General, with the Atlanta banking community used heavily for construction loans. No government money or land condemnation were used.

Some 45 acres were acquired for the Peachtree Center, to include office towers, a hotel, gardens, galleries, restaurants, museums and theatres, and apartments to live in. Portman's rule was that these coordinate urban units all be within seven and a half minutes walking time of each other—"the distance people will walk without thinking about wheels." He selected two horizontal connections between the buildings of the complex: one at 22 stories, by means of pedestrian passageways; the other at "the people or mall level." The latter is thwarted by Peachtree Street, which courses through the middle of Peachtree Center; Portman now hopes, however, that it may be possible to tunnel the traffic in connection with construction of the new rapid transit system, so that Peachtree Street too can be for people, not vehicles. "The whole idea is to get back to the idea of the European village where people can walk to work, school, church, shops, or theater," he said, "except that here we will have that village in the heart of a great city."

The jewel of the Peachtree Center is Portman's Regency Hyatt House Hotel, which no visitor to Atlanta now dare miss for its vast sunlit open central court, surrounded by 22 stories of rooms, dramatized (as if that were necessary) by glass-bubble elevators festooned with lights, and a 70-foot fountain. Portman planned it as the antithesis of what he calls "the typical hotel, where you go into a lobby with a fairly low ceiling and you get into a closed elevator and go to your room by way of a narrow corridor." The Hyatt House was designed with a fairly plain exterior and a dark entrance corridor. But as Portman explains his concept, this was no accident: "You walk in a front door that I call 'the people scoop.' It's 20 long paces, painted dark so it will come down on you. And then you come into the center of the building, and suddenly there it is—an explosion of space in all directions." Portman obviously relishes the dramatic effect on visitors: "You can always spot the first comers, when their heads fly up and their mouths fly open when they enter that space." But he insists that the hotel is really not as expensive as it may appear; the only materials used to any great extent are concrete and carpet. "We played with simplicity; it's the architectural design that diverts you from the plainness of the material." The central space, Portman said, was envisaged as a place where people would have contact with people, "like a small town square."

Portman saved a second surprise for those who take the glass elevators up to the glowing blue dome of the cocktail lounge on top of the hotel. "In that glass elevator, you literally 'go through the roof' because the lounge is two or three stories above it. This works on people's emotions," Portman said. He's right, of course, and while some critics say Portman's work is too stagy and flamboyant, the fact is that its rejection of monumentality to appeal to people's feeling and emotion is the most humanizing influence that any architect has yet brought to bear in this age of glass, steel, and high-rise architecture.

Portman has tried to apply the principles of coordinate urban units and vast lighted inner spaces to the other projects his fame has brought him, including a second Hyatt Regency at Chicago's O'Hare Airport, a Dallas suburban center, a hotel in San Francisco's Embarcadero Center, and the desperately needed 32-acre waterfront complex Henry Ford is financing for the city of Detroit. He also has huge hotels underway in Los Angeles and New York's Times Square, and a trade mart in Brussels. In Atlanta, Portman's encores for the 1970s include the tallest hotel in the world (70 stories) and an equally high World Trade Center. The hotel, Peachtree Center Plaza, rises on the spot where the Henry Grady Hotel, named after the 19th-Century editor, stood for 48 years, housing legislators, lobbyists, and, according to Bruce Galphin, "frolicsome ladies in waiting." The new hotel will consist of a spectacular bronze-glass cylinder, set upon a seven-story atrium lobby complete with typical Portman touches like a lake and waterfall and peninsulas on which people can eat and drink. As for the trade center, also part of the Peachtree Center, it will provide space for foreign consulates, world commerce offices, and the like—a symbol of Atlanta's intent, after becoming a prominent national city in the 1960s, to become an important international city in the 1970s.

The Omni International planned by Tom Cousins, who has become Portman's archrival in spectacular Atlanta development, nevertheless shows the influence of Portman's concepts. As designed by Atlanta architect Thomas W. Ventullett III, it will feature a totally enclosed environment in which a multiplicity of activities and people-to-people contacts can take place—in this case, an interior space of 8 million cubic feet, four times the magnitude of the Regency Hyatt House's atrium. Offices, stores, restaurants, a large hotel, 10 movie houses and a trade pavilion will all be under the 14-story roof, the various activities joined by walkways and plazas. Among other embellishments, the Omni will have the world's longest continuous escalator (200 feet, eight stories high) and eerie laser sculptures to enhance the decor. The cost of this single "megastructure" will be $65 million—heady stuff for this city that some people still call an overgrown Southern country town.

Atlanta, Peachtree, Blacks, and Politics

Every great city is a potpourri of the beautiful and the ugly, the exalted and the depressed, and Atlanta is no exception. It has no grand central plaza, no master plan by a Pierre L'Enfant or (as we will note later) Savannah's James Oglethorpe. But Atlanta does have a central artery, of immense variety and vitality: Peachtree Street. Atlantan William Schemmel has called its 20 miles "America's longest running road show." Peachtree begins at Five Points, the historic heart of Atlanta now synonymous with high finance. Then it wanders north and northeasterly, sprouting left and right at various angles with 27 circles, streets, and avenues with Peachtree in their name. Peachtree is the retail jugular of the South, with everything from department stores and posh specialty shops to fading junk stores. As one goes north, one passes the flashing brilliance of Portman's Peachtree Center. But soon afterwards, there are shabby boarding houses and schlock stores. Then the pedestrian office structures from which the feds rule the South. Between 10th and 11th Streets, there are the hip shops of the new youth culture, called The Strip. Atlanta's hippie population began to increase by leaps and bounds in the late 1960s, with attendant "law and order" problems.

Now one is in the section called "midtown" these days (the definition has kept changing, with the expansion of the city). Here is a half-century-old neighborhood with dignified churches, substantial apartments, medium-sized office buildings. The old community of Ansley Park, which was rather geriatric and a little seedy a decade ago, has been "discovered" by young professionals who have spruced up the gracious old homes. At 14th Street, there is the "micropolis" of Colony Square, where a modern-day entrepreneur, James E. Cushman, has been constructing two million square feet of buildings and shops, the whole adorned with the sculpture and landscaping which is *de rigueur* for first-class Atlanta development these days. At 15th, one sees the gleaming Atlanta Memorial Arts Center, built in the 1960s with private funds matched by an anonymous donor (which turned out to be Robert Woodruff and his family's foundation). Within the museum stands a bronze cast of Rodin's "The Shadow," that brooding sculpture, a gift of the French government in memory of the 122 members of the Atlanta Art Association who perished in a plane crash in Paris on June 3, 1962—a day not soon to be forgotten in Atlanta.*

Upper Peachtree is melanges of new hostelries and older, sedate residences, of shopping centers and luxury apartment towers, of movie houses and auto lots. Finally, it reaches a point where the Indians had a crossroads, and there was a single peachtree, and from thence the long street's name. The northernmost reaches of Atlanta, where Peachtree has been leading all the

* The presence of the Arts Center does not mean Atlanta is distinguishing itself in matters cultural. There are a few bright spots, including Robert Shaw's leadership of the Atlanta Symphony. But *Atlanta Magazine* echoed a widely held opinion when it reported in 1972 that "Atlanta's arts remain imitative, traditional, funded by few of the social set." On the other hand, pop music recording and movie making are now flourishing in the city.

time, harbor the poshest residential sections where many of the "power structure" live in mansions at the end of long, gated driveways.

I recall a first visit to Atlanta, before the architectural explosion of the '60s. It was April, and I drove along Peachtree, and the brilliance of the dogwood and azalea and manicured perfection was like a mecca of loveliness after long hours of driving through the impoverished, red-dirt country of rural Georgia. "When you're in Atlanta," an old saying goes, "you can forget you're in Georgia."

On that first trip, like many a visitor before and after, I caught scarcely a glimpse of the "other Atlanta" of grimy slums, some filled with white folks, others with black folks, a low-slung excrescence of the worst of the South. When I returned a decade later, to start gathering notes for this book, Alex Coffin of the Atlanta *Constitution* kindly took me for a tour of the city's less known face. Most of the slums lie south of the center of the city, a familiar Southern phenomenon, because that is the sewer side of the city. On Atlanta's southeast side, you can literally see a sewer flowing through. (The high ground to the north, by contrast, is occupied by the more affluent society.) Through the glittering 1960s, Atlanta still could not bring itself to pave its last 250 miles of dirt roads—some in startling proximity to its heart. Only a few blocks east of the Capitol, an old structure, still resplendent under its gold-plated dome, one comes on all-white Cabbagetown, filled with rundown single-family houses, an area threatened by highways, commercial developments, and the feared black onslaught. (Cabbagetowners in the '60s kept shotguns near the door, threatening to "shoot any nigger who tried to move in.")

Directly adjacent to the big Atlanta Stadium built in the '60s at Ivan Allen's instigation, one comes on the Model Cities area—3,000 acres with 48,000 people in six neighborhoods (four all black, one white, one in transition). The streets are narrow and muddy, the housing ranges from mediocre to shanties fit only for demolition. Coffin also showed me Dixie Hills, where a three-day racial uprising occurred in 1967, a place of fairly decent looking two-story apartments but hemmed in by freeways, crowded, without a tree in sight. And then there was Buttermilk Bottom, one of the worst slums, with magnificent vistas of the bold new Atlanta skyline. There one finds a street called Currier Place, incredibly gutted, cluttered with wrecked and abandoned autos, infested with dogs. Some of the unpainted shanty houses are propped up with cinder blocks. And the slum of Vine City—Martin Luther King, Jr., lived on its outskirts—offers blocks of high-density, ugly single-unit clapboard housing, much of it standing on stilts, with junk surrounding the houses.

That such scabrous housing needs removal, all agree, and as a matter of fact the city of Atlanta, by official action, destroyed 22,545 housing units, most of them serious slum dwellings, between 1960 and 1970. Many units were torn down so that Atlanta could have its stadium. But only 5,656 replacement units were put up by government agencies during the '60s. Atlanta still has a substantial inventory of public housing, which began with the Techwood project in 1936 near downtown. But the demand for decent low-income housing has long since outrun the supply. The Atlanta area has plenty of middle- to upper-income housing, with more coming on the market all the time. If you want a suburban rambler, you will have no problem, and if you'd like an apartment in one of the complexes for the young (presumably swinging) singles, the competition for your dollar is intense. (The Atlanta papers have run ads depicting a heavy-lidded blonde with this message: "Love thy neighbor. These apartments rated X, adults only.")

Getting a home if you're poor and have a large family is another matter. There are 23 housing authorities in the metropolitan region, but only one —Atlanta's—is actively pursuing a program, and it has run into violent objections over proposed project sites and faces a federal court order insisting that public housing projects go into white as well as black neighborhoods. Outside of Atlanta proper, there are very few black neighborhoods; usually blacks are found only as a remnant of the rural and small-town mixtures of once isolated communities where some blacks were needed as servants or laborers in times past. According to Reese Cleghorn, in *City* magazine, nowhere in the Atlanta area is there even one large and substantially integrated neighborhood that is stabilized racially; the metropolitan region as a whole is more segregated now than it was two decades ago. The city proper is absorbing more and more blacks, as young whites go to the suburbs. In 1960, 38 percent of Atlanta was black. By 1970, the figure was up to 51 percent (in a total population of 496,973). By 1980, the black percentage will probably be 60 percent.

The school system moved even more rapidly to black dominance Back in 1961, Atlanta had received favorable publicity when it became the first place in Georgia to start school integration. In the familiar American pattern, however, massive resegregation followed, until the system was 80 percent black in 1973. Just before he stepped down as school superintendent, Dr. John Letson said: "If, after 12 years of turmoil, we wind up with a segregated city, what will we have achieved?" But integration no longer seemed high on the priority list of black leaders in Atlanta, who agreed to drop their longstanding desegregation suit in exchange for having a black succeed Letson, and blacks appointed to half the school system's administrative posts. Proponents said the plan would defuse the busing issue and possibly diminish white flight to the suburbs. But some poor blacks attacked it as "trading off quality education for a few big jobs for a few big Negroes."

In the midst of Atlanta's black neighborhoods, one discovers the brick buildings of the Atlanta University Center, the largest center for Negro education in the world. There are four undergraduate colleges (Clark, Morehouse, Morris Brown, and Spellman), the Interdenominational Theological Seminary, and a graduate center, Atlanta University. Founded in the years after the Civil War, these institutions began as elementary and secondary schools where new Southern Negroes were prepared for higher education. Churches were the principal sponsors, and Spellman received a large portion of its funding from John D. Rockefeller, Sr., and his family after him. Overall, they are feebly financed, and until the late 1960s they had received less than $1.5 million from Atlanta sources in their entire history. Yet all are fully accredited, and their contribution to Negro life in Atlanta and the country has been immeasurable. When he was a professor at Atlanta University in the 1890s, W. E. B. DuBois began his trailblazing studies of Negro life, contradicting the counsel of Booker T. Washington to accept the segregated way of life. DuBois later wrote that "between 1896 and 1920, there was no study of the race problem in America which did not depend in some degree upon the investigations at Atlanta University." The influence of the university was instrumental in formation of the first biracial committee in the nation in 1918, an organization which became the Southern Regional Council in 1944. Today several organizations at the cutting edge of black study and action, including the Institute of the Black World, are in Atlanta because of the presence of the university.

The colleges have produced thousands of Negro leaders in education, government, business, and religion. Nowhere has their contribution been greater than in Atlanta itself, where they formed the elite of the nation's most competent black community. And more than competent, I would say —also uniquely self-assured. Martin Luther King, Jr., was the primary example of that, but there have been (and are) many others, including the leaders of the black Atlanta business community and political figures like Leroy Johnson, Julian Bond, and Mayor Maynard Jackson. Some have left the South, to make a contribution far afield; I think, for instance, of King's Morehouse classmate, Dr. Charles V. Willie, who is one of the nation's leading black sociologists, the vice president of the house of deputies of the Episcopal Church, and vice president for student affairs at overwhelmingly white Syracuse University in New York. In such men one sees unique dual qualities—the capacity to represent the black community (when it is, indeed, willing to let anyone represent it) and also to be so confident of their own abilities that they can move as full equals of their peers in the white world, with neither a chip on the shoulder nor any sense of inferiority. Some of the militants who have disrupted affairs at the University Center in recent years may be oblivious of the degree of *real* black power that has had its genesis there.

Consider, for example, the Rev. William Holmes Borders of the Wheat Street Baptist Church, born in a slum shanty in Macon in 1905, graduate of Morehouse, a kind of patriarch to the city's black community whom Ivan Allen once called "one of Atlanta's all-time, truly great citizens." Borders was a leader and negotiator in countless civil rights battles. He put his own body (and a massive, impressive one it is) on the line to defy, and then break, Jim Crow laws. As interstate roads and urban renewal threw poor Atlanta blacks out of their frame and tarpaper shacks in places like Buttermilk Bottom, Borders first felt himself helpless to stem the trend. But then he learned about federal long-term, low-interest loan programs for new housing, and his church sponsored a handsome 500-unit apartment complex.

Loansharks upset him so much that he started a credit union in 1955 with $45 seed money; by 1970, its assets were $270,000. His congregation ended up owning a shopping center, supermarket, and laundry, running day nurseries and Head Start classes, and generally providing invaluable services to the black community. One of the great ironies of Borders' career, Joseph Dabney reported in *Atlanta*, was the day in 1970 that this grandson of a slave stood on a platform at the base of Stone Mountain to deliver the invocation for the memorial carvings of those Confederate demigods, Robert E. Lee, Stonewall Jackson, and Jefferson Davis.

Atlanta has long held the largest pool of black capital and corporate wealth in the United States, centered in the Negro-owned and -operated banks, insurance companies, and stores along Auburn Avenue (now slightly seedy but long called "the richest Negro street in the world") and nearby Hunter Street. As early as the 1890s, a group of former slaves had begun this first American demonstration of black capitalism. Today the Atlanta Life Insurance Company, founded by ex-slave Alonzo F. Herndon in the early 1900s, is the largest stock life insurance company owned and operated by blacks anywhere. It operates in 11 states (half of them outside the South) and has assets of some $80 million. Herndon's son Norris, now in semiretirement, was ranked by *Ebony* magazine as America's richest Negro in the early 1960s; his personal wealth has been estimated as high as $15 million. Jesse Hill, the man who runs Atlanta Life today, is a prominent civil rights leader, spokesman and mediator on racial matters, treasurer of the Atlanta Chamber of Commerce (which admitted its first Negro, and then apparently by mistake, in 1962), and a member of the board of the mass transit agency.

Among black-owned banks, Atlanta has the largest in the U.S.: the Citizens Trust Company, with $34 million in assets, now located in a gleaming new 15-story building it constructed. Two of the most successful black entrepreneurs anywhere are the brothers Robert and James Paschall, who started in 1947 with a tiny restaurant on Hunter Avenue, near the Atlanta University complex. They expanded the restaurant constantly and in 1960 opened their La Carousel lounge, which features top modern jazz performers and draws a 60 percent white clientele. In 1967 they added a motel for which Citizens Trust provided construction financing and Atlanta Life long-term financing of more than $1 million. With additions, the motel now has 270 rooms. By drawing substantial white business, the Paschall brothers overcame the barrier that still frustrates black banks and life insurance companies—the inability to get much business outside of the black community. The Atlanta black who has done the very best in the white business world is Herman Jerome Russell, a native of the city's Summerhill slum section. Russell is a highly successful plastering contractor with several hundred employees (a quarter of whom are white). He claims that "99.1 percent of my business is from the white market."

Many of the black business leaders are as conservative in their own way as white businessmen—an understandable phenomenon when one thinks of it but a source of frustration to younger, more militant blacks. The older bankers and insurance and real estate men are criticized for paternalistic policies, for failing to take enough risks to advance the black cause. To all that, the established leaders have some interesting responses. Lorimer Milton, one of Citizens Trust's founders a half century ago, said in the 1960s: "There's been a lot of loose talk about black capitalism, black this and black that, black everything. All capital is green." What may be most important is the confidence of so many Atlanta blacks that they *can* succeed. Jesse Hill, who represents a more progressive trend among black businessmen, put it this way in a 1971 newspaper interview:

> Black men and black women can take on the system and negotiate it in business and economics, in government and politics, in religion, in education, in sports, in law, in health and medicine, in science and music. You name it, we can do it. Sure the system has excessive racists, bigots and discrimination, but I disagree with those among us who urge in indiscriminate fashion for us to "sock it to America." I say, "Sock it to the evils and bigots of America." I say develop our own goals, strategies, and priorities. I say the system can be had.

The black success class of Atlanta is so large that it fills large sections of extremely attractive housing on the southern and western flanks of the city—doubtless the most extensive, poshest Negro settlement in the United States. Some of the houses are set in parklike settings, surrounded by tall pines; many are in the $50,000 to $60,000 bracket, complete with double carports and swimming pools. One of these handsome residences is occupied by Xernona Clayton, a prominent exception to the "male only" rule of black successes in Atlanta. In the late 1960s, Mrs. Clayton was invited to be hostess of the first black TV show in the American South, carried in prime time each Sunday by WAGA-TV, the local CBS outlet. Petite and vivacious, she was an instant hit—gladly accepted in the black community and a real educator for whites, both in Atlanta and outlying rural Georgia, about black life and culture. Many prominent Atlanta blacks were "introduced" to the broader Atlanta community on her show. Mrs. Clayton started her television show even while holding down another fulltime job, community affairs director for the Atlanta model cities program. Her late husband, author Edward Clayton, was a friend, colleague, and biographer of Martin Luther King, Jr.; Mrs. Clayton has much the same relationship with Coretta King.

"Atlanta," Maynard Jackson told me in an interview a few months before his election to the mayoralty, "is the best city in the country for black people—and when I tell you that, I'm not shuckin' and jivin'. I'm as serious as I can be." Jackson named the city's physical attractiveness, its role as a center of black wealth and thought, its capacity to deal in race relations through formal and informal communications between black and white, the rich and the not-so-rich. Sitting in his downtown law office—he is a member of Georgia's first black law firm, one of the largest black law firms in the country ("which is kind of a joke, because there are only nine lawyers here")—Jackson said: "My roots are here. My mother was born two miles from here. I'm a fifth-generation Georgian. It may be deeper than that, but they didn't keep our records before 1865." And most important for the tenor of black and white relations, and the pride of the black community, Jackson said, is the memory of Martin Luther King, Jr. "He's buried here. His legacy is still living here. It still influences decisions here."

One of the most momentous occasions of Atlanta's history was the warm April day of 1968 when the fallen King's body was borne through the city streets on a wagon drawn by mules—symbols of the black man's sad heritage in the South. Half a million persons from every walk of life crowded into the center of the city, hundreds of thousands of them marching 30-

abreast for five hours. Mayor Ivan Allen, Jr., was one of those marchers; the moment he learned that King had been shot, Allen had rushed to the Kings' home, bringing with him Mrs. Allen—an important symbolic act in the South—and Atlanta's very progressive police chief of the 1960s, Herbert Jenkins.* "There is a deep sense of reverence and respect by a large majority of Atlanta people for Martin Luther King, Jr.," Allen said. For the first time in history, every man on the Atlanta police department was on duty at the same time that day—but the real reason that order and reverence were maintained, while 20 burning cities elsewhere in America became King's funeral pyre, was that the black people of Atlanta wanted it to be that way, and that the white leadership (except for Lester Maddox, who kept the State Capitol an armed garrison) showed they really cared. "There was more love in this city than I've ever seen in my life," reporter Alex Coffin observed.

A memorial center for King is now being constructed in a four-block area including his birthplace and the humble three-story Ebenezer Baptist Church, which served as the base for his activities and where his father, the Rev. Martin Luther King, Sr., has been the pastor for four decades. It will contain the simple tomb of the great apostle of nonviolence and winner of the Nobel Peace Prize. There will also be a Freedom Exhibition Hall, housing a Library Documentation Project and the Institute for Nonviolent Social Change which is presently located at the Atlanta University Center.

As I noted in the introduction to this book, Atlanta in the 1960s was the fountainhead of civil rights activity for the entire Southern United States. Dr. King's Southern Christian Leadership Conference operated out of headquarters on Atlanta's "sweet Auburn," sparking the battles of Montgomery and Birmingham and Selma and countless little towns that never made a headline in the North, but transforming the life of black people all across the South. Atlanta was headquarters, too, for the Student Nonviolent Coordinating Committee, which provided the blue-denimed foot soldiers for so many of those struggles. SNCC's leader in its most productive and turbulent years—1963 to 1966—was John Lewis, one of the most personally courageous men the civil rights movement ever produced. Forty times Lewis was arrested; at Selma he suffered injuries including a possible skull fracture and requiring hospitalization, but he still completed the entire 50-mile walk to Montgomery. But Lewis never forsook the principle of integration—a position that caused his ouster as SNCC's chairman (in favor of Stokely Carmichael) in 1966.

An amazing portion of the civil rights activity directed from Atlanta was centered in 5 Forsyth Street, a dingy old red building that had once housed the offices of the Atlanta *Journal* and *Constitution*. The first civil rights ten-

* Jenkins served as a member of President Johnson's Commission on Civil Disorders, and was even reported to be one of the more liberal members of that group. I went to see him in 1969 and found a genial, silver-haired professional with a keen sense of the political pressures in his community. He was working hard at community relations programs ("even though it makes us into a kind of family welfare service") and interested in upgrading educational levels in his department. Jenkins first recommended putting blacks on the force in 1948, and by the time he retired as chief more than 20 percent of the Atlanta police were black. The whites, however, include many young Georgia "crackers" in from the countryside, men with initially deep racial prejudices to overcome. Jenkins related his experiences and observations of police work and Atlanta's desegregation story in a book, *Keeping the Peace* (New York: Harper & Row, 1970).

ant was the late, lamented Episcopal Society for Cultural and Racial Unity, which moved in in 1960. (ESCRU took up quarters at 5 Forsyth after the building superintendent for its former offices refused to let the black secretary of the executive director use the ladies' room.) ESCRU was eventually followed by the Southern Regional Council and its Voter Education Project, The American Civil Liberties Union, the National Sharecropper's Fund, the Law Students Civil Rights Research Council, and the Atlanta Council on Human Relations. In 1971, when 5 Forsyth was vacated to prepare for the wrecker's ball, James Wooten observed in the New York *Times* that as a result of the projects, campaigns, lawsuits, and pamphlets produced by the black and white men and women who had worked there, "schools and a variety of other institutions have been integrated, a million black people registered to vote, elections won and lost, white politicians tempered, black candidates encouraged and supported, and popular racial traditions challenged and changed."

Often with altered roles, several of those organizations continue to operate out of Atlanta in the 1970s, scattered through buildings in the downtown section. The most concrete program remains that of the Voter Education Project, now headed by John Lewis. VEP is trying to knock down the last official barriers to black voting and particularly to get still unregistered Southern blacks to exercise the franchise won for them in the battles of the '60s. Maynard Jackson observed that there no longer is "a civil rights movement as we knew it in the 1960s. It has evolved into a political movement —which is what it fought to establish."

Nowhere is the new phase of the movement more apparent than in Atlanta itself. Blacks first became a vital factor in the city's politics in the first years after World War II and abolition of the white primary. Mayor Hartsfield, who had been as much a segregationist as other white leaders when he first won office in 1937, began to court the black vote—at first exclusively through a wealthy Negro lawyer, Austin T. Walden, who for years headed the bipartisan Negro Voters League.* A kind of deal was struck, under which blacks supported Hartsfield, and Ivan Allen, Jr., after him, in return for a relatively liberal course in city government including city help in building low-cost public housing. The power elite of Atlanta—the banks, utility companies, major retail stores, a few outstanding real estate dealers and lawyers, and the heads of the big home-based industries like Coca-Cola, Scripto, Delta, and Colonial Stores—in effect chose the city leadership, delivering election-time support from the middle- and upper-class whites who live on the north side of the city. The blacks were junior partners in picking candidates, but as time went on they delivered a greater and greater share of the votes. This alliance easily outvoted the working-class whites, mostly residents of central and southside Atlanta. In 1957 and 1961, Lester Maddox ran for mayor as the champion of the working-class whites. In 1957, Harts-

* Austin Walden was one of those early civil rights battlers who used the courts to win freedoms that blacks after him would use and enjoy. The son of ex-slaves, he got his law degree from the University of Michigan and returned to Georgia to defy white threats on his life because he dared, as a black man, to appear as a lawyer in court. It was Walden who, after a protracted legal fight, finally got the white primary declared unconstitutional.

field beat him with 63 percent of the vote; in 1961, Allen repeated the feat with 64 percent.

Allen had to cope with a rising tide of black militancy during his eight years in office but managed the situation with grace and courage that few men could have mustered in his situation. Events, not self-generated virtue, transformed Allen, the courtly, mild-mannered patrician, into a determined integrationist. In 1953, as a successful businessman, he had said: "Negroes have got to learn to respect the traditional rights of segregation." But in 1960–61, when he headed the chamber of commerce, students from the Atlanta University complex staged a major sit-in at Rich's lunch counters, protesting the tight segregation there and in other downtown stores and cafeterias. All were arrested, refused to put up bail, and remained in jail for months while the crisis boiled to a head. Allen, A. T. Walden, and others then negotiated a settlement to drop charges against the students and open up the lunch counters within a few months; when some Negroes protested the delay, Martin Luther King, Jr., stepped in to insist that the "first contract" ever written with the white man be honored. The episode won Allen solid black support, and Mills Lane and his other business friends and colleagues gave him the financial support he needed to win election. Once in office, Allen desegregated the fire department, gave Negro police the first authority to arrest white offenders, and led the first group of blacks into the still segregated City Hall cafeteria.

In 1963, at the request of President Kennedy, Allen went to Washington to testify for the public accommodations proposal that would eventually become part of the 1964 Civil Rights Act. Twenty of 24 local blacks he consulted urged Allen not to take the risk of testifying on the bill, on the theory that if he did, he couldn't be reelected. But Allen went, and returned to what he called "a holocaust" of white indignation in Atlanta. Nevertheless, within six months the white business community was saying he had done the right thing. In 1965 he was reelected with 61 percent of the vote.

A year later, Allen responded to rioting in the Summerhill ghetto by going to the scene of the action and dealing with the situation personally. "I had watched the Watts riot in Los Angeles, and thought how poorly it was handled," Allen told me at the end of his term. "I knew I had a greater responsibility—that I must be personally at the scene of the action and confront it. I was scared, I'll admit. I thought to myself, 'I'm going to make the riot come over to me, until it overwhelms the city.'" Allen broke up fights, exhorted from the top of an auto, and when the mob began rocking the car, had to hop off. He finally ordered use of tear gas—and got a heavy dose himself. But he had ordered an aide to call up 25 of Atlanta's leading Negro clergymen (including the Rev. Martin Luther King, Sr.), and they helped to cool tempers before excessive damage was done. Allen's intervention also succeeded because he had made a point of regularly walking the streets of the ghetto (before John Lindsay and other mayors got that idea). And "the word went out across the Negro community about police restraint," Allen said. "Instead of cries of 'police brutality,' the shoe was on the other foot."

By Allen's last year as mayor, his office was crowded with silver and gold shovels used to break earth for one big building project after another during his incumbency. He was proudest personally of the stadium, which drew big-league teams. Some critics said Allen's racial moderation was just a device to keep profits rolling in for his big business buddies. But I would prefer to take the word of Martin Luther King, Sr., when Allen retired: "You're coming down as John F. Kennedy did. You have, like him, touched even the hearts of children. My grandchildren said to me, 'Grandpa, are we going to lose our mayor?' I want you to know, I will die being your friend."

The black vote, 29 percent of the city total when Allen first ran, was up to almost 41 percent when he retired in 1969—and turning out in higher percentages than whites. Up to this point, blacks had rarely won citywide elections in Atlanta. The first breakthrough had been in 1953, when Dr. Rufus E. Clement, president of Atlanta University, had received the business establishment's blessing to win a place on the city board of education. Another was in 1965, when Q. V. Williamson, a highly regarded black businessman, was elected to the board of aldermen—over opposition of more than two-thirds of the poorer whites of Atlanta. But in 1969 there was a breakthrough of even greater importance. Maynard Jackson, then 31 years old, was elected vice mayor, winning by getting almost 100 percent of the black vote. But in that same year's election, a respected black member of the board of education, Dr. Horace E. Tate, failed to make it to the runoff for mayor. He had the support of figures like Julian Bond and Ralph Abernathy, but most "regular" black political leaders felt it was too soon to elect a black and backed instead vice mayor Sam Massell, Jr., the self-proclaimed "liberal Democrat" in the nonpartisan race. In the runoff, Massell defeated alderman Rodney M. Cook, a moderate Republican leader who had the support of Allen and much of the business leadership.

Massell, Atlanta's first Jewish mayor, proved to be "nobody's man" in his first years in office. He pleased the business establishment that had opposed him by breaking a strike of predominantly black garbage workers, but he made few friends when his brother was accused of Mafia ties, and organized crime activity accelerated in Atlanta. Massell made a black man (Franklin Thomas) the city government's personnel director and set a goal of 50 percent blacks in city jobs by 1974. Blacks were still heavily concentrated in laborer-service type positions, but of Massell's new appointments to department head posts, three-quarters were black.

A major change was clearly in store in Atlanta politics in the 1970s. While the grand coalition of the mass of black voters allied with affluent or liberal whites might continue, its basic nature would be altered. Instead of the white power structure dictating the man blacks would vote for, the blacks would be moving to the front of the political bus, stipulating which candidates would be chosen to lead Atlanta.

If any metropolitan area in the South was ready for an era in which blacks win election to office based on their capabilities, and not exclusively on a black bloc vote, Atlanta was that place. The Rev. Andrew J. Young proved the point in 1972 when he became Georgia's—and the South's—first black Congressman since Reconstruction. The Atlanta area district which elected Young, extending from predominantly black south Atlanta up to the affluent white northside and well out into the surburbs, had only 80,000 blacks (38 percent) among its 210,000 registered voters. Young had long since established his credentials among blacks, working as executive vice president of the SCLC under King, leading the 1963 demonstration in Birmingham when Bull Connor set dogs on the marchers, and proving his major skills as a negotiator in racial crises. In the two years between a losing 1970 race for Congress and his successful run, he was executive director of the Atlanta Community Relations Commission. Many young liberal whites worked for his election, and Young went beyond exclusive black concerns to oppose a freeway that would decimate white neighborhoods and to urge a clean-up of the Chattahoochee River so that its banks could be preserved for recreation as a national park. On election day he got 53 percent of the total vote, adding substantial support in affluent and even not-so-affluent white communities to his overwhelming black vote.

In a newspaper interview immediately afterwards, Young said, "I lost Old South voters and picked up New South voters." The New South voters, he said, were young Georgians more liberal than their forebears. "Working-day desegregation" in Atlanta helped his cause, Young observed. "I first began to notice the difference when I would go into cafeterias and see white and black persons lunching together—out of choice." "I believe in this city," Young said. He believes there really is "an Atlanta mystique" of progress and understanding.

In 1973 a black advance of even more importance was made: the election of Maynard Jackson as Atlanta's first black mayor. Eleven candidates competed in the first election that year, including such well known figures as Mayor Massell, Charles Weltner, and Leroy Johnson. The city's blacks, making up 48.5 percent of the electorate, solidified behind Jackson. He received 47 percent of the total vote in the first election, just short of the majority needed. Massell narrowly edged out Weltner for second place, and faced Jackson in the runoff. Jackson's issue was that Massell had presided over "an administration of neglect," permitting a sharp rise in the crime rate. Massell resorted to a quite racist campaign, warning of a "black takeover" and trying to associate Jackson with the controversial civil rights activist Hosea Williams, who was running for president of the city council (a powerful position created by a new city charter). Massell said there would be a "white flight" to the suburbs if the "racist team" of Massell and Williams—who actually ran quite unconnected campaigns—were elected. "Atlanta is too young to die," Massell's campaign advertisements declared. But the voters, it turned out, were quite able to tell the difference between Jackson and the more fiery Hosea Williams. They gave Jackson 60 percent of their vote, a victory which Jackson attributed to "a vote of confidence from a significant part of the white community and one hell of a turnout from the black community." But at the same time they elected Wyche Fowler, a white liberal, over Williams with a

64 percent vote.* Maynard Jackson—who at six feet, four inches in height and close to 300 pounds is as formidable physically as he is politically—became the first black mayor of a major Southern city and the first black to preside over a state capital anywhere in the United States. Taking office in January 1974, he was joined by a board of education with a black majority and a city council evenly divided between whites and blacks.

Clearly it was no overnight change of heart which permitted Atlanta, the commercial and cultural center of the old Confederacy, to move with such comparative amity into an era of black political rule. And at least some of the credit for the relatively smooth transition must go to the seeds of racial sanity and understanding planted over many years by the late Ralph McGill. McGill was editor of the Atlanta *Constitution* from 1942 to 1960, its publisher from 1960 until his death in 1969, and throughout an impassioned columnist-editorialist who deserved to be called, as he was by many, "the conscience of the South." McGill was rarely quite as far ahead of his region on race matters as the invective thrown at him by Dixie segregationists would have led one to believe. But he did show compassion where others had been blind, and he did on occasion deliver wrathful and rightful judgments. Eugene Patterson, editor of the *Constitution* during the 1960s, wrote that McGill "spoke for the Negro, the one-crop tenant, the linthead of the Chattachoochee valley and the children in the threadbare schools. By starting the conversation he broke paths for progress. . . . He may well have been the most influential newspaper editor who ever wrote in a region rich with Wattersons and Gradys."

McGill's reputation was so glittering that one would have expected the news coverage of the *Constitution* and its evening companion, the *Journal*, to be on a par with great regional newspapers like the Los Angeles *Times*. Sad to report, such has not been the case for many years. The reason has been the parsimonious control of Jack Tarver, president of the Atlanta Newspapers, Inc., who has been preoccupied with maximizing profits for the absentee owners, Cox Newspapers, which are owned by the three children of former Governor James M. Cox of Ohio. (Tarver himself also owns a substantial piece of stock in the local corporation.) No *Journal* or *Constitution* writer was sent to cover the Selma march of 1965, or James Meredith's march of 1967, or even to Memphis after Martin Luther King, Jr.'s assassination. The Washington bureau was so thinly staffed that it had little time to cover anything except the Georgia congressional delegation. In disgust over the low salaries paid, many young newsmen of exceptional talent quit (to be replaced, regularly, by eager young Southern writers arriving in Atlanta and glad to work for $100 a week). One of the alumni told *Newsweek:* "The *Constitution* had a chance to become a great national newspaper when the civil rights movement broke. The paper was sitting right in the middle of it, but it was too concerned about its profits." Just to make matters worse, many staffers of the papers charged that management made them water down or alter stories to appease local advertisers.

* Citizens of both races were showing a flexibility that confounded those who predicted unadulterated bloc voting. Jackson, for instance, received about a fifth of the white vote, while Fowler got almost a third of the black vote.

This is not to say that the Atlanta papers have not been, even beyond their editorial pages, a positive influence. Their eagle-eyed coverage of state government, for instance, has prevented serious corruption there. Writers like Margaret Shannon, who writes for the papers' Sunday magazine, have dug down to the roots of Georgia life. The editorial leaders of the *Constitution* today are young, enlightened Southerners the paper should be proud of—Reg Murphy and Hal Gulliver. But the tightfisted budgets go on.

Many of the newspapers' graduates migrated over the years to *Atlanta Magazine,* the monthly magazine put out by the Atlanta Chamber of Commerce which is at once a glossy advertisement for the opulence of the new Atlanta and the repository of much of the best writing done on the city. *Atlanta* had a crisis in the late 1960s, when the chamber cracked down on it for stories it considered too freewheeling and critical of the hand that fed it. Many heads rolled, and advocacy journalism disappeared from *Atlanta*'s pages. But the quality of writing about city problems still exceeds most city magazines. Atlanta's managing editor is Bruce Galphin, an ex-*Constitution* writer, book author, and journalist of stature.

Atlanta: Going Metro

If there is a great deal distinctive about Atlanta, the opposite can be said of its suburbs. Reg Murphy observed that there is little to distinguish them from the suburbs of any northern city. They are a place, he noted, of real cultural deprivation, especially for college graduates. They grow, in part, by a kind of homing instinct—people wanting to get back to the soil, or at least to own a quarter acre of it. The suburban American, Murphy said, is in a way the forgotten American—"but don't they *want* to be forgotten?" The new Atlanta suburbanites, almost invariably white, would certainly like to be forgotten by the blacks who now crowd the center city. They also want to get away from Atlanta's crime rate, which has more than doubled since 1965. By 1972, Atlanta had the highest homicide rate in America. The 225th and last murder of that year took place on New Year's Eve when a traveler from Florida phoned his wife from a booth to let her know he had arrived safely and that she should not worry about those stories of crime and violence in Atlanta. His last words to her, according to news reports, were: "He's got a gun . . . no, you're not going to . . ."

Atlanta has no natural boundaries, no great bodies of water or mountain ranges to constrain its growth, so that the suburbs have expanded, without obstruction, to all compass points. While the population of Atlanta proper remained static at just under 500,000 in the 1960s, the suburban counties added 363,000 people—up 69 percent in a single decade. DeKalb County, the biggest (and wealthiest) bedroom of them all, ended the 1960s with 415,000 people. Clayton, Cobb, and Gwinnett, essentially rural places when the postwar era began, had 367,000 people by 1970; if they grow as fast in the 1970s as they did in the 1960s, those three counties alone will have an aggregate population larger than Atlanta proper. In 1973, the federal government suddenly added 10 counties to the Atlanta standard metropolitan statistical area, more than doubling its geographic size to 4,326 square miles and adding more than 200,000 new residents. The new metro population total was estimated at 1.75 million. In a way, the expansion only confirmed what was really known about the economic influence of metropolitan Atlanta, which was already drawing commuting labor from no less than 48 counties.

Expressways and interstate highways, gutting parts of central Atlanta and then poking every which way into the suburban hinterland, reshaped the region during the 1960s. In 1969, work was completed on a circumferential route, Interstate 285, which loops around Atlanta for 63 miles, its flanks dotted with shopping centers, office and industrial parks, warehouses, discount stores, and apartments. "Functional it is, pretty it is not," an Atlanta newsman wrote of the new road.

The office parks, especially numerous north of Atlanta, symbolize a new real estate trend geared to a mobile society in which the white work force that fled the city for suburban life can now work in the suburbs too. The office park is ideally located for a company operating regionally, since it is right on the interstates and has easy superhighway access to the airport. The seemingly omnipresent computer of modern business has something to do with the phenomenon, too: it is simply cheaper and easier for a company to get the special electric connections and humidity connections it needs in a new office park structure than in a downtown office building. Atlanta has not experienced the severe drain of companies to the suburbs that many northern cities report, but there has been some loss—including the Atlanta corporate offices of firms like Sinclair and Shell Oil, Avon Cosmetics, and Monsanto. As for the industrial parks, they offer less crowded conditions than the city, the same convenient road connections, and access for the new suburban labor market (though not, of course, for the inner-city blacks who suffer from chronic high unemployment levels).

Atlanta was the last big American city to resist the trend to large suburban shopping centers. The reason seems to have been that Rich's department store so dominated the field that no downtown store was willing to take the suburban plunge until it did. Board chairman Richard Rich told *Atlanta Magazine*: "I said I wouldn't open up any branches until four conditions had been met. I wanted population to reach a million in the metropolitan area; the expressways to be finished; a 1,250-car parking garage built adjacent to our store; and a complete remodeling of the downtown store so it wouldn't look rundown in comparison with the new branch." The conditions were finally met in 1959, when Rich's opened its first suburban store; now it has seven. But the retail activity downtown has remained brisk. If retail moguls in other cities had set the same conditions Rich did, there might be fewer sick center cities in the country today.

All the growth of the '60s, however, created two monstrous headaches for Atlanta—one fiscal, the other physical. Sam Massell explained the fiscal problem this way: "The 1970 Census showed us that in the decade, 60,000 whites had moved out of the city of Atlanta, and 70,000 blacks had moved in. The average family income of the people who moved out was

$13,000 a year; of those who moved in, under $9,000. This is intolerable for a city. It's getting more poor people, which means services have to increase. Yet being limited to the property tax, with no funds from the commuters, we end up in the impossible situation of taxing the poor to pay for the poor." Another part of Atlanta's problem is that half of the property within its limits is tax exempt (government, church, and educational institutions).

For years, it has been clear that some kind of annexation would be needed to solve Atlanta's problem. No one quite dared to propose that wealthy DeKalb be fastened to Atlanta, but the remainder of Fulton County—an area rich with the new office parks and industrial concentrations—seemed like a feasible suggestion. But a city-council consolidation proposal lost in a 1966 referendum, and several later attempts to do the same by act of the legislature came to naught. One reason was that black legislators feared losing their inner-city clout; from their newly won majority position in Atlanta proper, they would slip to less than 40 percent in the whole county. White suburban legislators feared being attached to the city. Sam Massell was against annexation or consolidation when he ran for mayor in 1969, but the problem of his constricted tax base soon made him change his mind. Massell came up with a so-called "two city" plan for Fulton County. Atlanta would double its land area by annexing all unincorporated areas in north Fulton—a step that would only reduce the black population share from 51 to 47 percent. Simultaneously, a new city of South Fulton, heavily white with many blue-collar people, would be created. The proposal picked up major support from both racial groups and sailed through the state house of representatives. But Lester Maddox was able to block it in the senate. An enraged Massell uttered a string of blasphemies about Maddox, which were later engraved on a plaque that I discovered, a year later, hanging above the toilet in the washroom of the mayor's office. The likelihood is that the same plan, or a version of it, will be revived and passed in the near future.

The metropolitan area as constituted up to 1973 had a mishmash of five county governments, 45 municipalities, 38 water systems, and 23 sewer systems. An early metropolitan planning commission—dating from 1947—made some progress in regional coordination, but in 1971 a major step forward was made when the legislature set up the Atlanta Regional Commission. It replaced all earlier areawide agencies and was charged with preparing comprehensive guides for planning and developing highways, transit lines, parks, sewers, and some community facilities. A combination of 23 elected officials and private citizens sits on its board. With its power to pass on plans of area governments that have regional implications, and to monitor federal funds going to the localities, the commission may become a real power in the next years.

Atlanta's physical headache has to do with the horrendous traffic jams, some of which extend many miles out of center city at rush hours. The superhighways have not cured the traffic glut; in fact, they have exacerbated it. In 1962 there were 465,000 registered motor vehicles in the Atlanta metropolitan area; today there are more than 800,000. (In 1950 there were only

215,000.) New auto registrations, in fact, have risen twice as fast as the population. More than 50 percent of the land in the central business district is now dedicated to the movement and parking of automobiles. More than 80 percent of air pollution in the city comes from motor vehicles. No one seriously disputed Massell's prediction that the increase in motor vehicles, in the absence of a competitive means of transit, "would surely strangle the inner city."

The idea of rapid mass transit for the Atlanta region was first raised in 1952, but it was not until the mid-1960s that the legislature passed a bill to make a mass transit system possible. The law required referenda approval in the counties involved. The Metropolitan Atlanta Rapid Transit Authority (MARTA) was created in 1966, but two years later a hastily drawn plan for a 21-mile rail system to be financed by property taxes and uncoordinated with bus lines, was rejected by voters. After that, MARTA regrouped and came up with a transit plan which finally passed—albeit by the skin of its teeth—in the two key counties, Fulton (Atlanta) and DeKalb, in November 1971.*

The new Atlanta plan is a masterful combination of integrated public transportation, innovative financing, service to all sectors of the community, and supersalesmanship. It is probably the best ever devised in the United States, and many of its features are likely to be copied by other American cities in the '70s. The reason is that priority was placed on social benefits, rather than technological innovation, and that the public could be promised immediate benefits, not just the dividend of a "perfect" system several years in the future.

A key feature of the plan, for instance, is closely integrated bus and rail service. When the 50-mile rapid rail line is completed in 1979, some 1,500 miles of bus lines will feed into it. Sam Massell said that 90 percent of the people and 90 percent of the jobs within Atlanta's perimeter boundaries in Fulton and DeKalb Counties will be within walking distance of scheduled service. But as soon as MARTA purchased Atlanta's privately owned bus line in 1972, improvements were initiated. Orders were placed for almost 500 new buses, to beef up the fleet by 60 percent. Among the first 10 new bus lines were three—one to a hospital cluster, one to an industrial park, one to a new shopping center—designed to give center-city low-income black people access to jobs in the suburban ring.

The MARTA plan pioneers by making public transportation a low-cost, frankly subsidized service, like street maintenance or fire protection. The voters were promised that the day MARTA took over the bus lines, the fare —with transfers—would be lowered from 40 cents to 15 cents. The promise was kept, and MARTA expects to hold the fare that low until the late '70s. Massell originally wanted to have free fares, but 15 cents is presently the lowest in the country (except, I guess, for the Staten Island Ferry in New York and the Charles Street trolley in New Orleans). "I'm predicting free

* Clayton and Gwinnett Counties defeated the referendum, and will not be included in the new system unless they choose to have the lines extended to them later. Cobb County had already voted itself out.

fares in the next 10 or 15 years," Massell said. "You can take all your great rapid transit systems—in Montreal or San Francisco, by monorail or subway, and talk about modern equipment, or frequency and safety—but what no one had done, and what we did, and what will set the stage for the future, is the subsidized fare. Then you're talking about a governmental service." The result of low fares or free fares, Massell said, is to assure "man's fifth freedom—mobility." It is a freedom many people take for granted, he said, but one all too often denied the young, the poor, the aged, and the handicapped. In the first few months of the low fare, ridership of the Atlanta buses went up 27 percent.

Another important innovation of MARTA is its financing. Instead of a property tax surcharge, it is financed by a 1 percent local sales tax. The tax has several advantages. First, its yield is so high that it will cover not only operation of the bus lines, and later the rail lines, but so much of the capital costs that the system's peak accumulated debt, even when the rail line is being built, will probably not be much more than $200 million. And all bonds will be paid off in 15 years. (A huge but often unpublicized feature of all new mass transit systems, of course, is the massive federal subsidy under the Urban Mass Transportation Assistance Act of 1970. In Atlanta, that aid is expected to cover two-thirds of the capital costs.)

The sales tax feature was absolutely crucial to acceptance of the plan by Atlanta's suburbanites, who could have been expected to oppose (as they did in 1968) any plan to increase their property taxes. Massell admitted that the sales tax is regressive but claimed that the lowered fare saves an average working-class family $3 a week, compared to an increase of only 73 cents in its average weekly sales tax. The work mobility factor for low-income people, of course, will increase greatly when the system is finished. In the meantime, MARTA hires many more black bus drivers than the old private system, and will provide thousands of jobs in its $1.3 billion capital program—the biggest public works project in the South since the TVA.

MARTA's backers used a hard sell on dubious suburbanites, pointing out that they could save hundreds of dollars a year on reduced commuting costs—perhaps even sell their second car—and that downtown and the entire area would be much pleasanter with reduced traffic congestion and air pollution. Massell even campaigned for the transit referendum from a helicopter hovering over stalled freeway traffic, addressing the motorists through a bullhorn: "Frustrated? How'd you like to be riding 65 miles an hour in an air-conditioned train instead? If you want to get out of this mess, vote yes." All the proponents' arguments were necessary, because opponents were arguing that a region-wide subway would simply transport inner-city muggers and drug pushers to suburbia. Lester Maddox took out personal ads in the local papers to damn "this corrupt, inefficient and immoral idea." In Fulton County, the favorable vote was only 50.2 percent, in DeKalb 52.2 percent. However close the vote, Atlanta had made an historic advance in mass transit planning and financing in America—an achievement for which Massell, despite his reelection defeat, should long be honored. Significantly, the Atlanta financing system was quickly considered by other cities. In 1973 the voters of Denver, Colorado, endorsed a comprehensive rapid transit system financed by a metropolitan-wide sales tax remarkably similar to Atlanta's.

The rapid rail plan now on Marta's blueboards calls for nine miles of subways, most of which will be in the center of downtown Atlanta, all converging on Five Points. There will also be 16 miles of elevated rail and 25 miles of surface rail (plus 14 miles of fixed exclusive busways). The lines will go to all four major points of the compass, with several major spurs. Taking advantage of Atlanta's historic convergence of railway lines, MARTA will be able to build 65 percent of its rail system along existing rights-of-way. Alan F. Kiepper, MARTA's manager, said only 1,800 homes and businesses would be forced to relocate, compared to 23,000 families in the six-mile stretch of Chicago's proposed cross-town expressway. Another advantage of MARTA is that its directors are not insisting—as the directors of San Francisco's Bay Area Rapid Transit system did—that the rapid rail system score technological breakthroughs. The BART system encountered major technical problems when it opened in 1972, because its very advanced automated equipment had not been sufficiently tested. MARTA expects to avoid that error by using only technologically proven equipment. "We hope to learn from BART's travail," Kiepper said.

MARTA has already made some mistakes of its own, but so far they are mostly in the public relations area—including an ill-timed decision to grant extremely generous retirement benefits to its executives, years before the first rapid transit car moves. But Kiepper is a hard-driving and ultra-efficient manager. Now in his mid-forties, he already has behind him four years as Fulton County manager (a post in which he hauled the county government into the 20th century) and a stint as city manager in Richmond, Virginia. Kiepper is an intellectual who sees much farther than the next bus or transit stop:

> We'll take conscious and full advantage of the potential the MARTA system will provide for the redevelopment of this community. From the Toronto and San Francisco experiences, we know that a public transportation system, if it's sensitively designed, can have a profound effect upon the development of a community. It can serve as a catalyst for new growth. It can change living patterns. It can provide a meaningful transportation option for people.
>
> Since World War II, every community in the United States has been developed with the basic assumption that the auto will be the basic means of transportation. We believe the MARTA system will provide a real alternative. It means that development doesn't have to be oriented to suburban shopping centers and parking lots. What you see in Toronto is cluster development—high-density development around stations, with living facilities, recreation, and shops all right there. People are then able to meet their needs in these complexes, and then to use the rapid transit system to get to their places of employment.
>
> So the impact on the future development of the community becomes very great.

Kiepper's enthusiasm is shared by John Portman, who believes rapid transit will help return downtown Atlanta to people use—and let the downtown designer-builders like himself continue their fantastic transformation of the old inner city. "Before MARTA was passed," Portman said in 1973, "there was only one big building coming on stream. Atlanta was developing hardening of the arteries. MARTA was a way of giving new vessels to the heart."

Those are chamber of commerce words, however, and they need to be balanced with MARTA's potential role in giving better jobs and mobility to the poor people of Atlanta. In the 1960s, black and white in Atlanta began to work together for the first time. Now they face a decade when the city will be beset by all the problems that rapid growth can bring, from over-suburbanization and inner-city fiscal woes to traffic jams. But one feels the problems will eventually be solved, because of Atlanta's extraordinary spirit. Early in the 1970s, a black Atlanta alderman was quoted as saying: "We survived Sherman's fire and we can survive getting big. We're going to make it and we're going to make it together, black and white, and we'll probably be better off than anybody around."

Second-Tier Cities: From Savannah to Rome

After Atlanta, the story of urban Georgia turns quickly to Savannah on the seacoast, the place where the state began. The Founder was General James Oglethorpe, who arrived to found Savannah with his band of 125 English settlers in 1773. Before then, the white man's touch with Georgia had been limited to brief Spanish explorations, starting with Hernando de Soto's search for gold in 1540 and some Franciscan missions on the offshore islands Except for a thriving Indian culture, Georgia was essentially untouched when King George II granted Oglethorpe a royal charter "for the settling of the poor persons of London." The English planned Savannah to be the capital of their last and poorest New World colony, a military buffer between the thriving Carolinas and the Spanish in Florida, and a repository of the unfortunate souls of England's debtors prisons, whose cause Oglethrope had made his own.

Oglethorpe went up the Savannah River some 10 miles from the sea, found "a healthy situation" for a town on high land where the river formed a half moon, and there, he reported to his English trustees, "I have laid out the town." No one knows for sure, Anthony Wolff reported in *American Heritage,* what the genesis was of Oglethorpe's town plan. But the plan was so felicitous that Philadelphia's urban planner Edmund Bacon has called it "exalted . . . one of the finest diagrams for city organization and growth in existence." Others have suggested it was tragic that so few settlers of the American interior passed through Savannah, since its plan might have saved hundreds of American towns from the gridiron conformity that could only lead to urban sprawl in later times.

Oglethorpe's plan was deceptively simple: a series of modular units, called "wards," each with public buildings and some 40 residential lots and with a public square at the center, laid out one beside the next neatly across the landscape. The public squares were the secret genius of the plan, because each became a quiet oasis of green at the front doorstep, or almost so, of every house, the equivalent of the green in a New England village.

The plan succeeded so brilliantly because it allowed order and diversity to flourish together. As architectural critic Wolf Von Eckardt wrote:

> It is an unusual and almost dreamlike experience to walk the nearly two-and-a-half square miles of Savannah's Historic Landmark District on a sunny spring day. The shaded streets are of a most agreeable width that is at once airy and intimate. They are lined by all manner of houses, some free-standing, some in rows, that display a variety of architectural styles, materials and colors, a variety unified by the buildings' common desire to be polite, to speak softly, as it were, in a melodious Southern murmur. . . .
>
> Most [of the squares] are roofed by the leafy branches of huge old oaks, heavily hung with Spanish moss. All the squares are comfortingly enclosed by buildings. . . . These are urban parks, elegant outdoor salons.

Six wards were begun during the 10 years that Oglethorpe remained in America, and eventually 24 by 1856, when the city's common land was exhausted. Each retains a certain individuality and role, like Johnson Square, first ever built, where the banks and brokerage houses now stand, or Wright Square, the center for government buildings, or Forsyth Park, Savannah's heart, which has a reproduction of the fountain in the Place de la Concorde in Paris.

Nineteenth-century Savannah grew and prospered with King Cotton, as millions of tons each year passed through the factoring houses along the Savannah riverfront, there to be loaded on ships. By 1819, Savannah was the 16th largest city in America, and slaves to tend the cotton fields made up 41 percent of the population—even though slavery was not introduced at all to Georgia until 1750. But the golden age of Savannah came to an abrupt halt in 1895, when cotton prices collapsed, and the city had little to fall back on. Some cotton still moved through the port, along with quantities of tobacco and naval stores, but the dynamism was gone. A sleepy, indifferent ruling class controlled the life of Savannah, and little heed was paid to the life of the destitute blacks who inhabited a ring of dilapidated wooden structures, some dating back to the days of slavery, which surrounded the historic central area on all sides save its face to the river. The city government had a low reputation, and Savannah suffered the embarrassment of a very low bond rating.

Industries began to move in, most notably a mill of the Union Camp Corporation that was enticed in 1935 through city promises to protect it from property taxes and antipollution lawsuits. Eventually, the mill became the biggest paper bag producer in the world (35 million a day) with 5,000 workers on its payroll, but there was a price to pay: heavy pollution of the Savannah River, and a rotten egg stench befouling the city. Another industrial recruit was American Cyanimid, which dumped about a million pounds of acid wastes into the river each day. (The ecological sins of these two corporations were aired to the world in a 1970 book by Ralph Nader's raiders, *The Water Lords;* among other things, Union Camp—which is known locally as "The Bag"—was charged with causing 70 percent of the river's pollution and thus being largely responsible for a severe cutback in the oyster beds and shrimp and fish populations in the Savannah area. Another culprit was the city of Savannah itself, which dumped the raw sewage of 150,000 people into the Savannah River. Through state and federal regulatory efforts, most of these conditions were being corrected by 1973. The holdout was American Cyanimid, which refused to install pollution control equipment and suffered state-imposed fines [initially $500 a day] as a result.)

The economy of the Savannah area began to pick up after World War II, but the growth was almost all in the suburbs, not in the city proper. Between 1960 and 1970, for instance, the population of Savannah proper declined 21 percent, to 118,349, while that of surrounding Chatham county grew by 78 percent, to 69,418. Suburban subdivisions prospered, and a multimillion-dollar suburban shopping mall went up. Old Savannah seemed to slumber on, no one showing interest in "improving" it via the urban renewal bulldozer. A couple of the park squares were demolished for a highway, but the greater danger to the historic district was decay and piecemeal demolition.

Then, in 1955, the seeds of a grand renewal were sown. A lost battle to save the historic old vegetable and fish market was the catalyst. Mrs. Anna C. Hunter, one of the city's *grandes dames*, got together with six other women who saw that if the historic district were not protected in its entirety, it would be destroyed bit by bit. They formed the Historic Savannah Foundation, which began to buy up priceless old homes as they came on the market and then resell them quickly under protective covenants that required the new owners to restore the exteriors in harmony with the architectural heritage of each structure. All 2,500 buildings in the historic area were researched and judged for architectural merit, and eventually 1,100 of them were rated worthy of preservation and eventual restoration. By the early 1970s, 800 of those buildings had been restored, many by young middle-class families, some by Northerners who saw an opportunity to move into a community with roots and delightful ambiance. The foundation's efforts inspired others, including Mills B. Lane of the Citizens & Southern Bank, who landscaped several squares and sponsored some two dozen restorations. A long publicity campaign culminated in 1968 with a referendum which approved historic zoning. Congress even enacted a law ensuring that federal urban renewal funds could never be used to tear down any of the old houses.

Some mistakes have been made in Savannah, including an undistinguished Hilton hotel, a high-rise apartment tower that disturbs the skyline, and a $10 million civic center which may inspire conventions but is too bulky to harmonize with the low-key architecture of its neighbors. But the success of the restored historic district is so great that Savannah has a new and thriving industry: tourism. The city also no longer needs to be ashamed of its municipal government; a big reform fight was won in the late 1950s, and Savannah has since had an outstanding city manager.

The historic district renewal has done relatively little for Savannah's 53-000 black people or its lower-class whites; some, in fact, were forced out of their neighborhoods by the restoration process. What has helped is the "Savannah Plan" which the ebullient Mills Lane started in 1968. Through his lifetime, Lane had been a political conservative with segregationist leanings, but his outlook was radically altered after he helped organize a bank in Jamaica in the late '60s. Back home, he drove around Savannah's slums and was appalled. "It's high time," Lane said, "that we get around to emphasizing who a person is, not what he is." The answer: a C & S bank project to promote self-help projects for blacks and poor whites. The first big splash was a widely publicized "spring cleaning" in two of the worst Savannah slums. Lane went to two local colleges (one black, one white) and nearby Fort Gordon to get volunteers for the clean-up; in all, 10,000 outsiders and residents of the ghetto itself turned out for a day of work picking up and hauling away countless loads of junked cars, old beds, abandoned washing machines, and other trash. Then C & S, at Lane's instigation, set up a community development corporation to make first- and second-mortgage loans to poor families so that they could buy or renovate homes, and also for loans to low-income entrepreneurs. The program got a strong start in Savannah and later spread to many other cities around Georgia where C & S does business; by 1972, according to Bill Van Landingham, the bank's executive vice president in charge of what became known as "the Georgia Plan," $3 million in capital had been made available, which combined with other loans from C & S generated a total of some $10 million. "Only a bank," Mills Lane said, "has the capacity to tackle the victimization of low-income people. The poor man's problem is money. And we're the money people."

Several thriving minority-owned businesses in Savannah—a soul food restaurant owned by a former cook for the longshoremen on the waterfront, an auto agency run by a former power company worker who moonlighted as a salesman, a grocery store owned by a former bread salesman—got off the ground with loans from the C & S development corporation. Almost 200 such businesses have been started around the state. C & S also bought one of the worst black slum blocks in Savannah and got one of the minority companies it helped finance to do the remodeling work. At an isolated Savannah waterfront location, the development corporation took over a crime-ridden 133-unit white housing slum where the apartments were heated by kerosene and there had literally been evictions at night at gunpoint. (The owner, according to Van Landingham, had been a director of the Port of New York Authority.) After the houses had been bought by C & S for $250,000, the interiors were gutted and a complete renovation begun. In the first year of the new ownership, crime calls dropped by 86 percent.

And it has all been done, Lane likes to boast, "without a penny of federal money." That very fact, of course, has made the projects more palatable politically.

In Savannah and the other cities involved, C & S followed up its first-year clean-up campaigns with a second-year program to build 250 playgrounds with $325,000 worth of playground equipment in them. Again, local youths and Army volunteers helped to get the job started. In towns like Macon there have been new dental clinics for kids who have probably never seen a dentist before—"Project Smile." In other places, neighborhood libraries have been built and stocked. And in Savannah, C & S began a "support your schools" project designed to restore confidence in the schools after the crisis of desegregation. The schools project was badly needed, because there had been outbreaks of violence in the Savannah junior and senior high schools after a busing plan went into effect in 1971. Students, black and white alike, reported that they might be able to work out the problem on their own, but that white parents' opposition was keeping the situation tense. The C & S contribution was to provide matching funds for local school committees of parents, teachers, students, and neighbors, to let them study the needs of their particular school and identify specific projects to improve it. In an indirect way, the program was likely to get attention off the race problem and onto school improvements that would benefit both races.

Savannah was not only Georgia's first city but its most heavily populated for 140 years. Then, in the 1870s, Johnny-Come-Lately Atlanta overtook it, and in the past decade, the cities of Columbus and Macon surged ahead of Savannah, both on the basis of big annexation programs. Neither, however, can hold a candle to Savannah in historic lore, present-day beauty, or culture.

Columbus (1970 population 154,168) is located some 90 miles southwest of Atlanta, just across the Chattahoochee River from Phenix City, Alabama. The garish neon signs proclaim that Columbus is an Army town, and indeed it is: nearby is Fort Benning, one of the biggest Army bases anywhere, a place called "the university of the Army" because it houses schools for Infantry, Airborne, Rangers, and officer candidates. Benning makes Columbus one of the marryingest places in America, as girls from small towns all over Georgia and Alabama float in, in hopes of catching a young officer or noncom—and often succeed. Benning also made Columbus an international dateline with the celebrated 1971 trial of 1st Lt. William L. Calley, Jr., on charges of murdering 102 Vietnamese civilians in a hamlet called Mylai. The day after Calley's conviction, President Nixon decided he could leave the stockade and live in his bachelor quarters on post until a final decision was made on his appeals. In the meantime, other soldiers sweat it out in the Fort Benning stockade for offenses infinitesimal in comparison. The Vietnam war took a heavy toll of casualties of fighting men from families living in Columbus, but this remained one of the most militant of American cities to the end.

Beneath the military gloss, Columbus remains a low-wage Southern textile mill town, with all the problems of same. The civil rights battles of the 1960s seemed to pass it by, but in 1971 the smoldering black resentment over schools, employment, and housing hit the flash point as sniper fire broke out and hundreds of cases of nighttime arson were reported. Some of the original agitation came from blacks on the police force, who were—in the words of an organizer from the Southern Christian Leadership Conference who came in to help them—"tired of being black overseers on the white man's plantation." Part of the problem was a distinct communications gap between some of Columbus' traditional black leaders, including members on the Metro Council and school board, and younger, more militant members of the black community.

The racial eruption in Columbus could have been much worse if Maj. Gen. Orwin C. Talbott, who took over command of Fort Benning in 1969 after a tour of duty in Vietnam, had not striven to reduce tensions between blacks and whites on the base. A biracial committee (three blacks, two whites), with both officers and enlisted men, was established to monitor race problems on post and also the problems of soldiers in Columbus and Phenix City. The committee worked on problems like discrimination against black troops by local businesses, and then reported back to Talbott at least once a month. Businesses that were the targets of frequent complaints were placed off limits.

Columbus' governmental merger with Muscogee County is one of the purest examples of city-county consolidation in the country. (Others are Jacksonville, Florida, and Nashville, Tennessee.) The city administration has improved immeasurably since consolidation, partly because its revenue sources are so much better. And old sin-related corruption, part of the exploitation of military personnel, has abated. J. R. Allen, the mayor until his death in a 1963 plane crash, was a millionaire and also a lay preacher who was trying to improve race relations—as his aides put it, to correct "the injustices of the past."

The same could certainly not be said of Ronnie Thompson, the suave young firebrand who has been mayor of Macon (population 122,423) since 1968 and topped a number of other excesses in 1971 when he got on the police radio during a period of race tensions and, clearly for the benefit of blacks he hoped might be listening, exhorted a sergeant to broadcast the test-firing of a submachine gun. When the demonstration was finished, Thompson told the sergeant he should have done the test-firing "in the neighborhoods"—clearly referring to the black neighborhoods—and said there were a "lot of unpatriotic people and radicals out there." Thompson is a Republican, with ambitions to run for statewide office one day (though he lost a race for Congress against Representative Williamson Stuckey in 1972). Many Republicans consider Thompson too unstable; former state senator Oliver Bateman, a respected Macon Republican, said the submachine gun incident "had caused some people to have some genuine concern about his stability." There is, however, a touch of Populism in Thompson (he likes to say his support comes "not from the chamber of commerce or the industrial leadership, but from the man on the street, the blue-collar working people") which, combined with his acknowledged personal honesty and what one observer has called a "blend of gospel-singing unctuousness and political know-how," may make him difficult for other politicians to control.

Macon started out as a cotton town, boomed on textiles, and now has a number of thriving diversified industries (Keebler Biscuit, Armstrong Paper, etc.). Its biggest employer is Robins Air Force Base. The downtown area has a pleasant appearance with broad streets, buildings ranging from antebellum to modern high-rises, and several large gingerbread-style churches. The major annexation undertaken in the early 1960s added a lot of ghetto-type areas but also more affluent sections to the north. The annexation set the stage for consolidation with surrounding Bibb County, a likely development when the political climate is right.

One of Georgia's fastest-growing cities is Albany, in South Georgia, a town that had only 19,055 people in 1940 but 72,623 by the time of the 1970 Census. Albany's strategic location, in a part of the state with few major cities, is one reason for its success; long a peanut and pecan farming center, it has been drawing the excess farm folk to town to work in its many thriving new industries. A good water supply helps the industry to grow. Georgia's first artesian well was drilled there in 1881, a tremendous breakthrough in semitropical south Georgia, where so many of the surface streams are contaminated. In addition, the city operates its own electric and gas systems, a touch of socialism that industries happily overlook because it helps to keep taxes down. Then there are the positive inducements offered new industries; in 1967, for instance, Firestone Tire and Rubber decided to open a plant in Albany with 1,500 job openings, and the entire $53 million plant cost was borne by a county development authority through an industrial revenue bond issue. Not without reason did Raymond C. Firestone, the rubber company's board chairman, say he was "impressed with the attitude of the people in the Albany area. They make us feel we're wanted."

Civil rights workers remember Albany as the town that dealt Martin Luther King, Jr., his first defeat in an attempt to break segregation. The year was 1961. The police chief, Laurie Pritchett, forbade his men to use brutality, locked up some 1,500 demonstrators, and closed parks, libraries, and swimming pools as racially mixed groups tried to use them. Not until passage of the 1964 Civil Rights Act was the rigid segregation of Albany broken. (Today, Pritchett is police chief in High Point, N.C., and denies ever having been a segregationist: "The power structure in Albany made the law, and I had to enforce it or quit. I enforced their law, but . . . I didn't agree with their philosophy," he told a New York *Times* reporter in 1971.)

Albany is likely to grow some more in the next few years. No superhighway goes near it now, but it will be on the route of a proposed Georgia toll road that will run from west of Atlanta, past Columbus and Albany, and thence into Florida.

While Albany, an obscure town by national standards, is growing, the Savannah River city of Augusta, founded by Oglethorpe and kept famous by the annual Masters tournament of the Augusta National Golf Club and until recent years by General Eisenhower's visits, is in a state of serious decline. White people are rapidly fleeing this once proud "Garden City of the South," where six men lost their lives in 1970 in one of the worst race riots of modern Southern history.* Augusta has a festering 130-block ghetto, where blacks are crowded into one- and two-story unpainted houses, afflicted by low incomes, high illiteracy, and high unemployment. Early in the 1970s, blacks moved into the majority in Augusta; the city now has fewer than 60,000 people—11,000 less than in 1960. In the meantime, the unincorporated areas of surrounding Richmond County, fed by Fort Gordon, a plant of the Atomic Energy Commission, and burgeoning industries, grew by 58 percent

* Both whites and blacks were guilty of brutality in the Augusta riot, though it is worth noting that all the casualties were black, that three of them were innocent bystanders, and that all were shot by the police. The explanations of the riot were predictable. Grady Adams, one of four Negroes on the 16-man city council, said it was "decades of racism." Lester Maddox said it was "a Communist conspiracy."

(to more than 100,000) during the 1960s. Less than one out of five suburbanites is a Negro. Not surprisingly, a proposal for city-county consolidation was voted down in 1971.

Augusta is the home base of one of Georgia's most powerful politicians and rabid segregationists of all time, Roy V. Harris. Harris' power began at home, where for years he was the head of the so-called "Cracker party," once described by the Associated Press as a "malignant dictatorship . . . which produced boss-rule more arrogant than Tammany Hall in New York, more domineering than Boss Crump in Memphis." Opponents of Cracker rule, according to Robert Sherrill, "were likely to wind up in jail or with their taxes tripled."

There was a moderate side to Harris in his early years; as speaker of the Georgia house for several terms three decades ago, he got through measures like free schoolbooks and aid for the needy aged. But for the most part, Harris' interests have been (1) political kingmaking and (2) white supremacy. A skilled manipulator of the old courthouse rings, he was instrumental in electing Herman Talmadge and Ellis Arnall as governor, and he ran George Wallace's 1968 campaign in Georgia. For years he was the state's most powerful lobbyist, and he became president of the Citizens Councils of America. Once, according to Sherrill, Harris tried to break up a bus strike with a shotgun; on another occasion he beat up an editor in court. As a regent of the University of Georgia, he tried to suppress the student newspaper, saying it was "time to clean out all of these institutions of communist influences and the crazy idea of mixing and mingling of the races which was sponsored by the commie party." Now in his declining years, Harris still publishes a screaming segregationist tabloid, *The Augusta Courier*. It costs only $4 for a year's subscription, but the visitor can pick up a free copy any week in Lester Maddox's office at the State Capitol.

After Augusta, no Georgia city tops the 50,000 mark to qualify it as center of a metropolitan area. But note might be taken of three cities, all with quite progressive leadership these days and special qualities to recommend them. Athens (population 44,342) is prospering because it is home of the University of Georgia; the town also harbors some of the most beautiful homes in the South. Down in south Georgia, the farm trade center of Valdosta (32,303) is so physically attractive and well managed that the children don't want to leave. And up in northwestern Georgia, Rome (30,759) has been saved from periodic floods, courtesy of the Army Engineers and their dikes, and a long-term decline of the downtown has been turned around. The flavor of Rome is very much that of the mountain people of the Appalachian hills about it.

Rural Georgia: The Black Belt

Georgia has the greatest land area of any state east of the Mississippi and a geography of fantastic diversity. To the north, there are the hills and mountains; then there is a broad swatch of rolling plateau and the state's famous red clays; finally, to the southeast, lies a 150-mile shelf of coastal flatland that lay beneath the sea in prehistoric times. Writer Bruce Galphin provided a glimpse of Georgia's present-day variety in his book about Lester Maddox:

> Throughout the summer of 1966, a fatigued white station wagon crisscrossed the roads of Georgia—from the enervating heat of its vast southern pinelands to the welcome chill of evenings in the lower Appalachians, from dying cotton kingdom crossroads to the mushrooming metropolis of Atlanta, to cotton mill towns, beach resorts, pre-Revolutionary towns dreaming of past splendor, military base towns glaring with neon promises of pleasure, and young cities flexing industrial muscles.

Of the two million people in rural and small-town Georgia, about a quarter live in the black belt. This was preeminently old plantation land, the stronghold of slavery and then the tenant farmer system. By latest count, there were only 6,000 tenant farmers left in Georgia—a pale shadow of the 174,000 back in 1930. Driving through the black belt, one sees many abandoned houses, from shacks to plantation homes. A high proportion of the blacks—and many of those who used to be called the "white trash" too—have moved to nearby towns or the big Georgia cities. And the black belt supplied the lion's share of the 600,000 Negroes who left Georgia altogether between 1940 and 1970. A special pathos attaches to the blacks' departure, because no small part of the exodus was white-induced: not just the changes in agriculture that made the field hand obsolete, but denying him food or welfare for fear of what his vote might soon do, and the refusal to make any new economic move that would give purpose and dignity to those who had nurtured the heat-shimmering landscape and tended the white people's homes and children so long. Leaving was not as easy as the outsider might glibly assume. As Pat Watters wrote:

> This place, this land was home, and these white people, with whom in a lifetime through generations these Negroes were intimately bound. . . . these white people were part of home, too. In the curious and twisted ways that human love finds expression, these Negroes loved these white people. . . .
>
> The cruelest thing was the driving of the Negroes out, to end forever the perverted but human bond and disappoint forever that hope some of the Negroes had always had—as unfounded and majestic as the will of people without food or warmth not only to keep alive but send the children to school—that wistful faith that some day the whites would be all right.

Today the era of lynchings (491 Georgia Negroes were lynched between 1882 and 1952) is over, and also the worst kind of police brutality and "accidental" jail killings so well documented by the U.S. Commission on Civil Rights in its early years. But still, the poverty lingers on. Georgia newsman Remer Tyson told me of visiting black belt towns like Sparta and Wrightsville and seeing "unbelievable numbers of families"—mostly black but some white as well—crowded into one-room shacks. "The best thing that could happen to a kid there," he said, "would be to be kidnapped and carried away somewhere. The only good thing is that this is not run-of-the-mill anymore, even in rural Georgia. There's been great progress since World War II." Nevertheless, the 1970 Census found that the per capita income of black belt Georgians was barely half that of people living in the Atlanta area; for Negroes only, the figure was below $1,000 a year—about one quarter of the national average.

The thought of black belt towns and places, indeed, conjures up so many visions of what was best and what was worst of Georgia traditions, and of the painful, inexorable progress now being made toward a more equitable society. At Washington, Georgia, for instance, there is such a delightful variety of great old 18th- and 19th-century homes—from old plantation houses to Federal-style rectangular clapboards and even former slave shacks—that it has been called "a kind of private, un-self-conscious Williamsburg." But in Washington, as in most Southern towns, writer Ken Sobol reported in the early 1970s, the blacks, who make up a little more than half the town population of 4,094, are still as "psychologically invisible" to the controlling white power structure as they were in the 19th century.

At Pine Mountain, north of Columbus, lie the 12,500 mountain acres of Callaway Gardens, where miles of pathways through azaleas, camellias, magnolias, and other flowering plants and flowers testify to what man can do to beautify the natural habitat. Founder Cason J. Callaway created both a prime tourist attraction and and experimental gardens that have made findings of real help to Georgia farmers.

Close to Pine Mountain, and also in the black belt, is Warm Springs, the town Franklin D. Roosevelt made famous. Not only did FDR have a home there, and die there, but Warm Springs may have played a greater role in history than its residents ever dreamed. Roosevelt biographers agree that his friendships with Warm Springs people, together with his observations of the crushing rural poverty of the area, were touchstones of many of the social reform measures of the New Deal. In our time, journalist James T. Wooten wrote recently, Warm Springs is "a skeleton of its old self, the town struggling for survival. Like so many small towns in America, its older citizens are dying, its young people are leaving, and tomorrows are not as bright as those promised by Mr. Roosevelt."

Southeast of Columbus lies Webster County, one of the poorest in the nation; the 1970 Census found that 68 percent of its black people, who make up a majority of the population, were living in poverty, and that their per capita income was only $875 a year. In the late 1960s, when the Georgia welfare department tried to administer a food distribution program for the poor people of Webster, county officials balked and the U.S. Department of Agriculture began distributing food directly. The blacks of Webster have yet to elect a single one of their race to public office. In Worth County, near Albany in southwest Georgia, a 14-year-old black girl at a white school accused of starting a disturbance on a school bus was stuck in a reform school in another county; the fact that her parents were engaged in civil rights work probably had something to do with the harsh judgment meted out to her. Worth County's rigid white power structure consists of bankers, farmers, real estate people, and the tobacco and cotton warehousemen—a typical pattern in black belt and south Georgia. But the white man's advantage is not universal. Indeed, there are thousands of *poor* whites in the black belt, and at least one black man—farmer John Hunter of Jakin, in Early County—who owns 1,000 acres of prime farm land and grosses nearly half a million dollars a year raising steers for market. Thirty-five years ago, Hunter was sharecropping 200 acres of another man's land.

Hancock County, an economically barren spot 85 miles southeast of Atlanta in Georgia's red clay country, in 1968 became the first biracial county in the Deep South, or all America for that matter, to come under black political control. Despite a black population of more than 80 percent, Hancock had been a die-hard bastion of white supremacy. The blacks, many of whom live in tenant shacks on shabby farms, were rigorously consigned to separate but unequal facilities, and the county seat newspaper, the Sparta *Ishmaelite*, reserved its back page for "Colored News." But the white minority control began to disintegrate when blacks, in the wake of the 1965 Voting Rights Act, started registering in impressive numbers. In 1966 they sent the first members of their race ever to fill posts in the dowdy Faulknerian edifice called the county courthouse. By 1968, their control was complete.

The man who galvanized Hancock's blacks into political action was John L. McCown, a South Carolina native and itinerant civil rights worker who moved into the county in 1966. The old white power structure viewed McCown as a demagogic troublemaker; funeral home owner T. M. (Buck) Patterson, mayor of Sparta (which has a white majority), told visiting reporter Joe Cumming of *Newsweek*, "You talk to that nigger all you want. I've got no comment." McCown became, in fact, the political boss of the county and purged the first black county commissioner, whom he viewed as an Uncle Tom. He formed a local nonprofit cooperative that brought in more than $8 million in federal and foundation money for projects like a 357-acre catfish farm and processing plant, a concrete block manufacturing plant, and a 150-unit apartment project.

Race tensions in Hancock reached fever level in 1971 when the white city council of Sparta bought 10 submachine guns for its police force and the black county commission upped the ante by ordering 30 rapid-fire weapons. Governor Jimmy Carter finally stepped in to end the arms race, and since then tempers have cooled some. For the first time, blacks have been invited to join the chamber of commerce, and local civic leaders set up a steering committee to investigate ways of bringing industry into the county. Despite the fierce resentment against him on the part of Hancock's whites, and many blacks as well, McCown thinks things are looking up. "The mere fact that they [whites] are talking about working together with blacks—they may not be the ones I would have wanted—is what counts," he said.

South and Coastal Georgia

South and southeast of the black belt, and stretching to the sea, lies the region called simply south Georgia. About half a million people live in the rural counties here. Historically, south Georgia was something less of a plantation area—in fact, it was still heavily timbered, and only lightly populated, when the plantation owners of the black belt propelled Georgia into the Confederacy. So it is that south Georgia still has a Negro population of less than 30 percent, compared to the black belt average of about 50 percent. The physical image is one of millions and millions of slash pines. Pines grow fast in the hot climate, and the timber is used in many ways, with paper and boxes the chief products. All across the region, one sees giant smokestacks of the pulp and paper mills. Most are new enough to have modern antipollution equipment.

In small towns, the mills exercise an oppressive control over local politics. A prime example is St. Marys, which was a dying seacoast town of only 300 souls when the Gilman Paper Company moved there from Vermont in 1941. Today St. Marys has a population of 3,408, and 1,700 people work at the mill, which registers annual sales of more than $70 million. In 1970 a local physician, Carl Drury, dared to challenge the local state representative, who was amazingly at the same time the attorney for the city, the mill, the county, and the city housing authority. Drury accused the mill of evading taxes, polluting, and generally abusing its power. He won, but soon afterward found himself the victim of an incredible campaign of persecution, ranging from false charges of rape to physical assault. The town divided into bitter camps, and some people feared for their lives: a striking illustration of how, under the thin veneer of prosperity and civility in Southern towns, the region's heritage of elemental violence lives on.

Like most of rural Georgia, these southern reaches have literally pulled themselves out of the mud since the 1930s. (Georgia's *first* concrete road was built in 1919.) Remer Tyson recalled that when he was growing up, 10 miles from Statesboro in south Georgia, it took an hour to get to town because the roads were so muddy—and impassable in heavy rains. Now there's a paved road, and the folks can go to town a few times a day if they like. (This is *not* to say that Georgia is a leader among states in its road and highway development; indeed one study in the early '70s showed it near the bottom in terms of surfaced mileage as a percent of the total, primary roads that were four lanes or more, and the like.)

Like the black belt, south Georgia still has grinding poverty. But for many, there is a newly won affluence; the question now is not whether one eats well or not, but how well, what the cut of meat is. Only a small percentage of the people still live on farms, and even if they do, they supplement their income elsewhere.

A lot of thought is being given these days to rejuvenation of south Georgia and other rural sections of the state—a central interest of Senator Herman E. Talmadge, who has spoken frequently of slowing down or halting the "farm to factory" march that has robbed the small towns of their people and future. (Just between 1950 and 1970, Georgia's rural areas sank from 55 to 40 percent of the state population.) The federally supported Coastal Plains Regional Commission has made a number of recommendations, and the University of Georgia has begun to concentrate on the problem. In 1972 the United States' first state-operated rural development center opened at Tifton in south Georgia. It is looking for new crop possibilities, ways to process more of Georgia's agricultural products inside the state rather than outside its borders, development of small towns, and manpower training. One south Georgia county, Bacon, in the early '70s became the nation's first rural community to receive Model Cities status—a device it is hoped will give it needed start-up funds to attract various federal development programs. The objective is to stem the population outflow that occurs when farms increase in size, local merchants lose much of their business, tax revenues stagnate, and public services fall off.

The casual driver through south Georgia is likely to remember the profusion of Stuckey's emporiums (which began as a single pecan stand on U.S. 23 in 1936), America's most vicious speed trap in Long County, and perhaps the quickie marriage mills of Charlton County on the Florida border. Nature has left some wonders for those with curiosity, however. One of these is the vast and intriguing Okefenokee Swamp, the bog the Indians called "the land of the trembling earth." It was formed, naturalist Peter Farb has explained, when a low barrier of land emerging from the gulf isolated a portion of the coastal plain. The depression became choked with plants that act like a sponge, soaking up the water; when the sponge is full, the runoff goes to the sea by way of the Suwannee or St. Marys Rivers, both of which have their headwaters there. In the swamp, one finds great moss-bedecked cypresses, pines, hollies, and magnolias; the rich variety of fauna runs from bears and bobcats to threatening cottonmouth moccasins and the biggest alligators on the continent. The Okefenokee Swamp Park is operated tastefully by the city of Waycross, Georgia.

Georgia's window to the Atlantic is less than 100 miles long, running from Savannah on the north to the little fishing city of Brunswick on the south. But the coastline is a priceless asset of still largely inviolate marshlands and what the first explorers called the "Golden Isles of Guale"—Wassaw, St. Catherines, Blackbeard, Sapelo, St. Simons, Sea Isle, Jekyll, and Cumberland. Wealthy Northerners bought the barrier islands after the Civil War, as the antebellum plantations of rice, indigo, and sugar cane melted back into the primordial landscape. Anxious for privacy, the new owners kept the islands quite untouched, and only one island—Jekyll, earlier a resort of millionaires, since 1948 a state property—has been exploited so seriously as to strip it of its ecological importance. The question for the other islands is whether developers will get their hands on them as owners find it necessary to sell them off to pay taxes. A great victory for the public interest was won when Congress in 1972 made most of the wild, lush wilderness island of Cumberland into a National Seashore. The island has a gently curving white beach, 18 miles in length, and the acquisition almost doubles the length of Georgia beach open to the public while preserving the flora and a selection of wildlife that runs from egrets and blue heron to alligators, giant turtles, deer, and boar. The rejected would-be developers of Cumberland included the owner of Hilton Head, South Carolina, who wanted to open a second home community there, and a group of Camden County, Georgia promoters who had visions of a Coney Island.

The state of Georgia has slowly awakened to the need for preserving its unique coastline and islands. Governor Maddox wisely rejected a proposal by Kerr-McGee Corporation of Oklahoma to strip-mine underwater state lands for phosphate, and in 1970 the legislature set up a coastal marshlands protection agency that requires a permit before anyone can dredge, fill, or drain any marshlands within the estaurine area.

North Georgia

The rural counties of northern Georgia bear striking similarity to the other Appalachian hill areas of the South. Farms are small, in many places a kind of hillbilly culture (complete with moonshining) prevails, and poverty used to be endemic. The region has had pockets of Republicanism ever since the Civil War, a conflict that north Georgia people did not identify as their own. There were many "Scalawags" here during Reconstruction, and later supporters of Populist agrarianism in the 1890s. This is the whitest of all areas in Georgia; in fact there are three counties without a single black resident, and several with minuscule percentages.

Atlantans (and some Chattanoogans) are now flocking into north Georgia for sports and spring-to-autumn scenery, and buying vacation homes too. There are some big real estate operations and even a ski slope (usually iced by machine). Just north of Buford, the sparkling waters of the Chattahoochee River have been dammed up to create Lake Sidney Lanier, which lays claim to the country's largest inland sailing fleet (including 300 houseboats) and more visitors each year (11 million-plus) than any of the other water-resource playgrounds operated by the Corps of Engineers. The Chattahoochee is less fortunate when it reaches the Atlanta area, where civilization has made it into a polluted mess.

The little north Georgia city of Dalton (population 18,872) is the tufted textile capital of America, turning out more than 60 percent of the country's tufted carpets. Textiles, and also food processing, are important in Gainesville (15,459), the backbone of Georgia's big poultry industry. In fact, a quite high percentage of north Georgia's working population now has jobs in manufacturing plants. Wages are well below national averages, but the industries have helped to push per capita income far ahead of black belt and southern Georgia.

North Georgia is a prime example of how multi-county planning and development districts—one of the least heralded but most vital innovations in local government in modern America—can do for an entire region of a state what no single county could do for itself. The idea of planning and development districts was born in Georgia in the 1950s and later spread across the country.* Its intellectual godfather was Philip Hammer, the economist I quoted earlier about Atlanta who was then a young city planner there. As allies, Hammer enlisted J. W. Fanning, a vice president of the University of Georgia, and Frank Hood, the chief of industrial development for the Geor-

* John Fischer provided a detailed account of the local development district phenomenon in an article, "Georgia: Mother of Social Invention," in *Harper's Magazine* for March 1972.

gia Power Company. They reasoned that most of Georgia's 159 counties were too small and poor to compete intelligently for new businesses or get federal grants. The ideal solution would have been to abolish most of the counties, creating regional governments in their stead, but the determined opposition of local officeholders made that idea politically unfeasible. The alternative was to persuade a group of counties to form a local development district that could hire a professional to study the economic potential of the entire area and then work for improvement. Hammer and his cohorts got the legislature to authorize such districts in 1960, and the movement has gathered speed since.

The Georgia Mountains Planning and Development District, set up in the mid-1960s, has helped its 13 counties and 39 municipalities to get some $20 million in federal funds for parks, water, and sewer facilities, roads, health clinics, and like projects—the kind of improvements a substantial new industry will demand before it moves into a new community. Many new industries and tourist facilities were attracted, and employment in the area grew by 20 percent in five years. The development district had professional leadership in a young Ph.D. in economic geography, Sam Dayton. But it was politically feasible because most of its 26 board members were local elected officials, who could see to it that any item planned went into an appropriate local budget. In John Fischer's words, "the Magna Carta of all development districts in the country" was a 1971 order from the federal Office of Management and the Budget requiring federal departments and agencies to channel their aid to localities through local development districts. That meant that people like Sam Dayton would have life-and-death power over *all* federal loans or grants to local units, approving and coordinating federally assisted projects in more than 100 listed programs—even those of that sacred cow, the Army Engineers. Unless a proposal fitted into the overall regional development plan, it could be rejected. And the development district was supposed to deny any projects that could be harmful to the environment.

Virtually all of Georgia's counties are now in development districts. Many districts lack the professional quality of the mountains district or its foresight in pressing for such reforms as countywide zoning to prevent the ravages of fast strip development in the wrong places. The big-city counterpart of development districts are bodies like Atlanta's Regional Commission, or the COGs (councils of government) in urban areas across the country. Such metropolitan organizations may grow in importance in the next years, but they are unlikely to have an impact in any way comparable to that of the development districts in less- developed and easier-to-plan rural regions, where there is still time to determine the patterns of employment, the growth of towns, and protection of the environment—the factors that will have most to do with the very quality of life there in future years.

SOUTH CAROLINA

FOSSIL NO MORE

Should anyone doubt that the historic experience of an American state can shape and direct its existence, even in these days of cultural homogenization, the case of South Carolina proves the point. The roots go deep here. In spirit, in culture, and in finance, South Carolina was the center of the South when Mississippi was still Indian territory. In the 19th century, South Carolina leaders virtually created the South as a self-conscious region, and they led it out of the Union. Bleak years of poverty and pervasive Confederate nostalgia and general intellectual stagnation came between the Civil War and World War II. It was then that South Carolina truly was a "fossilized" society. But in the 1960s it was South Carolina that showed the South the way toward racial integration with dignity.

So it is that from the peculiarly aristocratic nature of the early planter class and the intellectual life of old Charles Town, to the era of John C. Calhoun and professed paternalistic care for slaves, to Fort Sumter and Reconstruction and the upcountry textile culture and the unique political roles of men like James F. Byrnes and J. Strom Thurmond and Ernest F. Hollings, the themes of a unique civilization come ringing down the corridors of history. Violence there has been too, from the bloody suppression of early slave rebellions to countless lynchings in the middle years to the massacre at

Orangeburg in 1969. But those have all been exceptions to a rule. Primarily, South Carolina has always practiced a softer kind of coercion, the kind directed from fine salons and board rooms rather than a "redneck" cabin. Most often, it has come less out of raw hatred between black and white people than in the interest of the hegemony of the ruling classes.

Small wonder, then, that journalist Jack Bass would use the phrase "Good Manners" to keynote his book on South Carolina, *Porgy Comes Home*. South Carolina, *Newsweek* Southern correspondent Joseph B. Cumming, Jr., suggested to me, is a state obsessed with "keeping the corners muted." Like Orientals, he said, South Carolinians worship their ancestors and eat a lot of rice. "But above all, they save face. Even the segregationists are offended by extreme activities like bus dumping. Everything is ordered and controlled. It is all run with a surface grace but with enormous emphasis on control—like a plantation or a cotton mill."

South Carolina in 1970 entered the fourth century of its history with a long list of disabilities. Its land, continuously under cultivation for centuries, had lost much of its fertility. Manufacturing remained heavily weighted toward textiles, one of the lowest paid industries in the country and a major reason that South Carolina ranked only 47th among the states in its factory wages. Per capita income was only 75 percent of the national average and less than that in 46 other states. Health and nutrition problems were among the most serious in the United States, accounting for one of the shortest life expectancies. Poverty was still rampant, affecting 12 percent of the whites and 50 percent of the blacks. (Negroes made up 30.5 percent of the population, the highest proportion of any state except Mississippi.) A deficient educational system was responsible for a high rate of functional illiteracy. Only one other state (Kentucky) had a lower level of educational attainment among its adult population.

On the bright side, there had been an immense increase in industrial investment, a large portion outside the textiles field, during the 1960s. Per capita income had increased 112 percent in a decade, an important advance even taking inflation into account and a far cry from 1929, when South Carolinians had earned only 38 percent of the national average. A wave of concern about hunger in the coastal counties, sparked by Senator Hollings, was leading to increased food stamp programs. Years of serious effort in vocational and technical education were bearing fruit in a more skilled labor force, and the average level of schooling increased by two years in the 1960s alone.

Statistics tell only part of the story, however. A new generation of politicians, more interested in solving social and economic problems than refighting the leftover battles of the Civil War, had risen to power. To its ancient value of *courtesy*, South Carolina was now adding *concern* about the underprivileged—both as persons and as potentially contributing citizens. Governor John C. West put it best in his inaugural address in January 1971, when he said, "The time has come when South Carolina for all time must break loose and break free from the vicious cycle of ignorance, illiteracy, and poverty which has retarded us throughout our history."

Political reality had much to do with the change: the fact that black people, for the first time in the 20th century, were voting in significant numbers and were a vital factor in the political balance of the state. But blacks made up only a quarter of the voting pool and would not have become an important force if hundreds of thousands of whites had not decided to give up voting along racially polarized lines. Racism still dictated the votes of many South Carolinians, but not a majority in most elections. V. O. Key, if he had been writing his *Southern Politics* again, would no longer have been able to make the flat assertion he did in the late 1940s about South Carolina—that "whenever the going gets rough, when a glimmer of informed political self-interest begins to well up from the masses, the issue of white supremacy may be raised to whip them back into line." There were those who still tried to raise the issue, but they were now generally on the losing end.

The Heritage Forms

Large portions of the Deep South states were rough-hewn frontier country until the early 1800s or, in the case of Louisiana, an outpost of Spanish and French culture. Not so South Carolina, and especially Charles Town and the surrounding coastal Low Country first settled by the English in 1670. Dependent from the start on slave labor, great plantations cultivating a single crop—first rice or indigo, then cotton—were thriving by the early 1700s. The settlement came years after that of regal Virginia to the north, but as Richard Hofstadter wrote in *America at 1750*, "South Carolina in its heyday enjoyed a prosperity that surpassed anything seen in the other colonies. . . . By comparison with Charles Town's elite, old Boston's upper crust looked poor and flimsy, and the hedonistic life of the South Carolina capital put the other seaboard towns in the shade." The peculiar attribute of early South Carolina, he noted, was that it lacked a substantial middle class, a phenomenon in sharp contrast to the colonies to the north.

New Englander Josiah Quincy probably exaggerated when he said that South Carolina was "divided into opulent and lordly planters, poor and spiritless peasants and vile slaves." But a society of vivid class contrasts was certainly what the first South Carolinians had in mind. The English philosopher John Locke was commissioned to draw up laws for the Lords Proprietors appointed by King Charles II, and his "Grand Model" provided for three orders of nobility; barons, caciques, and landgraves, each with large landed estates. The Church of England would be the established religion. The proprietor system was abolished in 1707, but the idea of a titled nobility living at ease upon the labor of others would be reflected in the planters who appointed overseers for their plantations and lived in comfort in Charles Town. Many of the early settlers came from Barbados, bringing with them the West Indian slave plantation concept and aspirations to form a sharply tiered society. Not even the later addition of Huguenots (whom the Anglicans tried to stop from voting, in a first attempt to impose second-class citizenship), or of Swiss and Germans, would seriously alter the aristocratic English and Bar-

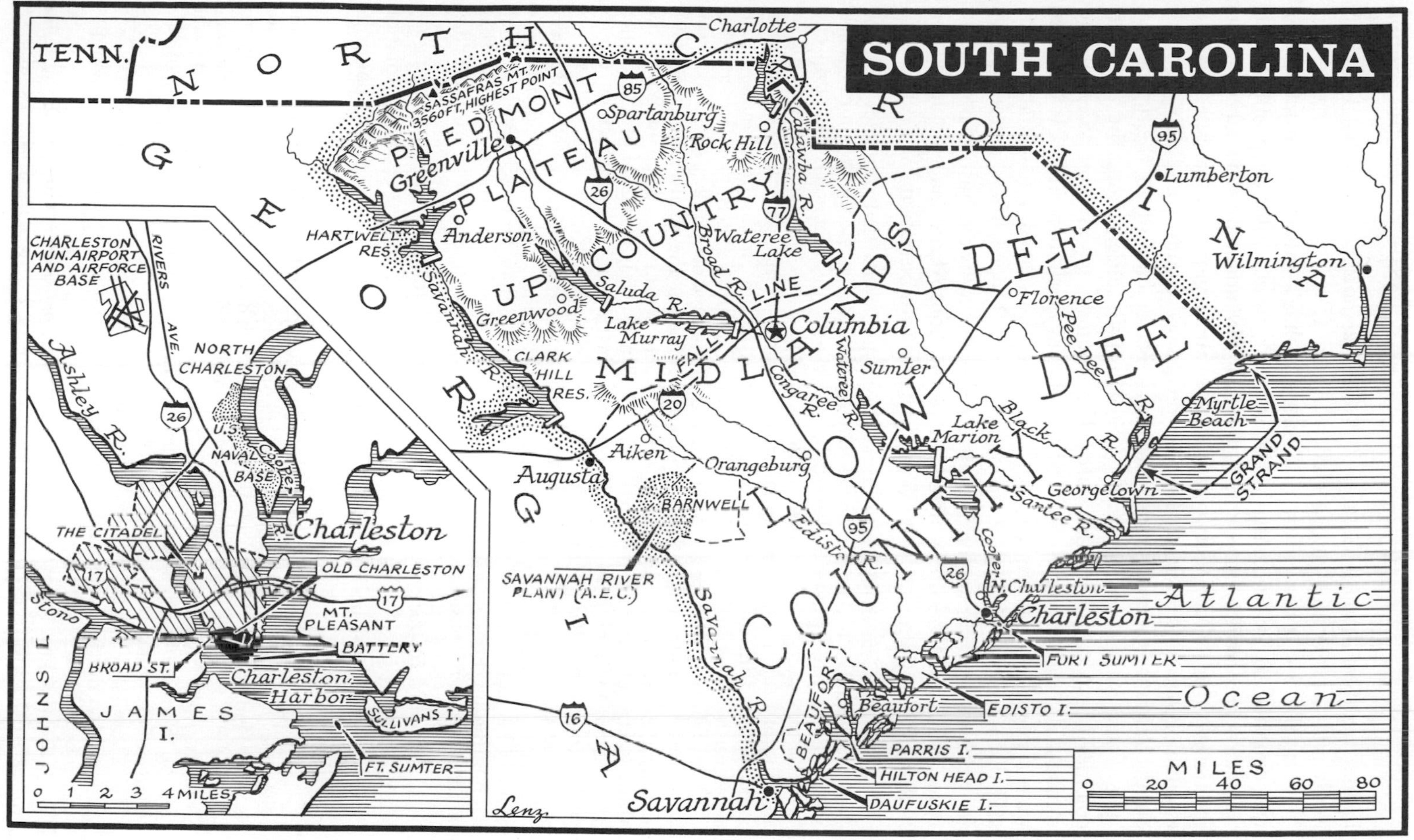
SOUTH CAROLINA
TENN.
NORTH CAROLINA
GEORGIA
Charlotte
SASSAFRAS MT. 3560 FT., HIGHEST POINT
PIEDMONT PLATEAU
UP COUNTRY
MIDLANDS
FALL LINE
PEE DEE
LOW COUNTRY
Spartanburg
Rock Hill
Greenville
Anderson
Greenwood
HARTWELL RES.
CLARK HILL RES.
Lake Murray
Wateree Lake
Columbia
Sumter
Florence
Lumberton
Wilmington
Myrtle Beach
GRAND STRAND
Georgetown
Lake Marion
Aiken
Augusta
Orangeburg
BARNWELL
SAVANNAH RIVER PLANT (A.E.C.)
N. Charleston
Charleston
FORT SUMTER
EDISTO I.
Beaufort
BEAUFORT
PARRIS I.
HILTON HEAD I.
DAUFUSKIE I.
Savannah
Atlantic
Ocean
Catawba R.
Broad R.
Saluda R.
Savannah R.
Wateree R.
Congaree R.
Pee Dee R.
Black R.
Santee R.
Edisto R.
Cooper R.
85
26
77
95
20
16
MILES
0 20 40 60 80
Lenz
CHARLESTON MUN. AIRPORT AND AIRFORCE BASE
RIVERS AVE.
NORTH CHARLESTON
U.S. NAVAL BASE
Cooper R.
Ashley R.
THE CITADEL
Charleston
OLD CHARLESTON
MT. PLEASANT
BATTERY
BROAD ST.
Stono R.
Charleston Harbor
SULLIVANS I.
FT. SUMTER
JAMES I.
JOHNS I.
0 1 2 3 4 MILES

badian tradition. "South Carolina," Hofstadter noted, "developed the most lordly and most leisured ruling class in America."

For the first half century of South Carolina's existence the settlement was confined to a thin coastal strip, some 15 to 20 miles deep, filled with waterways and great swamps which proved—with adequate slave labor—ideal for the growing of rice. Between that tidewater region and the fall line, the essential geographic dividing line between Low Country and Up Country South Carolina, German and Scotch-Irish began farming in the 1720s and '30s. Then, in the 1750s, waves of Scotch-Irish settlers from the northern colonies began to fill up the state's Up Country, mainly composed of the rolling hills, ragged woods, and red-clay dirt of the Piedmont Plateau. They were a fiercely Calvinistic lot, small farmers who owned a few if any slaves and disdained the effete Low Country culture. Indeed, there are few states in which the geographic divisions attracted such starkly contrasting population types. They were colorfully described in the South Carolina volume by the Federal Writers' Project of the Work Projects Administration (WPA):

> The Low Countryman may live in Charleston, a city that competes with the New Jerusalem in his dreams; or he may live in a drafty Georgian country house with a three-tiered piazza, hidden behind live oaks and magnolias that drip curtains of gray moss above blazing azaleas, wisteria, and camellia japonicas; or he may live in a cabin near a swamp infested by swarms of malaria-bearing mosquitoes, and look out with dull eyes over acres he must till for an absentee landlord. But wherever he is, his attitude is keyed to leisure, he thinks in terms of ease, and has a philosophical contempt for long ordered hours of daily work. . . .
>
> In this country where natural growth borders on the semitropical, and midday heat in summer is prostrating except where sea breezes creep in under the thick foliage of live oak and myrtle or between the tall trunks of longleaf pine, there seems to be no hard grinding necessity for thinking too much about money in the bank, fine clothes, and weathertight houses. . . .
>
> The Low Countryman cannot forget his leadership before the War Between the States (or the Confederate War, as it is also called). Though his diet may be skimpy, his clothes old and worn, his schooling negligible, he walks with head high among the big houses, graceful churches, and tumbledown forts, with more than a bit of scorn for those whose forebears came to the state 50 or 100 years after his.

It is hard to believe that description was written just over 30 years ago—a reminder of how recently South Carolina emerged from its long isolation from the national mainstream. The same writer then continued about the Piedmont people:

> The Up Country South Carolinian . . . will exhibit more physical energy and a greater desire to accumulate a bank account. His forebears . . . chose an isolated inland region. He has worked his own small farm for generations. Fortunately for him, enterprising businessmen came in and established cotton mills. . . . Into the mills came the Up Country farmer who was barely making a living, and out of the mountains came the barefoot man and sunbonneted woman, to take charge of the spindles and looms. . . .
>
> The vitality of the pioneer is still in his veins—but he isn't all energy. Depending too much on corn and hog meat, he is prone to fall into the apathy produced by pellagra. . . .
>
> Like the Low Countryman, he prefers his personal standards of right and wrong to those prescribed in the courts of law. . . . In some cases, he also believes in ghosts and witches.

The differences between the Up Country and Low Country, between the small democratic farmers of the frontier and the planter and merchant slaveholders of the coastal reaches, created a conflict in pre-Revolutionary days that would endure into the 20th century. By the late 1700s, the white population of the Up Country was a majority, though the Low Country had the vast preponderance of the slaves. The Low Countrymen, who had controlled the colony from the start, realized they would have to make some kind of compromise if they wanted to preserve the unity of South Carolina. They compromised to the extent of moving the capital from Charleston (the less British name form adopted in 1783) to Columbia, on the border of the fall line. But the state constitution of 1790 rigged the scheme of representation to assure continued Low Country control of the legislature. "That body," Bass commented, "operated as a ruling committee of the landed gentry and for the next 70 years provided in South Carolina an aristocratic republic."

South Carolina played an important role in the winning of American independence and sent distinguished delegates—men like Christopher Gadsden, Charles Cotesworth Pinckney, and John Rutledge—to the Stamp Act Congress, the Continental Congress, and the Constitutional Convention. The battle of Kings Mountain in northern South Carolina was a turning point in the Revolutionary War. In fact 137 military engagements took place in South Carolina, more than in any other state.

All that proud heritage, however, was soon to be eclipsed by the state's obsession with the slavery question. In the 1770s enough Scotch-Irish and other whites had poured into South Carolina to create a white population majority for the first time in half a century. Slavery had seemed to be on the wane, and there were a number of societies dedicated to freeing slaves. But in 1793 the Yankee Eli Whitney invented the cotton gin and the cultivation of cotton—with slavery in its wake—spread into the Up Country. The slave trade was reopened in 1804 and by 1820 South Carolina would again have a black majority in its population, a condition that would last until the 1920s. "The lust for the new money crop and the greed it generated," Bass wrote, "produced a closed society in which defense of slavery could not be questioned and questioning of slavery would not be tolerated." Those who tried—like the courageous Grimke Sisters, Sarah and Angelina, members of an aristocratic Charleston family—were forced into exile after they joined the Abolitionist movement. (If they had remained, they might well have been lynched.) The slave codes of the 1820s marked the zenith of the most dehumanizing aspects of the system of slavery.

South Carolina's great John C. Calhoun wrote as early as 1837: "Many in the South once believed that it [slavery] was a moral and political evil. That folly and delusion are gone. We see it now in its true light, and regard it as the most safe and stable basis for free institutions in the world." * One may spare himself the details of the elaborate defenses of the "peculiar institution"

* Calhoun's memory is still revered in many South Carolina circles, but certainly not universally. My Greenville physician friend, Donald G. Kilgore, president of the South Carolina Medical Association, considers him to have been a "catastrophe" and dug up the interesting fact that Calhoun, aside from all the slavery and tariff battles for which he is known, also led the fight against United States acceptance of James Smithson's legacy to start the Smithsonian Institution (in whose hallowed halls, in fact, a major portion of this book was written).

which Southerners, with South Carolinians in the forefront, constructed from then until the Civil War. South Carolina historian David Duncan Wallace was certainly right when he wrote: "Few more barren fields of intellectual effort exist than the volumes of defense of the constitutional right to continue a system that the whole course of civilization had doomed."

Bellicosity, nullification, finally secession—these were the chief contributions of South Carolina to the national political culture during the first half of the 19th century. Calhoun was one of the so-called War Hawks in Congress who urged declaration of the War of 1812, and later 1,100 South Carolinian volunteers happily went off to fight against Mexico in 1846. The Citadel, South Carolina's military college at Charleston, was founded in 1824 in response to the danger of slave uprisings; later a detachment of volunteers from its cadet ranks manned the Charleston batteries that fired the first shots of the Civil War. The tariff begun in the 1810s seemed to South Carolinians a particular injustice to their regional interests, and in 1830 the state made a formal declaration of States Rights principles, enacting an ordinance nullifying the act of Congress which imposed tariffs. Calhoun resigned as Vice President under Andrew Jackson to enter the Senate and fight for nullification; the state mobilized for war, and conflict was barely averted through a compromise on the tariff. But the burning issue of a state's right to nullify federal acts or secede from the Union remained unresolved, and it was on December 20, 1860, that a convention in Charleston adopted the Ordinance of Secession—the first state to take that fatal step. A Charleston newspaper headline the next day read: "Union Dissolved." It reflected South Carolina's lofty view of itself—as if, when one man withdraws from a law firm, it is dissolved. But the other Southern states soon followed suit, and everyone knows of the volley of shots against the federal ship, the *Star of the West*, as it tried to bring reinforcements to Fort Sumter in Charleston Harbor on January 9, 1861. The fatal deed was done, and in the great war that ensued, South Carolina would lose a quarter of the 63,000 men it sent into the battles. When General William Tecumseh Sherman's troops arrived in Columbia in 1865, they devastated the city with no compunctions, for they remembered which state had first broken the bonds of Union and begun the conflict.* In fact, Sherman's troops cut a path of destruction 50 to 60 miles wide across the state, leaving a trail of destruction and vandalism and a legacy of bitterness in the hearts of South Carolinians that lingers to this day.

One can argue about the precise date of South Carolina's fall from greatness. In the view of Gedney Howe, a brilliant and urbane Charleston lawyer, "we ended our lives with the slave codes, because we became so exclusionary." (Note the word "we" in Howe's comment, as if present-day South Carolinians were the same people who enacted the slave codes. I can think of no American state where the sense of historic connections runs so deeply, where family trees remain such a vital concern, and where there is a feeling that all

* Sherman's famous march had taken him from Atlanta to Savannah, and then to Columbia, skipping regal old Charleston. South Carolinians believe (whether true or not) that Sherman spared Charleston because he had a mistress there.

the state is still an encapsulated society of blood ties and common experience, passed down through the generations.)

Jack Bass believes South Carolina's fall began at the moment of secession, when the state became just another member of the Confederacy, no longer a threatened catalyst for the dissolution of the Union. In the view of many South Carolinians, it was Reconstruction, an era of "organized hell, . . . villainy, anarchy, misrule, and robbery," which harmed the state the most. Modern historians admit many of the abuses of the Reconstruction period, which lasted from 1868 to 1876, but point out that "the conditions imposed by the North were not satanic." There was widespread graft and corruption during the period, but the 1868 constitution was perhaps the best in the state's history. The Reconstruction legislature, the only one in the South with a majority of black members, established the state's first public school system. Such an embellishment would have been irrelevant for the antebellum planter aristocracy, which sent its own young to private academies and considered education of the masses, especially Negroes, more a threat than a blessing.

Regardless of the moment that South Carolina ceased to be a vital national force, there is no question that slavery, above all else, occasioned the downfall. Before the war, about half of the white people belonged to slaveholding families, a larger proportion than in any other state. Historian Daniel Hollis of the University of South Carolina has pointed out that South Carolina ranked high among the states in per capita wealth before the war chiefly because it possessed $400 million in slave property. After the war, there were still 400,000 Negroes in the state, but instead of representing millions of dollars of wealth, they made up an almost entirely illiterate population mass whose per capita wealth was zero. Their entry into the 1870 Census as individual citizens put South Carolina near the bottom of the statistical tables. South Carolina had not only lost a war, it had lost its greatest capital "asset." Thus it was "naive," Hollis observed, for South Carolina "to believe in 1865 that it could return to the Union with the power and prerogatives it had possessed in 1860." In matter of fact, the power and prerogatives have never returned.

The Bleak Middle Years

Both physically and spiritually, it took South Carolina a long time to recover from the ruination of war. When the legislature approved "Carolina" as the official state song in 1911, it accepted the lyrics penned by the Laureate of the Confederacy, Charleston's Henry Timrod, which read in part:

> Hold up the glories of thy dead;
> Say how thy elder children bled,
> and point to Eutaw's battle-bled,
>   Carolina! Carolina!
> Girt with such wills to do and bear,
> Assured in right, and mailed in prayer,
> Thou wilt not bow to despair,
>   Carolina! Carolina!

Straight down to the 1940s, South Carolina had a lot to despair about. The curtain had been drawn on the plantation system during the years of conflict, when South Carolina could no longer export any of its cotton or rice. Afterwards, when the landowners had no capital and the laborers no land, sharecropping became prevalent and even the independent small farmers survived only by placing heavy liens on their prospective crops. South Carolina had once produced half the country's rice, but in the postbellum years this production was lost entirely to competition from states to the west. Tobacco was renewed as a crop of some importance from the coast to the fall line, and corn and livestock were important too. But basically South Carolina agriculture subsisted on cotton, the crop best suited to sharecropping and tenancy but a continued obstacle to healthy diversification. In 1880 owners and tenants were about equal in number (47,000 each), but by 1935 the boll weevil and the harsh realities of the cotton economy had driven the number of farm owners down to 11,000—compared to 103,000 tenants. Millions of acres of land were so worn out that they were no longer fit for cultivation.

South Carolina had been well on its way to creating a diversified manufacturing base—in pottery, brick, lumber, and iron—when Whitney's gin set off the mad scramble for cotton profits in the early 19th century. The tariff and slavery issues compelled Calhoun and his contemporaries to condemn manufacturing as a threat to States Rights and the South's most treasured institutions. To accuse a man publicly of owning mill stock, for instance, was inviting personal combat or a libel suit.

A few South Carolinians dissented, including William Gregg of Aiken County, who was distressed to see cotton hauled to Charleston, shipped to New England, made into cloth, shipped back to Charleston, and then hauled again to the interior to sell at a high price to the very farmers who had produced it. Gregg was also concerned about the destitute lower classes of whites created by the slave system. In 1844 he wrote, "Shall we pass unnoticed the thousands of poor, ignorant, degraded white people among us, who, in this land of plenty, live in comparative nakedness and despair?" Soon afterwards, he established the first large-scale cotton mill in the state, at Graniteville in the Horse Creek Valley (along the fall line). Gregg's compassion for the lower classes did not deter him from using child labor. The plantation mentality held down the number of cotton mills, and by 1860 the total employment in them was only 891. After the war, there was no industrial capital for a time. Serious expansion in textile mills came in the 1880s, however, and the number of mill jobs rose to 47,000 by 1910 and 89,000 by 1939. The hallmarks of the system were as Gregg envisioned: employment was restricted almost entirely to whites, and a large part of the production took place in company towns. The industry was centered in the Piedmont, which could attract outside capital because of cheap water power and a labor force content with paltry wages. High profits for the owners, crumbs for the workers, a dependence on cotton, and a strict color line—it was the plantation system reincarnate. John Gunther observed in the 1940s that the "lintheads" (mill workers) were "among the most poverty blanched and backward folk in America."

The burden of the past rested just as heavily on the political system. Reconstruction was ended and native white rule restored in the "Red Shirt" campaign of 1876 that brought South Carolina's revered war hero, General Wade Hampton, to the governorship. (The "Red Shirts" were led by Confederate officers who had earlier organized "rifle" and "sabre" clubs to defend white interests against black militia—a refined version of the Ku Klux Klan, also active at the time. The Red Shirts terrorized Negroes and on election day, according to one account, "voted again and again, riding from one precinct to another as long as their horses would carry them.") Armed conflict almost broke out when the Reconstruction government refused to vacate office, but Hampton's Bourbon Democrats triumphed in April 1877 when President Hayes withdrew Union troops. The Reconstruction government had run up a huge debt, and the Bourbons were dedicated to parsimonious government and encouragement of manufacturing.

The impoverished whites of the Up Country, however, were not long content with the conservative rule of the old planter class. An agricultural depression hit the state in the 1880s, and the Populist themes popular across the rest of the country were championed in South Carolina by Benjamin R. Tillman. A colorful stump speaker, Tillman attacked the "aristocratic oligarchy" that had dominated the state since the Lords Proprietors and declared: "These broken down aristocrats paraded their Confederate glory in order to monopolize high office while the needs of the farmer went unheeded." Elected governor in 1890, he tried to help the poor farmers, then reeling from rock-bottom cotton prices, by advancing agricultural and vocational education. But his electoral appeal rested in large measure on violent racism. The Bourbons had permitted a number of Negroes—whose votes they often controlled—to continue voting. In 1890 there were still several Negro legislators and one Negro Congressman. Tillman would have none of that, and he proceeded to disenfranchise the black man. This was accomplished at an 1895 constitutional convention which instituted a poll tax and literacy test; from then until the 1940s, all South Carolina elections would be decided in a lily-white Democratic primary. As governor, Tillman once said: "I would lead a mob to lynch the Negro who ravishes a white woman."

The South Carolina aristocracy despised Tillman as a mouthpiece of the hoi polloi, but the masses saw him as a hero who finally brought Jacksonian democracy (half a century late) to South Carolina. Free silver was a burning issue of the day, and in his 1894 campaign for the Senate, Tillman opposed President Grover Cleveland on the issue and promised to jab the President with his pitchfork. From then on, he was "Pitchfork Ben." He won the election and stayed in the Senate until his death in 1918. But in his later years, he sold out to the Bourbons on issue after issue. "The fire-eating radical," V. O. Key wrote, "became a conservative of the conservatives, yet he was still a Democrat and a Negro-baiter." It was a familiar scenario in the South.

South Carolina's masses were duped even more egregiously by Coleman L. Blease, a racist demagogue elected governor in 1910. Historian Francis Butler Simkins noted that Blease not only inherited Tillman's following among the poor farmers and mill hands but also "Tillman's enemies—the corporations, the aristocrats, the newspapers, the preachers, the political rings—all who by reason of superior culture or craft had made themselves into the better classes." Yet in fact, "Coley" Blease offered his "wool hat" supporters nothing more than an unmitigated diet of racism, opposing regulation of factory working conditions or any kind of governmental program that might really benefit them. "Perhaps so nonrational a politics," V. O. Key observed, "can be practiced only when some diversionary issue, such as race, lies handy for use." Blease's work was made even easier by the ignorance of the thousands of mill hands fresh in off the farm. "When the mills were built," Key said, "often a first act of the new mill owner was to build a church, put the pastor on his payroll, and reap the profits of a theology propagating the doctrine that the meek shall inherit the earth."

Despite a couple of mildly progressive governors in the early 1900s, there was in fact no major political leader between Tillman's earlier years and the 1930s who really tried to do anything for the disadvantaged. South Carolina offered one of the most sterling examples of all time of how a one-party system can be manipulated to serve the ends of the privileged classes and prevent legitimate debate about issues. The Tillmans and Bleases sold out quietly to the people with wealth, there was no competition of parties for the votes of the poor people, and since everyone belonged to the Democratic party, the party itself stood for nothing.

Using the usual racial hyperbole to get elected governor in the 1930s, Olin D. Johnston did make a greater effort than any recent predecessor to do some thing for "the rag tags, lintheads, and poor farmers." Later he went to the Senate where he voted such a liberal line (except on civil rights) that blacks, as they began to vote, gave him their support. But lest anyone consider old-style South Carolina politics a simple matter, consider this: J. Strom Thurmond, later to be the 1948 Dixiecrat candidate for President, was a New Dealer in his early days and was opposed for governor in 1946 by conservatives who hinted darkly that he might be getting CIO money. Not long after Thurmond took office, he tried to get a mob convicted for lynching a hapless Negro. He even lent the dignity of the governor's office by sitting with the prosecution on the opening day of the trial. All of the alleged lynchers were officials or members of the CIO textile workers union. Thurmond as governor also led a successful campaign to repeal the poll tax. Journalist Earl Mazo, a native South Carolinian, told me the story of the 1950 Senate primary in which Johnston and Thurmond clashed. Johnston, "the great liberal," attacked Thurmond for appointing a highly qualified black to the state board of medical examiners. Thurmond, Johnston said, should have appointed a good Confederate descendant in the place of that "big black buck nigger."

Years later, when both Johnston and Thurmond were in the Senate, they rose one day to contribute speeches in a filbuster against a civil rights bill. After Johnston had made his obligatory remarks, he listened through a crack in the cloakroom door as Thurmond attacked the measure from stem to stern. Ruminating mostly to himself—he had a kind of subconscious flow that came out like a current—Johnston said: "Listen to ole Strom. Just listen to him. He really *believes* that stuff."

If the reader considers these crosscurrents confusing, consider the plight of the poor South Carolina voter during the long years of one-partyism when racism and its nuances colored every political debate. For more than 250 years, Jack Bass noted, preoccupation with race "not only subordinated other political issues, but for most of the period stunted the growth of the state economically, culturally, and intellectually and forced thousands of the most ambitious natives of the state to seek their fortunes elsewhere."

Palmetto Politics: Democrats and the Race Issue

South Carolina politics have evolved so rapidly from their one-party, white-party base that astute observers like William E. Rone, Jr., of *The State* in Columbia have been led to suggest that the state really belongs now more properly to the "Upper South" class of states like North Carolina, Tennessee, and Virginia than it does to the old "Deep South" grouping. The reasons are several.

Because of the white primary and other restrictions, an infinitesimal number of black people were registered to vote in South Carolina until the 1940s. Even when the Supreme Court in 1944 found the white primary unconstitutional, the South Carolina Democrats managed by subterfuge to exclude blacks for almost four more years.* But even as V. O. Key was writing of "The Politics of Color" in his classic *Southern Politics*, Federal Judge J. Waities Waring of Charleston was writing a decision that would forever alter the nature of South Carolina politics: "South Carolina is now the only state which now conducts a primary election solely for whites. . . . I cannot see where the skies will fall if South Carolina is put in the same class with [all] other states."

South Carolinians did not take kindly to Waring's admonition on voting rights, and were even more upset when he ruled, before the Supreme Court's *Brown* decision, that the "separate but equal" doctrine for schools was invalid because the schools for blacks were in fact *not* equal. Waring's life was threatened and he was socially ostracized in Charleston, where his family had lived for eight generations; in the face of those pressures he resigned from the bench and left the state.†

* South Carolina's response to the 1944 decision was to repeal all its statutes relating to primaries. This reduced the Democratic party ostensibly to the status of a private club, and primary balloting was not even secret. To become a Democratic voter, one even had to take an oath pledging to uphold white supremacy.

† Jack Bass records that at Judge Waring's 1968 funeral in Charleston, fewer than a dozen white persons were present, but there was a motorcade of more than 200 Negroes.

For more than a dozen years after Waring's 1947 decision, difficult registration laws restricted Negro voting very severely. The U.S. Commission on Civil Rights found that in 1958 only 14.8 percent of the voting-age Negroes in the state were registered—the lowest figure of any states except Mississippi and Alabama. But South Carolina's whites did not resort to crude intimidation or actual violence to stop Negro registration. Outside of a few university towns, the civil rights movement of the early 1960s did not catch fire in South Carolina with the visibility it did in other more violence-prone parts of the South. As a result, there was less polarization and more of an opportunity for subsequent coalition politics. From a level of 37 percent registration of voting-age blacks in 1964, the year before the Voting Rights Act, the figure rose to 58 percent in 1972. But South Carolina whites are so lax about registering, or one might say they have become so relaxed about blacks accompanying them to the polls, that only 63 percent of them have registered, one of the lowest figures in the entire country.

Now representing a full quarter of the registered voting pool, blacks are a vital factor in any close election. Even though only four blacks sit in the legislature, many white members owe their seats to black votes and since the mid-1960s have been appropriately sensitive to black demands on such issues as a liberalized registration law, passage of a compulsory school attendance law, a statewide food stamp program, and new bonding authority for a black state college. Either the NAACP or its close ally, the Voter Education Project, can pass the word at meetings on how blacks should vote in statewide races, and they respond. A virtually unanimous black vote for Ernest F. Hollings assured his election to the U.S. Senate in 1966. (There were about 100,000 black votes that year, and Hollings won by only 11,000.) Negro support was probably also decisive in the 1966 election of Democrat Robert E. McNair to the governorship (he won by 72,000) and definitely the margin of victory for Democrat John C. West for governor in 1970. (He won by 29,000.)

The alliance between blacks and the Democratic white leaders has been made possible by the skill of both—and a dash of traditional South Carolinian courtesy. Long past now are the years when, in the words of the Rev. I. DeQuincey Newman, who for years was NAACP field secretary in the state, "white politicians courted black leaders as a white businessman visits his paramour." Fully integrated delegations went to the 1968 and 1972 Democratic National Conventions and were not challenged for alleged racial imbalance, as so many others from the South were. At the 1970 state Democratic convention, 200 of the 900 delegates and alternates were black and a Negro was elected as a party vice chairman for the first time in the Democrats' history. The convention voted down a platform plank calling for a return to the days of "freedom of choice" on school integration. That year in Beaufort County, the party elected its first black county chairman.

There has been some black discontent with the Democrats—a feeling that the Democrats are longer on oratory about racial harmony than on concrete changes in state policy to aid black people, that too few blacks have been elected to office, and that white Democrats have left the blacks isolated in the support of Democratic Presidential candidates in recent years. A black-oriented United Citizens Party was actually formed in 1970 as a focal point of the protest. If the South Carolina Republicans would show any legitimate interest in black needs, they might be able to peel away some of the black vote. Newman is only one of many black leaders, now allied with the Democrats, who were once Republicans. "The situation in South Carolina is not stabilized," Senator Hollings told me. "If the Republicans nominated Nelson Rockefeller for President, bam, the blacks would be going in droves over to the Republican party."

To date, however, the newly enfranchised black vote has been an almost exclusively Democratic commodity. The present-day Democratic party of the state bears at least a surface resemblance to the ruling coalition in Atlanta, where Negroes have worked closely with an established business leadership that is interested first and foremost in preserving an atmosphere of stability and nonviolence. In South Carolina, of course, it is different because the Democrats still claim residual loyalty of the blue-collar workers in the Up Country and have a base of control in the county courthouses that one can hardly equate with Atlanta's metropolitan-style politics. Still, one might say that a broad-based Democratic party, ranging from the old gentility and pragmatically minded business leaders to women and the blacks, may have a brighter future in South Carolina than in practically any other Southern state.

If that occurs, the low-keyed and polite way that South Carolina Democratic leaders handled the race issue in the 1960s will have to be regarded as the starting point. The crucial event, that would set the tone for future years, came early in the decade when federal courts were insisting on the admittance of a Negro, Harvey Gannt, to state-run Clemson College in the Piedmont. As governor from 1959 to 1963, Hollings was committed to resisting desegregation but was realistic enough to know that integration in the colleges and schools was really inevitable. Touring the state in 1961, he later said, "People thought I ought to have some magic to stop the monster that was about to gobble us up, or else they expected me to go to jail. It looked to me like it was high time we started sobering people up before it turned out to be too late." In an off-the-record press briefing early in 1962, he told newsmen: "Before 1962 is past, South Carolina's legal defenses will fall like a house of cards. You might as well start preparing your readers for the inevitable. We are not going to secede."

At the same time, Hollings was cooperating with a group of South Carolina's most influential powerbrokers to effect a peaceful transition. They included Charles Daniel, a self-made millionaire and ultraconservative construction company owner; Edgar A. Brown, chairman of Clemson's board of trustees, president pro tempore of the state senate, and a longtime power in South Carolina politics; Robert Edwards, Clemson's president and an ex-textile executive; and John Cauthen, executive vice president of the South Carolina Textile Manufacturers Association and one of the most skilled and respected lobbyists in any American state in recent times.

Between them, and with the assistance of incoming Governor Donald S. Russell, this power structure quietly neutralized the most outspoken segregationists in the state,* arranged a series of statements by public leaders condemning any kind of violence and calling for peaceful acceptance of federal law enforcement, and saw to it that Harvey Gannt, when he arrived to register at the Clemson campus on January 28, 1963, would be greeted by nothing more sinister than a horde of curious newsmen on the lookout for violence that never occurred. Of all the public statements preparing South Carolina's people, perhaps none was more important than Hollings' in his farewell address to the legislature January 9. "As we meet," Hollings said, "South Carolina is running out of courts. This General Assembly must make clear South Carolina's choice, a government of laws rather than a government of men. We must move on with dignity. It must be done with law and order. The state's institutions and all law-enforcement agencies have been charged with their responsibilities."

In part, South Carolina was aided by the horrible example of what had happened on the campus of the University of Mississippi in Oxford only four months before. Shortly after that, a reporter had cornered Hollings and asked him if he would be willing to go to jail to prevent integration of a South Carolina school. "If it works out like Mississippi," Hollings replied, "jail would certainly be the safest place."

South Carolina was lucky, Cauthen said, not to have a Barnett or Wallace in the governorship, promising to "stand in the schoolhouse door." (A. W. "Red" Bethea, South Carolina's most vocal segregationist politician, had run in the 1962 gubernatorial primary but received only 5.3 percent of the vote.) Just as importantly, Cauthen added, "the business people and the people in education took the burden off the politicians. The politicians in effect stood aside to let things improve." When I asked Cauthen what might have happened if Thurmond had been governor, he shrugged his shoulders and said, "Who knows? Strom was frightened to be seen with the leaders of industry when race progress was being made. He is not representative of the course of government within the state for the past two decades."

Race tensions have not, of course, disappeared in South Carolina since the early 1960s. As recently as 1968, there was the terrifying incident at South Carolina State College at Orangeburg, in which the state police, called to quell an unruly campus demonstration, shot pointblank into a group of students, killing three and injuring 27 others—a story later documented masterfully by Jack Nelson of the Los Angeles *Times* and Jack Bass of the Charlotte *Observer* in their 1970 book *The Orangeburg Massacre*. The Orangeburg killings, according to Matthew J. Perry of Columbia, the state's leading civil rights lawyer, "resulted in sharp indignation and horror and anger among Negro citizens," who viewed it as one of the worst racial incidents in South Carolina's history. "The state authorities," John Cauthen told me,

* The individual the peacemakers were most concerned about was Marion Gressette, the second-ranking man in the state senate and chairman of the state committee set up to "discourage" integration. Gressette was known as "Mister Segregation" in the state and had called on the South "to rally to the support of the Great state of Mississippi" in its integration crisis. But Clemson president Edwards was able to influence Gressette on the effects of violence. A large national manufacturer had made overtures about building a multimillion-dollar plant in Gressette's county. "Senator," Edwards told Gressette, "if there's a ruckus at Clemson those people won't even plant scrub oak in Calhoun County." So Gressette issued a statement: "Peace and good order must be maintained both on and off the college campus."

"should have had a blue-ribbon investigation—to get the facts on the table. Instead they hid behind the FBI investigation, and most people in the state never saw the facts documented." The Nelson-Bass book corrected that, but only two years after the fact, and there was general agreement that Orangeburg was the low point of the generally progressive administration of Robert McNair, the governor of the late '60s who had been the first chief executive of South Carolina to appoint Negroes to boards and commissions.

Perry, who became the NAACP's chief counsel in the state in 1958 and handled numerous cases, including Gannt's application to Clemson, said a chief accomplishment of the '60s was to effect, by court order, the removal of the laws which subjected Negroes to stiff fines and prison sentences for using parks, beaches, or playgrounds reserved for whites. Throughout the '60s, he said, many school boards—especially in the Low Country, where the fight was the bitterest of all—demonstrated intransigent opposition to desegregation of the schools. Gressette and his house counterpart, representative Joseph Rogers, Perry said, were responsible for many repressive laws designed to stop integration or weaken the public school system.

As a civil rights lawyer, Perry said, he did not fear touring any area of the state; racism was generally "more genteel" than actual physical violence. But he did receive many threats and harassing phone calls all during the small hours of the morning. Activity by the Ku Klux Klan, he said, was apparent during the 1950s and hit an all-time peak around 1962 or 1963, subsiding thereafter. Likewise, the (white) Citizens Councils were powerful from the 1950s into the early '60s, especially in the ring of counties southeast of Columbia—Sumter, Clarendon, and Orangeburg. The Councils eventually receded, but the John Birch Society remained a factor throughout the decade, especially in Orangeburg. Most of the counties with the worst racial troubles were those with black majorities. Scarcely any whites remained in public schools in the Summerton school district in 62-percent-black Clarendon County. From a base of 15 to 20 private schools in the entire state in 1964, the number rose to 111 by 1972. They enrolled 25,000 white students and virtually no blacks; were subject to no state standards or control; frequently used transferred equipment and buildings that belonged to the public schools; and in many cases were run by church denominations, the Southern Baptists in particular. About half the "seg-academies" were relatively prosperous and seemed likely to last; another half were marginal enterprises of dubious longevity. And despite their growth during the most trying years of school integration, they still enrolled only 4 percent of the school children in the state. By 1973 the vast majority of the students in the state were attending integrated public schools, and thousands of whites had in fact accepted the idea of attending schools with a majority of black enrollment.

The public school system underwent its most severe test in 1970, when massive desegregation, including the use of cross-district busing, was effected. When Greenville's 58,000-pupil system faced a midyear court desegregation order, Governor McNair paid a personal visit to the city and gave his support to community leaders trying to effect a peaceful transition. McNair went on television to say that South Carolina had "run out of court, run out of time, and must adjust to new circumstances. I will oppose any attempt to close down public schools. The only way South Carolina is going to continue to grow is through its educational programs. We're going to have to maintain, support, and strengthen our public school system. . . . I don't think the people of this state will want to defy the order of the court after we've run the course legally." It was the first time any Deep South governor had spoken out so frankly on the school issue.

The transition to a unitary school system came smoothly in Greenville although the schools there were disrupted temporarily by unruly demonstrations amidst reports of actual or threatened violence by students of both races. In Lamar there was another blotch on South Carolina's reputation for moderation when a mob of angry whites attacked and overturned school buses bringing Negro children to a previously all-white school.

In the long run, though, the Lamar incident proved to be a healthy catharsis. Republican Congressman Albert Watson, running for governor, had appeared in Lamar nine days before the bus-dumping to address a mass "freedom of choice" rally. Watson virtually invited the subsequent violence by saying, "*Every section* of this state is in for it unless you stand up and use *every* means at your disposal to defend [against] what I consider an illegal order of the Circuit Court of the United States." Afterwards, there was a wave of revulsion in the state against the violence, and the issue backfired badly on Watson. Democrat John West did not mention the Lamar incident during his campaign, but afterwards he said it had been a strong factor in his election. He noted that an all-white jury had convicted the bus-dumpers of common law rioting. "There is still a lot of hardcore segregationist sentiment in South Carolina," West told me. "But South Carolina people are basically law-abiding and won't tolerate violence." As the chief issue of politics, West said, "the race issue is dead. The election showed it. It's a dead horse that's been whipped enough. I think people are saying let's get on with the important business—like housing, and hunger, and health."

(As recently as 1956, it is worth noting, South Carolina Governor George Bell Timmerman, Jr., had been calling for federal transportation of Negroes to Northern states where people favored "race mixing." That way, he said, "peace and good will will be restored" in the South.)

West's assumption about the subsidence of the race issue may be severely tested in the remainder of the '70s, and perhaps beyond. But if it is true anywhere in the Deep South, it is true in South Carolina. Despite all the problems, Matthew Perry said, he detected "a noticeable upsurge of good feelings between the races." * When I asked Senator Hollings if people in South Carolina still felt that their state and region were being "put upon" by federal civil rights enforcers, he replied: "They still have that feeling but they're not worked up. A lot of us feel we've done pretty well, and we're pretty far down the road, and it's been a traumatic experience in the '60s,

* In 1972 Perry, who had taken more than 10 cases before the U.S. Supreme Court and won all but one of them, was endorsed by Governor West and the state chairman of both the Democratic and Republican parties for appointment by the legislature as a circuit judge, the highest level of trial judge in the state. Perry would be the first black in the state's history to be a circuit judge.

and we're all satisfied we're going to live pretty well together, and now the trouble is going to come in Boston and Detroit and New York."

There are also some indications that economic issues are beginning to transcend the racial in South Carolina politics. In the early '70s Tom Turnipseed of Columbia, formerly national campaign director for George Wallace, became executive director of the South Carolina Taxpayers Association, a biracial Populist organization challenging the state's established powers on such issues as electricity rate increases. Turnipseed still had connections with segregated private schools, but in 1973 he addressed the state NAACP convention, saying: "The entire history of black people in America is one of exploitation by those who have always tried to grow rich and powerful at their expense. . . . These powerful men don't care a bit about you or your needs or mine either, for their exploitation of us transcends color."

In 1971, Louis Harris & Associates conducted a detailed survey of South Carolinian attitudes on economic growth in which a great majority expressed a desire for new industries and better wages. On some questions, there were marked differences between the races. Asked if blacks still suffered job discrimination, for instance, 68 percent of the blacks, but only 27 percent of the whites, answered "yes." But on the question of whether good race relations were important for the economic development of the state, 86 percent of the blacks and almost as many of the whites—83 percent—answered that they were.

. . . and Now the Republicans

When one speaks of the Democratic dominance of the "old" South Carolina, it is easy to forget how incredibly overwhelming it was. Between 1900 and 1944, the Republicans never got more than 7.01 percent of the state vote for President and often slipped down to showings like 1.4 percent in 1936 and 1.9 percent in 1940. How then did South Carolina become the fountainhead of the Republican party's "Southern strategy" of our times?

The story began in 1948, in the person of the amazingly durable figure still central to Republican fortunes in South Carolina—Strom Thurmond. Thurmond, as we noted earlier, had been a New Dealer in his early days, and he supported President Harry S Truman on rent controls and other administration moves. But something snapped inside Thurmond when he heard the young mayor of Minneapolis, Hubert H. Humphrey, give his now historic speech at the 1948 Democratic National Convention in Philadelphia: "It is now time for the Democratic party to get out of the shadow of states' rights and walk forthrightly in the bright sunshine of human rights." After that speech, a strong civil rights plank was adopted and a number of Southern delegations walked out of the convention. Meeting in Birmingham later, the States Rights party was organized and Governor Thurmond became its candidate for President. That was the year he told the nation: "We believe that there are not enough troops in the Army to force Southern people to admit the Negroes into our theaters, swimming pools, and homes."

Thurmond was on the 1948 ballot as the Democratic Presidential candidate in South Carolina that year, and he carried the state with 72 percent of the vote. The motivation for his vote was 99 percent racial, but at the same time industrialization was forming a new middle class—managerially oriented people, opposed to the national Democratic party on economic, not racial grounds. Over the next years it would grow, especially in the suburbs of cities like Columbia, Greenville, and Charleston, and to a lesser degree in Spartanburg, Florence, and Anderson, providing what is today the surest base of Republican strength in South Carolina. But because the national Democratic party was becoming more and more identified with black peoples' interests, state Democratic leader and political scientist Donald Fowler noted, "the race issue against the national Democrats and the economic base for the GOP worked hand-in-hand."

In 1952 the Republican cause in South Carolina—and across the South—was given an immense boost forward when Governor James F. Byrnes, a revered figure who had been the state's most influential member of Congress and the Cabinet since Calhoun, invited Dwight Eisenhower to speak at the State House and endorsed him for the Presidency. The old stigma against Republicans—which Thurmond attributes to the fact that "Republicans were in control of the national government in 1866 when the South was put under military rule"—held Eisenhower to 49 percent of the South Carolina vote. But it was still a momentous breakthrough for the GOP. Four years later, Adlai Stevenson carried the state for a second time, but only by a plurality, since the combined vote for Eisenhower and an independent slate of electors pledged to Senator Harry Byrd of Virginia was actually greater. Republican fortunes were set back by President Eisenhower's dispatch of federal troops to Little Rock in 1957, but, even after that, John Kennedy was able to defeat Richard Nixon in South Carolina in 1960 by less than 10,000 votes.

Early in 1960, South Carolina began to play a central role in the Republican party's new national strategy. Senator Barry Goldwater spoke at the Republican state convention and took the delegates by storm. The reception he received was so warm that when he returned to Columbia as the party's Presidential candidate in 1964, he would say: "I wouldn't be standing where I am today if it had not been for a state convention here four years ago." South Carolina's 16 votes, in fact, put Goldwater over the top at that year's Republican convention, and it was in the autumn of 1964 that Strom Thurmond switched to what he called "the Goldwater Republican party," * charging the national Democrats with leading the country toward socialistic dictatorship. Even James Byrnes took the stump for Goldwater. And when the smoke had cleared, Goldwater had won 33 of South Carolina's 46 counties and taken 59 percent of the total state vote.

Four years later, Thurmond's influence seemed to hit an apogee. He made the famous Atlanta motel room agreement with Nixon on federal policies. He

* Thurmond now says he used that phrase "more or less to help Barry." But only a few weeks after he made his switch in 1964, he suggested he would feel more at home in the Republican party if some liberal Senators like Jacob K. Javits of New York and Clifford P. Case of New Jersey would "move over" to the Democrats. Thurmond said he favored a realignment to make the GOP "the true, great conservative party."

persuaded Southern Republicans to "vote with your heads, not your hearts," thus heading off a very strong Dixie drive for California's Ronald Reagan that could well have cost Nixon the nomination. He let Nixon know that a liberal Vice Presidential running mate would not be acceptable, and the nomination of Spiro Agnew was a result. In the fall, Thurmond campaigned assiduously for Nixon in the Southeast and could take credit for the Nixon-Agnew victory, not only in South Carolina but to some degree in Florida, Tennessee, and North Carolina as well. The only reason Nixon's 38 percent of the South Carolina vote fell so far behind Goldwater's was that George Wallace was running, sharing the resentment vote against the national Democrats. (Wallace got 32 percent of the state vote, showing his greatest strength among the blue-collar workers of the Piedmont, faithful national Democrats up to then.)

The Nixon-Thurmond relationship was not uniformly happy during Nixon's first term. In fact, Thurmond took the Senate floor one day in 1970 to denounce the administration's school desegregation policies and accuse the President of a "breach of faith" that might cost him Southern support in the future. Thurmond was particularly upset by an Internal Revenue Service denial of tax exemption for the South's private segregation academies and the "proposed invasion of 100 carpetbagging Justice Department lawyers" ordered South to monitor school desegregation. His warnings had effect, however, as the Nixon administration appeared to back down on both policies. Thurmond later said he was convinced that the President had lived up to substantially all the points of the Atlanta agreement, including appointment of "strict constructionists" to the Supreme Court, opposition to school busing, and regulation of the growth of textile imports which had been harming Southern mills. Nixon's appointment of South Carolina's Clement Haynsworth to the Supreme Court—even though rejected by the Senate—was perhaps the most dramatic evidence of the administration's debt-paying to Thurmond. And all the while (until his resignation in 1972 to become general counsel of the Republican National Committee) Thurmond's former aide, Harry Dent, sat in the White House as political adviser to the President. Another former chief aide to Thurmond, J. Fred Buzhardt, was made general counsel of the Defense Department and later special Presidential counsel on the Watergate affair. (Buzhardt also maneuvered discreetly from his White House post to encourage the plea bargaining and resignation as Vice President of a scandal-tainted Spiro Agnew—the first man to resign the Vice Presidency since John Calhoun.) In all, twenty-odd Thurmond friends and associates were inserted into key Nixon administrative posts. Thurmond must have been pleased: rarely in American history has a political debt been so handsomely, consistently paid off.

In 1972 it all seemed to bear fruit as Nixon (helped along by Wallace's absence from the ballot) swept South Carolina with 71 percent of the vote, and Thurmond himself won reelection for a second time on the Republican ticket, garnering 63 percent. The only South Carolina voters who showed any appreciable support for George McGovern were the state's black people. Indeed, just viewing the Presidential and Senate election figures, one could have concluded that Thurmondism had reached ultimate perfection with virtually all the whites voting Republican and the blacks isolated in a hopelessly minority Democratic party.

In fact, that was not the case in any voting except the very "top of the ticket." The performance of South Carolina Republicans at the grass roots, where future leadership and long-term strength is built, has been perplexingly disappointing. Even after the great Nixon-Thurmond landslide of 1972, only 15 percent of the seats in the state legislature were held by Republicans. Only two of the state's six congressional seats were in Republican hands. And the party still held only about 100 offices at the county and municipal level.

What was the reason for the poor performance at the grass roots? Strom Thurmond explained that when South Carolinians vote Republican for President, "they feel that's way out yonder and if they vote Republican there won't be any stigma. But in state elections, especially among the less enlightened people, there's still that stigma against Republicans that goes back to the military rule of 1866 to 1876." By the very fact that the Democrats control the machinery at the local and state levels, Thurmond said, up-and-coming politicians see their best chance to be elected as Democrats, not Republicans. Senator Hollings offered a slightly different explanation. The Democrats keep their iron grip, he said, because Democratic state legislators "have been habitually good public servants. A textile leader knows he's got good support and following among them. It's given him a good business climate, and he doesn't want to upset that good applecart." Anyway, Hollings said, the Democratic party in South Carolina "is more conservative than it is liberal," so that Republicans attacking from the right lack ideological ground in which to maneuver.

The Republicans are unquestionably advanced from their condition of earlier times, when many of them were called "letterhead Republicans" because their organization existed chiefly on paper, a vehicle for a narrow group to reap patronage when the GOP controlled the White House. (Even as late as 1952, the Republican state chairman had a full-time job as chairman of the Board of Public Welfare in the District of Columbia. He kept a room in his mother's house in Pickens, South Carolina, which was his official voting address.) After the first Eisenhower election, retired industrialist David Dows of Aiken began building a Republican organization in the state, drawing on a mix of support from Democrats disaffected on the race issue (some of the old Bourbons), Republican businessmen who had moved into the state, bringing their party loyalties with them, and a small reform element upset with the generally unprogressive one-party Democratic rule. After the 1962 election, the organization work was sparked by J. Drake Edens, who began to build a more ambitious organization, down to the precinct level in some counties. But even in recent years, Democratic chairman Fowler noted, "the Republicans are intensively organized, but not extensively. They're great organizationally in the white upper-middle-class areas. But if you get out into the rural areas, the black precincts, and the blue-collar precincts, you just don't find a Republican organization." Republicans were also criticized for failing, through 1972, to hold an open primary that would give their candidates more exposure. Instead they nominated by convention, seeming to lend credibility to the Democratic charge that Republican candidates were hand-picked by a few party leaders.

The first Republican state legislator of the century was elected in 1961, and in 1962 William D. Workman, Jr., a veteran State Capitol reporter, ran against Olin Johnston for the U.S. Senate and got a very respectable 43 percent of the vote. In 1965 the Republicans got their first Congressman when Albert D. Watson, who had endorsed Barry Goldwater while running as a Democrat the year before, resigned his seat and won election as a Republican in a special election. In 1966, with Thurmond heading their ticket for the first time, Republicans advanced to 25 seats in the state legislature and almost defeated Ernest Hollings in the race for Johnston's unexpired Senate term. The Republican gains of '64 and '66 stunned the Democrats, who had long believed they needed only a loose organization to conduct primaries. The Democrats set up a permanent staff organization with regular headquarters, headed from 1967 onwards by Donald Fowler, a student of political patterns with a bent for practical organization. The new Democratic effort, combined with the segregationist cast that Thurmond and other leaders gave to the GOP in the very years that the Negro vote was expanding most dramatically, cut the GOP to eight legislators in 1968 and reduced their vote against Hollings, who was running for a full Senate term, to a mediocre 38 percent.

In 1970 Republicans saw a golden opportunity to seize the governorship. Strom Thurmond was riding high in the Senate, Harry Dent was in the White House, and the school segregation issue was boiling to a head. Brushing aside a more moderate contender who favored appealing for Negro votes, the Republicans chose Congressman Watson, an extreme segregationist, as their candidate. Thurmond nominated Watson at the state convention and for the first time put the full weight of his office and prestige behind another state Republican office-seeker. Vice President Agnew was brought in to campaign for Watson too. But that was the year of the Lamar bus-dumping, when proper South Carolinians recoiled at the prospect of a racial extremist in the governor's chair. Hollings campaigned as hard for John West as Thurmond did for Albert Watson, and the Democrats won.

The 1970 results were not good news for Thurmond. Noting the source —a high Democratic officeholder who asked that his comments be off the record—I found this description amusing:

> Thurmond had his day at bat in 1970 in that Watson race. And boy, when Watson was defeated, Strom was terrified. He put a black on his staff. He got the speaker of our house [Solomon Blatt] talking sort of Republican and then got Blatt's son appointed as a federal judge. He started playing catch-up ball all around. In 1972 he wouldn't put the word "Republican" on any of his literature or anything else. Before that, he had been Mr. Southern Republican, the Southern Strategy man, he got Richard Nixon in Atlanta, and he was Mr. Republican around everywhere. But he ran in 1972 as Mr. Independent—the great friend of the Democrats.

The same source said that if Thurmond had run as a Democrat in 1972, he would not have made it even past the primary—that the black and moderate voice was too great in the Democratic party for Thurmond to have a home there any more. Thurmond disagreed: "I could have been reelected as a Democrat. The people of our state will vote for a man on what he stands for, not the party he belongs to."

It is known that after the 1970 defeat, Harry Dent—a man of cooler temper than his erstwhile boss—took Thurmond aside and told him he would have to back away from a strong segregationist appeal. It was on Dent's urging that Thurmond put the black man, former Voter Education Project official Thomas Moss of Orangeburg, on his staff. The strategy, Dent told an interviewer, was to get Thurmond "in a position where he can't be attacked like Watson by liberals as being a racist." When Thurmond appealed openly to blacks, the white moderates who had been afraid of Watson were reassured. Thurmond won the 1972 election with ease, and in the sweep for him and Nixon, the state GOP boosted its legislature total back to 24 and elected a second Congressman.

Future Republican gains, it was clear, would have to be built on hard organization and economic issues, not on dazzling breakthroughs based on racism. A "postracial" South Carolina was no longer taken by the race issue. And the Louis Harris poll taken in 1971 showed that in terms of basic party identification, 51 percent of South Carolinians still considered themselves Democrats. Another 22 were independents, and only 11 percent were willing to say they were Republicans.

South Carolinians and National Power

From John C. Calhoun to James F. Byrnes to Strom Thurmond, South Carolina seems to have exerted an influence in national affairs far greater than its population—now just 1.3 percent of the national total—might justify. Some notes on a few major figures of the last decades:

When James Byrnes died in Columbia in 1972, at the age of 92, President Nixon said that "no man in American history has held so many positions of responsibility in all branches of our government with such distinction." The list of offices was indeed impressive. Starting in 1911, Byrnes served seven terms in the House and two in the Senate, becoming a key Senate troubleshooter for his friend Franklin Roosevelt in the 1930s. Roosevelt appointed him to the Supreme Court, but he remained there only 16 months before accepting appointment as Director of Economic Stabilization in World War II, a position Byrnes said "conferred on me greater authority than a President had ever previously delegated." He accompanied FDR to Yalta and President Truman to Potsdam, and was Secretary of State for two years. As one of Truman's most trusted advisers, he helped formulate the fateful decision to drop the atomic bomb on Japan, a step he thought would permit the U.S. "to dictate our own terms" in postwar relations with the Soviet Union. (One historian has suggested Byrnes was "the forgotten man of cold war history.")

Byrnes was disappointed, however, when he was passed over for the Vice Presidential nomination in 1940 and again in 1944, and he eventually fell out with President Truman, took issue with the national Democrats on the issue of civil rights and the "welfare state," and became a very embittered man. He said he personally liked Negroes but ended up as a diehard segregationist in his four years as governor of South Carolina (1951–55). It was the race issue that led Byrnes to propose a 3 percent sales tax when he took office, to equalize the quality of school facilities in the state. "We should do it because it is right," Byrnes said. "For me, that is sufficient reason. If any person wants an additional reason, I say it is wise." Byrnes obviously hoped that a good-faith effort could stave off a Supreme Court edict forbidding school segregation because the schools, if separate, were certainly not equal. But one of the five cases involved in the Supreme Court's 1954 *Brown* decision, which shocked Byrnes so deeply, came out of Clarendon County, South Carolina.* When Byrnes forsook the Democratic party to back Eisenhower in 1952, he said two of the reasons were Adlai Stevenson's support of fair employment practices and avowed intent to influence Congress to bar Senate filibusters. It all seemed incongruous to national observers, who had accepted "Jimmy" Byrnes as an urbane man of moderate persuasions. They did not know that Byrnes in his early days had been a close friend of "Pitchfork Ben" Tillman.

A distinguished South Carolinian told me: "Byrnes' sins were sins of omission. South Carolina has its inferiority complex, but when Byrnes made good on the national scene, he came home as a saint. He could have done anything for this state—constitutional revision, for instance, or improved race relations. But he didn't."

South Carolina's present junior Senator, Ernest Hollings, is a man few could accuse of sins of omission. In race relations, in economic development for his state, and in attacking the problems of the poor and hungry, he has done as much at each stage of his career—and sometimes more—than might be called politically judicious. He was born in 1922 into a Charleston family with deep Germanic roots—and Charleston's Germans, it is worth noting, were never part of the old slaveholding aristocracy or Charleston's natural elite, and had to scramble for status, using the political system, like Boston's Irish. When "Fritz" Hollings first ran for the state legislature in 1948, the idea was not to solve the world's problems but rather to enhance his career as a lawyer. But in his own methodical, conscientious way, he showed an immense capacity for growth over the years that followed.

In the legislature, Hollings became Jimmy Byrnes' floor leader and helped to push through the sales tax that started to pull South Carolina public schools out of the middle ages. He became lieutenant governor in 1954, broke with Byrnes when Byrnes pushed Thurmond for the Senate that year, and in 1958 advanced to the governorship. In that job, he undertook a massive industrialization campaign and kept race relations cool as tempers rose to a boiling point in other Southern states. He helped John Kennedy eke out a Presidential victory in South Carolina in 1960, was sobered by a defeat for the Senate at the hands of Olin Johnston in 1964, but came back to win the seat (now dis-

* B. O. Butler, who was made principal of a black elementary school in Clarendon County—his first job after graduation from South Carolina State at Orangeburg—recalled years later: "It was root pig or die then. We got no supplies. The students paid tuition to buy coal for heat. The buildings were dilapidated." Pleas to the Clarendon school board for help went unheeded.

avowing any close connection with the Kennedys) in 1966. Knowing he would face the voters again for a full Senate term two years later, Hollings compiled one of the most conservative voting records of all Southern Senators and even voted against confirmation of Thurgood Marshall for the Supreme Court. Yet as Lee Bandy, veteran Washington reporter for *The State*, reported in September 1968: "Hollings has been forced to parrot Thurmond and hew the conservative line more often than he desired. But if he is granted a new lease on his political life, Hollings will undoubtedly emerge as a member of the 'new progressive South' and become the kind of Senator he would like. He will tackle such national problems as mass transit, water and air pollution, poverty, education, and so forth." It turned out to be a remarkably accurate prediction, as Hollings in 1969 became his own man, to the immediate benefit of sick and hungry people in South Carolina and across the nation.

The metamorphosis in Hollings' thinking is important, not only because of the man but because it might prove a guideline for future Southern politicians. As governor, he later said, he had pushed for investment in new industries on the theory that "the money would trickle right down to the humblest man in the state." By the late '60s, he had learned that the theory was a bad one. "My myopia lifted and I saw hunger face to face," he later wrote, on a cold January morning of 1968 when he toured a Charleston slum ghetto and began to see that "the hungry are not able-bodied men, sitting around drunk and lazy on welfare. They are children. They are abandoned women, or the crippled, or the aged."

The next night he saw some 700 adults, almost all black, studying late at night in a schoolhouse to learn the rudiments of reading, writing, and arithmetic. "They weren't a bunch of drunks there that night. And they sure weren't shiftless."

A week later, at the invitation of civil rights leader I. D. Newman, he toured the "Black Bottom" area of Columbia, a destitute black and white slum not far from the Governor's Mansion he had once occupied. "Here," he recounted, "the weather was even colder than in Charleston—down to 18 degrees. The water spigots were left open to drip when frozen. I will never forget the four children and crippled man we saw piled on a bunch of old mattresses and trash. No heat, no electricity. . . . On one street there was an outhouse serving 38 families. Filth was everywhere."

That year, Hollings heatedly opposed a proposed South Carolina tour by Senator Robert Kennedy's subcommittee looking into hunger problems. (Kennedy, he said, "was as popular in South Carolina as Earl Warren. Once the Kennedy name was attached to hunger in South Carolina, everything I was trying to accomplish would go down the drain.") A Kennedy visit would also have endangered Holling's reelection chances, and it never took place.

When Hollings returned to the Senate in 1969, however, he was free to become the most vocal advocate in that entire chamber for expanded food stamp programs and more federal money to provide medical care and housing for the destitute. He made more "hunger tours" in South Carolina, including Beaufort County on the seacoast (which we will discuss further later in this chapter). He involved many local officials in his tours and was free to write in his 1970 book, *The Case Against Hunger*, of his region's "hunger myopia:" *

> Within a 40-mile radius of Timmonsville, South Carolina, there are 40 farmers who each received last year over $40,000 from the United States government—for not working. This doesn't affect the character of the farmer. He's still as red-blooded, capitalistic, free enterprising, and patriotic as ever before. But give the poor, little hungry child a 40-cent breakfast and you've destroyed his character. You've ruined his incentive. You've taught him bad habits. You have developed a drone society. "This food stamp program is a plot of the Communists." There are too many people all over America who believe this.

There are an especially large number of them in Hollings' native Charleston, I might add. In February 1969 Thomas R. Waring, editor of the Charleston *News and Courier*, was kind enough to take me to a cocktail party of distinguished, mostly aging, *crème de la crème* of old Charleston society. There was an almost universally hostile reaction to Hollings' revelations about hunger in South Carolina. Some assigned it to plain politics (Hollings' allegedly wanting to run for Vice President with Teddy Kennedy in 1972); others said they just couldn't believe there was real hunger—if anyone wanted to eat, he could. "After all, I have a hard time getting domestic help, so there's no shortage of money for those who really want to work," one dowager said. What seemed to concern many of the oldtimers was the buying up of South Carolina lands by the big paper mills. They bemoaned the fact that the possibilities for unrestricted hunting were fast evaporating.

Hollings carefully documented how malnutrition of a pregnant mother and a newborn child can cause irreparable brain damage that blights the chances of a child to become a fully intelligent, productive member of society. In the familiar poverty cycle, he argued, there was no more effective place to break in than by providing adequate nutrition:

> I'm convinced hunger can be eliminated. I'm convinced that this is an *economy* move, but how in the world can you convince people of that. . . . It is cheaper to feed the child than it is to jail the man. You leave them hungry, they get diseases, they get bad habits, they get frustrations, they get belligerent. They don't learn to turn the page of the book they get in the first grade. . . . They hit half the grades and by the sixth grade they drop out. . . . And then we talk about delinquency. And then the government goes into high gear. We get the truancy officer, we get the guidance counselor, we get the child psychiatrist, we get the vocational educator, and that's costing millions and millions of dollars.
>
> It'd be so easy to give them a decent meal, a hot breakfast in the school building. . . . Once you do that you eliminate $65 a day in a hospital room when they become ill. For $65 I can feed a family of four or five for a couple of weeks. I'm convinced that this just costs too much later on in welfare payments and rehabilitation programs and penal institutions and health problems.

Nationally, Hollings said, hunger was a problem for more poor white people than Negroes. In South Carolina, he found whites suffering from hunger in Columbia and Charleston and many rural counties. But predominantly,

* "Thank goodness," Hollings said in a magazine interview about that time, "for the six-year term, because at least you've got some chances to let the brickbats fall all around and work on through on the different programs."

it was a problem for black people in South Carolina, and that raised the specter that in some future election year an opponent could destroy his political career with an unmitigated racist appeal. He told me he was betting that the racial climate of his state had advanced far enough so that would not happen. He was trying to defend his political flank by emphasizing more popular South Carolina issues like protection of the textile industry. He held a seat on the Commerce Committee, which deals with textile problems, and while denied a seat on Armed Services (he got a slot on the powerful Appropriations Committee instead), he had compiled a promilitary voting record equaled by few and was preparing to wage his 1974 reelection campaign on "what I think is the primary function of government—and that's national defense."

Combining those traditional South Carolina causes with his daring excursion into the political quagmire of the hunger issue, Hollings seemed to have a chance to fulfill his professed ambition—"to be the best Senator South Carolina's ever had."

To our earlier reportage on Strom Thurmond, some personal notes should be added. Chronologically past his 70th birthday, he has the physique of a man half his age (Harry McPherson once wrote that he was "shaped like a medium-range missile"). He is a veritable physical fitness zealot who jogs two or three miles a day, performs enough morning push-ups to make one wince, never touches alcohol or cigarettes, and keeps healthy on fruit juice and vitamin pills. He cherishes his image as a states' rights scrapper; in fact he holds the record for the longest filibuster speech on record (24 hours, 18 minutes, against a civil rights bill in 1957). He once wrestled burly former Senator Ralph Yarborough to the floor outside a committee hearing room. He still believes that the South was profoundly wronged in the Civil War. "When the Southern states seceded from the Union," he told me, "slavery of course played a part, but the Southerners were more interested in the philosophy of government and thought that if they had joined the Union voluntarily, they had the right to withdraw voluntarily. Well, force said they did not."

Despite Thurmond's adamant opposition to every civil rights bill and virtually every piece of social legislation proposed since he went to Washington, he has assiduously claimed credit in the past few years for channeling big benefits to South Carolina for housing and welfare programs he initially voted against as "socialistic" and "dangerous." In 40 years of public life, he has only been defeated once (in 1950); he is the only man ever to win election to the Senate on a write-in vote (in 1954); and he is the only modern American politician to have run for office four ways—as a Democrat, a States' Righter, an independent, and a Republican.

Harry Dent and a number of other friends warned Thurmond of "political suicide" when he told them in 1968 that he was going to marry Nancy Moore, Miss South Carolina of 1966 and a girl 40 years his junior. But Thurmond went ahead and made great political hay out of the two cherubic infants who followed in due course—undercutting any arguments that he might be too old for reelection. When I asked in 1973 how Thurmond was viewed in Charleston, a local sage replied: "As far as we're concerned, Ol' Strom walks on water, and those two little babies just buoy him up."

Few South Carolinians have exercised national power on a scale with the late L. Mendel Rivers, a Charleston Congressman who spent the last five years of his life as chairman of the House Armed Services Committee, raising armies and launching navies and spending billions in the name of Constitutional authority. "I could defeat Strom Thurmond any day of the week," Rivers was once quoted as saying. "But I don't want to be a South Carolina Senator. I've got the most powerful position in the U.S. Congress."

Theoretically, Rivers' job as Armed Services chairman was to cast a critical and suspicious eye on Pentagon requests; in fact he acted as an unbashed proponent of virtually any request or weapons system proposed by the military and the industrial complex that fed it. For Rivers, the fighting forces were somehow the mystical body of the nation, and when the national mood shifted in the late 1960s to criticism of the military-industrial complex, Rivers asserted: "This is antimilitarism gone berserk." Rivers had an encyclopedic knowledge of military hardware and installations, plugged for higher military pay and benefits, and was a hard worker who plunged into his workday at about 6 A.M. each morning. He was the picture of the autocratic committee chairman, running most deliberations behind closed doors, cutting off critical committee members or witnesses. But he had broad support in the House as a whole and rarely lost a battle.

Rivers was not only for amassing military power but for using it. He wanted the atomic bomb dropped in the Korean War, and he favored an invasion of Cuba in the early '60s. "Words are fruitless, diplomatic notes are useless," he said of the Vietnam war. "There can be only one answer for America: retaliation, retaliation, retaliation!" When a group of distressed wives of Vietnam war prisoners visited him, he said of the Hanoi leaders: "We've been powerfully patient while this bunch of heathens have toyed with these ladies' tender feelings. Let them know war is hell. . . . Let them witness what would happen to have one of their cities disappear from the face of the earth." A Republican Congressman on Rivers' committee said it was fortunate the military itself knew how to exercise restraint: "If Mendel was running things we'd be in World War V."

Rivers was a tall, thin man with a mane of silver hair bunched up at the back of his neck and a florid Old South speaking style. His political hero was John C. Calhoun. He loaded so many military installations into his native Charleston that his predecessor as Armed Services chairman, Carl Vinson of Georgia, once said: "You put anything else down there in your district, Mendel, it's gonna sink."

The military returned Rivers' favors in abundant measure. At a snap of his fingers, an Air Force plane would be on hand to take him anywhere in the world, and when he went on alcoholic binges (a habit he finally kicked in the mid-1960s) he could recover in military hospitals. Charleston could not wait for Rivers' death to honor him: in 1965 a bust of him, mounted on a seven-foot granite shaft, was dedicated on Rivers Avenue, near the Navy Yard, and dozens of generals, admirals, astronauts, Congressmen, and Cabinet members flew in (at taxpayer expense) to honor him.

There was another side to Mendel Rivers, less noticed by the nation at large. He was born in 1905 as the son of a turpentine still operator near a rural crossroads called Gumville, in the Hellhole Swamp section of Berkeley County—an area, Jack Bass has noted, "known as a breeding ground for politicians and moonshine whiskey." His widowed mother took him to Charleston as a young boy, and he achieved a little bit of class by marrying a Charleston debutante. In 1940, he first won election to Congress by defeating Fritz Von Kolnitz, an aristocratic banker supported by an entrenched "Charleston machine." Rivers roamed the dusty crossroads of the eight rural counties attached to the Charleston district, roaring that "the only banker I ever knew was the one who foreclosed the mortgage on my Mama's farm after my daddy died." He lost Charleston in a big way but squeaked through to victory by virtue of the country vote. In that campaign he promised to come home each year to hear people's problems, and he never failed to spend a day a year hearing constituents in each county seat. A close associate described it "as the savior coming home."

Though matters military preoccupied Rivers, he never shook off his own humble background. He had the most liberal voting record of any member of the state's delegation, supporting antipoverty legislation, food stamps, and other social welfare measures. "I had an awful hard time living when I was a young fellow," he said once. "I knew poverty like nobody in the South Carolina delegation did. When I can help the man in the street, I'll do it, 'cause I remember it."

The people never forgot him either. When the "Swamp Fox" died in 1970, thousands filed past his casket—the powerful and influential, but also men in work clothes, bearded youths, elderly people, and blacks as well as whites. Then Rivers' casket was driven out through the moss-draped Low Country for burial in a pre-Revolutionary War cemetery, not far from his birthplace.

Low Country people think in such a dynastic way that they elected Rivers' 28-year-old godson, Mendel J. Davis, to succeed him, and there has been talk that Mendel L. Rivers, Jr., may run for the seat in the next few years.

The other Coastal Plains district got a real shock in 1972 when the 74-year-old curmudgeon who had represented it since 1938, John L. McMillan, was finally defeated in a Democratic primary. "Johnny Mac," as he was known back home, survived all those years on an electoral coalition of tobacco farmers and warehousemen (whom he helped as a high-ranking member of the House Agriculture Committee), courthouse and city hall politicians, and some old-line Negro politicans. He was regarded as a benevolent figure by the people of his dirt-poor district and did not meet his Waterloo until the image was shattered by a strange deal he made with an erstwhile primary opponent. Organized labor, black organizations, and the youth vote all played a role in McMillan's defeat at the hands of a progressive young state legislator, John Jenrette. But MacMillan supporters had their revenge in the general election when they helped a conservative Republican, farmer-businessman Ed Young, win the seat by a margin of more than 10,000 votes.

The cheering when McMillan went down was the loudest in the nation's capital, where he had been the chairman of the House District Committee for 24 years, squashing every home rule effort and doing his best to run Washington like a South Carolina plantation. Home rule, McMillan said, was backed by "Communist sympathizers" who hoped to take over the city. In 1970 columnist Jack Anderson summed up the suspicions of many Washingtonians when he wrote that McMillan "accepts favors from used-car dealers, parking-lot barons and liquor lobbyists" in return for "obstructing public parking, welfare payments, and home rule." Reporters were never able to prove McMillan took a crooked dollar, but his patronizing attitudes toward black people and his conduct of District Committee Affairs, which ranged from dilatory to dictatorial, were a matter of public record.

William Jennings Bryan Dorn, Representative from an Up Country textile district, is the most influential member of the delegation in the view of Lee Bandy of *The State*. He is the chairman of the Veterans' Affairs Committee, helps all areas of the state from an influential post on the Public Works Committee, and is a leader of the Southern "textile group" in fighting for restrictions on foreign imports. Textile lobbyist John Cauthen called him "our most effective spokesman."

It is Dorn's human quality that makes him most interesting, however. His family not only named him after the great Nebraska Populist (to whom he now bears a striking physical resemblance) but decided when he was an infant that he would be a politician. Though largely self-educated (he never went to college), he is well read and a fountainhead of Southern, United States, and world history. He is a great raconteur, a man of immense energy, and hires a young and well-educated staff (all under 30). He owns a fancy house and hobnobs with textile magnates but has scarcely any of the bank holdings or business interests typical of politicians; as the often critical Ralph Nader Congress Study noted, Dorn's public financial report "seems more like a filing for bankruptcy on a small farm."

Dorn seems the typical Southern Congressman with florid oratory and white suits, and he used to vote against civil rights bills. But there does not seem to be an ounce of personal bigotry in him. In 1971 he was the only South Carolina House member to vote for funds to establish a Washington memorial for Mary McLeod Bethune, a noted Negro educational leader and South Carolina native. Even more significant, he voted for federal funds to help areas (of which there are several in his district) which must bus school children to achieve integration. When some constituents objected, he replied: "How do you want to get there [to school]? You want to walk?"

Dorn used to be considered a strong conservative, and in 1962, was on a reported "purge list" compiled by Kennedy administration officials. By the early 1970s, he was still casting more conservative votes than liberal, but the populism of his namesake shone through in support for bills to help unemployed workers and victims of black lung disease. His change on civil rights seems to have begun in 1964, when he rode Mrs. Lyndon Johnson's "Lady Bird Special" campaign train through the South. In Columbia, Dorn recalled later, "the hate was so thick I could see it in their faces." After that, he said, "I took off and started talking. Mostly I talked with young people. High schools and colleges. Sometimes three and four speeches a day. I talked good manners, respect, and our heritage of tolerance." As early as 1966, he was saying: "I don't want to see this state get into a situation again where a buffoon like 'Pitchfork Ben' Tillman can take command of the people—decent people, even the aristocracy—because of racism."

After 13 terms in the House, Dorn returned home to become a leading gubernatorial candidate in 1974.

State Government: Farewell to the "Barnwell Ring"

In the annals of American state government, there is scarcely a parallel to the broad and lasting power exercised by Edgar A. Brown and Solomon Blatt, denizens of the little Low Country county of Barnwell and leaders of South Carolina's fabled "Barnwell Ring." Edgar Brown was first elected to the South Carolina house in 1920, and to the state senate in 1928. There he would remain until his retirement in 1972, at the age of 84, having spent 30 years in the two most powerful posts in the senate—president pro tem and chairman of the finance committee. Brown's power was so great that V. O. Key suggested half seriously that South Carolina go to a cabinet system of government and make Brown its prime minister. Solomon Blatt, a resident of the same little town and county of Barnwell, was elected to the house in 1932 and then served with only a four-year break as house speaker from 1937 to his retirement from the speakership in 1973. Brown and Blatt had their personal differences, but they agreed on two things—the need for balanced budgets, and the desirability of rural control of the legislature. When these two conservatives opposed Strom Thurmond, then in his New-Dealish period, for governor in 1946, Thurmond coined the nickname of the "Barnwell Ring"—and it stuck.

Part of the Ring's mystique, writer Roger M. Williams has suggested, was that Barnwell County was one of South Carolina's most lightly populated (17,176 in 1970). Williams described it as "a pleasant, lightly rolling country of neat little houses, battered shacks, unadorned Baptist churches, and towns whose names are unknown elsewhere." Once Barnwell County was wealthy cotton plantation country, but by the time Brown and Blatt first went to the legislature, it had declined to a collection of poor farms and dirt roads. Only since World War II has it begun to revive, with the Savannah River atomic energy project and assorted industries. But the county seat of Barnwell still bespeaks the rurality and sleepiness of the preatomic Old South.

Both Brown and Blatt came from poor circumstances. Brown's father had been a small farmer; Blatt's father was a Russian immigrant who made his start in America selling combs and corsets. Brown was a Protestant, at once an easygoing backroom politician and a stern manager of the state's fiscal affairs who became nationally known as Democratic National Committeeman from his state. Blatt was Jewish, a political curio in a Protestant, aristocratic state.* An intense individual, so resolutely provincial that he disliked spending a night outside of Barnwell County, he lacked Brown's gregarious, storytelling ways but shared Brown's skills as a manager of men.

Brown and Blatt expanded their influence far beyond the borders of Barnwell County by leading the rural bloc which controlled South Carolina until reapportionment came in the 1960s. "We had 25 counties," Brown said, "and they kind of looked to me for leadership." A second underpinning of Brown's and Blatt's power was their attentiveness to the economic interests of South Carolina's big powers—the planters, textiles, utilities, and banks. Brown once said he steered South Carolina state finances in such a way that "the big fellows like DuPont, Stevens, Deering-Milliken, Fiberglas, Textron, Chemstrand, Lowenstein, Burlington, Bowaters, and others . . . have confidence in our stability." He took great pride in South Carolina's Triple-A credit rating. Blatt, according to Robert Sherrill, devoted his "highly paid" legal skills to representing such groups as the South Carolina Textile Manufacturers Association, the South Carolina Electric and Gas Company, and most other private power companies.

"Money," Blatt told me in a 1969 interview, "is our greatest problem in state government. We need it to attract and hold new industries, so that we can do more for schools, higher education, a good medical college, mental health, corrections, and the like. Thus it all returns to the problem of finances—and finding new taxes which will not hurt business and industry."

He returned to the same themes in his 1973 farewell address as speaker, an almost classic definition of what he and Brown stood for:

> We emerged from the depths of the Depression with complete knowledge that economic disaster can overtake the whole nation with a suddenness so acute that it came almost overnight, starting with the crash on Wall Street. We learned that paying our own way with balanced budgets should always be a way of life in government and private affairs. It is my hope that this legislature and those who follow will continue rigidly to respect that financial philosophy. . . . We have worked hard for good, honest, sensible government for many years and we cannot afford to backslide by supporting policies which may sound good on a short-term perspective but will not stand up under the test of time.
>
> In my opinion the greatest thrust for progress in South Carolina has resulted from the close understanding between government, labor, business, and industry. . . .
>
> While I have stepped down as speaker, I have not resigned from the house and I will be a candidate for reelection in Barnwell County next year and I will be on the floor and will not play dead. I shall be an active representative of the people and . . . shall use every ounce of my strength to help defeat every piece of legis-

* Two centuries before Blatt, however, Francis Salvador II was a member of the Provincial Congress of South Carolina (1775). Salvador was the first person of Jewish ancestry elected to public office in the western hemisphere. Later he was killed in the service of the American colonies during a skirmish with Indians in the Revolutionary War. According to Eli N. Evans, in *The Provincials: A Personal History of Jews in the South,* nearly half the Jews in America in 1800 lived in and around Charleston. In the 17th century South Carolina granted Jews the right to vote—the first community in the modern world to do so.

lation that will be harmful to and against the best interests of the people of our state and especially those who have invested their millions in South Carolina, giving employment to thousands of our good people who earn a good livelihood and have given a good day's work for a good day's pay.

Both Brown and Blatt were segregationists—in the customary quiet style of South Carolina. Brown helped smooth the way for integration at Clemson, though he once had to be physically restrained from going out of his law office in Barnwell to pursue with his cane the black rights organizer, the Rev. I. DeQuincey Newman, during a street demonstration against voter registration practices in the county. Blatt called himself a "segregationist in moderation," but in 1966 when a bill to restore the state's compulsory school attendance law was being debated, he won a racist reputation with South Carolina's Negroes by declaring in an emotional outburst: "You may want a 16-year-old so-and-so to sit by your granddaughter, but Sol Blatt will fight and die to prevent it from happening to his granddaughter." (Over Blatt's opposition, the compulsory attendance law, which had been repealed during the "massive resistance days" of the '50s to reduce the number of young Negroes integrating white schools and to free white parents to keep their children out of school altogether, was finally restored.)

Slipping physically, Brown finally relinquished his senate seat and leadership in 1972, carrying with him into retirement only one great regret—that he had never realized, despite three tries, his lifelong ambition to be a U.S. Senator. (One of his defeats had been at the hands of Strom Thurmond in 1954.) Reapportionment and the rise of a generation of younger, more progressive legislators weakened Blatt's power, but by a compromise he held on to his speakership until July 1973. Then, in an emotional farewell speech, he noted the presence of the four black legislators (first elected in 1970) and expressed pride in a state "where no longer a man's religious views, political affiliations, or the color of his skin in any wise prevent him from walking the road of life to a distance far beyond that which he expected in the years gone by." He was succeeded as speaker by Rex L. Carter of Greenville, a progressive Democrat and supporter of the liberal social programs of Governor John West, many of which Blatt had opposed to the end.

Edgar Brown's successor as president pro tem of the senate was none other than Marion Gressette, the state's erstwhile massive resistance spokesman. A man of powerful presence and sometimes scalding oratory. Gressette was once described by Jack Bass as "the 20th-century embodiment of the conservative lawyer-planter class who ruled South Carolina before the Civil War." But Gressette's politics, especially on race issues, are not what they used to be. About the time that reapportionment arrived in the mid-1960s, his legislative segregation committee passed out of existence. Gressette even learned how to campaign for (and get) black votes in his expanded home district. In 1972, when he succeeded Brown, old Columbia hands were flabbergasted to see a score of invited Negro guests among the crowd that attended a champagne reception at the Wade Hampton Hotel to celebrate his swearing-in.

The leadership changes in the General Assembly suggest that the familiar scenario of South Carolina government over the past years—generally progressive governors making proposals that ran aground on the shoals of legislative opposition—may be ameliorated. But the prospect is by no means certain, for there is still no state in the Union where the legislature holds such preeminent power vis-à-vis the governor. The governor is only one of a committee of five which draws up the state budget.* The legislature, rather than the governor, names all members of the public service commission (which regulates utility rates) and boards controlling social services and employment security. The state board of education and the immensely powerful highway commission are elected by legislative delegations from the 16 judicial circuits. And all state judges are elected by the legislature—usually from the ranks of its own alumni. The governor's power is further restrained by his limitation to one term, though he does have a veto power over legislation.

The legislative dominance has slipped a bit in recent years, with appointment of more officials and control of federal grants passing into the governor's control. Reapportionment has undermined the system by which the senator from any county was automatically its political boss, in control of the county budget and the appointment of most local officials. But still, the legislators exercise power that would be the envy of their counterparts in almost any other state.

Fitting the Brown-Blatt doctrine of fiscal conservatism, but going back long before them, South Carolina's "legislative government" meant parsimonious government designed to save taxes for the entrenched powers of the state and, of course, to exclude labor unions. The result is all too clear when one compares South Carolina's per capita expenditures for education, highways, welfare, and other services with the levels in other states. South Carolina is far below the national average in each category. During the 1960s, for instance, South Carolina ranked lowest in the country (except for Mississippi) in teacher pay and per-pupil school expenditures, even though its illiteracy rate (5.5 percent in 1960) was the second highest in America. In the early 1970s, the South Carolina Education Association became so exercised about low teacher salaries that it threatened to impose sanctions if sizable increases were not forthcoming. Until a $500 increase was granted in 1973, the average teacher pay was $1,400 below the Southeastern average.

Part of the reason for low government expenditures surely lies with the low average income levels of the state. Another explanation is that local property taxes are scandalously low. In 1970 one study indicated South Carolina could collect $165 million more a year in property taxes and $31 million more a year in personal income taxes and still not exceed national averages; on the other hand, the state sales taxes (which fall most heavily on poor people) were found to be $36 million above the national average. In the early 1970s, South Carolina's tax effort—all state and local tax collections as a percentage of personal income—ranked only 42nd among the states.

There were governors who sought much higher levels of state expendi-

* The other members are two legislators and the independently elected state treasurer and comptroller general.

tures to meet a whole array of pressing social needs. Among these have been the three outstanding governors of the past decade and a half—Ernest Hollings, Robert McNair, and John West. Hollings was perhaps the most outstanding of the group. Having served 10 years in the General Assembly, including leadership positions, he steered around Brown and Blatt to get a remarkably broad legislative agenda passed. Over the opposition of the textile industry, he got approval of the two-year post-high school technical education program, which has been the basis of much of South Carolina's recent industrial growth.* He obtained approval of a major new tax program (principally for education), instituted the state's outstanding educational television system, reorganized and revitalized the state industrial development board, put in a committee on higher education, instituted a securities commission, and revamped the insurance department and the penal policies of the state. Thurmond, in the late '40s, pushed through a number of progressive programs—partly because he succeeded in ousting Solomon Blatt as house speaker for four years. Even James Byrnes, despite his general conservatism, made more money available through the sales tax (the preferred tax of the industrial interests) and took a great interest in mental health. To get the state mental hospital at Columbia cleaned up, Byrnes took the whole legislature for an afternoon's visit to the hospital, showing them beds jammed together, people sleeping on concrete floors, the shortage of physicians, and the poor food. The legislators immediately voted a bond issue for a greatly improved mental hospital.

Yet even to this day governors have to exert extraordinary moral leadership to get some of the changes they want in state government. A case in point was the difficulty Governor West—who had promised a "color-blind" administration in his 1971 inaugural—experienced in getting state agencies to submit affirmative action plans to end discrimination in state employment. A 1972 report by research staffs at the University of South Carolina and predominantly black Benedict College had concluded that "black employment statistics appear to reflect modern vestiges of historic discrimination . . . and only token integration in the state government now." Only 12 blacks were found to occupy classified job positions with a starting salary of $12,700 or more, and 51 percent of those employed received less than $4,000, the official poverty level for a family of four. When the state human affairs commission, set up under West, tried to get fair employment action plans, many state agencies ignored the request. West finally felt compelled to call in the agency heads and warn that if they did not take a voluntary action, he would ask the federal government to step in and enforce compliance

* Hollings himself has many ties to the textile industry, which he says has been, "by and large, a good influence in the state." But the textile interests initially opposed technical training because they wanted to keep a large, relatively untrained work force available at their own beck and call. As Hollings explains it, the textile industry habitually operated on a cyclical basis in employment, going from employment peaks of six-day weeks around the clock to valleys of a single shift just one day a week. "At the peak," Hollings said, "they wanted to reach out and get all those employees. They didn't want anybody competing and certainly not training them to higher skills and going off to higher pay. So we had quite a struggle in actually instituting our technical and industrial arts program. Every textile and chamber of commerce man in South Carolina now is proud of our industrial training. But they were the ones who resisted it at first."

with the 1964 Civil Rights Act. In a state with a strong executive, such a threat would never be necessary.*

The mildly progressive program of a governor like John West has minimized the age-old conflicts between South Carolina chief executives and the legislature, but a strong core of conservatism remains in the General Assembly, especially on the senate side. Yet it may have been a sign of the times that the 1973 legislature, the first after the demise of the Barnwell Ring, was the most liberal in memory on various social welfare issues. Reapportionment is bringing an increasing number of younger, better educated, and generally more progressive legislators into office, and they are generally proving far more responsive to gubernatorial leadership than their predecessors.

Innovations: Educational TV, Computerized Registration

South Carolina has come out very low in political scientists' listings of the American states in terms of programmatic innovations. But two efforts are truly unique and deserve recognition.

The first is the South Carolina Educational Television Network, which started on a pioneer basis in the late 1950s and subsequently developed into the nation's first statewide open and closed state television system with multichannel capacity. The South Carolina effort is of immense importance because of the low educational attainment levels of the state and the lack of sufficient skilled teaching personnel occasioned by low teacher pay levels. Centered in a complex production-transmission center in Columbia, the network had developed by the early 1970s to include five broadcast stations at various locations in the state and the multichannel, closed circuit system which reached almost 300 schools and technical education centers. The course enrollment—ranging from elementary school programs to the postgraduate courses and continuing education for physicians, teachers, businessmen, law enforcement officers, and the personnel of state agencies—was about half a million each year.

For example, secondary schools are supplied with series in languages, mathematics, science, social studies, vocational education, health, art, music, sewing, and driver education. There have been special projects for teacher certification, an innovative three-year Master's in business administration from the University of South Carolina, clinics for medical personnel on such subjects as pediatric cancer and strokes, the nation's first statewide training program for law enforcement officers, a monthly youth forum sponsored by the alcohol commission, a child-rearing series for the mental health

* George Hamilton, a black man whom West appointed to head the human affairs commission, deserved credit for pursuing the employment problem until West made his warning. Hamilton had already proven his mettle as director of a community action program for a four-county area in the state. When he wanted to start a Head Start program, he couldn't get any whites to enroll. Yet the project had to be integrated to obtain federal funding. About that time a white woman applied for a job with the CAP. Hamilton knew her husband was a member of the Ku Klux Klan, and told her she could get the job if she could get her husband to obtain permission for Hamilton to address a meeting of the local Klan. The permission was obtained, and Hamilton ended up recruiting 48 white children and five white volunteers.

department, and documentaries for the arts commission on the native South Carolina crafts of basket weaving and Catawba Indian pottery. Public affairs programs have included a program on the success of school desegregation in one of the state's larger counties and a four-night-a-week newsmagazine which allows viewers throughout the state to call in questions to the evening's guest. The network received an Emmy Award for its "Job Man Caravan," a regular program providing employment and job training information for disadvantaged people.

A second area in which South Carolina got a jump on all other states of the Union was the institution, in the late 1960s, of statewide computerized voter registration. Before then, registration had been exceedingly difficult in the state. Registration offices were open only three days a month, long lines always formed, and the voter lists carried large numbers of names of deceased and moved persons. An ancient story told concerned two men copying down names from Charleston tombstones for entry on the registration books. One man said, "Here's one long enough to make two names out of." To which the second man replied, "Now lookie here, I don't mind helping you, but if you're going to do something crooked like that, I'm going to quit."

The new system, by contrast, makes registration exceedingly easy, efficient, and corruption-proof. The counties report all registrations to a central state office, which enters them into computers (together with a voter identification number). In return, each county is regularly supplied with precinct-by-precinct voting lists. Deceased persons are regularly removed by reports from the bureau of vital statistics. Dual registrations by locality are immediately spotted. Jury selection is greatly simplified. And anyone can get a copy of the voter lists for political organization work. The listings are amazingly comprehensive, showing not only each person's name and registration number, but also his or her race, profession, and age. The only item excluded is party affiliation, since state law does not provide for registration by party. In addition to all this, registration hours have been vastly expanded.

Sadly, the new technology has not inspired a very high rate of voting in South Carolina. In 1968, the first year under the new system, only 46 percent of the voting-age population actually cast ballots for President (a ranking of 49th among the states). Four years later, South Carolina's turnout dipped to an abysmal 39 percent (worse than all but Georgia). About the best one can say about the turnout is that it is better than it was back in the old one-party days. As recently as 1940, for example, only 10 percent of the state's adults bothered to vote for President, and not many more in the state's contested Democratic primaries.

The Economy: Textiles Plus

"In my lifetime," textile association executive John Cauthen observed, "South Carolina has moved from a one-product agricultural economy to a diversified, advanced industrial economy." Indeed, when one views the spectacular growth of industry in the last decades, it is hard to believe that the state will long remain mired in some of the lowest personal income levels of the nation. The growth is not only impressive but is accelerating. In the 1950s, 72,000 new jobs were added, but in the 1960s there were 170,000. Personal income growth, less than 50 percent in the 1950s, jumped by 130 percent in the decade of the '60s.

Serious economic change in South Carolina began with World War II, when the textile industry branched out into synthetic fibers and companies like DuPont and Celanese added their weight to the hundreds of smaller mills in the state. The flow of textile mills from New England, which had begun as a trickle in the 1890s, gained steam just before the war and then expanded greatly afterwards. Many antiquated plants were abandoned and efficient modern ones put in their place. (Cauthen claimed that South Carolina installed more modern textile-producing equipment than any other state.) The industry began to diversify more into dyeing and finishing, synthetics and blends of cotton, wool, and other materials, stretch knit goods and carpets.* Especially in the synthetic fiber plants, more highly skilled jobs were created and salaries rose more sharply. Chemical and eventually petrochemical fiber plants enriched the mix.

Some of the mills were owned by South Carolina investors, including Spring Mills and Greenwood Mills. But the biggest operations were imports from New England. The largest of all was J. P. Stevens Company, headed for many years by Robert T. Stevens, who gained national prominence as Secretary of the Army during the Eisenhower Administration, and Deering-Milliken, under the direction of Roger Milliken. Each had scores of mills, scattered across the state (though concentrated in the Piedmont); both became pioneers in researching new methods of texturing, new weaves, and new end products. Roger Milliken became a big contributor to the state's Republican party—"Daddy Warbucks," some nicknamed him. Milliken contributed $84,000, part of it secretly, to President Nixon's 1972 re-election campaign. He had been among those named by columnist Jack Anderson as being involved in "a direct link between a campaign payoff to President Nixon and his efforts to restrict textile imports." Back home, Milliken also had an archconservative reputation. (His name was on stationery of the John Birch Society, though he denied actually being a member.) But in matters industrial, Milliken was anything but a reactionary. *Fortune* reported in 1970 that Milliken could "take credit for much of the technical progress that the textile industry has achieved since World War II." At his research center outside Spartanburg, for instance, Milliken's technicians pull apart and analyze every new weaving and knitting machine that goes on the market. "When we get through with a piece of machinery," a Deering-Milliken official said, "we know more about it than even the manufacturer."

Tremendous labor efficiencies were made possible by new textile-producing machines and the improvement of old ones. As one account noted, "the

* South Carolina has about 30 percent of the U.S. textile industry, and leads the nation in spinning, weaving, and finishing. North Carolina, by contrast, is bigger in the knitting industry, and its total textile output is somewhat larger.

old-fashioned textile mill, characterized by rows of sweating, lint-covered workers attending clanking machinery," has generally been replaced by "clean, air-conditioned plants of modern design, housing automatic, high-speed equipment that requires only periodic checks by trained technicians." Nevertheless, the industry has expanded so rapidly that total South Carolina textile employment inched forward from 130,000 at the end of World War II to 156,000 in 1973. During the same years, the value of textiles produced annually in South Carolina rose from $800 million to $4 billion. The allied garment industry also grew by leaps and bounds, as many farm women went to work in the hundreds of small plants, earning pitiful wages but still generating enough income to keep many marginal farmers on the land. In 1947 there were 9,000 garment workers, and by the start of the 1970s, over 44,000.

There has been a lot more to South Carolina's industrial growth than textiles and garment making, however. A vital turn came during Hollings' term as governor. Under him, Jack Bass noted, "the state development board was transformed from a group of cronies to a scientifically oriented, business-minded agency that worked hand-in-hand with potential new industry." Professional marketing and labor surveys, reliable statistical data for each county, and specialists in plant sites were all made available. The technical education program, also inaugurated under Hollings, provided 13 training centers around the state. Area vocational high schools also offered special programs for illiterates who hoped to prepare themselves for better jobs.

Even more impressive in the eyes of any industry planning to set up a new plant in South Carolina, or expand operations there, the state's committee on technical education routinely set up special schools to train the required number of new workers under simulated plant conditions. The particular company's plant engineer and foreman were even put on the state payroll for a period of time to make sure the training procedures complied with the firm's production methods. Few if any other states provided such an attractive and practical form of subsidizing for new industry.

The effort paid off handsomely. Nearly $4 billion was invested in new manufacturing facilities in the state during the 1960s, and the expansion was not only in textiles but also in such diversified fields as tool and die work, electronic design and assembly, chemical technology, and precision metalworking. Large plants were started by such blue chip industries as General Electric, DuPont, Carolina Eastman, Westinghouse, Union Carbide, Dow Chemical, Kimberly-Clark, Allis-Chalmers, and Lockheed. Significantly, there was also a major influx of foreign investment—actually $1 billion of the estimated $15 billion total in this country. One example was the $50 million, 700-worker Georgetown Steel Plant, a subsidiary of Korf Industries of West Germany, begun in 1969. Even other state governors were impressed. Governor Linwood Holton of Virginia told me, "When you get a state like South Carolina, that has acquired foreign investments and job facilities worth so many millions of dollars in the last few years, you're not looking at an antebellum South Carolina anymore." He might have added that one was not looking at an industrial mix so heavily weighted to textiles anymore. By 1972, textiles accounted for only 43 percent of the total manufacturing jobs—compared to 65 percent at the end of World War II.

By the start of the '70s, South Carolina leaders were emphasizing their desire for capital-intensive new industry, rather than the labor-intensive type the state had previously sought to soak up its large unskilled labor market. Governor West said: "In the early 1960s, two factors—cheap labor and the absence of unions—were the draws, but no more."

West was probably overstating the case. In 1973 executives of two foreign firms investing in new plants in Orangeburg—Peter Mayer of Mayer & Cie, Inc., of Tailfingen, Germany, and Masao Hayashi, of Koyo Seico Co., Ltd., of Osaka, Japan—offered very candid reasons for their choice of South Carolina. Speaking at a conference on foreign investment sponsored by the Southern Growth Policies Board, they cited such factors as availability of land and labor and high worker productivity, low taxes and free state training for their workers. They also listed the South Carolina right-to-work law and the fact that overall labor costs were already cheaper in South Carolina than in Germany, and in the long run would probably be cheaper than in Japan as well. Mayer explained that it was virtually impossible to operate a non-union plant in Germany, and Hayashi noted that wages were increasing at the rate of 20 percent a year in Japan. The Japanese executive also said his company was impressed by traditional South Carolinian politeness and manners, noting a similarity between Southern and Japanese hospitality.

Some South Carolina textile interests, however, have been less than hospitable toward new factories—foreign-owned or otherwise—which might disrupt their labor supply or force them, through competition, to raise their wages. (In 1972, Southern textile workers still earned $44 a week less than the average for U.S. industrial workers.) A case in point was the reaction to the 1973 announcement of the Michelin Tire Corporation, a French-owned multinational firm, that it would build two plants in the upper Piedmont—its first in the United States—with an initial employment of 1,800 workers. Governor West said the Michelin investment, expected to be over $300 million, was the largest by any foreign company in South Carolina's history and would "immeasurably increase our tax and economic base and provide welcome diversification." The textilemen of the Anderson-Greenville area were openly hostile, however. Noting that the rubber plants would pay wages several dollars an hour higher than textiles, they feared their workers would be lured away and that replacement labor would be unavailable in an area with an unemployment rate of less than one percent. (The state development board had tried to interest Michelin in the South Carolina Low Country, which has a labor surplus, but Michelin insisted on the upstate area, where there were trained workers accustomed to an industrial atmosphere.)

The textile complaints were given public exposure by William D. Workman, Jr., editorial analyst for *The State* in Columbia. He feared for "the old, established plants which have meant so much to the state" over the years and warned of serious economic dislocation in a tight labor market. J. Bonner Manly, then head of the state development board and himself a former

Deering-Milliken textile executive, wrote the newspaper: "You do a disservice. Almost 60 percent of the state's work force earns $4,000 or less, ranking us 47th in the nation. You are concerned about an 'overdose' of industry. I suggest the average South Carolinian is concerned about an underdose of income."

The traditional antiunion sentiment in South Carolina is a major reason for the state's exceptionally low manufacturing wages. Textile spokesmen like John Cauthen attribute it to "the nature of the workers themselves, who came off farms and out of the mountains and dislike being organized." But it is also true that hostility to unions has been ingrained into South Carolinians over years through the news media, in schools, and in churches. Only in Charleston, with its high numbers of longshoremen, iron, sheet, and electrical workers, have the unions made important inroads. Time after time—in the 1930s, in the big Operation Dixie right after World War II, and in recent years—have textile unions launched big, costly organizing campaigns. Despite some increases since the late '60s, the overall results have been pitifully meager. In 1972 the South Carolina work force was still only 9.0 percent organized, and the figure in the textile industry was estimated at only 7 to 10 percent. Blacklistings, harassment, and plant closings have all been used to stop unionization. In 1956, when the workers at Deering-Milliken's textile mill in Darlington voted for organization by the Textile Workers of America (TWUA) in an NLRB election, Roger Milliken imately called his directors to town and voted to shut down the mill in retaliation. The case lingered before the NLRB and before the courts for 13 years until Deering-Milliken was finally ordered to make restitution to the laid-off workers for the hardships they suffered. As late as 1973, not a dollar of the restitution payments had been made as Deering-Milliken continued to argue with the TWUA over exactly how much pay was involved and whether the company should pay interest on it. Some observers thought the payments might still be years off—while a few of the 550 affected workers had never again obtained employment, and as many as 100 had died, a glaring case example of justice delayed meaning justice denied. The company has never reopened the disputed mill. The TWUA has been no more successful with J.P. Stevens mills, losing every organizing election. In several cases, the NLRB found Stevens workers were fired because of union activities. Until the TWUA gets a toehold in one of the big companies, its future in the South will remain bleak.

Many textilemen claim that the higher wages which would come with unionization would drive them out of business because they have been so hard-pressed in recent years by foreign competition. But their reaction—especially after the import limitations on Oriental textiles worked out by the Nixon administration in 1971—is probably more visceral than rational. In 1973, for instance, Eugene Stone III, president of a large Greenville textile company, complained to the newspapers that the new Michelin plants might be susceptible to unionization. It would be, he said, "just like a cancer; once they [the unions] get a foothold, it tends to spread."

Low-wage and antiunion policies may return to haunt the textile industry, however, especially in the era of industrial diversification now dawning in South Carolina. Without competitive wage scales, the industry will find it harder and harder to exercise discipline in its plants or win employee loyalty. TWUA president Sol Stein noted in 1972 that labor shortages were hampering expansion of the Southern textile industry. Textile workers were so dissatisfied with their working conditions, he said, that the typical plant had to refill half its positions every year. The answer, he suggested, lay in wages and fringe benefits comparable to the mainstream of American industry, plus "cooperation and teamwork with employees through a union of their own free choosing."

In part, the unions have themselves to blame for the excruciatingly slow pace of organization. Several independent sources in South Carolina told me that there were many incompetents in the ranks of the union organizers. Nevertheless, among South Carolinians as a whole, antiunion sentiment is subsiding. The 1971 Lou Harris poll found that a large majority of South Carolinians felt quite strongly that they were not getting an equal break on wages. Asked if they agreed with the statement, "Industry is just running away from labor unions by moving South—we should unionize here too," 44 percent agreed and only 30 percent disagreed. Only 29 percent went along with the statement, "If labor unions get in here, new business will stop coming." The most insistence on higher-grade, better-paid jobs, and the least hostility to unions, was found among young people.

It is worth noting that federal equal employment legislation and labor shortages have combined to open up significant numbers of textile jobs to black people, for the first time in South Carolina history. The old state law that effectively barred Negro employment in the textile industry was declared unconstitutional by the state attorney general in 1960.* Even after that, black employment remained under 5 percent. The big break came after the 1964 Civil Rights Act. Black employment jumped to 17 percent by 1968 and 25 percent in the early 1970s. The transition was facilitated by the simultaneous movement of many trained white workers to higher-paying jobs in industries like chemicals and electronics. As a report from the federal Equal Employment Opportunity Commission noted: "The textile mill industry may serve as a training ground for Negroes in the future as it has for whites in the past. Though the industry has low pay scales, . . . it does provide a medium through which workers can move from an agricultural to an industrial way of life, . . . and perhaps to move on to higher paying jobs as opportunities present themselves." The government does not judge such things, but it is also possible that blacks will present the last and best chance for unionization of the textile industry.

Industry continues to eclipse agriculture as the chief income source of South Carolina, and the state's people seem to like it that way. In the Harris

* The action was taken quietly in typical South Carolina fashion. As John Cauthen later recalled, "We knew the old law was class legislation and unconstitutional anyway. But we feared a try for repeal, because we had enough little demagogues in the legislature, always looking for an issue. We also knew we would catch all holy hell from the textile workers on a straight repeal bill. Finally, the attorney general, Daniel R. McLeod, talked to me, saying there were enough court decisions to make the old law invalid. So Dan just wrote me a letter declaring the law null and void, and I quietly mailed a copy to each of the mills. There was no public announcement."

poll, 55 percent agreed, "It's a healthy thing for the state not to have to depend on farming and agriculture." In 1971 the value of farm goods was $466 million, compared to $3.6 billion for manufactures. During the 1960s alone, farm employment dropped from 188,000 to 78,000, and the number of farms from 86,000 to 53,000. Cotton is scarcely an important commodity anymore —the total crop value was barely $20 million at last count. Tobacco is first— about $100 million a year—followed by soybeans at $50 million. Many former cotton lands have been converted into rich grazing land for cattle, and there is a big, prospering poultry industry. The state produces more peaches than any state except California; in fact, Spartanburg County has a bigger peach crop than the entire state of Georgia. Only 4 percent of the state's 2,590,516 people were found living on farms in the 1970 Census.

Since the Atomic Energy Commission in 1950 announced its big Savannah River Plant in Aiken and Barnwell Counties, South Carolina has become one of the most advanced states in nuclear technology. The Savannah River facility, operated by DuPont on a nonprofit basis, has several nuclear production reactors and massive concrete buildings which house the reprocessing of plutonium and tritium—two key elements of atomic and hydrogen bombs. There are several nuclear power generating facilities, including a $700 million Duke Power Company plant in the upper Piedmont, and the Navy opened an assembly plant for Polaris missiles near Charleston. Military establishments at Charleston, Sumter, Columbia, and Myrtle Beach have accounted for some of the most significant population increases of recent years. Another important economic factor has been the growth in foreign trade, symbolized by Charleston's growth from the 65th largest U.S. port in cargo in 1947 to 13th in recent years. Most cotton for the mills is now imported directly through Charleston, and in a switch from the old pattern of bitter textile competition with the Orient, a highly successful textile mission to Japan was organized for executives of some of the largest South Carolina mills in 1972. They came back with large orders for such items as carpets, upholstery, drapery material, sheets and towels for the booming new hotels of the Orient.

Despite the diversification and growth of its economy, South Carolina has serious obstacles to overcome if it ever hopes to raise its personal income levels to the national average. One reason is that it shares with states like Alabama some of the highest percentages in the country of workers in blue-collar as opposed to usually higher-paying white-collar jobs. The state has three metropolitan areas (Columbia, Charleston, and Greenville-Spartanburg), but no big, thriving city that would serve as a major headquarters and communications town. Governor West said several times, "We don't want any Atlantas." He would prefer to concentrate development in the impoverished rural areas. That philosophy, however, places a damper on making any kind of great leap forward into a postindustrial era.

Notes on the Environment, Hilton Head Opulence, and Rural Destitution

Especially in its coastal regions, South Carolina has many wonders to offer the visitor, and hundreds of thousands come each year, spending more than $400 million. They come to enjoy the 281 miles of coastline and the seemingly endless miles of white sandy beaches, to view the Low Country's intriguing swamps of cypress and gum, to visit the landscaped parks and antebellum mansions, and to soak up the historic wonder of old Charleston and other venerable towns.

Some of the coastal resort areas, particularly the 50-mile Grand Strand centered on Myrtle Beach, have been subjected to the neon strippery and rank commercialization Americans seem to accept or even desire in their seashore vacation spots.* By contrast, there are only two or three resorts in America comparable in beauty and tastefulness to the modern development of historic Hilton Head Island near Savannah, a verdant subtropical 12-mile strip of land that is actually the largest island south of Long Island. Hilton Head is an Eden of seaside forests with picturesque Spanish-moss-laden trees, wildlife (birds and alligators), and spotless broad beaches. Since the early 1950s, the island has received close to $100 million in vacation-retirement homes, low-rise condominiums, and hotels, the whole designed to blend harmoniously with the natural environment. Charles Fraser's Sea Island Plantation became a model and guidebook for second-home developers in the country, and his resort is perhaps the choicest retreat of the rich and near-rich on the entire Atlantic coast. Its "Harbour Town," where an inviting circular yacht basin is surrounded by two-to-five-story condominiums that recall both a Mediterranean village and Charleston's Rainbow Row, has become the jewel of the Intracoastal Waterway and one of the most delightful spots I have ever seen on a seacoast.

The American experience has yielded few more dramatic contrasts than the opulence of the Hilton Head resorts and the abject poverty and deprivation of the surrounding coastal regions of Beaufort and Jasper Counties. The area's woes were thrust into bold relief in the late 1960s through the testimony of Dr. Donald Gatch, a courageous local physician, that 75 percent of the children were infected by worms, and Senator Hollings' investigation of hunger and malnutrition among the natives. "In Beaufort County," Hollings reported, "I visited a shack in which 16 persons lived and there was no light, no heat, no running water, hot or cold, no bath, no toilet. The entire store of food consisted of a slab of fatback, a half-filled jar of locally harvested oysters, and a stick of margarine. Dr. Kenneth Aycock, our state health official, who was accompanying me, tentatively diagnosed a man in the house as suffering from pellegra, a disease supposedly nonexistent in this country.

* The name "Grand Strand" is actually a promoter's idea, later accepted by the state legislature, to designate the wide beach near the North Carolina border. The area's diversions include surf and deep-sea fishing, many golf courses, and family camping. There are many inexpensive seafood restaurants that serve up the abundant fresh catch from the Atlantic.

In the same house, one small child had rickets and another was recovering from scurvy."

From Harbour Town, for instance, one can look across the water to the shore of Daufuskie Island, where a colony of black people (125 at latest count) have lived an incredibly isolated existence since the last century. In the 1960s they were found to be drawing their water from a single contaminated well, suffering from parasites, and living out their lives in one-room shacks sustained by meager welfare checks. No road is paved on Daufuskie, and the oxcart is still the principal means of transportation. Pat Conroy, a spirited young white who taught in the one-room schoolhouse there for a year (before the Beaufort County school board summarily fired him for insubordination), wrote in his book *The Water is Wide* that when he arrived not one of his 18 pupils knew the name of his or her country or state, or that it was the Atlantic Ocean that washed the shores of the island. Fourteen of them thought Daufuskie was one of the nine planets and that nearby Savannah was the largest city in the world.

Daufuskie is not too far from the county seat, Beaufort, second oldest town in South Carolina. Again, there is the stunning contrast of cultures. As Betsy Fancher wrote in *South Today:*

> The town's tortured and venerable history is concentrated at the Point, a colony of iron-filigreed and columned homes with tall verandas. . . . The gentlemen of the Point, men of exquisite courtesy and taste, are wrapped up in their professions, their homes with their rare antiques and leatherbound books, their patterned gardens of azaleas and oleanders, the conviviality and bounty of their tables (fine Madeiras, gumbos and sauces, and lemon-scented finger bowls), their clubs, and the education of sons trained in a South Carolina militaristic tradition that dates back to the Revolution. . . .

The elite of Beaufort (pronounced Bew-fuht) did not welcome the news of hunger in their midst, or react particularly when the federal government stepped in to set up the Beaufort-Jasper Comprehensive Health Services Project, which turned out to be one of the more imaginative, innovative health services programs under OEO funding (akin, in many ways, to the Tufts-Delta project at Mound Bayou, Mississippi). By 1973 there was a staff of 206 under a strong-willed black layman, Thomas C. Barnwell, Jr., whose family had lived in the area for two centuries. The project was providing everything from standard medical care to helping people build wells and privies for their shacks. Interestingly, though, Charles Fraser of Sea Pines Plantation—symbolizing the "new" wealth of Beaufort County—spearheaded a fight against intestinal parasites before the health services project was even conceived.

In 1969 Beaufort County and Hilton Head in particular became the focal point of a dramatic struggle of another kind—over the natural environment. In that year the American subsidiary of the West German dye and chemical giants, Badische Anilin- & Soda Fabrik (BASF), a corporate offshoot of I. G. Farben, quietly bought up a huge tract of land on the mainland, just four miles from Hilton Head, and then suddenly surfaced with the word that it would build a $200 million chemical-industrial complex there. Governor

McNair and the rest of the South Carolina political hierarchy were overjoyed at having landed what would be the largest single industrial development in the state's history. They were joined in their enthusiasm by the Beaufort area NAACP, the director of the local poverty program, and the Beaufort Chamber of Commerce. BASF promised to employ 1,800 workers to construct its plant and to hire several hundred at high wages thereafter. The company suggested that satellite industries would create another 7,500 permanent jobs nearby. It looked like the best news for the impoverished natives of the coastal region—a third of whom earned less than $2,500 a year—since Hilton Head's golden era as the capital of a sea island cotton kingdom before the Civil War.

Hilton Head developers Fraser and Fred Hack saw it quite differently. Unspoiled Port Royal Sound, they feared, might be filled with fouled water from the vast chemical complex, with a pall of fumes drifting over their valuable investments. They enlisted other resort owners and local black shrimpers and oystermen on their side, raised a war chest reported at $200,000 (a proof of how well money can fight money), and stirred up so much adverse publicity that BASF postponed and finally canceled its plans altogether. The fight even stirred up some local interest in the poor local Negroes, descendants of several thousand slaves left behind after Union troops quit the island they had captured at the end of the Civil War. Fraser, for instance, launched a hookworm study on the island and backed local antipoverty efforts.

It was not long after the denouement of the BASF affair that the Lou Harris poll zeroed in on the question of public attitudes toward new industrial growth. Over 60 percent of the people endorsed South Carolina's program to recruit new factories, and 65 percent said that given a choice between more major industry and some danger to the environment and character of the state, they would pick the new industry. Big majorities of the respondents favored more large manufacturing plants, more nuclear power plants, and oil refineries. But they wanted to have their cake and eat it too. On another question, 73 percent said that they felt air and water pollution was a serious problem in South Carolina. Harris suggested that the environmental issue, like the issue of better wages, was one that South Carolina officials would have to address more and more in the next years.

In 1971 the South Carolina legislature did correct its lackadaisical antipollution laws by creating a new pollution control authority with powers to set standards for air and water pollution control and see that they are enforced. But through 1973 it had still failed to pass legislation to zone—and thus deter filling and other forms of destruction—in South Carolina's 450,000 acres of tidal marshes, the most of any state on the Eastern seaboard. Dangers to the marshes range from proposed offshore oil development to the immediate threat of dredging and building as real estate developers move north from Florida. The tidelands provide an ecosystem returning oxygen to the environment, and are extremely productive spawning grounds of fish, shrimp, crabs, and oysters.

Piedmont and the Midlands

The historic differences in landscape and the temperament of the people between South Carolina's Low and Up Country remain sharp today, reflecting the lasting divisions between a land that ranges from semitropical swamps and beaches along the Atlantic to the foothills of the Blue Ridge Mountains. Some refinements on the Up Country-Low Country contrast are necessary. An account is incomplete without mention of the 10-county Pee Dee basin that overlaps the fall line in the northeastern part of the state, a tobacco-growing region that bears a great resemblance to neighboring North Carolina. Then there are the 14 Midlands counties, centered on the capital city of Columbia, an area rapidly shifting from agriculture to industry.

While the eight-county Low Country coastal plain, including Charleston, is sure to intrigue the visitor the most, the real economic muscle of modern South Carolina is in the 14 Up Country counties of the Piedmont. The major cities there are Greenville and Spartanburg, linked today by a 30-mile stretch of Interstate 85 that has all manner of modern, diversified industries along its flanks. During the 1960s some half billion dollars of new industrial investment went into the Greenville-Spartanburg area, ranging from textiles (in which the cities excel) to synthetic fibers, apparel, electronics, chemicals, pharmaceuticals, and metal fabricating. The I-85 corridor, as we noted in the Georgia chapter, is the economic lifeline of the New South.

The center city populations of Greenville and Spartanburg are relatively small—61,208 and 44,546 respectively. But the total population of their two counties and neighboring Pickens, part of the Greenville-Spartanburg metropolitan area, is now approaching half a million, more than half again the figure before World War II. Suburban shopping centers and new housing subdivisions abound, and steel-helmeted construction crews seem omnipresent. Downtown Greenville now has the tallest office structure in South Carolina. The city likes to call itself "the buckle of the Bible Belt" and is indeed the home of fundamentalist Bob Jones University, where the students are forbidden to smoke, drink, dance, hold hands, kiss, or even go on dates without chaperones. Many of its graduates go on to become missionaries or Southern pastors—or, if female, wives of pastors. Things are a bit more relaxed at Furman University, founded a century and a half ago by the great-grandfather of Judge Clement F. Haynsworth, the Greenvillian who almost made it to the U. S. Supreme Court. Greenville's politics are rather conservative, but from 1969 to 1971 the city had a mayor, Republican Cooper White, Jr., who tried to mobilize public support for the schools during court-ordered desegregation and busing. White refused to endorse Albert Watson for governor in 1970, accusing his fellow Republicans of trying to polarize the races in South Carolina. In his own contest, White had captured half the Negro vote, an unusual feat for Republicans anywhere in Dixie. He was succeeded by Max Heller, a Jewish immigrant who escaped Hitler's Europe and was elected mayor with bipartisan support. Heller is a Democrat and, by Greenville standards, a liberal.

The capital city of Columbia hangs exquisitely in the balance between old and new, between the Low Country and the Piedmont, between model civic progress and sins of omission that could ruin its prospects for a bright future. It is a city of fantastic contrast between broad, attractive streets and despicable slums, historic old structures in tree-shaded settings and blocks of small service shops. Two blocks from the handsome State Capitol one can see old, unpainted Southern shanties—yet, a block farther, the gleaming new coliseum of the University of South Carolina. A number of new private and state office buildings brighten the downtown scene, but directly opposite the Wade Hampton Hotel and across from the Capitol there is a pawnshop which advertises "diamonds, pistols, radios, and watches."

The Columbia metropolitan area, with a population of 322,880 that rose 24 percent in the 1960s alone, is a picture of robust health in terms of the growth in personal income, retail sales, construction, and industrial payrolls. To the extent that South Carolina has a center of banking, distribution, education, and of course government, Columbia is the place. But there is incredible fragmentation between the governments of the city proper, surrounding Richland County, next-door Lexington County, the unincorporated towns, and the school districts. Problems of public transportation, zoning, streets and highways, public housing, pollution, and sewers all receive belated and inadequate attention because of the confusion of governments. Yet in 1972 a modest proposal for consolidation of Columbia with Richland County was turned down by the voters.

During the 1960s Columbia made a brave effort to kick off the image of blatant white supremacy that had marred its past. An active community relations group made serious efforts to improve relations between the races. With cooperation of the business leadership, public accommodations were voluntarily desegregated, a year ahead of the 1964 Civil Rights Act. Later the established powers sponsored an exemplary employment guidance center which placed Negroes in more than 1,000 "breakthrough" jobs in its first three years of operation. Harbison, a racially and economically integrated "new town" on the model of Reston, Virginia, and Columbia, Maryland, was planned for 1,000 areas of land northwest of the city made available by the United Presbyterian Church. Yet in 1970 a study by the Central Midlands Regional Planning Council showed advanced degrees of blight in all but four of 25 predominantly black neighborhoods. Most suffered from substandard housing, serious health problems, high crime, and high welfare levels. In the wake of thorough school desegregation, achieved in 1970–71, there was a white exodus to private schools or to the overwhelmingly white suburban school districts. Though blacks make up only a third of the city population, they now account for well over half the school enrollment.

Columbia's old families, its established elite, have moved over to let the business leadership, centered in an unusually progressive chamber of commerce, run the show in Columbia. Part and parcel of the leadership group is *The State*, an excellent newspaper owned primarily by the descendants of Wade Hampton, the "redeemer" governor of South Carolina. *The State*'s associate editor, Charles H. Wickenberg, Jr., served as chamber of commerce president in 1972 and unveiled an ambitious master plan for redevelopment of the old inner city of Columbia. Two Columbia-based planning firms with national repute and an international company, Doxiadis Associates, worked together in development of the 30-year blueprint, which calls for blending restoration with new construction and such attractions as housing along the riverfront and a multilevel mall on Main Street.

Yet there is fear that all this might come to naught if the Columbia area fails to solve its problems of chaotic government structure and an increasing concentration of the area's poor blacks in the center city. And unless those problems can be solved, Columbia's future will remain murky. In an enlightening review of Columbia's problems and prospects for *City* magazine, writer John Egerton quoted an anonymous (but obviously well-informed) long-term resident of the city:

> Columbia has not yet come to an either-or situation. It's headed toward the same mistakes the big cities have made, but it hasn't arrived there yet, and it still has time. But there's no sense of urgency. We do a little and feel proud, put out a fire and then relax. The style is low-key, casual, deliberate, subtle, polite, courteous, and passive. The aristocracy, the ruling class, says "Look how far we've come," but not many people say, "Look what we're doing to ourselves." There are too many vested interests to control where we're headed, so nobody pushes, and the long-range problems and needs don't get serious attention until they become clear and present dangers, and then it's too late. This could be a great city —I hope someday it is—but it's not now, and in many ways it's not even headed in that direction.

Charleston: Motherstone of the South

We end our South Carolina story with Charleston, the quintessential city of the Old South and even today perhaps the most proud and self-possessed city of these United States. The hubris of Charlestonians is stunning, though in its more urbane citizens sometimes laced with a touch of humor. I caught the spirit first in a talk with the city's charming mayor, J. Palmer Gaillard, Jr., whose familial roots extend deep into antebellum times. (His great-great-grandfather, in fact, was removed from the mayoralty by the Northern military authorities in 1865.) "Charleston," Gaillard began, "is the historical center in this part of the United States and in some respects the historical center of the nation. This is where South Carolina was born. Charleston has supplied the leaders of this state from the founding right up to now." Attorney Gedney Howe put it much the same way: "Charleston is the spiritual center of the South. Even an Atlantan will tell you that. Everybody in the South agrees Charleston is the best. It's a bunch of bull, but everybody agrees on it."

Right or wrong, Southerners seem to regard Charleston as a kind of holy place, and when they come to visit it (as countless thousands do each year) it is with a reverence that implies the Holy Grail of their Southernhood is somehow enshrined there. "Charleston," in the words of Atlanta writer Bill Winn, "is the mother colony of the South." The historic legacy makes it that, and we touched on some of it earlier—the first South Carolina settlement in 1670, the golden era of trade and leisured planter aristocracy in colonial days, leadership in the Revolution, the city's preeminent role in the era of nullification and finally secession, and the events in Charleston Harbor in 1861, which drew down the curtain on the old South—and immortalized the myth of what Southerners imagined it to have been.

"Our city," editor Thomas R. Waring of the Charleston *News and Courier* noted, "was dead economically from the Civil War to the Navy Yard boom in World War I." And there was not really much activity until the Second World War, when Navy Yard employment ballooned from 1,000 to 2,500 employees and the groundwork was laid for the fantastic military-industrial boom which L. Mendel Rivers did so much to engineer. Indeed, Rivers claimed credit for 90 percent of the additions: a Polaris submarine base, a Sixth Fleet ammunition and supply depot, a mine warfare center, an Air Force base, a Marine Corps air station and the Parris Island recruit depot, an Army supply depot, and two Navy hospitals. After he became Armed Services chairman in 1965, plants of Lockheed, J. P. Stevens, McDonnell-Douglas, Avco, and General Electric arrived. By 1970 the Defense Department was spending almost $400 million a year in the Charleston Area. With the exception of San Antonio, Norfolk, and perhaps San Diego, Charleston had become probably the most defense-dependent metropolitan area in the country.

Charlestonians do not regard all of this as an unmitigated blessing. The Defense Department accounts for more than half the economic activity of the area, and there is concern about the trauma of a sudden pullout. "The military," Gaillard noted, "brings in people, brings money, and pays no taxes. It is wonderful now; it will be tragic when it leaves." And then there is the sociological worry about extreme transiency in a city which, above all, prizes stability. "Some of our leading citizens," Waring lamented, "are birds of passage." There are few metropolitan areas in Eastern America, Vance Packard noted in *A Nation of Strangers*, where so many residents pull up stakes and leave each year. The annual Charleston district phone disconnection rate, he discovered, was 37 percent. The esthetic consequences of all that Rivers wrought are also unpleasant. North Charleston, where most of the military personnel live, is a disordered mess of trailer parks and cheap tract housing and beer joints cheek by jowl with $50,000 homes—all without benefit of zoning. Rivers Avenue is North Charleston's connector, providing mile after mile of what Packard aptly described as "unrelieved visual mayhem—junkyards, three-minute car washes, used-car lots, shopping centers, fried chicken stands, and mobile-home emporiums." In the words of E. Kenneth Aycock, the state health officer, "North Charleston is a veritable smorgasbord of pollutants, including chemical plants, paper mills, and metal processing plants." He might have mentioned the petroleum and fertilizer plants there too.

During the 1960s, as the Charleston metropolitan area population expanded by a fifth to 303,894, the city extended its borders for the first time in 111 years, taking in a large chunk of land across the Ashley River on its western flank. What it got there, on land that until a few years ago was reserved for cabbage and potato farms, was yet another uniformly characterless suburbia. The area does, however, include Old Town, the site of the first European landing. It is set in a Spanish-mossed forest that was made into a joint state-city park in honor of Charleston's 300th anniversary in 1970. (For lovers of flowers and the ghostly magnificence of Low Country swamps, resplendent with tall pines and cypress and great live oak, the parks of the Charleston area are a veritable paradise, especially at blossoming time in the early spring. Some, like 250-acre Cypress Gardens, are then closed with arrival of the summertime heat and mosquitoes.)

Like Manhattan, Charleston is waterbound by two rivers and a harbor; the revealing ancient geography lesson of Charleston children holds that "Charleston is the place where the Ashley and Cooper Rivers meet to form the Atlantic Ocean." And fabled old Charleston, the home of its aristocracy, is crowded into an area at the very tip of the peninsula, only 412 acres running from around Cumberland Street ("south of Broad Street" is a euphemism) to the Battery. Along the labyrinthian streets one discovers one architectural treasure after another. The city has more than 70 buildings that predate the Revolution, over 200 built before the War of 1812, and more than 850 constructed in the days before the Civil War. There is an 18th century and English flavor to it all, the chief concession to the subtropical climate being the exterior galleries, or piazzas, generally faced southward to catch the breeze. The styles are too diverse, however, to conform to simple summary, and the variety is all the more enhanced by wrought-iron gateways in high brick walls, affording glimpses of gardens that bear flowers practically all months of the year. All of this was in dire danger of disintegration until 1931, when Charleston adopted the United States' first planning and zoning ordinance to protect an historic district. In subsequent years the Historic Charleston Foundation, headed by a tireless civic leader, Mrs. Frances Edmunds, has saved countless buildings from destruction and done more than $4 million worth of restoration work.

The buildings of old Charleston, having gone through a cycle from grandeur to slums to restoration, differ from a place like Williamsburg because they are lived in and used. The historic district encompasses not only residences but buildings that house Charleston's chief banks and law firms (the latter centered on Broad Street). As New York *Times* architectural critic Ada Louise Huxtable noted, "the historic Charleston district is no roped-off, stage-set enclave; it is downtown, and it is alive."

The residents of these hallowed precincts constitute an encapsulated old society with barriers to entrance as formidable as those of Boston. In 1762 their forebears formed the St. Cecilia Society, which still thrives two centuries later and remains, as Mayor Gaillard put it, "the gauge." There is a grand ball every year, but it is no longer true that a Charleston girl cannot be a debutante unless a daughter of a St. Cecilia member. As much as the proper Charlestonians cherish their traditions, however, they are not a stuffy lot. They tend to be gracious and witty, patrons of the arts, and jet-setters in many cases. Several I met had just returned from Spain or Portugal or Britain, and were also part-time residents of New Orleans, Washington, and sundry other American cities.

The old Charlestonians also care passionately about their city. For example, Mrs. Charles H. Woodward and her Philadelphia-born husband personally made available the funds to restore nine old homes threatened with decay and destruction, gave the money to landscape and plant a piece of property on the waterfront (thus creating a small park), and contributed to studies of planning and zoning for the overall betterment of the city. That I learned from a third source, but in a conversation Mrs. Woodward told me of her concern about the plight of poor black people in South Carolina and said many of her old-line Charleston friends considered her almost Communistic for her views on race. She also told me how young Charlestonians of the better set were volunteering their own time to help with such projects as an Episcopalian all-black rural parish, in improving living conditions there.

Regardless of their social views, old Charlestonians seem superbly attuned to leading well-ordered, leisured lives. The days are past when all the businessmen of the old set took siestas or went home early, but editor Waring said there were many like himself who still return home for two hours sometime after 1:30 P.M., enjoying a glass of sherry, a dinner, and a short nap before returning to work.

One would like to know more about this extraordinary breed of Americans; as Jack Bass wrote, "the great novel about Charleston, that proud and complex city of graceful charm and a hint of wickedness, is yet to be written." The "wickedness" theme Bass wrote of harks back to the Up Country suspicion of the aristocracy and the solid Baptists' aversion to a city that has always liked its liquor. Mayor Gaillard referred to the theme just before the state passed a law relaxing prohibition statutes to the extent of allowing mini-bottles of liquor to be served in public places. "Liquor by the drink is a big headache for me," he said. "What the hell am I going to do when for 200 years we have been going in taverns and getting a drink in Charleston? And we had perfectly fine liquor until the state came in and 'cracked down,' making a damn fool of themselves too. You have to remember, certain things are just accepted in Charleston."

Until 1930, virtually all of Charleston's elected officials were of the aristocracy. Since then, the old families have been obliged to adjust to the political facts of life as a number of persons of less select birthlines, including natives and a number of former military officers of outside origin, have won office. A lot of power in the city these days is exercised by what Waring called "the managerial crowd" of executives sent in by national corporations. The most powerful banker is Hugh Lane, president of the Citizens and Southern Bank of South Carolina. Like his more flamboyant brother Mills, who until recently headed C & S in Georgia, Lane comes from Savannah. Governor West made Lane head of the state housing authority and he won a measure of fame with a big "add-on bathroom" campaign to assure minimal sanitation for the housing of destitute black people in South Carolina.

The Charleston *News and Courier*, which until the 1950s seemed to be edited exclusively for the city's 400 most aristocratic families, is an important power factor in the city. It remains adamantly conservative, though Waring as editor has moved to a significantly more moderate position in recent years. In 1964 the *News and Courier* attacked the Johnson administration's war on poverty legislation because it would "implement the Civil Rights law by establishing integrated labor camps in rural areas" and "give $1,500 to every needy farm family" in return for votes for President Johnson.

There are only 7,000 Jews in all of South Carolina, but especially in Charleston they have exercised influence far out of proportion to their numbers. Figures like merchant Edward Kronsberg are among the commercial elite of Charleston. And the city's Democratic party depends heavily on Jews for money and organizational work. Charleston's diversity of character is underscored by the fact that more than half of the 40,000 Roman Catholics of the state reside there, and that in this overwhelmingly Baptist-Methodist state, a high proportion of the 43,000 Episcopalians are concentrated in Charleston—and in the city's elite.

The story of Charleston blacks—who today make up 45 percent of the city population—is as old as that of the colony itself, and perpetually intertwined with that of the whites who brought them to the Carolina shores as chattel and used and exploited them over the three centuries that followed. Many Charleston blacks are Gullah Negroes, speaking a peculiar dialect, spoken in triphammer fashion and unintelligible to all but Low Country ears, which was imported from Barbados and even put its stamp on the distinctive accent of the Charleston whites. Among the city's bitter memories is that of the black men's 1822 insurrection led by Denmark Vesey, a free mulatto from the West Indies. It cost 35 Charleston blacks their lives. A century later DuBose Heyward, one of the most distinguished Charlestonian authors, spotted a one-paragraph story in the *News and Courier* about Sammy Smalls, a crippled Negro goat-cart beggar who was arrested for firing a gun at a woman. The story idea was that the man everyone knew as a beggar had a vivid, unknown life of his own after dark, and Heyward translated it into the first South Carolina novel that depicted the Negro as neither a comic nor a brute. There was a Pulitzer Prize-winning stage version in 1927, and then the globally acclaimed 1935 folk opera, *Porgy and Bess,* for which George Gershwin wrote the music. Yet it would not be until 1970, in connection with South Carolina's Tricentennial celebration, that *Porgy and Bess* with its all-black cast would receive its first staging in Heyward's native Charleston. The showings turned out to be a tremendous success.

Charleston blacks appreciated the gesture, but it did little to relieve the monotony and poverty of the lives of most of their number in the ramshackle districts north of Calhoun Street, in the city's industrial neck, or in the primitive precincts of nearby James and Johns Islands. Modern Johns recalls the story of the black man, Esau Jenkins, who rose out of poverty and ignorance to be a successful businessman and leader of his people's struggle for justice. But it was also there that Senator Hollings and Governor West, reviewing conditions of malnutrition and hunger in 1971, discovered a windowless and unpainted shack where 15 children lived. In the next shack they learned that the older children had returned from school one day to find their mother dead, clutching an infant still trying to feed from her breast. The report was that she had died of starvation.

Yet it is only fair to record that in an area called Heritage Park, to the west of central Charleston, black professional people live in houses that cost upwards of $50,000.

The poor blacks of Charleston were not at the forefront of the civil rights movement of the early 1960s, but they did make interesting contributions before and after. In 1946 they staged a strike of food and tobacco workers and picked as their theme song the great hymn that would later be adopted by the movement—"We Shall Overcome." (It was borrowed, ironically, from a white Baptist hymnbook.)

Then, in 1969, when the South-wide rights movement was almost spent, several hundred poorly paid Charleston hospital workers—most of them women working as nurse's aides, orderlies, kitchen help, or maids—went on strike, demanding recognition of their union. The Medical University of South Carolina and the Charleston County Hospital curtly refused to have any dealings with a union, and Charleston seemed to be at the brink of a major conflagration. Thousands of National Guardsmen were called in, 900 arrests took place, and a curfew was imposed. Outside help came from the Southern Christian Leadership Conference, backed up by the AFL-CIO and United Auto Workers. Ralph David Abernathy came to town and was packed off to the Charleston Jail, and Mrs. Coretta King arrived to take his place as the major speaker at rallies—just a year after her husband's assassination in Memphis. Walter Reuther marched arm in arm with Mary Moultrie, the 27-year-old local leader of the struggling Retail, Wholesale and Department Store Workers.* And the blacks were pleasantly surprised to receive support from predominantly white South Carolina labor groups.

The Charleston press attacked "outside agitators" and Columnist Frank B. Gilbreth wrote in the *News and Courier*: "What guarantee is there, if the hospital strike were settled tomorrow, that the Reverend Abernathy and Mrs. King wouldn't be back in town again in two weeks, demonstrating for higher pay for garbage collectors, colored teachers or port workers? Or for kindergartens or for the reverse income tax for poor people?" Mr. Gilbreth was right about the long list of grievances of Charleston black people but wrong about the continued strength of the civil rights movement. After some 100 days, the women did win part of their demands from the local hospitals. But the SCLC had spent itself and many people believed it would never again mount a major campaign in the Southland.

There is a quality of resilience and everlastingness about Charleston that makes one conclude that even more black and white confrontations will not break the spirit or uniqueness of this quite special place. The city has al-

* In contrast to South Carolina's white women, who generally seem to steer clear of public life, the state's black women have been playing a prominent role. One of the best known is Victoria DeLee, a powerhouse from Dorchester County in the Low Country. She is a member of the state's advisory board to the U.S. Civil Rights Commission, runs a day-care center that has been subjected to considerable harassment, and has even expanded her interests to the plight of the few remaining Indians in the state. In 1971 she ran unsuccessfully for Mendel Rivers' old congressional seat.

ways been, historically, able to accommodate itself to nearly any new reality. Charlestonians recall that in the American Revolution the British captured the city and were welcome for their stay of several years, and that after the Civil War, the Reconstruction governor of the state was even welcomed to the St. Cecelia ball. Among the vicissitudes from which Charleston has somehow emerged over 300 years have been attacks by the Spanish, the French, the Indians, the English, pirates, and the Yankees. Five times the city almost burned to the ground—in 1740, 1778, 1796, 1838, and 1861—but each time it rose, Phoenix-like, from the ashes. There was a shattering earthquake in 1886, a devastating smallpox epidemic in 1772, and in the olden days repeated bouts with those special Low Country diseases—yellow fever, dysentery, and malaria. And still there was Charleston.

And despite its conservatism, Charleston has always had an undertow of tolerance. Gedney Howe attributes it to the Anglican and cavalier society of the early days. "Here were people of a more wealthy and cultured background," he said, "who scorned the Pee Dee crackers on their one flank and the Savannah basin poor white on the other. Within the structure of Anglican control was deep culture and high intellect and even a certain number of people who rejected the brutality of slavery, and still reject outright racism today." If it were not for that tolerant character, Howe said, he would not be able to defend every Charleston Negro accused of rape and not have it hurt his law practice. "Charleston may differ on what I stand for," he added, "but they're not going to try to throttle it."

One finds some evidence of Howe's thesis at venerable St. Michael's Episcopal Church, where George Washington and the Marquis de Lafayette reserved pews on their visits to Charleston. In the graveyard, not far from each other, lie the remains of two Charlestonians who espoused diametrically opposed views. One is Robert Y. Hayne, a noted nullification statesman. The other is James Louis Petigru, the indomitable Unionist who was perhaps the greatest South Carolina lawyer of his day. Woodrow Wilson, a President who spanned North and South, requested a copy of Petrigru's epitaph at the 1919 Peace Conference in France. In part, it reads:

Unawed by Opinion,
Unseduced by Flattery:
Undismayed by Disaster,
He confronted Life with antique Courage:
And Death with Christian Hope:
In the great Civil War
He withstood his People for his Country:
But his People did homage to the Man
Who held his Conscience higher than their Praise;
And his Country
Heaped her Honours upon the Grave of the Patriot,
To whom, living,
His own righteous Self-Respect sufficed
Alike for Motive and Reward.

FLORIDA

THE MAN-MADE STATE

ALTHOUGH THE LIFE PATTERNS of the Deep South linger on in northern Florida, the state as a whole has broken so sharply from its region that most of its ties to the Deep South today are an accident of geography. In 1940, less than two million people lived in Florida; in 1972, the count was 7,441,-545—a cumulative growth rate of 192 percent in 32 years.

Why this phenomenal boom? A big part of the answer can be traced to Americans' increased longevity and the affluence that lets them buy a retirement bungalow or apartment under the warm Florida sun. Floridians wince at the notion, but the Census figures prove it: this is the old folks' state par excellence. Just between 1960 and 1970, while the numbers of Floridians under 65 rose 32 percent, the ranks 65 or over went up 78 percent (an increase of 435,000, up to 989,000). Overall, 14.5 percent of Florida's residents are presently 65 or older, compared to 9.9 percent nationally. No other state has a comparable percentage of senior citizens; in California, once thought of as a great retirement mecca, the figure is only 9.0 percent. In St. Petersburg, 30.6 percent of the people are 65 or older; of the permanent residents of Miami Beach, 48.7 percent match that description.

The retirees, of course, are only one part of the Florida boom. Tourism has been growing by leaps and bounds, and in a recent year 25 million visitors came, enriching the economy by $5.5 billion. There are big, permanent military installations at Pensacola, Key West, Jacksonville, and many spots in the interior, the Space Center at Cape Canaveral has brought billions of dollars into Florida, manufacturing has made great strides, and a quarter of the world's entire citrus production still comes from Florida orchards.

Driving from Miami Beach along the Gold Coast to Fort Lauderdale, one sees a continuous, virtually unbroken wall of hotels and high apartment buildings that now face the Atlantic for 24 miles, a high proportion of them built within the past decade. And then going further north around 40 miles to Palm Beach, the concentration is almost as heavy; soon this area, too, will be 100 percent built up. Filling in the cracks and intruding into the hinterland are massive park- or village- type developments designed to hold tens of thousands of people when completed in the 1970s; the construction costs range as high as $800 million for a single project.

One is hard put to believe there could be enough wealth in the U. S. A. to pay for such gigantic playgrounds, but there they are, rising from the flat, sandy beaches before one's very eyes. In a way, they make sense. Given the fact that thousands upon thousands of Americans have the ready cash to pay hundreds or thousands of dollars for a winter vacation at a resort hotel (where a room for two in the high winter season easily runs $50 to $75 a day), they are often well advised to go ahead and buy a condominium. It is a hedge against future inflation, a good investment in its own right, it can be rented out when the owner is away, and it thus becomes depreciable-income-producing property for tax purposes. While one's there, of course, there is bright sun, a proximity to the Bahamas and Caribbean for quickie vacations, fishing, and all other manner of entertainment in the nearby resorts.

Neither luxury hotels nor condominiums are restricted to the Gold Coast, of course. One finds them scattered, in greater or lesser degree, all along the 1,350 miles of Florida coastline, from Jacksonville down to Key West and then up the Gulf Coast to Tampa–St. Petersburg and Pensacola. Florida has become—thanks to air conditioning, plus smart promotion—a year-round instead of a strictly winter vacation spot. One can now cross off as obsolete John Gunther's report on "a large proportion of the people living high for three months during the tourist season and then living low on fish and grits for the rest of the year." Amazingly, about a third of Florida's tourist volume occurs between June and August, months in which the north Florida resorts—Daytona Beach, Jacksonville Beach, Pensacola, and Panama City—do their biggest business. Yet even in those dog days of summer, incredible numbers of people, lured by cut rates and intensive advertising, still seem willing to shell out hundreds of dollars for vacations in the suffocating heat and humidity of places like Miami Beach.

Increasingly, the line between vacationer and retiree blurs, especially as jets make it possible to virtually commute in and out of Florida if one has the money, and people buy houses or apartments into which they gradually retire over time. But there are still the instant retirees—usually poorer—who suddenly descend on Florida with lifetime savings to try and soak up some post-retirement sunshine before the final line is drawn. In Sarasota, I visited

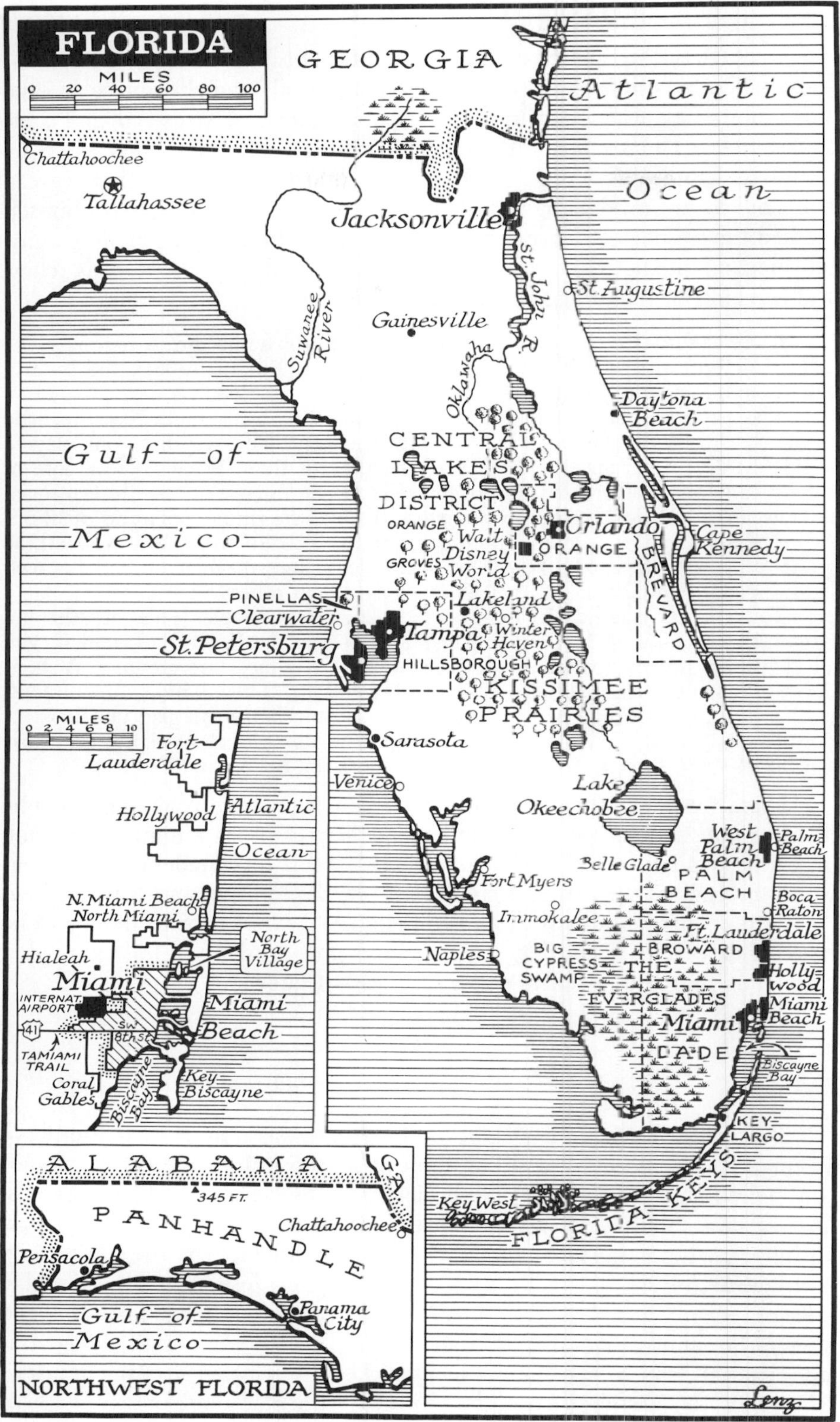
FLORIDA
MILES
0 20 40 60 80 100
GEORGIA
Atlantic
Ocean
Chattahoochee
Tallahassee
Jacksonville
St. John R.
St. Augustine
Suwanee River
Gainesville
Oklawaha
Daytona Beach
Gulf of Mexico
CENTRAL LAKES DISTRICT
ORANGE GROVES
Walt Disney World
Orlando
ORANGE
Cape Kennedy
BREVARD
PINELLAS
Clearwater
St. Petersburg
Tampa
Lakeland
Winter Haven
HILLSBOROUGH
KISSIMEE PRAIRIES
Sarasota
Venice
Lake Okeechobee
West Palm Beach
Palm Beach
Belle Glade
PALM BEACH
Fort Myers
Boca Raton
Immokalee
Ft. Lauderdale
Naples
BIG CYPRESS SWAMP
BROWARD
THE EVERGLADES
Hollywood
Miami Beach
Miami
DADE
Biscayne Bay
KEY LARGO
FLORIDA KEYS
Key West
MILES
0 2 4 6 8 10
Fort Lauderdale
Hollywood
Atlantic
Ocean
N. Miami Beach
North Miami
North Bay Village
Hialeah
Miami
INTERNAT. AIRPORT
41
SW 8th St.
Miami Beach
TAMIAMI TRAIL
Coral Gables
Biscayne Bay
Key Biscayne
ALABAMA
GA
345 FT.
PANHANDLE
Chattahoochee
Pensacola
Panama City
Gulf of Mexico
NORTHWEST FLORIDA
Lenz

one of their closest observers and sternest critics, the author MacKinlay Kantor. Kantor's home is in a luxuriant subtropical junglelike piece of land along Siesta Key, where only a few hundred souls lived 30 years ago, and some 10,000 today. He is not a little resentful about all the new population; he would be happier if things would stay peaceful and quiet "so that we can live close to the mockingbirds and the raccoons." But Kantor (who himself crashed the 65-year barrier in 1969) adds: "Even a savage old square like myself must admit that the lives of so many are so much better." Of his fellow and less affluent senior citizen compatriots, he says:

> I feel so sorry for them. . . . So many just dissolve and die. A few have the head and the heart to adjust to their new existence. But many lack the built-in self-discipline system.
>
> The happiest ones are in trailer parks. Camp living is more like the little towns they knew in Ohio and Indiana and Michigan. You see them out playing shuffleboard together and they're having the time of their life. They're a core of elderly humanity who are already harmonized to each other. True small-town social life develops. New folks are easily accepted. It's like the simple openness of life in Agony, Oklahoma, or wherever they came from. They're with their own ethnic group—the same kind of people a man may have known when he had his own hardware store up north. And they all appreciate each other. . . .
>
> Those in the subdivision homes—they know less people. They are the unhappy faces you see in the supermarkets. You go into the Kwik-Chek, and they're all glowering at everybody else and each other. Their faces are gloom. "Well, it doesn't cost this much up in Akron, I can tell you that." They're rude, discourteous, unobliging, their attitude being "You Florida people better be glad you have us down here spending our hard-earned money. You don't treat us right—you raise our taxes—then there's always California, there's always Arizona."

More fortunate are the elderly with enough money to take up a hobby like boating; they are forever refurbishing their boats or joining yacht club or power-squadron activities, and there's the special camaraderie of the boat world to brighten their lives. A special danger, Kantor says, awaits the retirees "without enough gumption to start something new, but enough money to lie back on their cans. Then they get bored and start drinking in the morning. I used to do that and in that way lies madness—I know."

Geography and Ecology

Before the synthetic civilization came, there was only natural Florida—a remarkable peninsula, extending more than 300 miles south of the major continental land mass, a great green mat, often broken by lakes and swamps, floating in a deep blue sea. The further south one looked, the more remarkable it was. From north to south, this was the view: first, the low-rolling, pine-covered hills of the north and the panhandle, close kin to the red clay hills of neighboring Georgia and Alabama, a land of magnolias and the languid Suwannee River, live oaks and Spanish moss. Then came the central lakes district, later to become the heartland of Florida's great citrus industry. After this, the Kissimmee Prairies, covered with grass and patches of palmetto, where the great cattle ranges would later be developed.* These lands drain into Lake Okeechobee, one of the largest lakes on the North American continent and certainly the largest of the 30,000-odd that dot the Floridian landscape. In primeval times, Okeechobee was shaped like a shallow saucer with short legs branching out where muddy waters from the northern prairies drained into it; today the shape is more regular, since a levee has been constructed around the lake to prevent its waters from escaping in a hurricane, and drainage canals have been built around it to reclaim the rich soils for intensive vegetable and sugar cane cultivation.

Okeechobee has no single outlet, but rather flows southerly toward the ocean as the land tilts ever so slightly down to the south through that remarkable sea of grass known as the Everglades. (The dominant sawgrass is hardly grass at all, growing 10 feet tall with edges set with teeth.) Over 5,000 square miles stretch the Everglades, the muddy waters draining imperceptibly below, the level stretch broken only by occasional "hammocks" where the underlying limestone protrudes to the surface and trees have grown. That same limestone, underlying almost all of southern Florida, also has a higher elevation along the coasts, saving stretches like the Atlantic beaches from degenerating into total swamp.)

As the ocean is reached, along some of the keys and the coast of southwestern Florida, the mangrove forests appear, constantly building land out of water until hurricanes occur to demolish their work. Nowhere else in America does one come on a plant like the mangrove, its gnarled roots reaching down into sea water which would be lethal to most land plants, forever spreading by dropping seedlings into the water which float off to find new homes.

Also unique geologically, across the face of North America, are the Florida Keys, a fantastic coral-built archipelago stretching 200 miles south and southwesterly from Miami. Naturalist Peter Farb points out that while corals are found on other North American shores, the conditions for reef-building—shallow seas with temperatures over 70° and currents strong enough to bring the little coral animals a constant supply of food—are present only at Florida's southern tip. Even now, a new living wall of coral is being built under the indigo waters.

Finally, one should mention the long, sandy buffer spits or islands lying just off the Atlantic Coast and part of the Gulf Coast. Not only did they provide most of the fabled Florida beach front, but behind their banks a safe Inland Waterway could be created.

Florida's record of stewardship of this land is mixed. The state has one of the most impressive state park systems in the nation, covering 177,000 acres and consisting of some 22 historical memorials and 61 parks. The effort to preserve state property began in 1915 when the Florida Federation of Women's Clubs acquired an area that became the nucleus of the massive (1.5 million acres) Everglades National Park, established in 1947. The system of

* Florida is forever boasting about its huge, growing cattle industry. However, its cattle population (1.8 million in 1970) ranks only 23rd among the states, and its total livestock marketings only 26th ($374 million in 1969). It had no more cattle in 1969 than it did five years before.

state parks now draws close to 8 million visitors each year.

But the drive to remake nature into a synthetic environment has been costly to the ecology, and now nature is beginning to hand in the bill. As one observer noted, Florida's "500-mile-long peninsula has been cut and channeled, bulldozed and bulkheaded, scraped and scissored to a point where the principal life resources have been threatened." An example: for some 80 years, men have been building drainage canals around Lake Okeechobee for land development and diverting fresh water for use in the coastal cities. In 1971, when a fierce drought hit southern Florida, the Everglades suffered massive fires, covering some 500,000 acres of scrub and fertile muckland—fires which the land, deprived of its own natural moisture, was unable to withstand. The Gold Coast was darkened by heavy clouds of ash and smoke, its first serious air pollution crisis. In the Everglades, many snakes, turtles, and alligators were trapped and destroyed by the flames. And as the natural water level dropped, there was a serious danger of salt water from the Atlantic seeping inland to contaminate Florida's fresh water supply. Arthur R. Marshall, a noted ecologist at the University of Miami, said: "It's unbelievable to me that while the fires burn at this moment across the parched Everglades, dredges are building more canals to drain away more water."

During the 1960s the Kissimmee River, which flows from central Florida into Lake Okeechobee, was converted from its original meandering, marshy condition into a canal for flood control. But then, as the population soared with developments like Disney World, sewage and silt and other pollutants flowed unchecked into Okeechobee, and the federal government contemplated the long, hard process of undoing its own project.

Water drainage problems, as serious as they appear, are only one of the dangers to Florida's environment. Tampa Bay's estuaries are so polluted that algae growth dies and produces massive amounts of hydrogen sulfide which bubbles to the surface and gives off the odor of rotten eggs. The bay also was hit by a serious oil spill (10,000 gallons) in 1970, a reminder of that constant threat to Florida's beaches. Like many freshwater lakes in Florida, lovely little Lake Thonotosassa near Tampa was virtually killed by wastes which rotted and choked off the oxygen necessary to sustain fish life. Lake Apoka (50 square miles of water), one of the nation's great freshwater fishing lakes, was so ravaged by sewer and industrial wastes that the Florida Air and Water Pollution Board drained the lake and cleansed its bottom in sunlight.

Escambia Bay near Pensacola became so polluted with wastes from factories, sewage from several cities, and pesticides from upstream farms in Alabama that its seafood industry was severely damaged: shrimp almost disappeared, oysters were declared off limits, blue crabs did disappear, and the shores were littered with millions of dead menhaden.

Pollution hit the Florida Keys, and the breathtaking beauty of Biscayne Bay remains in constant threat from the thermal pollution of the generators (conventional in operation, nuclear under construction) of the Florida Light and Power Company, the state's biggest utility. The Miami River is badly polluted, largely by industrial and sewage wastes from Miami International Airport and from boats docked in the river. Much the same condition prevails in the St. Johns River in Jacksonville. Indeed, one can say that most of the rivers and lakes in Florida, and much of its coastline, have been seriously damaged by the discharge of untreated industrial and municipal wastes.

Florida also has its own brand of strip mining—principally for phosphates, a prehistoric marine life laid down some 25 million years ago. This industry has left several hundred thousand acres open to the sky.

The early 1970s brought two important turnabouts on the environmental front. The first was the Presidential decision, in January 1970, halting construction of a 39-square-mile jetport in Big Cypress Swamp, just north of Everglades National Park. But conservationists were deeply concerned that the federal government was moving too slowly on plans to create a Big Cypress National Freshwater Reserve that would enhance Florida's ecological stability by safeguarding the major source of surface water for the Everglades.

The second major turnabout came a year later, in January 1971, when President Nixon stopped further construction on the Cross-Florida Barge Canal—for years a favorite pork-barrel project of the Florida congressional delegation. The canal, 107 miles long, would have run from Jacksonville on the Atlantic to the Gulf of Mexico near Yankeetown. It would have cost $200 million and benefited a handful of shipowners. It would also have destroyed the Oklawaha River and been one of the biggest boondoggles in the already mottled history of the Army Corps of Engineers (but brought vast profits to the construction industry and allied banks, which were its chief backers). Some 25 miles, costing $50 million, had already been built when the stop-work order came, but maverick Republican Congressman C. W. Young of the state spoke well when he said: "I'd a lot rather have a 25-mile ditch that isn't worth anything than a 100-mile ditch that isn't worth anything."

New environmental problems may be posed by the prospective development of Florida as a major oil-producing state in the 1970s. There are indications that enough oil reserves to make Florida a kind of "South Slope," corresponding to Alaska's North Slope, may be found in a geologic formation that begins about 60 miles northeast of Pensacola and runs offshore parallel to a spot just south of Sarasota, and then inland in a big curve to the Big Cypress Swamp. Offshore oil drilling could pose grave perils to Florida's beaches, and drilling in the swamp would be yet another danger to its role as the Everglades' water supply.

Discovery and Development

Except to the Seminole Indians, the land called Florida was unknown until the Spanish conquistador Don Juan Ponce de Leon came upon it in April of 1513 while following a commission from the king of Spain to "explore and colonize Bimini." The Spanish had no idea they had hit upon the North American mainland, but they did learn quickly of some perils. Even before they could land, a tropical squall came up and almost wrecked their ships on a promontory that would later become known as Cape Canaveral, four centuries later man's departure place for the moon. But before all that could happen, the whole region had to be named, and Ponce de Leon did that on the evening of April 2, 1513, selecting the name *Florida* because —as the royal chronicler later wrote—"it has a very beautiful view of many cool woodlands, and it was level and uniform; and because, moreover, they discovered it in the time of the Feast of Flowers (Easter season)." A day later, Ponce and his men landed at what would become St. Augustine, looking for the fountain of youth (as so many after them); in 1565 there was indeed a permanent settlement at St. Augustine, and the serious peopling of the continent had begun.

Between Ponce's discovery and formal U.S. proprietorship, 308 years were to pass. But the Spanish were continually harassed by competing French and English colonists, and when they finally relinquished the land in 1821, there was little to show for all their efforts except the small towns of St. Augustine and Pensacola. Most of the Spanish flavor one finds in Florida today—Tampa, with its Ybor City and Spanish restaurants, Miami with the big Cuban colony—dates from comparatively modern times. And as for Florida's early years under U. S. rule—the winning of statehood in 1845, Indian wars, involvement on the Confederate side in the Civil War, Reconstruction—they have been well depicted as a "faint duplication" of life elsewhere in America in those times.

The real history of modern Florida awaited the 1880s and the arrival of the first big promoters—hotel and railmen Henry M. Flagler and Henry B. Plant. Shocked by the primitive hotel accommodations Florida had to offer, Flagler in 1885 began to build the fabulously opulent Hotel Ponce de Leon in St. Augustine. Stung by Flagler's success, his west Florida rival, Plant, spent more than $3 million building the Tampa Bay Hotel, opened in 1891. But Flagler, who had already made millions as a partner of John D. Rockefeller, was not to be outdone. Thousands of affluent East Coast residents began to travel down to Florida on the posh all-Pullman train he put into service. First St. Augustine was the southernmost point; then Flagler decided on a southerly extension to Palm Beach, which he literally "made" with its sumptuous new hotel, The Breakers. Soon the private railway cars of the ultrarich could be seen on the Palm Beach sidings, and large private homes called "cottages" were erected near the Breakers. "In the evenings," historian Marjory Douglas recorded, "the music from the hotel ballrooms mingled with the rustling of palm fronds, glittering in moonlight, and the winds from the sea."

In those days, Miami was just a frontier village with a few sand trails and makeshift wooden shacks, but one of its first genteel Northern settlers, a young widow named Julia Tuttle, had a vision of its future. After a savage frost in the winter of 1894–95, which destroyed the citrus crop of middle Florida, Mrs. Tuttle was able to send Flagler sprigs of unharmed orange blossom to prove that Miami was south of the frost line. Within a year's time, the railroad was extended to Miami, and out of the "tangled mass of vine, brush, trees and rocks" Mrs. Tuttle had once described to a friend, there began to grow a great city—starting, of course, with a Flagler hotel.

But this was the era of Manifest Destiny, and Flagler dreamed of an even greater city, at the very tip of the continent, Key West. And true enough, from 1904 to 1912, the work went on to construct the Overseas Railroad across the subtropical keys. Huge engineering obstacles, mosquitoes, blazing summers, and three hurricanes had to be endured, and 700 men were washed away by storms. But in 1912 an 82-year-old Flagler—only four months from his own death—could ride the first train, all the way down from Jacksonville, over the bridges and viaducts and the sea, and into Key West. Florida's eastern coast had been conquered, and the frontier was no more. (A raging hurricane in 1935 swept away key sections of the Key West line, and a whole train with its passengers, but Flagler's roadbed was used to extend U. S. 1 across the keys on the Overseas Highway of today.)

Just a few years after Flagler's death, the great Florida land boom of the '20s was on. Hundreds of thousands of land speculators poured into the state—2.5 million people in the year 1925 alone—and prices zoomed to many times real value. But in the spring of 1926, the bubble broke; banks began to fail; paper millionaires became paupers overnight. And in the autumn of that year, hundreds died in one of the worst hurricanes of recorded history. Marjory Douglas, an eyewitness, recorded that the hurricane, rushing in from the Atlantic without advance warning, struck exposed Miami, "vulnerable with flimsy boom-time buildings, real estate shacks, garages, with the explosive force of a vast bomb." And when the 125-mile-an-hour winds abated in the light of early morning and people began to pour out into the streets to view the wreckage, they were caught by the steely winds and rains of the opposite side of the storm center, and many more lost their lives. After that, Miami adopted a new building code, drafted with an eye to potential hurricane effects, and this code later became a model for all of Florida.

But Florida seems to prosper through all adversities. Half a million permanent new residents were noted in the 1920s, even though the Depression had arrived in Florida a few years early. Despite the crash of 1929 and national depression, another 430,000 people found their way to Florida by the eve of World War II. Tourism fell off abruptly with the war, but right afterward a little big boom ensued as people tried to spend their wartime savings, lots of ex-GIs decided to mix some sun with their GI Bill studies, and the Social Security generation began to hit its stride. But the great boom of all Florida history—the one which continues, little abated, to this day—began around 1950. Lavish hotels began to spring up everywhere; air travel made it easy for Northerners to spend quick vacations; the retirement communities boomed and air conditioning arrived in a serious way. From 2.8 million people in 1950, the population spiraled to 4.9 million in 1960, a 78.7 percent increase unequalled by any other state. In the 1960s, everything accelerated even more, with NASA's $2 billion expenditures enriching the economy as well. The decade brought another 1.8 million people, an increase of 37.1 percent unmatched among the larger states. There was some slackening with the recession around 1970, but no one expected the economic downturn to last long. Some of the reasons:

- Tourism bolstered by a growing national population and increased personal income; earlier retirements with ever more generous pension and Social

Security benefits (now reaching even to groups like trade unions that buy retirement communities for their members); Florida's ever hucksterish promoters, intent on squeezing maximum profits out of every market. Over 60,000 Floridians make their living in hotels (compared to 20,000 in 1950), and 387,000 are employed in all sorts of services, many of them tourist-related; then there are 165,000 working in the construction industry, closely tied to tourist and retirement-home construction. The only threat would seem to lie in foolhardy overbuilding that outpaces real hotel and residential demand.

▪ Agriculture. The state's farm products sell for about $1.4 billion a year, produced on relatively few but huge farms. The leader is citrus; Florida boasts it sells even more grapefruit than California does oranges. Two-thirds of the crop is now processed into frozen concentrates, easily preserved and shipped all over the country. (The frozen orange juice craze has taken on so strongly it's hard to get a glass of fresh orange juice—in Florida!) To avoid dangerous freezes, more and more citrus planting is in south Florida, in a wide circle around Lake Okeechobee. There are now a million acres of citrus planted in the state—about three-quarters oranges, the rest grapefruit, tangerines, and limes. But the industry is nervous it may have overplanted and would like the federal government to bale it out by purchasing frozen orange juice for school lunch programs.

Florida also runs a respectable second to California in winter vegetables like tomatoes, white potatoes, celery, cabbage, sweet corn, cucumbers, watermelons, lettuce, and snap beans, with great concentrations from Dade County (Miami) up to Palm Beach and the Okeechobee area, as well as south of Tampa. On display in the winter markets, however, the displays of vegetables and fruits are of strictly mediocre quality, especially in comparison to what California offers at the same time of year. Sugar cane is also an important crop, and cattle as a result of successful crossbreeding of Angus and Hereford with India's Brahmin, more resistant to heat and pests. In a related field, Florida markets about $40 million worth of fish, oysters, and shrimp each year—but the industry is in grave peril from pollution and land-filling.

▪ Manufacturing. Florida is just beginning to establish itself as an important manufacturing state, and its 330,000 manufacturing employees are still less than half the number in Massachusetts, which trails in overall population. But the highly diversified Florida industries have moved from a gross output valued at $116 million in 1940 to $2 billion in 1960 and close to $4 billion in recent years. Products range from food products, chemicals, paper and pulp to printing, metals, cigars, fashions, electronics, and aerospace—a base, it would seem, for continued healthy growth. And aside from its military bases, the state also does well in defense contract awards, which have been close to $1 billion a year of late.

▪ Mining. Some $300 million worth of minerals are taken out of the Florida earth each year, the biggest being phosphate (used for fertilizer and other products). The dual problems of pollution control and outside competition are starting to imperil this industry.

The essential question of Florida's economy is whether it is too overheated—expanding too fast, gobbling up the natural Floridian environment. Some staggering figures on new housing starts in 1972 illustrated the problem. There were 282,000 new houses and apartments in Florida that year—more than in any other state, and over 13 percent of the total for the entire United States. Two million new Floridians were expected during the 1970s, and sensitive Floridians began to fear an ecological Armageddon. By 1973, the state department of commerce had stopped spending any money to attract people to live in Florida. That same year 65 experts and scholars, at a conference sponsored by the Florida Defenders of the Environment, recommended an official state policy to limit population growth and even resettlement from overpopulated areas. Other recommendations included discouraging land speculation and a bar against incompatible development in such environmentally sensitive areas as flood-prone lands, marshes, and intertidal zones.

In 1972 the legislature did approve a water and land management act which was hailed by Gov. Reubin Askew as "a giant step toward controlling our growth." The law set up a mechanism—starting with local land-use control, and then with a staircase of ascending planning controls to regional levels and then to the state government itself—by which new developments (housing, airports, incursions on the seacoast, or whatever) could be controlled, and by which certain lands could be declared environmentally endangered. But the legislature failed to provide enough funds to staff the bureaucracy needed to administer the program. The state seemed to be losing its race against avaricious growth as developers rushed to get their new projects underway before restrictions on growth took effect.

Several Florida communities were considering an absolute limit on the number of housing units they would permit within their borders. The wealthy oceanfront city of Boca Raton was the first to actually do that, but the idea was even gaining ground in Miami. One could almost hear old Henry Flagler turning over in his grave.

Old and New Politics in the Retirement State

The demographic profile of Florida has been so completely transformed by northern migration that there is little profit in reviewing old political patterns other than to note that the state was implacably Democratic from Reconstruction to the late 1940s. The flood of new postwar voters has created, in the words of University of Florida professor Manning J. Dauer, "a giant suburbia" where the people have little awareness of past politics and few local ties. On the map, one can identify a conservative urban belt that looks like a horseshoe and votes like a midwestern suburb. It runs from Fort Lauderdale and West Palm Beach on the east up the coast to Daytona Beach and the Cape Canaveral area, then across through Orlando in center-state to St. Petersburg on the west and down the Sun Coast to Fort Myers and Naples. The exception in the pattern is Tampa, with an industrialized-unionized economy fairly unusual in the state today. In the far southeast, there is Miami, which votes strongly Democratic for President, supports liberals in Democratic primaries, and can be characterized politically, as Dauer puts it, as "a piece of Manhattan Island which floated off 1,000 miles to the south and is warmed by the waters of the Gulf Stream." And up in the northern Florida, conservative-segregationist politics on the model of neighboring Deep South states are still practiced. Northern Florida also differs from metropolitan Florida as a place where one still hears people talk about "my [state] senator," "my representative," "my [county] commissioner."

Florida's political structure up to 20 years ago, as V. O. Key put it, was "an incredibly complex mélange of amorphous factions," virtually all centered in the one (Democratic) party. Anyone who got the itch and was willing to pay the filing fee could file for governor; the proof of political pulverization was offered in 1936 when 14 men entered in the first Democratic primary for governor and the winner had only 16 percent of the whole. Not until 1970 did Florida Democrats coalesce into a unified state organization —a reaction to stinging defeats the party had suffered in 1966 and 1968.

Ideologically, Florida's Democrats have been a mixture of conservatives and middle-of-the-roaders with an occasional maverick liberal enlivening the scene. A typical conservative was Sen. Spessard Holland, governor in the 1940s and Senator from 1947 to 1971. Holland was a states' righter, a citrus and big-business man, a chief sponsor of legislation giving the states title to tidelands. But he also led the fight against the poll tax, which he helped abolish in Florida in 1937 and for the U.S. through constitutional amendment in the 1960s. Claude Pepper, who held one of the state's Senate seats from 1937 to 1951, was a strong liberal—but by 1950, as it turned out, just a little too far left for the state. George Smathers challenged and defeated Pepper in the primary, accusing him of "softness" on communism and being an advocate of "treason." *

Florida's Democrats rarely engaged in the demagogic race-baiting typical of many Deep South states. But in the postwar era many of their candidates found ways to tap the strain of ultraconservatism evident in Florida life —a kind of mixture of fiscal conservatism, antigovernmentalism, opposition to any kind of welfare, nationalistic patriotism, and mild racism. Outside of the Miami and Tampa areas, the Democratic congressmen have been well to the right of center. Through the mid-1960s, most Democratic governors were in the same mold, the major exception being LeRoy Collins (1954–60), a native of Tallahassee who nevertheless made every effort to smooth the way to peaceful integration in the state and backed other progressive

* This was the same campaign in which Smathers reportedly told an audience of yokels: "Are you aware that Claude Pepper is known all over Washington as a shameless extrovert? Not only that, but this man is reliably reported to practice nepotism with his sister-in-law, and he has a sister, who was once a thespian in wicked New York. Worst of all, it is an established fact that Mr. Pepper, before his marriage, practiced celibacy." (Smathers now disputes authenticity of the speech, but not everyone is convinced.) Twelve years later Pepper made a comeback as a Congressman from Miami, a liberal stronghold where his strong social welfare stands are welcome. Smathers stayed in the Senate for three terms, working unremittingly for special economic interests and against migrants and other unfortunates, becoming a confidant and business partner of Bobby Baker and standing up for the likes of Dominican Republic dictator Rafael Trujillo—a record brilliantly and scathingly reviewed by Robert Sherrill in his *Gothic Politics in the Deep South* (New York: Grossman, 1968). The Long Island newspaper, *Newsday*, reported in 1971 that shortly after Smathers left the Senate in 1969, he paid $20,000 for $435,000 worth of stock in Aerodex, a Florida defense contractor frequently accused of "shoddy work, poor records, and fraud." Smathers reportedly "led a behind-the-scenes Congressional campaign" in 1967 to prevent cancellation of a big Air Force contract with Aerodex.

measures. (In 1968, when Collins ran for the U. S. Senate, he beat a more conservative opponent in the Democratic primary but was subsequently tagged as "liberal LeRoy" by his Republican opponent, Edward F. Gurney, and decisively defeated.)

Florida's governor from 1965 to 1967 was Haydon Burns, a former mayor of Jacksonville, who made the big time by campaigning against the Civil Rights Act of 1964 and defeating Miami's liberal mayor, Robert King High, in the 1964 primary. In office, Burns arrogantly channeled state purchases and insurance business to his campaign contributors, accepted a loan of an airplane from a grocery chain, and engaged in similar shenanigans. Even an avowedly racist line in the runoff primary failed to save Burns from defeat by High in 1966. But High lost the general election to Claude Kirk—the first Republican governor of the century.

For the Republicans, there has been little danger of an ideological split, since virtually all their supporters are avowed conservatives. Modern Florida Republicanism got its start in the 1940s under C. C. Spades, the first state chairman with interests broader than waiting for a Republican President to pick up local patronage. Major effort was put into the urban counties receiving the big migration from the North, with the first payoff in 1948 when Dewey carried Pinellas (St. Petersburg), Sarasota, Palm Beach, Broward (Fort Lauderdale) and Orange (Orlando). With Eisenhower leading the ticket, this urban base was expanded on for solid Republican victories in 1952 and 1956, and with Nixon heading the ticket, again in 1960 and later in 1968. Pinellas County was the seedbed of the Republican renaissance and the place which elected a young William Cramer to Congress in 1954, the first Republican Congressman from Florida since 1875. In 1962, a second Republican Congressman was added, and by 1972 the GOP's total was four. Kirk's election as governor came in 1966, and Gurney's Senate win in 1968. At the same time, the Republicans had taken over local offices like county commissions, school boards, and sheriff's positions in several urban counties; in the wake of reapportionment, Republicans upped their membership in the Florida legislature from 8 percent to 35 percent between 1965 and 1967. By 1973, however, the GOP figure had not risen much beyond that point.

Between 1950 and 1972, Republican registration in Florida grew by a 14-times factor, from 61,000 to 874,000, while Democratic registration more than doubled, from one million to 2.39 million. The Democrats still represented 72 percent of the registered voter pool and outnumbered GOP registrants in all but two counties (Sarasota and Pinellas). But survey data showed that 40 percent of the voters really considered themselves independents and registered with either party in order to participate in the closed party primaries for local city and county elections.

One factor sustaining Democratic registrations was increased total Negro enrollment—up from 48,157 in 1946 to 320,640 in 1971. Incredibly, the Republicans had less black registrants in 1970 (11,961) than in 1946 (15,877).*

* For this, the Republicans would seem to have no one to thank but themselves. No significant effort has been made to include Negroes in party activities, or to shape policies friendly to them. The 1964 GOP gubernatorial nominee, Charles R. Holley, campaigned on statements such as these: "Government's function should be limited to protecting the possessors of property against those who

Blacks represent only 1.5 percent of the Republican registration, but 14 percent of the Democratic, making them a factor to be reckoned with in the Democratic primary. Happily gone are the days of repression of would-be black voters. In 1951, the state NAACP chairman, Harry T. Moore, was killed by a dynamite explosion that destroyed his house, and as late as 1964, two of the 67 counties—Lafayette and Liberty, in north Florida—had not a single black registered. Now, black registration lags only 2 percentage points behind the percentage of the statewide voting age population that is Negro. The gap is attributable to cultural-educational factors rather than repression.

Another sign of political maturity is increased voter participation. The turnout in Presidential years hovered between 30 and 40 percent of eligible adults through the 1940s, but then rose rapidly to 50.0 percent by 1960 and 55.8 percent in 1968. It dropped to 50.6 percent in 1972, but that figure was still the highest among the southeastern states and a vast improvement over earlier years. Both the Negro vote and increased party competition have contributed to the change.

According to Professor Dauer's studies of recent voting patterns, the type of county most likely to go Republican is urban, high-income, with higher proportions of northern retirees in the over-65 age bracket. The exceptions are Dade County (Miami) and Hillsborough County (Tampa), where there is a heavy labor union vote. On the whole Democrats continue to do best in counties with low urbanism, low per capita income, low levels of education, and less retirees. The Democrats continue to do well in local and congressional elections (holding 11 of the state's 15 U.S. House seats, for instance). But Humphrey got only 30.9 percent of the Florida vote in 1968, and McGovern only 27.8 percent four years later. The Republican Presidential winning streak has been unbroken since 1952 except for 1964, and even then Goldwater got 48.9 percent of the vote and would probably have won if he had not upset many retirees on the Social Security issue.

Given their strong upward surge in the urban counties that now dominate Florida politics and their election of a governor in 1966 and a Senator in 1968, the Republicans had all right to face the 1970s in a spirit of high expectation, anticipating a total take-over of Florida government. But instead, they bombed out in the 1970 elections, losing the governorship, failing to win a U. S. Senate seat that seemed all but assured them early in the campaign, and slipping in the legislature. Part of the reversal had to do with the Democrats' newborn unity and nomination of politically moderate nominees, fresh faces on the statewide scene who could not be tarred and feathered as "ultraliberals" like the losing statewide Democratic candidates in 1966 and 1968. But more than anything else, the Republican defeat was attributable to fierce internecine battles—a culmination of the pettiness and factionalism that had afflicted the Republican organization for several years—and the mercurial, buffoonish personality of Claude R. Kirk, Jr.

---

possess nothing." Governor Kirk, who long appeared to give at least tacit support to civil rights progress, in 1970 saw it to his political advantage to defy the federal courts and engage in a crude form of interposition to delay school integration in Manatee County. After a pseudocomical struggle with federal marshalls for physical control of the school-board offices, Kirk was slapped with a federal contempt of court order and threat of $10,000 a day fine and finally backed down.

The Kirk story is a sad one, because of all he might have accomplished for his party and for Florida. He is a man of immense energy and native brilliance, who in fact opened the way for several innovative and promising new directions in state government—a story we will review later. But in the end, it would all be vitiated by the quixotic, flamboyant, and seemingly irresponsible way Kirk handled himself. Born in 1926 in California, educated in Illinois and Alabama, Kirk moved to Florida in the 1950s, made $500,000 exercising stock options for the American Heritage Insurance Company of Jacksonville (a firm he helped found), and in 1960 started in politics as state chairman of Democrats for Nixon. After that he switched parties, ran against Senator Holland in 1964, and lost badly, but bounced back to win the governorship in 1966 with virtually no program.

It did not take Floridians long to discover that their new governor was a master of surprise and showmanship. He appeared at his inaugural ball with a beauteous blonde whom he introduced only as "Madam X." She turned out to be Erika Mattfeld, 32, a German-born Brazilian divorcee, whom he married not long after and took off to Europe for a whirlwind honeymoon (as it later turned out, paid for out of state development funds). Within hours of taking office, Kirk announced he would launch his own private "war on crime" by hiring former FBI agent George Wackenhut and his detective agency; by the time this unique foray in private lawmanship was finished, there was an embarrassing debt of $550,000 Kirk had to cover from private contributions, although the episode helped persuade the legislature to set up a bureau of law enforcement and a number of Florida's worst local officials, including sheriffs, were forced out of office. In August 1967, when H. Rap Brown appeared at a Jacksonville "black power" rally, Kirk showed up unexpectedly, grabbed a microphone from Brown, and said, "Welcome to Florida. Are you here in good spirits? . . . I don't want any talk about guns." Brown's angry message was effectively defused and even the young blacks in the audience were captivated by the governor and his smile—which has been described as having "50,000 candlepower." Some likened Kirk to the gregarious flamingo, known for its scarlet wings and theatrical flair. Kirk's reputation as a ladies' man and drinker (with big bags below his eyes, bespeaking a life of dissipation) did nothing to detract from the image.

Kirk refused to let his life-style be limited by an official $36,000 state salary plus contingency funds of $13,000 and $159,000 to operate the governor's mansion. A rented Palm Beach house, Duck's Nest, cost him about $1,000 a month. Soon he was jetting all over the U.S. in chartered aircraft (generally Lear Jets) in a quest for the Republican Vice Presidential nomination. The Florida Development Commission placed a $90,000 contract with William Safire, a Madison Avenue public relations expert and political strategist, in a thinly disguised effort to get Kirk on the national ticket. And for a time, the Florida Republican party was intoxicated by Kirk and gladly paid his mounting bills for the Lear Jets, entertainment, hotel suites, and flowers for politicians' wives. Then the party cut Kirk off, and as the bills kept pouring in, the Miami *Herald* reported that money raising had become almost a full-time job for some of Kirk's staff and friends. A 1969 state audit of the governor's office disclosed controversial expenditures such as overpayment for travel and spending without statutory authority for flowers, credit cards, Christmas cards, and food. Some $1 million to $3 million "campaign funds" were collected by Kirk in his first three years in office, and even the official records of a $500-a-year "Governor's Club," which a court forced him to disclose publicly, showed receipts of $420,680 between April 1968 and January 1970. The 233 contributors to the fund included 47 who received Kirk appointments to state boards, committees, and commissions, 18 who were liquor licensees, 31 architect-engineers (most with state contracts), and 20 construction contractors eligible for state road projects.

The irony of it all, as Miami *Herald* writer Clarence Jones observed in late 1969, was that Kirk was the one politician who might have "beaten the system"—the commonplace Florida practice of governors turning to private contributors with a stake in state action, or a desire for contracts, in order to run their offices and political machines. Kirk had entered office with few commitments. His 1966 primary was a low-cost walkaway; in the general election the big-money people were eager and anxious to contribute to Kirk's cause just to make sure that Robert King High, who had defeated conservative incumbent Haydon Burns in the Democratic primary, wouldn't win. Just by upsetting High, Jones observed, Kirk had "paid off the mortgage, free and clear." Yet within two years he was struggling with huge debts and forced to accept money from special interests on a scale rarely paralleled among American governors. (By 1973, coincidentally, Senator Edward Gurney, the other leading GOP statewide officeholder and President Nixon's prime defender on the Senate Watergate Committee, would also be in deep trouble because of $300,000 in unreported campaign funds and alleged kickbacks for federal housing contracts involved in fund-raising on his behalf.)

The final denouement of the Drama Kirk came in 1970, when he became the would-be kingmaker in an attempt to make defeated U. S. Supreme Court nominee G. Harrold Carswell of Tallahassee the Republican nominee for the U. S. Senate. Already running was Rep. William C. Cramer, the eight-term St. Petersburg Congressman and virtually the founding father of the present-day Republican party in Florida. Kirk had long been jealous of Cramer's power and at one point attempted, unsuccessfully, to purge him as Republican national committeeman. Gurney also had good reason to resist the elevation of the more prestigious and more able Cramer to the Senate. So only a few days after the Senate rejected Carswell, Kirk and Gurney held long conversations with Carswell and put him into the Senate race.

At first, Carswell's entry looked like a brilliant move, and many Florida Democrats and Republicans saw Carswell sweeping triumphantly to election on the wave of bitter Southern resentment about the Senate's rejection of his court nomination. But Carswell turned out to be a paper tiger, unskilled in the ways of politics, and ideologically, it was impossible to get to the right of Cramer.

So it came about that Cramer crushed Carswell 2–1 in the Senate primary. In the meantime, the Democrats did an unusual thing. They rejected several old party war-horses (like former governor Farris Bryant, running for the Senate, or former attorney general Earl Faircloth, running for governor) in favor of two bright young state legislators: gubernatorial candidate Reubin Askew, from Pensacola on the northern panhandle, and Senatorial candidate Lawton Chiles, from Lakeland in the citrus belt. Askew appealed to many voters by arguing that the tax laws favored corporations and special interests, at the expense of the little man, and should be changed. (A teetotaler once likened to a "warm Presbyterian elder," Askew was about as different a public figure from the Kirk mold as one could imagine.) Chiles decided the voters had become frustrated by slick advertising campaigns and remote politicians. So he made a calculated decision to spurn large newspaper and television advertising; instead he undertook a walking tour, over 1,000 miles from one end of Florida to the other, meeting some 45,000 common citizens.* As he explained after his election: "The common theme of everyone I talked with—young and old, rural and city, black and white—was that 'no one listens to me, my vote doesn't count, no one cares any more, government is so big and far away.' My walk did say to these people that I cared." Chiles, of course, was no fool; he knew his walking tour would get him a lot of free time on television news programs, and it did. But the fact remains that in the year of the homogenized, prepackaged, standardized slick media campaign, a man who rejected it all could win.

Cramer ran an orthodox campaign based on heavy television advertising and importation of big Republican names to campaign for him, including Attorney General John and Martha Mitchell and President Nixon himself. But the tone of the Cramer campaign was strongly negative—asking voters to "join the fight to stop cop killers, bombers, burners and racial revolutionaries who would destroy America."

Chiles and Askew both won strong victories (53.9 and 56.0 percent respectively), built on an amazing combination of the rural cracker vote from northern Florida and the support of cosmopolitan Dade and several other urban counties. (Only two counties with any significant population—Orange and Sarasota—voted for both Kirk and Cramer.) The new-found Democratic unity was underscored by the fact that the first governor from the panhandle in living memory was elected, joining in a ticket with three successful nominees for cabinet posts from Miami. It was the first time Dade County had elected *anyone* to the cabinet, and two of its successful nominees were Jewish as well.

Florida voters seemed to be moving to the right again in the state's 1972 Presidential primary, which featured no less than 11 Democratic and three Republican contenders. There had been a Presidential primary on Florida statute books since 1904, but the contest had never drawn the national attention that Florida's big-state status would seem to merit. One reason may have been that it involved only election of delegate slates (often pledged to a favorite son); another was the late date in the primary season (late May). But the 1971 legislature session changed the law fundamentally. Under legislation sponsored by House Speaker Pettigrew, provision

* The visitor to Chiles' Washington Senate office finds a memo of the celebrated walk—a pair of old hiking boots, with holes worn in the soles—adorning his mantle.

was made for a true preference poll, with the Florida secretary of state, subject to review by a bipartisan committee, placing the names of all potential Democratic and Republican Presidential nominees on the ballot. To stay off the ballot, a prospective candidate has to swear in an affidavit that he is not running and does not intend to run. Delegates, also elected in the primary, must vote for the preference poll winner in their own congressional district (or in the case of at-large delegates, the statewide winner). Most interesting of all, the primary date was set for mid-March, so that it would be second only to New Hampshire in drawing early attention in a Presidential election year.

The Presidential candidates who descended on Florida in spring 1972 found the voters in a worried, skeptical, even grumpy mood. The list of concerns was long—crime in all the big cities, sulfurous air pollution in Jacksonville, traffic jams on Interstate 95 in Miami, high taxes, rising prices, drugs, the Vietnam war, and perceived abuses of the welfare system. But above all, Floridians were up in arms about school busing to achieve integration. That single issue eclipsed all others, made useless many of the hundreds of thousands of dollars invested in saturation television advertising by the various contenders, and permitted the man who had made the issue his own, George Wallace, to win the Democratic primary with 42 percent of the vote. Hubert Humphrey, the runner-up, got a lot of black and Jewish support, but still only 18 percent of the total; Washington state's Henry M. Jackson, running as a kind of white-collar Wallace, was third with 13 percent. Edmund S. Muskie, who up to then was regarded as the front-runner for the nomination, was far behind at 9 percent—his total possibly depressed, it later turned out, by deliberate sabotage of his campaign by political agents acting under White House orders. Mayor John V. Lindsay of New York, George McGovern, Congresswoman Shirley Chisholm, and several lesser candidates did even worse. On the Republican side, it was President Nixon in an 87 percent walkaway, swamping his right-wing opponent, Ohio Congressman John Ashbrook, who got 9 percent, and the challenger from the left, California Congressman Paul McCloskey, who received 4 percent.

The regional distribution of the vote on the Democratic side was predictable enough. Wallace scored the most heavily in northern and central Florida and made his weakest showing in Dade County and the rest of southern Florida; Humphrey's pattern of support was precisely the opposite.

An interesting primary sideshow surrounded a set of straw votes on the ballot regarding school integration. One straw vote, proposed by two Republican state senators and put on the ballot by the legislature, asked voters if they approved a constitutional amendment to "prohibit forced busing and guarantee the right of each student to attend the appropriate public school nearest his home." Predictably, it won overwhelmingly. But Governor Askew opposed it, and got the legislature to put another straw vote on the ballot. It asked voters if they favored "providing an equal opportunity for all children regardless of race, creed, color or place of residence" and whether they opposed "a return to the dual system of public schools." The Askew amendment also won overwhelmingly, vitiating the antibusing amendment to some degree.

It was a risky course for Askew to take, and in a later interview he acknowledged it might harm him some in future elections. Busing, he said, was a difficult and misunderstood issue that had become "a code word." The issue, he thought, would be solved "when it ceases to be a political football, so that we can get on with the real issue, which is to provide equal opportunity education on a quality basis." Busing, he said, had been unworkable in some situations. But in others it had succeeded and was "indisputably the most effective process we've had in dismantling a dual system of public education." Where the use of busing had helped, Askew said, he didn't want to remove it and force a community to start all over again. "And where busing has proven unworkable," he added, "then we should be looking for an alternative good faith solution. Congress could enact some guidelines the courts would appreciate and honor, if it was clear that Congress was trying to deliver a constitutional guarantee rather than thwart a court remedy." By HEW standards, he said, Florida was 95 percent integrated by 1972. "I tried to take some leadership when it looked like we could have some real violence in the schools. I respect the viewpoint of others, but somehow we're going to have to break this circle of discrimination or else we're going to give a legacy of inequality to our children that will be with us for many years."

It was an exceptional—and courageous—position for any Southern leader to take (and one that would get a first-class test when Askew faced the voters again in 1974). He sought to put the problem in perspective in a 1972 speech in which he said that "if the people remain divided against themselves on the race issue, they'll have no time to demand a fair-shake on taxes, on utility bills, on consumer protection, on government services, on environmental preservation, and other problems."

State Government: Demise of the "Pork Choppers" and a New Constitution

Florida's state government, just a decade ago one of the most archaic and unrepresentative in the Union, has recently undergone fundamental reform in both the legislative and executive branches and can face the 1970s with renewed confidence in its capacity to deal with fundamental problems.

The malapportionment of the legislature, based on restrictive provisions of the state constitution, was so egregious that by the 1961 session, 12.3 percent of the state's people could theoretically elect a majority of the senate and 14.7 percent a majority of the house. The five most populated counties accounted for more than 50 percent of the population, but only 14 percent of the senate membership. In the house, every county was guaranteed at least one representative; this meant that to have equally populated districts, because some counties were so lightly populated, the house would have to have been expanded to 1,600 members.

The infamous Florida "Pork Chop Gang"—a name brilliantly conceived by Tampa *Tribune* editor James Clendinen—emerged in 1953 when 22 rural senators, enough to exercise control, banded together to fight any reapportionment which would imperil their seats. Their districts encompassed about half of Florida's land area but only 18 percent of the population; for the most part, they came from counties along the Georgia and Alabama borders and in central Florida. Not only did they succeed in blocking reapportionment efforts (which began in earnest under Governor Collins in 1955), but they put their mark on broad areas of state legislation. According to a 1962 estimate, Pork Chop counties with 18 percent of the population accounted for about 15 percent of state taxes but received 30 percent of state disbursements. State racetrack revenues were apportioned on an equal basis among the 67 counties, which in some small counties was enough to pay all county government expenses; big landowners, of course, were among the principal beneficiaries. Road funds and state institutions were both channeled in disproportionate amounts to thinly populated counties, and the Pork Choppers blocked legislation authorizing urban renewal and government reorganization.

In addition, the Pork Choppers were closely tied to special interests—banks, private utilities, truckers, the liquor industry, timber and paper mills, small loan companies, and the like—and were easy prey for the lobbyists, since they lacked sophisticated constituencies that could catch them in irregularities.* There was a glaring absence of effective lobby registration or conflict of interest legislation, and Senator Chiles (who was then in the state legislature) recalls that when such matters were first brought up in committee, they were just laughed at. When he proposed making a statewide district for clean air and water regulatory purposes, a pulpwood lobbyist told him exactly how many votes he would get in committee—three out of 11. Seven of the eight who voted against the bill had a pulpwood plant in their districts.

Between 1955 and the mid-1960s, nine special legislative sessions were devoted primarily to reapportionment. But rural control held solid until a court test was finally resolved by the U. S. Supreme Court. A three-judge federal court then ordered new elections, in 1967, under a one-man, one-vote reapportionment plan proposed by Professor Dauer of the University of Florida. Under the new formula, there was a maximum population variation of 5 percent between the districts. Now legislators from urban areas are frequently elected to the house speakership and senate presidency, both powerful officers with authority to appoint all committees. The first house speaker in Florida history from Dade County, Richard Pettigrew, a progressive in the Askew-Chiles mold, was elected in 1971. In contrast to its past paralysis on the reapportionment issue, the legislature drew up new district lines in 1972 with amazing dispatch. By 1973, there were still only seven women and three blacks in the 160-member legislature, but progressives

* Some urban legislators, notably from Jacksonville and Pensacola, anxious to get in on the gravy train, also felt themselves politically secure enough to join the Gang.

took heart in 1972 when four veteran senators considered the darlings of the special interests were defeated for reelection.

It would be naive to think, of course, that the influence of special interest lobbies has withered away in the wake of reapportionment. Lobbying may be lower-keyed, and there has been some drying up of the supply of free drinks and meals and other forms of "entertainment" to legislators in Tallahassee. But there is increased contact by business and labor groups in members' home areas and campaign contributions are more important than before. On the conservative side, the most potent forces are Associated Industries, the big utilities (Florida Power Corporation, Florida Power and Light), the Farm Bureau, bankers, liquor interests, chain stores, the race tracks, and the phosphate council. Much weaker in influence, but still real factors, are the Florida Education Association, the AFL-CIO, and representatives of retired people. The new legislature, Professor Dauer reports, reflects the wishes of urban areas—but the suburban areas in the urban counties, far more than core-city liberal groups, which are a distinct minority on a statewide basis. There is no big urban state in America where organized labor is so weak as in Florida. Only in Miami, Tampa, and Jacksonville are there enough union members to have any appreciable political impact, and overall only 13.9 percent of the nonagricultural workers are organized, ranking Florida 46th among the 50 states on a scale of unionization. Florida in 1944 became the first state to enact a right-to-work law, and most of organized labor's legislative effort is to hold the line and if possible improve the levels of workmen's compensation. Labor officials told me they were often headed off in the legislature by conservatives' threats to put more teeth into the right-to-work law, thus impeding the small level of unionization achieved to date. Union officials have little influence over their members in elections; in 1968 there were some industrial plants where 100 percent of the work force seemed to be for Wallace (sometimes, of course, with the approval of conservative local union leaders).

Reapportionment has, however, brought fundamental reform in state government that would have been inconceivable before 1967. Governor Kirk, to his lasting credit, called the legislature back into session three times until it finally approved a brand-new constitution for submission to the people in November 1968. The new charter, replacing an antiquated 1885 version amended more than 150 times, was approved and went into effect in January 1969. It created an office of lieutenant governor, permitted the governor to seek a second four-year term, gave official status to the elected state "cabinet" (of which more shortly), provided limited home rule for cities and counties, required the consolidation of almost 200 executive agencies and boards into no more than 25 departments, and made the legislature a continuing operation with annual sessions, the power to appoint standing committees, authorize special studies, and the like.

By 1969, the legislature was operating smoothly with regular presession meetings to deal with prefiled legislation; it had one of the most competent legislative staffs in the country (working both for a legislative service bureau and on permanent staffs of the standing committees), and a sophisticated computer tracking system on all current bills, cross-keyed to existing Florida statutes. In 1971, when the Citizens Conference on State Legislatures issued its index on the capacity of legislatures "to perform in a functional, accountable, informed, independent and representative manner," Florida actually scored fourth highest among 50 states—an unthinkable achievement a half decade before.

In 1969, with Kirk's encouragement, the new legislature enacted the most far-reaching reorganization of the executive branch since the Civil War. Acting under the mandate of the new constitution, the multitudinous state boards and commissions were consolidated under 22 departments. The powers of the governor were greatly increased by giving him executive authority over half the departments. In other states, that might have seemed a minor reform, but in Florida the elective cabinet has had extraordinary power, vis-à-vis the governor, because its members are not only elected directly, but have a right of succession (which the governor lacked until 1969) and also sit ex officio on many boards and commissions. Some called it the "seven governor" system, because the six others—the secretary of state, attorney general, comptroller, state treasurer, superintendent of public instruction, and commissioner of agriculture—could and did build their own independent political bases, served an average of 12 years, knew the bureaucracy and legislative maneuvering better than the average governor, and could oblige him to share responsibility with them as a collegial executive. Like the malapportioned legislature, the system was tailor-made for entrenchment of special interests. The comptroller, with wide regulatory power over banks, was often supported by them in campaigns and thus indebted to those he was elected to oversee. The same was true of the state treasurer in respect to the insurance industry, the attorney general in regard to the bar, the agriculture commissioner in regard to big farming interests, and the like.

The reorganization, enacted into law by a coalition of Republicans and urban Democrats, could not and did not abolish the cabinet, but it greatly enhanced the governor's powers by making several major departments and functions his sole or primary responsibility. Kirk used these powers to put outstanding people into key posts like pollution control; Askew, in turn, took the bold step of appointing a black woman, Mrs. Athalie Range, to head the new department of community affairs. Under Kirk, it is worth noting, political influence in road building was vastly curtailed by staggering the terms of highway commission members and putting a professional engineer in charge of day-to-day operations. Florida became the eighth state to set up a transportation department, and Kirk started "Operation Concern" to attack problems of the poor in the big cities. As Roger Williams observed in *The Nation* in 1970, Kirk turned out "ideas and programs as a pinwheel gives off sparks."

The Askew administration, in contrast, was left with the more difficult job of increasing the quality of state services and effecting a reform of the highly regressive Florida tax system. Askew was the first governor of modern times to run on a platform advocating new taxes (specifically on corporate income), an act of candor and courage which alone should win him a place in the history books. Once in office, Askew first got the legislature and then the people in a statewide vote to authorize a corporate income tax.* Even that reform, however, will be just a first step. Florida is prohibited by its own constitution from levying taxes on personal income, and it has a high sales tax. The sales tax is often advertised as a way to put the bite on tourists, but the fact is it also penalizes low-income families and relieves richer people of the major tax burden that even a flat-rate income tax would effect. Florida also lacks any state inheritance tax, and for those over 65, there is a homestead exemption (property that cannot be taxed) of $10,000. Not until 1971 did Florida place even a moderate severance tax on its phosphate industry or other minerals.

The net result of all this is (1) gross inequality and (2) inadequacy of tax base and services. A 1969 study showed that the share of various taxes paid by Florida families earning less than $3,000 a year was $10.3 million for higher education, but their children received only $6.4 million in benefits. The tax share for education of families earning more than $10,000 was more —$25.7 million—but they received back $41.5 million, or 161 percent of what they paid in, in benefits. When one thinks of the squalor in which many of Florida's poor live, the appropriation of their meager incomes to educate rich people's children is little short of criminal.

There is little doubt that Florida could raise its taxes, assuming they were appropriately apportioned, without great pain. State and local tax collections as a percent of personal income in the early 1970s were only 9.6 percent, ranking 38th in the nation. The level of services delivered is accordingly low: on a per capita basis, 47th in the U.S. for public welfare, 41st for highways, 30th in support of local schools, 41st in support of higher education. Low teacher salaries triggered a statewide teachers' strike in 1968, finally prompting Kirk to ask for and get an increase in the sales tax to 4 percent to increase public school spending. The state has done quite well in the junior college field, providing 25 two-year institutions for college and vocational education, located within commuting distance of practically every home in the state. About 140,000 students are enrolled. But state university expenditures have risen very slowly by national standards and the American Association of University Professors reported that the University of Florida has become "not a state-supported but a state-assisted" institution, which depends on foundations and Washington for more than half its budget. Concerned about the whole educational system of the state, Askew appointed a blue-ribbon committee to devise a plan to "restore public confidence" in education. It recommended many changes, including abolition of the cabinet-level post of elected commissioner of education and a shift to a gubernatorially appointed commissioner with a lay board to guide the overall system. Presently the cabinet is, in effect, the board of education, a phenomenon leading to lackadaisical or overly political management.

Florida was also one of the last states to commit itself to the Medicaid program and, until 1969, funded it at the most minimal level. Effective regulation of public utilities has been hampered by lack of funds to investigate

* The affirmative popular vote on the tax was an unprecedented 70 percent, leading knowledgeable observers to rate Askew the strongest governor of modern Florida history

rate structures, and the legislature turned Askew down when he asked for an ombudsman-like consumer advocate to take the public's case before the industry-dominated public service commission, which regulates telephone and electric utility rates. The legislature has permitted innovations such as metropolitan government for Jacksonville and on a more modest basis for the Miami area, but the state constitution puts very strict millage limitations on real property taxes and the cities are desperate for more financial aid from the state government—which is slow in coming. Not until 1969 was general authority given for local governments to undertake urban renewal. But a progressive drift in Tallahassee was reflected in two innovative "no-fault" bills passed in 1971—no-fault divorce and no-fault auto insurance.

The prison system is regarded by many as the most shockingly deficient area of Florida government. Caught in a population boom that has placed heavy demands on all levels of government, Florida found it easy to put last priority on prison development and has begun to reap the whirlwind. Despite the population rise and a spiraling crime rate, no new prison construction took place between 1960 and the early '70s. (Florida ranks third in the nation in per capita murders and other violent crimes, eighth in crimes against property.) In 1967, a wooden barracks of World War II vintage at the state prison farm in Jay caught fire, killing 38 inmates; the subsequent state investigation, however, led to no new funds for prison construction. In 1971, the state prison at Raiford, designed to hold 2,400 prisoners, held 3,600. Many cells were packed with twice as many prisoners as their design capacity. Hundreds of men slept on the floors and the problems of sexual assaults and other violence reached crisis proportions. When a rebellious group of 700 prisoners staged a sit-down on the prison recreation field, guards peppered the convicts with birdshot and some machine-gun bullets, wounding 63. Of this "Lincoln's Day massacre," as the inmates called it, Florida corrections director Louie L. Wainrights said: "I gave the order to shoot. . . . I did it to protect the inmates themselves." Now corrections officials are asking for two new 600-man state prisons, costing $21.5 million.

Askew and the state attorney general, Robert Shevin, have taken a special interest in the prisons and pressed hard for new construction and reforms including work-release programs, more vocational training, improved medical services, conjugal visits for inmates, overhaul of the restrictive parole system, abandonment of the old road-camp system, and state take-over of local jails. The latter proposal gained new supporters in January 1971 when a 17-year-old runaway was strangled to death at the vastly overcrowded Dade County Jail. A local judge declared that the jail was a "jungle . . . where living conditions are unsafe" and ordered local officials to move out a third of the prisoners within 10 days. Later, when the state prison population soared to more than 10,000 (despite a safe capacity of no more than 8,300) prison officials refused to accept new inmates. The legislature, which once ran prisons as a kind of farm subsidy program, began—belatedly—to appropriate money for new facilities. "In spite of all our best efforts," Askew told me in spring 1973, "the prisons remain a very serious problem." He was pleased, however, with the judicial reform, including a streamlined and speeded-up trial court system, which he got approved as a state constitutional amendment during his first year in office. One part of the reform was a requirement that governors select judge appointees from recommended lists submitted by bar associations and laymen, a sharp break with the political patronage policies of the past.

The Sunshine Laws

To wind up a review of Florida government, two bright spots may be noted. The first is nicknamed, quite literally, the Sunshine Law. Enacted in 1967, it stipulates that any meeting between Florida officials must be open to the press. Decisions made at secret meetings, either at the local or state level, are simply illegal. According to court interpretations, there are *no* exceptions to the law outside of limited "judicial deliberations." Some mayors and state officials even had the doors removed from their offices so that they could not be accused of holding secret meetings in violation of the law. There has been some thought that Florida may have gone overboard with its Sunshine Law, but it is certainly a fresh change from the secretive ways that continue in many parts of American government—generally to the disadvantage of the public.

Secondly, there is Florida's "Who Gave It?–Who Got It?" campaign finance law, first enacted in 1951 and a pioneer state statute in trying to get to the roots of money in politics. Interest in the law began when word spread that Smathers and Pepper, though they said they had spent only $100,000 each in the 1950 Senate primary, actually spent in the neighborhood of $1 million each. Then came the Kefauver Crime Committee hearings and a revelation that three men had met in a Jacksonville hotel room to split the $450,000 cost of the 1948 gubernatorial campaign of Fuller Warren. One was W. H. Johnston, a race-track operator with connections to the Al Capone mob; the second was C. V. Griffin, one of Florida's most prosperous citrus growers (an industry that seems always to receive favorable treatment at the hand of state government); the third was Miami Beach multimillionaire Louis E. Wolfson, who would later serve nine months in jail for a stock registration violation.* The St. Petersburg *Times* took up the crusade for a full disclosure law and almost single-handedly embarrassed the legislature into passing the 1951 law.

Twenty years later, what is the law's record? Certainly, the voters have been given an impressive body of knowledge of where money comes from and goes to in campaigns. Candidates must designate exclusive campaign treasurers to receive and disburse all money in their behalf; campaign contributions must be put in a designated depository bank within 24 hours of receipt; frequent public disclosure of money received and spent must be made, and there is a prohibition against last-minute contributions to avoid publicity. Though the state government simply receives and files the reports, the press has open access to them and prints frequent stories on candidates'

* Wolfson's conviction was not for stock manipulation, as erroneously stated in numerous press reports and in the Florida chapter of *The Megastates of America.*

budgets and support. Enforcement, left somewhat in limbo when the law was first passed, later was tightened up when individual citizens were permitted to file complaints. The attorney general was obliged to decide in each case if prosecution of violators was warranted.

What the 1951 law did not do was set dollar limits on campaign expenditures, and as time went on, they climbed and climbed. In 1960, Farris Bryant won the governorship at a cost of $768,000, but in 1964, Haydon Burns's election expenses were $1.1 million. In the two 1966 primaries, Burns spent another $1.4 million in an unsuccessful effort to win renomination for a full four-year term. In 1970, Republican Jack Eckerd spent $1.1 million trying to upset Kirk in the primary. But by this time, the weight of expenditures was getting to be too much, even for the politicians. The secretary of state, Tom Adams, helped some to blow the whistle when he pulled out of the 1970 gubernatorial campaign, announcing that to raise the needed money to become governor, he would have needed to commit himself to so many privilege-seekers that his hands, as governor, would be tied.* And then Adams named the interest groups: road contractors who can profit from contracts and work-change orders, polluting industries anxious to avoid installing expensive control equipment, suppliers of automobiles and other major equipment to the state, land developers interested in having road interchanges or new roads built near their property, industries looking for tax breaks, liquor license applicants, engineers and other professionals anxious to snag state business.

Thus the way was paved for a 1970 law setting strict limits on expenditures: in gubernatorial and U. S. Senate races, $350,000 for any candidate in the primaries, and a like amount in the general election; for other statewide offices, $250,000 in each category; for the U. S. House, $75,000 in the primaries and the same in the general election; for legislative, county, and city offices, $25,000 in each category. Any individual was prohibited from giving more than $1,000 for local, $2,000 for congressional, or $3,000 for statewide contests. The legislation was further strengthened in 1973, and a bipartisan commission was given charge of its enforcement. It is likely to have a major dampening effect on escalating campaign costs in the future.

No one pretends that the Florida statutes tell all and control all in the campaign money field. More money than reported doubtless gets spent. Cash contributions and outlays are exceedingly difficult to trace. Contributors of record may simply be conduits for other people's money. Nevertheless, no state has yet enacted a better law than Florida, "the land of the fast buck and the quick deal."

Lingering Poverty

Few states can match Florida's stark contrasts between wealth and poverty, opulence and squalor. It came home to me most clearly when I

* Adams ran for and was elected lieutenant governor instead, but turned out to have some ethics problems of his own when the Florida house censured him for using state employees for his personal benefit, allegedly to the tune of more than $200,000.

spent a morning touring the Kennedy Space Center facilities, where billions were being poured into the moon shots, and that same afternoon saw a sick farm laborer's child, flies swarming around its little body, lying on a bed at the Old Top Labor Camp near Winter Haven. From the glitter and ostentatious consumption of Miami Beach, one need not travel far to find thousands of retirees waiting in their drab, sun-drenched little towns for the next Social Security check. From select and sumptuous Palm Beach, it is but a few miles to some of the most wretched migrant labor camps in all America. Within the same state are places like Coral Cables, Boca Raton, and Naples, where the *average* home value is more than $30,000, and scrubby north Florida or Panhandle counties like Liberty or Holmes, where the average value is around $5,500.

Florida's net income has crept up steadily, from 74 percent of the national average in 1928 to 88 percent in 1960 and close to 95 percent today. But much of the rise can be attributed to the tremendous wealth of a narrow cross section of upper-income Floridians—a privileged 15 percent of the population. The average Florida worker gets substantially less pay than the national average, partly because over 50 percent of the work force is in three low-paying industries—agriculture, retailing, and services. And a quarter of the state's households have cash incomes of less than $3,000 a year—a higher incidence of poverty than 40 other states.

In a way, the poverty that lingers on from one end of Florida to the other is a kind of legacy or remembrance of the days when Florida was so much more a Southern state. But today, the worst ravages of poverty are to be found among a newer class: the migrant workers. Their life of deprivation was an almost secret one to most Americans until that Thanksgiving weekend of 1960 when Edward R. Murrow's familiar face appeared on CBS stations across the country, proclaiming a *Harvest of Shame* that in historical perspective seems like a kind of introduction to the poverty wars of the 1960s. With a dusty road and battered trucks and milling people behind him, Murrow intoned:

> This scene is not taking place in the Congo. It has nothing to do with Johannesburg or Capetown. This is a shape-up for migrant workers. The hawkers you hear are chanting the going piece rate at the various fields. This is Belle Glade, Florida. This is the way the humans who harvest the food for the best-fed people in the world get hired. One farmer looked at this and said, "We used to own our slaves, now we just rent them."

From Murrow that night, America learned that every ambitious plan of the New Deal and Fair Deal and all of America's postwar affluence notwithstanding, there were still in America "the forgotten people, the under-protected, the under-educated, the under-clothed, the underfed . . ."

Ten years later, in 1970, another television crew and commentator—this time from NBC—visited Belle Glade. For all the rhetoric of the 1960s, little seemed to have changed. There were heart-rending scenes of migrants telling how "we 'bout starved to death down here in Florida," of mothers without money to feed their children or buy them shoes to go to school, of the degradation and shame all felt in their poverty. And still, the raw statistics: average migrants' annual income of $891, or $2,700 for a family of four, $900 below the official poverty line; migrant worker camps, filled with decrepit shacks lacking running water or toilet facilities, many long since condemned but still in operation; illegal child labor in the fields, with half the migrant youngsters failing to get to seventh grade, 80 percent never seeing a high school classroom; a migrant farm worker's life expectancy of 49 years, compared to 70 for other Americans. Estimates of the number of Florida migrants who work the long eight-month growing harvest season of the state range from under 100,000 to 200,000; of these, NBC reported, 55 percent are Negroes driven there when machines replaced them in the cotton fields of the Old South, another 35 percent are Mexican-Americans migrated from Texas.

Some white Northerners are migrants, too, and each winter several thousand cane cutters are brought in from Jamaica, Saint Lucia, Barbados, and other islands of the British West Indies. They are allegedly recruited because American workers are not interested in cane cutting, but critics charge that the planters prefer the "Biwis," as they are called, because they are so easily cheated on wages and meekly submit to life in wretched barracks without running water or any of the amenities American workers demand.

A few of the "Biwis" have been more fortunate. One of the most delightful characters I met in Florida was Ralston O'Connor, a genial, in-charge Jamaican who bossed a racially mixed migrant camp near Winter Garden, his personality obviously overcoming any resentments the Anglos and Mexican-Americans in his camp might have felt against him as a black man. O'Connor's camp was a thoroughly human place, with some showcase families like Felix Sanchez and his family from Nebraska, who make $500 a week during the height of the season and live in pleasant, middle-class surroundings in their $24-a-week rented house . . . or almost as well off, Mrs. Edna Thompson, a proud and dignified black woman with doilies and flowers on her color television set and pictures of Jesus, Martin Luther King, Jr., and Robert F. Kennedy on her walls.

For every happy story, there seem to be a dozen sad ones. Many of the worst have come out of Immokalee, Florida, a flat, sprawling town a few miles inland from Naples on the southwest coast. This self-proclaimed "watermelon capital of America" has been visited by congressional investigating committees and the Collier County officials are finally consenting to food stamp programs, seeking subsidized government housing and supporting a drive for a hospital. But no reforms were in sight as recently as 1969, when the New York *Times*'s Homer Bigart preceded the first Senate investigators and reported on Smith's Camp, "a dozen or more windowless plywood shacks, all without toilets or running water, all painted a dull green and facing a dark slough choked with bottles and trash." There were two privies, he reported, but "the latrines are unspeakably filthy, seats and floors smeared with dry defecation. So the people use the woods. . . . A spigot planted in the ground provides water [which] is foul smelling and foul tasting. The only apparent amenity is the naked electric light bulb hanging from the ceiling of each shack." In 1968, when outpatient examinations were given to a sample population of 23 migrant children in the Immokalee area, two were found to have pneumonia, one tuberculosis, 14 upper-respiratory infections, 11 ironic deficiency anemia, one otitis, three diarrhea, three impetigo, one ascariasis, one sickle cell trait, and one hydrocephaly.

One of the terrors of migrant life, one learns, are the crew leaders, who have power of life or death over each migrant's job, often misrepresent working conditions and pay a worker can expect, make big profits personally and have been assailed by a spokesman for migrants as "thieves, con men, fraud artists and alcoholics—any one or combination." In winter 1973 groups of farm laborers were discovered working under conditions of virtual peonage at Homestead and La Belle. The black crew leader at Homestead, Joseph L. Brown, was charged with "imprisoning" 28 black migrant workers, siphoning off virtually all their pay for inflated food and shelter charges, and then threatening and beating them when they threatened to leave. He was arrested at the Far South Labor Camp, described in press reports as "a squalid, reeking collection of 9-by-9 cement block cubicles clustered amid the tomato fields and mango groves." Police seized Brown as he walked to his 1973 Cadillac clutching a bag containing $43,786 in cash.

On many big Florida farms and orchards, the familiar form of enslavement is the company store, which extends credit to workers, sells groceries and other essentials at a markup, and in effect holds men in bondage to the end of each season.

The work of a citrus picker is no easy one; a man must be in top condition, able to go up a 30-foot ladder and handle a 90-pound bag on his shoulder. If he hurts himself, or becomes ill, he has none of the recourses—unemployment compensation, hospitalization, disability insurance—available to other workers. Work in the cane fields can be even tougher. There, some growers transport workers in large cage-type trucks normally used for sugar cane, with up to 120 men standing upright on a single load. A few years ago, one of these trucks turned over and 20 men died. Now legislation forbids the practice, but it reportedly continues in some areas.

Normally, there are plenty of jobs around January of each year for the migrants where the winter vegetables are maturing around the shores of Lake Okeechobee, south of Miami and in Collier County. But in 1971, the crops failed to mature at all—the result of a year-long drought that had lowered the water table in southern Florida and, even more serious, unusual hard freezes in the vegetable fields. Suddenly, 15,000 or more workers, recently arrived from Texas or the Deep South, where they had lived during the autumn months, found themselves without a hope of income. Then, three amazing events occurred. First, the state's new governor, Reubin Askew, appealed to President Nixon for assistance under the Diaster Relief Act—legislation earlier used only in the event of calamities like floods, hurricanes, and earthquakes. Second, a fledgling farm workers' organization—the Organized Migrants in Community Action (OMICA)—sent 500 migrants to Key Biscayne to demonstrate near President Nixon's winter White House, where he was relaxing for a weekend. The result was a spate of news coverage by the White House press corps, which could hardly miss the incongruity of starving farm workers assembling at gold-soaked Key Biscayne. Peaceably, the migrants knelt in prayer to ask "God and President Nixon" for help "because we are desperate," and then piled into their 10 old buses and 15 ancient cars and chugged back to their labor camps. The third amazing event was that President Nixon actually released several million dollars in disaster funds to tide the migrants over their emergency period.

Thus an immediate emergency was averted, and the Florida migrants began to learn the advantages of organization. OMICA is not technically a labor organization, but its leader, 35-year-old Rudy Juarez, has increasingly been referred to as "the César Chávez of the Florida migrant workers." Chávez himself has been active in the state. Friends of the migrants maintain that wages could be *doubled* for pickers and marketplace prices raised only a penny for a dozen fruit or for an average pound of vegetables. The trend also seems to be toward less and less annual migration of the field workers to the north; as this trend continues, it will be easier to school and organize the migrants, and easier for them to demand more in their permanent home communities. The 1971 legislature began some response to migrant needs by placing all agricultural workers under workmen's compensation and establishing mandatory standards for farm labor contractors. A planter-backed bill designed to kill off farm unions was rejected by the legislature in 1973.

Another hopeful straw in the wind is the newborn feeling of corporate responsibility on the part of some of the big companies who own thousands of acres of Florida groves and vegetables lands. The biggest of these is the Coca-Cola Company, which bought out Minute Maid orange juice in the early 1960s and owns or controls more than 30,000 acres of Florida citrus groves. Coca-Cola was mightily disturbed to find the slumlike conditions in some of its Florida worker camps revealed in the 1970 NBC News special. After complaining bitterly to the network, Coca-Cola quickly made public an ambitious program to put proper plumbing and other improvements in its housing, to establish permanent social-service centers for child care and preschool training, and raise the wages of its 300 full-time grove workers to $2 an hour. In 1972, Minute Maid also became the first Florida farm organization to sign a contract with Chávez's United Farm Workers Organizing Committee. Critics pointed out that it should hardly have taken 10 years for Coca-Cola to learn about the problems of its own workers, but the fact was that the company was indeed finally taking action—and that it might well set a standard for the entire industry.

Metropolitan Florida

Florida's most explosive growth has come in four distinct sections: the Gold Coast, Jacksonville, Tampa–St. Petersburg and Orlando. These population figures tell the story:

Metropolitan Areas	*1940 Population*	*1970 Population*	*Increase*
Gold Coast			
Miami (Dade County)	267,739	1,267,792	+ 374%
City of Miami	172,172	334,859	+ 95
Fort Lauderdale–Hollywood (Broward County)	39,794	620,100	+1,458
Fort Lauderdale	17,996	172,196	+ 857
Hollywood	6,239	106,923	+1,614
West Palm Beach (Palm Beach County)	79,798	348,753	+ 337
West Palm Beach	33,693	57,375	+ 70
North			
Jacksonville metropolitan area	210,143	528,865	+ 151
Jacksonville	173,065	528,865	+ 206
Orlando (Orange, Seminole counties)	92,378	428,003	+ 353
Orlando	36,736	99,006	+ 170
West			
Tampa-St. Petersburg (Hillsborough, Pinellas counties)	272,000	1,012,594	+ 272
Tampa	108,391	277,767	+ 156
St. Petersburg	60,812	216,232	+ 256

Outside of these, smaller pockets of growth have occurred in Brevard County (home of Cape Kennedy), which rose 1,325 percent—from 16,142 to 230,006—between 1940 and 1970, more than half that growth in the 1960s alone; Escambia County (Pensacola), up 326 percent to 243,075 in 1970; Leon County (Tallahassee), up 227 percent to 103,047; and Alachua (Gainesville), up 171 percent to 104,764. But the most significant growth has been on the Gold Coast, which in 1940 accounted for 20 percent of the entire Florida population, in 1970 for 33 percent. From an estimated 2.4 million people in 1973, the three Gold Coast counties were expected to grow to 3 million by 1980 and at least 5.6 million by the end of the century. The excruciating question was whether such a relatively small and ecologically fragile area could support a population of such magnitude. Arthur Marshall, director of the division of applied ecology at the University of Miami, was quoted as saying in 1973: "I'm convinced the only way we're going to solve the problems of Dade County is to get a quarter of a million people out of here. Our resources are overloaded. North Biscayne Bay has an assortment of pollutants—sewage, runoff waste from the streets and construction sites, garbage from marine users to a certain extent. Also overutilized are the county water supply, streets, schools, parks, jails, courts—even the air. Municipal budgets just can't provide solutions for these problems and, as a result, the quality of life here has been declining."

Back in 1940, the Census figures showed, four out of every 10 Floridians lived in an urban area. In 1970, with the state population practically tripled, seven out of ten lived in an urban area. The sunshine state, it turned out, was also a very urban state, suffering all the ills of urbanism in exaggerated forms because of the delicacy of its ecology.

Miami Metro, the Beach, and Crime

The image of Miami and its satellite communities has been described as one of sun, sand, sex, and sin—depending on one's age and proclivities, possibly sin, sex, sand, and sun. Arnold Toynbee, in his *Cities of Destiny,* lumped Miami together with Los Angeles as a hive of "renters," a place without singleness of vision, an eruption that has yet to attain even "the rudiments of soul." It is certainly the newest of the great cities of America—only 40 years ago it was just coming out of its wild boom-and-bust days of real-estate speculation, and not many decades before that it had been a mere assemblance of tents and sun-warped wooden shacks on the bank of a muddy tropical river. The carnival atmosphere of the 1920s still holds on, especially across the bay in Miami Beach; there the chief huckster of recent years has been Hank Meyer, whose flamboyant promotion ideas culminated in the Miss Universe contest of the 1960s and in persuading Jackie Gleason to produce his shows at the Beach. Meyer is an engaging man with a quiet flash to his clothes who can perform that marvelous feat of talking on two telephones simultaneously; with my own eyes I saw him do it, and Gleason was on the end of one of the lines.

But the Hank Meyer of today has some surprising observations, chief of which is that Miami is about to receive a great infusion of creative talent in medicine, the law, and arts—"not the kind of razmatazz I've thrown out for 20 years." Some believe this is already happening, and point to the strong efforts of Miami University to build its reputation in marine science, law, medicine, and inter-American studies and cast off its image as "Sun Tan U" for rich kids from the North. In the public education sector, the most startling development has been the Miami-Dade Junior College, which sprang into being in the 1960s and had close to 40,000 students (the most of any junior college in the country) by 1973. Another sign of Miami's coming of age was the reorganization of the Greater Miami Chamber of Commerce in the late '60s. The organization abandoned its willy-nilly growth for growth's sake attitude, added Negroes, labor officials, and women to its board of directors, and became concerned about problems relating to the *quality* of life.

Efforts at consolidation of government functions by the 27 separate municipalities of Dade County have led to more political participation and maturity. Acting under broad new home-rule powers granted by the state government, the county in 1959 enacted a form of metropolitan government—a sort of truce between those who wanted full consolidation and some local governments showing prickly independence. The metro government got wide powers over functions like sewers, water supply, transportation, and central planning, while the municipalities were allowed to keep their own departments like police, fire, garbage collection, parks, and that most delicate and important of all—zoning. Schools, hospitals, and airports had been put under countywide supervision more than a decade earlier. During the early years of metro, a coalition of municipalities tried to destroy the system. But it was saved by a coalition that included the areawide newspapers, the downtown chamber of commerce, the League of Women Voters, and even some members of the academic community. They not only turned back the attack but strengthened the metro charter in 1963. There are nine council members elected directly by the people (from separate districts); one of these serves as the metro mayor. A professional county manager runs the show on a day-to-day basis. In a 1969 report, the University of Miami faulted the metro government on inadequate water, sewer, and tax equalization policies, but praised it for having "transformed an obsolete and anachronous commission form of government into a first-rate, high-caliber administration" which had undertaken many valuable public projects.

Miami's very newness and lack of encrusted power structure may have made it possible for the area to embrace metro government. The mobility of population, the tourist atmosphere, the no-party system, the weak position of labor and minority groups, and the dominance of the big Miami papers all made possible an important step forward that older American cities were rejecting left and right in the same years.

The metro government's duties will expand dramatically in the next years as it builds a 59-mile-long aerial rapid transit network. The project —which involves electric trains running on a guideway some 15 feet off the ground, with 54 stations and a total cost of $805 million—will tie together downtown Miami, Miami Beach, and the Miami International Airport. It should help to alleviate the city's serious traffic and air pollution problems. Voters approved it in 1972, along with broad new bonding authority to upgrade the metropolitan area in such areas as sewage disposal, health care, libraries, and recreation and cultural activities.

Economically, Miami is much more mature now, too. Tourism remains king, bringing in hundreds of millions of dollars each year and supporting about a fifth of the population. Retirees, many people of substantial wealth, provide an important source of external income. Huge construction and service payrolls are associated with hundred-million-dollar apartment and shopping center complexes like Century 21, Fontainebleau Park, and Leisuretown. There are several *thousand* small manufacturing plants. The Miami International Airport, one of the busiest in the world, is the hub of travel with Latin America, the Bahamas and Caribbean. Miami benefits doubly from the airport because of the huge aircraft-maintenance facilities there; the airlines in fact qualify as Dade County's biggest employer. Latin-American visitors help swell Miami's $3 billion in annual retail sales, and amazingly, many of them also come for a visit to the Miami Beach hotels. In the past several years Miami has been outstripping New Orleans and Mobile as a magnet for Latin-American trade (doubled to more than $2 billion a year since the mid-1960s) and investments (some $100 million a year). Latin visitors anxious to avoid taxes or currency restrictions in their homelands also bring huge sums of "suitcase money" to invest in Miami banks—some of which offer secret numbered accounts on the Swiss model. Starting with Georgia's Citizens & Southern Bank in 1969, several banks headquartered in other states have set up Miami offices under a federal law that permits outside branches for the purpose of doing foreign business.

By virtue of three advanced scientific installations—the Oceanographic Laboratory of the Environmental Sciences Administration, combined with the U. S. Bureau of Commercial Fisheries' Tropical Atlantic Laboratory and the University of Miami's Institute of Marine Sciences, Miami sees itself as the world's leading center of undersea study. To all of this one can add huge incomes from horse and dog racing, the business generated by the Orange Bowl game each winter, Dade's standing as the fourth-richest agricultural county of Florida, and one has the picture of one of the luckiest metropolitan areas, in terms of economic growth, anywhere in the U.S.

Befitting its newness, Miami lacks an entrenched power structure. Of the 17 leading white community figures the University of Miami identified in its 1969 report on "Psycho-Social Dynamics in Miami," only four had been raised in Florida. The rest came from assorted places from the northeast to as far west as Minnesota. They identified the Miami Club—the city's only club with a limited membership—as the place where the most significant "behind the scenes" decisions were made. Everyone agrees that the Knight-owned and -run Miami *Herald* is one of the most influential papers in any U. S. city (and one of the best, too).* Other influential organizations in Miami include Florida Power and Light, Southern Bell Telephone Company, and the wealthy independent operators like Mitchell Wolfson, whose business holdings range from television stations to bottling plants.

With all these things going in their home town, Miamians are prone to complain when outsiders dismiss the entire city as a tinseled tourist haven or old folks' home. But that appurtenance across the bay, Miami Beach, still fits the old billing. Since 1915, the Beach has grown from a sand bar and clotted mangrove swamp, two-thirds inundated at high tide, into a Babylon on the sea such as the world has never seen—362 hotels, 29,627 rooms, a permanent population of 87,027, a peak winter population of close to 1,000,000.

Driving across Biscayne Bay toward Miami Beach of a summer afternoon, seeing the huge cumulus clouds and thunderheads blown in by the trade wind and the line of gleaming white hotels below, there is a feeling of pristine beauty about the Beach. Closer up, one has to be pleased with the hundreds of thousands of flowering plants that border every street, the lovely lagoons and waterways, the snipped perfection of everything. But then comes the realization: this is no longer a beach, it is a teeming city. The great hotels are packed together so closely the Atlantic is not to be seen beyond them. Collins Avenue, the main drag, becomes a traffic-snarled nightmare, and on some stretches, neon is everywhere. And inside the big hotels, there is the grotesque lobby decor, the very worst our civilization has produced in ostentation and bad taste; one needs only to think of the Fontainebleau, too haughty to put up a sign outside with its name, announcing in its blurbs that

* The morning *Herald* and evening *News* share joint production facilities in a handsome bayside building informally dubbed "the Taj Mahal of U.S. journalism." The *News*, a Cox-owned paper, has only a fraction of the *Herald* circulation (almost 400,000 daily, covering the entire Gold Coast and Florida down to the Keys).

it is "in all the world . . . in any season . . . the most beautiful resort hotel . . . anywhere!"

For many years after the war, each season would bring the grand opening of a new hotel extravaganza . . . the Deauville, Eden Roc, Doral, Americana, Carillon, Casablanca . . . the list goes on and on. Then, in the mid-1960s, the applications for new hotel building permits suddenly fell to zero. The building that did take place was in condominium apartments. The recession starting in 1969 began to cut back on business. People began to worry about the South Beach slum where—as the Miami *Herald* wrote "aged Jews have come for many years to die in the sun, where Cuban immigrants are now settling, and where governments park buses and garbage trucks along the bay." Below Eighth Street the average income is less than $2,500 a year, about 80 percent of the population is Jewish—and two-thirds elderly—and Social Security checks are the principal source of income. Some residential hotels are filled exclusively with people from single neighborhoods in New York's Brooklyn or Bronx; the residents come not only for the warm climate, but to escape the crime of the big city.

Starting in the late '60s, the constant erosion of the beach—none at all remains in front of some of the poshest hotels—developed into a hot political issue, with the mayor of Miami Beach, Jay Dermer, openly fighting for public access to all beaches and for a $35 million beachfront reclamation project by the Corps of Engineers (with at least part of the cost paid by local bonds). The hotels finally backed down and agreed to permit public beach access in return for the Engineers' reclamation project, which will create a 15-mile strip of beach 200 feet wide—greater than ever before.

And then there was the worry about competition. Neighboring island resorts like the Bahamas and Jamaica could offer American tourists a touch of the truly exotic, uncrowded beaches and casino gambling.

In a super resort city like this, the question inevitably arises of hotel owners' manipulation and control of politics. Observers find it passing strange that councilmen often spend $50,000 to win offices that pay only $7,000 a year, and that so many zoning variances are made for high-rises to go up without the legally required parking spaces. Hank Meyer, long close to the hotel interests, claims that their owners often live elsewhere and have but a shadow of the political clout of the Beach's retiree class. "Anyway," he says, "the hotels are so affluent and have such big egos that they end up fighting with each other" instead of putting up a strong common front. Mayor Dermer saw it differently, calling himself "the first mayor not controlled by the hotels." Dermer retired voluntarily in 1971 and was succeeded by former Dade County Mayor Chuck Hall, a man less likely to tangle with the hotel interests.

A new chapter opened for Miami Beach when the Republicans decided to hold their 1968 National Convention there. There was without question a numbing effect from the indulgent world of sun bathing and pool loafing and girl watching and rich eating at the Beach that made it not difficult for the Republicans to bypass the burning issues and choose a bland new Richard Nixon as their candidate. But what looked like a bizarre convention city choice in 1968 became commonplace when both the parties decided to hold their 1972 conventions at Miami Beach. The 1972 conventions were relatively trouble-free, but Miami Beach decided the delegates had been too tightfisted and that the gatherings were not worth the major cash inducements demanded by the parties. "I will never again solicit, work for, or encourage a political convention if it costs the city one red cent," Mayor Hall said.

A Republican official who spent months in Miami Beach planning for the 1968 convention told me that the political establishment of Miami Beach met in the back room of Mendelsohn's kosher meat market to make its decisions, like determining that Elliott Roosevelt would be mayor of Miami Beach, and then a few years later, that Elliott Roosevelt would no longer be mayor. The Fontainebleau, he said, was the scene of some very fancy gambling where thousands of dollars changed hands—but it was all in private, not house games. (Condoned gambling has largely disappeared from the Beach since the Kefauver investigations two decades ago.) The prostitutes, my source said, were certainly in evidence, but as far as could be determined, on their own. The Miami Beach owners and managers, Jewish in background like 80 percent of the Beach's population, were out to make all they could off the convention but acted honorably, kept their commitments, and did not engage in gouging. The real offender was organized labor, which did all service work on double time and got its pound of flesh from everyone. Electricians, for instance, insisted on charging $18 an hour for overtime—just on standby! One had only to talk a few minutes with one of these privileged workmen to find he was a rabid Wallaceite, railing against "them niggers" and all their sins.

Just north of the Beach is the gaudy, unincorporated strip known as North Bay Village, a glaring example of the kind of vice and corruption that has long existed through the presence of Mafia hoodlums living and operating openly in Florida. Illegal activities centered around the 18 motels of North Bay Village's "Motel Row" were the subject of a 1968 state legislative investigation and subsequent suits filed by the state's attorney general. The legislative investigation found that North Bay Village had become nationally known as a place for prostitutes to operate with virtual impunity, that underworld figures could live or meet there safely, and that the police department was so corrupt that it should either be overhauled from top to bottom or abolished altogether, with the police function turned over to the Miami metropolitan public safety department.

But to hear the story told by Florida law enforcement officers, North Bay Village is but a small part of the Mafia story in southern Florida. Miami has become the home, vacation spa, meeting place, and retirement goal of a large assortment of top underworld figures. Some are the lesser lights: the two-bit hoodlums sent south while things cool off in Boston or Baltimore, the Mafiosi rank and file being rewarded with a brief vacation. But the distinctive figures in Miami criminal circles are the major leaders of syndicated organized crime in America—practitioners of the kind of crime that involves a large organization, top accountants and lawyers, national- and international-scale operations. They have not selected Miami as a place for an especially great amount of overt criminal activity, but rather as their rest and retirement center, and as a place to invest in quite legitimate business ventures. A favorite investment property is Miami hotels. Florida law enforcement officials told me that close to 100 corporations have acted as holding companies for Mafia activities in the area, and that at least 50 hotels and more than 30 restaurants and cocktail lounges belong to those corporations. The hotels and restaurants provide a good way to consolidate ill-gotten gains, to buy a little respectability, to divert attention from illicit activities—and to make more money in the process.

Miami does have its share of serious crime. Not only is the city a major distribution point of stolen goods from the whole East Coast, but in the last few years it has become the premier American entry point for smuggled heroin and cocaine. In January 1972 federal agents at Miami made the largest heroin seizure in the history of American antismuggling efforts—$47 million worth. They arrested two Cubans, five Puerto Ricans, and an Argentinian in the seizure.

Florida's top hoodlum for many years has been Meyer Lansky, the Bernard Baruch of syndicated crime in the U.S.A. Born Maier Suchowljansky in Russia in 1902 and brought to this country by his parents in 1911, Lansky is not a member of the Mafia establishment at all because of his Jewish birth. But he has amassed a personal fortune estimated at between $100 million and $300 million; as Nicholas Gage wrote in *Atlantic* in 1970, Lansky in his chosen field of work "is as much a visionary and innovator as Andrew Carnegie, Henry Ford and John D. Rockefeller were in theirs." Until a two-year hiatus in Israel in the early '70s, Lansky lived unobtrusively in a Miami beachfront apartment near the Fontainebleau, constantly watched by the FBI (on whom he actually depended for protection). One reason for the sudden move abroad, it seemed, was Lansky's anticipation of a federal grand jury indictment in March 1971 accusing him and three others, including Morris Lansburg, Miami Beach's biggest hotel operator, of illegal gambling in connection with the Flamingo Hotel in Las Vegas. Israel eventually deported Lansky, however, and when no other country would grant him asylum, he returned to the U.S. to find a small army of federal agents awaiting him.

The Miami area has also had its share of ordinary political corruption. In March 1973, the mayor of North Miami and a councilman there were indicted for bribery. Only two weeks later, the mayor of Miami itself, David Kennedy, was indicted along with two Dade County judges and three other local figures on bribery charges relating to reduced sentences of convicted felons. Kennedy had played a national political role the year before, supporting first Hubert Humphrey for the Democratic Presidential nomination and then becoming a vice president of John Connally's Democrats for Nixon organization.

Miami: City Proper and the Cuban Story

The habitable area of Miami and its surrounding cities is confined to a narrow strip of high-lying land bordered by the Everglades on the west and Biscayne Bay on the east. Aside from Miami Beach, the big attractions of Biscayne Bay are beautiful Virginia Key and the self-proclaimed island paradise of Key Biscayne, the latter made famous in recent years by the aforementioned Richard M. Nixon. Biscayne Bay literally swarms with pleasure craft of every description and also has man-made Dodge Island, where the big cruising ships, increasing sharply in number in recent years, tie up after their runs to Nassau, San Juan, and St. Thomas.

Nixon's Key Biscayne property, substantially increased in value by improvements for "security" paid out of the federal Treasury, is next door to that of his longtime, loyal companion, Miami businessman Charles Gregory (Bebe) Rebozo—the same man who played a major role in the financing of Nixon's other estate at San Clemente, California. Rebozo controls the only commercial bank on Key Biscayne, a monopoly preserved by two Nixon administration decisions to reverse recommendations of federal bank examiners which would have let in a competing bank. Late in 1973 Congress began to inquire into a never-disbursed "campaign contribution" of $100,000 in cash sent Rebozo by billionaire recluse Howard Hughes in 1969 and 1970. Rebozo let the currency sit untouched in safe deposit boxes until the spring of 1973, when he returned it to Hughes.

Right beside the docks is Miami's verdant Bayfront Park, remembered as the spot where Franklin Roosevelt barely escaped assassination in 1933. Behind that, one sees the high white buildings, old and new, which constitute "downtown Miami"—a rather disappointing center, now aging and almost incongruous in a region where everything else is so new and filled with exciting modern architecture (like the startling buildings of the University of Miami campus). Downtown Miami, like parts of the Beach, recalls the culture of the first waves of retirees, a generation ago now.

Back from downtown and the bay, the city of Miami proper stretches toward the Everglades in a monotony of white stucco checkerboard blocks. Through the heart of this, headed due west on its way toward Tampa, is the Tamiami Trail, Route 41; within the city limits it is S.W. 8th Street, which with nearby West Flagler Street forms Little Havana, the heart of the Cuban exile colony in the United States. Dade County's Spanish-speaking population—90 percent of which is Cuban—was only 22,000 in 1959, when Fidel Castro stepped off the Sierra Maestra and into power. Today it is more than 300,000. Cubans now make up 24 percent of the county population and 45 percent in the city of Miami itself. "Cuba has been relocated here," some say. The immigration has also had a profound impact on the city. Before the Cubans came, the downtown area was in financial decline, much property vacant, landlords and businessmen retrenching. Quickly, all that changed, as tens of thousands of Cubans poured in, renting and beginning to restore old buildings, starting their own shops and little businesses, adding a new vibrancy to Miami's life. Important recognition of the Cuban culture came in spring 1973 when Dade County, to the delight of the Cubans, was made officially bilingual and bicultural through action of the county commission.

One reason for the Cubans' success has been the $300 million and more that the federal government has poured into relocation assistance. But the more important reason has been the Cubans themselves. Literally, they are the cream of Cuban society. Of those who worked in Cuba before the revolution, the average annual income was four times the average on that island. Over 12 percent had been to college, almost two-thirds lived in Havana rather than small towns and villages, and they included a disproportionately high percentage of doctors, lawyers, teachers, and other professional people. Among these educated Cubans, the period of menial labor in Miami—lawyers washing dishes, engineers tending gardens, physicians working as lowly helpers in hospitals—was short-lived indeed. And then the entrepreneurial middle-class Cubans went to work, and by 1971 there were some 4,500 Cuban businesses scattered along Miami's palm-lined streets, ranging from cigar factories, boat yards, restaurants, gas stations, and repair shops to markets, bakers, undertakers, cinemas, night clubs, auto dealers, and chemists. The Cuban labor pool suddenly propelled Miami to third place in the U.S. (after New York and California) in garment manufacturing. A special Census report released in 1971 showed a stunningly low Cuban unemployment rate of 2.0 percent—compared, for instance, to rates three times as high for Mexican-Americans and Puerto Ricans.

Miami's gain from the Cuban influx has been more than economic; one might say the Cubans have brought spirit to a pretty soulless city. A new center for Cuban studies prospers at the University of Miami. Music conservatories, ballet schools, and exile theater groups teach culture with a Latin accent to Cuban and American youngsters alike. And then there is the gastronomic input. What other city, Frank Soler of the Miami *Herald* asks, boasts over 70 restaurants that serve *congri, paella,* and *frijoles negros con arroz?*

Gone now are the days when the Miami Cuban colony seethed with plots and vainglorious schemes to reconquer the homeland and drive Castro from power. The Bay of Pigs, in matter of fact, settled that, and despite their bitter disappointment, the Cubans know it, and more and more are readjusting to a new and probably permanent life in the United States. Hope of a return to Cuba delayed Cubans' entry into the mainstreams of American politics, but now, as more and more pass the five years' residency requirement and obtain their American citizenship—and thus the right to vote—this is changing. At first it had been assumed Cubans would simply support all anti-Communist candidates—one reason Richard Nixon won a clear majority among them in his 1968 and 1972 campaigns (and also a reason that a handful of their number were misled into involvement in the Watergate bugging case). But in the 1970 elections, Miami's Cubans cast about 60 percent of their votes for the Democratic candidates for Senator and governor, indicating a strong ingredient of social liberalism.

Miami is flanked on the south by the exclusive, independent city of Coral Gables (42,494) and the once-independent town of Coconut Grove, a Bohemian-flavored enclave of winding streets and estate homes. The metropolitan area has 189,763 Negroes, largely confined to three areas including the Liberty City-Brownsville district where rioting broke out during the 1968 Republican Convention. The city's record on race relations is a strangely mixed one of token integration and heavy community-police tensions, perhaps fitting to Miami's character as a half-Southern, half-Northern city.

Up the Gold Coast, and Beyond

The major landmarks as one moves up the Gold Coast are Fort Lauderdale, now one of the great yachting centers of the Western world and growing in affluent splendor, and that exclusive island, Palm Beach, where the cream of Eastern society still winters.

Fort Lauderdale was such an insignificant speck on the map at the end of World War II that Gunther felt free to omit any mention of it in *Inside USA*. Most national news coverage about the town has centered around the annual springtime inundation of tens of thousands of college students who come to sun, frolic, and sometimes riot on its beaches. "While here," one news report of the late '60s read, "the collegians will swim; stroll; boy and girl watch, sunbathe; drink beer; engage in volleyball, touch football, weight lifting, tug-of-war, swim and dance contests, for 'valuable prizes' offered by the city; enjoy the 'world's biggest hot dog roasts' or just loll and listen to three rock bands." Given the $2 million the kids leave behind each year, city fathers have been willing to overlook outside criticism of sex orgies and alcoholic-drug binges. But they do keep close tabs on the visitors and try to prevent recurrences of 1967 when 817 young people were arrested after a melee triggered by police breaking up a group of boys tossing bikini-clad coeds in blankets.

Behind all that hoopla is the fact that Lauderdale, doubling its population every five years or so, has flowered into one of the most magnificent resort and retirement cities in America. It does have its faults, especially the Galt Ocean Mile where oceanside hotels and condominiums are packed together in tasteless fashion akin to Miami Beach. But there is also a superb six-mile stretch of public beach, acquired by farsighted city commissioners and closed forever to the developers. Moreover, starting at center city and spreading out some 35 miles are 300 miles of navigable canals and waterways that help to make this the yachting capital of America. The huge Bahia-Mar Marina, which has space for 425 yachts of various sizes on a handsome in-city 35-acre tract with its own post office, stores, hotel and restaurant, is highly prized by the nation's leisure boatmen. Up the canal is the even newer and some say more glamorous Pier 66, the creation of retired Phillips Petroleum board chairman Kenneth S. ("Boots") Adams.

Such facilities play no small part in the leisure pattern of East Coast and Midwestern business executives, now numbered in the tens of thousands, who in earlier decades (when their numbers were a small fraction of today's affluent) might have gone to established, old hotels or built their own retirement estates. The yachting crowd that made Fort Lauderdale in the postwar years, Stephen Birmingham observes, were so heavily from the industrial Midwest that Lauderdale "could have been kiddingly likened to a Cleveland-by-the-Sea." But with an admixture of Eastern boatmen

Fort Lauderdale has become—again in Birmingham's well-chosen words—"as glittery as Palm Beach without the latter resort's pomp and formality and endless emphasis on clothes and parties." Lauderdale also has the swank new Club International which charges a fat $1,000 initiation fee but surprisingly gets away with a policy of no religious or racial restrictions. Instead, it offers celebrities in the likes of Joe Namath, Elke Sommer, Dinah Shore, *et al.*, apparently strong drawing cards for a more adventuresome younger set.

All the yachts, forever in need of repairs or refurbishing, help sustain a $125-million-a-year marine industry in Fort Lauderdale. Just to the south is Port Everglades, the deepest harbor between Norfolk and New Orleans and now port of call for many Caribbean cruise ships.

About the only cloud on Lauderdale's horizon, except for slight and temporary slowdowns in recession periods, is pollution. Out from the Inland Waterway, past Port Everglades and into the Atlantic, flows a stream of filthy water; unless something is done about the situation, the city's famous beaches might have to be closed by the mid-1970s. The effluent of the affluent civilization, in fact, is causing severe problems all up and down the Gold Coast. Palm Beach pumps its wastes only a mile out to sea and will be saved only by a tie-in to new treatment facilities in West Palm Beach. The situation is probably the worst in Dade County, where the major waterways are grossly polluted because of septic tanks and the inefficiency of some 114 separate sewage plants. Even the surf at Miami Beach sometimes has coliform bacteria counts exceeding minimum standards as a result of two ocean outfalls discharging raw sewage offshore.

Cast in much the same mold as Fort Lauderdale, but lacking its special character, are Hollywood on its southern flank and Pompano Beach to the north, all sharing in the region's scarcely credible population growth as northern vacationers and retirees pour in and everyone else goes to work servicing them. Boca Raton (Spanish for "rat's mouth"), a few miles further up the Gold Coast, had 447 inhabitants in 1930, less than 1,000 in 1950, and 41,000 by 1973. It had a spotted history of boom and bust, now practically all boom as it rakes in income from its $4 million convention center, year-round tourism, the construction of more and more apartments, and the introduction of light industry. The population cap decreed in 1973 (40,000 housing units, or about 100,000 people) was championed by the wealthy white upper classes of the community—a brand new phenomenon in urban politics.

The northern anchor of the Gold Coast lies in the vicinity of that most aristocratic of all American resorts, Palm Beach. It is actually an island, 14 miles long and no more than two miles wide, occupied by some 9,000 persons year-round and an estimated 36,000 during the high winter season. It was just a narrow sandspit, much of it swamp, when the inimitable Henry Flagler came upon it in 1890 and decided this would be the place to build his ultimate resort hotel. (The first resident, a Confederate draft dodger, had moved onto the island only 25 years before. But the palms were already growing, the result of a wreck of a Spanish barque loaded with coconuts in

1878. They had washed ashore, starting the turn of Palm Beach into South Sea loveliness.) Flagler's hotel, the Royal Poinciana, was the largest wooden structure in the world and must have been quite a sight to see; it is gone now, but his second hotel, The Breakers, still stands, impressive enough in its capacity (415 rooms) and rates (up to $95 a day for a single person).

Long since past are the days when as many as 80 private railroad cars would arrive at Palm Beach for the winter (though jet travel substitutes nicely), and gone too are some of the grandiose mansions, fallen prey to the progressive income tax. But wealth incomprehensible to average man still winters here, and so do some names of European royalty that always make me flinch when I read of Palm Beach as the acme of the American Dream. Writers have always had a field day with the Palm Beach theme, right up to a 1971 description by Tom Buckley in the New York *Times Magazine:*

> In financial Palm Beach, recessions and depressions happen to other people. . . . Such unemployment as exists in Palm Beach is mainly what might be called discretionary. "One of the first things I learned when I came here," said a lively woman from the Midwest, "was never to ask the man next to you at the Bath and Tennis Club what he did. Most of them don't do anything." . . .
>
> As it stands now, Palm Beach is unquestionably one of the most beautiful towns in the country. The obtrusive ugliness of billboards, big neon signs and aluminum siding has been banished. The streets are quiet and immaculate; big trucks are a rarity. A slow drive on the road along the shore past the geometrically clipped private hedges, the palms and pines that shield most of the great houses from the eyes of the curious is pleasant enough to calm the stings of envy. . . .
>
> Palm Beach society is a gerontocracy, a Golden Age Club with real gold, and its ruler is Mrs. Marjorie Merriweather Post, who just celebrated her 84th birthday, has five marriages behind her, and is still going strong. Her residence, Mar-A-Lago, is a fantasia of imported building stone, gilded 30-foot ceilings, inlaid marble tables, columned cloisters and bubbling fountains, surmounted by a 75-foot tower. [Editor's note: Mrs. Post died in 1973, two years after this account.] . . .
>
> Mrs. Post's heiress apparent is Mrs. Stephen (Laddie) Sanford. . . . While Mrs. Post is remote, Mary Sanford is regarded as a ball of fire, raffish and approachable, who roughs it up with a staff of seven. . . .
>
> In Palm Beach the generation gap becomes an abyss. Aside from the sleek beachboys and pretty playmates, one is not conscious of the presence of many young adults. A young woman who has visited here under impeccable social auspices says that she will never come back. "It's a wicked, awful place, totally degenerate. . . . You can't have a relaxed, natural moment. Everyone is dressed by 10 or 11 in the morning. . . . There's a total emphasis on status, clothes, cars and who you know." . . .
>
> Time and change are enemies, and the purpose of the endless round of social ceremonies is to deny their existence. The only cloud in the Palm Beach sky is Old Mortality.

Perhaps the best known of all Palm Beach home owners is Mrs. Rose Kennedy, mother of the late President; for years the most illustrious Palm Beach guests were the Duke and Duchess of Windsor. But Palm Beach is not as immutable as many would like to have it; just in the past few years there has been an influx of condominiums lining the beaches and such very nonexclusive hostelries as Howard Johnson and—yes, a Holiday Inn.

Across Lake Worth lies West Palm Beach, the city Flagler built "for my help." A quarter of West Palm Beach's 57,375 people are Negro, many descendants of Flagler's servant class. It used to be that a Negro caught on Palm Beach at night without a good excuse would face a beating or a night in jail, and Palm Beach sometimes shudders at the thought that the blacks might decide to invade the privileged island sanctuary and right old scores. But West Palm Beach has a lot of other thoughts on its mind, including the making of money from its own resorts, agriculture, and the payrolls of advanced technological firms located nearby (Pratt & Whitney, Minneapolis Honeywell, RCA, etc.).

The Palm Beach newspapers, together with newspapers in Dayton and several other cities, were owned until 1969 by John H. Perry, Jr., a vigorous man in his early fifties who decided to give it all up—at a sales price of $75 million, to Atlanta's Cox papers—so that he could make a full-time profession of his hobby-turned-avocation: building submarines. "I went in for skindiving after the war," Perry explains, "and when I had been out shooting fish a shark followed me in and I tried to shoot the shark and shot myself through the hand instead. I got a tetanus shot but was paralyzed for a week. So I decided to build myself a small sub—starting work in my garage—so that I could shoot sharks without getting hurt. After several false starts, I realized it was getting too expensive, so I formed a corporation, and we've sold over a dozen submarines at prices from $50,000 to a half million." In the process, Perry became fascinated with the possibilities of oceanography. "Two-thirds of the global envelope is water," he points out, and there are immense ways the ocean can be tapped to help mankind find new sources of food and raw materials. Florida, he says, has the best access to the ocean of any state with its warm climate, thousands of miles of coastline, its position on the Gulfstream and closeness to the Bahamas with the world's clearest waters. So Perry has turned his wealth and idealism to new fields in creative ways that the old Palm Beach millionaires probably find, at the least, incongruous for a man of established wealth.

North of the neon-lined Gold Coast, Florida's flank to the Atlantic begins to take on much of the untouched air of pre-Flagler days. Only occasional seaside villages and small cities disturb the sight of ocean pounding onto uncluttered sandy shores. But there are exceptions: Cape Kennedy (with its urbanized spinoff around Cocoa Beach), Daytona Beach (striving for metropolitan status, but still offering a magnificent 23-mile arc of beach that rates among the hemisphere's best), St. Augustine (steeped in Spanish history), and finally the new metropolis of Jacksonville (not far south of the Georgia border). How long the still undeveloped, pristine shores of the central eastern coast will remain that way is doubtful. *Florida Trend* magazine trumpeted the news in the early '70s: "Big money, big people, big projects are moving in—and things will never again be the same." International Telephone and Telegraph Corporation, for instance, staked out a 100,000-acre expanse between St. Augustine and Daytona Beach. The conglomerate promised a planned new city of 750,000 people there by the end of the century—"a city the size of Philadelphia with the density of Beverly Hills." All of this will take place in Flagler County, which had only 4,454 residents in the 1970 Census.

Out at the tip of Cape Canaveral, which juts like a sharp elbow into the Atlantic, stands the delightful old Cape Canaveral Light House, flashing its warnings to ships at sea as it has for more than a century. Vacationers of times past tell of threading their way through stretches of scrub oak, slash pine and palmetto, skirting mangrove swamps, to find camping sites on the lee of grass-covered dunes. But all of that began to change in 1948 when the government decided to use the Cape area, which for the most part is flat, sandy land carved into irregularly shaped pieces by the Indian and Banana Rivers, as a base for launching long-range guided missiles.

The first missile launch took place in 1950—a modified German V-2 rocket as the first stage, with a U.S. WAC Corporal as the second stage. A primitive gantry of iron tubing cradled the rocket for firing. Before launch preparations could begin, an advancing line of jeeps scurried around the test site to scare snakes away, stirring up swarms of mosquitoes. The launch was a success, and the Cape was on its way to becoming one of the best-known spots on earth.

It was given an official name, the Air Force Missile Test Center, which later would be changed to the Cape Canaveral Air Force Station. New rockets were developed and tested. Some of the launches went well; others did not. An early Army Redstone missile headed erratically toward a nearby industrial area before diving into a patch of palmetto scrub. Another day, a Navy Polaris missile veered close to the local town of Cape Canaveral before a range safety officer could blow it up, showering fragments over a trailer court. Then, on December 6, 1957, while millions watched and listened, a Navy Vanguard missile, carrying America's hopes of regaining some world prestige after the surprise of Sputnik, misfired on its launching pad and exploded in a burst of flames. But seven weeks later, on January 31, 1958, the first American earth satellite, Explorer I, was launched from the Cape.

That same year, the National Aeronautics and Space Administration was created and a massive program of expansion and construction got underway at the Cape. Unmanned satellites and space probes, bearing such names as Echo, Tiros, Telstar, Early Bird, and Explorer, were launched. In 1961, President John F. Kennedy proclaimed the national goal of landing a man on the face of the moon before the end of the decade, and manned space flight progressed through Projects Mercury and Gemini to Project Apollo. The guided missiles came to be called launch vehicles. And they got bigger and bigger, starting with Redstone, which developed 78,000 pounds of thrust at liftoff, and growing into the awesome Saturn V, which developed 7.5 million pounds of thrust at liftoff. A Redstone launched Alan B. Shepard, Jr., America's first man in space, on his May 1961 suborbital flight. A Saturn V launched Neil A. Armstrong, Edwin E. Aldrin, Jr., and Michael Collins for the July 30, 1969, lunar landing by Armstrong and Aldrin, who thus became the first human beings to walk on the moon.

The impact of the Space Age on the Cape was tremendous. A local newspaper began to carry a daily banner line: "Fastest Growing County in the U.S.A.," and, indeed, it was. Brevard County's population soared from 23,653 in 1950 to 111,435 in 1960; by 1970, it had more than doubled again, to 230,006. In 1950, there were 9,500 housing units, in 1970, 77,700. But even at that some workers were commuting from as far away as Daytona, Vero Beach, and Orlando with round-trip travel each day of up to 150 miles. Schools had to resort to double, even triple sessions as enrollment rocketed from 4,163 to 59,000.

The burgeoning Brevard population was due not only to NASA's own personnel, but workers for the multitude of contractors working on various stages of the rockets—companies like Boeing, North American Rockwell, Bendix, RCA, McDonnell Douglas, IBM, General Electric, the Martin Company—plus TWA and Pan American for base maintenance. Riding up and down the elevators inside the huge Vehicle Assembly Building, one had the feeling of viewing America's whole aerospace industry, working on the Saturn stages in layer-cake fashion.

In a national paroxysm of memorialitis after the assassination of President Kennedy, Cape Canaveral was summarily renamed Cape Kennedy, thus expunging from the maps a name dating from the earliest Spanish explorations. And the Cape gradually found itself forced to share the glory of the space age with NASA's Manned Spacecraft Center in Houston, which directed the design, development, and testing of manned spacecraft, plus selection and training of astronauts and earth control of manned flight. The Cape was reduced to playing the role of a glorious launching pad. According to one scarcely credible story long in vogue at the Cape, Houston's selection for manned space flight control was part of the arrangement under which Lyndon Johnson, of Texas, agreed to become John Kennedy's running mate in 1960. The least expensive alternative might well have been to locate the manned flight control at the Goddard Space Flight Center in Maryland, which was already laden with sophisticated satellite control equipment.

The character of the astronaut crews changed as the manned space program matured in the 1960s. The original seven, one old Cape hand told me, "were seat-of-the-pants flyers, test pilots, men who had to have guts. Except for John Glenn, they were hell-raisers. At one point they all had Stingrays which they'd race around the motels at 3 A.M." Later, the astronaut corps was filled with a new breed of more restrained professionals—men with highly technical backgrounds, several with advanced degrees in engineering.

As the U.S. entered the decade of the '70s, there were rapidly mounting doubts about the need for post-Apollo manned space flight, the appropriateness of vast expenditures for a space program in the face of great unmet human needs on earth, and the future role of the Cape, where the government, by now, had invested some $1.5 billion in facilities. The result was a long, slow letdown in the national space program. NASA and its contractors, which had a peak employment of 26,500 working at the Cape in 1967–68 (the height of Apollo flight preparation), slipped to 15,000 by early 1971. And the Brevard County economy seemed headed for a tailspin. Actually, it was averted, and the outlook for the '70s made fairly bright when a big effort was made to resell the surplus housing for retirement homes and new industries were recruited to fill up the half-empty office buildings and shopping centers. The tourist influx—with 14,000 people a day visiting the historic moonport—also began to fill the scores of motels between Cape Canaveral, Cocoa Beach, and Satellite Beach, where newsmen and scientists had encamped before. In December 1972, when Apollo 17 made what would probably be Americans' last trip to the moon in this century, there was nostalgia—but not panic—at the Cape.

On a reduced scale, NASA operations were to continue: for the Skylab program, for joint flights with Soviet cosmonauts, and the multi-billion dollar space shuttle program with its inaugural flights around 1978.

Regardless of NASA's future, local residents of all political persuasions made one point clear: they wanted the Cape's old name back. Some historians, indeed, believe it was Ponce de Leon himself who first assigned the name of Cape Canaveral—translated as "a place overgrown with canes or reeds." And indeed, in 1973, while the Kennedy Space Center retained its name in memory of the late President, the federal government ordered that the Cape would become Cape Canaveral again.

Jacksonville (World's Largest City), North Florida, and Panhandle

The largest city in the world, in terms of area, is Jacksonville (1970 population 528,865), once the famed "Gateway" to Florida in the heyday of the passenger railroads, now desperately seeking a new identity and a new future.

Jacksonville is an oddity. It is isolated in the northeast corner of the state; tourists fly over it on the way south instead of passing through it in train or car. It serves the back country of northern Florida and not much more. It is dominated by the conservative attitude of nearby southern Georgia. Yet the city embarked on a daring experiment in consolidated metropolitan government with a strong mayor-council form of government. What Jacksonville has already done, many other cities are likely to copy in the 1970s. Few American cities have had such a renewal of spirit in recent times.

It was not always so. After World War II, Jacksonville experienced a steady decline, with urban white population moving to the suburbs and abandoning a deteriorating center city to low-income blacks. The governments of Jacksonville and surrounding Duval County were so fouled up that the area had the reputation of being one of the worst governed in the nation. All Jacksonville high schools were disaccredited in 1964 for lack of financial support. Property was assessed for tax purposes at only 20 percent of fair market value. And then, in 1966, came the final blow to Jacksonville's self-esteem: television station WJXT investigated city insurance dealings and disclosed practices which led to the indictments of two of the five city commissioners, four of the nine city councilmen, the city auditor, and the recreation department chief. The city tax assessor discreetly resigned.

With that, the public rebelled. Citizen leadership brought about establishment of a local government study commission, which proposed merging Jacksonville (pop. 200,000) with surrounding Duval County (pop. 325,000) in a consolidated metropolitan government. A group called Citizens for Better Government recruited 1,000 workers to push doorbells for the proposal, and it carried on Aug. 8, 1967, by a 2–1 margin. In a twinkling, Jacksonville grew from 30 to 827 square miles.

Under Mayor Hans Tanzler, a raw-boned, six-foot, five-inch dynamo, the city moved on race relations (once among the worst in the state), tax relief, improved fire and police protection, ambulance service, and cleaning up the horribly polluted St. Johns River, which bisects the city. Rebuilding of the moldering downtown, which had actually begun a few years before, proceeded apace, and now both banks of the river gleam with new buildings.

A television station polled citizens in March 1969 and found that 64.1 percent accepted the new government. In March 1970, the figure had risen to an astounding 78.8 percent.

There had been fears in the black community that its political power would be severely diminished by consolidation; blacks constituted 44 percent of the city before the metro plan and only 23 percent after. Yet a majority of blacks supported consolidation. In the old city council, there were two blacks. In the new city council, consisting of 19 members (14 elected from districts, five at large), there were four blacks, including one elected at large. Two of the blacks were women, the first ever to serve

The success of blacks in elective politics is all the more amazing in light of Jacksonville's long history of racial violence. The Ku Klux Klan, its membership fed by rural migrants from south Georgia and north Florida, was strong in the city and sent shock troops to St. Augustine, 35 miles to the south, when Martin Luther King, Jr., was demonstrating there for open accommodations legislation. Jacksonville synagogues were frequent targets of terrorists in the early 1960s. And in 1971, Panther-type organizations of young blacks were involved in ugly clashes with local police accused of brutal tactics by both blacks and some responsible white leaders. A breadth of antiblack sentiment was evident in George Wallace's winning 36.3 percent of the Jacksonville vote in the 1968 Presidential election. Yet when massive school busing went into effect in 1971 under court orders, it proceeded with many less disturbances or problems than had been widely expected.

The most powerful man in Jacksonville and arguably in Florida is Edward W. Ball, head of the billion-dollar Alfred I. DuPont estate, long an archconservative and potent force in Florida politics. Juanita Green, the Miami *Herald's* outstanding urban affairs editor, once described Ball as "arch conservative, segregationist, antilabor, antibureaucrat, anti-big government." He is also against the income tax and all forms of government regulation, both of which have caused him no little trouble.

"Mr. Ball," as even longtime friends call the octogenarian, had the good fortune to be the brother of a schoolteacher who married Alfred I. DuPont.

Things were never the same again. DuPont feuded with his brothers in Wilmington and left to do good works with some $30 million in Florida in the late 1920s. DuPont died in 1935 and Ball took over as dominant trustee of an estate that came to own vast holdings of timber land throughout the state, the Florida East Coast Railway, a telephone company, and 30 banks in the Florida National group. The late Mayor Robert King High of Miami once testified: "You can hardly drive 50 miles in Florida—in any direction—without encountering some facet of the DuPont estate."

Ball guided the estate with a heavy hand and saw it increase in value to well past the billion-dollar mark, perhaps twice that. He was the key figure behind George Smathers' defeat of Claude Pepper in 1950, close to Governors Farris Bryant and Haydon Burns, and helped Edward Gurney beat Leroy Collins for the Senate in 1968. Ball was also a leading figure in getting Florida to adopt a sales tax instead of any kind of income tax, and thus can be given important credit for the state's regressive tax structure.

His intractability finally caught up with him in the late 1960s. During a long strike by railway workers, unions complained to Congress of the feudal character of the DuPont estate which, among other things, held 30 banks under an exemption to the Bank Holding Company Act of 1956. The act forbids companies owning two or more banks from simultaneously holding nonbanking businesses, and it defines ownership as having an interest of 25 percent or more. In 1966, following a bruising battle behind the scenes on Capitol Hill, Congress closed the loophole and Ed Ball lost his biggest fight for the estate.* Ball's wealth and holdings (including the railroad) remained immense, however.

A feeling of the Old South, in the look of the land, in race attitudes and politics, pervades northern Florida from Jacksonville west and, in large measure, out across the panhandle as well. Here are miles and miles of Dixie-style piney woods and a great pulp farming industry, tobacco and peanut farms, and still those languorous rivers of yore. But like the rest of the South, this region is changing.

Consider the case of Gainesville (1970 population 64,510), home of the University of Florida. The old Southern trappings are there. Visit in the springtime, for instance, and you will find dogwoods, redbud trees, and azaleas in bloom, new leaves pushing out on the moss-laden oaks which shade the residential streets. Until a few years past, to be a Negro in Gainesville was about the same as being a Negro in Savannah, Georgia. The town had been officially dry since 1905. The university's national reputation was strictly mediocre.

But after World War II, things began to change. An expansion program at the university added greatly to enrollment, and academic standards began to rise. In the 1950s a medical school was added, and by the late 1960s the university had close to 20,000 students (due to reach 25,000 in 1975) and an annual budget on its way toward $100 million. Integration came to

* To his credit, Jacksonville Congressman Charles E. Bennett voted to eliminate the exemption that benefited Ball. Bennett, who holds the congressional record for the longest unbroken string of roll-call votes, is so strong on the ethics issue that some have dubbed him the "Eagle Scout" of the Florida delegation.

the university, and then blacks actually started to eat in Gainesville restaurants and attend the theaters of whites. In 1967 the town finally voted to go wet, ending the heyday of the moonshiners and whisky runners. Reporting on some of these developments in 1968, reporter Nixon Smiley of the Miami *Herald* also recorded the shock it had all been to one local merchant: "It's a godless place. The niggers, the hippies and the Communist professors and students are taking over this town. But don't put my name in your paper. I'll be bombed."

But Gainesville's change continued. In 1948 the county (Alachua) had gone for Thurmond's Dixiecrat party for President; by 1968, the university-research complex was strong enough to make it one of only four Florida counties carried by Humphrey. In 1970 Gainesville received an all-American City Award for the way it had used vigorous housing code enforcement to effect rehabilitation of 1,637 slum homes. Similar action—and the reward—would have been terribly unlikely a decade before.*

The same kind of revolution in basic attitudes and practices is quietly taking place in Florida's charming old capital city of Tallahassee (population 71,897). The city has a very conservative and dignified power structure; this is a town, I heard, where the old families "reign," and the last thing they want is any kind of commotion.

Tallahassee is renowned for its parklike hills lined with giant oaks and antebellum mansions. Its Capitol Center, consisting of the Capitol and several other big government buildings, has a class many states fail to match. The old city has begun to hum in recent years with huge condominium and recreational projects and thousands of new hotel rooms—and the familiar problems of urban sprawl. Life is also added by Florida State University, a onetime women's college turned coeducational in the late 1940s. Florida State is experiencing the same burgeoning enrollment and construction reported at Gainesville. Together with the other six predominantly white schools of the state university system, they will be governed by a regents decision, made in 1973 under government and federal court pressure, to increase black enrollment from 4.5 percent to 8.8 percent and add 321 black professors by the autumn of 1977. An uncomfortable problem is what to do about formerly all-black Florida A & M University, about a mile from FSU in Tallahassee and still vastly inferior in facilities, qualifications of faculty, and alumni support.

Moving out across the panhandle, one finds the Old South flavor leavened with more cosmopolitanism, perhaps because there is beach here—miles and miles of beautiful white sand and, with it, the tourist trade. There is also a heavy military component (Navy at the big airbase at Pensacola,

* This is not to suggest a millennium, especially at the University of Florida. Its president, Stephen O'Connell, was chief justice of the Florida Supreme Court when it issued rulings to keep the first blacks out of the university, and he has shown amazing insensitivity to demands of black students for an increase in black enrollment, more black faculty and administrators, curriculum changes, and a variety of attitudinal changes. Hundreds of white students and the faculty of the College of Arts and Sciences supported the blacks' cause, but the university administration responded with an ugly show of force in the spring of 1971. About a third of the black students and half the black faculty then took the rather self-defeating course of resigning from the university. In 1972 O'Connell tried to get rights of prior censorship over the student newspaper, *The Florida Alligator,* but was rebuffed by both the state attorney general and the university regents.

Air Force at Fort Walton Beach), heavy lumbering (first paper pulp mill was built at Panama City in 1931), and small farming. Panama City is a sort of Atlantic City South with its roller-coaster and convention hall. But something far more important happened at the old Panama City courthouse a few years ago. Here Clarence E. Gideon got a retrial, on direct orders from the U.S. Supreme Court, because he had been unable to afford a lawyer at his trial and was not furnished one by the government. The Gideon case, of course, became a landmark in the civil rights decisions of the Warren court.

Pensacola, so far west it seems within a stone's throw of Alabama, is another one of those Florida cities with a long Spanish history but little to show for it today. In fact, there is no special Spanish flavor to the city at all. The Naval Air Station has been the mainstay of Pensacola's economy since 1914, permitting slow, steady growth toward a 1970 total of 59,707 people. Pensacola got a great bonanza in the late 1940s, however, when the federal government turned over to it Santa Rosa Island with its 55 miles of virgin beach. The beach is connected to Pensacola by a causeway and has become a big tourist magnet.

Politically, northern Florida usually votes conservative-segregationist. It was overwhelmingly for Goldwater in 1964, Kirk in 1966, Wallace and Gurney in 1968. But given a chance—that is, when the Democratic candidates don't appear to be "liberals"—the north will vote Democratic. In 1970 the essentially moderate Democratic governor and Senate candidates, Askew and Chiles, swept north Florida with close to two-thirds of the total vote. One reason for the high Democratic vote, of course, may have been that Askew was from Pensacola. Not in the memory of living man had northern Florida elected a governor, and the "friends and neighbors" vote for Askew must have been strong. His election, some believed, might also help break down north Florida's old feeling of being a stepchild on the Florida scene.

Central Florida: Orlando, Disney World, et al.

Central Florida is preeminently citrus Florida, mile after mile of orange and sometimes tangerine and grapefruit orchards, the greatest concentration of citrus in the world. The largest city is Orlando, grown from a trading post on a cow range in the late 19th century to a booming metropolis of some 100,000 people with 330,000 more in its immediate hinterland. Citrus and the prosperity of a well-to-do retirement center gave Orlando its initial thrust; military bases, electronics, aerospace, and the proximity to Cape Kennedy 65 miles distant have propelled it forward in the past two decades; all these advantages plus the prospect of immense profits from the new Disney World have led to projections of a metropolitan population of a million by the end of the 1980s. Some see a second Florida megalopolis, rivaling the Gold Coast, coming into being on the axis of Orlando to Tampa–St. Petersburg and then down the coast to Sarasota and Fort Meyers; already some 2½ million people live in this region.

Physically, Orlando is far more attractive than many of the more celebrated coastal areas, the city proper and the land for miles around dotted with blue lakes contrasting with the evergreen foliage in gently rolling countryside. High buildings, including the Florida headquarters of several large insurance firms, are giving a focus to the sprawling city proper. Almost 30,000 blacks are crowded into a west side ghetto, but that community has developed some strong leadership and found ways to work with the white establishment of the city. Among the technologically oriented companies that have fueled the local economy are Martin Marietta's aerospace division, General Electric, Xerox, and Control Data Corporation. Several of these firms devote their Florida activity to research and are located in a prospering "clean" industrial park established in 1963. There are also big payrolls at Orange and McCoy Air Force Bases and Naval recruit training facilities.

In a pattern akin to San Diego, California, the combination at Orlando of affluent retirees, the military, and a staunchly conservative newspaper all add up to a strongly Republican voting pattern. In 1970, Orange was Florida's only metropolitan county to go Republican for governor—and did so with a whopping 65.3 percent vote.

Democratic Senator Lawton Chiles attributes Orange County's strong Republicanism to an informational "iron curtain" thrown up by the *Orlando Sentinel*, a property since 1956 of the Chicago *Tribune*. As a Democrat, Chiles claims, "you're not only hit on the editorial page, but you're slanted out of the news." The huge Republican vote, he says, can be traced to the circulation of the *Sentinel*. Orange County's conservatism predates the Chicago *Tribune's* purchase of the local paper, however. The former *Sentinel* owner, Martin Anderson, was a Florida-type Colonel McCormick who practiced a very personal brand of journalism. As early as 1960, GOP Presidential candidate Richard Nixon carried Orange with 71.0 percent of the vote. This was the congressional district that sent archconservative Republican Edward J. Gurney to the U.S. House in 1962 and then helped boost him into the U.S. Senate with a 72.0 percent vote in 1968.*

Sixteen miles west of Orlando, on a huge drained swamp, rises the latest and perhaps the greatest American monument ever to the gods of fun and escape: Walt Disney World. The great Disney himself, before his death in 1966, had personally set in motion the plans for Disney World and announced the idea.

In some respects, Walt Disney World is simply in the genre of the original California Disneyland, complete with fairyland castles (Cinderella's castle is 18 stories high with gold turrets), the plaster mountains (Space Mountain is 30 stories high), the animated animals, the monorails, the boat rides. But Walt Disney World (27,400 acres) is vastly larger than Disney-

* In the 1968 campaign, Gurney's forces circulated thousands of pictures of his opponent, former Governor Collins, walking arm-in-arm with Martin Luther King, Jr., during the Selma, Alabama, confrontation, when Collins was the head of the federal government's Community Relations Service. The racist pitch helped Gurney carry northern Florida, which had never voted for a Republican—except Goldwater—before.

land (230 acres) and it is far more than an amusement park. It has several hotels (American, Asian, Polynesian, Venetian), three golf courses, bridle trails, picnic grounds, lagoons and a big lake, beaches and campgrounds on a 2,500-acre Vacation Kingdom, a 100-acre Magic Kingdom with six fantasy-lands ranging from Frontierland to Tomorrowland—and, eventually, a planned community with 20,000 or more persons living, as Disney decreed, "a life they can't find anywhere else in the world today."

Land-buying for the project began in secret in 1964, a year before Disney announced his plans. Disney did not repeat the mistake he had made at Disneyland, where the small amusement park is surrounded by non-Disney enterprises which are parasitic on the tourists and their dollars. Frontmen bought up thousands of acres on all sides to protect the main project. But that did not prevent other entrepreneurs from starting an array of amusement parks some miles distant—Sea World and Wild Kingdom and Wild West and the like—all riding the coattails of Disney. As no less than 10 million people poured through Disney World's gates during its first year of operation, massive traffic jams occurred and the city of Orlando found itself faced with a grave shortage of housing for the thousands of new service workers. Auto congestion, street crime, and taxes all soared. Disney officials liked to say they had warned the Orlando area but had not been believed.

Where it really counted to them, however, the Disney operatives had won many concessions from the dazzled Florida legislature long before the official opening in 1971. Disney's chartered town, Buena Vista, was given powers exceeding those of any county commission in the state. Disney World received a 40 percent markdown on sales taxes on attractions constructed in California and shipped to Florida. And the legislature changed state trademark law to prohibit the opening of a "Micky Mouse Restaurant" or a "Snow White Motel," for example, and to forbid any business in the state from advertising itself as a given number of miles from Walt Disney World.

An early environmentalist, Disney ordered his planners to preserve as much of World in its natural state as possible. Cars must be left in parking lots while visitors ride around in vehicles powered by steam or compressed natural gas. Waste from hotels and restaurants is collected through underground pneumatic tubes, baled, and burned in an incinerator which emits almost no smoke.

Beyond the hotels and golf courses of Vacation Kingdom, beyond the gilded castles and plaster mountains of Magic Kingdom, lies Disney's ultimate vision, of an Experimental Prototype Community of Tomorrow (EPCOT). Disney saw it as a planned community, an "exceptional" new city, designed perhaps in concentric circles without vehicles on the streets, with all transportation by monorail and trams. It will be many more years in the planning by Disney's "imagineers" (as he called them), and one will watch with fascination to see what comes of the world's first city started with Mickey Mouse money and done with mirrors.

If Disney World is the ultimate in calculated and programmed amusement for the millions, Cypress Gardens—at Winter Haven, some 60 miles southwest on the way to Tampa—is Florida's best indigenous specimen of how one uses publicity, cheesecake, and pure nerve to make something worth millions out of virtually nothing. In this case, the nothing was a tangled muck swamp that the engineers had given up on draining in the 1930s; the something is Cypress Gardens, one of the most fabulously successful tourist attractions in the U.S.A. and the creation of a single master promoter, Dick Pope. Pope and his imitators are the type who make it possible to state seriously: *Florida is the state man made.* God may have supplied the sun and sand and rains and swamps, but more than in any other state, the hand of man was needed to make a place (1) habitable, and (2) an attraction for millions. Brad Byers, a writer for *Southern Living*, caught the spirit of it a few years ago when he recalled that Cypress Gardens had tied with the Grand Canyon in a vote of the country's travel agents and writers as the most photogenic spot in the U.S.A. "Using the Colorado River as her tool," Byers wrote, "nature carved the Grand Canyon. It took six million years. Using men with shovels and buckets, Dick Pope built Cypress Gardens. It took three years."

Pope himself is a bouncy, ruddy-faced extrovert and enthusiast who is given to rainbow-colored sports jackets "because I'm a little fellow (five feet, five inches) and it's the only way they can remember who I am." He got Cypress Gardens built with WPA men working at one dollar a day to create walkways and floral displays around a grove of cypress trees growing out of a lake. Pope's real genius was in publicity. As soon as the gardens opened, mountains of pictures of speedboats on the lake and pretty girls posing beside cypress and flowers and purple prose about the "inconceivably beautiful gardens" were flowing to the nation's newspapers—which, lacking anything better for their space, printed without charge. Hundreds of newsreels featured news about Pope and his gardens, with every excuse from the crowning of some kind of queen (he once crowned seven queens in a day) to water-skiing extravaganzas. Then there were numerous movies filmed at the gardens, and television shows, and celebrity guests by the hundreds. From 186 guests paying 25 cents a head on opening day in 1935, the gardens advanced to 1.5 million visitors a year, each adult paying $2.75 a head, in the late 1960s. The annual gate doubled after the opening of Disney World, but Pope was still pouring over $400,000 a year into promotion and advertising, and as much on maintaining the flowers.

In World War II, Pope enlisted in the Army, firmly convinced that "publicity could win the war." He had hoped that on classification, he'd get at least a colonel to decide his duties. "But I got an acting corporal. He couldn't find public relations in his little book. But he was on the page for "p" and put me down for pole line construction." So Pope spent the war putting up and taking down telephone poles. When he came home, there was a problem with the bougainvilleas—begonias coaxed to grow on high displays. "We found that if we put them on a tree, they'd break it down; if we put them below, they'd be in the shade." Quickly, the solution came to Pope: use poles. "Now we mount the bougainvilleas on 55-

foot giant black diamond poles. People think these are trees, but if you look in back, you'll always find a pole. If I could find that acting corporal, I'd give him a Cadillac. I don't care how dumb he was, he was the man responsible for us rising to a helluva position in life."

A cynic might question how much floral gardens are helped by pretty girls in antebellum dresses sitting around every curve, but Pope has a good reason: "Everyone else advertises girls on their booklets. We have them there. This is truth in advertising." As for true horticultural skills, Pope admits that when he started out he couldn't even spell "azalea." His wife supplied botanical knowledge and inspiration. "For a generation or more," he recalls, "none of the great botanists came here." Finally, a leader in modern botany, Frederick Olmstead, phoned and asked if Pope could give him half an hour of his time to show the gardens. "I was so damned honored it was pitiful," Pope says. "Nothing like this ever happened to me before, and I'd been in the business 20 years."

Now about 70, Pope is still going strong. His slogans sum up a lot of Florida the state and Pope the man: "If it ain't fun, the hell with it."

But Florida is a many-cultured state, and mention might be made of two other central Florida personalities. One is Willis McCall, sheriff (until his defeat in 1972) of rural, citrus-growing Lake County near Orlando. For 28 years, McCall symbolized an almost legendary terror to the blacks of the county. In 1972 he was acquitted of a second-degree murder charge over the death of a black prisoner in his jail.

And then there is Charlie Smith, who runs a candy and soft-drink store in Bartow, near Lakeland. Smith claims that he was lured onto a slave ship in his native Liberia at the age of 12, and his age—131 in 1973—has been substantiated by an 1855 bill of sale of a Negro boy in the New Orleans slave market. He wound up on a Texas plantation owned by a man named Charlie Smith, whose name he adopted. He was freed during the Civil War and spent years as a cowpuncher, bootlegger, gambler, and outlaw. Both the American Medical Association and the Social Security Administration have certified Charlie Smith to be the oldest living person in the United States.

Down the Sun Coast, on to Key West

The big population center on Florida's western flank is around Tampa and St. Petersburg, the northern anchor of the so-called Sun Coast which covers some 120 miles on the Gulf of Mexico, down through Bradenton and Sarasota to Fort Myers. In spots, the Sun Coast is sprouting forth with tall seafront condominium apartments. But it will be years before this becomes another tightly packed Gold Coast; on the stretch from Sarasota south to Fort Myers, for instance, there are beautiful beaches where one can still walk for miles and not see a soul.

Tampa, western Florida's biggest town, "does its share of pickin' Yankees," as an old Florida saying goes, but essentially it is an industrial and distributing center, quite unlike most Florida cities. There are big, masculine industries like beer brewing (Schlitz, Budweiser), steel, and cigar-making. The port of Tampa is one of the most important in the southeastern U.S. and the world's largest export point for phosphate, which is mined only 40 miles away.

Spanish explorers and pirates wrote a colorful early page in Tampa history in the 1500s, but serious settlement waited until 300 years later. A blockade and shelling in the Civil War, followed by a yellow fever epidemic in 1873, almost decimated the town. But then things began to look up with discovery of the big phosphate reserves nearby, the arrival of Henry Plant's South Florida Railroad in 1884, and the appearance two years later of Vincente Martinez Ybor's cigar factory, which moved lock, stock, and barrel from Key West and brought a dash of Spanish-Cuban culture which endures to this day.

Good fortune has continued to smile on Tampa. It shared in the real estate boom of the 1920s, got in on the floor of the citrus industry as a shipping and processing point, boomed as a shipbuilding center in World War II, and has since added a multitude of small industries to supplement beer, cigars, and the port. Florida's biggest shrimp fleet harbors at Tampa, and just south of town is McDill, one of the country's largest Air Force bases. An $80 million Tampa International Airport, opened in 1971, uses fast trainlike cars to whisk travelers between satellite buildings and a central terminal and appears to be America's latest word in pleasant and efficient passenger handling.

Tampa became Florida's first urban renewal city, leading to a great face-lifting for the old waterfront, where railroad lines and old warehouses were torn out to make room for a $4.5 million convention center, a splendid new library, and a hotel. The central business district has been rejuvenated with new high-rise office buildings and hotels. Ybor City, which still has the country's largest cigar factory, has been revived as a center of Spanish culture. First came demolition of old slumlike buildings, then construction of 400 low-income family apartments in a Spanish design, and finally, to lure tourists, a four-acre Spanish walled city. Despite a heavy Negro influx, Ybor City has been able to sustain its Spanish atmosphere through the architecture and, more particularly, some of the world's finest Spanish restaurants. The proprietor of the Columbia Restaurant, an engaging Latin bon vivant named Cesar Gonzmart, deserves major credit for inspiring the renewal of Ybor City. The Columbia got its start around the turn of the century when Cuban immigrants working in the cigar factories would pay $5 a month for lunch and supper. To this day, the original old room is in operation, supplemented by more opulent dining halls. Gonzmart likes to boast of his great mix of clientele —local workers, kids from the universities, and "the high-class, diamond-perfume trade"—a unique brand of gastronomic egalitarianism.

Tampa has made good use of its elected representatives in Washington and Tallahassee. Stephen M. Sparkman became chairman of the U.S. House Rivers and Harbors Committee in the 1910s and was instrumental in getting Tampa Harbor substantially deepened so that the big phosphate ships could come in. Sam M. Gibbons, the present U.S. Representative, performed two cardinal services when he was in the state senate a decade ago. The first was obtaining authorizing legislation to let Tampa take advantage of urban renewal; the second was to win approval of a state university for Tampa (now called the University of South Florida, with a 17,000-acre, $34 million campus that enrolls 16,000 students). Neither feat was easy in the old days when the pork choppers still held sway in Tallahassee. The rural legislators long opposed any state university in an urban area; before Tampa got its state university, for instance, the only two were in lightly populated northern Florida—Gainesville (the University of Florida) and Tallahassee itself (Florida State University). The first state-supported university in Miami's history, Florida International, opened in 1972.

In Washington, Gibbons went on the House Education and Labor Committee, and it was probably no accident that Tampa got the first federally funded experimental program for preschool children (a forerunner of Head Start) and was one of the first cities selected for the Model Cities program. Half a million dollars of Model Cities funding went into one of the country's finest neighborhood service centers in a black neighborhood of West Tampa.

One reason that Tampa's poverty and Model Cities programs won a reputation as being among the best in the U.S. was that they were always run through local governments—which, in turn, showed unusual sensitivity in including minority representatives in planning and operations. A fundamental change in the tone of local politics, occurring over the past two decades, made this possible. In the 1930s, Tampa was plagued with organized crime and rigged elections that even necessitated calling out of the National Guard on one occasion. Since then, local government has become both honest and progressive. As late as the mid-1950s, there was strict segregation in Tampa. Not a single Negro had anything more than a janitorial job in city or county government, and one would never see a Negro in a white restaurant, movie house, or theater, or, of course, in a white school. But around 1960, public accommodations were rapidly and completely integrated. Living conditions for a vast majority of the blacks remained deplorable, contributing in no small measure to a destructive riot in 1967. But gradually, Negroes were admitted to more and more government jobs, if not in proportion to their share of the population (20 percent of the city, 14 percent of Hillsborough County), at least in comparison to the total exclusion of earlier years. School integration even proceeded to the point where substantial busing was resorted to, thus reducing the incidence of racially lopsided schools.

The moderate tone of local politics has been reflected in broad community acceptance of the various federal antipoverty programs, a phenomenon all the more exceptional when one recalls that a large segment of Tampa's population is made up of white Southerners from Georgia, Alabama, and South Carolina. They were probably responsible for George Wallace's strong showing (33.0 percent) in the county in 1968. But the area is also 20 percent Latin (Spanish, Cuban, and Italian *) and has elected two Latin mayors and a Latin state senator in recent years. The Latins are fairly well off economically and progressive politically. Except for Presidential elections, when it is fighting territory, Tampa tends to vote Democratic, just as one would expect in a workingman's town.

Basking in the sun on the seaward side of Tampa Bay lies St. Petersburg, removed from Tampa by just a few miles of open water but its diametric opposite by almost any standard you can think of.

Tampa is a rich ethnic stew; St. Petersburg has people from everywhere in the U.S.A., but predominantly it is white, middle-class America.

Tampa has 3 percent less old folks than the Florida average; St. Petersburg has twice as many (30.6 percent) and sometimes thinks it succeeded too well in its early slogan—"St. Pete, the Perfect Retirement Center."

Tampa lives off its port and old-style factories; St. Petersburg lives off the pension checks of its retirees and a sprinkling of electronic-aerospace companies which have filtered in since the 1950s.

Tampa is Democratic; St. Petersburg pioneered with present-day Republicanism in Florida.

Tampa is a leading antipoverty city; St. Petersburg has little patience for such programs and in the late 1960s angrily drove a girls' Job Corps Center out of town on the basis that the federal government was running a "disorderly house."

Tampa seems to be trying to build bridges between its white and black communities; St. Petersburg rather callously broke a 1968 strike by Negro sanitation workers who had the temerity to suggest that salaries as low as $3,890 a year were not enough to support a worker and his family in the modern U.S.A.

But when it comes to newspapers, the pattern suddenly reverses:

The Tampa *Tribune*, property of the Richmond, Virginia, papers, is generally conservative; The St. Petersburg *Times*, owned by local publisher Nelson Poynter, is liberal and sometimes downright crusading. (Poynter's chosen successor is Eugene Patterson, Pulitzer prizewinning veteran of the Atlanta *Constitution* and the Washington *Post*.)

St. Petersburg's role as a retirement-vacation center has been well set since the 1880s, when the *American Medical Association Journal* said the climate made it the healthiest place in the world to live. How that judgment could have been made only a decade after nearby Tampa was ravaged by yellow fever remains something of a mystery. But St. Pete has always been expert in the art of self-promotion. Since 1910, the *Evening Independent* (now owned by the *Times*) has offered a free newspaper any day the sun fails to shine, and it has had to pay off on an average of only four times a year.

In 1918 St. Petersburg became the first city in the world to hire a press agent, and the succeeding years have been filled with all manner of

* Many of Tampa's Italians, oddly enough, speak Spanish. They came first to work in the cigar factories, where Spanish was the commonly spoken language.

promotion campaigns. The latest, in the 1960s, tried to downpedal the city's reputation as a geriatric heaven and emphasize instead the glowing opportunities for investment, family vacation, and business relocation. A number of the fabled green benches, where the old folks congregate to exchange reminiscences and snooze in the sun, were removed, as were two other favorite gathering spots of the oldsters—the old rococo stucco Municipal Pier building and the Tourist Information Center. A modernistic six-story dining-recreation-shopping building rose at the Municipal Pier, and the city can now boast of a $5 million Bayfront Center auditorium and arena, a new art museum, library, and municipal marina all in the million-dollar class, a new Hilton hotel, and a $5 million federal building.

There is still a lot to attract the senior citizens, however, including shuffleboard courts, afternoon band concerts in Williams Park, and quick one-dollar blood pressure tests in local drug stores.

Depending on their economic status, St. Pete's elderly are to be found in stately old hotels, $50,000 retirement homes in posh sections, dingy downtown rooming houses, or in infinite rows of little white cottages surrounded by palm trees and tropical flowers. The big middle-class elderly vote was an early foundation of the Republican revival which brought GOP control of most local government positions and, starting with the 1954 election, Florida's first Republican Congressman of the 20th century. But the St. Petersburg–Pinellas area is not irrevocably Republican. In 1964, when Goldwater ran and many of Florida's redneck areas turned Republican for the first time in living memory, Pinellas rebelled and gave Lyndon Johnson 55 percent of its vote. The implied Goldwaterian threat to the Social Security card was just too much to contemplate. In 1970, in a wave of revulsion against the swashbuckling Claude Kirk, the county gave 54.7 percent of its vote to Democrat Reubin Askew for governor. In the 1972 Presidential primary, St. Petersburg and Tampa were relatively weak for Wallace and strong for the liberal contenders, suggesting that as far as Democratic primaries are concerned, the area now rivals Miami as a bastion of liberalism.

One activity in which the Tampa Bay area seems to have an edge on the rest of Florida is baseball winter training. St. Petersburg has the St. Louis Cardinals and New York Mets, Tampa the Cincinnati Reds, Clearwater the Phillies, Bradenton the Kansas City Athletics and nearby Sarasota the Chicago White Sox. Florida cities bid anxiously to get these teams, since the exhibition games can be a great boon to late winter tourism.

Sarasota used to have another form of winter training: the circus. Now the great Ringling Bros. and Barnum & Bailey has migrated a few miles south to the town of Venice, where animals, trainers, clowns, acrobats, and all the rest go through their paces each winter before heading north in March.* In matters of arts and the intellect Sarasota seems to lead all Florida. MacKinlay Kantor is only one of several well known authors and cartoonists in residence, and the area has a plethora of art schools and shows, little theater and concert

* Sarasota is not likely to soon forget its circus association. Area Congressman James A. Haley married into the Ringling family and once managed the circus; he was the man who took responsibility for the great Hartford tent fire and served a term in jail as a consequence. Sarasota now has a delightful Ringling Museum of Art with outstanding Baroque and Renaissance collections.

groups. Some renowned architects have designed local schools, homes, and churches. On the university front, New College is taking only the brightest youngsters and hopes to become the "Harvard of the South." I. M. Pei designed buildings for New College, where the administration building is the old Ringling mansion. A roomier and lower-keyed city than most others in Florida, Sarasota may have a bright future if it can keep its population growth in bounds. In 1950 the city had 18,896 people; in 1970, 40,237. Many of the "quieter" well-off select it as their retirement home.

At remote Cape Haze, a few miles south of Sarasota, a new town named Rotonda West is being built and may eventually accommodate 50,000 people. The shape of the town will be an interesting one: eight wedge-shaped slices, separated by canals, each with its own 18-hole golf course, all converging on a commercial center. Harvard University Business School professor Philip David, who is chairman of the company developing Rotonda West, claims "it's really a Renaissance plan and was developed hundreds of years ago for security. One of the big advantages is that it gives people today a greater sense of security and more internal participation."

Several miles farther south, at Fort Myers, two huge communities designed to attract retirees have been erected on pine and palmetto flats beside the Caloosahatchee River. Lee County, where this development is located, grew from 54,539 people in 1960 to 105,216 in 1970.

By contrast, Collier County, directly to the south, has only 38,040 (a third of them in the city of Naples with its posh retirement community). After that, all that remains of the southwest coast are swamplands including the Ten Thousand Islands (of mangrove) and Everglades National Park.

Then, across Florida Bay, lie the Keys, dotted with resort areas of every stripe. The fever pitch of recreation-area development has threatened to engulf the Keys; in 1972, in fact, a dredge-and-fill moratorium was imposed to prevent ecological disaster along the dazzling coral reefs.

Key Largo, on the northern end of the Keys, offers visitors the country's first continental underseas park (Pennekamp Coral Reef State Park) and also the luxurious accommodations of the Ocean Reef Club (a combination hotel, yachtsmen's haven, and vacation-retirement home development where a lot alone can set one back $39,000). At the Keys' southern tip is the old city of Key West, where the Census takers found 27,563 people in 1970. The city's real days of glory, though, were around 1880, when it had 9,890 people and was the largest city in Florida. The prosperity came from being the world's largest cigar manufacturing center and from profits of the "salvage" crews which used to go to the "rescue" of ships wrecked on the reefs and shoals surrounding the Keys. Eventually, both these sources of income dried up—the salvaging by government decree, cigar producing by Ybor's move to Tampa. But Key West kept the ethnic mix of its early years: many Cubans, "Conchs" who trace their ancestry back to Cockney English settlers in the Bahamas, Yankee sailing men, Virginia merchants, and a number of native Bahamians.

Flagler's railroad brought serious tourism, but by the 1930s Key West seemed to have reached the end of its rope. The depression had hit hard, and then the 1935 hurricane swept the railroad into the sea. Only the Naval activity of World War II (chiefly in defense of the Panama Canal) returned prosperity. In recent decades, the Navy has been key to the city's life, and Key West suffers intermittent pangs of fear of a pullout of the military installations.

A big factor in putting Key West back on the map after World War II—outside of the Overseas Highway, a precondition to meaningful tourism—was all the publicity stemming from President Harry Truman's frequent visits to his "little White House" there. But then, in 1959, came Castro's revolution in Cuba and an end to the bustling ferry and air service to Havana that had been a major reason many tourists chose to come all the way to Key West at all. During the 1960s, the city's population dropped a full 18 percent, while the rest of Florida boomed. Distant, isolated, so totally exposed to the sea, with its own distinctive mix of nationalities and ways of making a living, Key West has always been a place set apart from greater Florida. It doubtless always will be.

ACKNOWLEDGMENTS

THESE BOOKS HAD TO BE, by their very character, a personal odyssey and personal task. But they would never have been possible without the kind assistance of hundreds of people. First there were those who encouraged me to go forward when the idea was first conceived: my wife Barbara (little imagining the long curtailments of family life that would ensue, and whose encouragement was vital throughout); my parents and other relatives; my editor, Evan W. Thomas, vice president and editor of W. W. Norton & Co.; John Gunther, my agent, Sterling Lord, and his assistant at that time, Jonathan Walton; Richard Kluger, Bernard Haldane, Roan Conrad, Joseph Foote, and William B. Dickinson; Richard M. Scammon, director of the Elections Research Center and coauthor of *The Real Majority;* and D. B. Hardeman, professor of political science and biographer of the late House Speaker Sam Rayburn. A fellowship at the Woodrow Wilson International Center for Scholars provided intellectual and physical sustenance.

My very warmest thanks go to those who read the draft manuscript in its entirety: Evan W. Thomas; Russell L. Bradley; Jean Allaway; Frederick H. Sontag, public relations consultant of South Orange, N.J.; and copy editor Calvin Towle at W. W. Norton & Company. In addition, each of the state chapters was submitted to several persons living in, and having extensive knowledge of, the state in question. The returning corrections and amendments were immensely helpful. The names of those readers appear in the longer list of names below; I choose not to list them here lest someone hold them responsible for something said or unsaid in one of the chapters, and of course the full responsibility for that lies with me.

Various friends and associates helped with many of the details of research, and for that I am especially indebted to Thomas Ward, Judith Kolberg, Oliver Cromwell, Geneva Torrey, Barbara Hurlbutt, Prentice and Alice Bowsher, Anne Gault, and DeMar and Claudia Teuscher. And without the cheery and efficient services of my typist, Merciel Dixon, the manuscript would never have seen the light of day at all. Rose Franco of W. W. Norton helped in innumerable ways; I am indebted to designer Marjorie Flock and production manager Ancy Marasia of Norton; and credit goes to Russell Lenz, former chief cartographer of the *Christian Science Monitor,* for what I feel is the superb job he did on the state and city maps.

Across the country, people gave generously of their time to brief me on the developments of the past several years in their states and cities. I am listing those from the seven Deep South States below, together with many people who helped with national and interstate themes. The names of some officials are included whom I had interviewed in the year or two prior to beginning work on this project, when the background from those interviews proved helpful with this book. To all, my sincerest thanks.

PERSONS INTERVIEWED

Affiliations of interviewees are as of time of author's interview with them.

AINSWORTH, Robert A., Federal Judge, New Orleans, La.
ALLBRIGHT, Charles, Winthrop Rockefeller & Associates, Little Rock, Ark.
ALLEN, Ivan, Mayor of Atlanta, Georgia
AMRINE, Michael, Former Aide to Gov. Winthrop Rockefeller of Arkansas, Washington, D.C.
ASHDOWN, Sam, Special Assistant to Lt. Gov. Tom Adams (Fla.)

ASKEW, Reubin, Governor of Florida
AYERS, Harry Brandt, Editor and Publisher, Anniston *Star,* Anniston, Ala.
BALDING, Marvin, Press Secretary to Sen. John J. McClellan (Ark.)
BALDWIN, David G., Director, Public Affairs Division, American Medical Association, and Former Correspondent, New Orleans *Item,* Washington, D. C.
BANDY, Lee, Washington Correspondent, *The State* (Columbia, S. C.)
BARTLEY, Numan V., Professor of History, University of Georgia, Athens, Ga.
BASS, Jack, South Carolina Correspondent, Charlotte *Observer,* Columbia, S. C.
BATES, Lester, Mayor of Columbia, S. C.
BAXLEY, Bill, Attorney General of Alabama, Montgomery, Ala.
BECKER, J. Bill, President, Arkansas State AFL-CIO, Little Rock, Ark.
BEIMAN, Irving, Business Editor, Birmingham *News,* Birmingham, Ala.
BELSER, Heyward, Chairman, South Carolina House Judiciary Committee, Columbia, S. C.
BENEDICT, Howard, The Associated Press, Cocoa Beach, Fla.
BENNETT, Charles E., U.S. Representative from Florida
BILLINGSLEY, Orzell, Attorney and Civil Rights Leader, Birmingham, Ala.
BIOSSAT, Bruce, National Correspondent, Newspaper Enterprise Association, Washington, D. C.
BLACKWELL, Clinton, Managing Editor, Gulfport *Daily Herald,* Gulfport, Miss.
BLAKEY, Durward, M.D., Director, Division of Preventable Disease Control, Mississippi State Board of Health, Jackson, Miss.
BLATT, Solomon, Speaker, South Carolina House of Representatives, Columbia, S. C.
BOGGS, Hale, U.S. Representative from Louisiana (deceased)
BOHNING, Don, Correspondent, Miami *Herald,* Miami, Fla.
BOYD, William J. D., Assistant Director, National Municipal League, New York City
BRODER, David S., Correspondent and Columnist, Washington *Post,* Washington, D. C.
BROWN, Tom Watson, Attorney, Atlanta, Ga.
BUSBY, Horace, Former Presidential Assistant, Washington, D. C.
BUSSIE, Victor, President, AFL-CIO State Council, Baton Rouge, La.
CANNON, Lou, Correspondent, Washington *Post,* Washington, D. C.
CARR, Andrew, Plantation Owner, Clarksdale, Miss.
CARR, Oscar, Jr., Plantation Owner, Clarksdale, Miss.
CARTER, Hodding, III, Editor, *Delta Democrat-Times,* Greenville, Miss.
CARTER, Jimmy, Governor of Georgia
CASSELLA, William N., Jr., Executive Director, National Municipal League, New York City
CAUTHEN, John K., Executive Vice President, South Carolina Textile Manufacturers' Association, Columbia, S. C.
CHADWICK, John R., Editorial Writer, Birmingham *News,* Birmingham, Ala.
CHILES, Lawton, U.S. Senator from Florida
CHOATE, Robert, National Institute of Public Affairs, Washington, D. C.
CHRISS, Nicholas C., Southern Correspondent, Los Angeles *Times,* Houston, Tex.
CHUBBUCK, James, Professor and Director, Institute of Politics, Loyola University, New Orleans, La.
CLARK, Timothy B., Executive Editor, *National Journal,* Washington, D. C.
CLECKLER, Robert M., Administrative Assistant to Gov. Albert Brewer, Montgomery, Ala.
COCKRILL, Sterling R., Jr., State Representative, Little Rock, Ark.
COFFIN, Alex, City Hall Reporter, Atlanta *Constitution & Journal,* Atlanta, Ga.
CONLEY, Bill, Director of Press Relations for Gov. Winthrop Rockefeller (Ark.)
COOPER, Jerome A., Attorney, Birmingham, Ala.
COOPER, Owen, President, Mississippi Chemical Corporation, Yazoo City, Miss.
CORPORON, John, Former News Director, WDSU-TV, New Orleans, La.
CROSS, Edward, M. D., Department of Health, Education and Welfare, Washington, D. C.
CUMMING, Joseph B., Jr., Southern Correspondent, *Newsweek,* Atlanta, Ga.
DANIEL, W. John, President, Delta & Pine Land Co., Scott, Miss.
DASTE, Verdun R., Publicity Manager, Board of Commissioners of the Port of New Orleans, New Orleans, La.
DAUER, Manning J., Professor of Political Science, University of Florida, Gainesville, Fla.
DAVIS, Ovid, Vice President for Governmental Affairs, The Coca-Cola Company, Atlanta, Ga.
DeLAUGHTER, Jerry, Director, Institute of Politics in Mississippi, Millsaps College, Jackson, Miss.
DENT, Harry, Special Counsel to the President (Richard Nixon) and Former Aide to Sen. Strom Thurmond (S. C.), Washington, D. C.
DIXON, Mrs. Margaret, Managing Editor, Baton Rouge *Advocate,* Baton Rouge, La. (deceased)
DOMINICK, Richard, State Senator, Birmingham, Ala.
DONALD, Leroy, State Editor, Arkansas *Gazette,* Little Rock, Ark.
DUNAWAY, Edwin E., Former Justice, Arkansas Supreme Court, Little Rock, Ark.
DURR, Clifford, Former Commissioner, Federal Communications Commission, Wetumpka, Ala.
DURR, Mrs. Virginia, Wetumpka, Ala.
DuVALL, Leland, Business & Farm Editor, Arkansas *Gazette,* Little Rock, Ark.
ELLIS, Dorothy, Institute of Politics, Loyola University, New Orleans, La.
EMMERICH, J. Oliver, Editor, McComb *Enterprise & Journal,* McComb, Miss.
ESSER, George, Executive Director, Southern Regional Council, Atlanta, Ga.
EVERS, Charles, Mayor of Fayette and Democratic National Committeeman, Fayette, Miss.
FALKENBERRY, Roswell L., Publisher and Editor, Selma *Times-Journal,* Selma, Ala.
FLOWERS, Walter M., U.S. Representative from Alabama
FOWLER, Donald, Executive Director, Democratic State Committee, Columbia, S. C.
FOX, Al, Political Reporter, Birmingham *News,* Birmingham, Ala.
FRANCIS, Norman, President, Xavier University, New Orleans, La.
FRASIER, Waldo, Executive Vice President, Arkansas Farm Bureau Federation, Little Rock, Ark.
FREE, James, Washington Correspondent, Birmingham *News,* Washington, D. C.
GAILLARD, J. Palmer, Jr., Mayor of Charleston, S. C.
GARDNER, Ellis B., President, Ingalls Shipbuilding Corp., Pascagoula, Miss.
GARDNER, The Rev. James Edward, President, Alabama Christian Movement for Human Rights, Birmingham, Ala.
GASTON, Paul M., Professor of History, University of Virginia, Charlottesville, Va.
GEORGE, Elmer, Executive Director, Georgia Municipal Association, Atlanta, Ga.

GIBBONS, Sam M., U.S. Representative from Florida
GILLIS, James, Director, State Highway Department, Atlanta, Ga.
GILLIS, Jim, Columnist, New Orleans *Times-Picayune,* New Orleans, La.
GLASS, Andrew J., Congressional Correspondent, *National Journal,* Washington, D. C.
GODFREY, John M., Financial Economist, Federal Reserve Bank of Atlanta, Atlanta, Ga.
GONZMART, César, Proprietor, The Columbia Restaurant, Tampa, Fla.
GOODWIN, George, Bell & Stanton, Inc., Public Relations, Atlanta, Ga.
GORMIN, Kenneth, Public Relations, New Orleans, La.
GUIDRY, Father Joseph, St. Gabriel's Catholic Mission, Mound Bayou, Miss.
GULLIVER, Hal, Associate Editor, Atlanta *Constitution,* Atlanta, Ga.
GUNTHER, John, Author, New York City (deceased)
HALEY, James A., U.S. Representative from Florida
HALL, Cody, Executive Editor, Anniston *Star,* Anniston, Ala.
HALLGREN, Art, First Vice President, Florida AFL-CIO, Miami, Fla.
HAMMETT, Earl, Senior Vice-President, Ingalls Shipbuilding Corp., Pascagoula, Miss.
HARDEMAN, D. B., Professor of Political Science and Former Aide to House Speaker Sam Rayburn, Washington, D. C.
HARRIS, David, Public Affairs Director, Redstone Arsenal, Huntsville, Ala.
HARRIS, Gordon, Public Affairs Director, John F. Kennedy Space Center, Kennedy Space Center, Fla.
HATCH, John, Director, Community Health Services, Tufts-Delta Health Center, Mound Bayou, Miss.
HAVARD, William C., Dean, Virginia Polytechnic Institute and State University, Blacksburg, Va.
HEALEY, George, Jr., Executive Editor, New Orleans *Times-Picayune,* New Orleans, La.
HEARIN, Robert, Chairman of the Board, First National Bank, Jackson, Miss.
HESSER, Charles, Correspondent, Miami *News,* Miami, Fla.
HILL, Lister, Former U.S. Senator, Montgomery, Ala.
HOBBS, Sam Earle, Attorney, Selma, Ala.
HOLLINGS, Ernest F., U.S. Senator from South Carolina
HOPKINS, Sam, Correspondent, Atlanta *Constitution & Journal,* Atlanta, Ga.
HOWE, Gedney, Attorney, Charleston, S. C.
HUSSEY, Ruth, Public Information Office, Environmental Protection Agency, Washington, D. C.
JACKSON, Maynard N., Vice Mayor of Atlanta, Georgia
JACOBSON, James, Assistant Managing Editor, Birmingham *News,* Birmingham, Ala.
JENKINS, Herbert T., Chief of Police, Atlanta, Ga.
JENKINS, Ray, Editorial Page Editor, *Alabama Journal,* Montgomery, Ala.
JOHNSON, Charles A., Executive Secretary, Mississippi Education Association, Jackson, Miss.
JOHNSON, Frank M., Jr., Federal Judge, Montgomery, Ala.
JOHNSON, Kenneth E., President, City Council, Huntsville, Ala.
JOHNSON, Leroy R., State Senator, Atlanta, Ga.
JONES, Carlisle, Director of Public Affairs, Aerospace Industries Association, Washington, D. C.
JONES, Robert E., U.S. Representative from Alabama
JOSEPH, Stephen, M. D., Department of Health, Education and Welfare, Washington, D. C.
KANTOR, MacKinlay, Author, Sarasota, Fla.
KELSO, Iris, Correspondent, WDSU-TV, New Orleans, La.
KEY, Jack, Florida Bureau of Law Enforcement, Miami, Florida
KIEPPER, Alan F., General Manager, Metropolitan Atlanta Rapid Transit Authority, Atlanta, Ga.
KILGORE, Donald G., Jr., President, South Carolina Medical Association, Greenville, S. C.
KIRKLAND, Lane, Secretary-Treasurer AFL-CIO, Washington, D. C.
KLAPPER, Dr. Margaret, Associate Dean, University of Alabama in Birmingham, Birmingham, Ala.
KNOWLES, Robert P., Wisconsin State Senator and Arrangements Director, 1964 and 1968 Republican National Conventions
LANDRIEU, Moon, Mayor of New Orleans, La. (Interview conducted by Timothy B. Clark and William Lilley III of the *National Journal*)
LANE, Mills, President, Citizens & Southern Bank, Atlanta, Ga
LANG, Raymond, Miami Metro Publicity Bureau, Miami, Fla.
LEMANN, Stephen B., Attorney and Civic Leader, New Orleans, La.
LEWIS, John, Executive Director, Voter Education Project, Atlanta, Ga.
LIDDELL, Wesley James, Sr., Mayor of Mound Bayou, Miss.
LYONS, Marvin L., Executive Director, Louisiana Municipal Association, Baton Rouge, La.
MADDOX, Lester, Lieutenant Governor and Former Governor of Georgia
MASON, Gilbert, M. D., Biloxi, Miss.
MASSELL, Sam, Mayor of Atlanta, Georgia
MATTHEWS, Charles D., Chairman, Arkansas State Democratic Committee, North Little Rock, Ark.
MAZO, Earl, Journalist, Washington, D. C.
McCLUNG, Dan, Executive Assistant to Mayor Moon Landrieu, New Orleans, La.
McDERMOTT, John, Correspondent, Miami *Herald,* Miami, Fla.
McGHEE, John, President *The State,* Columbia, S. C.
McMANUS, Charles, Law Clerk to Judge Frank M. Johnson, Jr., Montgomery, Alabama
McPHERSON, Harry C., Jr., Special Counsel to the President (Lyndon B. Johnson), Washington, D. C.
MEEK, Edwin, Director of Public Information, University of Mississippi, Oxford, Miss.
MERVIS, Mrs. Helen, Civic Leader, New Orleans, La.
MEYER, Hank, Hank Meyer Associates, Miami Beach, Fla.
MINOR, Wilson F. (Bill), Mississippi Correspondent, New Orleans *Times-Picayune,* Jackson, Miss.
MITCHELL, Mrs. Frieda, The Penn Center, Fragmore, S. C.
MOORE, Powell, Press Aide to Sen. Richard Russell (Ga.)
MORGAN, Cecil, Founder, Public Affairs Research Council of Louisiana, New Orleans, La.
MORGAN, Charles, Jr., Southern Director, American Civil Liberties Union, Atlanta, Ga.
MORRIS, Earle E., Jr., State Senator and Former Democratic State Chairman, Pickens, S. C.
MORRIS, James A., Commissioner, South Caro-

lina Commission on Higher Education, Columbia, S. C.
MURPHY, Harry H., Jr., Director of Public Information, University System of Georgia, Atlanta, Georgia
MURPHY, Reg, Editor, Atlanta *Constitution,* Atlanta, Ga.
NELSON, Jack, Bureau Chief, Los Angeles *Times,* Atlanta, Ga.
NETTLES, Bert, State Representative, Mobile, Ala.
NICHOLSON, John B., American Bankers Association, Washington, D. C.
NOLAN, Fred, Director, Jackson Urban League, Jackson, Miss.
O'BOYLE, Ted, Reporter, Gulfport *Daily Herald,* Gulfport, Miss.
O'CONNOR, Ralston, Manager, Harlem Heights Station Farm Labor Camp, Winter Garden, Fla.
PARR, Rex, Manager, Old Top Labor Camp, Tildenville, Fla.
PAUL, Robert, General Manager, The Masonite Corporation, Laurel, Miss.
PAYTON, Benjamin F., President, Benedict College, Columbia, S. C.
PEPPER, Claude, U.S. Representative from Florida
PERKINS, John, State Representative, Meridian, Miss.
PERRY, John, Jr., President, Perry Publications, Inc., West Palm Beach, Fla.
PERRY, Matthew J., Attorney and Civil Rights Leader, Columbia, S. C.
PETERSON, Dr. John, Administrator, Arkansas Employment Security Division, Little Rock, Ark.
POOLE, Victor, President, Bank of Moundville; Member, State Board of Education, Moundville, Ala.
POPE, Richard, Owner, Cypress Gardens, Winter Haven, Fla.
PORTMAN, John C., Jr., Architect, Atlanta, Ga.
POWELL, Jody, Press Secretary to Gov. Jimmy Carter (Ga.)
PRIDE, Don, Press Secretary to Gov. Reubin Askew (Fla.)
RADNEY, Tom, State Senator, Alexander City, Ala.
RAMSAY, Claude, President, Mississippi AFL-CIO, Jackson, Miss.
REED, Clarke, Chairman, Mississippi Republican Party, Greenville, Miss.
RENWICK, Edwin, Institute of Politics, Loyola University, New Orleans, La.
RICHARDSON, Mrs. Martha, Civic Leader, Huntsville, Ala.
RICKER, William, Executive Director, Operation New Birmingham, Birmingham, Ala.
ROARK, Dr. Donald B., Personnel Director, Mississippi Chemical Corporation, Yazoo City, Miss.
ROCKEFELLER, Mrs. Jeannette, Morrilton, Ark.
ROCKEFELLER, Winthrop, Governor of Arkansas (deceased)
ROGERS, Lee, Public Relations Director, Lockheed-Georgia Co., Marietta, Ga.
RONE, William E., Jr., Editorial Page Editor, *The State,* Columbia, S. C.
ROSE, Frank, Former President, University of Alabama; President, L. Q. C. Lamar Society, Washington, D. C.
ROZZELL, Forrest, Executive Secretary, Arkansas Education Association, Little Rock, Ark.
RUFF, John, M. D., Magnolia, Ark.
SANCHEZ, Felix, Migrant Farm Worker, Winter Garden, Fla.
SCAMMON, Richard M., Director, Elections Research Institute, and Former Director of the Census, Washington, D. C.
SEIBELS, George G., Mayor of Birmingham, Ala.
SHOCKLEY, Ray, Executive Vice President, South Carolina Textile Manufacturers' Association, Columbia, S. C.
SIMMONS, William, Director, The Citizens Council, Jackson, Miss.
SIMMS, Leroy, Publisher, Huntsville *Times,* Huntsville, Ala.
SIMS, The Rt. Rev. Bennett, Bishop, Episcopal Diocese of Atlanta, Ga.
SLATTERY, Bart J., Jr., Public Affairs Director, Marshall Space Flight Center, Huntsville, Ala.
SMITH, B. F., Executive Vice President, The Delta Council, Stoneville, Miss.
SMITH, Doug, Reporter, Arkansas Gazette, Little Rock, Ark.
SMITH, Henry, Public Information Office, Bureau of the Census, Washington, D. C.
SMITH, Robert, Manager, News & Publications, Board of Commissioners of the Port of New Orleans, La.
SMITH, Robert L. T., Sr., NAACP Leader, Jackson, Miss.
SOLER, Frank, Correspondent, Miami *Herald,* Miami, Fla.
SPICER, Don, Secretary of Commerce, State of Florida, Tallahassee, Fla.
STAFFORD, Charles, Washington Bureau Chief, St. Petersburg *Times,* Washington, D. C.
STAGG, Tom, Former Republican National Committeeman, Shreveport, La.
STARR, Douglas, Director of Information and Research, Florida Department of Commerce, Tallahassee, Fla.
STARR, John Robert, Associated Press Bureau Chief, Little Rock, Ark.
STEIMEL, Edward, Executive Director, Public Affairs Research Council of Louisiana, Baton Rouge, La.
STEPHENS, W. R. (Witt), Chairman of the Board and President, Arkansas-Louisiana Gas Company, Little Rock, Ark.
STERN, Edgar, Jr., Business Leader, New Orleans, La.
STOUDEMIRE, Robert H., Professor, Bureau of Governmental Research & Service, University of South Carolina, Columbia, S. C.
STREET, Bruce, Aide to Governor Winthrop Rockefeller (Ark.)
STREVEL, Howard, Alabama State President, Steelworkers of America, Birmingham, Ala.
SUTTER, Donald, Executive Vice President, The Hancock Bank, Gulfport, Miss.
TAYLOR, Dr. Charles, Director of Research, Federal Reserve Bank of Atlanta, Atlanta, Ga.
THOMPSON, Edna, Migrant Farm Worker, Winter Garden, Fla.
THOMPSON, Ruby, Statistician, Mississippi Department of Education, Jackson, Miss.
THURMOND, Strom, U.S. Senator from South Carolina and 1948 States Rights Party Presidential Candidate
TOWNSEND, Vincent, Sr., Assistant to Publisher, Birmingham *News,* Birmingham, Ala.
TROVILLION, Frank, Florida Citrus Mutual, Lakeland, Fla.
TUREAUD, A. P., NAACP Counsel, New Orleans, La. (deceased)
TYSON, Remer, Political Editor, Atlanta *Constitution,* Atlanta, Ga.
VANCE, Robert S., Chairman, State Democratic Executive Committee of Alabama, Birmingham, Ala.
VANCE, Sarah, Researcher, Public Affairs Research Council of Louisiana, Baton Rouge, La.
VAN LANDINGHAM, Bill, Director of Public Affairs, Citizens & Southern Bank, Atlanta, Ga.
VENUS, Dr. Charles E., College of Business Ad-

ministration, University of Arkansas, Little Rock, Ark.
WAGNER, Dr. Kenneth, Director, Mississippi Research & Development Center, Jackson, Miss.
WALL, Marvin, Voter Education Project, Atlanta, Georgia
WALLACE, George C., Governor of Alabama
WARING, Thomas R., Editor, Charleston *News & Courier,* Charleston, S. C.
WATTERS, Pat, Author and Editor for the Southern Regional Council, Atlanta, Ga.
WEBER, Palmer, Former CIO-PAC Representative, Charlottesville, Va.
WEEKS, Barney, President, Alabama Labor Council, AFL-CIO, Birmingham, Ala.
WEEKS, Dr. David, Associate Director, Tufts-Delta Health Center, Mound Bayou, Miss.
WEST, Jay W., Editor, Laurel *Leader-Call,* Laurel, Miss.
WEST, John C., Governor of South Carolina
WISENBURG, Karl, Attorney, Pascagoula, Miss.
WILLIAMS, John B., Governor of Mississippi
WILLIE, Charles V., Professor of Sociology, Maxwell Graduate School of Citizenship and Public Affairs, Syracuse University, N. Y.
WILTSEE, Herbert L., Director, Southern Regional Office, Council of State Governments, Atlanta, Ga.
WINSLETT, Merrill, Administrative Assistant, Office of Sen. Spessard Holland (Fla.)
WINTER, William, Lieutenant Governor of Mississippi
WOODWARD, Mr. and Mrs. Charles H., Civic Leaders, Charleston, S. C.
WORKMAN, William, Editor, *The State,* Columbia, S. C.
YOUNG, Sinway, President, South Carolina State Labor Council (AFL-CIO), Columbia, S. C.

BIBLIOGRAPHY

DESPITE THE EXTENSIVE INTERVIEWS for these books, reference was also made to books and articles on the individual states and cities, their history and present-day condition. To the authors whose works I have drawn upon, my sincerest thanks.

NATIONAL BOOKS

Barone, Michael, Ujifusa, Grant, and Matthews, Douglas. *The Almanac of American Politics—1972.* Boston: Gambit Publishing Co., 1972.

Birmingham, Stephen. *The Right People—A Portrait of the American Social Establishment.* Boston: Little, Brown, 1968.

Book of the States. The Council of State Governments. Published biennially, Lexington, Ky.

Broder, David S. *The Party's Over: The Failure of Politics in America.* New York: Harper & Row, 1972.

Brownson, Charles B. *Congressional Staff Directory.* Published annually, Washington, D.C.

1969 Census of Agriculture, Bureau of the Census, Washington, D. C.

1970 Census of Population, Bureau of the Census, Washington, D. C.

CBS News Campaign '72 handbooks—Democratic National Convention, Republican National Convention, various primary states, and general election. New York: CBS News, 1972.

Citizens Conference on State Legislatures. Various studies including *The Sometime Governments: A Critical Study of the 50 American Legislatures,* by John Burns. New York: Bantam Books, 1971.

Congress and the Nation, 1945–64, and Vol. II, *1965–68.* Congressional Quarterly Service, Washington, D. C., 1967 and 1969.

David, Paul T., *Party Strength in the United States,* 1872–1970. Charlottesville: University Press of Virginia, 1972.

Editor and Publisher International Year Book. New York: Editor and Publisher. Published annually.

Employment and Earnings—States and Areas, 1939–71. U.S. Department of Labor, Bureau of Labor Statistics, Washington, D. C., 1972.

Encyclopedia Americana. Annual editions. New York: Americana Corporation. (Includes excellent state and city review articles.)

Farb, Peter. *Face of North America—The Natural History of a Continent.* New York: Harper & Row, 1963.

Fodor-Shell Travel Guides U.S.A. Fodor's Modern Guides, Inc., Litchfield, Conn. (In several regional editions, the best of the travel guides.)

From Sea to Shining Sea—A Report on the American Environment—Our National Heritage. President's Council on Recreation and Natural Beauty, Washington, D. C., 1968.

Gunther, John. *Inside U.S.A.* New York: Harper & Row, 1947 and 1951.

Jacob, Herbert, and Vines, Kenneth N. *Politics in the American States: A Comparative Analysis.* Boston: Little, Brown, 1971.

Life Pictorial Atlas of the World. Editors of *Life* and Rand McNally. New York: Time, Inc., 1961.

McPherson, Harry. *A Political Education.* Boston: Little Brown, 1972.

The National Atlas of the United States of America. Geological Survey, U.S. Department of the Interior, Washington, D. C., 1970.

Pearson, Drew, and Anderson, Jack. *The Case Against Congress.* New York: Simon & Schuster, 1968.

Phillips, Kevin H. *The Emerging Republican Majority.* New Rochelle, N.Y.: Arlington House, 1969.

The Quality of Life in the United States: 1970, Index, Rating and Statistics, by Ben-Chieh Liu with Robert Gustafson and Bruce Marcy. Kansas City, Mo.: Midwest Research Institute, 1973.

Rankings of the States. Published annually by the Research Division, National Education Assn., Washington, D. C.

Ridgeway, James. *The Closed Corporation—American Universities in Crisis.* New York: Random House, 1968.

Saloma, John S. III, and Sontag, Frederick H. *Parties: The Real Opportunity for Effective Citizen Politics.* New York: Knopf, 1972.

Sanford, Terry. *Storm Over the States.* New York: McGraw-Hill, 1967.

Scammon, Richard M., ed. *America Votes—A Handbook of Contemporary American Election Statistics.* Published biennially by the Government Affairs Institute, through Congressional Quarterly, Washington, D. C.

Scammon, Richard M., and Wattenberg, Ben J.

The Real Majority—An Extraordinary Examination of the American Electorate. New York: Coward-McCann, 1970.

Sharkansky, Ira. *The Maligned States: Policy Accomplishments, Problems, and Opportunities.* New York: McGraw Hill, 1972.

State and Local Finances. Published periodically by the Advisory Commission on Intergovernmental Relations, Washington, D. C.

State Government Finances. Published annually by The U.S. Department of Commerce, Bureau of the Census, Washington, D. C.

Statistical Abstract of the United States. Published annually by the U.S. Department of Commerce, Bureau of the Census, Washington, D. C.

Steinbeck, John. *Travels With Charley—In Search of America.* New York: Viking, 1961.

Survey of Current Business. U.S. Department of Commerce, Bureau of Economic Analysis, Washington, D. C., monthly. April and August editions contain full reports on geographic trends in personal income and per capita income.

Thayer, George. *The Farther Shores of Politics.* New York: Simon & Schuster, 1967.

These United States—Our Nation's Geography, History and People. Reader's Digest Assn., Pleasantville, N.Y., 1968.

Tour Books. Published annually by the American Automobile Assn., Washington, D. C.

Uniform Crime Reports for the United States. Published annually by the U.S. Department of Justice, Federal Bureau of Investigation, Washington, D. C.

Whyte, William H. *The Last Landscape.* Garden City, N.Y.: Doubleday, 1968.

Williams, Joe B. *U.S. Statistical Atlas.* Published biennially at Elmwood, Neb.

The World Almanac and Book of Facts. Published annually by Newspaper Enterprise Assn., Inc., New York and Cleveland.

REGIONAL BOOKS AND SOURCES

No region of America has been as exhaustively and continuously examined by writers as the South. Of the multitudinous writings available, I found these the most useful: *A History of the South,* 4th ed., by Francis Butler Simkins and Charles Pierce Roland (New York: Alfred A. Knopf, 1972); *Southern Politics in State and Nation,* by V. O. Key, Jr. (New York: Alfred A. Knopf, 1949); *The Changing Politics of the South,* edited by William C. Havard (Baton Rouge, La.: Louisiana State University Press, 1972); *The South and the Nation,* by Pat Watters (New York: Pantheon Books, 1969); *Haunted by God: The Cultural and Religious Experience of the South,* by James McBride Dabbs (Richmond, Va.: John Knox Press, 1972); *A Mind to Stay Here,* by John Egerton (New York: Macmillan, 1970); *Human Geography of the South,* by Robert B. Vance (Chapel Hill, N. C.: University of North Carolina Press, 1935). Especially good regional bibliographies are included in the Havard, Simkins-Roland, and Vance books. A pamphlet completely devoted to Southern bibliography was the American Historical Association's *The South in American History* (Washington: 1965).

The Mind of the South, by W. J. Cash (New York: Alfred A. Knopf, 1941); *The Burden of Southern History,* by C. Vann Woodward (Baton Rouge, La.: Louisiana State University Press, 1960); *The Legacy of the Civil War,* by Robert Penn Warren (New York: Random House, 1961); *The New South Creed: A Study in Southern Mythmaking,* by Paul M. Gaston (New York: Alfred A. Knopf, 1970); *The Strange Career of Jim Crow,* by C. Vann Woodward (New York: Oxford University Press, 1955); *Gothic Politics in the Deep South,* by Robert Sherrill (New York: Grossman, 1968); *From Thurmond to Wallace: Political Tendencies in Georgia, 1948–1968,* by Numan V. Bartley (Baltimore: Johns Hopkins Press, 1970); *The Southern Strategy,* by Reg Murphy and Hal Gulliver (New York: Scribner, 1971); *Change in the Contemporary South,* edited by Allen P. Sindler (Durham, N. C.: Duke University Press, 1963); *The Old South,* by John Osborne and others (New York: Time-Life Library of America, 1968); *The South Central States,* by Lawrence Goodwyn and others (New York: Time-Life Library of America, 1967); *The Emerging South,* by Thomas D. Clark (New York: Oxford University Press, 1961).

Report of the United States Civil Rights Commission—1959 (Washington: Government Printing Office). Includes the best review of state laws restricting the right to vote in the post-Civil War period, voting registration figures in the 1950s, and a good review of various states' reactions to the 1954 *Brown* decision of the U.S. Supreme Court. *Climbing Jacob's Ladder: The Arrival of Negroes in Southern Politics,* by Pat Watters and Reese Cleghorn (New York: Harcourt, 1967); *An American Dilemma: The Negro Problem and Modern Democracy,* by Gunnar Myrdal (New York: Harper, 1944); *Negroes and the New Southern Politics,* by Donald R. Matthews and James W. Prothro (New York: Harcourt, 1966); *The Shameful Blight: The Survival of Racial Discrimination in Voting in The South,* by Washington Research Project (Washington: Washington Research Project, 1972); "John Lewis: Keeper of the Dream," by Archie E. Allen, *New South,* Spring 1971; *Radicalism: Southern Style—A Commentary on Regional Extremism of the Right,* by Reese Cleghorn (Atlanta: Southern Regional Council, 1968).

Plantation Politics: The Southern Economic Heritage, by J. Earl Williams (Austin, Texas: Futura Press, 1972). *The Tax Structure of the Southern States: An Analysis,* by Eva Galambos (Atlanta: Southern Regional Council, 1969); *The Advancing South: Manpower Prospects and Problems,* by James G. Maddox (New York: The Twentieth Century Fund, 1967); *Let Them Eat Promises: The Politics of Hunger in America,* by Nick Kotz (Englewood Cliffs, N.J.: Prentice-Hall, 1969).

"That New South," by John Egerton, *The Progressive,* April 1972; "Some Reflections on the South," by George Esser, *New South,* Winter 1973; "The Changing South: National Incorporation of a Region," by John C. McKinney and Linda B. Bourque, *American Sociological Review,* June 1971; "A Hesitant New South: Fragile Promise on the Last Frontier," by Peter Schrag, *Saturday Review,* Feb. 12, 1972; " 'The Mind of the South,' " by Joseph B. Cumming, Jr., *Newsweek,* April 10, 1972; 'Dabbs Adds to Insights into Mind of South," by Jack Bass, Charlotte *Observer,* April 15, 1973; "From Where I Live," by Eudora Welty, *Delta Review,* November-December 1969.

"Southern Bloc Losing Grip on Congress," by Richard L. Strout, *Christian Science Monitor,* Nov. 25, 1972; "Old South of Russell Is Yielding to the New," by James Reston, Washington *Evening Star,* Jan. 22, 1971; "The State of the Opposition," an editorial in the Washington *Post,* Jan. 21, 1973; "South's Power Periled," by Kevin Phillips, Washington *Post,* Aug. 10, 1971; "Senate's Solid South: Gone With the Wind," by Spencer Rich, Washington *Post,* Dec. 2, 1972.

"Whatever Happened to the Solid South?" by Numan V. Bartley and Hugh D. Graham, *New South,* Fall 1972; "Politics, Race and the Law: The Southern Strategy," by Charles Morgan, Jr., *Black Politician,* Winter 1970; "The GOP and the South," by Michael S. Lottman, *Ripon Forum,* July-August 1970; "Southern Strategy Pays Off," by Clayton Fritchey, Washington *Post,* Oct. 14, 1972; "The New Strategy for Dixiecrats," by Rowland Evans and Robert Novak, Washington *Post,* Jan. 8, 1973; "Why Judge Haynsworth," an editorial in the Washington *Post,* Aug. 19, 1969; "Populism in Office or, Whatever Happened to Huey Long," by James Clotfelter, *New South,* Spring 1973.

"King's Political Legacy," by David L. Lewis, *Focus,* January 1973; "Martin Luther King: A Fusion of Two Worlds," by Max Lerner, Washington *Evening Star,* Jan. 19, 1970; "Remembering Martin Luther King," by Roger Wilkins, Washington *Post,* April 4, 1972; "King, Not Kennedy, Is Man to Remember," Garry Wills, Philadelphia *Inquirer,* April 11, 1972; "Is Martin Luther King Irrelevant?" by Samuel D. Cook, *New South,* Spring 1971; "Whites' Resistance Slows Gains of Negro in South," by Roy Reed, New York *Times,* Feb. 7, 1970; "Decade of Change in South Gives Negroes High Hopes," by Thomas A. Johnson, New York *Times,* Aug. 16, 1970; "More Black Americans Return to the South From 'Exile' in North," by Bernard E. Garnett, *Wall Street Journal,* Nov. 10, 1972; "Blacks Start Reverse Migration as Changes Increase Lure of South," by William L. Chaze, Philadelphia *Bulletin,* Dec. 8, 1972; "Black Power at the Dixie Polls," *Time,* June 15, 1970; "A Rural Politician Looks at the South," by Felton J. Capel, *Black Politician,* January 1971; "Black Poverty Keeps State Poor, Baxley says," by Carol Nunnelley, Birmingham *News,* May 12, 1973; "A Race Against Racialism in the Deep South," by Peter Jenkins, *The Argus* (Cape Town, South Africa), Oct. 6, 1972; "School Matters," Letter to the editor of the *Atlantic Monthly,* June 1973, by Edna McA. Watts; *It's Not Over in the South: School Desegregation in Forty-three Southern Cities Eighteen Years After Brown* (report by several civil rights organizations, Washington, 1972).

"The New Rich South: Frontier for Growth," *Business Week,* Sept. 2, 1972; "The Looming Money Revolution Down South" by Richard Armstrong, *Fortune,* June 1970; "South's Taxes Hit Poor Hardest," by Bob Anderson, *South Today,* November 1969; "Welfare Reform: The Southern View," by Tom Herman, Winston-Salem *Journal,* Dec. 15, 1970; "Family Assistance Plan Seen Harmful to Economy of South," by Kevin P. Phillips, Washington *Post,* July 25, 1970.

LOUISIANA

Several excellent books on Louisiana have appeared in recent years and were helpful in preparing the chapter:

Ten Flags in the Wind: The Story of Louisiana, by Charles L. Dufour (New York: Harper & Row, 1967); *Huey Long's Louisiana: State Politics, 1920–52,* by Allan P. Sindler (Baltimore: Johns Hopkins Press, 1956); "Louisiana: Resistance and Change," by Perry H. Howard, chapter of *The Changing Politics of the South,* ed. William C. Havard (Baton Rouge: Louisiana State University Press, 1972); "Louisiana: The Seamy Side of Democracy," chapter of *Southern Politics in State and Nation,* by V. O. Key (New York: Random House, 1949); *The Louisiana Elections of 1960,* by William C. Havard, Rudolf Heberle, and Perry H. Howard (Baton Rouge: Louisiana State University Press, 1963); *Huey Long,* by T. Harry Williams (New York: Alfred A. Knopf, 1969); *The Earl of Louisiana,* by A. J. Liebling (New York: Simon and Schuster, 1961); *Louisiana: A Guide to the State* (New York: Hastings House, American Guide Series, 1941); *The History and the Government of Louisiana* (Report of the Louisiana Legislative Council, 1964). Other sources: Regular coverage of the New Orleans *Times-Picayune, New Orleans Magazine,* and the specific articles cited below:

ECONOMY, ENVIRONMENT *Industry Rates Louisiana* (Baton Rouge: Public Affairs Research Council of Louisiana, 1971); "Louisiana Battles for Its Gas Reserves," *Business Week,* Feb. 3, 1973; "Oilmen at Sea: Life on South Marsh Island 73," by Leo Janos, *Time,* March 1, 1971; "Offshore," by Leo Janos, *Atlantic Monthly,* August 1972; "Where Search for Natural Gas Is in Full Swing," *U.S. News & World Report,* Dec. 13, 1971; "Small Oil Slicks Rise, Pose a Worse Threat than Major Blowouts," by James C. Tanner, *Wall Street Journal,* Feb. 10, 1971; "Oil Industry Fights Polluted Image," by Philip D. Carter, Washington *Post,* Oct. 21, 1971; "Oil and Garbage May Kill the Gulf of Mexico," by Roger Gallagher, *Intermountain Observer,* July 18, 1970; "The Mississippi Highway of Pollution," by Roy Reed, New York *Times,* Dec. 8, 1971; "Seacoast and Superports: A Supercatch for the Pelican State?" by P. J. Mills, *State Government,* Summer 1973.

"Louisiana Opens the Bayous to the Alligator Men," by James Wesley Pruden, *National Observer,* Sept. 23, 1972; "Big Louisiana Swamp Is Slowly Dying," by Roy Reed, New York *Times,* Oct. 22, 1970; "Sweetening the Harvest," *Time,* Nov. 13, 1972; "Tied to the Sugar Lands," by Peter Schuck, *Saturday Review,* May 6, 1972; "The Big Shakedown in Baton Rouge," by A. James Reichley, *Fortune,* August 1969; "The Hullabaloo About Hadacol," by J. D. Ratcliff, St. Louis *Post-Dispatch,* Sept. 8, 1951; "La. Sen. D. J. LeBlanc Dies," by Tom Huth, Washington *Post,* Oct. 23, 1971; "Louisiana," by Susan Fenwick, *New Orleans Magazine,* December 1970; "Cajuns Find Their Tongue in Louisiana," by Nicholas C. Chriss, Los Angeles *Times,* April 12, 1973.

POLITICS *20 Years of Louisiana Politics 1950–1970* (Baton Rouge: Public Affairs Research Council of Louisiana, October 1970); *Primary Election November 6, 1971,* and *Second Democratic Primary Election December 18, 1971* (Baton Rouge: Public Affairs Research Council of Louisiana, November and December 1971); "The Dean of Them All [Hébert] Talks About Politics," by Herschel Miller, *New Orleans Magazine,* October 1969; "Gumbo Politics: It's Election Day in Louisiana," by Nicholas C. Chriss, Los Angeles *Times,* Nov. 6, 1971; "Reformers Win Big in Louisiana Races," by David Snyder, Washington *Post,* Nov. 8, 1971; "Reform Candidates Seek Nomination for La. Governor," by Philip D. Carter, Washington *Post,* Dec. 18, 1971; "End of the Old Hayride," by Joseph Kraft, Washington *Post,* Dec. 14, 1971; "An Old Political Feud Stirs Up a Louisiana Hayride," by Wesley Pruden, Jr.,

National Observer, Dec. 18, 1971; "Edwards Apparent Winner in La.," by Philip D. Carter, Washington *Post,* Dec. 20, 1971; *General Election—February 1, 1972* (Baton Rouge: Public Affairs Research Council of Louisiana, February 1972); "Perhaps Beyond Conservatism," *Ripon Forum,* April 1971; "Wallace Will Run," by Leon W. Lindsay, *Christian Science Monitor,* April 9, 1971.

STATE GOVERNMENT *Targets for Action* (Baton Rouge: Public Affairs Research Council of Louisiana, 1971); *Property Tax Inequities* (Baton Rouge: Public Affairs Research Council of Louisiana, October 1971); "Louisiana Revision Alternatives Cited," *National Civic Review,* February 1970; "Gullibles Travails or Life in the Land of the Legislators," by Ken Dixon, *New Orleans Magazine,* August 1970; "Early Louisiana Desegregation Foe Repents in Legislature Speech," by Charles Layton, New York *Times,* June 6, 1972; "La. Attorney General, 4 Others Indicted in Loan Company Fraud," by Bill Lynch, Washington *Post,* Feb. 15, 1969; "LL&T Records Contained Gremillion's 1966 Letter," New Orleans *Times-Picayune,* Jan. 19, 1969; "The Little Man Is Bigger than Ever," by David Chandler, *Life,* April 10, 1970; "Louisiana's Little Man Denies Anything Illegal," Los Angeles *Times,* Sept. 9, 1970; "U.S. Abandons Attempt to Deport Mafia Figure," Washington *Post,* Dec. 23, 1970; "Tales of Rule by Mob Inspire Louisiana Panic," by Wesley Pruden, Jr., *National Observer,* Spring 1971; "Louisiana: 'Confidence in Government' to Be Theme of May Session," by David Snyder, *South Today,* March 1973.

CONGRESSIONAL DELEGATION *Ralph Nader Congress Project* reports on Russell B. Long, Hale Boggs, F. Edward Hebert, Otto E. Passman, Joe D. Waggonner, and John R. Rarick (Washington: Grossman, 1972); "Boggs: A Southern National Democrat," by Andrew Glass, *National Journal,* Jan. 23, 1971; "The Majority Leader—A Short History of a Controversial Man," by Rosemary James and Philip Moreton, *New Orleans Magazine,* July 1971; "Plea to Indict Long Rejected by Justice Dept.," by Leonard Downie, Jr., Washington *Post,* May 1, 1970; "Search for Boggs Is Suspended as Weather in Alaska Worsens," New York *Times,* Nov. 25, 1972; "Elegy for Hale Boggs: Effective Human Bridge," by William S. White, Washington *Post,* Dec. 9, 1972; "New Senate Patriarch," (Ellender), New York *Times,* Feb. 5, 1971; "Hard Scrabble's Favorite Son," (Ellender), by Jack Anderson, Washington *Post,* Dec. 21, 1971; "Arms and Mr. Hébert," by Orr Kelly, Washington *Star-News,* Aug. 13, 1972; "The New Strategy for Dixiecrats" (regarding Joe Waggonner), by Rowland Evans and Robert Novak, Washington *Post,* Feb. 8, 1973; "Free Speech and the Pentagon," by James H. Manahan, *Ripon Forum,* March 1973.

RACE RELATIONS "Bussing Rolls Along in Louisiana Schools," by John Dillin, *Christian Science Monitor,* Jan. 11, 1972; "School Fight Puts Judge in Middle," by Peter Milius, Washington *Post,* July 27, 1969; "Students' Demands for Change Stir Black Colleges in the South," by Paul Delaney, New York *Times,* Dec. 10, 1972; "Why Prisoners Riot—and Reform Fails," by Lawrence Mosher, *National Observer,* Aug. 31, 1970; "Louis Sirgo: A New Orleans Policeman Working Against the Odds," Washington *Post,* Jan. 15, 1973; "Mayor Signs Access Law," by James H. Gillis, *Times-Picayune,* Dec. 24, 1969; "Two Die as Police-Panther Wars Erupt Again," by Jack Wardlaw, *National Observer,* Sept. 21, 1970.

PEREZ "Louisiana County Controlled by Perez Stays Segregated," Washington *Star,* Sept. 1, 1966; "Leander H. Perez Dies at 77," Washington *Post,* March 20, 1969; 'Leander Perez: The Swamp's Gift to Dixie," chapter of *Gothic Politics in the Deep South,* by Robert Sherrill (New York: Grossman, 1968); "Leander's Legacy," by Clint Bolton, *New Orleans Magazine,* September 1972.

NEW ORLEANS—GENERAL "New Orleans Mon Amour," by Walker Percy, *Harper's Magazine,* September 1968; "New Orleans and Her River," by Joseph Judge, *National Geographic,* February 1971; "Spectacular Plans for New Orleans," by Charles E. Dole, *Christian Science Monitor,* July 6, 1973; "The Port of New Orleans . . . Is the Waterfront in Trouble?" by Hoke May, *New Orleans,* April 1968; "Superdome—Past, Present, Future," by Joey Morgan, *New Orleans Magazine,* January 1973; "New Orleans' Dome for All Seasons," by Parry D. Sorenson, *National Observer,* Jan. 22, 1972; "A Financial Hero in New Orleans," *Business Week,* Sept. 18, 1971; "Builders Take On New Orleans," *Business Week,* Jan. 27, 1973; "The Fight for the Queen, or Two Cheers for Congress," by Oliver Jensen, *American Heritage,* April 1971; "New Orleans Jazz . . . with a Foreign Accent," by Charles Suhor, *New Orleans Magazine,* November 1972; "Mardi Gras," special issue of *New Orleans Magazine,* February 1971; "Mardi Gras," chapter of *U.S. Journal,* by Calvin Trillin (New York: Dutton, 1971); "The Young Claim a Bit of Mardi Gras' Action," by Stephen Green, *National Observer,* March 1971; "The Diversity of Mardi Gras," by Sally Quinn, Washington *Post,* March 6, 1973.

NEW ORLEANS—POLITICS AND GOVERNMENT *Politics and Reality in an American City: The New Orleans School Crisis of 1960,* by Morton Inger (New York: Center for Urban Education, 1969); "When the Caucus Ruled the World," by Iris Kelso and Rosemary James, *New Orleans Magazine,* May 1971; "The Emergence of Coalition Politics in New Orleans," by James Chubbuck, Edwin Renwick, and Joe E. Walker, *New South,* Winter 1971; "Black Politics: A Concept in Search of a Definition," by Furnell Chatman, *New Orleans Magazine,* August 1971; "Mayor Moon Landrieu of New Orleans," *National Journal,* Dec. 16, 1972; "New Orleans May Get Liberal Mayor," by Roy Reed, New York *Times,* Jan. 17, 1970; "Liberal Cinderella Favored in New Orleans Race," by David Snyder, Washington *Post,* Jan. 26, 1970; "Moon Over New Orleans," *Newsweek,* June 14, 1971; "The Mayors' Revolt," *Newsweek,* May 24, 1971; "Jim Garrison: New Orleans Magazine's Man of the Year," by Rosemary James, *New Orleans Magazine,* January 1973.

ARKANSAS

The following books provided the most useful background on the state: "Arkansas: Independent and Unpredictable," by Richard E. Yates, chapter of *The Changing Politics of the South,* ed. William C. Havard (Baton Rouge: Louisiana State University Press, 1972); "Arkansas: Pure One-Party Politics," chapter of *Southern Politics in State and Nation,* by V. O. Key (New York: Random House, 1949); *Arkansas: A Guide to the State,* compiled by writers of the Writers' Program of the WPA (New York: Hastings House, 1941); "Orval Faubus: How to Create a Successful Disaster," chapter of *Gothic Politics in the Deep South,* by Robert Sherrill (New York:

Grossman, 1968); "Arkansas," by Claude Brion Davis, chapter of *American Panorama* (New York: Doubleday, 1960); *Accelerating Economic Growth in Arkansas* (publication of Arkansas Economic Expansion Study Commission, Little Rock, 1964).

Other sources: Regular coverage of the *Arkansas Gazette* as well as the specific articles cited:

POLITICS, GOVERNMENT, GENERAL "Arkansas Politics and Politicians," by Leland DuVall, *Arkansas Gazette,* June 22, 1969; "Arkansas First to Meet Jobless Aid Standards," *AFL-CIO News,* Feb. 13, 1971; "Arkansas Raise in Taxes Beaten," New York *Times,* March 16, 1969; "Legislative Improvement in Arkansas," by Cal Ledbetter, Jr., *State Government,* Spring 1973; "The Silent Fear in Little Rock," by Gertrude Samuels, New York *Times,* March 30, 1958; "Democrats End Arkansas Party Ban on Negroes," New York *Herald Tribune,* Sept. 23, 1950.

"The Choice for Governor," *Arkansas Gazette,* Oct. 15, 1970; "Bumpers Breathing Life into Party, Mills Tells Backers," by Ernest Dumas, *Arkansas Gazette,* Oct. 23, 1970; "Bumpers' Runoff Victory Blow to Machine Politics," by Ernest Dumas, Washington *Star,* Sept. 13, 1970; "Arkansas," by Barlow Herget, *Atlantic Monthly,* February 1972; "Bumpers Shies from a Slugfest in Arkansas Bout," by Nina Totenberg, *National Observer,* Oct. 12, 1970; "Arkansas' Bumpers: His Moderation Symbolizes Maturer Politics—but What of His Deeds?" by Ed Stainfield, *South Today,* May 1972.

"Arkansas: Strange Blend of Yesterday and Today," by Philip D. Carter, Washington *Post,* Aug. 4, 1971; "A River—and a State—Revitalized," by Joseph Kraft, Washington *Post,* Feb. 27, 1973; "End of Ozarks' Out-Migration May Signal National Trend," by George C. Wilson, Washington *Post,* March 11, 1973; "Arkansas: Education, Health Programs Pushed, but Federal Cutbacks May Postpone Budgeting," by Ernest Dumas, *South Today,* March 1973; "Energy, Medical Care Are Arkansas Challenges," by Doug Smith, *Southern Growth: Problems and Promise* (publication of the Southern Growth Policies Board, Research Triangle Park, N.C., 1973).

CITIES, RACE RELATIONS "All Is (Relatively) Well at Little Rock's Central High," by Reginald Stuart, *South Today,* January-February 1973; "Helena, Ark., an Embryonic Center of Music," by Roy Reed, New York *Times,* Dec. 6, 1972; "War Germ Facility Viewed as an Asset by Pine Bluff," by Roy Reed, New York *Times,* June 10, 1971.

"Mob Rule in Forrest City," *New South,* Fall 1969; "Anti-N.A.A.C.P. Bill Voted in Arkansas," New York *Times,* Feb. 19, 1959; "The Lid Goes On in Forrest City," by George Lardner, Jr., Washington *Post,* Oct. 12, 1969; "Widespread Racial Violence Persists in Eastern Arkansas Farming Area," by Roy Reed, New York *Times,* Oct. 10, 1971; "A Boycott Devastates Little Southern Town Bypassed by the 60s," by Neil Maxwell, *Wall Street Journal,* Feb. 24, 1972.

"Down South With Gerald L. K. Smith," by Paul Greenberg, *Newsday,* Aug. 27, 1970; "Gerald K. Smith Becomes Issue in Ozarks," by Ernest Dumas, *Arkansas Gazette,* Nov. 28, 1969; "An Update on Harding College," by Dudley Lynch, *New South,* Spring 1970; "America's Right Wing Propaganda Center," by Dudley Lynch, *Texas Observer,* Jan. 23, 1970.

ROCKEFELLER "A Blue Blood Finds Success in Bible Belt," by Nicholas C. Chriss, Los Angeles *Times,* July 7, 1970; "Winthrop Rockefeller: Buying Own Defeat?" by Phillip D. Carter, Washington *Post,* Nov. 1, 1970; "Governor Cites Arkansas Gains," New York *Times,* Dec. 6, 1970; "Arkansas Pins Orphan Status on Rockefeller," Los Angeles *Times,* Dec. 17, 1970; "The Transformation of Arkansas," *Time,* Dec. 2, 1966; "Winrock Goes to Little Rock," *Ripon Forum,* March 1970; "Winthrop Rockefeller Thinks Nation Wastes Its Ex-Governors," by Roy Reed, New York *Times,* July 22, 1971; "Winthrop Rockefeller of Arkansas Dies," by Bill Terry, Washington *Post,* Feb. 23, 1973.

PRISONS "U.S. Prisons Called Monster Factories," by Leonard Downie, Jr., Washington *Post,* March 5, 1969; "Ex-Official Tells of Brutalities in Arkansas Prisons," New York *Times,* March 5, 1969; "Too Cruel for the Cruel," *Time,* Feb. 2, 1970; "Arkansas Spares All on Death Row," New York *Times,* Dec. 30, 1970; "Critics Assail Arkansas Governor's Commutations," by Gene Foreman, *National Observer,* Jan. 11, 1971; "Dark and Evil World of Prison Life Is Ruled Too Harsh for Inmates," *National Observer,* Feb. 23, 1970; "Arkansas Prison Scandal," *National Observer,* Jan. 26, 1970; "The Shame of the Prisons," *Time,* Jan. 18, 1971; "One Year of Prison Reform," by Tom Murton, *The Nation,* Jan. 12, 1970; "Prison Youth Plan: One Day Brings Death," by Nicholas C. Chriss, Los Angeles *Times,* Dec. 13, 1971.

CONGRESSIONAL DELEGATION "Mourning Becomes Senator Fulbright," by Charles McCarry, *Esquire,* June 1970; "Can Fulbright Be Re-elected?" by Robert S. McCord, *The Progressive,* November 1967; "Washington's Cleanup Man," by Jerome Beatty, *The American,* June 1951.

"McClellan-Kennedy Team Is Set for Season's Biggest Investigation," by James Y. Newton and Cecil Holland, Washington *Post,* Feb. 22, 1957; "Senator Raps Highest Court," by John T. Dauner, Kansas City *Times,* April 3, 1970; "McClellan the Victor in Arkansas," by Bill Rutherford, Washington *Post,* June 14, 1972.

"The Most Important Man on Capitol Hill Today," by Julius Duscha, New York *Times Magazine,* Feb. 25, 1968; "Mills Tells Panel of His Conversion to President's Income Plan for the Poor," by Marjorie Hunter, New York *Times,* April 8, 1970; Wilbur D. Mills: A Study in Congressional Influence," by John F. Manley, *American Political Science Review,* June 1969; "An Idea on the March," *Time,* Jan. 11, 1963; "Even If Mills Stays On, Ways and Means Panel Faces a Loss of Power," by Albert R. Hunt, *Wall Street Journal,* July 10, 1973.

"Lawmaker Asks Study of Nursing Homes After Working in Some," New York *Times,* Feb. 24, 1970; "Snakepit Conditions in Nursing Homes," by Jack Anderson, Washington *Post,* Oct. 20, 1970; "A Congressman Lobbies for the Aged," by Nick Kotz, Washington *Post,* Jan. 4, 1971.

STONE COUNTY "Fiddles, Festivals and Folk," by F. J. Hurley, *Delta Review,* September 1969; "How Harold Keen Found Winthrop Rockefeller in Darkest Arkansas." *San Diego Magazine,* January 1970; "The Ballads of Bobby Lynn Blair," by Tom Dearmore, New York *Times Magazine,* June 30, 1968; "The Purest Folk Music in America," by Reg Murphy, Atlanta *Journal and Constitution Magazine,* July 19, 1970.

MISSISSIPPI

Mississippi is such a fascinating subject that many books of quality have been written about the state. Among the best, most helpful in preparing this book, were: ***The Past that Would Not Die,*** by Walter Lord (New York: Harper & Row, 1965); *Mississippi: A Guide to the Magnolia State* (New York: Viking Press, American Guide Series, 1938); *Mississippi: The Closed Society,* by James W. Silver (New York: Harcourt, 1964); "Mississippi: Unreconstructed and Unredeemed," by Charles N. Fortenberry and F. Glenn Abney, chapter of *The Changing Politics of the South,* ed. William C. Havard (Baton Rouge: Louisiana State University Press, 1972); "Mississippi: The Delta and the Hills," chapter of *Southern Politics in State and Nation,* by V. O. Key (New York: Random House, 1949).

OTHER SOURCES: GENERAL "State Boasts New Progressive Image," by W. F. Minor, New Orleans *Times-Picayune,* Dec. 24, 1972; "Mississippi: The Fallen Paradise," by Walker Percy, *Harper's Magazine,* April 1965; "The Worst American State," by John Berendt, *Focus,* November 1972; "A Mississippi Portrait," special 1969 edition of *The Reflector* (student newspaper at Mississippi State University); "Political Correlates of Social, Economic, and Religious Diversity in the American States," by John L. Sullivan, *The Journal of Politics,* February 1973; Publications of the Mississippi Agricultural and Industrial Board (Jackson).

RACE RELATIONS, POLITICS "Restore Image, Is Plea in Miss.," by W. F. Minor, New Orleans *Times-Picayune,* March 10, 1965; "Mississippi Metamorphosis," by Frank Morgan, *Wall Street Journal,* March 16, 1965; "Blacks Wary of Poverty Reforms in Mississippi," by Austin Scott, Washington *Post,* Sept. 18, 1972; "Delta Ministry Reconstructed," *Race Relations Reporter,* June 21, 1971; "Voices from Mississippi," by C. J. Wilson, *New South,* Spring 1973; "Conviction Shows Mississippi Shift," by Robert P. Hey, *Christian Science Monitor,* March 18, 1968; "James Meredith and Ole Miss: Decade After a Bloody Insurrection," by Wayne King, New York *Times,* Oct. 1, 1972; "Ole Miss Enters the '60s," *Newsweek,* March 30, 1970; "Cow College No More: Don't Look Now, but State's a University," *Freelance* (Starkville, Miss.), September 1969; "Meredith Sticks to Maverick Role," *Atlantic Constitution—Journal,* Feb. 20, 1972; "Leaders of Mississippi's Black Activists Confident of the Future," by Thomas A. Johnson, New York *Times,* Jan. 11, 1970; "Giant Step to Moderation," by Lewis Perdue, *The Reflector,* 1969; "Jackson State a Year After," by Stephan Lesher, New York *Times Magazine,* March 21, 1971.

"Pulpwood Strike," by Kathy Kahn, *South Today,* April 1972; "Strange Alliance," *Newsweek,* Nov. 8, 1971; "Evers Extends Hand to Interracial Drive," by Roy Reed, New York *Times,* Sept. 24, 1971.

"Mississippi Election Analysis," *Race Relations Reporter,* Feb. 17, 1972; "Blacks to Decide Mississippi Race," by Paul Delaney, New York *Times,* Aug. 22, 1971; "Evers' Confessions Add to Campaign Hurdles," by Philip D. Carter, Washington *Post,* April 12, 1971; "Ancient Southern Political Rites Begin at Unique Neshoba County Fair," by Jack Wardlaw, *National Observer,* Aug. 2, 1971; "Blacks Still Haunted by Fear, Threats in Mississippi Elections," by Robert C. Maynard, Washington *Post,* Aug. 15, 1971; "Mississippi Blacks Fail to Gain Control," by Jack White, *Race Relations Reporter,* Nov. 15, 1971; "How Much Power Do We Now Have?" *The Drummer,* December 1971; "In the Deep South, Blacks Have the Vote But Not the Votes," by Neil Maxwell, *Wall Street Journal,* Nov. 2, 1971; "Black Setback in Mississippi," *Time,* Nov. 15, 1971; "Letter from a Lost Campaign," by Thomas Powers, *Harper's Magazine,* March 1972; "Evers Expects Nixon to Get Big Black Vote," by Jack Nelson, Los Angeles *Times,* Sept. 21, 1972.

"Mississippi Democrats—A Black-White Mending," by John Dillin, *Christian Science Monitor,* Feb. 28, 1972; "Agnew, in Miss., Treads Tightrope in Endorsements," by Lou Cannon, Washington *Post,* Oct. 1, 1972.

ECONOMY "Deep South's Changes Have Come Recently," by Wilson F. Minor, *Southern Growth: Problems and Promise,* a publication of Southern Growth Policies Board, Research Triangle Park, N. C., 1973; "Mississippi in 1972," by William N. Cox, III, *Federal Reserve Bank of Atlanta Monthly Review,* September 1972; "The Stakes in the Rural South: Family Assistance," by Lester M. Salamon, *The Nation,* Feb. 20, 1971; "Per Capita Income Reflects Economic Health," by Janet Troskey, *The Reflector,* 1969; "Vocational Tech: 'You've Come a Long Way, Baby—To Get Where You Are Today . . . ,'" by Tom Greet, *The Reflector,* 1969; "BAWI: Help or Hindrance?" by Michael C. Horowitz, *The Reflector,* 1969.

STATE GOVERNMENT "Mississippi: Gov. Waller Urges Caution on Tax Cuts, But Legislators Prefer Them to Upgrading State Services," by W. F. Minor, *South Today,* March 1973; "'New' Legislature Sheds Foot-Dragging Image," by W. F. Minor, New Orleans *Times-Picayune,* April 12, 1970; "The Governor Leads a Charmed Life," by Austin Scott, Washington *Post,* Sept. 24, 1973; "Shifts in Federal Aid Alarm 'New South,'" by Jon Nordheimer, New York *Times,* March 19, 1973; "Despite Killings and Court Order, Mississippi Penitentiary Still Uses Armed Trusties," by Roy Reed, New York *Times,* Jan. 27, 1973; "Mississippi Urged to Revamp Prison," New York *Times,* Jan. 23, 1973; "Mississippi Asked by Governor to End Dry Laws of 1908," New York *Times,* Feb. 3, 1966.

CONGRESSIONAL DELEGATION *Ralph Nader Congress Project,* reports on James O. Eastland (by Don Colburn), John C. Stennis (by Gay Cook and Ann Adamcewicz), and Jamie L. Whitten (by Ann Millet) (Washington: Grossman, 1972); "Why the Pentagon Pays Homage to John Cornelius Stennis," by James K. Batten, New York *Times Magazine,* Nov. 23, 1969; "Stennis Shooting Stirs Gun Law Demand," by Spencer Rich, Washington *Post,* Feb. 1, 1973; "Key Voice for the ABM," by David F. Rosenbaum, New York *Times,* July 10, 1969; "A Poor, Hard Life on Eastland Plantation," by Nick Kotz, Des Moines *Register,* Feb. 26, 1968; "Rep. Jamie Whitten's Influence Attracts Nationwide Recognition," Editorial, Jackson *Clarion-Ledger,* Sept. 24, 1970; "Rep. Jamie Whitten Works Behind Scenes to Shape Big Spending," by Norman C. Miller, *Wall Street Journal,* June 7, 1971; "Pesticides Firms Aided Whitten Book," by Nick Kotz and Morton Mintz, Washington *Post,* March 14, 1971; "Rep. Colmer, at 81, a Powerful Voice on Hill," by Robert Gruenberg, Washington *Evening Star,* Feb. 17, 1971.

JACKSON "Jackson, Miss.—Too Polite, Comfortable for NAACP," by Richard Harwood,

Washington *Post,* July 5, 1969; "All's Quiet in Jackson," by Eleanor Clift, *South Today,* December 1971; "A Southern City Turns to Compromise," by Billy Skelton, Washington *Post,* Sept. 5, 1971; "Opening The Airways," by Phil Gailey, Washington *Post,* Feb. 12, 1973; "Viewers in Jackson, Mississippi See Something on Their TV Screens that Nobody Else in the Nation Does," by Reginald Stuart, *South Today,* December 1972; "In the Public Interest, Convenience, and Necessity . . . The Broadcasting Industry Meets the People," by Everett C. Parker, *Civil Rights Digest,* October 1972; "Dimout in Jackson," *Columbia Journalism Review,* Summer 1970.

GULF COAST, SMALL CITIES "End of an Era," *Newsweek,* June 7, 1971; "Senate Probe of Camille Aid Set," by Jerry DeLaughter, Washington *Post,* Dec. 4, 1969; "Camille's Cleanup Is Slow and Painful," by Nina Totenberg, *National Observer,* Jan. 19, 1970; "Jubilant Shrimpers Return to the Sea After Tragedy of Camille," by James T. Wooten, New York *Times,* June 8, 1970; "Shipyard Investment May Be Large Miscalculation," by Sam Love, *The Reflector,* 1969; "The Litton Ship Fiasco," by Rep. Les Aspin, *The Nation,* Dec. 11, 1972; "Litton Shapes Up a Ship Contract," *Business Week,* March 24, 1973; "Behind the Write-offs at Litton Industries," *Business Week,* Sept. 23, 1973.

"The Hard Traveler from Vicksburg," *Fortune,* January 1972; "Catching Up with Natchez," by Nicholas C. Chriss, *The Nation,* Dec. 6, 1971; "Natchez Among South's Fastest Growing Centers," by Jeanerette Harlow, Jackson *Clarion Ledger,* May 21, 1970; "Natchez, Where They Say, the Old South Still Lives," by Judy Klemesrud, New York *Times,* March 29, 1970.

THE DELTA "The Negro Exodus from the Delta Continues," by Hodding Carter III, New York *Times Magazine,* March 10, 1968; "In Darkest America," by Victor Ullman, *The Nation,* Sept. 4, 1967; "Cotton Boom Puts Smiles on Farmers," by Roy Reed, Atlanta *Journal-Constitution,* July 9, 1972; *Hungry Children,* Special Report, Southern Regional Council (Atlanta, 1967); *The Will to Survive,* by Anthony Dunbar, A Study of a Mississippi Plantation Community Based on the Words of Its Citizens (Southern Regional Council, Atlanta, June 1969); "28-Year Partnership for Health in Mississippi," *Ebony,* April 1970; "Sharecropper Plight Frustrates Doctors," by Stuart Auerbach, Washington *Post,* Sept. 15, 1970; "A Stir of Hope in Mound Bayou, Miss.," by Richard Hall, *Life,* March 28, 1969; "To Rural Negroes, Health Center Is Hope," by Sandra Blakeslee, New York *Times,* Aug. 28, 1970; *The Delta Ministry,* by Bruce Hilton (New York: Macmillan, 1969); *Where I Was Born and Raised,* by David L. Cohn (South Bend: University of Notre Dame Press, 1935, 1967).

ALABAMA

In preparing the Alabama chapter, I was fortunate to have access to an excellent unpublished manuscript on the state by Ray Jenkins of the Alabama *Journal* (Montgomery). The best standard references on the state include: *The Land Called Alabama,* by Malcolm C. McMillan (Austin, Texas: Steck-Vaughan, 1968); *Alabama: A Guide to the Deep South,* compiled by the writers of the Writer's Program of the WPA (New York: Richard R. Smith, 1941); "Alabama: Planters, Populists, 'Big Mules,'" chapter of *Southern Politics in State and Nation,* by V. O. Key (New York: Random House, 1949); *Alabama: Portrait of a State,* by Victor B. Haagan (Huntsville, Ala.: Wingate, 1968); *History of Alabama,* by Albert Burton Moore (Tuscaloosa: University of Alabama, 1934). Other sources: Regular coverage of the Birmingham *News,* Montgomery *Advertiser,* Alabama *Journal* (Montgomery), and the following articles and books:

STATE GOVERNMENT "The Deep South's Hottest Young Politician" (Bill Baxley), by Margaret Shannon, Atlanta *Journal-Constitution Magazine,* July 25, 1971; "Alabama: No Program in Sight, as Courts Force Issues, and Some Urge Wallace to Retire," by Ray Jenkins, *South Today,* March 1973; "50th Legislative Ranking Rankles," by Don F. Wasson, Atlanta *Journal-Constitution,* Feb. 7, 1971; "Wallace, Defeated on Funds, Belches Fire at Legislature," by Don F. Wasson, Montgomery *Advertiser,* May 9, 1971; "Alabama Cuts 33,000 From Welfare," by Bill Kovach, New York *Times,* Aug. 31, 1971; "Tax Indictments Name 4 Persons," Atlanta *Journal-Constitution,* Sept. 19, 1971; "Judges Order Redistricting," by Don F. Wasson, Atlanta *Journal-Constitution,* Jan. 9, 1972; "Special Session Urged in Alabama," New York *Times,* Oct. 29, 1972; "Acting Alabama Governor Will Follow Wallace Policy," *The Christian Science Monitor,* June 26, 1972; "Gov. Beasley for a While," and "Wallace to Implement Cost Findings," by Don F. Wasson, Atlanta *Journal-Constitution,* June 25 and Dec. 29, 1972; "Reorganization Proposals in New State Constitution," by Ralph Holmes, Birmingham *News,* April 29, 1973.

POLITICS "'Big Jim' Folsom, in a Last Hurrah, Seeks Protest Vote in Alabama Primary," New York *Times,* April 30, 1970; "State GOP Seeking That Certain Something," by James E. Jacobson, Birmingham *News,* July 19, 1970; "Building the Alabama GOP," by Bill Nettles, *Ripon Forum,* October 1970; "Labor Faction Role Boosted in Elections," by Don F. Wasson, Atlanta *Journal-Constitution,* Oct. 15, 1972.

"Black Politics in the New South," by Carlyle C. Douglas, *Ebony,* January 1971; "Multi-Party Races Shape; Wallace Still in Spotlight," by Don F. Wasson, Atlanta *Journal-Constitution,* Nov. 11, 1971; "Negro Democrats Put Up a Slate of 169 for Elections in Alabama," New York *Times,* Sept. 2, 1970; "Alabama Poll Tax Law Amended," *AFL News Reporter,* Jan. 8, 1954; "Black Party Backs a Candidate to Face Wallace for Governor," New York *Times,* Aug. 2, 1970.

WALLACE *Wallace,* by Marshall Frady (New York: World, 1968); "Compulsive Campaigner," by Ray Jenkins, *South Today,* 1971; "George Wallace, Fake Populist," by Kenneth Reich, *The Nation,* May 1, 1972; "Wallace Planning in Busy Silence," by Phil Garner, Atlanta *Journal-Constitution,* Feb. 16, 1969; "Showdown in Alabama; Wallace Fights to Save 'Movement,'" by James R. Dickenson, *National Observer,* April 20, 1970; "Applied Racism," *Race Relations Reporter,* April 19, 1970; "Wallace Drives to Home Town to Vote," by James T. Wooten, New York *Times,* June 3, 1970; "Elections: Wallace Victory May Affect '72 Race," New York *Times,* June 7, 1970; "Wallace Rides Again," by Michael S. Lottman, *Ripon Forum,* August 1970; "Nixon Gets Wallace's Silent OK," by Don F. Wasson, Atlanta *Journal-Constitution,* Oct. 22, 1972; "Man of the Year: Wallace," by David S. Broder, Washington *Post,* Dec. 31, 1972; "Wallace Faces Mounting Criticism in Alabama Over His Record, His Brother and His Aides," by Martin Waldron, New York *Times,* May 5, 1972.

COURTS "Alabamians Laud A Son—Hugo Black," by James T. Wooten, New York *Times,* July 19, 1970; "Black Championed New Deal, Civil Rights," by Alan Barth, Washington *Post,* Sept. 26, 1971; "'The Black Court': A Jurists' Legacy," by John P. MacKenzie, Washington *Post,* Sept. 18, 1971; "Hugo Black—'An Elemental Force,'" by Anthony Lewis, New York *Times,* Sept. 26, 1971; "The Making of a Judgeship 1971," *Ripon Forum,* February 1971.

CONGRESSIONAL DELEGATION *Ralph Nader Congress Project* reports on John J. Sparkman, by William Bridge, and Robert E. Jones, by Steven Saferin (Washington: Grossman, 1972); "Portrait of a 'Southern Liberal' in Trouble," by Robert Sherrill, New York *Times Magazine,* Nov. 7, 1965; "Dollars from Across the Nation Choose Sides in Alabama Race," by Nina Totenberg, *The National Observer,* Oct. 28, 1972; 'Loophole Is Used to Aid Sparkman," by James R. Polk, Washington *Star,* March 10, 1972; "The Sparkman-Blount Race," by Rowland Evans and Robert Novak, Washington *Post,* Sept. 15, 1972; "Sen. Allen Denies He's Wallace's Man," by Bruce Galphin, Washington *Post,* July 13, 1969; "Buchanan Rips KKK in Tarrant Speech," by Walton Lowry, Birmingham *News,* Nov. 9, 1965; "Flamboyance Marked Boykin's Career," by Nicholas Horrock, Birmingham *Post-Herald,* March 13, 1969.

RACE RELATIONS "Rosa Parks Wouldn't Budge," by Janet Stevenson, *American Heritage,* February 1972 (excerpted from her book, *The Montgomery Bus Boycott,* published by Franklin Watts, Inc.); *Cycle to Nowhere,* U.S. Commission on Civil Rights, Clearinghouse Publication No. 14; "Charlie: This Letter Is to Advise You," *New South,* Winter 1968; "A Threatened Alabamian Bows Out," by Carolyn Lewis, Washington *Post,* Sept. 28, 1968; "How Jay Cooper Did It," *South Today,* November 1972; "Homeboy's Dixie Returns Pays Off," by Alex Poinsett, *Ebony,* December 1972; "Two Blacks Returning to Alabama Take Office as Mayors," by Jon Nordheimer, New York *Times,* Oct. 5, 1972; "Letter from Tuskegee," by Roger Williams, *South Today,* May 1970; "60 Minutes," CBS Television Network (Segment on Tuskegee, Ala.), March 18, 1973; "Alabama Boycott Stirs State Raids," New York *Times,* July 29, 1957; "The South's Many Moods," by William G. Carleton, *Yale Review,* Summer 1966; "Alabama U. Rally Protests a Negro," AP dispatch in New York *Times,* Feb. 5, 1956; "New Beat in the Heart of Dixie," by Peter Schrag, *Saturday Review,* March 30, 1971.

ECONOMY "Government, Growth Go Together in Alabama," by Ray Jenkins, *Southern Growth Polices Board,* 1973; "Browns Ferry: Awesome Atomic Giant Rises in Alabama," by Frank Sikora, Birmingham *News,* Sept. 29, 1968; "The Golden Needle," by Thomas F. Hill, Birmingham *News,* Dec. 8, 1968; "Where the Chickens Come Home to Roost," by Gene D. Sullivan, *Federal Reserve Bank of Atlanta Monthly Review,* February 1972 "Striking Poultry Men Dejected in Battle With Big Processors," by James T. Wooten, New York *Times,* Nov. 22, 1970.

BIRMINGHAM *A Time to Speak,* by Charles Morgan, Jr. (New York: Harper & Row, 1964); "Birmingham of the Sixties," *Birmingham Magazine,* December 1970; "Face-Lifting Due for Birmingham," by Jack Rosenthal, New York *Times,* May 7, 1970; "Birmingham: 'The Gap's Getting Bigger,'" by Haynes Johnson, and "Birmingham's Congressman [John H. Buchanan, Jr.] Replies," Washington *Post,* Dec. 28, 1969, and Jan. 11, 1970 "Seibels Is Expected to Be Approachable, Inspire 'Go' Spirit," by Jerry Hornsby, Birmingham *News,* Nov. 1, 1967; "Voters Again Support Concept of Resurgent Birmingham," by Leon W. Lindsay, *Christian Science Monitor,* Oct. 29, 1969.

"Biracial View," by Leon W. Lindsay, *Christian Science Monitor,* Nov. 17, 1969; "Church Divides Over Blacks," by Betty Medsger, Washington *Post,* Nov. 8, 1970; "In Birmingham, a Baptist Church Drops the Color Line," *Life,* Nov. 5, 1971; "Precious in His Sight," *Newsweek,* Aug. 10, 1970; "Why Birmingham's a Medical Center," by Keith Coulbourn, Atlanta *Journal-Constitution Magazine,* Jan. 24, 1971; "UAB West Campus Blossoms with Buildings and Students," by Garland Reeves, Birmingham *News,* May 6, 1973; *Corporate Social Responsibilities,* by Clarence L. Walton (particularly Appendix II on United States Steel in 1963 racial crisis) (Belmont, Calif.: Wadsworth, 1967); "U.S. Steel, USW Cited in Discrimination Suit by Justice Department," *Wall Street Journal,* Dec. 14, 1970; "U.S. Steel Seniority Scrapped," by Peggy Roberson, Birmingham *News,* May 3, 1973; "U.S. Steel Authorizes $12 Million to Fight Air Pollution in Birmingham, Alabama Crisis," by Jim Montgomery, *Wall Street Journal,* May 17, 1971; "The Day They Shut Down Birmingham," by Patrick J. Sloyan, *Washington Monthly,* May 1972; "Law May Help Birmingham to Clean Its Air," by Kenneth Reich, Los Angeles *Times,* Dec. 6, 1971; "Anti-pollution Efforts to Pay Dividend in Fall," by Irving Beiman, Birmingham *News,* April 29, 1973.

OTHER CITIES "Huntsville Gets Chemical War Plant; Cost Over $40,000,000," Huntsville *Times,* July 3 1941; "Wernher von Braun, the Peripatetic Genius," by Phil Garner, *Atlanta Magazine,* August 1969; "Huntsville's Return to Earth," *Business Week,* Feb. 14, 1970; "'A Kind of Blindness' Blurs Vision of the New South," (regarding Anniston), by Philip D. Carter, Washington *Post,* Aug. 18, 1971; "Major Industries Located in Booming Mobile Area," by Sheldon Morgan, *Journal of Commerce,* June 19, 1967; "Montgomery: Testing Ground," by George Barrett, New York *Times Magazine,* Dec. 16, 1956; "Grover Hall, Jr., Editor in South," New York *Times,* Sept. 25, 1971.

GEORGIA

These books provided the most useful general background on Georgia in our time: *From Thurmond to Wallace: Political Tendencies in Georgia, 1948–68,* by Numan V. Bartley (Baltimore: Johns Hopkins Press, 1970); "Georgia: Static and Dynamic," by Joseph L. Bernd, chapter of *The Changing Politics of the South,* ed. William C. Havard (Baton Rouge: Louisiana State University Press, 1972); "Georgia: Rule of the Rustics," chapter of *Southern Politics in State and Nation,* by V. O. Key (New York, Random House, 1949); *The Riddle of Lester Maddox,* by Bruce Galphin (Atlanta: Camelot, 1968); *Georgia: A Guide to Its Towns and Countryside,* by writers of the WPA writer's project (Athens: University of Georgia Press, 1940); *This Is Your Georgia,* by Bernice McCullar (Northport, Ala.: American Southern, 1966); *Georgia Statistical Abstract 1972* (Athens: University of Georgia College of Business Administration, 1972). Other sources: Regular coverage of the Atlanta *Constitution* and *Journal,* and specific articles cited:

ECONOMY "Marching Through Georgia," by Bill Winn, *Atlanta Magazine,* March 1969; "Where the Chickens Come Home to Roost," by Gene D. Sullivan, *Federal Reserve Bank of Atlanta Monthly Review,* February 1972; "Georgia Farms? They're Alive and Well," by Ron Taylor, Atlanta *Journal and Constitution,* Feb. 9, 1969; *A Review of Georgia's Economy 1960–72,* Research Department, Federal Reserve Bank of Atlanta, September 1972; "Georgia Looks to New Revenue Sources," by Sam Hopkins, in *Southern Growth: Problems and Promises* (publication of Southern Growth Policies Board, Research Triangle Park, N.C., 1973).

POLITICS "Boss Rule Issue Up in Georgia with Vote to Extend County Unit System to General Elections," by Spencer R. McCulloch, St. Louis *Post-Dispatch,* Oct. 31, 1950; "Candidate or Not, Maddox Will Be the Man to Beat in Georgia Race," The *National Observer,* Dec. 22, 1969; "Peanut Farmer Stuns Experts to Lead Ga. Governor's Race," by Bruce Galphin, Washington *Post,* Sept. 11, 1970; "The Loser Who Won," by Robert Coram and Remer Tyson, *Atlanta Magazine,* November 1970; "Georgia's Top Democrats Like Convention Reforms," by John Dillin, *Christian Science Monitor,* April 11, 1972; "Senate Race in Georgia Centers on Who Is Furthest Right," by Richard L. Lyons, Washington *Post,* Oct. 31, 1972; "GOP Not Carpetbaggers, Shaw Says," by Harry Murphy, Atlanta *Journal-Constitution,* Feb. 14, 1971; "GOPs Re-elect Most Officers," by David Nordan, Atlanta *Journal-Constitution,* June 3, 1973; "Bidding for Majority Status," by Michael S. Lottman, *Ripon Forum,* July-August 1970; "Backlash and Black Power: A Reporter's Reflections," by Jack Nelson, *New South,* Winter 1967; "Whatever Happened to Charlayne Hunter?" *Ebony,* July 1972.

CONGRESSIONAL DELEGATION "Regression vs. Conservatism in Georgia," by Douglass Cater, *The Reporter,* Oct. 20, 1955; "They Venture Out on a Limb," by David Nordan, Atlanta *Journal-Constitution,* March 28, 1971; *Ralph Nader Congress Project* report on Herman E. Talmadge, by Anne L. Millet (Washington: Grossman, 1972); "Talmadge Twenty Years Later," by Robert E. Baker, Washington *Post,* Jan. 6, 1966; "The New Herman," by Phil Garner, Atlanta *Journal-Constitution Magazine,* Sept. 9, 1973; "The Senate: Richard Russell," *Newsweek,* Feb. 1, 1971; "Off the Record with Sen. Russell," by Charles Pou, Atlanta *Journal-Constitution,* Jan. 5, 1969; "Richard Russell Dies at 73," by Bob Hurt, Atlanta *Constitution,* Jan. 22, 1971; "Richard Russell, Senator of Influence," by Don Oberdorfer, Washington *Post,* Jan. 22, 1971.

STATE GOVERNMENT "Politics: Legislative Report Card," by Robert Coram, *Atlanta Magazine,* April 1972; "Politics," by Robert Coram, *Atlanta Magazine,* June 1969; "Equality Sought on Education," by Prentice Palmer, Atlanta *Journal-Constitution,* Dec. 3, 1972; "ABC's of Illiteracy in Georgia," by Robert Coram, *Atlanta Magazine,* April 1971; "Georgia Educator Requests More Funds," by Robert P. Hey, *Christian Science Monitor,* Feb. 27, 1968; "Will Georgia Be Fiftieth Again?" by Reg Murphy, Atlanta *Constitution,* Jan. 14, 1969; "Revamp His Middle Name," by Harry Murphy, Atlanta *Journal-Constitution,* Dec. 26, 1971; "Governor's Happy State," by Margaret Shannon, Atlanta *Journal-Constitution Magazine,* July 18, 1971; "Welfare Bugs the Voter," by Bob Fort, Sam Hopkins, and Nick Taylor, Atlanta *Journal-Constitution,* Sept. 24, 1972; "Battling Bill Burson," *Atlanta Magazine,* March 1969; "Welfare's Parham Starts on $230 Million Task," Atlanta *Journal-Constitution,* Jan. 24, 1971; "Criminal Justice Is a Failure," by Robert H. Hall, Atlanta *Journal-Constitution,* May 2, 1971; "Apathy Hurts Penal Reforms," by Gene Stephens, Atlanta *Journal-Constitution,* Feb. 28, 1971; "Maddox Hails Penal 'New Day,' " by Gene Stephens, Atlanta *Journal-Constitution,* Jan. 10, 1971; "State Mental Care: Half-Filled Cup," by Charles Seabrook, Atlanta *Journal-Constitution,* June 18, 1972; ". . . And in Georgia a River," by Jeff Nesmith, *South Today,* October 1970; "Pafford for the People," by Phil Garner, Atlanta *Journal-Constitution Magazine,* April 11, 1971; "Out of Small Emanuel County Will Likely Come One of the State Government's Top Three Officials —Again," by Hal Gulliver, *Atlanta Magazine,* September 1970; "The Gillis Dynasty," by Margaret Shannon, Atlanta *Journal-Constitution Magazine,* Aug. 18, 1968.

SAVANNAH "The Heart of Savannah," by Anthony Wolff, *American Heritage,* December 1970; "Saving Savannah," *Life,* May 7, 1971; "Black Capitalism," *Time,* May 23, 1969; "Contrast Marks Savannah Race Ties," by Bill Winn, Atlanta *Journal-Constitution,* May 26, 1968; "Georgia's Biggest Bank Wades into the Slums," *Business Week,* May 24, 1969; "Let Us Go to School Together in Peace," by Wendy Watriss, *Christian Science Monitor,* June 12, 1972; "Savannah, Key to Urbane Livability," by Wolf Von Eckardt, Washington *Post,* May 20, 1972; "Community Growth—Loans Aid Businesses," Savannah *News Press,* Feb. 9, 1969; "A Hosanna to Savannah," *Newsweek,* Feb. 7, 1972; "Nader's Raiders Study Stirs Kind of Fight Against Pollution Any City Could Make," by Neil McBride, *South Today,* April 1972.

OTHER CITIES "Black-White Issue Flares in Augusta Merger Vote," by Raleigh Bryans, Atlanta *Journal-Constitution,* May 23, 1971; "Witnesses to Augusta Riot Say 3 of 6 Killed Were Bystanders," by James T. Wooten, New York *Times,* May 17, 1970; "Augusta: Race Riot No. 1," *Time,* May 25, 1970; "What Makes Ronnie Run," by Roger Williams, *Atlanta Magazine,* January 1971; "Snipers, Nightly Firebombs Rend Georgia City," by Mark R. Arnold, *National Observer,* Aug. 2, 1971; "Army Town: Brides, Ricebirds and Hawks," by Jon Nordheimer, New York *Times,* Dec. 1, 1970; "Talbott Racial Idea Works at Benning," by Bill Montgomery, Atlanta *Journal-Constitution,* June 25, 1972; " 'Oreos' Aren't Cookies in Columbus," by Charles Wheeler and Harmon Perry, Atlanta *Journal-Constitution,* June 27, 1971.

TOWNS AND COUNTRYSIDE "Georgia's Private 'Williamsburg,' " by Ken Sobol, New York *Times,* June 4, 1972; "At Warm Springs, Happy Days Are Gone," by James T. Wooten, New York *Times,* April 13, 1970; "1,000-Acre Tycoon," *Ebony,* July 1972; "Hancock County Keeps Cool but Tension's Still There," by Bill Montgomery, Atlanta *Journal-Constitution,* Dec. 3, 1972; "Negro Takeover Jars Ga. County," by Paul W. Valentine, Washington *Post,* Dec. 22, 1968; "Hancock County," *New Republic,* March 6, 1971; 'A New Day for Rural Georgia," by Joseph H. Baird, Atlanta *Journal-Constitution Magazine,* March 26, 1972; "Bacon County: A Model," by Don Winter, Atlanta *Journal-Constitution,* Nov. 5, 1972; "Company Town: The Agony of St. Marys," *Newsweek,* May 22, 1972; "Jekyll at the Crossroads," by Margaret Shannon, Atlanta *Journal-Constitution Magazine,* June 18, 1972; "Ecologists Hope to Save Wild Islands off Georgia," by Jon Nordheimer, New York *Times,* July 4, 1972; "Most of Island off Georgia to Be National Seashore," by Bayard Webster, New York *Times,* May 8, 1971; "Everyone Seems to Covet This Island," by Peter T. Chew, *National Observer,* Jan. 5, 1970; "The Length and the Breadth and the Sweep of the Marshes of Glynn," *Life,* Nov. 14, 1969; "The Easy Chair: Georgia—Mother of Social Invention," by John Fischer, *Harper's Magazine,* March 1972.

ATLANTA—GENERAL A full review of Atlanta's history, arts, economy, and politics appeared in *Atlanta Magazine's* March 1972 issue marking the city's 125th anniversary; a dazzling view of the future appeared in the same magazine's August 1973 edition, entitled "Atlanta 2000." Other articles:

"Atlanta," by George Sessions Perry, *Saturday Evening Post,* Sept. 22, 1945; "Atlanta, Pacesetter City of the South," by William E. Ellis, *National Geographic,* February 1969; "The Agenda for Atlanta's Future," by Reg Murphy, Atlanta *Journal-Constitution,* Sept. 28, 1970; "Atlanta, Rising or Falling," by Jack Spalding, Atlanta *Journal-Constitution,* March 5, 1972; "Youth's New Mecca: Swinging Atlanta," by David W. Hacker, *National Observer,* Feb. 22, 1971; "Powderpuff Power," *Atlanta Magazine,* April 1971; "The City Is a Celebration of the Spirit," by Doris Lockerman, *Atlanta Magazine,* May 1971; "Deadly Way of Life," *Time,* Jan. 15, 1973.

"Atlanta's Mayor to Retire on Top," by James M. Naughton, Cleveland *Plain Dealer,* Feb. 26, 1969; "The Mayor Looks at His City," by Raleigh Bryans and Margaret Shannon, Atlanta *Journal-Constitution Magazine,* Feb. 16, 1969; *Mayor: Notes on the Sixties,* by Ivan Allen, Jr., with Paul Hemphill (New York: Simon & Schuster, 1971); "Atlanta's 'Power Structure' Faces Life," by Bill Schemmel, *New South,* Spring 1972.

The Atlanta Elections of 1969, by Charles S. Rocks (Atlanta: Voter Education Project, 1970); "Atlanta Elects a Black Mayor, First in a Major Southern City," by John Nordheimer, New York *Times,* Oct. 17, 1973; "For Atlanta: Racial Equity," by John Dillin, *Christian Science Monitor,* Oct. 18, 1973.

"The South Loses a Forceful Voice," by Eugene Patterson, The Washington *Post,* Feb. 5, 1969; "Why Atlanta Needs a Media Review," by Bruce Galphin, *Atlanta Journalism Review,* July/August 1971; "Crisis of the Constitution," by Arlie Schardt, *The Nation,* Dec. 23, 1968; "Constitutional Issue," *Newsweek,* Oct. 7, 1968.

ATLANTA—BLACKS "Black Atlanta: 'Name It, We Can Do It,'" by Haynes Johnson, Washington *Post,* March 14, 1971; "Atlanta: Mecca of New South's Black Wealth," by Nicholas C. Chriss, Los Angeles *Times,* Oct. 25, 1971; "God's Errand Boy on Auburn Avenue," by Joseph Dabney, *Atlanta Magazine,* September 1970; "Wealthy Atlanta Negroes . . . How They Did It," by Margaret Shannon, Atlanta *Journal-Constitution Magazine,* March 9, 1969; "South's First Black Since 1870 Is Elected to House by Georgia," by John Hemphill, New York *Times,* Nov. 9, 1972; "Blacks are Building," by Joseph Kraft, Washington *Post,* Nov. 26, 1972; "The Mediator," *Time,* Nov. 4, 1970; "Atlanta's Charmer," *Ebony,* December 1970; "Daring, They Came to Woo the Siren," by Bruce Galphin, *Atlanta Magazine,* 1971.

ATLANTA—ARCHITECTURE, BUSINESS "John Portman's Encore," by Bruce Galphin, *Atlanta Magazine,* November 1972; "Omni, Omnia, Vincit," by Bruce Galphin, *Atlanta Magazine,* November 1972; "City's Skyline to Leap," by Tom Walker, Atlanta *Journal-Constitution,* Feb. 13, 1972; "Underground Fun," *Holiday,* October 1969; "A City for Everyman's Tempo," *Atlanta Magazine,* May 1971; "The Companies It Keeps," *Atlanta Magazine,* May 1971; "Horatio Alger, Part II" (J. B. Fuqua), *Forbes,* Jan. 15, 1973; "Airlines: Amazin'-Dixon Line," *Time,* June 7, 1971; "A Georgia Cracker's Crackerjack Bank," by Rush Loving, Jr., *Fortune,* November 1969; "Atlanta's Beat Goes On," *Time,* July 24, 1972; "Portman: A New Force for Rebuilding the Cities," *Business Week,* Feb. 17, 1973; "The Money Injectors," by Reuben Smith, *Atlanta Magazine,* September 1970; "Wunderkind in the Wonderful World," by Robert Coram, *Atlanta Magazine,* August 1972; *The Big Drink: The Story of Coca-Cola,* by E. J. Kahn, Jr. (New York: Random House, 1950); "A New Life for Migrant Workers" (regarding Coca-Cola's Minute Maid), by Phil Garner, Atlanta *Journal-Constitution Magazine,* Jan. 23, 1972; "Life Improves for Florida's Orange Harvesters," by Philip Shabecoff, New York *Times,* March 19, 1973.

ATLANTA—METRO AREA "Atlanta," by Reese Cleghorn, *City,* January-February 1971; "Perimeter—Functional—But It's Not So Pretty," by Paul T. Beeman, Atlanta *Journal-Constitution,* May 9, 1971; "Office Parks: Beating the Money Market," by Tom Walker, *Atlanta Magazine,* February 1970; "Georgia Continues Move Toward City-County Link," by Bob Payne, Atlanta *Journal-Constitution,* July 11, 1971; "The New Metro: Now We Are 15," *Atlanta Magazine,* July 1973.

"Atlanta Offers Another Rapid Transit Plan," by Kenneth Reich, Los Angeles *Times,* Oct. 3, 1971; "A Win for Mayor Sam," *Newsweek,* Dec. 6, 1971; "Mass Transit: The Route to Change," by Joseph Kraft, Washington *Post,* Feb. 20, 1973; "The Mellowing of MARTA's Mover and Shaker," by Robert Coram, *Atlanta Magazine,* October 1972.

SOUTH CAROLINA

The best overview of present-day South Carolina is *Porgy Comes Home: South Carolina After Three Hundred Years,* by Jack Bass (Columbia, S. C.: R. L. Bryan, 1972). Other books that provided valuable background included *South Carolina: A Short History,* by David Duncan Wallace (Columbia, S. C.: University of South Carolina Press, 1961); *South Carolina: A Guide to the Palmetto State,* compiled by the workers of the Writers' Program of the Works Project Administration (New York: Oxford University Press, 1971); *South Carolina: Annals of Pride and Protest,* by William Francis Guess (New York: Harper, 1960); *Priorities for Progress in South Carolina,* Survey by Louis Harris & Associates (New York: October 1971); and *America at 1750,* by Richard Hofstadter (New York: Alfred A. Knopf, 1971).

Substantial coverage was gleaned from *The State* (Columbia), the Charlotte (N. C.) *Observer,* and the *Atlanta Constitution* and *Journal.* Especially helpful were the following articles from those newspapers and other publications:

LEGISLATURE, STATE GOVERNMENT "Two Old Men—In S. C., Brown and Blatt Are the Senior Partners," by Roger M. Williams, *South Today,* April 1971; "Times Have Changed and So Has Gressette," by Jack Bass, *Charlotte Observer,* Dec. 3, 1972; *The Bishop from Barnwell: The Political Life and Times of Edgar Brown,* by W. D. Workman, Jr. (Columbia, S. C.: R. L. Bryan, 1963); *Speaker Blatt—His Challenges Were Greater,* by John K. Cauthen (Columbia, S. C.: R. L. Bryan, 1965); "South Carolina: Gov. West Seeks Mildly Progressive Programs, and Urges Conservative Fiscal Policy," by Jack Bass, *South*

Today, March 1973; "State Jobs—'Only Token Integration,' " by Jack Bass, Atlanta *Journal-Constitution,* August 9, 1972; "Gov. West Threatens to Call Feds if State Doesn't End Job Bias," Atlanta *Journal-Constitution,* May 27, 1973; "State Public Television—A New Tool for the States," by John P. Witherspoon, *State Government,* Autumn 1971; "Near Perfect Performance Given by Voter Computers," by Hugh E. Gibson, *The State,* November 20, 1968; "Computerized Voter Registration in South Carolina," by O. Frank Thornton and James B. Ellisor, *State Government,* Summer 1969.

NATIONAL ROLE, CONGRESSIONAL DELEGATION *Ralph Nader Congress Project* reports on Strom Thurmond (by Richard Barnard), Ernest F. Hollings (by John Hancock), and W. J. Bryan Dorn (by Miles Hawthorne), (Washington: Grossman, 1972); "James F. Byrnes: A Manager of Men," by Alden Whitman, New York *Times,* April 10, 1972; "Byrnes Will Support Eisenhower as Best Qualified for Job," Washington *Evening Star,* September 19, 1952; "How Strom Thurmond Does It," by Charles Roberts, *Newsweek,* September 13, 1971.

"Senator Ernest Hollings: Education of A Conservative," by Robert Sherrill, *The Nation,* August 16, 1971; "A Conversation with Sen. Fritz Hollings, S. C.," *Atlanta Magazine,* July 1969; *The Case Against Hunger: A Demand for a National Policy,* by Senator Ernest F. Hollings (New York: Cowles, 1970).

"Ol' Man Rivers," by Charles McCarry, *Esquire,* October, 1970; "Rivers—A Farm Boy With Cunning," by Jack Bass, Charlotte *Observer,* December 29, 1970; "L. Mendel Rivers—King of the Military Mountain," by Robert G. Sherrill, *The Nation,* January 19, 1970; "Moved by Wives of Missing GIs, Rivers Urges Bombing of Enemy City," by Richard Homan, Washington *Post,* March 7, 1970.

" 'Red Sympathizers' Support Home Rule, McMillan Asserts," Washington *Post,* June 5, 1968; "Timber Lobby Friends," by Jack Anderson, Washington *Post,* March 1, 1970; "Two Challengers Bidding to Topple 'Johnny Mac,' " by Jack Bass, Atlanta *Journal-Constitution,* October 10, 1971; "Power on the Potomac: Johnny Mac Finally Got Scraattched," by Jack Kneece, *Washingtonian,* December, 1972.

"Dorn Happy to Be on Democratic Purge List," by Willard Edwards, Chicago *Tribune,* May 5, 1963; "W. J. B. Dorn—S. C.'s Political Enigma," by Dwayne Walls, Charlotte *Observer,* January 9, 1966.

POLITICS "South Carolina: The Politics of Color," by V. O. Key, chapter of *Southern Politics in State and Nation; Presidential Voting in South Carolina 1948–1964,* by Donald L. Fowler (Columbia, S. C.: University of South Carolina Press, 1966); "South Carolina: Partisan Prelude," by Chester W. Bain, chapter in *The Changing Politics of the South,* ed. William C. Havard (Baton Rouge, La.: Louisiana State University Press, 1972); "Republican Party in S. C. Is Certified," *The State,* July 20, 1950; "S. C. Court Backs Morris in GOP Fight," Washington *Post,* August 10, 1952; "Palmetto Test-tube for Two-Party System," by George McMillan, Washington *Post,* August 23, 1953; "President Warned About '72—Thurmond Rips Nixon Policies on Schools," by David S. Broder and Philip D. Carter, Washington *Post,* July 18, 1970; "South Carolina: Where It All Began," by Michael S. Lottman, *Ripon Forum,* July–August 1970; "Old South No More," *The Nation,* Oct. 15, 1973.

CIVIL RIGHTS "Integration with Dignity: The Inside Story of How South Carolina Kept the Peace," by George McMillan, *Saturday Evening Post,* March 16, 1963; "Negro Suffrage Fight in S. C. Almost Won," by Henry Lesesne, Washington *Post,* July 18, 1948; "Negro Political Influence Growing in S. C.," by Jack Bass, Charlotte *Observer,* November 17, 1968; "South Carolina: The 'Movement' Finally Arrives," by David Nolan, *The Nation,* May 26, 1969; "Massive White Flight in Summerton," by Jack Bass, *Race Relations Reporter,* May 1972; *The Orangeburg Massacre,* by Jack Nelson and Jack Bass (New York: World, 1970); "Seg Academies, with Much Church Aid, Flourish in South . . . ," by John Egerton, *South Today,* September 1973.

ECONOMY, LABOR "Industry Grows Up in South Carolina," *Business Week,* September 2, 1972; "South Carolina's 300 Years," prepared by the South Carolina Tricentennial Commission, advertising section in the New York *Times,* March 1, 1970; "Two Foreign Execs Explain Why They Like Palmetto State," by Jack Bass, Atlanta *Journal-Constitution,* July 1, 1973; "Excess of Industry Can Upset An Economy," by William D. Workman, Jr., *The State,* February 22, 1973; "Michelin Go Home," *The New Republic,* May 19, 1973.

"What the U.S. Textile Industry Really Needs," by Rush Loving, Jr., *Fortune,* October 1970; "The American Textile Industry," by William H. Wallace, *The Federal Reserve Bank of Richmond Monthly Review,* September 1969; "Textile Mission Highly Successful," by Jack Bass, Atlanta *Journal-Constitution,* September 24, 1972; "Darlington Textile Workers Keep Hopes Alive 13 Years," by Eugene A. Kelly, *AFL-CIO News,* May 3, 1969; "Industry in South Woos Negro Labor," by Roy Reed, New York *Times,* May 19, 1969; "Workers Have Waited 16 Years for Pay," by Bill Arthur, Charlotte *Observer,* June 24, 1973.

LOW COUNTRY, ENVIRONMENT "Conservationists Battle Industrialists in Hilton Head, S. C.," by Bruce Galphin, Washington *Post,* December 15, 1969; "Troubled Little Island," *Time,* January 26, 1970; "Hilton Head Is Wondering About Its New Neighbor," by Eugene Warner and John Carmody, Washington *Post Potomac Magazine,* April 26, 1970; "A New Plant Meets a New Age: A Southern Regional Council Report," by Betsy Fancher, *South Today,* June 1970; "Retreats to Luxury," by Diane Thomas, *Atlanta,* April 1973; "Discovering Harbour Town," by Philip Morris, *Southern Living,* March 1972; "Oil Issue Puts New Slant on Tidelands" and "They Hope Air Is Cleared," by Jack Bass, Atlanta *Journal-Constitution,* June 4 and Oct. 15, 1972.

"A Teacher: Daufuskie's Conroy Paying the Penalty," by Betsy Fancher, *South Today,* December 1970; "Daufuskie: Hope Fades After Teacher Is Fired," by Betsy Fancher, *South Today,* November 1970; "Healing the Poor of Beaufort-Jasper," by Natalie Davis Spingarn, Washington *Post,* February 25, 1973; "Esau Jenkins' Island," by William Winn, *South Today,* April 1971.

CITIES "Columbia, S. C.: A Southern Center Where There May Still Be Time," by John Egerton, *City,* Summer 1972; "Greenville Has Two Men of the Moment," by James T. Wooten, New York *Times,* August 20, 1969; " 'I Promised My Son I'd Bust Him,' " by Bill Collins, Atlanta *Journal-Constitution,* May 30, 1971.

"Charleston: Impressions of the Mother-City, or Part of It, Anyway," by Bill Winn, *Atlanta,* June 1969; "Booked For Travel: Carolina Swoon," by David Butwin, *Saturday Review,* April 15, 1972; *Freedom's Four Square Miles: The Story of America's "Harbor of History,"* by J. Percival Petit (Columbia, S. C.: R. L. Bryan, 1964); *A Nation of Strangers,* by Vance Packard (New York: McKay, 1972); "The City: Echoes of Memphis," *Time,* April 25, 1969.

FLORIDA

Books offering valuable background on Florida include: *Florida: The Long Frontier,* by Marjory Stoneman Douglas (New York: Harper & Row, 1967); "Florida: The Different State," by Manning J. Dauer, chapter in *Politics of the Contemporary South,* ed. William C. Havard (Baton Rouge: Louisiana State University Press, 1972); *Florida: A Guide to the Southernmost State,* compiled by the Federal Writers' Project of the WPA, American Guide Series (New York: Oxford University Press, 1939); *Gothic Politics in the Deep South,* by Robert Sherrill (New York: Grossman, 1968); *The Old South,* by John Osborne (New York: Time-Life Library of America, 1968); "Florida: Every Man for Himself," chapter in *Southern Politics in State and Nation,* by V. O. Key (New York: Random House, 1949); "Florida Republicanism: A House Divided," chapter in *Southern Republicanism and the New South,* by John C. Topping, Jr., John R. Lazarek, and William H. Linder (Cambridge, Mass.: Ripon Society, 1966); "Florida," by Budd Schulberg, chapter in *American Panorama* (Garden City, N.Y.: Doubleday, 1960); *Bean Soup—Or Florida with a Spanish Accent,* by M. Lisle Reese (Crawford, Jacksonville, Fla.: 1964).

Other Sources: Regular coverage of state and local events by the Miami *Herald* and St. Petersburg *Times,* and the following articles and reports:

GENERAL "Many Older Adults Moved Southward," by Jack Rosenthal, New York *Times,* March 29, 1971; "Industry, More Citizens? Some in Florida Veto Them," by Charles F. Hesser, Atlanta *Journal-Constitution,* Feb. 14, 1971; "It's Back: Divide Florida," by John Pennekamp, Miami *Herald,* July 21, 1970; "Florida Rides a Space-Age Boom," by Benedict Thielen, *National Geographic,* December 1963; "Having Fun With Florida," by Roger M. Williams, *The Nation,* Aug. 17, 1970; "Kirk Against the World," by Michael Lottman, *Ripon Forum,* August 1970; "Florida: The State with the Two-Way Stretch," by William L. Rivers, *Harper's Magazine,* February 1955; "Growth Plan Reversal Studied," by Charles F. Hesser, Atlanta *Journal-Constitution,* Oct. 10, 1971; "Florida Gets Growing Pains from Success," by Wade H. Stephens, III (in *Southern Growth—Promises and Problems,* Southern Growth Policies Board, 1973); "Florida's Superboom," *U.S. News & World Report,* June 11, 1973; "Florida Seeks to Curb Runaway Growth," by Jon Nordheimer, New York *Times,* Nov. 19, 1973.

ENVIRONMENT "Park-Rich Florida Is Getting Even Richer," by C. E. Wright, New York *Times,* March 8, 1970; "Indifference Builds a Gravestone for a Lake," Tampa *Tribune,* Jan. 31, 1969; "Keep Out People to Save the Glades?" by Richard Pothler, Miami *Herald,* Feb. 28, 1970; "Florida to Drain a Polluted Lake," by Martin Waldron, New York *Times,* Jan. 4, 1970; "Pensacola Is Paying for 20 Years' Abuse," by Mike Toner, Miami *Herald,* Dec. 6, 1970; "Biscayne Bay," *Audubon,* September 1970; "Miami River's Filth Blamed on Airport," by Don Bedwell, Miami *Herald,* Jan. 22, 1971; "Water Park Promoted to Save Florida's Ecology," by David W. Hacker, *National Observer,* Jan. 15, 1972; "Unmaking a Florida Canal," by John Dillin, *Christian Science Monitor,* March 24, 1973.

"President Blocks Canal in Florida," by Robert B. Semple, Jr., New York *Times,* Jan. 20, 1971; "Blocking Florida's Ditch," *Newsweek,* Feb. 1, 1971; "What Can Be Done with Part of Canal?" by Charles F. Hesser, Atlanta *Journal-Constitution,* Jan. 31, 1971.

"Everglades Jetport Barred by a U .S.-Florida Accord," by Robert B. Semple, Jr., New York *Times,* Jan. 16, 1970; "Florida," *Life,* July 4, 1970; "Everglades Jetport," by Luna B. Leopold, *National Parks Magazine,* November 1969; "Oil Exploration a Peril to Everglades," by Jon Nordheimer, New York *Times,* July 8, 1970; "Fiery Ordeal of the Everglades," *Life,* May 7, 1971; "Water Rationing, Raging Fires Plague Florida," *National Observer,* May 10, 1971; "Florida May Be Next Big Oil State," by Roberta Hornig, Washington *Star,* June 16, 1971.

MIGRANTS "Rate of Disease among Migrants' Children 'Startling,'" by Samuel Adams, St. Petersburg *Times,* April 4, 1968; "Migrants to Get Help in Florida," New York *Times,* Nov. 9, 1969; "OMICA: A Nonviolent Way to Equality," by Bruce Galphin, Washington *Post,* April 26, 1970; "Hunger in America; Stark Poverty Leaves Florida Migrants Vulnerable to Disease," by Homer Bigart, New York *Times,* Feb. 20, 1969; "Coca-Cola Says Migrant Reforms Planned," Washington *Star,* July 23, 1970; "Corporation: The Candor that Refreshes," *Time,* Aug. 10, 1970; "Migrants: Florida's Shame," *South Today,* September 1970; *Migrant: An NBC White Paper* (NBC broadcast of July 16, 1970); "President Orders Relief for Migrant Workers after Florida Crop Failure," Robert H. Phelps, New York *Times,* March 16, 1971; "Jobless Migrant Workers 'Ambush' President Nixon and the Press," by William Tucker, *National Observer,* March 22, 1971; "New Moves May End State's 'Harvest of Shame,'" by John McDermott, Miami *Herald,* Feb. 2, 1969; "Florida Cane Cutters: Alien, Poor, Afraid," by Philip Shabecoff, New York *Times,* March 12, 1973; Florida Peonage Charges Reflect Plight of Migrants," by Wayne King, New York *Times,* March 15, 1973.

POLITICS "Piney Woods, Urban Dade Went for Askew," by Juanita Greene, Miami *Herald,* Nov. 5, 1970; "Carswell Hits Liberals Who Killed Court Bid as He Runs for Senate," by Arlen J. Large, *Wall Street Journal,* July 30, 1970; "Carswell: Defeat from the Jaw of Victory," New York *Times,* April 12, 1970; "Florida's GOP Primary Tests Kirk and Carswell," by Bruce Galphin, Washington *Post,* Aug. 2, 1970; "Carswell's Campaign," *Newsweek,* June 29, 1970; "Chiles Walks to Prominence on Only a Shoestring Budget," by Hunter George, Miami *Herald,* Sept. 10, 1970; "Florida: A Battle of Styles," by Rowland Evans and Robert Novak, Washington *Post,* Oct. 19, 1970; "Carswell's Loss Blocks Kirk's Bid for Party Control," by Jon Nordheimer, New York *Times,* Sept. 10, 1970; "Governor's Office Returns to Demos as Kirk Leaves," by Charles F. Hesser, Atlanta *Journal-Constitution,* Jan. 10, 1971; "NAACP Chief: Black Voters 'Strike Out,'" Miami *Herald,* Aug. 23, 1970; "A Presidential Primary at the Beach," by Charles F. Hesser, Atlanta *Journal-Constitution,* April 4, 1971; "Florida Becomes a Primary Factor," by Stanley J. Hinden, *Newsday,* June 11, 1971; "Election Report: Florida's Changing Political Climate Makes Its Primary Crucial to '72 Campaign," by Gene Baro, *National Journal,* Sept. 4, 1971; "Paper Links Smathers to Deal With Contractor He Promoted," New York *Times,* Oct. 12, 1971; "Grumpy Mood of Florida Voters," *Time,* Feb. 14, 1972; "Busing Issue Overshadowing" and "Nixon-Agnew Expected to Win Easily," by Charles F. Hesser, Atlanta *Journal-Constitution,* March 5 and Nov. 5, 1972.

STATE GOVERNMENT "Cabinet, PSC Indebted to Those They Control," St. Petersburg *Times* and Miami *Herald,* Feb. 9, 1969; "Reorganization Bill Is Passed," by Martin Dyckman, Miami *Herald,* June 4, 1969; "Legislative Modernization—The Florida Experiment," by Fred Schultz, *State Government,* Autumn 1969; "Florida Prison Shootings Called Effort 'to Protect the Inmates,'" by Jon Nordheimer, New York *Times,* Feb. 28, 1971; "Judges, Goode Seek Better Jail," by James Buchanan, Miami *Herald,* Jan. 28, 1971; "Prison Reforms Coming?" by Charles F. Hesser, Atlanta *Journal-Constitution,* Feb. 21, 1971; "Florida Ban on Closed Meetings Merges Candor and Confusion," New York *Times,* Feb. 28, 1971; "All Secret Meetings Illegal, Florida's High Court Rules," by Susan Burnside, Miami *Herald,* Jan. 28, 1971; "Judicial Reform Program Is Set in Motion," by Charles F. Hesser, Atlanta *Journal-Constitution,* April 2, 1972; "'The Public Just Doesn't Care,'" by John Fialka, Washington *Evening Star,* Jan. 12, 1972; "I Man and 1 Vote Gets Speedy OK," by Charles F. Hesser, Atlanta *Journal-Constitution,* April 9, 1972; "Florida Regents Disclose 5-Year Plan to Desegregate University System," New York *Times,* June 27, 1973.

"Florida: The Limits of Public Disclosure," chapter in *Development of Campaign Finance Regulation, Electing Congress: The Financial Dilemma,* by The Twentieth Century Fund Task Force (New York: The Twentieth Century Fund, 1970); *Representation and Apportionment* (Washington: Congressional Quarterly Service, 1966); "Campaign Fund Cap Clears Legislature," by William Mansfield, Miami *Herald,* June 5, 1970; "2-Party System to Add to Dixie Campaign Cost," by Bruce Galphin, Washington *Post,* Oct. 3, 1969; "Florida: Reporting Law Helps," by Philip D. Carter, Washington *Post,* Nov. 22, 1970; "Election Law Reform," by Elston Ready, *National Civic Review,* April 1970.

"The Public Record of Claude R. Kirk, Jr.," *Congressional Quarterly Weekly Report,* Aug. 18, 1967, p. 1607; "Florida's Defiant Governor," New York *Times,* April 7, 1970; "Governor Kirk Fails to Stifle Controversy over Donations," Washington *Post,* March 19, 1970; "Florida Sunshine," by Ernest B. Furgurson, Baltimore *Sun,* Dec. 14, 1969; "War-Like Kirk Attacked Legislators' Integrity," by Bill Mansfield and Jim Minter, Miami *Herald,* April 25, 1969; "A Governor on the Go Carries a High Price," Miami *Herald,* Dec. 14, 1969; "Kirk Had Chance to 'Beat System,'" by Clarence Jones, Miami *Herald,* Dec. 18, 1969; "2nd County May Go to GOP," Associated Press dispatch in Miami *Herald,* Aug. 7, 1970.

"Gov. Askew In Profile," by Larry Vickers, *South Today,* November 1972; "Busing, Gov. Askew, and the Florida Primary," by Robert W. Hooker, *New South,* Spring 1972; "Florida's 'Supersquare'—A Man to Watch," by Jon Nordheimer, New York *Times Magazine,* March 5, 1972; "Florida: Cutbacks, Financial Uncertainty, Force Trimmings . . .," by Martin Dyckman, *South Today,* March 1973; "School Revamp Again Proposed," by Charles H. Hesser, Atlanta *Journal-Constitution,* Feb. 4, 1973.

"Ed Ball's Grip Is Felt by All," by Juanita Greene, Miami *Herald,* Sept. 22, 1969; "Florida Makes News by Not Passing a Bill," by Bruce Galphin, Washington *Post,* June 11, 1970; "Congress May Bounce Ed Ball from Grip on Florida Banking," by Charles Stafford, Miami *Herald* and St. Petersburg *Times,* March 23, 1969; "Mr. Ball," by Nixon Smiley, *Floridian,* May 5, 1968.

MIAMI *Psycho-Social Dynamics in Miami,* Report of a Summer Study Conducted under the Auspices of the University of Miami, Prepared for the Department of Housing and Urban Development, January 1969; "The Gleaming Shores of Miami," by Dick Schaap, *Holiday,* June 1968; "The Men Who Own Downtown Miami," by Juanita Greene, Miami *Herald,* March 16, 1969; "Miami Is Becoming a Major Winter-Cruise Port," by Jay Clarke, New York *Times,* Jan. 18, 1970; "A New Home for Miami's Booming Fleet," by Jay Clarke, New York *Times,* Nov. 1, 1970; "Discovering the Gold Coast," by June Kronholz, Miami *Herald Magazine,* Nov. 29, 1970; *Highlights of Greater Miami, Hollywood and Fort Lauderdale* (Mills Publications, Inc., Miami, Fla.); "The Climate Of Learning," by Peter Schrag, *Saturday Review,* March 15, 1969.

"The Junior College, Belittled in Past, Now a Major Force," by Jack Rosenthal, New York *Times,* Feb. 14, 1972; "Dade County Voters Approve Rapid Transit," *National Civic Review,* January 1973; "Miami Mayor and 2 Judges Among 6 Indicted for Bribe Plots," New York *Times,* April 8, 1973; "Money Games Under the Palms," *Forbes,* Feb. 15, 1972.

MIAMI—CUBANS "Havana, Florida: Cubans Thrive in Miami Area and So Does the City," by Yvonne Thayer, *Wall Street Journal,* Dec. 12, 1969; "Success Story: U. S. Cubans," by Haynes Johnson, Washington *Post,* March 28, 1971; *Cubans in Miami: A Third Dimension in Racial and Cultural Relations,* by John Egerton (Nashville, Tenn.: Race Relations Information Center, November 1969); "Cuban Refugee Aid Cost Spirals," by Charles F. Hesser, Atlanta *Journal-Constitution,* June 20, 1971; "Florida's Dade County Adopts Bilingual Policy," Los Angeles *Times,* May 7, 1973.

MIAMI—MIAMI BEACH "Miami Beach, the All-Too-American City," by Robert Sherrill, New York *Times Magazine,* Aug. 4, 1968; "Wish You Were Here," by E. M. Michel, Miami *Herald Tropic,* Nov. 15, 1970; "Miami Beach Oceanfront," by Morris David Rosenberg, Washington *Post,* Nov. 8, 1970; "The Sands of Time Are Running Out for Miami Beach," by Jay Clarke, New York *Times,* May 10, 1970; "Miami Beach: A Steel and Concrete Shore," by Susan Miller and Joseph P. Averill, Miami *Herald,* May 24, 1970; "Gambling Defeat in Poll Is Hailed," New York *Times,* April 26, 1970; "South Beach: Ripe Area for New Face," by Bill Amlong, Miami *Herald,* Feb. 22, 1969; "Face to Face with the G.O.P.," by Elia Kazan, *New York,* Aug. 26, 1968; "Miami Beach and Chicago," Norman Mailer, *Harper's Magazine,* November 1968; "Miami Beach Launches Tourist Drive," by Frank Eidge, UPI dispatch in Washington *Post,* Nov. 2, 1972; "Elderly Flee N.Y. for Florida's Peace," by Kenneth Reich, Los Angeles *Times,* Jan. 26, 1971; "Miami Blues," by Donn Pearce, *Esquire,* November 1972; "Miami's Last Political Roundup," *Business Week,* Aug. 26, 1972.

MIAMI—CRIME "The Little Big Man Who Laughs at the Law," by Nicholas Gage, *Atlantic,* July, 1970; *The Grim Reapers,* by Ed Reid (Chicago: Henry Regnery, 1969); "Lansky Is Indicted again in Miami," Washington *Post,* March 26, 1971; "Illicit Traffic of Cocaine 'Growing by Leaps and Bounds' in Miami," by George Volsky, New York *Times,* Feb. 1, 1970; "Faircloth's Law: A New Way to Nail Elusive Mobsters?" by Denny Walsh, *Life,* Oct. 24, 1969; "Florida Is Becoming Drug Traffic Center," by James M. Markham, New York *Times,* May 1, 1972; "Miami Drug Raid Nets $47 Million Worth of Heroin," UPI dispatch in Newark *Star-Ledger,* Jan. 6, 1972.

OTHER CITIES AND PLACES "Jacksonville: Emerging from Morass of Mediocrity," by Jeff Nesmith, Atlanta *Journal-Constitution,* Sept. 21, 1969; "Jacksonville Area Highlights Activity," *National Civic Review,* June, 1970; "Metro Aided

Jacksonville as Ship Nearly Swamped," by Les Seago, Chattanooga *Times,* April 12, 1970; "Newcomer to City Gave Impetus to Consolidation in Jacksonville," by Les Seago, Chattanooga *Times,* April 13, 1970; "Mayor Hails Merger in Jacksonville," by Ralph D. Olive, Milwaukee *Journal,* April 19, 1970; "The Jacksonville Story," by L. A. Hester, *National Civic Review,* February 1970; "Racial Unrest Hits Jacksonville Despite Efforts to Ease Tensions," by Martin Waldron, New York *Times,* June 21, 1971; "Jacksonville: So Different You Can Hardly Believe It," by John Fischer, *Harper's Magazine,* July 1971.

"The Gold Coast booms again," *Business Week,* July 12, 1969; "At Fort Lauderdale It's Water," by Stephen Birmingham, *Holiday,* December 1970; "Palm Beach Is . . .," by Tom Buckley, New York *Times Magazine,* March 21, 1971; "Heyday of Railroading in Florida Is Recalled," by Ward Allan Howe, New York *Times,* April 26, 1970; "Growing Pains In Palm Beach," by George L. Hern, Jr., New York *Times,* Dec. 6, 1970; "Florida's Burgeoning Boca Raton," by George L. Hern, Jr., New York *Times,* April 6, 1969; "A New Look at the Dynamic Florida East Coast," *Canaveral Missile,* January 1972; "ITT Subdivides Paradise," by Michael F. Toner, *The Nation,* May 1, 1972.

"Gainesville: In the Spring of Our Discontent," by Nixon Smiley, St. Petersburg *Times,* April 14, 1968; "Black Students Hit UF Policies," by John Edgerton, *Race Relations Reporter,* June 6, 1971; "Travel: An Economic Boom . . . in Tallahassee," *Atlanta Magazine,* May 1972.

"Will Science Parks Boost Economy?" by Robert M. Cour, Seattle *Post-Intelligencer,* Oct. 10, 1970; "Ghetto Youth Are This Doctor's Bag," *Ebony,* October 1970; "A Dream Gets Off the Ground," by Fred Andersen, Miami *Herald,* March 2, 1969; "Booked for Travel," David Butwin, *Saturday Review,* Feb. 6, 1971.

"Disney World Wakes Sleepy Orlando, *Business Week,* Nov. 14, 1970; "Florida's Manmade Magic," by Brad Byers, *Southern Living,* June 1966; "The Man Who Can't Stop Running," by Nixon Smiley, Miami *Herald Sunday Magazine,* Feb. 5, 1967; "Lot of Mickey Mouse Surrounds Disney World Development," by William Richards, Washington *Post,* Oct 22, 1972; "Animal Neighbors Ring Disney World," *Business Week,* Feb. 26, 1972; "Controversial Florida Lawman Defeated, Faces Further Inquiry," by Martin Dyckman, Washington *Post,* Nov. 10, 1972; "The 130-Year-Old Man," *Newsweek,* Oct. 2, 1972.

"The Richly Flavored Spell of Tampa's Cesar Gonzmart," by Bette Orsini, St. Petersburg *Times,* Sept. 29, 1968; "Superjet Airports Run into Trouble," *U.S. News & World Report,* March 22, 1971; "God's Waiting Room," *Newsweek,* April 20, 1970; "In St. Petersburg: A Profile Of Failure," by Edwin Stanfield, *New South,* Summer 1968; "Ringling Brothers and Barnum & Bailey Circus," by Bill Ballantine, *Holiday,* April 1970; "A City in the Round," by Charles E. Dole, *Christian Science Monitor,* June 26, 1970.

"Key West Fears Crisis if Navy Pulls Out," by Jon Nordheimer, New York *Times,* Oct. 31, 1970; "The Lower Keys, Florida's 'Out Islands,'" *National Geographic* January 1971; "Florida Keys Land Boom in Full Swing," by Charles Hillinger, Los Angeles *Times,* Sept. 12, 1972.

CAPE CANAVERAL "Blues at the Cape," by Thomas O'Toole, Washington *Post,* Jan. 31, 1971; "Cape Kennedy: Eclipse on the Ground," *Newsweek,* June 2, 1969; "Cape May Lose Out on Space Shuttle Shots," by Chuck Hoyt, Miami *Herald,* Jan. 24, 1971; "The Heron and the Astronaut," by Anne Morrow Lindberg, *Life,* Feb. 28, 1969; *Summary Report: NASA Impact on Brevard County,* by Annie Mary Hartsfield, Mary Alice Griffin, and Charles M. Grigg (Tallahassee: Institute for Social Research, Florida State University, 1966); *The Kennedy Space Center Story* (Kennedy Space Center, Fla.; National Aeronautics and Space Administration, 1968); "'Space Coast' Tightens Belt," by James Russell, Miami *Herald,* Oct. 11, 1970; "Floridians Ask Hill to Restore Name of Cape Canaveral," by William Greider, Washington *Post,* Nov. 25, 1969; "No Cape Kennedy Now—But Name Is Everywhere," *U.S. News & World Report,* Oct. 29, 1973; "And Now—How High the Cape?" *Newsweek,* Dec. 18, 1972.

INDEX

Page references in **boldface** type indicate inclusive or major entries.

Scale of Miles
0 100 200 300 400 500
CAN
WASH.
Seattle
Olympia
Spokane
MONT.
N.D.
Fa
Helena
Butte
Portland
Salem
ORE.
Eugene
IDAHO
Billings
Bismarck
S.D.
Aberdeen
YELLOWSTONE NATIONAL PARK
Boise
WYO.
Pierre
CALIF.
NEV.
Pocatello
Casper
NEB.
Great Salt Lake
Ogden
Oakland
Reno
Cheyenne
Salt Lake City
UTAH
Carson City
COLO.
Sacramento
Denver
KAN.
San Francisco
YOSEMITE NAT'L. PARK
Colorado Springs
Mt. Whitney
GRAND CANYON NAT'L. PARK
Wichit
Las Vegas
Farmington
Santa Barbara
Santa Fe
Oklah City
ARIZ.
Amarillo
Los Angeles
Albuquerque
San Diego
Phoenix
N.M.
Wichita Falls
Pacific Ocean
Tucson
Lubbock
Fort Worth
El Paso
TEXAS
Austin
San Antonio
U. S. S. R.
Kotzebue
ALASKA
Nome
Fairbanks
CANADA
U.S.S.R.
U.S.
Anchorage
Juneau
MEXICO
Bering Sea
MILES
0 200 400 600